AF518883

PEOPLE OF INDIA

HIMACHAL PRADESH

VOLUME XXIV

PEOPLE OF INDIA

NATIONAL SERIES

VOL. I	PEOPLE OF INDIA	AN INTRODUCTION
VOL. II	PEOPLE OF INDIA	THE SCHEDULED CASTES
VOL. III	PEOPLE OF INDIA	THE SCHEDULED TRIBES
VOL. IV	PEOPLE OF INDIA	ALL COMMUNITIES
VOL. V	PEOPLE OF INDIA	ALL COMMUNITIES
VOL. VI	PEOPLE OF INDIA	ALL COMMUNITIES
VOL. VII	PEOPLE OF INDIA	IDENTITY, ECOLOGY, SOCIAL ORGANIZATION, ECONOMY, DEVELOPMENT, PROCESS AND LINKAGES: A QUANTITATIVE PROFILE
VOL. VIII	PEOPLE OF INDIA	COMMUNITIES, SEGMENTS, SYNONYMS, SURNAMES AND TITLES
VOL. IX	PEOPLE OF INDA	LANGUAGES AND SCRIPTS
VOL. X	PEOPLE OF INDIA	THE BIOLOGICAL VARIATION IN INDIAN POPULATIONS
VOL. XI	PEOPLE OF INDIA	AN ANTHROPOLOGICAL ATLAS

STATE SERIES

VOL. XII	ANDAMAN AND NICOBAR ISLANDS
VOL. XIII	ANDHRA PRADESH
VOL. XIV	ARUNACHAL PRADESH
VOL. XV	ASSAM
VOL. XVI	BIHAR
VOL. XVII	CHANDIGARH
VOL. XVIII	DADRA AND NAGAR HAVELI
VOL. XIX	DAMAN AND DIU
VOL. XX	DELHI
VOL. XXI	GOA
VOL. XXII	GUJARAT
VOL. XXIII	HARYANA
VOL. XXIV	HIMACHAL PRADESH
VOL. XXV	JAMMU AND KASHMIR
VOL. XXVI	KARNATAKA
VOL. XXVII	KERALA
VOL. XXVIII	LAKSHADWEEP
VOL. XXIX	MADHYA PRADESH
VOL. XXX	MAHARASHTRA
VOL. XXXI	MANIPUR
VOL. XXXII	MEGHALAYA
VOL. XXXIII	MIZORAM
VOL. XXXIV	NAGALAND
VOL. XXXV	ORISSA
VOL. XXXVI	PONDICHERRY
VOL. XXXVII	PUNJAB
VOL. XXXVIII	RAJASTHAN
VOL. XXXIX	SIKKIM
VOL. XL	TAMIL NADU
VOL. XLI	TRIPURA
VOL. XLII	UTTAR PRADESH
VOL. XLIII	WEST BENGAL

PEOPLE OF INDIA

HIMACHAL PRADESH

VOLUME XXIV

General Editor

K.S. SINGH

Editors

B.R. SHARMA

A.R. SANKHYAN

ANTHROPOLOGICAL SURVEY OF INDIA

MANOHAR

1996

ISBN 81-7304-094-X

Published on behalf of ASI by Ajay Kumar Jain
Manohar Publishers & Distributors, 2/6 Ansari Road, Daryaganj New Delhi-110 002

Typeset by AJ Software Publishing Co. Pvt. Ltd, 305 Durga Chambers,
1333 D.B. Gupta Road, Karol Bagh, New Delhi-110 005

Printed at Rajkamal Electric Press, G.T. Karnal Road, Delhi-110 009

A NOTE ON THE SE

There exists an information gap on a very large ties in India, and whatever information on them or needs to be updated. The Anthropological launched a project on the People of India on objective of the project was to generate a brief, logical profile of all the communities of India, t change and development processes and the l together. This was in accordance with the o established forty-five years ago in December 19 pursuing bio-cultural research among different p its eight regional centres. Its objectives have bee resolution, adopted in 1985, which commits th survey of the human surface of India.

The identification of the communities and t long history which started from the early perio Manu. Regional lists of communities figured i dieval chronicles contained a description of th in various parts of the country. Listings in the undertaken on an extensive scale, after 1806. momentum in course of censuses from 1881 to lation of the lists of the communities of India un project, we drew upon ethnographic surveys, Castes and Scheduled Tribes drawn up by the the lists of backward classes prepared by Back sions set up by various state governments, and t Mandal Commission Report. We were able 6748 communities at the start. This list was ta and checked, and finally 4635 communities we ied.

Unlike surveys in the colonial period, whic and a few princely states, our project cove bringing within its ambit such parts that had not surveyed earlier or where the survey had been way. Each state and union territory was treate was decided to start with the investigation of th nities, and then move on to a field study of better-known ones. Investigators for the surv each area on the basis of their experience a

CONTENTS

investigators of the Survey, as well as local scholars, were set up for each state and union territory to plan the surveys, seek the co-operation of local scholars, generate and evaluate findings, etc., etc. Later, editorial boards consisting of local scholars — one or more of these were nominated as co-editors for each local volume — were set up for each state and union territory. We sought the co-operation of the state governments in implementing the project, and this we received in ample measure, particularly from the welfare and backward classes departments of the state governments, local officers of the Census of India, tribal research institutes, university departments of anthropology, other departments of local universities, etc. Local scholars participated enthusiastically in our project as well as in the seminars held by us.

The progress in the investigation and coverage of communities from 2 October 1985 to 31 March 1992 was steady and impressive. We were able to identify, locate and study 4635 communities in all the states and union territories of India, out of the 6748 listed initially. As many as 600 scholars participated in this project, including 197 from 26 institutions. About 100 workshops and rounds of discussions were held in all the states and union territories, and in these about 3,000 scholars participated. The investigators spent 26,510 days in the field, which works out to 5.5 days per community studied in the various states and union territories of India. Our scholars interviewed a large number of people, out of whom we have recorded only the key informants, i.e. 24,951. This works out to about 5 'informed' informants per community. Of the informants, 4981 were women. Our instruction to the investigators was to study a community at two or three places, and in at least two or three cultural regions into which the larger states of India were divided. Interviews in connection with the study of the communities were conducted in 3,581 villages, mostly multi-community villages, and in 1,011 towns and cities spread over almost all the districts of India, i.e. 421 districts and 91 cultural regions. We were thus, able, to study on an average a community at about two places. It should be noted that most of the smaller communities could be studied at only one place since they are not located in more than one area.

A major achievement of this project was the preparation of cartographic maps showing the distribution of the communities and the location where they were studied. About 4,000 maps were prepared. Yet another achievement was the visual documentation of the people of India as part of the field operations. About 21,362 photographs were generated, most of them in black & white, and a substantial number

A NOTE ON THE SERIES

There exists an information gap on a very large number of communities in India, and whatever information on them exists is either scanty or needs to be updated. The Anthropological Survey of India (ASI) launched a project on the People of India on 2 October 1985. The objective of the project was to generate a brief, descriptive anthropological profile of all the communities of India, the impact on them of change and development processes and the links that bring them together. This was in accordance with the objectives of the ASI, established forty-five years ago in December 1945. The ASI has been pursuing bio-cultural research among different population groups from its eight regional centres. Its objectives have been defined in the policy resolution, adopted in 1985, which commits this organization to the survey of the human surface of India.

The identification of the communities and their listing have had a long history which started from the early period of our history, with Manu. Regional lists of communities figured in Sanskrit works. Medieval chronicles contained a description of the communities located in various parts of the country. Listings in the colonial period were undertaken on an extensive scale, after 1806. The process gathered momentum in course of censuses from 1881 to 1941. In our compilation of the lists of the communities of India under the People of India project, we drew upon ethnographic surveys, the lists of Scheduled Castes and Scheduled Tribes drawn up by the Government of India, the lists of backward classes prepared by Backward Classes Commissions set up by various state governments, and the list that exists in the Mandal Commission Report. We were able to put together about 6748 communities at the start. This list was taken to the field, tested and checked, and finally 4635 communities were identified and studied.

Unlike surveys in the colonial period, which covered British India and a few princely states, our project covers the whole country, bringing within its ambit such parts that had not been ethnographically surveyed earlier or where the survey had been done in a perfunctory way. Each state and union territory was treated as a unit of study. It was decided to start with the investigation of the least-known communities, and then move on to a field study of the lesser-known and better-known ones. Investigators for the survey were identified for each area on the basis of their experience and expertise. Teams of investigators of the Survey, as well as local scholars, were set up for each state and union territory to plan the surveys, seek the co-operation of local scholars, generate and evaluate findings, etc., etc. Later, editorial boards consisting of local scholars — one or more of these were nominated as co-editors for each local volume — were set up for each state and union territory. We sought the co-operation of the state governments in implementing the project, and this we received in ample measure, particularly from the welfare and backward classes departments of the state governments, local officers of the Census of India, tribal research institutes, university departments of anthropology, other departments of local universities, etc. Local scholars participated enthusiastically in our project as well as in the seminars held by us.

The progress in the investigation and coverage of communities from 2 October 1985 to 31 March 1992 was steady and impressive. We were able to identify, locate and study 4635 communities in all the states and union territories of India, out of the 6748 listed initially. As many as 600 scholars participated in this project, including 197 from 26 institutions. About 100 workshops and rounds of discussions were held in all the states and union territories, and in these about 3,000 scholars participated. The investigators spent 26,510 days in the field, which works out to 5.5 days per community studied in the various states and union territories of India. Our scholars interviewed a large number of people, out of whom we have recorded only the key informants, i.e. 24,951. This works out to about 5 'informed' informants per community. Of the informants, 4981 were women. Our instruction to the investigators was to study a community at two or three places, and in at least two or three cultural regions into which the larger states of India were divided. Interviews in connection with the study of the communities were conducted in 3,581 villages, mostly multi-community villages, and in 1,011 towns and cities spread over almost all the districts of India, i.e. 421 districts and 91 cultural regions. We were thus, able, to study on an average a community at about two places. It should be noted that most of the smaller communities could be studied at only one place since they are not located in more than one area.

A major achievement of this project was the preparation of cartographic maps showing the distribution of the communities and the location where they were studied. About 4,000 maps were prepared. Yet another achievement was the visual documentation of the people of India as part of the field operations. About 21,362 photographs were generated, most of them in black & white, and a substantial number in colour, by amateur photographers.

At an early stage of our project in March 1985 we decided to transfer the data to a computer. We were subsequently able to develop probably the first software in the country — and one of the first in the world — in ethnography, in close collaboration with the National Informatics Centre. From 28 May 1988 we started transferring the quantitative data collected in computer format to floppies. Simultaneously, the transfer of descriptive data (abstracts etc.) on to the computer also started at almost all the regional centres. We succeeded in computerizing an enormous mass of data, and also in producing the first results of univariate analysis, by March 1990.

The descriptive material, running into 120 manuscript volumes, and the quantitative data contained in 157 diskettes, were released on 1 October 1990 by Sri Chimanbhai Mehta, Minister of State for Human Resource Development, in the presence of a distinguished audience in Delhi, for use by scholars at the Nehru Memorial Museum & Library, and at eight regional centres of the ASI.

The phase of more elaborate analysis started in July 1991, in collaboration with the Centre for Ecological Sciences, Indian Institute of Science, Bangalore. This resulted in a voluminous output of analyzed data, which have been presented in a comprehensive matrix consisting of the four categories of populations, the constitutional, religious, occupational and locational. These sets of data, together with a map, were released by Shri Arjun Singh, Minister of Human Resource Development, on 24 December 1991. The last workshop on the People of India project was held at the Indian Institute of Social and Economic Change in Bangalore, where the preliminary results of the analysis presented by the ASI were discussed by distinguished scholars.

It should be noted that the study of communities has been conducted in 3,581 villages and 1,011 towns situated in 421 districts of the states and union territories of India. The information was collected from about 25,000 'learned' informants by our scholars, 500 of them, over the period 1985 to 1992. Therefore, the observations relate to this limited time frame and to the universe of the ethnographic project entitled People of India. The percentages relate strictly to the responses made by the informants to the questionnaire contained in the schedule guideline and computer format, and to the queries made by the investigators at the places of investigation. The responses have been supplemented with the observations of the investigators, the secondary material has been checked and cross-checked at many levels with other sources of information by scholars, particularly local scholars.

We are presenting the material published under the People of India project in two parts which are interrelated. The first consists of the ten-volume national series, five of which contain an abstract on all communities across the length and breadth of the country. The data generated in this respect has been strengthened by the addition of information from census and other secondary sources. These volumes include two on the Scheduled Castes and Scheduled Tribes, prepared as part of the celebration of Dr. B.R. Ambedkar's birth centenary; three of all the communities of India, and two containing data on the languages and biological structures of Indian population. The remaining volumes contain description of the quantitative profile, communities and their segments, community-specific languages and the biological structure of Indian populations.

The second part comprises the state/union territory volumes based on a detailed write-up on each community of India. The contributors of the national volumes on the SC, ST and all communities are listed in the last volume, Volume VI. The Glossary given in Volume VI is common to all the national volumes. At the end of each account we have given references to the texts from which we have quoted, or references for further reading. This is only illustrative. An exhaustive bibliography appears at the end of the national volumes, in Volume VI.

The Oxford University Press has been publishing the national volumes. A consortium of publishers has been set up to publish the material on states and union territories. Seven volumes each for the northern states, southern states and the islands, the central and western states are being published respectively by M/S Manohar Publishers and Distributors (New Delhi), M/S Affiliated East-West Press Private Limited (Madras) and M/S Popular Prakashan Pvt. Ltd. (Bombay). The eleven volumes on the north-eastern and eastern states are being published by M/S Seagull Books Private Limited (Calcutta), which has also already published the introductory national volume.

I trust the series on the People of India, which is based on a comprehensive anthropological survey of the country, will be found useful by all sections of our people, including students, researchers, teachers, social activists, administrators and political leaders. I hope we have laid the groundwork for a comprehensive ethnography of the people of India which needs to be continually updated and built upon by successive generations of researchers and scholars.

K.S. Singh

FOREWORD

Himachal Pradesh emerged as a distinct territorial identity, after independence on 15 April 1948. The state was enlarged with the addition of Bilaspur state in 1954 and some areas from Punjab after the organisation of Punjab in 1966. However, various parts of the present-day Himachal Pradesh are recalled in folkore and history and have been associated with numerous episodes in the epics and the puranas. The Trigarta played a glorious role in the Mahabharata war. Both the Kaurvas and Pandavas are identified with the local gods, and Krishna became a dominant influence. The lower parts of Himachal Pradesh which consist of the plains became part of the kingdoms that rose and fell in the Punjab.

The Nag figure both as myth and as a people in the folkore of Himachal Pradesh from the very early times. The Nag rulers were transformed into local gods. The Nag are worshipped as the guardians of hills and streams, as village deities, as protector of crops and the symbol of fertility and sexuality. The peoples who have Nag totem are said to have descended from Nag and they are the Brahman and Rajput who have Kashyap gotra: they also have Nag as their title and the local variants of Nag such as Khadpa, Goslu and Pundrik as their gotras.

The state has three well defined eco-cultural zones which are intrinsic to the understanding of various ethnic identities. For instance, the upper niches of the Himalayas are dominated by the communities following the Mahayan tradition of Buddhuism or Lamaism, speaking languages belonging to the Tibeto-Burman family and practising pastoralism (9.48 per cent as against national average of 1.90 per cent), horticulture (15.52 per cent against 4.27 per cent), animal husbandry (40.52 per cent against 21.55 per cent), etc. The middle belt is dominated by the communities following terrace cultivation (25.86 per cent against 4. 75 per cent) and horticulture and some elements of pastoralism, following Hinduism (78.45 per cent against 76.35 per cent) and folk religions. Ethnically they belong to Khas, Kuninda and Kol, speaking the languages belonging to the Indo-Aryan family. The lower belt consists of the sub-mountainous ranges and plains peopled by the communities such as the immigrants (61.21 per cent against 59.98 per cent) with an exposure to the larger world practising settled cultivation (21.55 per cent against 35.12 per cent), business and trade (43.97 percent against 33.59 percent), speaking Pahari languages.

Himachal Pradesh has always evoked a sense of wonder and mystery. It is known for some of its communities, which are somewhat unique and have no parrallel elsewhere in the country. The Khas (Kanet) and Kinnaura are an autochthonous community. The Mawi a traditional warrior segment of Kanet community are noted for 'Dheeng'—war strategy. The Pangwal and Swangla are agriculturists and pastoralists, besides being bee-keepers. The Seok is an isolated Kanet group of Bhangal area of Mandi and Kangra districts, practising pastoralism and animal husbandry. The Malaneese are the most isolated people residing at an altitude of 2633 metres in Kullu. They are noted for their democratic village organisation which has been romanticised a great deal. The Malaneese as the first republic in the world, with its own executive and judicial system and bicameral legislature representing people and households, subject to the will of ultimate arbiter, the local god, as interpreted by *gur* are also noted for collecting and selling honey and wild medicinal plants. The Nar and the Beda are noted for the Narmedha ceremonies known as the Kahika and the Bhunda, respectively. The Sipi is a musician community of the lower social order speaking a language that retains Sanskrit characters. Many of the communities trace their descent to the Puranic and historical characters. The state has unique ethnographic traits such as widespread propitiation of village deities particularly the female deities, culminating in the unique Dussehara in Kullu.

Many communities of the present-day Himachal Pradesh particularly in the lower region were studied as part of the general ethnographic survey conducted in the north-western provinces including Punjab. However, it is for the first time that all the communities of Himachal Pradesh have been ethnographically studied in a compreshensive format by the scholars from the Anthropological Survey of India, Himachal Academy of Arts, Culture and Languages and other institutions as well as by independent scholars. The materials were discussed at a workshop held in Shimla in October 1989.

The total number of communities studied in Himachal Pradesh is 116. To these have been added 8 more communities later (see Appendix A). The analysis of the data presented in the format is based on the study of 116 communities only because the data for the communities reported later have not been included in the data set for Himachal Pradesh. Many of the identities are in a state of fluidity, and even overlap.

Populations of Himachal Pradesh have been extensively studied for different biological traits owing to their unique position. The All India Anthropometric Survey suggests that the hill people are generally short to below medium in stature (162.33 cms), have long (53.48 per cent) to round (25.76 per cent) head, narrow to below medium (48.17 per cent) nose and round (32.36 per cent) to long (33.11 per cent) face. However, the scheduled tribes have broad to medium facial profile. Dermatoglyphic studies indicate that loops (49-60 per cent) preponderate over whorls (36-49 per cent) in other communities, but show equal range in the tribal groups of loops (38-57 per cent) and whorls (37-60 per cent) except Mongoloid tribes where whorls (53 per cent) show relatively high frequency than loops (44 per cent). Pattern intensity index varies from 11 to 15 per cent in other communities, and from 13 to 15 per cent in tribal groups. Colour blindness has low incidence (0-6 per cent).

Though a small state, there are as many as 32 languages spoken in Himachal Pradesh. Out of these there are 6 belonging to the Tibeto-Burman family, 3 unclassified, 2 are foreign and the remaining 21 to the Indo-Aryan and or its Pahari sub-family.

The Pahari language alongwith the Bilaspuri is spoken by the largest number of communities (21), followed by Kangri (14 communities), Chambiali (9 communities), Urdu (7 communities), Kulvi (5 communities) and Mandiali (4 communities). The nine scheduled tribes speak Bhotia, Gadiali, Khampa, Kinnauri and Pangwali. The Chinali, Manchat and Sansi are unclassified languages. A smaller number, 29 communities are linguistically heterogeneous speaking different languages in different linguistic zones of the state.

According to 1981 census, Pahari/Hindi languages are spoken by the largest number of persons (3,797,702) followed by Punjabi (254,651), Kinnauri (52,674), Gorkhali/Nepali (45,848), Kashmiri (630,950), Dogri (21,310), Lahauli (18,097), Urdu (13,569) and Tibetan (10,999). Bhotia is spoken by 2,770 persons.

Hindi speakers are bilingual in English (266,349), Punjabi (47,013) and Urdu (40,224). Punjabi speakers are bilingual in Hindi (106,860), English (8,735) and Urdu (2,334). Other language speakers are also mostly bilingual in Hindi. Among the Scheduled languges, 3,873 Hindi speakers are bilingual in Dogri, 386 Kinnauri speakers and 194 Lahauli speakers are bilingual in Bhotia, and 265 Kinnauri speakers are bilingual in Tibetan.

Apart from the Devanagari and Perso-Arabic scripts, minor scripts like Tankri/Takri, Bhatakshri, and Tibetan are also used in Himachal Pradesh.

We will now discuss some of the ethnographic features of Himachal Pradesh which stand out in relation to the rest of the country. As most of the communities are located in the lower belt, they perceive themselves as regional (52.59 per cent against nationl average of 63.49) communities having linkages across the border of the state. With the growth of literacy, a number of communities also see themselves as part of national (30.17 per cent) communities. Most of them have their history (32.76 per cent) of origin and migration (61.21 per cent). A fairly large number of communities consider themselves as regional communities whose immigration is recorded in history (24.14 per cent against 12.41 per cent of national average).

Many communities have reported living in the conditions of extreme cold (12.51 per cent) at high altitude (19.83 per cent) with low humidity (89.66 per cent) in the valleys (61.21 per cent) and thin-forested terrains (81.90 per cent). There are 40 scheduled castes and 12 scheduled tribes which have been covered. A small number of communities do distinguish themselves by their dress (male 13.74 per cent), headgear, both male (13.79 per cent) and female (4.31 per cent), ornaments male (4.31 per cent against 2.89 per cent) and female (6.03 per cent against 6.82 per cent) and body marking for male (3.45 per cent against 2.65 per cent), etc. The Himachali cap has emerged as the distincive headgear of most Himachal communities.

Considering the ecology of the Himalayas, most communities (70.89 per cent) are non-vegetarian against 37.20 per cent national average with a very high (88.79 per cent) proportion of women non-vegetarian against national average of 72.25 per cent.

The meat commonly consumed is of ram and goat. Among other kinds of meat consumed is also pork (40.52 per cent against 29.92 per cent) of wild boar. Interestingly there are also communities which are pure vegetarian such as Agarwal, Jain, and some sections of the Brahmans. The staple cereals are wheat (99.14 per cent against 56.70 per cent national average), maize (80.17 per cent against 24.79 per cent) barley (27. 59 per cent against 4.81 per cent), and rice (87.07 per cent against 88.18 per cent). Among the pulses, the important one is urad (93.97 per cent against 63.04 per cent). Mustard oil (93.97 per cent against 48.89 per cent) is the medium of cooking. Roots and tubers are universally consumed at a level higher (86.21 per cent) than the national average (71.52 per cent).

Again consisdering the ecological conditions the consumption of alcohol among men (62.07 per cent against 52.27 per cent national average) and women (42.24 per cent against 22.37 per cent) is very high; so is the incidence of smoking which is much higher (92.24 per cent) than the national average (23.45 per cent). Conversely the consumption of betel (13.79 per cent against 76,48 per cent) and snuff (2.59 per cent againt 21.62 per cent is much lower like in the other north-western states. Interestingly, the shift form non-vegetarianism to vegetarianism (37.07 per cent against 9.02 per cent) is very high in the state largely because of influence of many relgious cults, such as Radhaswami, Brahma Kumari, and so on which enjoin vegetarianism. It is also reported that some sections of the scheduled castes are shifting to vegetarianism as part of the process of upward social mobility.

The Himalayan communities are highly stratified. The extent of social divisions reported is higher (87.93 per cent) than the national average (81.51 per cent) largely in terms of clans (41.38 per cent against 64.75 per cent), lineages (62.07 per cent against 29.43 per cent), segments, all hierarchically

(34.48 per cent against 22.57 per cent) arranged. Differentiation exists at levels which are higher than of the national average. For instance, social differentiation is more wide spread (87.07 per cent against 48.39 per cent). So is religious differentiation because of conversion to religious cults as also territorial differentiation (14.66 per cent against 11.69 per cent) within communities because they are occupying various terrains. Differentiation in terms of economy and occupation is much less (10.34 per cent against 12.60 per cent) because of slow economic development. Most of the social divisions regulate marriage (92.24 per cent against 80.82 per cent) or indicate descent (85.34 per cent against 42.61 per cent).

The Himalayan communities show much higher awareness (83.62 per cent against 68.46 per cent) of varna system, which is recognised by a large number of communities (71.55 per cent against 49.51 per cent) including both indigenous communities claiming Rajput (27.59 per cent againt 15.90 per cent) status, and immigrant Rajput communities, Brahman (13.79 per cent against 9.36 per cent) and others. The Vaishya category is relatively small considering the smaller scope for trade and business. Following from this, those placing themselves in high (31.90 per cent against 22.85 per cent) and is low (19.3 per cent against 28.85 per cent) categories are larger than the national average.

Most of the communities practise the norm of community endogamy (98.28 per cent against 96.16 per cent). There are, however, some communities which practise clan endogamy (5.17 per cent against 2.31 per cent) such as the Od and Badhai. Like all states of north-west there is more of village exogamy (59) and less of village endogamy (11). Gotra exogamy is extensively practised (56.90 per cent against 27.90 per cent). Notion of pravara is weak and almost non-existent except among some Brahaman groups (2.59 per cent against 1.12 per cent).

A unique characteristic of community formation in Himachal Pradesh is offered by the Gaddis and Pangwals. These are two communities which have both hypergamous and hypogamous relationships. Both are communities living at high altitude where immigration does not seem to have taken place in a normal course. These are territorial communities which broke up into various jatis such as Brahman, Rajput and others.

Himachal Pradesh is also unique in the sense that it had been the haven and refuge for the communities fleeing the plains and coming from the other regions of India following political upheavals. Such immigrants did not penetrate very deep into the Himalayan regions but they mostly remained confined to the sub-mountainous region.

Again like other north-western states, Himachal Pradesh has reported a very high incidence of hypergamy or hypogamy across commnities.

Consanguienous forms (18.97 per cent against 4.44 per cent national average) of marriage, of the paralleled cousin type are reported by some communities only. Cross and parallel cousin marriages are practised by the Muslims, etc. All forms of marriage except uncle-niece marriages are reported.

Like other parts of the north-western region, Himachal Pradesh records the highest level of junior of levirate (71.85 per cent against 30.33 per cent national average), junior sororate (92.24 per cent against 58.04 per cent) as also senior levirate (8.62 per cent against 4.21 per cent). Child marriage is relatively on a small scale (2.59 per cent against 7.10 per cent). Adult marriage is extensively practised (97.41 per cent against 89.06 per cent). The Himalayan folkore refers extensively to the Gandharva form of marriage. The present data set shows that Himachal Pradesh while reporting extensively marriage by negotiation (97.41 per cent against 97.26 per cent national average) also report other forms of marriage i.e. by capture (7.76 per cent against 1.81 per cent), trial (1.72 per cent against 0.32 per cent), elopement (19.83 per cent against 13.57 per cent), and exchange (54.31 per cent against 16.70 per cent). Himachal pradesh is unique in the institution of polyandry of both fraternal (4.31 per cent against 0.60 per cent) and non-fraternal (0.86 per cent against 0.11 per cent) types and to some extent in the polygyny of sororal type (2.59 per cent against 14.67 per cent).

Both bangles (56.03 per cent against 38.06 per cent) and vermillion (51.72 per cent against 54.63 per cent) are extensively used as marriage symbols together with finger ring (9.48 per cent against 9.06 per cent), nose ring (37.93 per cent against 8.72 per cent) and nose stud/pin (58.62 per cent against 9.64 per cent).

Penetration of the Brahamanical influence, explains the high incidence of kanyadan (64.66 per cent against 38.83 per cent national average) as one of the marriage rituals. Dowry is given by some mostly in kind (59 communities) and bride price is in vogue among smaller number of communities in cash in 11 and in cash and kind in 8 communities.

Most of the communities (116) practise the rule of patrilocal residence. There is high incidence of divorce (104) in Himalayan society, again with a higher level of social approval (43). The reasons for divorce, as reported, are maladjustment (88), impotence (39), cruelty (66), insanity (84) and even sorcery (29). Either party can divorce (92). This is also at much higher level. Children are the liability of father in cases of divorce. That the situation is in favour of women will be further evident from the fact that remarriage of widow is widely (98) allowed. Other changes in marriage practices are the increase in the age (87.07 per cent against 83.26 per cent) of marriage. Lesser observance of marriage rituals is now reported. Change from bride price to dowry is also reported in 44 communities. Himachal Pradesh also reports a much larger number of extended families (81.90 per cent against 49.09 per cent national average). Most of the communities report avoidance (84.08 per cent against 70.94 per cent) and joking (96.55 per cent against 77.41 per cent) relationship at a level higher than the national average.

In matters of property relations conflicts have been increasingly reported (108). Female right to property is non-existent; only twelve communities have reported equal and property rights for women. In terms of norms of inheritence and descents property goes to all sons (103) and daughters are nowhere in the picture in matters of sharing, barring the cases where there is no son in the family.

With growing urbanisation in Himachal Pradesh the numbers of nuclear family are rising (95), but the extended families (26) also exist along side. Himachal Pradesh reports a very large measure of women's involvement in all kinds of economic and household activities such as agriculture (91), animal husbandry (97), collection of fuel (103), etc. Women maintain a high profile role in social functions (112). They are going out into politics (53). There are however no women oracles. The status of women is considered equal in a surprisingly large number of communities (56) but it is still low in most of the communities (60), though it is not as low as in other parts of the country (51.72 per cent aginst 72.19 per cent). Women substantially contribute to family income and also control expenditure in a very large number of communities.

Pre-delivery (11) and puberty (1) ritual are not observed except among a handful of communities, and is kept a secret. However, post-delivery ritual is visible. Immersion of bones in water (83) and disposal of bones in snow is reported (2).

Most communities consider land (93) a primary resource followed by forest (16). Most of the resources are controlled by individual proprietors (87). Some (8) communities collectively control the forest resources. Considering the availability of land every community has some land. In this sense landlessness is less rampant. According to our data, hunting and gathering has almost become extinct. Shifting cultivation has ceased to exist. Horticulture is developing rapidly as a major occupation (18 communities). Communities have taken extensively to terrace and settled cultivation. Terrace (30 communites) and settled cultivation (56) are major mode of subsistence followed by animal husbandry (47) and pastoralism (11), sericulture, (4) bee-keeping (7) etc.

The government is the biggest employer, government services being returned as a major occupation by a large number of 94 communities. With slow growth of economy and industry, self-employment (83) is emerging as an important area of occupation. With the boom in the construction activity, masonry (13) has emerged as a major occupation, followed by the wood work (7), jewellery making (4) stone carving (3) metal work (7) etc. Textile spinning and weaving has been both a traditional and a modern occupation. Mining has been reported in 7 communities. There has been a rise in the number of labourers both skilled (18) and unskilled (15). The communities have been linked to the market particularly daily markets (110). Barter is reported on a small scale (5.7 per cent). Child labour is extensively reported particularly in pastoral activities (58.62 per cent).

Traditional caste and tribal councils exist extensively (82.76 per cent against 61.94 per cent) where election are held by consensus (75.86 per cent) or by voice votes. They are very active, and impose fine (98.10 per cent) and hand down punishment and awards (17.24 per cent).

Most of the communities are Hindus (91). There are also Muslims (19), Sikh (8), Jain (2), Buddhist (6), and Christians (3). Hinduism, in the state has strong folk roots with the higher number of village deities (82.76 per cent against 56.33 national average) being propitiated. There is a hierarchy of village deities and regional deities and the deities of wider pantheon. The roles of sacred specialists are very substantial in performing sacred rites (98.28 per cent against 77.26 per cent), curing ailments (59.48 per cent against 20.97 per cent), divination (61.21 per cent against 7.68 per cent), exorcism (79.31 per cent against 25.22 per cent), etc. This is largely because of the perponderance of deities (82.76 per cent against 65.33 per cent)

Many communities have reported socio-religious movements largely in terms of conversion to religious cults. Folk culture of Himachal Pradesh is most vibrant with the largest number of communities (112) reporting existence of oral traditions, myths and legends, etc. A variety of musical instruments, some of historical importance, are found. However, the disturbing aspect is that while both men and women still dance (32.76 per cent), there is lesser participation of men (3.45 per cent) in folk dances. Women (19.83 per cent against 10.59 per cent) still have a larger participation in the dance. The Himalayan society has its share of commensal restrictions across commnutites, which have broken down. Though untouchability has not disappeared, there is now much higher level of exchange of food (94.83 per cent against 89.54 per cent) and of water (80.17 per cent against 78.88 per cent) among communities in Himalayan society. There is also a higher incidence of inter-communities marriage (37.93 per cent against 23.80 per cent), a larger network of putative kinship (87.93 per cent against 34.43 per cent), etc.

Among the modern linkages the rise of entrepreneurs/businessmen (89.48 per cent against 55.99 per cent), etc. among all communities is particularly significant. More and more people are going into defence services, (51.72 per cent against 28.37 per cent). A new leadership has emerged at regional level (18.97 per cent). All communities of Himachal Pradesh have felt the impact of the process of change and development, even though it has been uneven. Like in most places, education is favoured more for boys (85 communities) and less for girls (27 communities) because of the economic role of the latter. But in case of Himachal Pradesh it is much less so. Reasons for girls drop out are more social (78.45 per cent against 64.40 per cent) than economic because the girls are attached to the household in their childhood.

There is preference for family planning albeit on a scale smaller than the national average (71.55 per cent against 76.35 per cent). The preference is for three (57.76 per cent against 34.48 per cent) or four children. Use of indigenous herbs as contraceptive is preferred by some people (15.52 per cent against 7.72 per cent). The modern methods have wider acceptance (70.69 per cent against 65.09 per cent). Somehow the methods have not been too successful among the women (6.03 per cent against 37.84 per cent) as is evident from the data, which may be because of non-availablilty of facilities for the women.

There are abundant water resources, particularly in the form of springs (50.86 per cent against 10.08 per cent), streams (28.45 per cent against 11.42 per cent) and rivulets (12.93 per cent against 8.37 per cent). Various communities of Himachal Pradesh report availablilty of drinking water. Popular sources for drinking water are stepwells (39.66 per cent against 4.29 per cent), piped or tap water (79.31 per cent against 55.21 per cent), etc. Various schemes of employment have made a greater impact here than elsewhere and activities particularly in agriculture (65.52 per cent against 46.06 pr cent), animal husbandry (49.14 per cent against 27.2 per cent), knitting and weaving (10.34 per cent against 8.44 per cent) and various other modes of self employment.

Considering the hilly terrain, there is surprisingly a higher degree of the impact of electronic media than the rest of the nation: radio (100 per cent against 96.89 per cent) and TV (80.17 per cent against 49.77 per cent) coverage. There has also been considerable extension of infrastructural facilities, such as roads (91.38 against 94.65 per cent national average). Being surplus in electricity (88.79 per cent against 74.28 per cent), Himachal Pradesh shows higher rate of consumption of electricity.

Again being a wooded country, dependence is much higher on traditional fuel resources such as firewood (96.55 per cent against 92.45 per cent), dung cakes (50. 86 per cent against 54.24 per cent) and sawdust. Gas and gobar gas (7.96 per cent against 4.85 per cent) as fuel resoures have yet to make an impact. Dependence on rainwater (71.55 per cent against 55.17 per cent) is higher in agriculture. Public distribution system (97.41 per cent against 94.63 per cent) has penetrated into remote areas. The integrated child development (89.66 per cent against 50.03 per cent) scheme has also made an impact, but the benefits of the programmes are yet to percolate to all sections of the people in a systematic and effective manner, particularly for those living in remote areas.

There are indications that natural resources are being severely depleted with deforestation which has resulted in erosion of top soil and impoverishment of people, mounting pressure on women who bear the main burden of supporting family and so on. However, with its very rich resources and small populations there is no reason why Himachal Pradesh cannot set an example of sustainable development. In fact, with its rich repertory of oral traditions and its rootedness in folk culture, Himachal Pradesh can well set an example of a happy blending of modernity and tradition.

K.S. Singh

ACKNOWLEDGEMENTS

We are grateful to various contributors for their contributions, namely Prof. V. Bhalla, Department of Anthropology, Panjab University, Chandigarh, Dr. P.C. Sharma (Kullu), Dr. Gautam Sharma Vyathit, Govt. Degree College Dharamshala, Kangra, Shri O.P. Shant, (Una) and Shri R.C. Rojhe (Solan). Other than one of the editors and State Coordinator (ARS) the main contributors from Anthropological Survey of India are Shri Rajendra Sarkar, Anthropologist (C), Smt. Vatsala Sarkar Anthropologist (C) and Dr. D.K. Chakraborty, Research Associate (C); Shri T.K. Ghosh, Asstt. Keeper, contributed two whereas Shri Mukul Hazra, Research Associate (C) and Shri Anand Saran, Sr. Technical Assistant (C) contributed one community write-up each. Shri D.S. Hooda (Cartographer) of the Survey prepared maps. Many notable scholars of Himachal Pradesh did a preliminary scrutiny of the write-ups, namely Shri C.R.B. Lalit, Director, Department of Language and Culture, Dr. H.R. Jasta, Asstt. Director, Department of Education, Shri Vidya Sagar Negi, Department of Bhoti, H.P. University, Dr. Anil Rakeshi, Hindi Department H.P. University (Evening Section), Dr. O.C. Handa, Curator, State Museum, Shimla; and Dr. V.C. Thakur, Distt. Language Officer, Mandi. Three scholars, Prof. L.R. Sharma, Department of Economics, H.P. University, Shri Tobdan, Shimla, and Mian Govardhan Singh, Shimla, kindly sent their thematic essays.

In addition to most of the above contributors, many local scholars participated in the workshop/seminar of the Anthropological Survey of India held at Shimla during October 26-27, 1989, locally organized by Dr. B.R. Sharma, one of the editors and the then Secretary, H.P. Academy of Arts, Culture Languages and, Shimla. Some of these scholars were Dr.S.S. Sashi, Director Publications Division, Ministry of Information and Broadcasting, New Delhi, Dr. Shammi Sharma, Kangra, Dr. Brahm Dutt Sharma, Hamirpur, Shri Amar Singh Ranpatiya and Shri Hari Prasad Suman, Chamba, Shri H. Hira, Director, Directorate of social and women welfare, Shri K.C. Suri, Shri Ramdayal Neeraj and Shri M.R. Thakur, the then Dy. Director Deptt of Language & Culture, Shimla and Shri K. Angrup Lahuli, Panjab University, Chandigarh.

We are obliged to the Chief Secretary and all other authorities at District, Tehsil, Block and Panchayat levels, various educational, social and cultural organizations and the Census Department of Himachal Pradesh for the generous help and warm reception accorded to our investigators. We are much indebted to all the informants and above all to all people of Himachal Pradesh who shared their information with our investigators.

ACKNOWLEDGEMENTS

INTRODUCTION

Geography and Ecology

'Himachal', or the land of the snow as it is called, lies in the lap of the Himalayas. It is bounded on the north by Jammu and Kashmir, on the south-east by Uttar Pradesh, Haryana on the south, and Punjab on the west. On the east it forms India's border with Tibet. It is located between 32^0 22'40" to 33^0 12'40" north latitude and 75^0 47'55" to 79^0 04'22" east longitude. The territory is totally mountainous with an altitude in the State varying from 350 metres to 7000 metres above sea level. It covers an area of 55,673 square kilometres and accounts for nearly 1.7 per cent of the total geographical area of the country. However, it has only 0.62 per cent of its population, at the rate of 77 persons per square kilometre as against the national population density of 208 persons per square kilometre according to the 1981 Census figures.

Physiographically Himachal Pradesh can be divided into four well-marked parallel zones differing from one another in orographical, hydrographical as well as vegetational features. These zones are:

1. Outer Himalaya or the sub-Himalaya or the Shivalik range;
2. Middle or Lesser Himalaya;
3. Inner or Great Himalaya; and
4. Trans-Himalaya or Tibetan Himalaya.

Outer Himalaya: It forms a continuous chain, parallel to the principal Himalaya and forms the southern part of the State, with height ranging from 600 metres to 1,200 metres. In ancient times the Shivalik ranges were known as Mainak Parbat. The word 'Shivalik' literally means the 'hairlocks of Shiva'. These ranges are somewhat steep and have cliff-like slopes in the south whereas they have gentle slopes towards the northern valley called *dun* or *duar*. Between the Ravi and the Yamuna rivers, the Shivaliks maintain a regular and conspicuous form. As a result of high deforestation the Shivaliks have been badly eroded. This enormous erosion has given birth to numerous *cho* which are torrential and seasonal streams and can be seen in abundance in the Una district.

Middle Himalaya: Between the Greater Himalaya and Shivalik ranges are found the middle or lesser Himalaya with an elevation of 2,000 metres to 3,300 metres. The series of parallel ranges are divided by longitudinal valleys (the only exception being the Kullu valley which runs at a right angle). The Kangra valley is a longitudinal trough or depression at the foot of the Dhauladhar range.

Going from east one finds a topography consisting of low, tangled and scrub jungles covering the hills. The Beas valley is quite wide near Mandi. Beyond Mandi, Beas has cut awe-inspiring gorges in Dhauladhar at Larji and Aut. Above the sulphur springs of Vashishta the valley shows signs of glaciation.

Inner Himalaya: This is the highest range of the Himalayas and forms a single mountainous range generally distinguishable by its many peaks. These mountain ranges attain an altitude of 5,000 metres to 6,500 metres above sea level. The great Himalayan range in Himachal Pradesh is the eastern extension of the mighty Great Himalayas starting from Nanga Parbat in the west. The Pir-Panjal range also joins the Great Himalayan range near Deo Tibba in Himachal Pradesh. Between these two ranges is situated the valley of Lahaul. The range is cut across by a gorge of the Satluj river which works as a water divide between the Spiti and Beas drainage systems. The range crosses the Satluj valley near Chini and Kalpa, where Kinnar Kailash is the highest peak (6,473 metres). In the east a high-level dissected plateau is centered at Pooh. Many remnants of past glaciation in this valley are found.

Trans-Himalaya: It lies behind the Inner Himalaya with a width of approximately 40 kilometres, and at places is cut by the rivers flowing in a southernly direction with their basins at an altitude varying from 3,000 to 4,300 metres above sea level.

Vegetation types: The zonal distribution of forest vegetation from the outer foothills through the middle Himalaya to the central ranges is determined primarily by the altitude, though geology, soil and other biotic factors exert a considerable influence. The altitude determines sub-tropical, temperate and alpine vegetation from the sub-mountainous tracts to the snowy ranges. The effect of the altitude varies with relative elevation and is further modified by other factors. In general, a rise of 270 metres in the hills corresponds to a fall of one degree centigrade in the mean temperature up to about 1500 metres, above which the temperature fall is more rapid.

The upper limit of forest growth varies from 4,000 to 4,200 metres which is more dry in the western Himalaya. Beyond these altitudes trees and shrub disappear and the mountains assume a rugged, wind-swept and frost-bitten character. The rainfall steadily diminishes to almost total absence.

Drainage: Five main rivers in Himachal Pradesh, i.e. the Satluj, the Beas, the Ravi, the Chenab and the Yamuna constitute the watersheds of Himachal Pradesh. The catchment areas of all these river systems are located in the snowbound areas (which being perennial in nature) play a significant role in the life and economy of the State.

The easternmost river, Yamuna which originates at Yamunotri in the Garhwal range of the Himalayas forms the eastern boundary with Uttar Pradesh. The Satluj, the largest among the five, originates beyond the Indian borders from Mount Kailash and enters in the Indian territory at Shipki in Himachal Pradesh. The Beas which forms the Kangra and Kullu vallies, originates from the Rohtang Pass. The Ravi originates in Bara Banghal on the snow-clad Dhauladhar ranges. Alpine zone or the dry-hill zone which corresponds to high-altitude ecological zone comprises Kinnaur district, Pangi sub-tehsil of Chamba district and Lahaul-Spiti district. The monsoon rainfall is almost negligible in the region, and the area is covered with snow for most part of the year.

Climate: Situated over 1,600 kilometres away from the Bay of Bengal, and between the Greater Himalaya in the north and Punjab plains in the south, Himachal Pradesh is distinguished from the adjoining Punjab plains by colder and prolonged winters, comparatively heavier precipitation and shorter and less oppressive summers. The southern sandy foothill tracts and piedmont plain areas experience hot and sub-humid tropical climates. With the increase in altitude the climate changes from temperate to cold alpine and somewhat arctic. Based on the principle of lapse rate, the low valley bottoms and other areas lying below 600 metres (above sea level) have hot and moist tropical climates. The climate of Kangra valley, Beas valley, Shivalik areas and Kiarda valley is quite severe in summers, but the winter is pleasant. Snowfall is rare.

From the floristic point of view there are three different altitudinal zones in the western Himalayas which more or less also correspond to the ecological zones. These are (i) Sub-montane zone, up to 1,500 metres; (ii) Temperate zone, from about 1,500 metres to 3,400-3,700 metres and (iii) Alpine zone, from 3,400-3,700 meters to 4,600 metres.

Sub-montane zone or the low and middle hill soil zone corresponds to the low altitude ecological zone that comprises the Paonta valley and Nahan tehsil and lower parts of Renuka and Pachchad of Sirmaur district, Kunihar, Arki and Solan tehsils of Solan district, Balh valley and Joginder Nagar area of Mandi district, Chamba and Bhattiyat tehsils of Chamba district, and Kangra and Palampur tehsils of Kangra district, Bilaspur, Hamirpur and Una districts.

Temperate zone or the high hill and mountainous soil zone which corresponds to the middle altitude ecological zone comprises the upper areas of Pachchad of Sirmaur district, upper Shimla hills, Chachiot and Karsog tehsils of Mandi district, upper parts of Kangra and Palampur tehsils of Kangra district and upper Churah and Bharmaur of Chamba district. These areas are over 2,000 metres above sea level and experience cool temperate climate. Higher up the climate is cold temperate up to an elevation of 3,000 metres. Still further up the temperature falls down rapidly till one reaches the snowline. This tract falls in the middle or lesser Himalayan ranges of Himachal Pradesh where the climate is pleasant in summers, very cold in winters and the snowfall is heavy. Above the snowline the climate changes from arctic to polar type depending upon the altitude. This forms a part of the Chandra Bhaga and Kinnaur valleys where the climate is temperate in the summer and semi-arctic in winters. Snowfall normally begins in October and after December the whole valley is under snow till March or April. Communications remain cut off and the villages become almost isolated.

History

The history and traditions of Himachal Pradesh go back to the dawn of human civilization. No major empire was ever established in the region now occupied by Himachal Pradesh State, which was primarily because of its complex physiography, extreme climate and inaccessibility. A few small principalities were annexed by various outside rulers at times, but they failed to keep those territories for long. Many famous scholars including the German scholar Warrel have considered the Himalayas as the original home of aboriginals and Himachal Pradesh has always been an integral part of the Himalayas. On the basis of historical evidence, the historical evolution of Himachal Pradesh can be traced through the following periods.

The Pre-Aryan and Aryan Period: The history of this period is mainly based on the epics like the Vedas, Puranas and the *Mahabharata.* In the *Rig Veda,* 10 rivers are propitiated and of these four, namely Asikni (Chenab), Purushani (Ravi), Arjikiya (Beas), and Satudri (Satluj) have been flowing through the region now falling in the State of Himachal Pradesh. There is no doubt that human habitation had been established in this region long before the Aryan infiltration. Of all these non-Aryan tribes, Dasa tribe had then assumed a significant place in this area, who were later defeated by the Khasa who invaded from the north-west. Koli, Hali, Dagi, Dhangri, Khasa, Kirat and Kinner were the other tribes who occupied this territory.

When the Aryans advanced in this region the non-Aryan tribes inhabiting this region opposed their advance. All the hill chiefs fought against the Aryans, but were defeated. Consequently, they fled to the still higher and inaccessible areas, where the Aryans could not pursue them. The Trigarttas (people of the present Kangra) and Audumbaras are the most ancient tribes and find mention in the *Mahabharata* and the Puranas as well as in *Rajatarangini.* Panini mentions several Sanghas or republics by name. One of these he names Trigartta-Shastha or league of six Trigarttas, which are believed to have been spread from the Ravi to the Beas in the hills. The tribe acquired its name from their geographical location, as was usual in ancient times. The land of their habitation was known as Trigartta, meaning "the land of the three rivers" or valleys, viz., Ravi, Beas and Satluj.

Audumbara, also known as Udumbara or Odumbara, were one of the prominent peoples of ancient India and Panini classified them among the Rajanya people. Numismatic evidence confirms their place to be around present-day Pathankot. Their name finds mention along with Kuluta and Kulinda in the *Ramayana* and *Vishnu Puran*. Kuluta were close to Audumbara with Kulinda as their eastern neighbours. The territory of the Kuluta was located in the upper Beas valley, now known as the Kullu valley. Kulinda were hill people and they lived in the areas lying in between the rivers Beas, Satluj and Yamuna (Shimla and Sirmaur hills and between Ambala and Saharanpur in the plains). The Kulinda are identified with the Kanet of the present time who now form a bulk of the population of Kullu, Shimla and Sirmaur.

Col. Jenkins and Harcourt have stated that while our ancestors were unreclaimed savages, and while the empire of Rome was yet in infancy, there was a Katoch monarchy with an organised government at Kangra. King Susharma Chandra of the *Mahabharata*, who sided with the Kauravas, was the founder of this ruling dynasty. Legend says that Bhim got married to Hidimba in these hills. Another hero of the *Mahabharata*, Vidur got married to Tandi, a niece of Hidimba. Vidur had two sons from Tandi, namely, Mukhur and Bhot. Mukhur founded the kingdom of Kullut (Kullu) while Bhot is said to have founded the Bhotia kingdom on the other side of Rohtang.

The Panini literature which was written sometime between seventh century B.C. and fourth century A.D., refers to the prosperous kingdoms of Trigartta (Kangra), Kulind (Sirmaur), Kullut (Kullu), Yugandhara (Bilaspur and Nalagarh), Gabdika (Chamba) and Audumbara (Pathankot). Thus, it is clear that by the first century B.C., the present territory of Himachal Pradesh had been divided into more than 100 principalities and feudal territories. It is also gathered that the mighty rulers of Maurya, Kushan and Gupta dynasties also had a hold on these areas for short periods. Besides the kings of the major states of Kangra, Kullu, Chamba, etc., the principalities and feudatories were ruled by Thakurs, Ranas and Mawis who never united to face any outside invasion. Often they were fighting amongst themselves over petty matters. Thus, these ever-warring Thakurs and Ranas had very limited areas under them.

Early Period: The outside invaders during this period exploited the internal strifes of the petty hill chiefs and started subjugating them one by one. They integrated the adjoining feudatories to form larger kingdoms as far as possible. During the period A.D. 629 to 644, several foreign invaders also invaded some parts of Himachal Pradesh. The Kir tribe of Yarkand invaded the kingdom of Chamba killing the ruler Luxmi Verman. Similarly, Tibet invaded Lahaul-Spiti, in which it was helped by the King of Kullu. In reward he was given three villages of Spiti. In this period the administration was also of the primitive type. The lack of kings' personal interest in the State work offered opportunities to Thakurs and Ranas to declare themselves independent. This was also a golden period of culture and civilization. Since the kings and their subjects had a deep faith in religion, many temples were built in different parts of Himachal Pradesh. During this very period Padam Shambhava propogated Buddhism in Tibet. Buddhism also spread in areas of Kinnaur and Lahaul-Spiti during this period.

Medieval Period: During this period the older, larger states of Kullu, Kangra, Mandi, etc., were broken and many new small states came into being. The small states of Guler, Siba, Datarpur, Handur, Koti, Bhajji, Kumarsain, Khaneti, etc., came into existence. During this period Muslims, Mughals, British, Dutch, Portugese and French invaded many parts of India. No doubt the Sultanate kings invaded parts of Himachal Pradesh at times, but because of difficult geographic conditions they could not establish a permanent hold on any of these areas.

The relations between Mughals and these hill states commenced with Akbar who sent Todar Mal to annex Kangra. History testifies that the erstwhile ruler of Kangra, Dharam Chand, accepted the sovereignty of Akbar. Later, in A.D. 1620, during the reign of Jahangir Kangra came under Mughal rule which continued for a long time.

While this was the state of affairs in Kangra, the other hill states of Chamba, Kullu, Lahaul-Spiti and Bashahr had internal strifes among themselves as a result of which the rulership of these areas changed hands repeatedly.

During the reign of Aurangzeb, when the foundations of the Mughal Empire started rocking under the pressure of Marathas, Guru Govind Singh, the tenth Guru of Sikhs, made efforts to unite these warring hill states and fortify the strategic locations of these hills with persuasion and force. But the hill rulers withdrew their support to Guru Govind Singh and instead accepted the superiority of the Mughals.

The Mughals never intervened in the internal matters of these hill rulers. The chief political characteristic of this period was that the hill rulers continued warring among themselves as usual. The victorious rulers used to dictate terms to the defeated ones.

After the death of Aurangzeb, the Mughal empire in India was on the decline and it was at this time that Ahmad Shah Durrani and Nadir Shah Abdali dealt a serious blow to the dying empire. At this juncture, Gurkhas, Sikhs and Marathas were emerging as strong powers on the political horizon of India. Many nawabs and kings in different part of India had declared their independence. Raja Sansar Chand on becoming a ruler of Kangra in A.D. 1775 made ambitious plans of regaining control over the Kangra fort, which he did in 1786. He also annexed parts of Mandi, Suket and Chamba, and made plans to annex parts of Punjab which was then ruled by Maharaja Ranjit Singh who made his efforts futile. Facing failure on this front, he annexed parts of Kahloor. By this act many hill chiefs and the ruler of Kahloor invited Gurkhas who were emerging as a new power in the second half of the eighteenth century. The Gurkhas conquered almost the whole of the western Himalayas by A.D. 1805.

People, however, soon got tired of the harsh and tyrannical rule of the Gurkhas. They united themselves and took a stand against them. Raja Sansar Chand fought severely with the Gurkhas from inside the Kangra fort for about four years, during which the economy of Kangra was badly shattered. He prayed to Maharaja Ranjit Singh for help. They jointly drove the Gurkhas beyond Satluj. For the help he gave, Maharaja Ranjit Singh, was handed over 66 villages of Kangra. The English, who with their victory in the battle of Plassey, paved the way for the British control of India, compelled the Gurkhas to leave the country.

British Period: After getting hold of the Kangra fort, Maharaja Ranjit Singh proceeded to conquer other hill states and annexed many of the Himachal principalities. In 1842, with the annexation of Ladakh by the Sikh General Zorawar Singh, the territory of Lahaul-Spiti became a Sikh possession. After the Anglo-Sikh War of 1845, the British took over the territories of Lahaul-Spiti and in accordance with the Lahore Treaty, Raja Gulab Singh was recognized as an independent ruler, both by the Sikhs and the Britishers. The entire hilly area lying between the Satluj and Yamuna rivers with the exception of Kullu and Mandi was awarded to him for his services rendered to the Britishers during the Anglo-Sikh War. In 1848 all the rulers of this area, tried to liberate their territories with the help of Sikhs, but were defeated and the rebel rulers were killed.

This caused great resentment among the chiefs. In 1857, they revolted along with some other princes, one of whom was Raja Samsher Singh of Bashahr. By the mid-nineteenth century, parts of Kangra, Kullu, Lahaul, Spiti, Kotgarh, Kotkhai, etc., had come directly under the British empire while other hill states were allowed to be retained under their native rulers. However, British Political Agents, Superintendents and Residents were stationed in these states for overall supervision. In fact the Britishers were the *de facto* rulers, whereas the native rulers had only *de jure* reins in their hands. But history bears testimony that with the passage of time these hill people also rose in arms against slavery and feudalism.

During the First World War some youths in the hills took part in Ghadr

Party, which advocated direct military and violent action against the British to throw them out of India. In 1939 at a session of All India State People's Conference held at Ludhiana, it was decided to form Praja Mandals in the hill states to devote special attention to these areas. This was set up with the efforts of people like Bhag Mal Sautha of Jubbal and Y.S. Parmar of Sirmaur, with its headquarters at Shimla. The leaders of the Praja Mandals were oppressed and their properties attached, but this did not effect the determination of the Mandals, who ultimately succeeded in throwing off the yoke of slavery.

While India became independent, the native Indian states remained under the yoke of feudalism, in spite of the appeal of national leaders for the merger of Punjab states and Punjab hill states. It was later on 26 January 1948, at a meeting held under the aegis of All India State People's Conference at Shimla, that a unanimous decision was taken urging the national leadership to merge all hill states to form one state. To attain this goal the Himalayan Prant Provincial Government was also formed. On 16 February 1948 a 48 hour ultimatum was given to Suket to merge with the Indian territory, but finding no response to the ultimatum, the Satyagrahis launched a 'dharna' and liberated Suket from feudalism on 18 February 1948. Subsequently, certain hill states were merged in 1948 and 1950. In 1954, Bilaspur, which was previously left out and kept under separate rule was merged with Himachal Pradesh. In order to carve out a greater Himachal, on 1 November 1966, Kangra, Kullu, Lahaul and Spiti and Shimla district of Punjab were integrated with it. Full statehood was granted to Himachal Pradesh on 25 January 1971 when it emerged as the eighteenth full-fledged state of the Indian Union.

Cultural Elements, Festivals and Festivities

It is believed that when the inhabitants of the Indus valley spread through the Saraswati and the Gangetic plains, they pushed back the Munda-speaking Kolarian people who used to inhabit this part earlier, but were forced to migrate to forests and valleys of the Himalayas. They lived in groups and had their own language and beliefs. During the Rig Vedic period, these people were called Dasa, Dasyu, Nishad, etc. Literary sources also refer to Kinnar, Nag and Yaksha who migrated to the hills of Himachal Pradesh during the post-Vedic period. The Kols are considered to be the original inhabitants of the area and possibly the Koli, Hali, Dum, Chanal of the western Himalayas and the Chamar and Damang of Kinnaur, Lahaul-Spiti are the remnants of the race.

The second and perhaps the most important element in the population of Himachal Pradesh is the Khasha, who penetrated from the north-west and settled in the mid-mountain belt. With the passage of time and alien influences, they split into numerous sub-sections. Kanet is one such important section, the other branches are Ghirath, Rathi, etc.

Rajputs and Brahmans entered Himachal Pradesh from the Indian plains from time to time for one reason or the other—either for adventure or in search of security. The other important reason of their migration was the location of the holy places in and around Himachal. Within the caste system, a process of upward mobility has been known to have occurred in the country. During periods of emergency, there were recruitments to the army, and people of lower castes who joined started calling themselves Kshatriya. It was the Brahman who dug out a lost genealogy for a wealthy and powerful patron, proclaimed him—and his lineage—as belonging to it, and invested him with the symbol of the high caste status and lineage. Some of the communities migrated to the hills during the Muslim invasion of north India between the twelfth and the sixteenth century.

The Mongolian-featured people who settled in the Himachal hills are mentioned as Bhot, and are akin to the people of western Tibet. It is believed that Lang-darma (836-42) in Tibet sent many Buddhist monks away from Tibet. A few of them took refuge in the border areas of Spiti and Kinnaur and were instrumental in strengthening the base of religion there. Their characteristic features include Tibeto-Burmese language and Lamaistic Buddhism.

Himachal Pradesh is one of the few states in India where Buddhism is followed by a sizeable number of the population (1.23 per cent of the total population of the state according to the 1981 Census). In Himachal Pradesh a majority of the population of Buddhists (82.85 per cent) is concentrated in the districts of Lahaul-Spiti (18,818) and Kinnaur (14,426), which accounts for 58.62 and 24.23 per cent respectively, of the Buddhist population of the state. These two districts are situated in between the Middle Himalayan and the Greater Himalayan ranges.

Looking at the distribution pattern of the communities, it can safely be inferred that the cultural regions overlap the geographical regions. The higher altitudes, which also border the international boundaries, are the home of the bulk of tribal populations. Those tribals which live near the international borders are Buddhists by faith—a faith which is practised in the adjoining area. Such tribals of the higher altitude who do not live near international borders are Hindus.

The middle altitude zone is the abode of the bulk of the indigenous Himachali population, whereas the lower altitude zone is inhabited by a mixed population of different faiths like Hindu, Muslim, Sikh, Christian and Jain because of their proximity with the plains of Punjab, Haryana and Uttar Pradesh, with whom they also share many cultural traits. In the upper reaches of Himachal Pradesh particularly in the districts of Lahaul-Spiti and Kinnaur, Buddhism is practised. This Buddhism combines the yellow and the red sects.

An account of Himachal's life will be incomplete without a mention of its fairs and festivals which serve the need of social cooperation not only for economic subsistence but also for cultural survival. The important festivals are Navratras, Baisakhi, Haryali, Rakhi, Cherwal, Pathom, Dussehra, Diwali, Lohri and Shivratri. Every fair and festival has a legendary origin which is the governing factor in each of these gatherings. The important fairs are Bhunda, Zat, Thodda, Sair, Minjar, Naina Devi, Kullu Dussehra, Lavi, Renuka, Shivratri, Manimahesh Jatra, Nalwari, etc.

Language and Dialect

Nearly 90 per cent of the people of Himachal Pradesh speak western Pahari dialects, popularly known as Pahari. It is an Indo-Aryan language which is more akin to Sanskrit and Hindi than Punjabi. In its forms of speech Pahari shows many variations in dialects in different areas separated from each other by mountainous ranges. A classified list of the various 32 languages/dialects spoken in Himachal Pradesh is as follows :

I. Indo-Aryan Family

A. Pahari/Himachali Group:

1. Bharmauri/Gadiali
2. Bilaspuri/Kehluri
3. Bushairi/Bushehri
4. Chambiali/Chameali
5. Gujjari
6. Hinduri
7. Kangri
8. Khaskura
9. Kulvi
10. Mandiali
11. Pahari/Himachali
12. Pangwali
13. Saraji/Siraji
14. Sirmauri

B. Other Indo-Aryan:

1. Banjari
2. Haryanvi
3. Hindi
4. Nepali/Gorkhali
5. Punjabi
6. Rajasthani
7. Urdu

II. Tibeto-Burman Family

1. Bhotia/Bhoti
2. Kanasi
3. Khampa
4. Kinnauri
5. Ladakhi
6. Lahauli
7. Manchat

III. Foreign Languages:

1. Khaka (Chinese)
2. Persian

IV. Unclassified Languages:

1. Chanali/Chenali
2. Sansi

The languages spoken in Lahaul, Spiti and Kinnaur and in the different valleys of these districts are different and are influenced by the Tibetan language. The dialects of these districts include Kinnauri (Kanaury Anuskad), Manchat and Bunan, among others.

Pahari in the old days was written in the Tankari or Thakuri script. The princely states kept records in the language. The Banias and other trading communities also kept their accounts in the Tankari script. Bhatakshri was also an earlier form of Tankri in Shimla and Sirmaur areas. But nowadays Pahari is frequently written in Devanagari script.

Demography and Census

According to the Presidential Orders of 1950, 1951 and 1956 and Section 28 (2) of the Central Act 31 of 1966, the Kinnaura, the Bhot or Bodh, the Swangla, the Gujjar, the Gaddi, the Pangwal, the Lahaula and the Jad Lamba and Khampa were declared scheduled tribes of Himachal Pradesh. Amongst these, the two most dominant ones are Gujjars and Gaddis, both of whom are pastoral tribes. The Gujjars are of Hindu and Islamic faith, where each of these two faiths follow their own religion, customs and beliefs, whereas the Gaddis are Hindus. A bulk of the Muslim Gujjars still continue to be pastoral while their Hindu brethren have opted for a settled life. Chamba, Lahaul-Spiti and Kinnaur are the major tribal districts of the state and contain the bulk of the tribal population. Besides, there are 56 scheduled castes mentioned in the state list which constitute a considerable portion of the state population. The majority of the population of Himachal Pradesh according to the 1981 Census is of Hindus (95.77 per cent), but Buddhists (1.23 per cent), Jains (0.02 per cent), Sikhs (1.22 per cent), Muslims (1.63 per cent) and Christians (0.09 per cent) also have a respectable place in the state.

In order to assist the Backward Classes Commission, the Census of India, gave an estimate of the population of each caste in 1951. There were 30 castes specified as scheduled castes in the Presidential Order of 1951, which subsequently went up to 56. This is primarily because of transfer of additional territory to Himachal from the erstwhile Punjab. Besides these, there were 112 other Hindu castes and 69 Muslim castes. Due to fusion and fission of castes, over a period of three decades, certain castes have merged, and so have a few communities. This has resulted in the lowering of the number of communities to 124 today, which have been studied for this project, *People of India*.

Religion and Sects

In areas where the terrain is rugged and climate inhospitable, agriculture becomes an unprofitable proposition and hence there is a great faith in the Almighty. The Himachalis are very god-fearing and it is their deep faith in the Hindu god that has given the name of Shiv Bhumi or Dev Bhumi to this territory.

Hinduism

Hinduism in various forms, and in some cases influenced by Buddhism, was predominant in Himachal territory since the early centuries of the Christian era, and persists even today more or less in its ancient form. The aspects of nature and the manifestations of physical force are manifold and have been allotted to a multitude of gods which are worshipped in each village of Himachal Pradesh. The reverence of the Brahman, strict adherence to caste rules, meticulous observance of personal purity and abstension from ceremonial pollution, were the moral features of this religion.

Himachalis are great worshippers of the great Hindu trinity—Brahma, Vishnu and Mahesh. It is observed that 'whoever abstains from meat is an esteemed Vaishnav without regard to the doctrine'. The Shaiva may worship Vishnu, and the Vaishnav Shiva, but the Vaishnav will not take meat while a Shaiva may take to meat and drink.

Shiva has 100 names, but the commonest of them all is Mahadev, Rudra or Shambhu. He is worshipped extensively by all the inhabitants and especially by people of the lower social order. The cult of Mahadev is another form of Shiva worship. Mahadev is the originator of many castes, generally of the lower grades, while Brahma is the progenitor of higher castes. In Himachal Pradesh Shiva is worshipped not only under that name, but two cults—those of Shirgul and Mahasu—are believed to be derivatives of Shaivism.

Closely connected with the worship of Shiva, and far more widely spread, is the worship of his consort, Devi. This goddess is called by many names. Durga, Kali, Gauri, Asuri, Parbati, Kalka, Mahesari and Bhavan Astbhuji are a few common names for Devi. The humbler divinities, Sitala (the goddess of small-pox), Masani and other goddesses of disease, are manifestations of Mahadevi, the greatest goddess. She is known by the places of her temples as Jawalaji, Mansa Devi, Chintpurni, Naina Devi and the like. The Himachalis celebrate all the days which are most holy to Devi, that is, the first nine days of waxing moon in the months of *Chaitra* (March-April) and *Asauj* (September-October). The *asthami* that follow in these months are considered holy and these immediately follow the annual *shradha* or commemoration of the dead. On these occasions the Devi is personified as a girl under ten years of age and offerings are made to her as if to the goddess.

The worship of Devi assumes the most diverse forms in the hills and it is common to find a Nag and Devi temple side by side as similar attributes are ascribed to both.

Next to the Shiva and Devi worship, the cult of Nag worship is most prevalent in Himachal. This seems to be the cult of common man's interest without any philosophical foundations. It is the faith in healing power of the Nag or their ability to cure disease and avoid harm that makes the cult so popular. Guga worship is another form of Nag cult and is associated with the Nag worship and has become especially popular as an effective cure for snake bites. All over the hills Jogis and Naths consider Guga as their foremost deity and sing ballads of his exploits. Guga ballads are also present in Rajasthan, Punjab, Haryana and parts of Uttar Pradesh. Wooden and stone images of Guga are very common in Kangra and Bilaspur districts.

The other popular deities are Ganesh, Hanuman and Bhairon. Ganesh is the 'obviator of difficulties and impediments'. He is the first god to be worshipped in holy rites. The worship of Hanuman or Mahabali is closely connected with that of Lord Rama, and is worshipped by all castes. Along with gods themselves, there are several demi-gods and *rishis* (saints) to whom special reverence is paid.

Buddhism

Buddhism has also left its impact on the populations of Himachal Pradesh. Only the people of Lahaul, Spiti and parts of Kinnaur profess Buddhism. It is believed that Buddhism entered Lahaul in the eighth century A.D.

Nearly every pious Buddhist has his own prayer wheel, which he twists round as he engages in conversation, and in all the monasteries are large vat-like cylinders that revolve on an iron axis. Often a stretch of land is enclosed or marked with loose stones, on which are inscribed the mystical *Om mani padmehum* or *Om shloka* (verses) in the Tibetan character. They are deposited as offerings by those who want to have some particular desire granted, or as thankful offerings for answers to one's expectations. In addition to the above, the *chorten* and *dungston* are also worth noting and are frequently found just outside the monasteries or large villages. The *chorten* dedicated to the holy Buddha is very similar in form to the *dungston*, which is a relic built in the honour of Buddhist saints.

Buddhism in its purer form exists in Spiti more than in Lahaul or Kinnaur. The head of this religion here is called head Gelong or the Avtari Lama under whom are five other Gelong; all the other priests being Lama or Chela. But in other areas it exists with the admixture of Hinduism. Though no human sacrifice now exists yet goats and sheep are offered to trees when water courses are opened in the spring, or during festivals at the start of the harvesting season. Buddhism which does not tolerate shedding of blood has never been able to entirely drive out this system of worship. This is contrary to the spirit of Buddhism. Hinduism and Buddhism are known to have certain points in common, and Buddha is said to have been the ninth incarnation of Lord Vishnu. The Lamas are the priests of Buddhists. The Buddhism which dominates Himachal belongs to the mixed sect of yellow and red caps.

The other religious segments of the Himachali culture are the Sikhs, Jains, Muslims and Christians. They live mostly in the areas adjoining the plains of Punjab, Haryana and Uttar Pradesh. The communities practising these faiths are not indigenous to the state but have settled here after the opening of the region and carving of the state and its reorganization. Only Christianity has been able to make its impact on some local people mainly residing in the Shimla and Sirmaur districts, who have taken to Christianity.

Economic Trends and Development Process

It should be noted that before the planning process started, 69.4 per cent of the net domestic product of Himachal Pradesh originated from agriculture, while industry and services (the non-agricultural sectors) accounted for the remaining 30.6 per cent. During the three decades (1950-51 to 1982-83), the structure of production underwent a change, with the share of the agriculture sector falling to less than half of the total (43.4 per cent) in 1982-83, while more than half (56.6 per cent) was accounted for by the non-agricultural sectors. Besides, the change in the production structure, another macro-economic shift which is usually associated with the rise in per capita income is the trend towards urbanisation It can be seen from the census data on distribution of population between rural and urban areas of Himachal Pradesh, that in 1951 the state was highly rural with only 4.1 per cent of the population then living in the urban areas. Even 30 years later in 1981, the urban population rose only to 7.6 per cent, which means that the state continues to be predominantly based on rural economy.

As is clear from the preceding paragraph, there has been a relative decline in the agriculture sector. The nature and extent of some of these changes are reflected in the change in the cropping pattern of the area, but if one looks at only the broad categories of land under cereal and non-cereal crops, the cropping pattern remains unchanged. A change is only discernible when one probes deeper and finds that the share of area devoted to wheat has risen from under one-third (in 1950-51) to nearly two-fifth (in 1982-83) of the total area sown. This is due to the adoption of new farm technology, with the other two main crops, i.e., maize and rice maintaining their share in the cropping pattern. Within the non-cereal (horticulture) category, there has been an increase in the share of area under fruits of all kinds, which increased substantially from 1 to 3 per cent during the three decade period from 1950-51 to 1981-82.

The predominance of cereals and pulses in the cropping pattern of Himachal Pradesh has only marginally fallen from 94.3 to 90.7 per cent from 1950-51 to 1981-82. It is interesting to note in this context that in 1950-51, the six important individual crops of the state were wheat, maize, rice, barley, potatoes and gram, which together accounted for 81.1 per cent of the total area sown.

It is also to be noted that Himachal Pradesh has a large potential for the production of temperate, sub-tropical and dry fruits, due to its peculiar geographical features. Consequently, the area as well as the fruit crops have registered much higher growth rates as compared to other food crops.

Besides the analysis of cropping pattern, an analysis of the seed-fertilizer-irrigation package is of great significance.

Available information relating to the growth of farm inputs in the state indicates an uneven growth of farm inputs over the years, with the gross area irrigated having recorded the slowest growth. There has, in fact, been hardly any growth in gross area irrigated in the two sub-periods. In 1977-78, only 16 per cent of the net area sown was under irrigation, which was the lowest figures amongst any of the states of India. The slow growth of this input would remain a constraining factor in agricultural development of the state. It is here that the paradox of scarcity amidst plenty finds illustration in the state. There is no dearth of water in the five rivers and numerous streams of the state. This water indeed irrigates the parched fields of Punjab, Haryana and even Rajasthan, yet it cannot be utilized in the area where it originated because of the problems of topography and terrain.

The estimates of the quantity of fertilizers used in the pre-1966 period is not very significant when compared to the later years. But it is clear that after 1966 the use of fertilizers has grown rapidly and between 1966-67 and 1982-83 the increase has been as much as eightfold. Still the state lags behind many other states. In 1981-82 the per hectare consumption of fertilizers in Himachal Pradesh was only 19.5 kg., as against the national average of 34.6 kg. The constraining factor obviously has been the lack of the complementary input, irrigation.

The information regarding the third component of the modern package, viz., high yielding varieties (HYV) of seeds is available only for relatively recent period. Between 1975-76 and 1982-83, however, the area under this input rose by nearly 36 per cent.

Thus, from the foregoing it is evident that while the area under irrigation has remained virtually stagnant, the use of other two inputs has increased impressively. Further, within the national perspective, Himachal Pradesh does not seem to have done badly in the matter of productivity growth in agricultural sector. As against the all-India average yield of foodgrains of 1.03 tonnes per hectare in 1981-82, the average yield in Himachal Pradesh was 1.24 tonnes, and only five other states have a higher yield.

Two broad changes have been witnessed in the production structure of the agricultural sector—which is the dominant segment of the economy—viz., first, a rise in the share of wheat and fruit crops in the total area sown and second, growth of the area under two modern farm inputs—HYV seeds and chemical fertilizers. But the impact of these has been more evident in the lower altitude areas than in the middle and higher altitude areas.

As Himachal Pradesh was formed by the merger of feudal principalities, it is obvious that a primitive economic system, with a woefully inadequate infrastructural and institutional framework existed during the time. So, for the purpose of ascertaining change, 1948 has been taken as a cut-off year, as this is the year when Himachal was formed.

According to the first census of the state in 1951, 7.5 per cent of males and 2 per cent of females in the state were literate, with the overall literacy percentage working out to 4.8 per cent, which was at that time lowest in India. There was in existence only one school per 70 square kilometres of area and per 2,700 people.

However, with the merger of the state and the impact of planned development, the picture of the state is completely changed today. With the lowest rate of literacy in 1951, it went up to 42.5 per cent in 1961-71 which was primarily because of the merger of the areas from the erstwhile Punjab, where the literacy rate was already high. The attitude of the Himachali people is in general favourable towards the education of boys, some of whom are sent for higher studies outside the state, whereas others study up to secondary or college level and then drop out, usually for economic reasons. Their attitude towards girls' education on the contrary is only partly favourable and in general they are not allowed to study beyond the secondary level for social reasons and for want of schooling facilities in the area. Furthermore, female education has remained more neglected in some districts of the state than in others. According to the 1981 Census, in 4 out of 12 districts, the literacy percentage among females was even less than 20.

In the sphere of medical and health facilities, the state was poor in medical institutions and medical practitioners. Between 1950-51 and 1982-83 the number of hospitals and dispensaries per 10,000 of population has more than doubled and the number of doctors and *vaids* has nearly quadrupled and the number of hospital beds nearly trebled. The attitude of the people towards modern medicine is favourable but they make use of both the traditional, modern and indigenous systems of medicare. The attitude towards family welfare schemes has been well accepted by the younger generation, who restrict their family to three to four children by using modern methods of contraception, or sterilization by either of the sexes.

Drinking water is available to the majority within the locality. In the high altitude areas natural springs and streams are the source of drinking water, whereas in the lower altitude areas piped water and step-wells and, only very recently, deep-bore hand pumps provide drinkng water.

In the sphere of employment programmes, Rural Employment Programme and Rural Employment Guarantee Scheme have been well accepted by the people of the state. Antyodaya scheme became popular and Jawahar Rozgar Yojna has been introduced recently. The people are generally employed in agriculture which is subsisted by animal husbandry. A few of them have also taken up jobs in government and other departments.

There has been much improvement in the infrastructural facilities, especially the roads. The interior areas, however, are not connected by metalled roads. This is partially because of the high cost and physical constraints in the construction of roads in the high hills. Though television facilities are not available in the interior areas yet video parlours have mushroomed all over the state. The people in the urban areas and those near the urban locales have access to all modes of recreation and communicational facilities but information and other recreational facilities available in the higher altitudes are primarily through radio sets and extension agencies. Electricity is available almost to all of the villages through hydroelectric sub-stations in the state.

A majority of the communities still continue to use firewood and cowdung cakes as fuel resources. Exception to this are those living near townships, who have access to liquified petroleum gas.

Though the majority of the people depend on agriculture, irrigational facilities are not available in many of the areas and people have to depend on rainwater. However, in the lower altitude areas bordering Punjab, Haryana and Uttar Pradesh, irrigation is available through *kuhl* (canal), tube-wells and lift irrigation. Consequently, this has also resulted in the low use of chemical fertilizers in the water scarcity areas.

A sizeable population avail themselves of the mid-day meal scheme for the children, and the Integrated Child Development Scheme facilities are availed all over the state. The facility of ration at subsidized rates in the tribal areas and its availability elsewhere has greatly helped the people.

Banking and investment facilities are important catalysts of economic growth. With merely four bank branches in 1951 the number of banks increased to 36 in 1965. This accounted for about two bank branches per lakh of population which in view of the widely dispersed population of hills was still very inadequate. The increase from 36 to 76 branches by 1965-67 was primarily because of enlarged territory of state due to the reorganization of the states. During the eight year period 1976 to 1984 bank branches increased by 85 per cent. This testifies to the fact that people have now a favourable attitude towards savings.

Thus it can be inferred that infrastructural facilities have contributed in some cases, directly or indirectly, to the promotion of social welfare.

Political Systems, Elections and Movements

Before the formation of Himachal Pradesh, the former princely states had a different system of administration and different sets of laws. These laws were primitive and were a hurdle in the way of general progress. With the exception of a few large states, administration was run on the whims and fancies of the rulers or their *wazir*, whose word was considered law. In such states the whole administration used to be in the hands of only one or two persons.

In March 1948, 30 odd princes of Shimla and Punjab hills met in Delhi and signed on a document and surrendered their century-old *raj*. Thus Himachal in the form of a unit came into existence on 15 April 1948. The territory was headed by a Chief Commissioner who was assisted by an advisory council.

The Government of India enacted the Government of Part 'C' States Act in 1951 which received the ascent of the President of India. This Act laid guidelines for constituting an elected assembly and the formation of a Council of Ministers, and to replace Chief Commissioner, by a Governor. Both the Governor and the Council of Ministers were under the overall control of the President of india.

The year 1956 marked a change in the history of the administration of Himachal Pradesh. After the promulgation of the States Reorganization Act of 1956, the State of Himachal became an Union Territory with effect from 1 November 1956; and Raja Bajrang Bahadur Singh of Bhadri assumed the charge of Lt. Governor from this date. The first general election to the Himachal Pradesh Vidhan Sabha was held in 1952 with Dr. Yashwant Singh Parmar being elected the first Chief Minister of the state.

Establishment of Panchayati Raj on a proper footing was started during the regime for the first popular ministry in 1963. Some 600 Gram Panchayats and an equal number of Nyaya Panchayats were later formed. The number of Gram Panchayats then rose to about 1,900 while the number of Nyaya Panchayats remained the same. The prolonged and peaceful struggle of Himachal leadership bore another fruit when it succeeded in getting Himachal Pradesh declared as the first full-fledged state of the Indian Union, on 25 January 1971.

Himachal is one of the classic examples of rapid transformation from the worst forms of feudalism to democracy, from a tiny hill area to a state bigger in size than Punjab, Haryana and Kerala.

As mentioned earlier, during the First World War some youths from these hills took part in the Ghadr Party, which had aimed at direct military and violent action against the British to throw them out of India. In 1939 the session of All India State People's Conference was held at Ludhiana in which it was decided to form Praja Mandals in the hill states and to devote special attention towards these areas. As a result of this, a general awakening grew among the highlanders. Praja Mandals were formed openly in these states and this led to a panic among the kings and the fedual lords and they started repression against the activists of the Praja Mandals. To coordinate the activities of different Praja Mandals working in different states, Himalayan Hill State Regional Council was formed, and this worked jointly in liberating these hill states from the yoke of feudalism.

Social Organisation

The people of Himachal Pradesh are colourful, humorous, lighthearted, simple, with very delicate and well-formed features. Except for a few towns, there is hardly any urban life in the hills. Even after 30 years of the formation of state, according to the 1981 Census figures, the urban population has risen to only 7.6 per cent from 4.1 per cent in 1951, which means that the state continues to be predominantly rural based.

Customs are the real mirror of the consciousness of the community and the expression of its character. The main feature of the Himachali customs is their continuity.

The child is named either by the parents or sometimes by the priest within the first year of birth as per the prevailing custom of the community. Among the Koli and some other communities, a child is named after the day or month he is born, e.g., Somu, Manglu, Budhu, Chaitu, Jethu, Baisakhi, etc. The people of the upper class have compound names. The suffixes communities use are Ram, Lal, Das, Chand whereas, Rajputs use the term Singh. In order to distinguish the family names from one another, some people use community names and family names, like Thakur, Verma, Sharma, etc. The people of Kinnaur use the suffix Negi with their names. The Rajputs who migrated from the plains use *gotra* names like Rathor, Chauhan, Parmar, Tomar, etc.

Earlier marriages in Himachal Pradesh were usually performed in childhood but nowadays marriages are performed on attaining adulthood. The most common form of acquiring a mate is by negotiation and is called *byah*. The other common forms are *batta-satta* (marriage by exchange), marriage by capture, elopement, etc. Payment of bride-price was an essential feature of Himachali matrimony but with the passage of the time, due to growth of literacy and a wider world view, this has given way to dowry which is mostly in kind. Among the Muslims, marriage is performed by *nikah* in consideration of *mehar* which is either a fixed Rs. 32.25 amount (silver coins) or at times is negotiable. The residence after marriage is patrilocal but soon the couple separate to set up their own house. Divorce is permissible in most of the indigenous communities primarily on account of maladjustment, cruelty, adultery, impotency, etc., by social approval. Though monogamy is the general rule, the practice of fraternal polyandry prevailed and still continues in a few communities in the border areas, the trans-Giri tract and in the outer Seraj area of the Kullu district.

A usual practice in Himachal Pradesh is keeping a common wife between two or three brothers; the division of conjugal rights is made through private, mutual understanding. This system is now on the decline and on the verge of disappearance. Widow and divorcee marriage is permissible for there is a belief in the higher hills that a woman is never a widow. Among the low communities a widow is free to marry in or out of her husband's family. A Himachali woman is sociable and carries the reputation of family and society with dignity. She is an indispensable part of the economy. These qualities have given her a status of the better half in reality, and she commands a place of honour and dignity in the Himachali society.

The happiness and well-being of a community lies in the preservation of its indigenous cultural traditions. The people of Himachal Pradesh have reasons to be proud of their rich cultural traditions which they have preserved for ages despite the inroad of alien influences. Singing and dancing are a mode of expression of joy, be it a social occasion or otherwise. The important dances of the Himachal are *Munjra, Naati, Gidda, Burah, Kayang, Bakayang, Chham, Birsu, Ghunghti, Chandrauli*, etc. These dances and songs are not community-specific but are common to a region. Songs are sung at all social, festive and religious occasions. Devotional songs sung in the honour of Shiva are called *Ainchli*, whereas other forms are *Bhet* or *Bharta*. These songs sung to the accompaniment of cymbals and drums, trace their origin to the rich folk traditions. Their themes are love, chivalry, village gossip, sacrifices, prayers and seasons. Most of the songs are based on love themes which surpass the community barriers. The important folksongs of Himachal are *Suhi, Chhinj, Chanjhoti, Laman, Jhuri, Naati, Har,* etc.

Folkdances are an important medium of entertainment and are performed during the leisure time of the Himachal people, especially during winter months. The most popular type of the hill folkdrama are *Kariyala, Banthara, Jhanki, Swang, Haranater* and *Bhagat.*

Himachal has been the cradle of several arts and crafts. It has the distinction of being the originator of the Pahari styles of paintings. The important craft forms are the Chamba *rumals*, Chamba *chappals*, basketry, etc. Himachalis are good weavers, and they weave *patoi, gardu, kamli, thdoi,* Kullu *topi* and shawls, etc.

Ballads are also fairly common in Himachal Pradesh, and their charm lies in the story they tell. These are mythological and historical. The most popular ballads are *Bharatrihari, Guga, Asa Hinduan, Hari Hinduan, Sadhrata, Ramayan, Puran Bhagat, Pandrayan, Jhere* (heroic ballads), etc.

As the bulk of the community still lives in the rural setting, inter-community linkages are more rigidly adhered to here in comparison to the urban setting. In matters of commensality and acceptance of food, the hierarchy among the communities is quite visible and is formed more on the basis of concept of ritual purity and pollution than on anything else. *Kachha* food which comprises boiled food preparation can only be accepted from one's own communities and communities ritually superior to one's own, whereas *pucca* (cooked/fried) food can be accepted from other clean and artisan communities. But a middle order community accepts *pucca* food from an *asavarna* community provided it is cooked at a separate place either by a Rajput or a Brahman. Though the people of scheduled caste community accept all types of food from the non-scheduled caste people, the latter would only accept *sukka* (raw grains) food from them. The people of the *savarna* and *asavarna* communities may or may not share water sources, cremation grounds, religious shrines and so on but the old commensal restrictions are breaking down.

It is a custom in the hills for men to exchange turbans or caps and for women to exchange goods or handkerchiefs which they tie round the head. This exchange of head dress makes them brothers or sisters. To tie *kangna,* a thread on the wrist is another type of ceremonial bond especially in the lower hills. The relationship thus established is regarded as good as a blood tie. Such putative bonds are a common feature at the time of marriage.

As the life in the hills is tough, activity is generally not possible without mutual cooperation in the various fields, and as such people have symbiotic relationships. The specialized services of certain artisan communities make their role important in different spheres of their social and economic life for other communities with whom these communities have *jajmani* (patron-client) relations.

The traditional caste rigidity in the rural settings has loosened in the urban locales primarily on account of urbanization, education, etc., and due to the development of a wider world view.

A.R. Sankhyan

ABDAL

The Abdal, also pronounced as Badal, is a small Muslim community. In Persian the term Abdal means 'lieutenant' or chief. Rose (1919) refers to the Abdals as the wandering Muslim saints who occupy the fifth place in the Sufi hierarchical order issuing from the Great Qutb. The community traditionally comprises the singers who play on *sarangi* (a string musical instrument) and sing *bar* or *birlap* (mourning songs) while putting on the clothes of a Raja killed in a battlefield and precede the funeral procession of their masters. They used to seek alms for this act from the royal kinsmen and were also known as Darbesh. The community chiefly inhabit the districts of Bilaspur, Mandi, Sirmur, Kangra and Chamba, but their exact population is not known. The Bilaspur district (study area) is located in a hilly terrain of the Himalayan foothills amidst seven hill ranges called *dhar* and is drained by seven major streams or the tributaries of the river Satluj. The hill ranges are covered with thin forests of pine trees and are infested with wildlife. The climate of the area is warm and temperate with seasonal moderate rainfall and low humidity. The community is known by this name at the regional level. They speak a local dialect Bilaspuri (or Kehluri) of the western Pahari language and communicate in Devanagari script. Their religious communications are in Urdu language written in Perso-Arabic script. Traditionally, they used to wear a *churidar pyjama* and a *kurta*. Men wear a cap, traditionally a *safa* (turban). Women do not wear *burka* (veil). Traditional ornaments of women are silver *choora* (wristlet), *mahel* (bracelet), conical *chak* (scalp ornament) and a *murki* (coiled nose ring).

The Abdals are non-vegetarian in food habits and eat fish, eggs and halal meat but not beef. The staple food is wheat, rice and maize along with various pulses like gram, *urad, moong* and beans alongwith potatoes and vegetables cooked in mustard oil or vegetable *ghee.* Some men occasionally consume country liquor purchased from the local market and also smoke tobacco. Milk and milk products are consumed frequently but fruit intake is occasional and mainly seasonal consisting of apples, guava, peach, bananas and mangoes.

The Abdal community in Bilaspur is segmented into small exogamous *got* (clans) like Qureshi, Saketru, Mirane, Tadialu, etc. According to Rose (1919), they have twelve *toli* (sects) in Kangra. But hierarchical stratification is lacking. In the regional Muslim social hierarchy they are treated at par with the Faqirs, Mirasis and Bharais, but below the Raeens, the Sunhaks (the Chandel Muslims) and the Pathans. The community is generally endogamous but sometimes marriages do take place between this community and the Mirasis and the Bharais. Village, Mohalla and clan exogamy is practised. Marriages occur in adulthood and through negotiation. Exchange marriages as noticed among the Faqirs, do not generally occur. A golden *tili* (nosepin) is regarded as the marriage symbol along with glass bangles. The bride lives patrilocally. Monogamy is the usual practice but bigamy may occur in cases of childlessness or when there is no male issue from the first wife. Consanguineous marriages occur at the cross-cousin level, i.e., father's sister's daughter and mother's brother's daughter. Widow remarriage may occur but junior levirate is not practised. A widower may marry junior sororate. Divorce may occur as per the Islamic prescriptions and only men have the right to divorce on the ground of adultery or maladjustment. Children are the liability of the father in such cases and compensation is given to the divorced wife. The payment of *mehar* occurs at the marriage and is equivalent to the traditional silver coins of rupees thiry two and a quarter i.e. about Rs 1,500. It is said that the amount of Rs 32.25 was fixed as a *mehar* in the case of the wife of prophet Mohammed, Fatima Bibi. Both male and the female divorcees may remarry.

The family pattern is becoming predominantly nuclear although vertically extended joint families are still present. Avoidance relationship of the *lari* (son's wife) exists with her *saurah* (husband's father) and *jeth* (husband's elder brother). Informal and occasional joking relationship exists between *devar-bhabi* (husband's younger brother and elder brother's wife) and *jija-sali*(sister's husband and wife's sister). The inheritance pattern is usually as per the rule of male equigeniture but daughter may claim a part in her father's property. The succession pattern is patriarchal and the eldest son succeeds the father. The status of women is comparatively low and normally they are not employed in job or money-earning pursuits. This can be attributed to illiteracy and household work. They are usually confined to domestic chores like the collection of fuel and firewood and fetching potable water. They participate in social and religious ceremonies but have no role in the political sphere and mechanism of social control.

The life-cycle rituals are observed as per the Islamic tenets. Pre-delivery rituals are not observed but pre- and post-delivery restrictions on the mother exist. The post-delivery pollution is observed for 40 days but first purification ceremony is observed on the seventh day by taking *sarbat* (juice) when the naming ceremony is also performed by some but this not a regular feature. *Sunnat* or *khatna* (circumcision) in boys is the only and the major ritual in childhood, usually performed between three to eight years of age. It is performed by a member of the community and a Maulvi (priest) recites *kalma* (excerpts) from the Quran. The Maulvi is consulted to fix a date of marriage which may occur in all months except during Ramzan and Muharram. The *batna* (turmeric and oil) and *mehndi* (henna) ceremonies, as among the Hindus of the area, precede the major marriage ritual, *nikah*. At this time the amount of *mehar* is decided and paid and then the Maulvi takes the *kaul karar* (consent) of the boy and girl three times in the presence of witnesses for acceptance of the marriage. The marriage is then contracted. The *nikah* takes place at the bride's residence whose parents gives a feast to the groom's party. The latter also feast the *ladhar* (persons accompanying the bride) at their place. The nuptial ceremony occurs at the bridegroom's place on the day following the marriage. Death rituals are observed as per the Islamic prescriptions. The dead are buried and ancestor worship is observed for 40 days during the pollution period with intermittent rituals observed on the tenth, twentieth and the thirtieth day. On the *chalhia* (fortieth day) the Maulvi is given alms in the name of the dead and the community is served a meal.

The Abdals are basically a landless community. The traditional occupation of seeking alms on death and festive occasions is now a practise of the bygone days and is followed only by few. They have presently taken up various miscellaneous occupations, like those of *kasai* (meat and fish sellers), masons, contractors, tailors, barbers, grocers and petty shopkeepers. A few are taxi-drivers. Some are also employed in Government departments on lower cadres. The links with the market are direct and the market is fully regulated and payments are made in cash. Child labour exists.

Social disputes are resolved by the elderly members of the community and major problems regarding marriage and divorce are taken up in the Islamic committee elected by a voice-vote. The statutory Gram Panchayat in the village and the Municipal Committee in the town, perform the usual functions of social welfare and may also levy cash fine on the guilty. But the Islamic committee does not have powers of punishment through fine. In addition, the Islamic committee also preaches Islam and encourages the study of Urdu. The Abdals belong to the Sunni sect and worship one God or Allah. However, some have family affiliations with pirs and local deities like Nahar Singh, Guga, Lakhdata and Balak Nath. The sacred specialist (Maulvi) is from the Faqir community or the one appointed by the Islamic committee. They have faith in the local magic-men also who treat ailments caused by malevolent spirits. The festivals of socioreligious importance are mainly Id and Bakrid. But they also celebrate local regional festivals of Hindus or prepare festive food, particularly on Diwali, Lohri, Baisakhi and Sair. The main fairs visited by the Abdals are the Nalwari cattle fair annually held in the town and various fairs of the Guga and Lakhdata. Sarangi is the traditional musical instrument of the community usually played on death and while seeking alms. Various local regional Pahari folksongs, tales and lores are shared but the *bar* and *birlap* are peculiar to the community.

Traditional commensal norms are mainly confined to Muslim communities like Bharai, Mirasi, Teli, Faqir, etc. They accept food and water from

Hindus except from a Chamar, Dumna and Julaha. They give uncooked cereals and pulses, that is *sukka* or *sidha* to an upper caste Hindu having social exchange with the Abdals or they may arrange a *suchchi rasoi* (clean food) cooked by a Brahman or a Rajput.

In respect of the modern developmental programmes, formal education has made some impact on the community. They send their children to school and formal school education is favoured for boys and girls. But boys hardly receive college education due to economic reasons. The goal of the girls is to get married rather than to acquire education. In the sphere of health and medicare, both modern and traditional methods are used. Attitude towards family planning is becoming favourable and couples do not prefer more than three children, though desire for one or two male children is still dominant. Some persons have adopted sterilization for family planning. Potable water through pipelines is available at their doorsteps. Provisions of Integrated Rural Development Programme (IRDP) exist but they are generally self-employed. Electricity and modern mass media (radio, television and cinema) and road and post office facilities are available or easily accessible. The fuel energy resources are cowdung cakes, coal, sawdust and kerosene oil. Nutrition programmes for children (mid-day meal) and immunization, public distribution system through fair price shops are available. Only a few have a favourable attitude to savings but many still depend on the local moneylenders and shopkeepers.

A.R. Sankhyan

ACHARAJ

The Acharaj are the Brahman who seeks *dan* (offerings) in the name of the dead by performing death rites—*kirya karam* for various Hindu communities. The etymology of the name is from word 'Acharya' meaning teacher, and Acharya is also used as a synonym as well as a title for the Acharaj or Charaj community. The Acharya while performing ancestor worship establishes links with the departed soul through chanting Sanskrit *shloka* and methods of worship of the *preta* (spirit of the dead). The community seems to be as old as the Hindu caste system. A legend goes that the community originated from the *panch* (five) Gaur and *panch* Dravida Brahman (Rose, 1919) because they accepted *dan* within thirteen days of the death of a person and this *dan* was considered polluted, and as such they were excommunicated and grew into a separate community, the Acharaj. A section of the Acharaj who performs the death rites of the dead in the community itself is called Mahacharaj or Parcharaj, who are also known as Mahabrahman or Brahman of Brahmans. Rose (1919) mentioned the Mahacharaj as a subdivision of the Gargacharaj, a Garga *gotriya* section of the Acharaj community.

The Acharaj live in small numbers in almost all the districts of Himachal Pradesh. However there is a good number of them in Bilaspur, Mandi, Shimla and Kangra. They occupy the hills and dales of the sub-Himalayas experiencing warm and temperate climate, with low humidity and medium rainfall.

They speak local Bilaspuri, Kangri, Mandiali, etc. dialects of the Pahari and communicate in Devanagari script within and outside the community. Men wear white dress, a *kurta* and *dhoti* with a *parna* (piece of red cloth) on the shoulders while performing ancestor-worship. The dress of the woman is shirt, *salwar* and a *dupatta* or *chadru* (shawl). Traditional ornaments are golden *chak* on head, *murki* (nose ring), *laung* or *tili* (nose-studs), silver *mahel, gajra* or *kangan* (wristlet), *tore* or *jhanjar* (anklets), etc but presently some of these ornaments are rarely used.

The Acharaj are vegetarian in their food habits. Their staple food is wheat, maize and rice which is eaten with different pulses like gram, *urad, moong, kulthi, masur*, peas and beans, etc., cooked in vegetable *ghee* or mustard oil or groundnut oil. Various seasonal vegetables, roots and tubers are consumed in plenty. The fruit intake is moderate and seasonal. Milk and milk products are consumed regularly. Some men occasionally consume country liquor. They also smoke *bidi*, cigarettes and loose tobacco in the indigenous *hookah*(hubble-bubble). The non-vegetarian food, gram, *heeng* (asafoetida), onion and oils are not consumed in the event of a death on *patak* (pollution) days. Festive foods are *khichri* on Lohri, *babru* (fried wheat cakes) on Baisakhi, *seviyan* (vermicelles), *bhalle* (cakes of pulses) and *halwa* on Sair, and *ankloo* (rice cakes) and *ankli* (rice paste bread) on Diwali.

The Acharaj have various *gotra* like other Brahman such as Bhardawaj, Sandil, Modgil, etc., which help them to regulate marriage alliances. The Mahacharaj or Parcharaj is a section of the community endogamous with the Acharaj but maintains a religious superiority over this community as they officiate in the death rites of the Acharajes and are revered as *guru*. Otherwise the Mahacharajes are considered a socially inferior section and their visit to the house is considered inauspicious. The Acharajes have to offer *dan* to the Mahacharajes to their full satisfaction and their demands have to be fulfilled otherwise it is feared that their annoyance would bring misfortune to the family. In view of this, on the death of a family member the Acharajes, it is said, remove costly articles from his house before the Mahacharajes visit their house. The social status of the Acharajes in the regional social hierarchy is not high and they are regarded as an unwanted but unavoidable people.

The institution of marriage in the community is similar to that of other Brahmans and Rajputs. The community is endogamous and practises *gotra* and village exogamy. Earlier, child marriages were prevalent and the marriage of a girl before attainment of puberty was considered a *dan* called *kanyadan. Kanyadan* is still followed formally but now the age of marriage has increased to above 16 years for the girls and above 20 for the boys.

Marriages occur through negotiation but a few decades back *batta-satta* (exchange of sisters) marriages were quite common. Presently, however, *dharam punya* (without any gain or compensation) marriages are socially respected and followed, and the girl is given dowry in kind consisting of household articles, clothes, ornaments and special items like television, radio, watches, etc. The symbols of marriage are *sindur* (vermilion), glass bangles, golden nose and ear pin, stud or rings. Monogamy is the rule. The bride lives patrilocally. Widow remarriage or levirate marriages are not practised but a widower may remarry a junior sororate. Divorce is also not permitted socially. But if the spouses are maladjusted, they can seek judicial assistance or legal approval and the wife is paid compensation or maintenance expenses/ allowance. The grown up children are the liability of the father in such cases. Both of the legally divorced spouses may remarry.

The family pattern is both nuclear as well as vertically extended joint system. Usually the sons do not separate as long as the father is alive or all sons have been married. Avoidance relationship exists between *lari* and *saurah, jeth* and with any other elderly members of the village. Informal relationships exist between *devar-bhabi, jija-sali, nanad-bhabi* (husband's sister - brother's wife) and *jija-sala* (sister's husband's-wife's younger brother). The inheritance is on male lines and as per equigeniture rule, and succession goes to the eldest son.

Conflicts may occur on the distribution of paternal property, especially when all the sons do not contribute equally to the family income. Traditionally, however, the junior members are obliged to obey the elders and respect the traditional norms. There is a trend towards breakdown of the joint family system in the wake of persons employed outside their hometowns. The status of women continues to be low and barring a few educated ones, they do not contribute much to the family income and are less privileged in the matters of making decisions, social control and the political sphere. They, however, do all the domestic jobs, including animal husbandry in rural areas and collection of fuel and fodder, bringing potable water, participating in social functions and religious ceremonies. They also control the family expenditure.

The life cycle rituals of the community are similar to those of the other categories of Brahmans. Pre-delivery rituals have lost their significance and are not observed but post-delivery restrictions as well as pollution called *sutak* are observed for 40 days with intermittent purification ceremony called *guntral* (taking cow's urine) on the eleventh day. The naming ceremony is observed and the name is given as per the horoscope of the child. *Annaprashan* (cereal-taking) ceremony is also observed when the child starts taking solid food. *Mundan* ceremony (tonsure) is observed for the boys and is conducted by the *mama* (mother's brother) of the child on any odd year of the birth before the child attains five years of age. A *jatra* (religious procession) is led to Nahar Singh (local deity) and a goat is offered on the birth of the first son. The *yagopavit* (sacred thread wearing) ceremony was observed before marriage, but presently, it is performed on the elder brother's marriage. The marriage rituals are observed as per the Hindu Sanatana tenets and performed by their own community priest. At this time, the clan deity is propitiated and *saand* and *samuhat* ceremonies are conducted, nine planets worshipped and a *havan* for peace is performed. At bride's place the *lari* (bride) and *lara* (bridegroom) circumambulate the sacred fire and take oath for an ideal life. The bride's parents give a feast to the groom's party. Later a *pipal* tree is worshipped at the groom's place and circumambulated to propitiate lord Brahma who is supposed to be represented by the tree. The marriage ends with fun and frolic and the gathered kith and kin are served meals. The bride returns to her parents the same day and the groom comes to the in-laws' house at night. He takes the bride with him on the next day. This ceremony is called *muklawa*. The death rites are also similar to those of Brahmans. The dead are cremated and the ashes are immersed in Ganga at Hardwar and *pind dan* is offered to the *panda*. Ancestor worship is conducted by way of reading scriptures, especially from the Narada and Garud Puranas which depict the journey of the departed soul to Yamraj—the Lord of death. This is arranged for ten days during the pollution period called *patak*. On the eleventh day the

Mahacharaj officiates to perform purification *havan* (offerings to fire) and seeks offerings in the name of the departed soul. On the sixteenth day which is called *solia*, the family priest performs *havan* and seeks offerings. The kith and kin are served with meals. Annual death rite called *barkhi* and *chabarkh* (fourth annual rite) are similarly observed to propitiate the ancestors.

The Acharaj community is largely landless and thrives on the traditional occupation of seeking offerings on death. Presently, the educated ones are variously employed in government services as doctors, engineers, administrators, teachers, bank managers, etc. Some are also business entrepreneurs and some deal with general merchandise. Some who have small landholdings in rural areas also attend to agricultural work. The links with the market are direct and the market is fully regulated. The Acharajes usually sell the offerings received in kind to the local shopkeepers for cash. The community's social control is maintained by its own Acharya Sabha (council) which has its headquarters at Sundernagar (Mandi district). It is a formal body with officebearers and a *pradhan* (president) elected by a voice vote or through secret ballets. Every household pays an annual subscription for the growth of this Sabha. This Sabha regulates the jurisdiction of earning in different areas. This community is also aspiring to achieve the constitutional status of Backward Class for statutory benefits. Socio-economic disputes of the village are taken up in the statutory Gram Panchayat which performs the usual welfare and developmental activities of the village.

The Acharaj follow Sanatan Dharama and are not involved in socioreligious movements of their own. They have different family or clan deities like Nahar Singh, Sohni Devi, Naini Devi, and Ghagas Devi, which are also local and village deities. Other village and local or regional deities propitiated by them are Guga, Lakhdata, Balaknath, etc. which are propitiated from time to time and particularly during their annual fairs. They celebrate various local and national Hindu festivals like Sair and Chiran (local), Diwali, Krishan Janamashtami, Ramnaumi, Lohri, Baisakhi, etc. Various Pahari folk songs, tales and lores, music and dances are shared.

They accept *kachcha* and *pucca* food from the upper caste Hindus. In the social ceremonies of the upper caste Hindus the Acharajes eat while sitting in a separate row or get a *pariha* (meal for home). They serve a *suchchi rasoi* cooked by a Brahman or a Rajput to the upper caste Hindus.

The Acharaj have favourably responded to modern developmental programmes. Formal education has increased considerably irrespective of sex and children get higher education up to post-graduate level, though many may not go in for higher education partly due to economic limitations or other reasons. They favour and avail themselves of modern health and medicare facilities but also utilize traditional medicare. Attitude towards family planning has become favourable and modern methods of family restriction like sterilization and vasectomy are now adopted. Drinking water is available through taps but traditional sources like *bauri* (step well) are also used in the periods of inadequate piped-water supply. Provisions of IRDP (Integrated Rural Development Programmes) exist but people deny having availed themselves of any facility under these programmes. Most of them are self-employed and are busy with their traditional occupation. Their houses are electrified and they avail themselves of modern mass media (radio, television, etc.) facilities. The road communication and postal facilities are within reach. Energy sources are different in rural and urban areas.

A.R. Sankhyan

ARD POPO

The Ard Popo, also pronounced as Arar Popo or Harar Pop or Ard Pop, is a small community of Dakaut Brahman who subsist traditionally on the alms and offerings earned by practising palmistry. Rose (1919) traced the etymology of the word Harar Pop from *thag* or money grabbers. They are also known as *jyotshi* (astrologers) and move from place to place in search of clients. In Kangra the Bujrus or Bojrus who also sometimes earn by practising palmistry also subsist mainly on alms for the evil stars like Saturn, Rahu and Ketu. Bhole Brahman is also an uncommon synonym for the Ard Popo in Una district. Commonly, they call themselves Gaur Brahmans. Similar in the profession of palmistry is another group of Dakaut Brahman known as Bhatra or Bhatre, who are generally found in Punjab and are vagrant *sadhu* who trace their origin from Madho Mal, a Brahman saint (Rose 1919). Ard Popos are distributed in different parts of Bilaspur district and suggest their migration from Punjab plains during India's partition in 1947 or earlier. They are presently allotted some land and have settled. The Bhatras are found in the areas along the Punjab borders. The community is aware of its distribution at the regional level. They occupy the hilly terrain of the Siwaliks and its valleys that receive warm and temperate climate, low humidity and medium rainfall during most of the year.

The Ard Popos speak Bilaspuri and Kangri dialects of the western Pahari and Punjabi (in the areas adjoining Punjab), and write in Devanagari script. Men wear a white dress including a shirt, *dhoti* and *pagri* (turban) and put a *tilak* (mark) on forehead either of turmeric or *chandan* (sandal wood). Women wear *kurta* and *salwar* and a shawl or *dupatta*.

The Ard Popos are occasional non-vegetarians. Their staple food is like that of other people of the area and includes maize, wheat and rice along with pulses of various types like grams, *urad, moong, kulthi*, peas and beans and different local seasonal vegetables, roots and tubers. The cooking medium is either mustard oil or vegetable *ghee*. They take milk and milk products but this mainly depends on their earnings as they are dependent on the agricultural communities for these items. Men consume country liquor occasionally and smoke loose tobacco or *bidi* or cigarette.

The Ard Popos, Bujrus and Bhatras are different sections of the broader Dakaut Brahman community. There is no hierarchical differentiation among the different sections but they have some *gotra* which are used for regulating matrimonial alliances. They claim Gaur Brahman status but other people hesitate to accept them as such. The community is endogamous and practises *gotra* and village exogamy. Earlier, pre-puberty marriages were quite frequent but now the marriage age has increased and girls are usually married some years after attainment of puberty, between sixteen and eighteen years and the boys at or around their twenties. Marriages are negotiated. Exchange of sisters may also occur. Monogamy is practised. *Sindur, koka/tili/nath* (nose stud/pin or ring) are the marriage symbols. They practise *kanyadan* and do not accept bride-price but give some dowry in the form of household articles, clothes and ornaments. The bride lives patrilocally. Divorce is a rare event and occurs only in certain circumstances of maladjustment. The spouses may dissolve the marriage through social or judicial approval. Compensation is given to the wife and the children are regarded as the liability of the father. The divorcees may remarry. Widow remarriage is generally not practised but a young widow may be allowed to remarry. A man may remarry a junior sororate.

The family pattern is predominantly nuclear and the married sons quite often establish new households. In a joint family, avoidance relationship exists mainly between the *lari* or *nuh* and *sauhra.* Joking relationships, exist between *devar-bhabi, jija-sali* and *jija-sala.* The property is inherited on male lines and as per equigeniture. The succession goes to the eldest son. Conflict in a family may arise on property matters. The women do not inherit paternal property. Their status is lower than that of the male members and they do not contribute to family income but do have some control over expenditure. They also participate in agricultural work and animal husbandry (wherever these people have small landholdings), bring potable water and collect fuel. They also participate in social and religious ceremonies.

The life-cycle rituals are performed by their community priest. Pre-delivery restrictions on women exist. Post-delivery pollution called *sutak* lasts for 40 days. The name is given to the child by consulting the horoscope. *Annaprashan* is observed by some. The *jatlu* or *mundan* among boys is performed by the *mama* before the fifth year of age and a *jatra* is led to Baba Balak Nath or other patron deity on the birth of the first son. The *karan bedhan* (ear-piercing ceremony) is ignored. The *yagyopavit* has lost its pre-marriage significance but is observed at the time of marriage. Marriage rituals are observed at the bride's place. The *lara* and *lari* circumambulate the sacred fire and a golden idol of their clan deity. Some also circumambulate and worship a pipal tree at the bride's place. The marriage feast is given by the bride's parents. The *muklawa* occurs on the following auspicious day of the marriage.

The death rituals are also performed by their community priest. The dead are cremated and the ashes are immersed in the Ganges at Hardwar or in the Beas river at Kangra. On the cremation ground, a bronze plate containing some wheat puddings is kept in the name of the departed soul. Ancestor worship is observed for 11 days, after which they become pure from the *patak* (death pollution) by performing *havan* and by giving alms to the priest.

This community is semi-nomadic and subsists primarily on alms and offerings by practising palmistry and astrology. Some have small landholdings and keep some cattle but most of the people are landless and non-agriculturists. A few are engaged in petty business and run small shops. Some are electricians or mechanics and a few also work as attendants at shops. They also render priestly service at times. The linkages with the market are direct and the market is fully regulated. Child labour exists. The community social control is maintained by its informal caste council. Usually the elders of the community resolve social disputes. The Gram Panchayat resolves the economic disputes of the village over land and water, which is empowered to punish the guilty through cash fine as well.

The Ard Popos worship gods of the Hindu pantheon in various local and regional forms. Naina Devi, Balak Nath and Nahar Singh (in Bilaspur) are family as well as village and regional deities. They have their own sacred specialists and or also employ magic-cum-medicine men from other communities for seeking relief from the evil spirits.

They celebrate various festivals like Holi, Lohri, Diwali, Navratre, Sair and Rakshabandhan, and visit local fairs of the regional deities.

The Ard Popos have little social interaction in terms of commensal and connubial norms. They accept food and water from various communities except that *kachcha* food is not accepted traditionally in social gatherings from castes like Chamar, Dumna and Julaha, but *sidha* or *sukka* may be accepted. The Ard Popos may have putative kinship-based friendship with other castes. The traditional water sources like *bauri* or springs are commonly shared and so are cremation grounds. A member of this community is working as a school teacher in Bilaspur. Modern developmental programmes have made little impact on the Ard Popos at large. The facilities for formal education are exploited by a few and are generally fewer for girls who usually are educated only up to the primary school level due to social and economic reasons. The boys hardly go for college education and seek only secondary school education. They also drop out due to economic reasons or because of no guidance, incentives or interest. Both indigenous and modern systems of medicare are utilized but modern facilities are expensive and not everyone can have an access to them. Magic men are still favoured and consulted. Attitude towards small family is favourable because of economic compulsions. This community does not use family planning measures though at times resorts to sterilization methods. Drinking water is available through pipe lines in the vicinity but traditional sources of water are still used due to inadequate supply. Provision of Intensive Rural Developmental Programmes (IRDP) does exist but only a few actually get its benefits. The modern mass media (radio, television) facilities are availed of by a few but are accessible to all in the neighbourhood. Nutrition programmes for children (ICDS) are partly availed of though the immunisation facilities are availed of widely. They also have access to public distribution system. Most of them, however, live in poor economic conditions and in mud-walled and straw-thatched huts and are dependent on local money-lenders.

A.R. Sankhyan

ATISHBAZ

The Atishbaz, also known as Barudgir, deal with fireworks. Traditionally they have been involved in manufacturing explosives. Recalling their history from Akbar's time, they claim that their ancestor named Shahbuddin came from Gora, a place in Iran, to join Akbar's army as the general of the artillery. Later, during the reign of Shahjahan, they were given some land and villages in Haryana, which is still referred to as Patti-i-Sheikh (Rose, 1919). From here, some of them migrated to Sirmaur (Himachal Pradesh) because the then Raja of Sirmaur invited them to manufacture explosives. It was customary in those days to arrange firework and shoot canonballs to welcome British officials. Since then, the manufacture of explosives has continued from one generation to another.

The Atishbaz speak Haryanvi while talking among themselves, but with outsiders they use Hindi and the educated ones make use of English as well. The script used is both Perso-Arabic and Devanagari. In dress habits they are in no way different from others. Women wear *salwar*, *kameez* and *orhna* while men sport *kurta, pyjama* and also wear pant and shirt.

The Atishbaz are non-vegetarian but do not take beef and pork. The use of the latter is tabooed. Their staple food comprises wheat, pulses of *masur, channa, urad* and seasonal vegetables. The medium of cooking is mustard oil. Men smoke and drink but are not fond of betel and tobacco chewing. Fruit consumption is occasional.

The Atishbaz claims the status of Sheikh and belong to the Quresh *khandan* (lineage). In the social heirarchy they are grouped along with the Muslim occupational castes. They are aware of the varna hierarchy but do not accept it. Though endogamous, marriages can be contracted outside the community, but within the Muslim fold. Marriages are settled through negotiation. The usual age at marriage is between 18 and 20 years for girls and between 22 and 25 years for boys. Another form of marriage, namely exchange marriage (locally referred to as *batta-satta*) may also take place. Consanguineous marriages between all types of cousins are both practised and prescribed, but nowadays, in the selection of the match, they prefer to go outside consanguineal kinship. A second marriage in the lifetime of the previous wife is permitted under Islamic prescription, but is rarely practised.

Remarriage of widow, widower and divorcee is permitted. Levirate and sororate are also practised. The rule of residence for girls after marriage is patrilocal. There is no bride-price, but dowry exists in the form of gifts given to the daughter at the time of marriage. *Mehar* (dower) is settled at the time of marriage and is payable to the wife at the time of the divorce. Divorce is granted on grounds of adultery, cruelty and maladjustment, however, only men have the right to divorce. Children remain in the custody of the father, but infants may stay with the mother as long as they need her care.

Joint family system is more prevalent, though nuclear families also exist. Married brothers sharing a common roof have normally separate kitchens. The eldest male member heads the household. The relationship among the members of the household is cordial though conflict and confrontation do occur mostly over property. Married women observe purdah (veil) in the presence of the senior male members of the husband's household, while joking relationship exists with the husband's younger brothers and sisters. Inheritance and succession is patrilineal. All sons inherit the property equally; the daughters are also entitled to a share as per the Islamic law but they invariably surrender their share in favour of the brothers. The succession is from father to the eldest son.

Women do not enjoy equal privileges in comparison to men despite the fact that they perform all the domestic chores like bringing water and fuel, and are equally responsible for the satisfaction of the economic needs of the family. In the domain of household management they have ample freedom to exercise their will but economically they are dependent on men. In matters pertaining to religion, they have little say and cannot address any religious gathering nor assume any religious office. They can nevertheless participate in religious festivals and rituals. Political consciousness is on the rise among women also, but their participation in the political life is minimal.

The life-cycle rituals of birth to death are common with those of other Muslims. The birth of the male child brings more joy and happiness to the family. As soon as the child is born, an *Imam* is called, who whispers *azan* (the verses from the holy Quran) into the child's ears. Post-birth pollution is observed for 40 days. Purificatory bath is given to the mother and the child on sixth, eleventh, twentieth and finally on the fortieth day. The woman and the child are then taken outside the house, this is known as *tara dikhana,* symbolising the fact that she is ritually pure to start her normal schedule. *Khatna* (circumcision) is the most important ritual for boys and can be performed anytime from early infancy to the fifth year. *Aqiqa* ceremony is also observed and it is customary to sacrifice a goat on this occasion. Two goats are sacrificed for a male child.On this occasion the head of the child is also shaved off.

Nikah ceremony takes place at the bride's house and a *maulvi* presides over the occasion. Before the actual marriage ceremony one more ceremony known as *tel* and *mehndi-ki-rasam* takes place at both the bride's and the groom's place. *Tel* (oil) and turmeric are applied to the bride and the groom by the female relatives of the respective sides. *Mehndi* is also applied a day prior to the wedding. At the groom's house another important rite takes place, wherein the groom is lifted by the maternal uncle after he has been given a bath and dressed as a bridegroom. The Nai then ties a *sehra* (ceremonial headgear made of flowers) around the boy's head. The boy goes to the mosque for seeking divine blessings. Marriage songs are sung on this occasion. On the marriage day, the bridegroom, accompanied by his near and dear ones and friends come to the bride's home where *nikah* is performed. The guests are given a feast by the bride's side.

The dead are buried and the pollution lasts for 40 days. The important death rites are performed on the third (*tija*), tenth (*daswan*) and on the fortieth (*chaliswan*) day. The woman, on being widowed, observes *iddat* (a period of three and a quarter month of confinement and seclusion). During this period, she not only remains confined to her house but also does not cook or does the normal household work. It is only after the *iddat* that she can remarry. Another rite, *rasam pagri* (turban tying) is also observed, where the eldest son symbolically assumes the responsibility of head of the house after the death of his father. Ancestor worship is also conducted.

Traditionally, the Atishbaz have been associated with the manufacture of gunpowder and explosives which were earlier used in warfare and now a days required in mining operations. This trade has suffered a setback because of the stringent licencing policy for explosive manufacturers and also because the old gunpowder technology has been replaced by the new gelatine technology which is by far superior and advanced in nature. The secondary sources of the community's income are agriculture, business, service and self-employment. A small percentage is also represented in the white-collar professions such as teaching, law and medicine. They are fully dependent on market supply which is regular and organized. They depend on middlemen for marketing the product and for maintaining intra-State and inter-State supply of their goods. The terms of exchange are mostly by way of cash. There are no reported cases of bonded labour and child labour, though the possibility of the latter cannot be completely ruled out.

The people have access to courts of law and statutory panchayats. However, domestic issues are first settled by the elders of the community. In case of any discrepancies, these can be referred to their association, *Anjuman,* which is an effective body for the implementation of social norms. Punishment is by way of cash fine only.

The Atishbaz abide by Islamic beliefs and practices. They belong to the Sunni sect. They visit mosques and *dargah* and celebrate the various Muslim rituals from time to time. Id, Bakrid, Shab-i-raat are some of the well-known festivals.

Belief in supernatural powers, evil spirits, magic, charms and amules is widely prevalent. Visiting *dargah* (tombs) of well-known saints for paying tribute and for wish fulfilment, is a common practice. The community shares the regional oral traditions in respect of music, dance, folklore and folktales.

The traditional patron-client linkages based on mutual obligations have considerably weakened in view of the new economic, socio-political linkages that are based on the modern belief in the principles of *quid pro quo*. This is becoming more apparent in the urban context. Not all Muslims irrespective of their occupation and social position, observe distinction in respect of exchange of food and water with their fellow members. However, in practice, food is not accepted from Chuhra and those involved in other unclean occupations. The Hindu communities accept any food from them, but during feasts, if cooked separately by a Brahman/Rajput. In the urban context such norms are not followed so rigidly. Connubial relations are however, limited within the *biradari*, but marriages can be contracted with the other Muslim communities of similar socioeconomic ranking. Instances of intercaste marriages are more common in the urban situation. Cases of intercommunal marriages are rare and are seen only in very progressive section of the community. Putative kinship may also exist with certain castes only. Politically they are conscious and also participate at the local level. Political leadership has emerged at the regional level.

The impact of developmental progammes is witnessed in the sphere of electricity, means of transport, communications, water supply and irrigation facilities . Literacy and health standards have improved. Medical facilities by way of hospitals, family planning centres and Integrated Child Development Scheme are availed of by the people. Postal services, banking facilities, fair price shops are also made use of. For economic development, this community strongly feels that their traditional trade of explosive manufacture has immense potentialities of expansion but due to Government's stringent policy in granting licences, people are dissuaded to take it up on a large scale. Besides, they do not get any subsidy or loans because firework is considered among luxurious goods under the Indian Explosives Act. Nevertheless, loans under the Integrated Rural Development Programme and Employment Guarantee Scheme are being given to the people.

Vatsala Sarkar

BADHAI

The Badhai or Barhai are a community of woodcutters and carpenters popularly known as Tarkhan. The word Badhai denotes cutting or felling down, and is related to the Hindi word *badhna.* In some areas they are considered part of the Dhiman community and this term is used by the members of the community as their surname. This community is also known by other names like Khati, Tryal, Kondal, Ramgarhia (Rose, 1919). The surname Dhiman is also used by the Lohars in the lower hills but in Kullu hills the Lohar community is considered an outcaste. Rose (1919) denies that the Badhais in Kullu form any separate caste, but holds that the Kolis or Dagis who use the axe have been renamed as Barhai. He further states that the Barhai clan is also found among the Rathis of Kangra. But Badhai/Tarkhan in the outer Saraj area of the Kullu district (study area) claim to be Dhiman and trace their origin from Vishwakarma and are treated an upper caste whereas the Lohars are regarded as a scheduled caste. The Badhais attend to woodwork only. The community is spilled over in almost all districts of the State, living in varying climates. In the study area, they live in a difficult, hilly terrain near the snowline. The climate remains cold during most of the year with moderate annual rainfall and low humidity. The terrain is covered with thin to thick deodar and pine forests. Their houses are made of wood and thatched with slates. They generally live in the second storey of their houses and keep their animals on the ground floor. They speak local dialect called Saraji *boli,* a local variation of the Kulvi dialect of the western Pahari. The script used is Devanagari both within and outside the community. The community dress or ornaments are similar to that of the other hill people. Men wear a coulourful cap called Kullu *topi*, a *kurta* with a woollen coat, *pyjama* and woollen shoes. Women wear a scarf on head *dhatu, kurta* and flared trousers and a woollen jacket. Typical ornaments are small nose and ear rings.

The people are non-vegetarian in their food habits and meat is frequently eaten. Wild boar may also be hunted. Staple food is maize, rice, wheat, bajra and barley along with pulses of different types, like *urad, moong, kulthi,* and peas and beans. Seasonal vegetables are consumed. The cooking medium is *desi-ghee* (clarified butter) or vegetable *ghee* or oils. Fruit intake is seasonal and fruits like apples, peaches, plums and apricots are taken in plenty. Home-made liquor is frequently consumed by both men and women. They also smoke *bidi* or loose tobacco. Milk and milk products are taken frequently. Festive food is *bhaturu /siddu* (baked cakes) and *halwa* (pudding) and meat with liquor. Food taboos may be observed during the death pollution. This community has become more vegetarian over time and the intake of fruits, vegetables and pulses has increased.

The Badhais have a single Dhiman clan which is synonymous with the community name. They observe a *gotra chhidra* ritual later performed by the Brahman priest to salvage them from the sins of marrying within a *gotra*. In the regional social hierarchy the position of the community is in the middle. The perceived descending order of the local social hierarchy is Brahman, Rajput, Kanet, Thavi, Barhai (Dhiman), Od, Lohar, Koli and Dagi. Although they claim parity with the Rajput/Brahman but they are placed among the Sudra by their neighbours.

They follow the norm of community endogamy but sometimes village exogamy is also practised. Consanguinity occurs at cross-cousin level, MBD (mother's broughers' daughter) and FSD (father's sister's daughter). The marriages occur at adulthood and through negotiation but *har* (elopement) also occurs and is socially approved. In the *har* type of marriage the boy and girl who love each other usually run away from their homes. This generally happens during fairs. Earlier, child marriages were common and bride-price was a common practice. But, presently bride-price is no more respected and taken except by the financially handicapped members of the community. Monogamy is practised. Marriage symbols are golden *phulli* (nose-rings), toe-ring and ear-rings. Dowry in the form of household articles, agricultural implements, clothes and ornaments is given. The bride lives patrilocally but *ghar jamai* (boy living with girl's parents) arangement is also practised.

Widow remarriage may be a junior levirate or she may marry any other man. Man may also marry a junior sororate or any other woman. Divorce is permitted socially on grounds of maladjustment, impotency, cruelty, etc. The compensation is paid to the aggrieved party. If the woman divorces and marries another man, the latter has to pay the compensation called *reet* to the first husband. The children are the liability of the father or mother as per decision of the Biradari Panchayat. Main changes in the marriage institution are increase in age at marriage, fading of the *reet* custom and a trend towards legalization of the process of divorce.

The family pattern is mainly vertically extended joint system and sons normally do not separate as long as their father is alive. But now there is a trend of breaking up of the families when the married sons become economically self-sufficient or when there is some conflict in the family on division of labour and discrimination in treatment to a particular son or his wife and on account of unfair distribution of property. Normally the inheritance occurs as per the rules of male equigeniture and the eldest son succeeds his father. Avoidance relationship is lacking but joking is permitted as in many Hindu communities of the region between *devar* and *bhabhi*, *jija* and *sali*, *jija* and *sala* and between *nanad* and *bhabhi*. Women enjoy almost an equal status as the men. They participate in economic activities and also have some say in decision-making. They attend to all domestic chores including agriculture and animal husbandry. They collect fuel and fodder and fetch potable water. They also participate in social and religious ceremonies and also have a say in political and social control mechanisms and regulate the family expenditure.

The life-cycle rituals are performed by a Brahman priest. Pre-delivery and post-delivery restrictions exist for the woman and delivery pollution called *skor* is observed for three days in case a girl is born and for five days in case of a son. The *suddhi* (purification) occurs by taking *sharbat* (juice) and cow's urine. The child is named after consulting a Brahman. A small feast may also be given to the villagers. *Julu* or *jatu* is the major childhood ritual for the boys and is performed by a barber at the Mahu Nag or Shamshar Mahadev temple on an odd year after birth. A small feast is also arranged by sacrificiing a goat. The *bajantris* (musicians) play music and greet the couple. The *janeu* (sacred thread) ceremony is performed at the marriage time.

The marriage is negotiated by a man called *kharodi*, who along with the boy's father goes to the girl's place for *barni* (fixing the marriage). On the marriage day a Brahman priest performs the vedic rites. Turmeric and oil ceremonies are observed. Major rituals occur at the bride's place, viz., *ved/ lagan* and *phere* in which the *lara* and *lari* circumambulate the sacred fire and *kanyadan* is perfomed by bride's parents. After this the dowry articles are given to the bride. The groom's party, his relatives and villagers are feasted. The bride enters the house of the groom after *deorhi pujan* (door worship).

The *daroja*, also called *pheru gheru* (a synonym for *muklawa*) takes place soon after the marriage in case of the so-called *ghar biah* (when the boy goes to girl's place and all rituals are observed there). It occurs on the following day in case of *dohra biah*, i.e., when the boy does not move to the bride's place and part of the rituals are observed at his place. Nuptial ceremony occurs at the groom's place. The boy's parents also give a ceremonial feast.

The dead are cremated outside the village and ashes are immersed in the Satluj river. But some well-off persons immerse them in the Ganga at Hardwar and offer *pind dan* to the Panda. Ancestor worship is observed by a Kartu or a Kareshtu, a local synonym for Acharaj, on the eleventh day and offerings are made in the name of the dead. The Brahman priest performs a purification *havan*. A ceremonial feast is given to the villagers which makes the exchange of food open.

Land and forests are the natural resources on which the Badhais survive. They thrive mainly on carpentry or woodwork which is a stable occupation as wood is the major constituent of a typical house in the hills. Besides, they prepare various types of furniture and agricultural implements. They also work in State forests for cutting timber. Agriculture, animal husbandry and horticulture are their supplementry occupations. Some persons possess sizeable land for horticulture. A few persons are also employed in Government jobs as teachers.

The market is located at some kilometres from the village and it takes a few hours to reach there, but a road link has also developed recently. The market functions daily and is fully regulated. Dealings occur in cash. Child labour exists. Development of horticulture has brought a major economical boost to the community.

The social control is in the hands of *sayane* (elderly members) of the village but community-specific formal council is lacking. The members of the statutory Gram Panchayat play an important role in solving socio-economic disputes of the villagers. Besides, people trust their local deities in resolving socioeconomic disputes. They worship the gods of the Hindu pantheon and local deities. Shamshar Mahadev, Mahu Nag and Jigeshwar Mahadev are the local male deities of special reverence. Other local and regional deities propitiated are Kulchhetar Mahadev, Panevi Nag, Pachhla and Kusumba Devi. Their shrines are visited on annual fairs as well as on festive occasions. The fairs include Jitrala, Dalash and Ani fair. Major festivals of socioeconomic and socioreligious importance are Dhogi or Buddhi Diwali, Diwali, Shivratri and Dussehra. Sacred specialists and magic men play a major role in social control and treatment of ailments. The people have various folk and oral traditions. Music and dances make their lives colourful. Nati is a popular dance in which both men and women participate and the *bajantris* play percussion and wind music. Various folksongs and lores are *Nati* songs, *Naihni, Bamnu* and *Lari Shanta*. Among folktales, *Baladhyalu, Minyo-Ranjha, Raja Bhoj, Kajhera*, etc. are popular. Their art and craft is linked with their wood work like carving and engraving.

They exchange *kachcha* and *pucca* food and water with other castes except the Kolis and the Lohars. Traditional water resources are shared with others. Their cremation grounds are separate but the religious shrines are common. Relationship also exists with the Lohars and the Kolis, the latter are the *bajantris* of the local deities and also render instrumental music on marriages and other festive occasions. There are members in teaching and defence services and business. Political leadership has emerged at the Gram Panchayat level. Modern developmental programmes have made a good impact on the community. The level of education has become high and some persons are getting even post-graduate education though the majority does not study beyond the secondary school level. Usually higher formal education is favoured for boys and only partly so for the girls, due to social and sometimes economic reasons and because colleges are very far-off. Both modern and traditional methods of health and medicare are followed and favoured. But adequate facilities for these are not easily available/accessible to them in the rural areas, hence the traditional magic-cum-medicine men have a considerable role to play. Family planning has not made much impact though they favour small families and a few have adopted vasectomy as a method of family planning. Socially, the community demands at least one son in the family. Their houses are electrified. Modern mass media facilities, except radio, have not yet reached nearby. But road communication has reached in the vicinity and postal services are also accessible. Piped drinking water is available in the locality though the traditional sources like springs are still used. General provisions exist under IRDP but not much help has reached them. The people are mostly self-employed. Fuel energy sources are firewood, cowdung cakes, sawdust and agricultural waste material. The source of irrigation is normally rain water though some people also use the natural springs wherever possible for irrigation. They use chemical fertilizers and organic manures. Immunization is availed under ICDS. Fair price shops are located in the vicinity to get ration on subsidized rates. Most of the people favour savings and are not dependent on local landlords or moneylenders.

A.R. Sankhyan

BAIRAGI

The term 'Bairagi' or 'Vairagi' indicates 'anyone unattached to the world or devoid of passion'. According to Ibbetson (1883) the people of this sect belong to ascetic and mendicant order and are placed in the category of Faqirs. The Bairagi community is of non-householders and religious people having no personal property. They are generally the worshippers of Rama, Krishna and Lord Vishnu. The Bairagi Sadhus are divided into several sections like Ramanandi, Radhabalabhi, Nimanandi and Ramanuja. About the Bairagis of Punjab the following account is available in Rose (1919 : 36):

> "In the Punjab only two of the four *sampardas* are usually found. These are (i) the Ramanandis, who like the Vishnuswamis are devotees of Ramchandr, and accordingly celebrate his birthday, the Ramnaumi, study the Ramayana and make pilgrimages to Ajudhia, their insignia being the *tar pundri* or trident, marked on the forehead in white, with the central prong in red or white.
>
> The only other group found in the Punjab is (ii) Nimanandi, who, like the Madhavacharis, are devotees of Krishna. They too celebrate the 8th of Bhadon as the date of Krishna's incarnation, but they study the *Sri Mad Bhagwat* and the *Gita*, and regard Bindraban, Mathura and Dwarkanath as secred places. On their foreheads they wear a two-proged fork, all in white." The Bairagis of both the orders live in Himachal Pradesh, in addition to some Shiva worshippers.

The history of the community is traced back to the eleventh and twelfth centuries, to the times of Saint Ramanuja. Saint Ramanuja preached Vaishnavism in the South. The Bhakti movement of Vaishnavies reached late in the North and it is said that Shri Anand, the twelfth disciple of Guru Ramanand founded the Bairagi sect of ascetics.

Though the Bairagis are considered devoid of passion and worldly attractions, yet in the later period some of these saints became ordinary peasants and householders, with belongings and immovable property, so their progeny, inherited their property and formed a part of the society of householders. In various parts of the State the Bairagis are associated with the Brahmans. Though with the passage of time, this community adopted farming, yet, even today, the Bairagis exercise a wholesome influence as pious people knowing Sanskrit, ways of worship, meditation and *tantra-mantra*.

In Una District, the Bairagis live in Malangar, Dharampur, Kangad, Badhera, Lalehri, Nangal Khurd, Basdehra, Takka, Sanaur, Nangal Kalan and Saloh (study area) villages. In addition, they also inhabit parts of other districts such as Kangra, Mandi, Kullu, Hamirpur and Solan. The Sanyasi Bairagis do not have landed property and stay in various temples or Maths. They have *akharas*, and are keen to take part in religious festivals like Kumbh and Mahakumbh arranged at various *tirathas* in the country. The Nath Bairagis of Chamba district are famous for their mystic powers and till recently they performed an important role at the time of *Kumbhsnan* (pious bath at the time of the Kumbh festival).

The Bairagis of village Saloh in Una District relate that about a century ago, one of their ancestors, Baba Asanand, was brought in a palanquin to have *darshna* of Lord Radha Krishna at Swami Ka Bagh near Nangal. He was the *guru* of the ruler of Garha State whose boundaries touched Nangal. The capital of Garha State was at Swamipur Bagh. As the legend goes, the Rani of the State had a separate *guru* and was jealous of Baba Asanand. She so manipulated that both *gurus* had to exhibit their spiritual powers by remaining under the earth for a specific period. Baba Asanand accepted the challenge and both the *gurus* were buried under the ground. After 18 days, the Baba indicated that the Rani was feeding her *guru* through a tunnel. The ruler, on enquiry, found the statement to be true and got the tunnel closed. As a result of this, the *guru* of the Rani died of hunger and Baba Asanand was established as the *guru* of the royal family. Fearing vengeance by the Rani, he was later brought to Saloh by one of his followers and, as the story goes, entered in *grihasthashram* by marrying a woman from that area. Earlier, on reaching Saloh, he was given 43 *bigha* of land for establishing his *ashram*. The descendents of the Baba are agriculturists now. Baba Tota Ram, one of his disciples, was a famous saint who performed many miracles. He was the last to be buried and now the dead in the lineage are cremated. The village has only two *samadhis* of these two *gurus*. It was reported that at the Samadhi of Baba Tota Ram, a snake known as 'Ichhadhari' (literally, capable of changing forms) used to be seen every now and then. One day, a man belonging to the Dutta clan killed the snake by mistake and as a result of this, his house and family were destroyed in a devastating fire.

The Bairagi have no special dress but the male members wear *dhoti* at the time of rituals and special occasions whereas womenfolk wear *ghaghra, salwar* and *sarees*. Locally they are known as Bhat Brahmans and perform worship in temples. They are mainly Rama and Krishna worshippers but in Takka and Sanaur villages they also worship Lord Shiva.

The Bairagis have Vashistha, Bharadwaj, Kaundal and some other *gotra*. They prefer to marry within the community but also intermarry with other Brahman subgroups. Earlier, the Brahamans of superior *gotra* did not want to have marital relations with the Bairagis but the concept has now changed after Independence of the country. Among them a pregnant woman avoids going to abandoned places like cremation grounds. On the birth of a son, a *havan* is performed and songs are sung by the women of the neighbourhood. At the time of childbirth, the mother is kept in a separate room where she is accompanied by a midwife and some female members of the family. An iron weapon is kept underneath her bed as a safety measure to avoid evil influences of invisible spirits who are feared to haunt the place from time to time. After the childbirth, bread or hard food is not given to the mother for some days. A *purohit* is called to cast a horoscope and later the first letter of the name of the newborn is indicated according to the *janamrashi*. A purgative known as *ghutti* consisting of an extract of *saunf*, sugar, *banafsha* (voilets), rose leaves etc. is given to the child during the initial days.

The days of impurity due to childbirth in a family are called *sutak ke din* whereas those after the death are known as *patak ke din*. *Sutak* is observed for 11 days and *patak* for 16 days. During *sutak*, the mother is not allowed to touch anyone and she takes bath after 5 or 7 days according to her state of health. The purificatory ceremony is known as *guntrala*. On this occasion, the mother and other members of the family sip *gunte*r (cow urine). A feast is arranged after *havan* and *Satyanarayana ki katha* is read along with singing of folksongs for the long life of the child. Solid food is given to the child after about six months. This ceremony is called *khirpu* as *kheer* is served on this occasion. The *janeu* ceremony is assumed either at an auspicious time (*muhurat*) around the age of 10 or at the time of marriage of the boy.

Only *dharam punya* types of marriages are prevalent among the members of the community. The marriage of the girl is considered to be a great pious act (*punya*). Dowry is not demanded, but, if given in kind by the parents of the birde, is not refused. *Shanti havan, parsahi* (wearing ornaments with *sehra* by the bridegroom), *milni* (reception), *vedika* (performing the ceremony by pandits at the altar), *sirgundi, andron* or *andrera* and *pipal pujan* are important ceremonies at the time of marriage.

The Bairagis lead a very simple and pious life. They are pure vegetarian and do not consume drinks. There are very few smokers in the community. There are no social divisions among the Bairagis. Their staple diet is wheat, rice, maize, pulses and they use green vegetables grown in the fields or purchased from the nearby market. Their villages are neat and clean and they honour guests according to their capacity and financial position. They love joint family system and no case of divorce has been reported.

Krishna Janamashtami, Ramnavmi, Karwa Chauth, Diwali, Dussehra, Ahoi Ashtami and death anniversary of Baba Arjun Gir are a few of their festivals and ceremonies. Another saint, Baba Van Bihari, established a school at Saloh which has since been taken over by the Government and raised to the high school level. On Ramnavmi day, a great fair is organized in the school ground every year. *Sadhus* from various places visit this fair on this day.

Baba Kaladhari of Bedi clan, who established a *gurudwara* at Una, stayed at Saloh for quite sometime. There has been some connection between Sikhism and Bairagi sect. Rose (1919: 37) writes:

"The connection of the earliest form of Sikhism with the Bairagi doctrines is obscure, but it is clear that it was a close one. Kalladhari, the ancestor of the Bedi family of Una, was the predecessor of the Brahman Kalladhari *mahants* of Dharamsal in the Una Tehsil, who are Bairagis, as well as followers of Nanak, whence they are called Vaishnav-Nanak-Panthi. This community was founded by one Nakodar Das who in his youth was observed in the deity while lying in the shade of a banyan tree instead of tending his cattle, and at last, after a prolonged period of adoration, disappeared into the unknown. Another Bairagi, Ram Thamman, was a cousin of Nanak and is sometimes claimed as his follower. His tank near Lahore is the scene of a fair, held at the Baisakhi, and formerly notorious for disturbances and, it is said, immoralities. It is still a great meeting point for Bairagi ascetics. Further it will not be forgotten that Banda, the succesor of Sikh *gurus*, was originally a Bairagi, while two Bairagi sub-sects (the Sarandasi and Simrandasi) are sometimes classed as Udasis".

In the Bairagi community, the women almost enjoy equal rights as the men and control household affairs. The male members attend to agriculture and outside work including *jajmani*. *Jajmani* system is still prevalent and the Bairagi are invited as *purohit* to perform various rituals and social ceremonies. Some of them are experts in astrological predictions and some others are famous for diagnosing ailments relating to the effects of spirits and black magic. No change is noticed in ritualistic performances as these are based on Sanskrit scriptures and *purohits* have to follow the old traditions.

In the villages inhabited by the Bairagis, the control over land possessed by the members is exercised according to the revenue code applicable to all other communities, so there is no exception with regard to control over land, water, forest and other resources.

The Bairagis are not only a land owning community but they practise other occupations like treating the patients with herbal medicines and reading scriptures at the time of various social ceremonies. Besides, some of them are in business and Government service. The only change in their social set-up, visible after Independence is in marital relations with other groups and clans of Brahmans.

The community, like other communities in the region, is controlled by community panchayat as well as the village panchayat. The community panchayat is a Biradari Panchayat which keeps an eye over the deeds of an individual of the community and introduces punitive measures for evil deeds or unwanted behaviour. The punishment is in the form of fine, rebuking, segregating and direction to conduct *tirath yatra* as a penance for an undersirable act. After *tirath yatra* one is expected to feed the community a lunch, known as *yajna* or arrange a *Satyanarayan ki katha.*

There has been no famous artist in the community. It was found during the course of the survey that the members of the community are keenly interested in keeping the houses clean and using washed clothes which distinguish them from others. Their interest in growing flowers in front of their houses and maintaining kitchen gardens is also noteworthy.

The community is receptive to developmental schemes of the Government and has a high level of literacy and education. The parents consider it their duty to give good education to their children.

B.R. Sharma

BANGALI

The Bangali is a scheduled caste known for its peculiar traditions of snake-charming, wandering, hunting and gathering and eating the meat of a fox, bush-lizards and tortoise. Ibbetson (1883) and Rose (1919) offered three interpretations of the name Bangali : (1) A native of Bengal, (2) a tribe akin to the Sansis found in Kangra driven off by the passing of the Criminal Tribe Act, and (3) the Kanjar and Sapada or snake-charmers of the plains. In Punjabi, *bangali* means a person, who lives by begging, exhibiting snakes and hunting etc (Rose, 1919). In Bilaspur, the Bangalis claim their origin from Bengal but their peculiar dialect is not akin to the Bengali language. They also claim their origin from the Meena tribe of Rajasthan and associate themselves as helpers of Rana Pratap during his difficult days. According to some their ancestors did not migrate from Bengal but in order to earn their livelihood resorted to magic tricks and charms and declared that they possessed the magic of Bengal. Hence they are called the Bengalis. They appear to have entered Bilaspur about a century back, as their population in Kehlur (Bilaspur) was recorded as only two persons by Kavi Ganesh Singh (1892). The total population of the community in 1971 in Himachal Pradesh was 617 out of which there were 74 persons in Bilaspur, 104 in Shimla, 208 in Kangra and 231 in Sirmaur (Singh, 1971). But the number rose to 1631 in 1981. They live generally in warm and temperate climate of low humidity in the hills and dales and amidst thin pine forests along the tributaries of the rivers where their game animals like fox,wild boar, hare, bush-lizards, fish etc. are found in plenty. In Kangra valley they have migrated from Punjab or its borders during the post-independence period.

The Bangali speak a dialect of their own at home and with their kin, which is not understandable to other people called Bangali Boli. But they also speak the local dialects, viz., Bilaspuri, Kangri, Panjabi, Sirmauri, etc. Devanagari script is used for communication. A Bangali is generally dark complexioned and wears a *kurta* and *tamba* (loin cloth) or *pyjama*, with a *pagri* as a headgear, whereas a Bangalin (female) wears *kurta, salwar* and *chadru*. The ornaments for women consist of a golden finger-ring, *koka* (nose-pin) and anklets of silver.

The Bangali are basically non-vegetarian and are noted for their characteristic food habit of eating the meat of fox, wild cat, tortoise and bush-lizards called *goh* or *sappar machhi* (rock fish). They also eat pork but not beef. Besides hunting these animals, they also hunt wild animals like wild boar, hare, jungle-fowl and birds like partridge, peacock and peahen. Their common staple cereal is maize, wheat and rice and pulses like *urad, moong* and gram. Their favourite cooking oil is mustard, *alsi* (linseed) and vegetable *ghee.* Animal fat is also used as a cooking medium. The roots and tubers eaten by them consist of radish, potatoes, *kachalu* (*Colocassia*), *zimikand* (yam), etc. Their vegetable intake is occasional. The fruit intake is also very occasional and limited to the seasonal mangoes, banana, guava, apple, peach and some other wild fruits. People of both the sexes are used to drinking country or home-made liquor and smoking *bidi* or tobacco in some areas. Milk is consumed very occasionally and tea is a common drink. Food taboos are not observed and usual local festival foods are *khitchri* on Lohri, *kachauri-babru* on Baisakhi and *ankli* and *ankloo* of rice flour on Diwali, besides their own non-vegetarian dishes.

There is a recent trend of change in the Bangalis' traditional food habits (as observed in Bilaspur) and the younger generation, coming in contact with local communities, feel ashamed of eating the inferior quality meat, i.e., of fox and *goh.*

The Bangalis broadly constitute two groups, viz., the Hindus and the Christians. In Bilaspur, those claiming to be Hindus, have two sections, namely the Mormar and the Natue or Kalandar. The Mormar (peacock-killers) used to kill peacocks for feathers and skin as an occupation. Though this is no longer the case, however, the name Mormar continues. The Mormars consider themselves socially superior to the Natue. This hierarchy is, however, only based on occupation due to the fact that the Mormars abstain from eating the inferior quality meat of fox and lizard. This does not affect their matrimonial ties with the Kalandars and other sections or clans, such as Bhatti, Bajaniye and Mundhauk. In Kangra, the Bangalis divide themselves into four sections—Gharu, Gandhila, Bahmbi and Gawar. Some place Bahmbi at the top and Gawar, Gandhila and Gharu after them. Another clan of them Krichde is considered important as the persons belonging to this clan were considered warriors and fighters. They do not come under the purview of the Varna system but in Bilaspur they claim a Kshatriya status, which is, however, not acknowledged by other people. Those belonging to the Gandhila section at Bharmar in Kangra, do not attach themselves to Hinduism and some in Palampur tehsil have got converted to Christianity. In Kangra the Bengali community was kept under surveillance at Holta and the members could not go out without the intimation to the local police. Later, after independence they were rehabilitated and their wards admitted to St. Hilta's Girls School, Palampur and St. Paul School, Palampur for imparting education.

The Bangalis are endogamous and practise group/clan/*got* and village exogamy. They marry at maturity and marital relations are settled through negotiation. The boys and girls, however, have freedom in selecting their own mates. Very often this takes place when a camp or *dera* of the Bangalis comes across another *dera* and a boy and a girl fall in love with each other. Monogamy is practised. The *sindur*, glass bangles, bridal-ring and nose and ear pins or rings are considered marriage symbols for women. Earlier there was the practice of giving a bride-price in some cases, but now there is no such practice. Nominal gifts consisting of a few sets of clothes, some utencils, a small box, a cot and a bedding is given. There is a tradition of giving a dog and a snake in *daj* besides other things like transistor radio and watch, etc., according to the economic status of the family. The residence of the bride is patrilocal, but some cases of *ghar jamai* also exist among the Mormars. The dissolution of marriage is permitted socially by the Biradari Panchayat on grounds of maladjustment and cruelty. The panchayat assesses the compensation to be paid to the aggrieved party. The divorcee may marry again. They tend to seek judicial approval of divorce so that the woman gets compensation from the man. Minor children in such cases go with the mother. A widow may remarry but there is no social custom of junior levirate, though a widower may remarry a junior sororate. A few exceptional cases of inter-caste marriages are seen when some people from outside married Bangali women and are living with them.

Nuclear family is prevalent as the married sons separate from their parents. The elder members of the community are more individualistic and self-dependent and earn more by snake-charming, selling herbs (and sometimes, cheating people). But when moving in a camp for hunting a game, animal fox or pig they become cohesive. There is little interpersonal relationship based on mutual respect, love, obligation or fear of the elders. Conflicts and confrontations are common when a senior member tries to grab the daily earnings of the juniors. There is no avoidance relationship in the community. Informal joking relationship exists between *devar* and *bhabi*, among the boy's and girl's parents, *jija* and *sali*, and *jija* and *sala*. There is small immovable property to inherit, usually, a small home or a hut and a piece of land which is, however, inherited paternally as per the rule of male equigeniture. But sometimes the married/divorced/widow daughter may also claim a share of the father's property. The eldest son succeeds the father. The interfamily bonds are expressed only during festivities, marriage and death, and when they wander from one place to another in a camp for hunting.

The Bangali women enjoy a good deal of freedom and equal status in the family. They are nearly self-sufficient in earning their daily livelihood by selling herbs and also accompany the men in hunting. In addition, they collect firewood and fodder for their cattle (usually a mule). They have equal freedom in selecting and leaving their life partners. They participate in social and religious ceremonies. They are good housewives and work without hesitation.

The birth of a child takes place at home or in the camp and the delivery is performed by an old, experienced woman of the community. The birth of a child, whether son or daughter, is celebrated by the family and the kith and kin by consuming liquor. The *sutak* varies depending upon the health of the mothers and ranges between three and thirteen days, when they take cow's urine called *gunt* for purification—probably a borrowed custom from the local caste Hindus. Only *mundan* of boys is the major childhood ritual performed in an odd year from the birth. The haircut of the boys is done by mother's brother and some sweets are distributed among close associates.

About two decades back, marriage was a simple ceremony which was performed in the *dera* (camp) or at home and completed by a small feast and by amusement performed by professional *swangis* (folk artists) from the Chamar or Julaha community. The bridegroom's father was supposed to offer one or two bottles of liquor failing which the bride's father would abuse and give a thrashing with a stick. No services of *purohit* and *nai* were employed (in Bilaspur), but now they take the services of a priest of the Chamar community, who performs the Hindu Vedic rituals and the bridegroom and the bride circumambulate the sacred fire. In Kangra, the Gandhila Bangalis employ a priest of their community who also conducts certain Vedic rituals and the bride and the groom circumambulate the fire. The Christian group performs marriage in a church. Marriage is consummated on the same day.

The Christian group bury their dead but others cremate them and the ashes are immersed in a nearby river. One of their ancestors (in Bilaspur) is said to have been buried and his little finger and *choti* (cue) were burned. The Gandhila section also bury the dead and pour water on the burial for three days. In Bilaspur, they observe impurity period for 10 days and perform ancestor worship with the help of an Acharaj. They also give a ceremonial feast on *solia* to the community. In Kangra they observe 40 days' pollution period and no festivities are arranged during this period, excepting a feast on the last day.

The Bangalis are still a hunting and wandering community and earn their livelihood by snake-charming, selling herbs and treating certain common ailments like tooth ache *kunanda,* ear ache and otorrhoea (ear blowing supposed to be caused by an insect called *bhudarwalu*). They also earn money by catching snakes from inside the houses of the rural people and are also trusted for treating snakebite. They sell *gidarsingi* (a horn recovered from the head of a fox) and a snake *mani,* which, according to them bring joy, prosperity and victory to the possessors. People often suspect that a Bangali deliberately leaves a snake near the houses of the villagers, and then he starts playing on his flute like instrument *been* and tells the presence of the snake expecting money for catching the same. They also hunt water birds, tortoise, *goh*, hare and catch fish. During the rainy season, greenary jackals and wild boars are easily available and hunted by them.

Earlier the community was landless but some land has since been allotted to them. There is, however, no bonded labour in the community. The children assist their parents in various activities but they do not work as labourers. The Gandhila section earn their livelihood by preparing and selling liquor also. Since they could not get considerable attention from the government for their rehabilitation their involvement in the extraction of illicit liquor and selling it by their women folk, puts the members of the community to legal and social difficulties on a number of occasions.

Some of the Bangalis still maintain their traditional vagrant occupation but the settled ones have adopted road and forest labour. Their children now also receive school education and dislike their ancestral vagrant tradition and snake-charming.

In Kangra, the Bangalis have their own panchayat called Bangali Sabha with a *nambardar* as its head. Elections to the Sabha are through a voice-vote. In Bilaspur, the headmanship of Bangali Sabha is different, as the elderly men of the community are empowered to excommunicate the guilty with *hukka-pani band* and he is readmitted to the *biradari* on payment of a certain fine in cash or kind and washing the feet of a *kanya* (virgin) and serving drinks to the community. The statutory Gram Panchayats help in settling the disputes over land and water.

In Bilaspur the Bangalis propitiate gods and goddesses of the Hindu pantheon. They worship goddess Durga as their patron deity. The other deities propitiated on other occasions are Deot Sidh (Baba Balak Nath) on the birth of a male child and Lakhdata Pir or (Pir Bhianu) on fulfilment of a wish. Snake god, Guga is specially worshipped by offering a *roat* (big loaf of sweetened bread) on Guga Naumi day during the month of Bhadrapada. They also worship lord Shiva. Nag Panchami is a major festival of the community in the Kangra region. They also celebrate other Hindu festivals like Dussehra, Diwali, Lohri, Baisakhi and Sair etc. Local fairs like that of Guga, Lakhdata (Bhianu), Devi, Deot Sidh, etc. are also attended to for the purpose of business and earning money by exhibiting snakes, selling herbs and treating various ailments. They also believe in magic and witchcraft, and a few of this community also practise them.

The Bangalis share various regional folksongs, folklore and folktales as well as music and dance. *Nagin* (snake) songs on *been* played by them have come to be associated with the Bangalis. *Gidha* and *nati* dances are also performed on festive occasions.

The Bangalis have little traditional social, ritual and occupational linkages with other local communities, but they survive with the help of the surrounding natives. The pace of interaction with other communities is very slow as they have different social traits that suit them only. A Bangali, however, traditionally avoids accepting water and *kachcha* and *pucca* food from a Chamar on social occasions. Some prominent Bangalis invite the caste Hindus to their social functions and offer them a *suchchi rasoi* prepared by a Rajput/Brahman or they serve them uncooked cereals. Barring exceptional intercommunity marriages, they have no connubial norms with other communities. Putative kinship-based friendships like *dharam bhai* and *dharam bahin* occur at the time of marriage. Normally, in view of the separate settlement of the Bangali located on the periphery of the village along a *choe* or streamlet, they have their own water resources but may also share the same with other communities. They have free access to schools, temples, houses (except the kitchen) and Panchayat Ghar etc. They have their own cremation or burial ground. Patron-client relationship is lacking. They participate in statutory activities of the Gram Panchayat and other political activities, but political leadership has not emerged from within this community. Modern inter-community linkages are yet to emerge.

There were no literate persons in the community about two decades ago but now some families send their children to schools, though none has received college education as yet. The Bangalis visit the local primary health centres only at a critical time as they first use indigenous methods of treatment. They are now receptive to family planning. Drinking water facilities are available to them at certain places and their houses are electrified. They listen to radio and also have access to television and cinema. Each of their family has since received free grants of Rs. 1,500 under IRDP schemes, for constructing houses and some land has also been allotted to them by the State Government. Their energy sources are firewood and cowdung cakes. Tap-water facility is available. Immunization, ICDS progammes are not utilized by them. The public distribution system as well as banking facilities are available to them. Most of them live from hand-to-mouth and are under debt to the local shopkeepers.

A.R. Sankhyan

BANJARA

The Banjara is also known as Lavana or Labana. But in Himachal Pradesh the Banjaras are listed as a scheduled caste with a population of 2100 persons according to 1981 Census. The Labana are not scheduled. The name Banjara is derived from the Sanskrit word, *vanijya* or *banijya-kara* meaning merchant (Crooke, 1896). They are widely spread throughout Central Western India and are also found in the South. In Himachal Pradesh, they are reported to have come from Rajasthan and Haryana. In dress and speech they resemble those from Rajasthan. Their dialect is a mixture of Rajasthani and Haryanvi dialects but they can communicate in Hindi also. Their dress pattern is changing because of men adopting the Western style of dress and women wearing *salwar, kameez* instead of the traditional *ghagra* and *choli.*

Though non-vegetarian occasionally, the Banjaras' staple diet consists of wheat or maize. They use rice, pulses, green vegetables cooked in mustard, vegetable oil or butter. Fruit consumption is occasional. Tea is their favourite drink. Men are fond of smoking and drinking. Elderly women are also sometimes seen smoking *bidi.*

There are Hindus, Sikhs and Muslims among the Banjaras. The Sikh Banjaras are also known as Charan Banjaras and the Muslim ones as Mukeri Banjara. The Hindu and the Sikh Banjaras may intermarry but the Muslim group forms a separate endogamous section. The Hindu Banjara group claim to have directly descended from the legendry Lakhi Banjara who possessed more than a lakh heads of cattle. They are further segmented into a number of clans and subclans. Some of these are the famous Rajput clans like Chauhan, Rathor, Tomar, Jadon, and Panwar. Each one is further subdivided into numerous *got* known as *khanp* like Kurpe, Minjraut, Udane, Banrot, Baratiye, Dhaiyot, Barasgane, Bhukiye and many other. These are exogamous units, whose purpose is to denote descent and to regulate marital alliances.

Marriages are settled through negotiations at the behest of middlemen. Marriages are now being performed at the age of maturity and these are settled outside the *gots* of the parents. Earlier, child marriages were common and *muklawa* ceremony was performed five to seven years after the marriage. Monogamy is the general practice but the second marriage can take place in the event of the barrenness of the first wife. Symbols of marriage for the women are vermilion and nose-pin. The bride lives patrilocally. The practice of giving bride-price was present some two decades back, but now dowry in the form of gifts of domestic use is generally given to the daughter at the time of marriage. Divorce can be obtained on grounds of adultery, impotency, cruelty and practice of sorcery. The divorcee can remarry. A widow and widower can also remarry. Junior levirate and sororate marriages are practised. A widow at the time of remarrying, however, does not need to have a regular ceremony but only a *karewa* in which the bridegroom presents a new pair of clothes and a nose-pin to the woman in the presence of her close relatives. A widower's remarriage on the other hand is celebrated with full marriage ceremonies.

Joint family enjoys social support whereas nuclear families, though slowly emerging, are the result of domestic discord and therefore looked down upon by the elders of the community. The eldest male member is the head of the family and is consulted on important issues. Women observe purdah in the presence of the senior male relatives of the husband's household whereas with husband's younger brothers and sisters, joking relationship prevails. Division of property is based on the principle of male equigeniture. Daughters are eligible to receive a share in the absence of a son. Succession rights are transferred from father to son.

Women do not enjoy an equal status in the sphere of economy, religion and politics but in the discharge of domestic affairs, they exercise considerable control. Women are hard working and take equal share of the economic workload in addition to the domestic chores but ironically they do not have economic independence. Though women take part in the rituals and festivals, yet they do not hold any religious office. In politics they are gradually showing more interest and are taking part in the activities of the Mahila Mandals which are set up in each block to hear the grievances of the women.

The life-cycle rituals commencing from birth to death are common with the other Hindu communities. At the time of the birth of the child the mother is given a separate room. A purificatory bath is given to her and the child on the sixth day i.e. *chhatti pujan*. Thereafter on the tenth or eleventh day (*dasthon*) the house is plastered with cowdung and the water of Ganges is sprinkled to purify it. A *havan* is performed and relatives and friends are given sweet dishes. Pollution is observed for 40 days following birth and after that the mother can attend to her normal activities. The mother and the child are taken out on the following Sunday. *Mundan* is usually performed at the temple of the goddess during the *navratra* (nine days devoted to the worship of goddess Durga in the months of September-October). Investiture or *janeu* ceremony is not observed among the Hindu Banjara.

Marriage consists of a number of important ceremonies and rituals. The actual marriage ceremony consisting of *kanyadan* and *phera* takes place at the bride's house. When marriages were performed at a young age, another ceremony known as *muklawa* used to be performed at a later date and sometimes five to six years after the marriage but now this is performed immediately after the marriage because of the upward change in the age at marriage.

The dead are cremated and the pollution lasts till the thirteenth day in the case of male and till the twelfth day in the case of a woman. The eldest son performs the funeral rites of the parents. He is to observe certain restrictions on food and movement, for instance, he eats only once a day and pours water over the village deity known as Khera Devta. An Acharaj officiates the funeral rites. On the tenth day and thereafter on the thirteenth day twelve Acharajs are given the funeral feast. Ancestor worship is performed annually during the *shradha* (a special fortnight dedicated to the commemoration of the ancestors).

Traditionally the Banjaras have been associated with carrying grains and salt from one place to another in their characteristic bullock carts and supplied commodities to armies in the battlefield. But because of the modern means of transport their trade has suffered a great deal. This has probably necessitated a shift from trade to settled agriculture. Majority of them have agricultural land to subsist on. Business and service are the other subsidiary occupations. Elsewhere, outside the State of Himachal Pradesh, the Banjaras are also carrying on trade in cattle and are mostly seen bargaining during the *pasu mela* (cattle fairs). Besides, there are others who are engaged as labourers in road and construction work, rickshaw-pullers, vendors and the like. There is no weekly market system. People procure the essential supplies from the adjoining town markets or from small general merchandise shops in the vicinity of each village. Barter used to be a popular mode of exchange but nowadays commodities are mostly bought and sold on cash payment. However, children are seen assisting their parents in the economic activities.

As a mechanism of social control, the traditional Biradari Panchayat as well as the statutory panchayats are functioning simultaneously. Purely domestic issues such as intra-family feuds, cases of marital disharmony, divorce, etc., are first tried at their own level. The elders of the *biradari* as also of the neighbourhood are invited to intervene and reach an amicable settlement failing which the same is referred to the statutory panchayats and the law courts. In the present day context the role of the *biradari* councils is fairly constrained in view of the growing powers of the statutory councils and the general awakening for seeking justice through legal means. Criminal and economic offences are invariably tried by the statutory panchayats. The penalty is mostly in terms of money and the amount thus collected is utilized for the welfare of the community in general.

Though Hindu by faith, there is a considerable admixture of Sikh religious beliefs and practices owing to the frequent intermarriages between Hindu and Sikh sections. The Hindu Banjaras celebrate Hindu festivals and visit religious shrines and also take part in the Sikh religious congregations and visit their sacred centres and Gurudwaras. They have faith in the gods and goddesses of the Hindu pantheon but generally worship the local deities and the village deity. For the Banjaras of Sirmaur, among the regional deities, the names of Trilokpur Devi and Madanan Devi are of great importance. Madanan Devi is mostly worshipped by women and is held in great awe and respect because of the belief that displeasure of the deity with a wrongful deed may bring endless miseries to an individual or family. The village deity, known as Khera Devta, is said to have his abode in a pipal tree and is worshipped annually by all the communities of the village. The fairs and festivals celebrated are of the socio-religious significance.

The Banjarads share the folk art, songs, dances, folklores and tales of the region. The women are deft in the art of wall painting involving different floral and symbolic designs. The folktales are mostly related to the legendry hero Lakhi Banjara and his heroic deeds. The women participate in the folksongs and dances during festivals and social ceremonies.

The Banjaras maintain cordial relations with their neighbouring communities while observing certain caste norms of exchange of food and water. *Pucca* food is accepted from the majority of other communities excepting Chamar. The Brahman, Rajput and Vaishya have reservations in accepting food from them. A Brahman priest officiates during their social ceremonies but is given raw grain which he cooks separately by himself. Water is available through pipes as well as from *barma* (step wells) which is shared commonly with all excepting the communities at the lowest strata. The traditional patron-client relationship exists with artisan and communities such as carpenter, Jheevar and Nai but the system is less prevalent now and people prefer to give cash or kind whenever their services are required.

The Banjaras have access to the basic facilities of transport, electricity, water, literacy and health. Water is available through pipes which sometime do not function properly. Primary-level education is available but facilities for higher education are far from adequate as the colleges are located only in towns. Majority of the children leave their schooling after reaching primary or secondary level. The younger children get the facility of *Anganvadi* where there is provision for mid-day meals for both children and expectant mothers. Vocational centres for women are also being run to train them in stitching and embroidery. Sewing machines are given to the widows and destitutes by these centres. Dispensaries and hospitals exist and the paramedical staff remains on the move going from door to door for inoculation and immunization of the children. The Banjaras get economic aid by way of loans and subsidies under Integrated Rural Development Programme and Employment Guarantee Schemes. Facilities of irrigation, manure and improved seeds are availed of by them.

Vatsala Sarkar

BANSI

The Bansi or Bainsi, a scheduled caste is traditionally a community of flute (*bansi* in Hindi) players attached to the temple from where they derive their name. They inhabit only the Chamba district of Himachal Pradesh where their population in 1971 was only 553 which grew to 957 in 1981. They have been inhabiting the Chamba region since the remote past. During recent times they were given some land in lieu of the service rendered at the temples. They speak Chambiali, a dialect spoken largely by the people of the Chamba district. The script is Perso-Arabic but those who have attained formal education can write in Devanagari and English. Earlier, Tankari or Takri used to be the script widely used by the people of this region, though nowadays it is rarely put to use.

The prevalent dress for males is *kurta, pyjama*, jacket and a *topi* whereas women wear *salwar, kameez* and a *dupatta.* This, however, is also a common dress pattern of the people of Chamba in general.

The staple food of the Bansis consists of maize, wheat and *mah*. They are non-vegetarian and take the meat of goat, sheep, fish and chicken. Eating beef is taboo. Consumption of vegetables and fruits is moderate. They are fond of alcoholic drinks which are sometimes purchased from the market and also brewed at home. Tea is the most popular beverage. Smoking *bidi* and *hookah* is very much prevalent among the menfolk. Elderly women also smoke *bidi.* Women also consume alcoholic drinks on festive occasions.

The Bansis are divided into a number of exogamous *gotra* which regulate marital alliances. They do not have any other endogamous divisions. Since they are in small number there is a tendency to merge with larger groups such as Hali, Chanal and Sanhai. They are now allowing marriages of their boys and girls with their counterparts in these groups. The Bansis usually enjoy a caste status as is enjoyed by Hali and Sanhai. The Chanals are, however, reckoned low but they have also been accepted to be at par. The Bansis occupy a low position in the caste hierarchy but regard themselves above Chamar, Chuhra and Dom.

The Bansis are, by and large, monogamous with stray cases of polygamy reported on account of barrenness of the first wife. Marriages are settled through negotiation. Marriage by exchange is also reported which is locally known as *batta.* The usual age at marriage for the boy is 21 to 22 and for the girl, 18 to 20 years. A married woman puts on a nose stud which is regarded as the marriage symbol. A red *paranda* (pig tail) is also put on by the married women at least during the first year of the marriage. The residence for the girl after marriage is patrilocal. Earlier the community practised the custom of bride-price which is now giving way to dowry. The amount received as bride-price had to be returned to the husband in the event of dissolution of marriage by the wife. Both divorce and remarriage of widow and widower are permissible. This form of marriage is known as *ghadoj*. In this type of marriage a woman is simply given a *paranda* by the man who marries her. In some cases a feast to relatives and members of the community is also given. Levirate and sororate are both prescribed and practised.

The structure of the family is extended joint type, though nuclear families are gradually increasing. The family is headed by the eldest male member who is entrusted with the powers of decision-making. However the functioning of the family is more democratic. Property travels in the male lines with the exception that in the absence of a son, a daughter is entitled to a share and the son-in-law is invited to manage the property. In this case he is known as *ghar javantri*. Similarly, succession is also patrilineal. Mutual love and affection binds the members of the family which are best seen on occasions like birth, marriage and death.

Women do not enjoy the same status as men. On the other hand women work more than the men as they bring water, fuel and fodder for daily consumption, attend to household chores and also work in the fields wherever the family has a landed property. Despite their known economic potential, the womenfolk have no claim to the property. They have a low profile in political and religious life of the community.

The life-cycle rituals are patterned on Hindu religious beliefs and practices and are similar to those of other communities of the region. The birth of a male child is an occasion calling for jubilation and celebration. Post-birth pollution and purification is observed. The purificatory bath is given to the mother and the child on the sixth and eleventh day. The post-birth pollution lasts for 21 days. *Jattu* is performed for the child in either the first, third, fifth or seventh year. The first feeding of cereal is known as *khirpo* and this ceremony is observed when the child is six months old. A sweet rice pudding is made and the child is given a little of that to initiate him to the cereal diet.

The bridegroom goes to the bride's house with a marriage party where the marriage rituals take place. There are three different forms of marriage which are recognized. The regular or traditional marriage is known as *dan-pun vyah* and consists of Hindu rites. But in other forms of marriage such as by service or *har* (elopement), the marriage rites are greatly simplified.

The dead are cremated and the ashes are immersed in a river. Death pollution is observed for a minimum of seven days. Ancestor worship is also observed.

The economic activities of the Bansis revolve around the village temple.

Bansi are flute players and also play instruments like *nagara, ransingha* and *shehnai* (clarionet). They are required to play *nagara* (drum) and *bansi* (flute) once in the morning and in the evening when the head *pujari* of the temple makes his regular oblation in the temple. During the period of princley states, they enjoyed the patronage of the *raja* and were given land in lieu of their services. They were also frequently required to play the instruments for the royal clan and also on the occasion of various fairs and festivals; during royal marriage and birth ceremonies for which they were suitably rewarded. Ever since the temples have been handed over to a trust, they have become paid employees of the temple on a paltry sum. They are given a room to live in but free food twice a month. This, according to the people, is abominably low for any standard of living. Besides, with the growing emphasis on the modern brass bands, they have fewer opportunities to play their instruments at the time of marriage and other occasions. This has adversely affected their economic life. They cannot take to other full-time occupation since they have been traditionally associated with temples and so find it increasingly difficult to switch over to other alternative sources of income. Those few who have retained some land, do agricultural work as well.

For the effective management of social norms, the Bansis have their traditional caste councils to decide on cases of elopment, divorce, intercaste marital alliances, divorce, breach of caste rules, etc. With the enforcement of the Panchayati Raj Act in 1968 many village problems like encroachment and minor criminal cases are now being handled by the panchayats. Besides, the Gram Panchayats are also active in respect to the welfare activities in the village like making village paths, cleaning of *bauli* and repairing public buildings, etc. In urban areas people take recourse to courts of law only if effective solution is not reached at the level of caste councils or Gram Panchayats.

The Bansis worship all the major gods and goddesses of the Hindu pantheon. However, Shiva is their principal deity. A famous pilgrimage known as *jatra* is held each year on the fifteenth day after Janamasthami to Manimahesh situated at the height of 13,000 ft. in the Chamba district. This is the most famous pilgrimage to propitiate their presiding deity, Shiva. There are other fairs and festivals known as *jatras* and Sui-ka-mela, held at Chamba. On the *Sui-ka-mela* day women go to the temple of Naina Devi and worship goddess Sui or Naina who sacrificed herself for the welfare of the people of the town. It is said that Rani Naina was a queen of Chamba who dreamt one night that Chamba town would have a water channel only if someone from the royal family sacrificed him/herself for the cause. She offered to sacrifice herself for the purpose and water gushed from the source which is situated near by. A fair is held every year to commemorate this event. Similarly, the famous Minjar fair is held during July-August, when thousands of devotees make offerings to god Varun by floating *minjar* i.e. symbols of maize flowers in the river Ravi. There is, however, no specific fair which is particular to the community. By and large, people are god-fearing, have faith in supernatural powers, evil spirits and in the power of magic. In order to appease the evil spirits, the usual practice is to sacrifice a goat. Any prolonged disease, or personal loss is thought to be the result of some evil spirit and in order to put an end to this, they take the help of specialists known as *chela, bhagat* or *sayana.* The *chela* (the medium) is invariably a man from the Sippi community of the region.

They share the folksong, folklores, music, dance and craft or handicraft with other communities of the region, though they are interested in folk and performing arts and have preserved the old cultural traditions of music and dance.

The Bansis are regarded low in the regional caste hierarchy, and certain restrictions are observed in terms of commensal norms according to which Brahmans, Rajputs, Rathis or Khatris avoid dining with them. Similarly, there were restrictions on the Bansis regarding entering the houses of the high castes, but now these are gradually giving way to a more respectful attitude towards them. They now sit and take their meals with others at the time of public feasts. They are, however, rated higher than the Chuhras and the Doms, from whom they do not accept *kachcha* food but can partake *pucca* food. There are, however, no restrictions on their taking water from the common source, or sharing school, temple and other public buildings. The system of *jajmani* relationship does not exist with any other community.

The attitude of the Bansis towards the various developmental activities like education and literacy, health, drinking water, electricity and communication is noteworthy for the simple fact that though the basic civic facilities are provided but some of them are unable to make use of electricity and other facilities. In the field of education, they have lagged far behind in comparison to many others. Though freeship and scholarship are given to their children yet very few children really go beyond the primary school level. There is a provision for grants of subsidy and loan on low rate of interests since the Bansis are in the scheduled caste category, but only a few of them make use of these facilities for lack of information.

Vatsala Sarkar

BARD

The name Bard is variously pronounced as Barad, Barar, Burar or Berar (Rose, 1919) but its etymology is not clear. The origin and migration history of the community is not known, though this community is distributed in various districts viz., Bilaspur, Hamirpur, Kangra, Shimla, Solan and Kullu. Their population according to the 1971 Census was 2432 (Singh, 1971). In 1981 their population is given as 2843 (for Barad) and 416 (for Barar, Burar/ Berar). Their villages are located on rough and rugged hilly terrain of the Shivaliks with warm and temperate climate, low humidity and moderate rainfall. They speak local dialects of western Pahari or Himachali like Kehluri (or Bilaspuri), Kangri and Kulvi. The script used is Devanagari in communicating both within and outside the community. They share the local dress and ornaments etc. The community is classified as a scheduled caste.

The Bards are occasional non-vegetarian in food habits and eat fish, eggs, birds like *titar* (partridge) and *jangli murga* (jungle fowl). The intake of non-vegetarian diet is, however, relatively occasional in comparison to vegetables, tubers and pulses. Their staple food is maize *roti* in winter and wheat in summer. Rice is usually eaten on festivals and festivities. The fruit and milk intake is very low. Men are fond of alcoholic drinks, and country liquor is occasionally consumed by them, because it is not easier to afford it. Food taboos are observed on death and on certain festivals.

The Bards share the clans of the Rajputs, like Chandel, Pathania, Jammual, etc. and so claim a Kshatriya descent. But the community is well aware of its low social status and is placed among the Shudra in the Varna system. They, however, see themselves above the Chamars and do not eat with them except in religious gatherings.

The marriage rule is *got* (clan) and village exogamy and community endogamy. Marriages took place between 10 and 14 years for girls and between 12 and 16 years for boys in the recent past. The common mode of acquiring mates has been *satta-batta* through negotiations. Monogamy is practised. *Bindi* (mark on forehead) and glass bangles are marriage symbols but not adhered to strictly. The newly-wed girls generally wear a red suit (a *kurta* and *salwar* with a red shawl). Bride-price exists in some cases, where the boy is illiterate/or where there is no sister for exchange. The amount is decided by the Biradari Panchayat. The residence of the bride is patrilocal. Divorce is rare and permissible in cases of maladjustment and cruelty. The children in such cases are the liability of either of the spouses as per decision of the Biradari Panchayat. Judicial sanction is preferred for divorce as the divorced women are ensured of the compensation. Widow marriage with a junior levirate is permissible. A widower can remarry a junior sororate or some other woman.

The marriage institution has witnessed changes in respect of an increase in marriage age, a decrease of the bride-price and to giving of dowry.

The Bard families are predominantly nuclear ones, where a son starts living separately. The *lari* avoids the husband's father, elder brother and other elderly males of the village and community. Joking relationship exists between *devar* and *bhabi*, *jija* and *sali* and *kuram* and *kurmani* (boy's and girl's parents). The eldest son is the successor of his father but property is inherited patrilineally as per the rules of male equigeniture. The changes in family pattern show decline of the joint-extended system.

Their women are economic assets to the concerned families but their social status is regarded as lower than that of the men. They go from door to door to sell the winnowing fans they make and earn a living. They also sing greeting songs and get alms. They collect fuel and fodder, fetch potable water and do all agricultural and other household jobs, but political activities and mechanisms of social control remains the men's domain.

Pre-delivery restrictions on the expectant mother are observed. Post-natal delivery pollution, *sutak* is observed for 11 days and purification occurs by *guntrala* ceremony by taking cow's urine. Naming and cereal-taking ceremonies are ignored. The *mundan* ceremony is performed by the mother's brother before the fifth year.

The marriage rituals are performed by the priest of the community and no Brahman priest and barber are employed. The elder sister's husband acts as the *nai*. The community priest is given one rupee and twenty-five paise for this purpose. Music is provided by band masters of the community. The clan deity is worshipped. Brief Vedic marriage rituals are performed. The bride and groom circumambulate the sacred fire and parents perform *kanyadan* and also give feast to the groom's party. At the groom's place the bride and groom circumambulate a *pipal* tree. The bride returns to her parents followed by the groom on the same day. The marriage is consummated with *muklawa* on the next day. In case the girl is below puberty, the *muklawa* takes place after her attaining the puberty.

The dead are cremated and ashes immersed in a river nearby. Death pollution is observed for 13 days. The *dan* is given to *dhian* (married daughter) and no Acharaj/Brahman is employed but a learned person from the community does the job. On the sixteenth day, a feast is given to the community.

Traditionally, the Bards were landless and lived on basketry as well as begging. But now they have got small landholdings. The land allotted to them is, however, insufficient for their subsistence on agriculture and animal husbandry. So, they still survive on making mats and *chhaj* (winnowing fans). These are made of *surar* /sirki/reed (a kind of grass). The male members of the community seek daily-wage casual labour in road construction, forestry and sandstone quarries to supplement their income. Some also work as agricultural labourers with the village landlords. There is no bonded labour though children sometimes work as domestic aids. The community lacks persons in white-collar jobs and in business entrepreneurship. Market is located at a short distance and is of daily nature and is fully regulated. Dealings are both in cash and kinds by exchange of their produce.

The community has its own Biradari Panchayat whose headman or *panch* is elected through a voice vote. It settles domestic and social quarrels of the community and may, also punish a person by imposing cash fine or social boycott. It also ventures to uproot certain social evils and suggests changes in the living habits of the community. The general welfare programmes are taken up by the statutory village panchayat which also takes up cases not solved by the Biradari Panchayat. They may also go for other statutory measures for a solution of the economic disputes over land and water.

The Bards worship gods and goddesses of the Hindu pantheon. During the post-Independence period, many have taken to Radhaswami sect which emphasises little dependence on ritual and deities. They are iconoclasts who do not weep at the death of dear and near ones. They immerse the ashes of the dead in the Beas river. Their marriage rituals are also not as elaborate as that of the Sanatanis. They attend regular meetings called *satsang* of their *guru* at Beas in Punjab. Those who follow the Hindu Sanatna rules, propitiate family, village as well as regional deities. Deot Sidh, Guga, Lakhdata and Nahar Singh are propitiated as village and regional deities. Devi Sohni is their *kulja* (family/clan) deity. The sacred shrines of the regional deities are visited on annual fairs and festivals. The festivals like Holi, Diwali, Dussehra, Shivratri, Krishan Janamashtami, Ram Navmi, Rakashabandhan, Lohri and Baisakhi are celebrated by the community. Two local festivals of Chiran and Sair are also celebrated by them. The sacred specialists in their own or other communities are consulted for removing diseases caused by evil spirits.

There is a tradition of basketry and mat-weaving both as a craft as well as the occupation of the community. The regional folksongs, tales, music and dances are shared. Women sing some *vadhai* songs (greeting songs) by offering a small pinch of green grass called *drub dena* on festive occasions. Recently, some men have formed a brass-band musical party to provide music on marriage occasions and earn their livelihood. *Bhajan* and *kirtan* of goddesses are also common folksongs. Gidha dance is performed by women on festive occasions.

The Bards have little ritualistic and social interactions with the upper castes. But they have occupational linkages with other communities in the form of supplying winnowing fans, working as labourers, etc., and they depend much upon seeking alms or begging. They also have little commensal norms with other communities, except with the Chamars with whom they may exchange *kachcha* and *pucca* food particularly during their Radhaswami Satsang. Their water resources are either separate or shared with the Chamars. Cremation grounds are usually separate but temples and other public places are common with the upper-caste Hindus.

The Bards have favourably responded to certain modern developmental programmes. They presently give school education to their children but only up to the primary/middle standards, only a small number receiving school education up to secondary level. They have adopted modern methods of treatment, health and medicare but belief on traditional methods is still strong. Recently, sterilization has been accepted as a family planning method but incentives, more than the spirit of the scheme, attracts them. They have drinking water, electricity, roads and mass media facility accessible in the vicinity. They have received economic aids for house construction under the Integrated Rural Development Programme (IRDP) and availed of immunization under the Integrated Child Development Scheme (ICDS). The facility of public distribution system is also availed of. Their energy resources are cowdung cakes, wood and straw. They are mainly self-employed in basketry and general labour but remain from hand-to-mouth and indebted to the local shopkeepers and landlords.

A.R. Sankhyan

BATTARHA

In Punjabi etymology the word *battarha* is derived from *batta*, meaning stone, as occupationally they are the stoneworkers or dressers/breakers. They are commonly known as Mistri or Raj (masons) and in the profession of stonework they are similar to the Thawins of the hills. They also call themselves as Jammualiye Rajput in Kangra district (the study area) who came to the area from the Jammu during an earthquake that rocked the region during 1905. Somehow the name Battarha is not liked by the community and they prefer to hide the name and like to be identified as Rajputs or specifically as the Jammualiye Rajputs. However, a locality called Battahar Mohalla in Dharamshala town in Kangra district still popularizes the community name. Some persons of the Ghirath (or Chowdhary) community who have adopted the profession of stonework and masonry also claim to be the Battarhas though they are different from the Jammualiye Rajput Battarha and are also not accepted as such by the latter. This community chiefly inhabits Kangra district and only sporadically other places in Mandi and Chamba districts. They live in a hilly terrain and valleys of the sub-Himalayas near the snowline and so the winters are cold but summers are warm and temperate. Humidity is low and annual rainfall is moderate. The hill ranges are covered with thin forests of pines. They speak the regional Kangri dialect of the western Pahari within and outside the community and write in Devanagari script. Men wear a *kurta* and *pyjama* or pant and women wear a *kurta* and *salwar* and *chunni* or *dupatta*. Women wear ornaments of nose, *koka/tilli*, ear-rings, bracelet and bangles.

The Battarhas are non-vegetarian in food habits and eggs, fish and meat are occasionally consumed. Their staple food is maize, wheat and rice. Maize is more frequently eaten. Various types of pulses like *urad, moong, masur*, gram, peas and beans are consumed along with seasonal vegetables and roots and tubers. The cooking medium is mustard oil and/or vegetable *ghee*. Milk intake is occasional except for children. Tea is a common drink. Fruits are also occasionally consumed. Country liquor is consumed at times by men and is purchased from the local market. Men also smoke *bidi*, cigarettes and loose tobacco in the indigenous pipe called *kali* or *hukka*. Some persons chew tobacco and betel leaves. Festive preparations are *kheer, halwa, babru, ankli* of rice and *khichri* of pulses and rice. Non-vegetarian food is not consumed during death pollution.

The Battarhas recognize only small social units called *got* (clan) which regulate marriage alliances and denote ancestry/descent. These clans are like those of the Rajputs of the area, viz., Atar, Jaggi, Jammual, Chauhan and Pathania. These clans may also be used as surnames by some . They claim Kshatriya status but in the Rajput social hierarchy they are placed quite low.

The Battarhas are endogamous and regulate marriages by rules of *got* (clan) and village exogamy. The marriages are negotiated. Exchange of sisters is not allowed socially. Adult marriages occur and monogamy is practised. Marriage symbols are glass bangles, *sindur*, nose pin/stud and toe-rings. Widow remarriage is not approved of socially but a widower may remarry a junior sororate or other woman. Dowry, called *daj dan,* is given in the form of household articles and *kanyadan* is performed. The bride lives patrilocally. Divorce is socially not approved but in rare circumstances of maladjustment, either of the spouse may seek a legal sanction. The husband is liable to compensate the wife and support the children. Both the divorcees may remarry. Over time, the main change in the marriage institution is an increase of the age of marriage and judicial approval for divorce.

The Battarhas live in the nuclear as well as vertically extended joint families. The *lari/nuh/bahu* covers her face from and touches the feet of her *saurah*, *jeth*, *nandoi* and other elderly male members of the village. Informal joking relationship may exist between *devar-bhabi*, *jija-sali*, *nanad-bhabi* and *jija-sala.* The inheritance of paternal property occurs on male lines by the rule of male-equigeniture and the eldest son succeeds the father. Conflicts may arise on unfair distribution of paternal property. The status of women is usually low and they remain confined to the domestic chores. They collect fuel and fetch potable water and participate in social and religious ceremonies and rituals. They have no role in mechanisms of social control and in the political sphere. They do not contribute to the family income but control family expenditure.

The life-cycle rituals are performed as per the rites of Sanatan Dharm by a Brahman *purohit.* Pre-natal and post-natal restrictions exist for the expectant mother. Post-delivery pollution is observed for thirteen days and purification occurs by *gunt* (cow's urine) ceremony when some people also give a feast to the kith and kin and villagers on the birth of first son. Sugar-coated grams are distributed. Child's *nana* brings *jhaggu-topu* and *kangnu*. Naming and cereal-taking ceremonies are generally ignored by many people. *Jattu* or *mundan* of the boy is the major childhood ritual, performed by the *mama* of the child and *kulja* is propitiated and hair is offered to the deity. Wearing of a *janeu* occurs only at the time of marriage. The marriage rituals are similar to those of many upper-caste Hindus.

Clan deity worship, *sand, samuhat* and oil ceremonies are observed. The *ved* and *lagan* rituals are performed at the bride's residence when the *lara* and *lari* circumambulate the sacred fire and the bride's parents perform *kanyadan.* They also serve meals to the groom's party. At bridegroom's place *andrera* ritual is performed. Finally the bride and groom worship and circumambulate a *daran* (pomegranate) tree. Putative kinship-based relations are also made at this time and the marriage ends with music, dance and a community feast. The *muklawa* ceremony occurs on the next day after which the bride lives with the groom. The death rituals are observed as per the Garud Purana. The dead are cremated and ashes are immersed in the Ganges at Haridwar and ancestor worship is observed. The *patak* lasts for 13 days and a Charaj or Masku performs death rites and *havan* and seeks offerings. A Brahman priest also performs purification *havan* and seeks offerings. The gathered kinsmen are served meals on *solhia* (sixteenth day). Annual and fourth annual anniversaries are also observed.

The Battarhas are landless and traditionally thrived on the occupation of masonry or stonework. They also seek casual daily work or regular employment as skilled labourers in stonework or house buildings, construction of roads and dams and in forests. Only a few persons are employed in Government jobs as bus conductors, peons, chowkidars and clerks. A few are also teachers and in defence services. The links with the market are direct and the market is fully regulated. Child labour exists. The dealings are in cash.

The social disputes are settled by the Battarhas' own community people, the *sayane* (elders). Economic or village disputes are resolved by the statutory Gram Panchayat (or ward members) which deals with welfare and developmental activities. The Battarha are Hindus and worship gods and goddesses of the Hindu pantheon. Besides they have family/clan and village deities propitiated on birth, marriage and other festive occasions. In Kangra Bankhandi Devi is regarded *kulja* by some and Balaknath as a village deity. Other local deities are Brajweshwari, Jawalamukhi, Chamunda and Chintpurni whose religious shrines are visited from time to time and on the occasion of the fairs. Sacred specialists are employed from other communities whenever there is a need. They have faith in *bhoot* (ghost), and other evil spirits which cause certain diseases and only to be treated by *chela.* Various regional and national festivals of the Hindus like Lohri, Baisakhi, Sair, Shivratri, Navratre, Ramnaumi, Rakshabandhan, Diwali, etc., are celebrated. The Vishwakarma day is celebrated with great zeal on the day following Diwali when they observe rest and worship their tools. The community is not involved in any socioreligious movements. They share the regional Pahari or Kangri folksongs, lore, tales and music and dance forms. Some popular folksongs sung are *Kunju-Chenchlo, Kangre de fauji, Subhadro-Bajeer, Nurpure dia ghatia, Bhala Sipahiya dogria,* etc. Popular music is by percussion instrument (drum), and *kirtan* and *bhajans* are sung.

They are treated at par with the Rajputs and the Brahmans in exchange of *kachcha* and *pucca* food and water, except in some areas. Traditional water sources are likewise shared. Connubial norms are restricted to the community but putative kinship like *dharam bhai* and *dharam bahin* may occur with any community. The cremation ground is shared with the upper-caste Hindus. Religious shrines and other public places are common. They have persons holding white-collar jobs and in teaching and defence services. The political leadership has emerged only at the local level.

Modern developmental programmes have made some favourable impact on the Battarhas. Formal education is favoured for the boys who usually study up to the secondary school level; only a few receive college education. Formal education is less favoured for girls. Modern mass media (radio, television) facilities are availed of and their houses are electrified. Communication facilities like road, railway and postal services are available. They favour both modern as well as indigenous medical care methods. Attitude towards the small family norm has become favourable and sterilization is the common method for this purpose. However, at least one male child is very much desired by the family even at the cost of more children. Drinking water through taps is available to many but the traditional water sources like springs and *bauri* are also used at the time of water scarcity. There are no special provisions for employment and as such the people are generally self-employed in their traditional occupations and other professions. Traditional energy sources such as firewood, coal, sawdust and kerosene oil are used. Among the nutritional programmes for children (ICDS) immunization facilities are available free of cost. The facility of public distribution system is also available. Normally the people favour savings and put their earnings in banks and post offices, and only a few persons are dependent on the local moneylenders or shopkeepers.

A.R. Sankhyan

BATWAL

The Batwal and Barwala, though used as synonyms, are of different origins. The word Barwala seems to have been derived from *bara* or *baria,* a kind of wild grass used for weaving, whereas Batwal means a watchman or a guard (Rose, 1919), the position which many of them still hold today in Chamba district of Himachal Pradesh. The etymology of the term Batwal means 'son of a *beti'* (daughter). It is said that a Raja's daughter became enceinte by an illicit amour and was expelled from her father's kingdom. A Chuhra took her to his wife and she gave birth to a child who founded the Batwal caste. However, Dr. J. Hutchison notes that the Batwals of Chamba, "claim descent from Siddh Kaneri, a deified ascetic of whom they know nothing. Formerly employed as watchmen, a few are still enlisted in the State police" (Rose, 1919: 66).

In the upper hills they are known as Batwal whereas in lower hills they are known as Barwala. In certain parts of Kangra, they are known as Karoack, also a term used for a person whose duty is to call and collect persons. The fact that the Batwals are the watchmen is further strengthened by the following example:

> *Champapur ke purab me, Devi Sui bhai prakash, ardh mas iski jatar kare, nahin to huae banash, Chet mas ke ardh mein, mela sui pradhan, yah mela hai nari ka, ghat-ghat batwal hain, nar deva na jan.*
>
> (In the east of Champapur (now Chamba) goddess Sui is born, who is worshipped every fortnight, and one not worshipping her will have a bad end. In the middle of Chait (March), the main festival of Sui is held, which is a fair of women. It (the festival) is guarded by Batwals, who do not allow any man to go near it).

The present-day distribution of the Batwals is primarily in the districts of Chamba, Kangra, Bilaspur and Solan of Himachal Pradesh and in adjoining districts of Punjab, and Jammu and Kashmir. The Batwals live in separate localities along with members of other communities in the village. They mostly occupy the middle and low altitude hills of Himachal Pradesh, and lead a tough life, owing to the typical climatic conditions of the hills. The total population of the Batwal according to the 1981 Census is 10,290 in Himachal Pradesh including figures for the Karoack community.

The dialect spoken by the people of this community is Bharmauri or Gadiali (as they were originally in Brahmaur owing to the seat of the Raja), but now they speak in Chambiali with each other. With others, they speak

Hindi and the educated among them can converse in English too. The script used by them among themselves is Perso-Arabic, while with others it is Devanagari and English. The Batwals residing in other region speak the dialects of the regions concerned. The Batwals cannot be identified these days by their dress, but in earlier times they wore the same kind of dress as worn by the Gaddis, i.e. *chola* and *dora*. The community along with its counterparts, the Karaock, are included in the scheduled castes of the State.

The Batwals are non-vegetarian. They mostly take meat of goat, fish, sheep, wild boar and ghural. Their staple diet consists of rice, *rongi* (red beans) and *mah*. Wheat *chapati* (unleavened bread) are taken, and so are vegetables. The vegetables are either purchased, or are grown in their kitchen gardens. Edible roots and tubers are also taken. Mustard oil or hydrogenated oil are used as cooking media. There is a moderate consumption of fruits like plums, apricot and apples which are grown locally and are only available in certain seasons. Milk is available from the cows, which are kept in almost every house and there is rarely a situation when they need to purchase it. It is taken in its raw forms by infants, growing children and occasionally by invalids and the aged, while others take it in tea and in its various derivatives, like curd, *lassi*, butter and *ghee*. Alcoholic drinks are also consumed by menfolk and occasionally by women. They mostly prepare brewed liquor at home, but sometimes it is also purchased from the market. They also chew and smoke tobacco. Non-vegetarian food is consumed more frequently during winter, and this is also true for the consumption of alcohol. During inauspicious occasions taking non-vegetarian food is taboo.

The Batwals are divided into a number of exogamous *gotras* like Badial, Narial, Chattriyal, Bhardwaj and Kharontia. There is no hierarchy among these *gotras*. The name of a *gotra* signifies the saint from whom they claim their descent; members of the same *gotra* are regarded as blood relatives and the main function of *gotras* is to regulate marital alliance. Members of one *gotra* are obliged to render mutual help to their fellow brethren. Though the people perceive themselves equal to the Rajput in social and varna hierarchy, but this is not acceptable to members of other communities. They reckon them to be of low standing, but above the Dumna and Chuhra castes, and regard them as Sudra in the varna order.

Endogamy at the community level and exogamy at the *gotra* level are the common rules of marriage. Matrimonial alliances outside the community, sometimes result in excommunication. Hypergamous marriages are prohibited but hypogamous marriages meet with social approval. Prior to Independence, during the days of princely states times, the Batwal married their children at very young age but deferred their *gaona* (ceremony of consummation of marriage) till they had grown up. Nowadays marriages are held when the boy is around 25 years of age and the girl around 15 or above.

Mates are acquired either by negotiation (regular *byah*) or by *atta-batta* (exchange). Though monogamy is the general form of marriage, yet occasionally bigamy or polygamy is also resorted to when the first wife is unable to provide the family heir. In such cases the consent of the first wife is essential. Junior sororate and junior levirate are also practised. The latter practice is known as *ghadoj*.

Though marriage symbols are not strictly observed, yet nose-ring is a marriage symbol. Dowry is prevalent in the community and though earlier it was demanded in cash, it is now given by the bride's parents on their own. The usual form of residence after marriage is patrilocal, but in rare cases, where there is no male issue in the family the son-in-law comes to stay with the bride's parents and is known as *ghar javantri*.

Divorce is permissible in the community, and can be initiated by either of the spouses and is granted with the consent of the traditional panchayat. The common ground for divorce are infidelity and incompatibility. In the event of the husband divorcing the wife for his own fault, the dowry expenses have to be returned to the wife. The children of the divorced parents are the liability of the father. Widower and divorcee remarriage are allowed, but widow remarriage is prohibited outside the family. However, she can marry husband's younger brother with the consent of the panchayat.

Previously joint family was the prevalent form, but today it is being replaced by nuclear family system. This is primarily because of their moving into diversified occupations. Nevertheless, the family is still a strong social unit which binds the members together. The eldest male member of the house commands greater respect and his decision in all family issues is final and is ungrudgingly accepted, for more often than not, it is arrived at after mutual consultation with the other members. The daughter-in-law observes avoidance with husband's elder male relatives, by covering her face with a veil. Joking relationships also exist with the elder sister's husband, the husband's younger brother and the wife's younger sisters. The husband and wife avoid taking each others' name, and often they are addressed, as 'mother or father of so and so' (teknonymy) by each other.

Male-equigeniture is practised. A widow or a married woman has no right to inheritance, though she can act as a custodian of the property in the event of her husband's death and her children being small. In the event of there being no male issue, the practice of *ghar javantri* is resorted to, and only in such a case can the property be inherited by the girl. But should she fail to bear a male child, the property reverts back to her collaterals. This is known as the Mundaband law of inheritance. The eldest son succeeds as head of the family.

Women's status is lower than that of men. But they have an important role in the economic sphere, for they carry out all the agricultural activities in their fields except ploughing. Women of poor families also go to work in others' fields as agricultural labourers, to add to their family income. They also collects fuel and fodder for the animals. The women take part in all the social and religious festivals and rituals of the family, community and the region. They also take part in political activities, which is only limited to the casting of votes. The Batwal women are responsible for family management, and carry out all the domestic chores. They control the family expenditure, contribute to the family income but have no decision-making powers.

Post-natal observance of pollution is reported for a period of six days. On the sixth day, both the mother and the child are given a ceremonial bath and the house cleaned. At the end of one year of the birth of a child *ritan* (head shaving) ceremony is observed. In some of the families a *bodi* (cue) is also kept, as in other Hindus.

Marriage is solemnized by circumambulating an earthern pitcher placed at the centre of a canopy fixed on four poles. Brahmans do not officiate at their weddings. This job is performed by two elderly persons of the community. A feast is given by the bride's father. As a good omen, the food is first thrown to the crows, which the Batwals worship.

As a rule the dead are cremated, but such males whose *mundan* has not been performed are buried. The period of pollution remains upto the thirteenth day, when the Brahmans are given cash and *seedha*. The remains of bones are either taken to the Ganges at Hardwar, or Parmandal in Jammu, which is a pilgrim spot of the region.

When the king or any member of his family used to die, the Batwals were called, and it was their duty to carry fire and incense in front of the corpse and funeral procession, up to the cremation ground and to safeguard the corpse from being overpowered by any evil spirit.

The major resource of the Batwals is land, which is owned by individuals. The Batwals, today are mainly a landowning community. Those who meagre land take others' land on *ghar* (sharecropping). The traditional occupation of the community was to act as a watch and ward, which continued until the end of princely states. After the abolition of the states, their demand fell down and many had to take up other occupations. Some are still in the police department and some have taken to white-collar professions, government jobs, tailoring etc. Though the primary and subsidiary occupation differs from family to family, agriculture is the mainstay of the community. The community is totally dependent on market, as they have to market their produce, and purchase things which are not grown by them. They have direct links with the market, and employ no middlemen. The sale takes place on cash basis. Barter system is resorted to within the village, where one foodgrain is often exchanged for another.

Children below 15 years of age also assist their parents in agricultural activities. Girls assist their mothers in household work, and also in agricultural activities as labourers in others' fields where they are normally paid in kind but occasionally in cash.

For the maintenance of law and order the Batwals have their own traditional Biradari Panchayat, which is headed by a *mukhiya*, who is assisted by *up-pradhan, sachiv* and *panch*; all elected by voice votes on the basis of their ability to give an impartial judgement. The cases that come up before them relate to *ghadoj*, divorce, infidelity and breach of community rules. The guilty are punished by imposing fines, both in cash and/or kind, the amount of which is utilized towards defraying the expenditure on the panchayat. After Independence, the statutory panchayat maintains law and order and plans and implements welfare activities. Nevertheless, the people prefer their traditional panchayats.

The Batwals worship family deities. Each *gotra* has a mound of earth at a place which represents their temple and they prostrate before it, and offer sacrifice of a goat in the honour of the eldest son. This is known as *kulj* or *kuldeota.* Jalpa, Shakti, Shitala and Chamunda Devi are their regional deities. Nag Devta is represented as a village deity and is worshipped by all communities residing in the village. The Batwals' major sacred centres are Mani Mahesh at Brahmaur, Hardwar, and Parmandal in Jammu, and visit to these places in the lifetime of a person is believed to bring them salvation.

The Batwals' sacred specialists are the knowledgeable persons from their own community. They officiate at all the life-cycle rituals. The Batwals have to perform a very important role in the offering of *newala* to Shiva. Their presence as one of the nine persons required to officiate this occasion is a must. In the times of princely states, they were specially invited at such occasions to guard the sanctum-sanctorum, the canopy or the place of worship. *Newala* can be offered by any of the families in the area. In Sui mela the Batwals have to guard the entry of males, as it is primarily a fair for women, celebrated on the fifteenth day of *Chait* (March). Besides, they also participate actively in the Minjar fair, celebrated in the month of August and Manimahesh *yatra* in September. All these festivals have socio-religious significance.

Traditionally the Batwal used to prepare mats using a wild grass. Nowadays, this has been dispensed with. Most of the houses unlike other communities of the hills, possess *khadi* (loom) and the Batwals weave their own woollen clothes and blankets in their spare time.

The Batwals have oral traditions of folklore and folktales which are common with all the communities of the region. They sing and dance on occasions of betrothal, wedding and birth of a child. Men and women dance and sing separately. The women dance within the four walls of the house.

The traditional intercommunity linkages mostly existed with the princely

Rajput families of the erstwhile princely state, where they performed the duties of *chowkidar*, and with others, officiated at ritual performances in the offering of *newala* to Shiva and carried fire in front of the bier of the royal family members. They also had links with other communities like Lohar, Sippi and Dumna, who used to render their traditional services to their clients, in return of which they received fixed quantity of food grains at the harvest times.

A Batwal traditionally can accept both *kachcha* and *pucca* food from the Brahman, Khatri, Rajput, Rana and Rathi. On the other hand, all the castes from whom the Batwals accept *kachcha* food, cannot take either *kachcha* or *pucca* food in their houses. On social occasions, in the event of the food being cooked by a Brahman, they can accept *pucca* food only. The other communities however accept both *kachcha* and *pucca* food from them. Similar restrictions regarding acceptance of water are also observed. *Dharam bhai* or *sakhi* relations can be established with unrelated members of the same community. There is, however, no restriction on the sharing of water resources, entry into the common crematorium, temple, houses *etc.*

Their rising level of education has enabled them to take up white-collar professions and some of them today are administrative officers, police officers, doctors, engineers and teachers.

There is a greater awareness among the Batwals of various developmental progammes, but their impact has been varied. In the sphere of literacy and education, only very few in Chamba have been able to go beyond matriculation. The main reason for this is the non-availibility of school for higher education in the villages, except at tehsil district headquarters. Also the distances are great. Nevertheless, because of free education, and facilities like scholarships, books, stationery and uniform people have started sending boys and girls for primary education. Though the girls drop out for family reasons, the boys are allowed to continue as per the family's economic capability.

The Batwals living near urban centres are favourable to the Government allopathic dispensaries and hospital where the facilities are available, whereas in the villages, they resort to traditional home-made remedies at the first instance, and when not cured, avail themselves of hospital treatment. The younger and the educated people favour the small-family norms and adopt modern contraceptive devices, except sterilization, which is not preferred by either of the sexes. The older generation is averse to family planning.

Drinking water facilities are available in the urban centres, through piped supply, but in villages the people depend on natural snowfed streams. Similarly, electricity is available near the district and tehsil headquarters and urban conglomerations. The Batwals have obtained employment under various government schemes like rural employment programmes and jobs against quota and under self-financing schemes. They have availed themselves of the facility of setting up shops of general merchandise, tailoring and haircut, etc.

The district and some tehsil headquarters and urban conglomerations are connected by metalled roads, whereas, most of the villages have link roads which are *kachcha.* Post offices do exist but are far from the villages. Telegraph facilities are available in district and certain tehsil headquarters, whereas those in remote areas have wireless facility. Television is available at district headquarters. They use wood and kerosene as the fuel. Irrigation is through rainwater or on perennial snowfed streams. Chemical fertilisers and pesticides are used in smaller quantities and preference is given to the locally available organic manure. But people do avail themselves of high yielding varieties of seeds. Mid-day meal programme in school and nutrition progamme under Integrated Child Development Scheme is available at Balwaris and Anganwaris, and is availed of by expectant and nursing mothers and children. They avail of the public distribution system. Banking and investing facilities are available at the district and tehsil headquarters, and are availed of.

Rajendra Sarkar

BAZIGAR

The Bazigar or Bajigar is a scheduled caste. The name Bazigar is derived from the Persian word *bazi* (acrobatic activity). They are also known as Sirkiband or Sirkibaz after *sirki*, the reed-hut dwellers, as they used to make portable huts while wandering across the country for giving performances of their acrobatic skills and to collect money and eatables for their subsistence. Rose (1919) states that the Bazigars may be included in the broad group of Nats as an occupational category. However in Kangra, where the study was carried out, the community identifies itself by the name Bazigar even though they have now left their acrobatic ways. According to them, a Nat is a rope dancer whereas a Bazigar is an acrobat. They claim their ancestry from a legendary saint, Babe Lal, whose shrine is located at Udhoke in Batala (Punjab). The Bazigars are immigrants to Himachal Pradesh and entered the State from Punjab during the recent past. They still have matrimonial alliances in Hoshiarpur, Navanshahar and Amritsar, and speak Punjabi and write in Gurumukhi as well as in Devanagari script. They are mainly concentrated in Kangra (Nurpur and Indora tehsil) and Una districts. They live in the villages of the Shivalik foothills experiencing, in general, warm and temperate climate, low humidity and moderate rainfall. Their total population in Himachal Pradesh according to the Census of 1971 was only 663 (Singh, 1971) but after a decade it rose to 1144 in 1981.

Their food habits are similar to those of other people in Kangra. Their food consists primarily of maize and wheat, supplemented by rice. They are fond of local liquor and also smoke *bidi* or tobacco. Both men and women are non-vegetarian in food habits and occasionally eat eggs, fish, pork, flesh of goat and sheep and chicken but beef is not taken. Various types of pulses, roots and vegetables are consumed which are cooked in mustard oil or vegetable *ghee*. Milk intake is minimal except by children. Fruits are also occasionally consumed.

The Bazigars sometimes claim Gaur Brahman status (in Kangra) which is unacceptable to other communities. They distinguish many *gots* as smaller exogamous units, like Sandhu, Malike, Dashike, Dulchike, Namsol, Mashal, Karmuke, Morike and Vartiye. These denote their descent lines and are used as exogamous units. The Bazigar are endogamous and practise *got* and village exogamy. The age at marriage is about 16 years for girls and above 20 years for boys. Mates are acquired through negotiation and monogamy is the prevalent marriage form. Marriage symbols are *sindur*, glass bangles and *bindi*. No bride-price is given or taken but the practice of giving dowry exists. The bride lives patrilocally. Divorce is permissible through social approval in cases of adultery, maladjustment, impotency, cruelty, insanity, etc. and either of the spouses can divorce. But normally a man is responsible for children. Remarriage is permissible on divorce, death of the spouse and in the absence of an issue or a male child. Junior levirate is permitted but normally does not occur. Junior sororate may also occur.

The families of the Bazigars in Kangra are predominantly nuclear ones. Avoidance exists in joint families between *bahuti* and *saurah* and *jeth* but this relationship does not last long and ceases to exist after a few years of marriage. Joking relationship between the bride and others is similar to that in other regional communities. Inheritance is on the male lines as per the rule of male equigeniture and the eldest son succeeds the father. The significant change in the Bazigar family pattern seems to be the decline of joint extended families.

The Bazigar women are an economic asset to their families. Presently, when the community has lost the acrobatic occupation and has settled with a small piece of cultivable land insignificant for subsistence, some Bazigar women have virtually started begging. They participate in various economic activities, agricultural and animal husbandry (in some cases), collection of fuel and fodder, bringing potable water, family management, and in social, religious and ritualist ceremonies. They enjoy an almost equal status with that of the male members.

Post-delivery pollution called *sutak* is observed for 13 days and purification occurs by taking *gunt* (cow's urine). Naming and cereal-taking ceremonies may be ignored. *Mundan* ceremony is observed for boys on third/fifth year of birth and the hair is cut by a barber or the *mama* of the child.

The pre-marriage ritual is *karmai* (engagement) when a finger ring and clothes are given to the boy and the girl from both sides. The marriage rituals are performed by a Brahman priest as per Sanatan Dharam Vidhan but elaborate rituals are avoided. Marriage rituals are performed at the bride's place and a feast is given by both sides. The bridegroom and the bride circumambulate the sacred fire and also worship a mango tree and take its rounds. The *muklawa* ceremony occurs on the third day after the marriage.

The dead are cremated but a saintly person is laid down in a *samadhi* and his nails and *choti* (cue) are immersed in water. Immersion of ashes occurs in the Ganges at Hardwar and *pind dan* is offered to the Panda. Death pollution is observed for 13 days when the community is offered a ceremonial meal. No Acharaj is employed for death rites or ancestor worship, and the offerings may be given to the married daughters of the family.

The life-cycle rituals are becoming less important in the present times and are being curtailed due to economic contraints.

The Bazigar has been a vagrant community and used to perform acrobatic acts like jumping, rope dancing and gymnastics and subsisted on this occupation. But now most of them have lost the traditional occupation and became casual labourers, beggers, drum beaters, hawkers and agricultural labourers. Some of their women go to nearby villages to sell needles or petty items of domestic use like hawkers and virtually beg for cereals, bread, money, and clothes. During the post-Independence period they have been allotted land but which is barely sufficient for house construction and kitchen gardening and only a few have landholdings to do farming, or for rearing cattle. Child labour is prevalent. During some ceremonial occasions and wrestling matches, the Bazigar beats drum and seeks alms (so also known as Dholi). Market facilities are available in the vicinity.

The Bazigars have their own community panchayat constituted only by male members who elect a *pradhan* through voice vote with 20 to 25 executive members. There is subscription of a rupee every six months collected as *chulha* tax from each family. However, they contribute substantially for special gatherings of the panchayat in which, at times, over 400 persons assemble to solve certain disputed cases about marriage, divorce or some crime. If someone does not contribute to the panchayat he is called *dhonsia* and is socially outcast and reinstated only after he pays the desired amount.

The Bazigars (in Kangra) are Hindus but in Hoshiarpur (Punjab) they are also Sikhs who may intermarry with the Hindu Bazigars. They have family and clan deities. Some in Nurpur propitiate Deot Sidh as *kulja* and others propitiate Jawalamukhi as their clan deity. They also propitiate the regional deities like Lakhdata, Guga, Brajweshari Mata, Chamunda and Chintpurni, and the shrines of these deities are visited on occasions of marriage and birth. Babe Lal is specially worshipped as a community deity every year. Their sacred specialists are from other communities. The main festivals celebrated by the Bazigars are Shivratri, Baisakhi and Lohri.

There are some skilled singers among them. The Bazigars sing Punjabi folk songs, religious songs like *mata ki bhetan, kirtan*, and *bhajan* which are sung both by men and women. Percussion (drum) and valve (harmonium) musical instruments are commonly used. The folktale of Babe Lal is often cited.

The Bazigars may have *jal/chal* and exchange of *kachcha/pucca* food with other similarly placed castes. Putative kinship may exist with other communities. There is sharing of wells and water, schools, temples and cremation grounds.

The Bazigars in Kangra have a special role of beating drum in *chhinj* or wrestling matches similar to that of the Bharai in Bilaspur. Patron-client relationship does not exist except with a Brahman. The community lacks business entrepreneurs, scholars, teachers, administrators and engineers/ doctors, but there are some members in other services like the army and ministerial jobs. Political leadership has not emerged.

Developmental programmes have made little impact on the community. Their children avoid going to schools as they are avoided by other children owing to their poor hygienic conditions and their vagrant/begging way of life. But a few get secondary school education after which they may drop out due to economic reasons. Female education is little favoured. Modern health and medical care facilities are availed but they favour indigenous methods as well. They have adopted modern family planning measures, particularly sterilization. Drinking water (piped water) is available in the vicinity. They listen to radio and watch television in their neighbourhood. Postal, telegraph, road, railway and electricity facilities are also available. The public distribution system and banking facilities are available. Some have been benefited by IRDP progammes. Immunization is availed of under the ICDS. They remain dependent on local moneylenders and shopkeepers. They used to live in thatched huts whose walls are made of reeds called *sirki*. Presently, baked brickwalls have replaced the *sirkis*. Energy sources are firewood, cowdung cakes, sawdust and coal.

A.R. Sankhyan

BEDA (BODH)

The Beda is a professional musician of the Bodh group in the Lahaul and Spiti district, who specializes in playing flutes and drums. The community is concentrated in the Lahaul subdivision of the district. A community of the same name which professes Hinduism also lives in the Outer Seraj area of Kullu and the adjoining villages of Rampur Bushahr of Shimla district (See Appendix A). The Bedas of Lahaul and Spiti occupy the high altitude mountainous terrain, where climatic environment is extremely cold, rainfall scanty (mainly due to local precipitation), with semi-arid and arid conditions prevailing in different places, conforming to the mountain desert conditions. Vegetation is scanty, humidity is low and the forest is sparse. The region experiences heavy snowfall. Exact recent population figures are not available. The language they speak is akin to the Bhoti or the Tibetan group, with deviations areawise, where, in parts, mixture of Kulvi is also found. These include Boonun or Punan, Manchat or Tinan or Tinent, and Chinali. These tongues are spoken in different areas by the Beda and other low-caste groups. Their dress consists of the overall type of coat of knee or ankle length, tied by a metre long *sash* at the waist. They, however, may not wear the *Bhoti* cap usually worn by high class/caste Bodhs. The present-day change to trousers, shirts and coats (western type) is evident, but they wear the traditional dress on special occasions. In Lahaul-Spiti they form a part of the scheduled tribe population.

The Bedas are usually non-vegetarian. Wheat is their staple diet, supplemented with maize and barley, and occasionally rice. Their traditional intake is Thugpa/Thukpa (a sort of a wheat noodle in plenty of soup with meat and mixed vegetable pieces). *Mok mok* is another patty type of preparation from wheat but is steamed, instead of being baked. *Sattu*, a sort of powdered gram or barley is also consumed. Pulses, as such, are rarely taken. Cooking is done mainly in yak's fat or vegetable oils. Roots and tubers are regularly consumed. Fruit consumption is occasional as and when locally available. Buttered tea is regularly consumed. So are alcoholic drinks, *chhang* (local millet beer) and *arak* (whisky) prepared at home. They smoke the hubble-bubble or cigarettes. Yak milk and *churi* (cross between a yak and a cow) milk are also consumed whenever available, in a limited manner. There has been no change in their basic food habits, though outside foods have made their entrance and are making headway.

The landed aristocracy are the Tongpa. Artisan group, the Lakishes come after them. The Bedas come under the latter group, but remain confined to themselves. The community is considered low in status and they are aware of their social position. The Rajput Bodhs form the upper section of the social hierarchy here and among them and Thakurs are the landed aristrocrats. However, social distinction and discrimination are kept at a minimum.

The Bedas practise endogamy but *gyut* exogamy. Sororate junior and levirate exist. Marriage is delayed as girls are economic assets and the parents are not eager to part with the daughters. The marriage is traditionally polyandrous and negotiated. However, polygamous marriages are not accepted if the first wife is unable to produce offsprings.

Love marriage and marriage by capture and service are accepted. Today monogamy is gaining ground and polyandry is on the decline. Symbols of marriage are a female headgear of precious and semi-precious stones called *perak*. This is seldom worn and is adorned only on special occasions. Ear-rings, bangles/wristlets and necklaces are worn by the women. Marriage is usually accompanied by bride-price, because women are an economic asset. It is returnable on divorce. The marriageable age for girls is between 25-30 years. Two forms of traditional marriages are in vogue in the area. One is the *magpa*, wherein the boy goes and lives at his wife's residence, thereby acquiring rights. Such a marriage is resorted to in case the bride's father is without any son. In the *bagma* marriage, the girl goes to live with her in-laws and acquires rights thereby. In case of preferential marriages or marriage by mutual consent, the union is usually accepted but the residence may initially be neolocal. The traditional practice was fraternal polyandry. However, sometimes a man other than the brothers may be brought in as a husband in the polyandrous system. The Bedas practise this to keep their group big. In the present day, however, monogamy is preferred and is gaining ground. In marriage, village exogamy is practised as far as possible.

Divorce is permissible on grounds of adultery, barrenness and insanity. Either party can divorce. Children are usually the liability of the father, but can stay with their mother if so agreed upon. Compensation is socially decided upon. Widow, widower, male and female divorcee remarriage are all permissible. There has been no change in marriage rules except that the custom of polyandry is fast giving way to monogamy. Family types are nuclear, the mixed extended ones virtually coming to an end. Families are basically patriarchal, initially patrilocal and inheritance is patrilineal. Avoidance relationship is at the minimum. Joking is fairly common and without much inhibition. The society is liberal and conflict and confrontations on any matter are minimal.

Sons inherit equally, while daughters are given their share at the time of marriage.. On divorce, she again acquires some rights with her parental property, losing the same on remarriage. Unmarried girls enjoy the rights to the parental property. When there are no male heirs the daughters inherit. Succession is usually by the eldest son. There has been a rise in the formation of nuclear families. With monogamous unions nowadays, the succession pattern is being split up.

Women are subservient to the men in social, ritual and religious spheres. In political spheres, they play no role. However, a woman plays an important role in steering the economic activities and has her say indirectly in mechanisms of social control, which are, nevertheless, dominated by the menfolk. Women enjoy high status, and make their own contribution to the family income, and control the family expenditure.

In case of birth, pre-delivery restrictions are observed and the woman is separated, and confined to a room. Pollution period after birth is 7 days. In case of a male child, the first religious worship is done on the third day and for a female, it is done on the seventh day. Diet restrictions are observed. Purificatory ceremony is done on the third or the seventh day respectively. Confinement period is up to 30 days. A worship is arranged on the fifteenth day for the welfare of the child. Ceremonial tonsure of a boy is done between first and second years, in consultation with the *lama* (monk), on an auspicious day, with cash presentation by the guests. The naming ceremony is conducted therein by the *lama* or *labha* (witch-doctor). Names are given by them in consultation with the almanac. For the Bedas, marriage is a contract. Rituals are conducted at the bride's and the groom's residences. The groom does not accompany the party to the bride's residence but waits patiently at his own place for the party to return with the bride. The occasion is celebrated with a feast at both the places. Consummation of marriage takes place at the groom's residence. In case of polyandrous marriages, the consummation by the brothers is according to seniority. The dead are cremated in a sitting posture with fanfare. Pollution is observed and a special rite is observed after some days of the event. Another ceremony is observed at the end of the second month to ensure safe passage of the soul into the next life. Food and drinks are served on each occasion. Memorials for the dead may be prepared and the remains kept therein. The rituals are not as elaborate or strictly adhered to as they were traditionally. People spend less and lesser people attend these rituals. Even people in the remote areas find rituals becoming more expensive.

The Bedas are traditionally a musician group providing music on all occasions of celebration or to mark an event and that was their main source of income. Initially, they had to depend on it for subsistence or sustenance, the payment being in cash and kind. This was and is supplemented by agricultural or other type of labour. They do not possess much land of their own for cultivation and get their remuneration for services performed in cash and kind, which are enough for their daily needs. The community is mainly a landless community. Ritual begging is permitted by tradition. They used to move from village to village for this purpose. Traditionally, they had no permanent home and used to set up tents for night shelter. But subsequently, with lands donated by well-to-do patrons, they were able to settle down in permanent residences. Some land is devoted to growing vegetables or crops in limited quantities.

The marketing facilities for the community are irregular. Fairs and festivities take place at the monastery or religious sites. Both barter and cash are used for transactions. Otherwise, small shops at places or travelling salesmen cater to their needs. Children are rarely put to work. However, children over 15 years of age help with the family occupation. But fewer children are taking to this family occupation because of the economic poverty in the profession. They are now in the favour of educating themselves and finding employment in more renumerative professions. Hence, the population in the traditional service is fast dwindling.

Social control is exercised by the *goba*, the *lambardar* and village councils. All these consist of members from highly placed village families. The village panchayat, on voice vote basis, has been introduced, but has not been much functional. However, they deal with cases of minor disputes, and punishment is in the form of fines in cash or in the form of the guilty throwing a feast for the village. Thus matters are attempted to be settled amicably. Recourse to modern forms of justice has yet to develop sufficiently to replace the traditional ones.

In Lahaul-Spiti the community follows the Red sect of Buddhism whereas in other areas they follow an improvised form of Hinduism. *Lhu* is the traditional malevolent spirit of the area, who has to be appeased and propitiated. Chugma and Palmo Lama are the female deities providing them welfare and protection. Palmo Lama is equivalent to the mother goddess, Durga. Gyephan is the god of the snowy mountains, the patron deity of the whole of Lahaul and Spiti. The Buddha is their main god. Mahadeva is venerated as an incarnation of the Buddha. Festivals are of socioreligious significance to them and celebrated at different time and to mark the various occasions of the season and living.

The Moravian Missionaries started a Christian mission as a socioeconomic religious movement. Their activities were related more to social welfare and economic welfare than to religious conversion. Hence conversions were few, though welfare activities brought great success. The movement fizzled out with the forced departure of the missionaries by the authorities in the 1940s.

Except for the making of drums and other musical instruments required for their type of social and religious performances, the Bedas have not many other works of art to their credit. Only monastries specialize in carving out *mane* stones and religious paintings. Women do knitting, taught initially by the Moravian Missionaries, in various local designs. The musical instruments are nowadays often bought from traders in Manali and Kullu, where they are manufactured and sold on a commercial basis. The locals are thus left to the job of reparing them. Folklore and folksongs exist and are sung by both sexes on occasions. Occasional dances in the traditional style involve mainly males but sometimes females also.

Members descended from a common ancestor are known as *gyut* members, and do not intermarry. *Chaspun* relationship is formed between individual members from different families bound together by some religious promise to help each other. *Phasphun* are social brotherhood groups meant to help in time of need. They consist of a few families grouped together, worshipping a common deity and providing mutual help at all times. They share the same water sources, cremation grounds and religious shrines with other communities. Participation in traditional festivals and festivities with the rest is common. Triloknath is a major pilgrim centre for the locals.

The Bedas have a social obligation, i.e., to render the services of a musician to other communities of the area. They also provide physical labour on payment as and when required.

The Bedas have only musicians and labourers, and being socially and economically backward, they have not been able to make much headway in any other sphere.

Literacy and education is gradually spreading in the area. Children usually drop out by middle school. Attendance in schools is also irregular. The main drawback in children's education is that they also have to help the family in economic activities. They believe that formal education is only for the well-to-do under their circumstances.

Facilities of health and medical care are minimal, the locals rely more on the *amchi* (indigenous medicine men). Modern medicine is availed of rarely. In an area with sparse population and a tradition of polyandry, which was widely prevalent till some time back, family planning has no meaning. Local springs provide drinking water, as well as water for irrigation.

The Bedas listen to radio very keenly. The public distribution system is not widely prevalent. There are some banking facilities and some cooperative and credit societies to facilitate farming and export of potatoes. Since this affects the landed population, the Bedas are not concerned with them.

T.K. Ghosh

BHARAI

The Bharai or Bharyai is a small Muslim community of traditional drum-beaters. Rose (1919) suggested the origin of the name from *hara bhara* (evergreen) or from a place Parahin in Multan or from *chauki bharna* (to keep a vigil) by the followers of the Sakhi Sarwar deity propitiated by the Bharais. But it seems more appropriate to trace the etymology of the name from Hindi word *badhai* (greetings and blessings) as the Bharais visit the households of their clients on ceremonial occasions and convey their greetings by singing songs and beating drums. Rose (1919) and Ibbetson (1916) considered the Bharais an occupational group or a spiritual brotherhood that comprises many caste components or subgroups, mainly the Rajput Bharai and the Jat Bharai. The Bharais mainly inhabit the districts of Bilaspur, Kangra, Hamirpur and Mandi in the hills and dales of the Himalayan foothills experiencing warm and temperate climate, medium rainfall and low humidity. Pockets of thin forests may be seen in the seven hill ranges of the district Bilaspur drained by a network of seven streams, the tributaries of the major river the Satluj. A water reservoir named Govind Sagar which is the rich abode of fish has come up with the construction of the Bhakhra Nangal Dam and has contributed to reshaping the ecology of the area.

The Bharais may be identified from their typical insignia, viz., a *dhol* (drum) and a stick, a *khallar* (wallet) hanging around the neck by a string, and a *jagadhri* (tussel) on a long pole. Men wear a typical dress while beating drums, i.e., a white shirt and a *churidar pyjama* or *tamba*, a black jacket and a white turban along with a black *seli* (ribbon) of wool. They speak regional (Bilaspuri) dialect of the western Pahari and write in Devanagari script except in their socio-religious communications which may also be in Perso-Arabic script.

Their staple food is maize and wheat supplemented by rice. Various pulses, gram, beans, etc. prepared in mustard oil or vegetable/*desi ghee* are consumed. *Khajur* (date palm) is eaten during *roza* and other religious occasions. They are non-vegetarian in food habits and take *halal* meat but avoid beef. Men smoke *bidi*/cigarette or tobacco but do not take liqour.

The Rajput and Jat sections of the Bharais are distinguished by their clan names, namely Chauhan and Ghorwahe (Rajput) and Gill (Jat). The Jat clans may be more numerous among the Bharais as stated by Rose (1919), and these include clans like Dhillon, Deo, Rawal, Grewal, Mann, Randhawa, Jham, Karhi and Badecha. There does not exist any social hierarchy in the two sections and both can intermarry. The clans simply indicate their descent or ancestry and lack matrimonial significance as the Bharais may marry within a *got.* They also intermarry with the Faqirs and the Raeen Muslims; usually they take daughters from the Faqirs. They rank above the Mirasi and the Faqirs but below the Raeen and the Sunhak (Chandel Muslim) in the regional Muslim social hierarchy.

Village exogamy is practised. They prefer marriages of cross-cousins, but avoid *dudh ka sak* (milk relationship). Pre-puberty marriges were quite common a few decades ago but presently post-puberty marriages are more common. Marriage occurs through negotiation but *batta-satta* may also occur. Monogamy is the common practice, though bigamy may also occur. Glass bangles and nose-pin/stud are considered symbols of marriage. *Mehar* is paid at the time of marriage and ranges between Rs. 500 and Rs. 1500. Dowry in the form of household articles is also given. The bride lives patrilocally. Junior sororate, junior levirate, widower, widow remarriages may occur as per Islamic sanctions after *iddat.* Permission also exists for a divorcee's remarriage.

The family pattern of the Bharais is traditionally vertically extended, but nuclear families are on the increase. There exists avoidance relationship between *lari* and *sauhra* and *jeth*. Joking relationship are informal and are similar to those in many Hindu communities of the area. Inheritance is as per the rules of male equigeniture and succession goes to the eldest son. Junior members are obliged to pay respects to the elders but conflicts may arise on property matters. The families appear to be well interlinked on the occasions of festivals and sorrow. Women participate in domestic as well as agricultural and animal husbandry pursuits. They collect fuel and fodder and fetch potable water. They also partake in social rituals and religious ceremonies but do not play any role in political matters and mechanisms of social control. They also lack the power of decision-making and are placed lower than men in social status.

Life-cycle rituals are observed as per the Islamic tenents. Pre-natal and post-natal restrictions are observed. Birth pollution is maintained for 40 days. Naming, cereal-taking, *mundan* (tonsure) and *aqiqa* ceremonies are ignored. The *sunnat* or *khatna* (male circumcision) is the main childhood ritual performed by a Nai or Julaha or an Abdal who is offered a brass or steel plate, a hen and some cash which may range from Rs. 25 to Rs. 200. The community is given a *nyaz* (feast). *Nikah* is the marriage ritual when a *maulvi* takes *kaul karar* (consent) of the boy and the girl three times and the marriage is then contracted. The parents of the bride feast the bridegroom's party and the latter also reciprocate the same to the *laddhar* (persons accompanying the bride) at their place. *Muklawa* occurs on the day following the marriage.

Death rituals are also observed as per the Islamic prescriptions. The dead are buried and death pollution is maintained for 40 days and ancestor worship is observed on the third, seventh, tenth, twentieth, thirtieth and fortieth day known as *chaliha*. A Faqir is given alms, and a ceremonial feast is given to the gathered relatives.

The Bharais are settled agriculturists and are also involved in animal husbandry. They still maintain their traditional occupation of drum-beating and get *lag* (customary dues) particularly during the *chhinj* and cattle fairs. They are skilled in the cattle trade. Due to paucity of land to subsist on they also seek daily-wage casual labour. A few persons are in the government as electricians and forest rangers and in the army. Some are also petty shopkeepers. Links with the market are direct and of daily nature. Dealings are in cash. Child labour exists.

The Bharais' disputes are resolved in the community council and in the Islamic committee which is elected by a voice vote. The latter generally takes up more serious problems like marriage and also seeks to acquaint people of the Islamic tenets. Village disputes are resolved by the elders of the village or by the statutory Gram Panchayat which generally performs the developmental and welfare activities in the village, and is empowered to put a cash fine on the guilty in disputes over land and water. They propitiate Sakhi Sarwar as their patron deity. In addition, like Hindus, they also propitiate the local village and regional deities, namely Lakhdata, Balak Nath, Nahar Singh and Guga. They have a specific role of beating drums during Chhinj fairs frequently arranged in the name of Lakhdata every year in the area. Generally two festivals, viz., Id and Bakrid are celebrated with zeal but they also have reverence and celebrate various local Hindu festivals like Lohri, Basoa (Baisakhi), Sair and Chiran. They have traditional magic-cum-medicine men in the community, but the *maulvi* who performs life-cycle rituals is from the Faqir community. Like the Faqir the Bharais (men) also perform an ordinary *dhamal* dance while beating drums. Various Pahari including Bilaspuri and Kangri folksongs are sung and regional folktales and folklores are shared.

The commensal norms in terms of exchange of food (both *kachcha* and *pucca*), traditionally exist with the Muslim communities. Usually Hindu *botis* (cooks) prepare meals for Hindus in social gatherings. Marital linkages may occur with the Faqir. Putative kinship may occur with Hindus as well. Burial places are separate and located outside the village. They usually visit religious shrines of all regional deities. There is no discrimination in respect of an access to various public places. Traditional water sources are common but the Bharais would not touch the water pot of an upper caste Hindu. The members are engaged as shopkeepers or businessmen, persons in the defence services, etc.

Modern developmental programmes have made an impact in the spheres of literacy, health, etc. Children usually receive secondary school education, though due to economic reasons or lack of interest, boys do not receive higher education. Higher education is not favoured socially for girls.

Indigenous methods are still favoured though modern system of medicare is fully used. Modern family planning methods, predominantly vasectomy, are followed and people do not favour more than three or four children, though a male child is still desired even at the risk of having more children. Electricity and modern mass media (radio and TV) and communication facilities are available. Piped water for drinking is available but traditional sources like *bauri* are still used quite often when piped-water supply becomes irregular and inadequate. Rainwater is the chief source of irrigation. People use chemical fertilizers. Fuel sources are wood and cowdung cakes. There is no community-specific programme for rural employment/development but general facilities under IRDP and child development programme including immunization exist. The facility of public distribution system through fair price shops is available.

A.R.Sankhyan

BHARARE

The Bharara (singular) or Bharare (plural) is a localized group of Brahmans in Kangra. They write their caste as the Tugnait Brahman who claim to be Nag Brahmans by origin. The Tugnet is shown as a Bhatehru Brahman in Kangra by Rose (1919). The etymology of the word 'Bharare'/'Bharara' is related to a place named Bhardwin located in the vicinity of their present habitat. Also, another place Ghurada, located in Hoshiarpur distrct (Punjab) from where their ancestors had come in the recent past, is suggested to indicate the etymology of the community's name. 'Bharari' or 'Bhararu' is also a name assigned locally for an 'upland' locality, and therefore, may contain the explanation of the community name. Some learned persons of other communities suggest that the name Bharara has been derived from a local term *bharar,* meaning making a hole by tearing a piece of cloth. This is based on the fact that the Bharare, who used to cremate dead bodies in the area tear or take out the coffin of the dead person. The Bharare, however, deny that all of them do the job of cremation of the dead bodies and claim that they only render the priestly services on the banks of the river Beas at Kaleshwar Mahadev temple where the people of the area cremate their dead and perform death rites. Some economically well-off persons of the community dislike the name Bharara which they say has been imposed on them by other people, though they admit that some of the poor persons of their community carry on the cremation job. Instead of Bharara, they like to be respectfully addressed as Pandit ji.

They are also the *pujaris* (priests) of the Mahadev temple of Kaleshwar, but presently their grievances are that the management of the temple which was earlier in their hands is now with a *sadhu* from elsewhere. Also, their land which is the property of the temple is under litigation. Nevertheless, in view of their priestly services in performiing death rites and/or cremation of dead bodies, the Bharare appear to be akin to the Acharaj and Jogi. The latter also cremate dead bodies on the bank of Beas in Hamirpur district. In Sundernagar (Mandi district) their kin call themselves as belonging to a Rawal caste. The community known by the name Bharare is however localized in the Garli tehsil of Kangra district even though they suggest their kinship with temple priests in Kangra and Mandi districts. They are numerically small but an exact figure of their population is not known. They live in the hilly terrain of the Himalayan foothills experiencing warm and temperate climate, low humidity and medium rainfall annually. The terrain is covered with bushes and sporadic thin forests and is drained by monsoon streams meeting at the river Beas. They speak the regional Kangri dialect of the Pahari and write in Devanagari script. Some of the old men also know Urdu and Sanskrit. Priestly men wear a white *kurta* and *dhoti* and put on a *parna* on their shoulders. They also put a *teeka* (mark) of sandalwood and turmeric on their foreheads. On ceremonial occasions, the old men wear a white *safa*. Young men wear shirts and pants. Women dress in *kurta* and *salwar* and a *dupatta* or *chadru*. Traditional ornaments of women were a conical silver *chak* on head, golden *murki, kante, har, gajra* or *choora* and *jhanjar*.

The Bharare are occasionally non-vegetarian. Their staple food is maze, wheat and rice. Various types of pulses like *moong, masur, kulthi*, peas, *rajmah* and *raung* (beans) and gram are consumed. Different types of seasonal vegetables are consumed alongwith roots and tubers. Fruit intake is occasional. Festive foods are *kheer* and *halwa, sevian, babru, ankli/anklu, saag* (mustard leaves' spinach) and *khichri*. Food taboos are observed during death pollution, such as non-vegetarian foods, spices and *heeng* and milk are not consumed. Milk is particularly taboo for a person performing *pind dan*. Milk and its products are consumed regularly. The cooking medium is mustard oil or *desi ghee* or vegetable *ghee*. Men occasionally consume country liquor. In Mandi district, their kins, the Rawals, frequently consume a local homemade liquor called *ghanti* prepared of sugar molasses. *Bhang/sulfa* (Indian hemp) in almond juice is ceremonially consumed by some as it is considered the favourite intoxicant of Lord Shiva, their patron deity. Men smoke loose tobacco in an indigenous pipe called *hookah* or *kali* and also smoke *bidi*/cigarette.

The Bharare recognize only a few *gotra* divisions like Kaushal (at Kaleshwar in Kangra district) and Rawal in Mand district. The *gotras* regulate the marriage alliances and denote ancestry from a particular lineage of the Brahmans. In the regional social hierarchy the Bharare rank at par with the Acharaj/Masku and Jogi and other groups of the inferior Brahmans and other priests of the Shiva temples. They may intermarry with these communities but the Bhojkis (the temple priest of goddesses) in Kangra do not intermarry with the Bharare and consider them inferior to them. *Gotra* and village exogamy is adhered to as a rule in contracting marriages. The marriages occur through negotiation, but *batta-satta* is also practised. The girl is married after the attainment of puberty or at around 17 years of age and the boy's age is usually around or above 20 years. Some decades back, however, child marriage was quite common in the community and some people used to take the bride-price. Presently, however, there has been much change in social attitude and child marriages and bride-price no longer exist. The so-called *kanyadan* or *dharame pune* marriages are performed and *daj dan* is given in the form of articles for domestic use, ornaments and clothes. Monogamy is the rule but a man is socially allowed to marry another woman if the first wife is infertile or has not given birth to any male child. Marriage symbols are *sindur* and *bindi* (red mark on forehead) at a time, glass bangles and a nose and ear ornament (nose ring/pin/stud). The bride's residence is patrilocal. Widow remarriage and divorce have no social approval but divorce may occur on judicial approval on grounds of maladjustment. Either of the spouses may seek divorce. The compensation or maintenance expenditure is paid to the woman and the children are liability of the father. Such divorcees may marry again if they like. Widower marriage is permitted. He may marry either a junior sororate or any other woman.

Their family pattern is both nuclear as well as vertically extended. Sons usually do not get separated as long as the father is alive and or until all sons are self-sufficient and married. The family members are bound together by the convention of respect to the elders and obey them. However, quarrels and confrontations may arise in the famly on division of property, unequal distribution of family workload and due to traditional conservative social attitude of the *sas* (husband's mother) towards *lari/bahu*. The *lari* covers her face in presence of her *saurah, jeth, nandoi* (husband's sister's husband) and from the elderly male persons of the village. Joking relations are informal and may be observed between *devar* and *bhabi, jija* and *sali, nanad* and *bhabi* and *jija* and *sala*.

The property is divided as per the rule of male equigeniture and the eldest son becomes the successor of his father. Nuclear families are showing an increasing trend now. The status of woman remains low and they do not contribute to the family income and do not generally seek employment. The women, however, do all types of domestic and agricultural work except ploughing. They bring potable water and collect fuel and fodder. They also participate in various social and religious ceremonies but do not perform death or temple rituals. They also lack participation in the mechanism of social control and in political sphere and also have no decision-making powers but regulate family expenditure.

The life-cycle rituals are performed as per the Vedic tenets though some rituals like pre-delivery, cereal-taking and thread-wearing before marriage have lost significance and are ignored. Restrictions on the expectant mother as well as after delivery are observed. Post-delivery pollution called *sutak* is observed for 11 days when the mother takes bath and a *gunt* or *guntrala* ceremony is performed to purify her by tasting water of river Ganga and cow's urine. She, however, still does not cook for about 40 days. The birth of a male child is rejoiced over. Folksongs called *ranjhunana* are sung and sweetened germinated grams are distributed. The *nana* (mother's father) of the child offers *jhaggu-topu* and *kangnu* (wrist rings) to the child. A name is given to the child by consulting the horoscope and a small feast may be given to young children. The only childhood ritual is *mundan* or *jatlu utarna* observed only among male children on any odd year of birth before five years' of age. It is performed by the *mama* (mother's brother) of the child or any other person chosen as *dharam bhai* by the child's mother. A feast is given to young children and a *tola* (weighing of child with grains, metal pieces, coins etc.) is also performed to remove the effect of malevolent stars of the child. The *janeu* is put on the marriage only.

The marriage rituals are similar to those of other Hindu communities of the area. *Barni* or *karmai* (engagement/betrothal) is a premarriage ritual in which the girl and boy are given some clothes, sweets and some token money by the parents-in-laws. The marriage is contracted only if the stars of the both the boy and the girl match, which is assessed by the family priest. *Sand* and *samuhat* are the premarriage rituals observed two or three days before marriage after which the girl and the boy are bound not to go outside or cross a stream/or visit an inauspcious place or eat from others. The major marriage rituals are *lagan* and *ved* performed by the family priest at the bride's place. The *lari* and *lara* see each other's face at this time. They then circumambulate the sacred fire and finally the brdegroom keeps the hands of the bride in his hands called *pani grahan* and the parents of the bride perform her *kanyadan* or *sankalp*. They give a feast to the party of the groom side. At groom's place the first ritual is entering the house called *andrera*. The second major ritual is a tree worship which is either of a mango or *daran* (pomegranate) tree, according to the convention of different families. Finally the marriage ends with dance and music rendered by a brass band party. The *muklawa* of the bride occurs on the auspicious next day and the marriage is then consummated.

The death rituals are similar to those of other upper caste Hindus of the area. The dead are cremated at the banks of river Beas in the vicinity and ashes are immersed in its water. Sons shave off their heads on the death of the father. Death pollution lasts for 11 days when *kirya-karam* (ancestor worship) rites are performed by the Acharaj and offerings are made to him. The community is served a ceremonial meal on the sixteenth day called *soliha* and the family priest performs havan and gets offerings. The first *barkhi* (death anniversary) and *chabarkh* are also observed to commemorate the dead and ceremonial feasts are given. Every year a *shradh* of every dead person of the family is observed in the Hindu Pitri Paksha and a meal, usually with milk pudding, is given to the family priest and to the crows as *pitra poojan*.

The Bharare survive on their special service as temple priests of the Mahadeva and seeking offerings from the people for performing cremation and some death rituals. They also possess land but some of it is with the temple management and is presently under litigation with the local administration. They are also engaged in animal husbandry. Their income from charity collections of the temple is also not stable presently as they have been deprived of the sources by the temple management/trust, and so are facing an economic crisis. They have some earning hands in government services and also in private employment. A few persons are in the army. A small market is located in the village but the main market is about ten kilometres away in the tehsil headquaters approachable by road and a foot track. The dealings are in cash. Child labour exists in-as-much as they assist their parents in agriculture and animal husbandry and other activities.

A formal community council does not exist, but the *sayane* (elders), of the community resolve social disputes in respect of earnings from temple and cremation grounds. Other socioeconomic disputes over land and water are settled by the elders of the multiethnic village or by the statutory Gram Panchayat, which also deals with welfare and development activities. Economic disputes are also dragged to civil courts.

Besides, having faith in the Hindu trinity, the Bharare worship Shiva (Kaleshwar Mahadev) as a patron deity. Brajeshwari Devi at Kangra is propitiated as *kulja.* In addition to these the regional deities of special reverence are Jawalamukhi. Chamunda and Chintpurni. Their holy shrines are visited during the annual fairs or upon the fulfilment of a wish. They celebrate various Hindu festivals of socioeconomic and socioreligious importance such as, Lohri, Baisakhi, Chiran, Sair, Ramanaumi, Rakhi, Nag Panchami, Dussehra, Diwali, etc. Somawati Amavashya is specially celebrated and they observe fast on this day and propitiate Lord Shiva. Nag Panchami and Shivratri are also of special significance. They perform *Nag Puja* (snake worship) and have a place in the courtyard where an idol of the snake god is kept and propitiated. Their sacred specialists are from their own as well as from other communities. They believe in diseases caused by supernatural beings and use the services of some local oracle to treat them. Oral traditions notable among them in the Kangra region are *Jhanjoti, Dharmu, Subhadro-Bhajira, Bhala Spahiya dogria, Kangre de fauji, Nurpure da thana*, etc. Beside these they also sing *bhajan* (religious songs) and *kirtan. Gidda* dance is a favourite with women, especially young girls.

The upper castes traditionally do not accept *kachcha, pucca* and even *sidha* food and water from them but they may accept the same from the former. Traditional water sources are shared with the upper caste communities and the crematorium is also common as are the religious shrines and public places. Traditional *jajmani* (patron-client) relationship exists with Nai, Lohar and Charmar. Some members of the community are holding white-collar jobs and in defence services.

Modern developmental programmes have made some impact on the Bharare. The formal education is equally favoured for boys and girls up to secondary school level, but higher education is not favoured for girls, even though boys also normally do not seek college education due to lack of interest/or no security of an early employment. Girls are considered social liabilities and are supposed to be married off soon. General awareness towards a small family size has increased during recent years and steriliztion has been adopted as one of the methods for family planning. But desire for at least one son exists. Their houses are electrified. They avail themselves of or have access to modern mass media (radio, TV and cinema) facilities and they also are linked by road, and postal facilities, springs and *bauri*. No special provisions exist for the community under IRDP and only immunization facility is availed of under the ICDS.

A.R. Sankhyan

BHAT

Traditionally the Bhats were genealogists and while rulers moved from one place to the other or when they marched towards battle-fields, they followed the troops narrating family histories and heroic deeds of the rulers. The community is identified locally as well as at the regional level. The historical accounts show that they migrated to their present habitat. In Sirmaur, they are found distributed in the trans-Giri and cis-Giri tracts (the present study area). The climate of the area is moderate, with hilly terrain, low humidity, thin forests and medium rainfall. Among themselves the Bhats speak in Pahari dialect and use Devanagari script for writing. The Bhats are non-vegetarian and their womenfolk also take fish, meat and eggs. Their staple food is wheat and maize but those who can afford take rice also. They take pulses like *urd, moong, kulthi,* and *masur.* Mustard and vegetable oils are used as cooking media. They take roots and tubers with varieties of seasonal vegetables. The consumption of fruit is moderate. They use alcoholic drinks as well.

The Bhats call themselves Brahmans but the latter do not endorse it, as the former follow the *karewa* system. Their customs and rites differ from those of the Brahmans. The Bhats recognise *gotra.* The *khel* is a smaller group and is the regulatory mechanism for contracting matrimonial alliances. They do not have hierarchical differences but their status is maintained with their education, economic condition and occupational position. Some of them do write their surname as 'Bhat' but nowadays they have started writing 'Sharma' instead. The community is aware of the varna system and they consider themselves Brahmans of the highest order in the varna system.

The Bhats are endogamous, they permit marriage within the same *gotra* also. But marriage within the *khel* (nearest relations) is prohibited. Marital age varies between 20 and 25 years for boys and 15 and 20 years for girls. Life mates are acquired through negotiation and the Bhat are mostly monogamous. Their married women use *sindur* and nose-stud as marriage symbols. They do not have any tradition of dowry or bride-price but nowadays the parents of boys have started demanding dowry according to the education, occupation and economic position of the boy. They follow the rule of patrilocal residence for the bride. Both husband and wife have the right to divorce in case of maladjustment and can remarry. Children can live either with the mother or the father after divorce. Widow and widower remarriages are permissible. One can marry the wife's younger sister and also the elder brother's widow. There is no apparent change in the marriage rules except increase in the marital age.

In the rural areas vertically and horizontally extended family types are available but in the urban areas nuclear families are on the increase. In a family, the younger brother's wife maintains *purdah* (veil) in front of the husband's elder brother and other senior male members. One can joke with the elder brother's wife and also with the wife's younger brothers and sisters. The sons inherit paternal property but the eldest male member of the family succeeds to the headship of the family. The women of Bhat families involved in agriculture do not contribute much to agricultural activities. They however collect fuel, water and look after domestic animals. The women control family expenditure but they cannot take independent decisions as they do not have an equal status to men. They take part in social, religious and, in some cases, in economic activities.

The time of birth is noted for preparation of the *kundli* (horoscope). The name of a child is given by the family priest in accordance with the stars in the horoscope. On the name-giving ceremony, walnut or a mixture of seasam and rice with sugar is served. *Mundan sanskar* is held at the age of three and the child is given some cereals at the age of six months. *Janeu* ceremony is performed between 7 to 11 years of age, but some prefer to perform this ceremony at the time of marriage. The bridegroom goes to the bride's house with his friends and relatives at the time of marriage. After the death the Bhats observe pollution for 13 days and cremate their dead. Due to hardship, economic stringencies and fast life-style, the rituals are getting curtailed.

The Bhats' main occupation is cultivation. A few are also engaged as priests. They have a direct link with the daily market and their transaction is in cash. They lack a community council, though in villages statutory panchayats exist and these are heterogenous in composition.

The Bhats follow Sanatana religion. They have family deities, and also worship village and regional deities. Sacred specialists are from the same community. Hardwar, Vaishnodevi, Jawalamukhi, Kedarnath, Badrinath, etc., are the sacred centres, which these people visit occasionally. They observe the festivals of Bissu, Diwali, Holi, Shivratri, etc. They have oral traditions, which tell us about their migration and their glorious activities in their leisure time.

They accept water from almost all communities. They accept *kachcha* and *pucca* food from the Rajputs but they do not take *kachcha* food from the Vaishyas and other lower castes. They accept *sidha* from the the Chamar, Julaha, etc. communities. The Bhats also participate in all the village festivals, sometimes as a priest or sometime as a member of the area. as they are one of the affluent communities in the area, and also politically and economically very much advanced. They are engaged in white-collar jobs—many of them are engaged in teaching services in colleges and schools. Their children are becoming engineers, lawyers and doctors and have now started practising. Many of their boys are engaged in defence services.

The Bhats are very much aware of the need for their children's education. They allow their boys and girls to go to schools. Many of their boys complete their education from colleges and universities. They use both traditional and modern medicines. Their attitudes towards family planning is positive. People hesitate to go in for sterilization but they use other methods for family planning without any hesitation. Drinking water is now available within the locality. Though the Himachal Government has started various programmes for the self-employment, the Bhats have not benefited much from them. In the rural areas they engage themselves in agricultural work. Communication in general has improved, all-weather roads, both metalled and unmetalled exist in the area. The people listen to radio and see television programmes. They also visit cinema and the video shows. Economically well-off families use electricity for lighting. For cooking purposes they mainly use fuelwood and kerosene oil, but nowadays in the urban centres some people use cooking gas. For irrigation they have to wait for rains and in some areas cultivators use stream water.

D.K. Chakraborty

BHISTI

Bhisti is a Muslim community and is also known as Saqqa or Abbasi. Etymologically, the word is derived from the Persian word *bahisht* or Sanskrit *vasishta.* But Major Temple points out that *bihishti* in Persian does not mean water carrier (Rose, 1919), and suggests a derivation from the Sanskrit *vish*, which meant to sprinkle water. The Bhistis claim their ancestry from Abbas Alamdar, who was the first person sent to fetch water from the pond in a *mashak* (skin bag) to quinch the thirst of Imam Rasul of Damascus, who was restrained from drinking water during *jehad.* The Bhisti live mostly in Uttar Pradesh, Haryana and Punjab, where they carry on their traditional occupation of carrying water. In the Paonta tehsil of Himachal Pradesh, their advent has been recent: the first family moved in from Jagadhri in Uttar Pradesh in 1951. They do not have any idea regarding their dispersal in Himachal Pradesh, but claim that they mostly inhabit the territory adjoining the areas of Punjab, Uttar Pradesh and Haryana.

The dialect spoken by the Bhistis among themselves is Urdu mixed with Sirmauri, and with others is Hindustani and Sirmauri. The script used by them is Perso-Arabic both among themselves and with others. The younger generation has started writing in Devanagari also.

There are certain common features like keeping long, flowing beard by elderly men, wearing round cotton cap or turban, and a round mark on the forehead which the Bhsitis share with other devout Muslims.

The Bhistis are non-vegetarian, and they take meat of goat, chicken, fish and buffalo. Pork is prohibited by religion. Their staple food consists of rice, wheat or *makki chapati* (unleavened bread of maize), *masur* and/or vegetables. Non-vegetarian food is not taken daily. The cooking media are mustard/*til* (sesame) oil. Wild roots and tubers like *turar* and *sharar* are also taken. There is a moderate consumption of vegetables and fruit which are taken occasionally. Milk in its original form is generally taken only by the children and invalids, whereas the elders take milk in tea and in the form of curd and *lassi* (buttered milk). The Bhistis chew and smoke tobacco. Alcoholic drinks are normally not taken and are prohibited by religion.

Special foods like *seviyan* and mutton are specially cooked on Id and Bakrid and also on other festive occasions. Restriction on partaking food and water exists from sunrise to sunset during the 40 day period of *roza* during the month of *Ramzan.*

They are divided into 72 *firqa* (schools of thought), and all of them are considered to be on equal footing. Among the Muslims of the village, they rank second in social hierarchy, the first being Sheikh Ansari.

Other communities like Nalband, Mirasi, Muslim Banjara, Rangar (Muslim-Rajput) and Pinja are reckoned lower than the Bhistis. The communities which are socially lower testify the fact and admit that since the Bhistis supply water to all, and all can accept water from them, they are therefore socially superior.

The Bhistis are endogamous at the *firqa* level. Consanguinity is practised. Care is taken to avoid mother's milk. Marriage between brother and sister's children are permitted. Marriage with father's sister's daughter and mother's brother's daughter is preferred. Both junior levirate and sororate are practised.

Marriages are performed in adulthood by *nikah* in which the consent of the boy and girl is taken. Sometimes, instead of the consent of marriage partners, the consent of their parents is accepted as the consent of the intending partners. *Batta-satta* is also practised by exchanging girls between two families as brides. Though polygamy is the prescribed form of marriage, usually monogamy is practised. Second marriage is resorted to only with the consent of the first wife in case the first wife is unable to bear a child for the family.

Nose-pin and glass bangles are the usual marriage symbols but these are not observed strictly. *Mehar* is fixed at 152 *tolas* of silver. This is a deferred payment, and has to be paid in cash on annulment of marriage or before death. Though it is implied that the *mehar* amount should be paid immediately on the bride coming to the groom's house, yet this is rarely done. Usually, the wife exempts the husband from paying the *mehar*, but the husband has to formally offer her the *mehar* amount in cash or kind. The usual rule of residence is patrilocal, but in cases where the girl's parents have no son, the son-in-law is invited to stay with the in-laws and looks after the property. Such a son-in-law is known as *ghar jamai*.

Talaq (divorce) has social approval. Couple intending to divorce have to repeat the word *talaq* thrice in the presence of two *gawah* (witnesses) and the marriage is nullified. Later on moving the Biradari Panchayat or *anjuman* for compensation the divorced wife is paid the *mehar* amount and *daj*. The fine imposed by the *anjuman* on the offender is retained by the panchayat. But in the case of fault of the wife, the *daj* (gifts) and the *mehar* are forfeited. Divorce occurs on grounds of infidelity by either of the spouses, maladjustment and cruelty. Either of the aggrieved parties can initiate divorce. Children of divorced parents are a liability of the father. Divorcee, widow and widower remarriage are also possible. A widow (if young) can marry her deceased husband's younger brother in case his wife and he himself have no objection. This is known as *baithana*, and the *nikah* is once again performed. Though this is not essential, she can also marry outside the family. A widow before remarrying has to observe a period of *iddat* for 3 $^{1}/_{4}$ months. A divorced wife can remarry her divorced husband again but if she has been married to someone else and divorced again. In case of widower remarriage, preference is for the wife's younger sister, but the men of this community can also seek alliance from outside.

The family is of vertically extended type, but the households are nuclear. Father, mother, their married and unmarried children all share the same *chullah* cordially. The eldest male member of the house commands great respect and is the head of the family. His decision in all family matters which are arrived at after mutual consultations with the family members is final. Due regard is given to seniority in age. The daughter-in-law observes purdah (avoidance) in front of the husband's male relatives. Husband and wife address each other by teknonymy. The property is equally divided according to the number of wives and subsequently their shares are further subdivided according to their sons, who share the property equally. No share is given to daughters unless there is son in the family. The widower and unmarried children are the joint responsibility of all the sons. The eldest son succeeds as the head of the family.

The status of women is equal to that of the men. Normally the Bhisti women do not work outside the house, except in cases of extreme poverty. The women are supposed to stay back in the house, cook food, look after the young ones, and manage the household. A woman working in the agricultural fields is not held in high esteem. Though they do not have a direct role in agricultural operations, yet once the food grains are brought inside the house, cleaning and storing is done by the women. Women have a role in other economic activities also. They stitch clothes, knit woollen sweaters, do embroidery and weave *durri* (carpets), and sell them to other village families and earn money to supplement the family income. Women also have a role in rituals, religious spheres, and in social functions; but their contribution in the political sphere is limited only to casting of votes. They also do not have decision-making powers and role in the mechanism of social control.

For the enceinte mother the 40 days period of *chilla* (pollution) is observed. She can start working within the house three days after delivery. As soon as the child is born a *maulvi* (priest) is called and an *azan* is given in the child's ears; the child is named thereafter. Though no ritual ceremony is observed for naming, but the naming is so important that even the child who is born dead is first named and then buried. *Aqiqa* is observed on the sixth day of the birth, but in cases where it cannot be performed on the said date for economic reasons, it is deferred as per the individual's convenience, but has to be done on the same day and month in which the child is born in any year. In the event of the birth of a son two goats are sacrificed and in case of the birth of a daughter only one goat is sacrificed called *kurbani*. On the day of *aqiqa*, the head of the male child is also shaved off. *Khatna* or *sunnat* (circumcision) is performed for boys before the age of six years by the *jarrah* (barber surgeon) or as per the religious scriptures immediately after birth, but it is invariably deferred. Marriage is performed by *nikah* at the bride's residence. Immediately afterwards *nikahnama* (marriage agreement) is signed by two witnesses, who are normally the parents of the bride and the groom. The couple and the *maulvi* are given a copy of the same, but among the Bhistis of Newada, no written documentation is made and all arrangements are verbal. The *barat-ka-khana* (marriage feast) is given by the bride's parents, this is followed by a feast at the groom's residence, which is known as *dawat-e-walima.* The nuptial ceremony is observed at the groom's residence.

The dead are buried in a common burial ground and a *kachcha* or *pukka* tomb is erected over it. *Matam* (mourning) is observed for a period of three days. The death rituals vary from section to section according to the *firqa* (school of thought). Sunnat Jamati on the day of death after burial and reciting of *fatiha,* assemble in mosque and keep five kilograms of black gram in front, and 40-50 *maulvi* utter the *kalma* 1.25 lakh times. With this done the dead is believed to have received salvation. A Deobandi, however, will observe *tija, daswa, biswa* and *kul* on the third, tenth, and twentieth days after one month of the death. Food can be cooked in a Sunnat Jamati house after the *kalma,* but in the other *firqa* food cannot be cooked in the house for at least three days of *matam,* but provided to the bereaved family by friends and relatives. On each anniversary the Deobandis go to the *mazar* (tomb) and offer *chadar* (a sheet of cloth) , flowers and incense.

Traditionally, economic resources of the Bhistis were derived from supply of water, carrying the same in the *mashak* for door to door supply, when the sources of the same were meagre. Now also they continue their traditional occupation, but this is limited to the supply of water to vegetable sellers and at building sites. Finding their traditional occupation inadequate to support the family, many have taken to agriculture, business, services and religious teaching where they impart scriptural teachings to the younger generation in the mosques . The landholdings are very small and in majority of the cases the land has been acquired. Many continue to be landless. A few also do *batai* (sharecropping) on 1/2 the share or on *tehai* (1/3 of the share) on the fields of other landowners. The Bhistis are totally dependent on the market for buying things of need and selling their surplus produce. Cash is the usual mode of exchange. Children below the age of 15 years, especially boys, assist their parents in agricultural pursuits and also in tending the cattle. At times they also work as agricultural labourers in the fields for which they are paid in cash.

The Bhistis share their *anjuman* (council) with the other Muslims at Deoband in Saharanpur. The Deoband Anjuman has a secretary, treasurer and 40 to 45 members. All are elected to these posts. Cases relating to *dan* and *dahez*, *talaq*, family disputes, and theft are decided by the Anjuman as per the established norms. Cash fines are imposed on the guilty. The money thus realised is spent on the maintenance and manning of the religious *madarsas* (schools) . If one fails to pay the dues, he is excommunicated. He is, thereafter, also referred to the statutory panchayats, which have come into existence after Independence. The Gram Panchayat plan and implements welfare activities and dispense justice on matters of petty crimes.

The Bhistis belong to the Sunni sect. They venerate the *khera* (village) deity by offering sweets and incense and paying obeisance. The village deity is believed to be the caretaker spirit of the village, and safeguards the inhabitants during epidemic or other natural calamities. Their sacred shrines are the *dargah* (tomb) at Ajmer Sharif and Sirhind. The people themselves act as religious priests for them and as officiant-in-charge of rituals at the non-calenderical rituals. They also act as exorcists and give charms and amulets to the patient to relieve him of the sufferings.

The major festivals of the Bhistis are Shaberat, Idul Zuha, Idul Fitr and Moharram, all of socioreligious significance. The Bhistis also take part in the fairs held in the honour of Makdoor Shah, Nanu Gaza Pir and Sabir Mian at Paonta and offer their obeisances to him. On the *sukhna* (wish) being fulfilled a *chadar* is offered.

The Bhistis have their handicrafts. Their women do fine *kashidakari* (embroidery) on cloth. Body painting is also resorted to by women. Young and old, all paint their palms, and feet with exquisite designs by applying *henna. Alta* (red colour) is also applied by women on their feet, especially at marriage or other social ceremonies. Folksongs excepting Nad are common to all the community in the region and Bhistis also take part in them. Nad songs are specially sung by the womenfolk during Shaberat.

Traditional occupational linkages of Bhistis with most of the communities existed, whom they used to supply water, especially to the Muslim community in exchange of *kachcha* and *pukka* food. A Bhisti can traditionally accept both *kachcha* and *pukka* food from all Hindu communities excepting the Chamar and Chuhra. Ritual kinship is established with both the Muslims and other Hindu communities living in the neighbourhood. The Bhistis have access to the common water resources. Separate schools known as *madarsa* exist for imparting religious education to Muslim children. Girls go only to the *madarsa*, whereas boys also go to the regular schools for receiving formal education. The Bhistis share a common burial ground with other Muslims. Traditional *jajmani* relationship exists with Nai, Badi, Lohar, Faqir and Hafiz who serve them with their traditional skills, and receive food grains at each harvest. Near the urban locales people are more flexible in matters of acceptance of water and food from the Bhisti.

The attitude of the Bhistis towards literacy and education is favourable for boys and partly favourable for the girls who are sent only for scriptural learning and not for formal education. The boys study up to matriculation and beyond, depending upon the means of the family. The attitude of the Bhisti to modern medicine is partly favourable, but they also rely on the indigenous homemade remedies in the first instance. Belief in exorcism is also responsible for their half-hearted attitude towards modern medicine. Their attitude towards family restriction is not favourable for they believe children to be the gift of Allah.

Drinking water is available through pipes and wells. The Bhistis have been able to procure loans under the Integrated Rural Development Programme for the purchase of *khaddi*.

The Bhisti village of Newada is well connected with the main road by a two kilometre stretch of a *kachcha* link road. It is electrified, and has a post-office. Transistors and television form other media of communication. Firewood is the common fuel, though some families also use kerosene stoves. The use of chemical fertilizers and pesticides is limited. A scheme for providing nutritious food for the children in 0-5 age group, expectant and nursing mothers is availed of, through Balvadis. Public distribution system is also made use of. Those residing in urban areas avail of banking facilities.

Rajendra Sarkar

BHOJKI

The Bhojki is a community of priests of Devi temples. The etymology of the word Bhojki is from *bhoj* meaning to offer food, some eatables or other things to the deity. Since they are the *pujari* locally called *pajiale,* who keep offerings in the name of the deity and maintain the temple of the deity, they are popularly known as the Bhojki. Some ethnographic information is available on the community in old literature (Ibbeston,1916 and Rose, 1919). They are priests of the major Devi temples like Naina Devi (in Bilaspur), Brajeshwari Devi, Jawalamukhi and Chintpurni in Kangra. They live in the hills and dales of the outer Himalayan ranges. In Bilaspur, they live mainly on the top of the hill range of the Dhar Naina Devi, but in Kangra their shrines are also located in the valley region. They speak regional dialects of the Pahari. e.g., Bilaspuri and Kangri with Devanagari script. Their women wear *kurta* and *salwar* and a *chunni* or *chadru.* A few also wear *sari.* While in temple men wear a typical priestly Brahmanical dress — a white *kurta* and *dhoti* with a red *parna* (scarf) on the shoulders. They also put a *tilak.* Ornaments of women are not unique to the community but these include a golden *gut ka chak* (cup shaped ornament on the occiput), *kante or bali* (earlets/rings), *tili* or *nath* and a golden locket (necklace).

The food habits of the Bhojkis are similar to those of the other communities of the area. Their main staple food is wheat and maize supplemented with rice. All different types of pulses, locally available like *moong, masur, kulthi*, peas, beans and gram are consumed after cooking in groundnut or mustard oil or vegetable *ghee.* Various seasonal vegetables, mustard leaves, roots and tubers are consumed frequently. Fruit intake is moderate and fruits like apple, peach, guava, mango, banana, plums, etc., are consumed. They occasionally also eat eggs, fish and meat and are non-vegetarian in food habits. Widows do not eat non-vegetarian food. Milk and milk products are also consumed quite frequently. Men occasionally may consume liquor on festive occasions by purchasing it from the market. They also smoke *bidi*/cigarette and loose tobacco in the indigenous *hukka* (pipe). Festive food preparations are *kheer* and *halwa, babru, seviyan, ankli/ankloo, khichri,* etc. Non-vegetarian food is taboo during death pollution and festivities.

The Bhojkis have a social hierarchy. The Kangra Bhojkis consider themselves superior to the Naina Devi Bhojkis and also do not marry with the latter. There are 15 *gotra* divisions in the community, common being Kans, Gautam, Kaliye, Kashyap, Bhardwaj, Vats, Ghabru, which are sometimes used as surnames but are functional primarily to regulate marriages and indicate the lineage. The Bhojkis in general are treated as inferior in the Brahmanical hierarchy, and have little intercourse with higher Brahmans.

The community is endogamous and practises village exogamy. Monogamy is practised and marriage occurs through negotiation, *byah*. The age at marriage of the girl is around or above 16 years and of the boy is about 20 years or above.

Earlier pre-puberty marriages were common. Bride price is not taken and marriages occur as *dharma pun* through *kanyadan* and *daj dan* is given in the form of utensils, beddings, furniture, clothes and ornaments. Marriage symbols for a woman are *sindur*, *bindi*, glass bangles, nose and ear ornaments and pin/stud/ring. The bride lives patrilocally. Widow remarriage and junior levirate are not socially approved, but a widower may marry a junior sororate. Divorce is also not approved by the community but it may occur if either spouse takes a legal course on grounds of maladjustments, cruelty, etc. Man bears the compensation expenditure for woman and the children are also his liability. The divorcees may remarry. The main change in the marriage institution is the increase of age at marriage and the giving of dowry.

The family pattern of the Bhojkis is largely vertically extended. The family does not break in the lifetime of the head of the family. The junior members are to respect and obey the senior members of the family. Avoidance relationship of the *lari/bahuti* is maintained with her *saurah*, *jeth* and *nandoi*. But some younger women do not observe avoidance. Joking relationship may occur between *devar* and *bhabi*, *jija-sali*, *nanan-bharjai* and *jija* and *sala*. The paternal property is inherited as per the rule of male-equigeniture and succession goes to the eldest son. Points of conflict in the family may be on account of property or income of the individual family members if the same is not included in the common property of the joint family. Conflicts may also arise on account of unequal division of labour or non-sharing of family responsibilities. Also, there is some socially rigid attitude towards the new *lari* or tension may occur in the *sas* and *lari* and *jethani* and *darani* relationships. However, the joint family system is still continuing satisfactorily to a considerable extent. The status of women remains generally lower than that of men. Only a few of them contribute to family income through employment but the majority are confined to the domestic chores and bring potable water which is however in the vicinity. They participate in social and religious ceremonies but do not render priestly services. But in the sphere of social control, political matters and decision making their role is negligible. They, however, regulate the family expenditure.

The life-cycle rituals are performed as per the Vedic tenets but certain rituals like pre-delivery and cereal-taking ceremonies have lost significance and are ignored. Pre-delivery and post-delivery restrictions are observed and the woman is confined to an inner room called *obra/obri* of the ground floor of the house for delivery. The birth pollution called *sutak* is observed for eleven days when the woman takes bath and is purified by taking cow's urine and Ganga *jal* (water). This ceremony is called *guntrala.* Sweets or sweetened germinated grams are distributed in the neighbourhood. The ladies' folksongs called *ranjhunana* is arranged on a male child's birth. A small feast may also be given and a name is given to the child as per the zodiac sign in its horoscope. *Mundan* or *jattu* (tonsure) is the major childhood ritual of the male child and is performed at family or clan deity's temple by a barber where offerings are made. Young children are given a feast and some coins. Adolescent and puberty rituals are not observed but *yagopavit* ceremony occurs at brother's marriage or at an individual's own marriage.

Marriage is contracted only if the stars of both the boy and girl match in their horoscopes and is fixed for a particular auspicious month and date. In a per-marriage ritual *barni* or *karmai* ceremony, some clothes and ceremonial cash are given to the boy and the girl by their prospective parents-in-laws. Their own community priest performs the marriage rituals. Various observances prior to the marriage ceremony are *sand, samuhat* and oil ceremony. Actual marriage rituals are *lagan* and *ved* when the bride and the groom circumambulate the sacred fire. Finally, the parents of the bride perform *sankalapa* and *kanyadan* in which they formally give their daughter to the bridegroom. They give a feast to the groom's party. At bridegroom's place the first marriage ritual is *andrera.* The second major ritual is *pipal puja* or Brahman worship in which the bride and the groom circumambulate the sacred tree and tie a white thread around its stem. Putative kinship-based relations of bride and groom are also made at this time by a red thread in each other's wrists. The marriage finally concludes with a music of the brass band party, dance and a *dham* (feast). On the same evening the bride returns to her parental home which is followed by a visit of the bridegroom. Some rituals are performed there and the *muklawa* of the bride takes place on the next auspicious day and the bride lives with her husband patrilocally.

The dead are cremated and their ashes are collected on the third day. The sons shave off their heads in mourning and the ritual is called *bhadran* on father's death. The eldest son carries the *phool* and *asthi* (charred teeth and bones) in a packet for immersion at Hardwar in the Ganga and offers *pind dan.* Pollution called *patak* lasts for eleven days when ancestor worship is performed by an Acharaj or *sanyasi* who gets the offerings. A *havan* is performed by the family priest to purify the family and he takes *dan.* The family becomes pure for exchange of food and water on the sixteenth day called *solia,* when a ceremonial feast is given to relatives and friends. The first death ceremony and fourth death anniversary are observed and alms are given to a *sanyasi* and relatives and the villagers are invited for a ceremonial feast. Annual *shradh* is observed during *Pitri Paksha* every year and the family priest is served meals and crows are fed.

The Bhojkis are landless as ploughing is socially/religiously taboo for them. They survive on the alms and offerings to the temples. Their share in the income of the temple is 50 per cent and the other half goes to the trust/ management. The days on which different families act as priests in the temple are fixed on a weekly basis. Some also earn by rendering priestly astrological services to the people. The community also has persons in government services such as teachers and doctors who hold white-collar jobs, and also persons in military services. Some also do general merchandise business and run small *maniyari* shops within the temple complex. The market is fully regulated and is held daily, and dealings are in cash. The community has its own social council to resolve their social as well as economic disputes. Statutory Gram Panchayats exist to solve the village disputes over land and water but are of little concern to the community. Their social council is a formal body and its president is elected by a voice vote.

The Bhojkis have faith in pantheon gods and goddesses but their patron deities are goddesses or *devis* (reincarnations of goddess Durga/ the Shakti) such as Jawalamukhi, Brajeshwari, Chintpurni, Naina Devi, etc. Badoli Devi in Bilaspur is also a family/patron deity of some Bhojkis/Panda and they propitiate Kotila Sidh as a village deity and Baba Balak Nath as a regional deity. They are the devotees of these goddesses and maintain their shrines. The Naina Devi fair is very famous. They celebrate various Hindu festivals like Lohri, Diwali, Dussehra, Ramnavmi, Navratre and Rakshabandhan. The regional folksongs, tales and lores, viz., *Mohan, Gambri, Ranjhu-Phulmu, Bhala sipahiya dogria, Kangre de fauji, Subhadro-Bajira* and *Kunju-Chenchlo,* are shared with other people. They participate in religious songs of the deities like *Mata ki bhet, jagrata* and *bhajan* and *kirtan* and share regional music and dances. No community-specific tradition of art and craft is present but floor and wall paintings with floral designs are known to women.

The Bhojki generally have only the traditional linkages with various communities in the temple or outside. The caste Brahmans and Rajputs do not traditionally accept *kuchcha* and *pucca* food and water from their hands, but they accept food and water from them and from various Hindu castes. From the Chamar, Dhobi, Julaha, Dumna, etc. they accept only *sukka* or cooked by a Brahman/Rajput in social gatherings. Water sources, cremation ground, religious shrines and other public places are commonly shared largely without any social discrimination. They have members in general merchandise/ business, holding white-collar jobs, teaching, medical profession and in army/defence services. Political leadership has emerged at the local level.

Modern developmental programmes have made a good impact on the Bhojkis in the spheres of formal education, health and medicare, family planning and mass media and communication. Formal education is equally favoured for boys and girls and they also go for higher college, university and professional education. But some may drop out due to lack of interest or due to traditional priestly interests. Both modern as well as indigenous medicare facilities are availed and favoured depending upon the availability and effectiveness of the particular treatment. They do have faith in the oracles and other faith healers. They normally favour small family size and have adopted sterilization as the method of restricting family size. But socially there is a strong desire for at least one son.

Potable water is available through taps, but sometimes the traditional *bauri* are also used. There are no special provisions for the community under IRDP and ICDS, except for the immunization facility under the latter. Their houses are electrified and they use modern mass media including radio, television, cinema (in some places) facilities. Railway link is available at Kangra but road links and postal services are available to the community almost everywhere. They use firewood, cow-dung cakes, coal, sawdust, kerosene oil and liquid petroleum gas (LPG) in the urban areas. Fair price shops to supply ration on subsidized rates are located in the vicinity and this facility is used.

A.R.Sankhyan

BODH

The Bodh, Bhot or Chazang, as they are called are primarily distributed in the Spiti valley of Lahaul and Spiti district. They are a scheduled tribe and have been enumerated along with Jad, Lama and Khampa, the total population of which according to 1981 Census is 22,635. Though the history of the Bodh is not available, yet according to an account by the natives, those people of Tibet who came and settled here in the past i.e. prior to 1962 are called as Bodh or Bhot, whereas those who came after 1962 are known as Tibetans. According to another more plausible view, the people are the followers of Buddhist faith and hence are called Bodh.

The Bodhs live in an inhospitable terrain with little vegetation as the area falls in the arid zone. Spiti is referred to as the cold desert of Himachal Pradesh. It has very scanty rainfall. Stone boulders and loose rocks keep falling all over and on small patches of terraced fields, which are usually near the river beds. Bhoti is the dialect spoken by the Bodhs among themselves and their script is also Bhoti, but with outsiders they speak in broken Hindustani and the literate among them can also converse in English. Some of them can write in Devanagri and English scripts.

The male Bodhs wear *kera* or *cholu* with woollen trousers and *pattu* (band) on their waist. The females put on *cholu* and *jeptan* (a shawl around the shoulders). Each Bodh house has a *harsho* (flag) in the courtyard to ward off evil eyes that are cast on the house by invisible spirits. The staff is also a typical identity of a Bodh household.

The Bodh are non-vegetarian, taking all kinds of edible meat. They also eat yak and cow meat. They are very fond of locally brewed drink called *chhang* and *arak*, which are distilled in almost every house. Their staple food consists of *thukpa* and *momo* which is made from *maida* (fine wheat flour without bran) and mutton. Occasionally, they also take pulses, *rongi*, green vegetables and tubers. Fruits consumed are *chulli*, *bahemi*, grape and the like. Fresh milk is available in a small quantity and is usually kept for the infants. The adults take fresh milk occasionally. Mostly powdered mik is used in the preparation of sweetened tea. Salt tea is also taken frequently. Tobacco is chewed and smoked by both men and women. Special food and delicacies are cooked on festive occasions, but on solemn occasions non-vegetarian food and drinks are avoided.

The bio-anthropological information on the Bodhs reveals that the ABO blood group gene frequency is 0.2503 (p), 0.3100(q) and 0.4393(r) (Chopra & Sidhu : 1970), based on 306 samples. Chowdhury's (unpublished) data based on 100 samples show the gene frequency of ABO blood groups p, q and r as 0.223, 0.304 and 0.475 respectively. The MN blood group gene frequency is 0.706 (m) and 0.294 (n). The Rh gene frequencies are 0.182 (r), 0.075 (Ro), 0.097 (R_2), 0.637 (R_1) and 0.088 (R_z). PTC tasters and non-taster gene frequencies are 0.344 (t) and 0.656 (T). 1.45 per cent Bodhs are found to be colour blind. As per the demographic information, the sex ratio is 1007. The average age at marriage is 23.38 years for males and 21.50 years for females. The pre-natal mortality rate is 1.5%, infant mortality rate is 1.67% and offspring mortality rate is 3.17%.

Bodh is a generic term and is applied to people of the Buddhist faith. They are divided into six classes, viz., Lama (the priest), Nono (the ruling class) Kharpan (the *wazir* of the king), Chazhang (Rajput Bodh, the agriculturist class), Zo (blacksmiths) and Hesi/or Beta (goldsmiths and musicians). This division is on the basis of occupational specialization. In the entire valley there are only five houses of Nono and only two houses of Kharpan. The majority of the Bodhs calling themselves as Rajputs, are agriculturists and constitute the bulk of population. The Zos and the Hesi/Beta are included in the list of scheduled castes of the State.

The chief function of these social divisions is to regulate marriage except in case of Lamas who observe celibacy. Since there are only five Nono families in the valley, they have entered into matrimonial alliances with the well-to-do Thakur families. Similarly, the two Kharpan families have entered into matrimonial relationship with the Rajput Bodhs who are also known as Zad or Jad. The Zo and the Beta marry within their respective groups. They recognize their position in the social hierarchy according to their occupational categorization, and are placed in that order which is acceptable to all.

Endogamy is the rule of marriage, with the exception of the Kharpan and Nono. Marriage within the village is not looked down upon. Cross-cousin marriage is not frequent, nevertheless it is practised, while parallel cousin marriage is totally absent. They also do not marry blood relatives. Junior sororate and levirate marriages are resorted to. The most popular form of acquiring mate is by *reje* (marriage by negotiation), the other form being *khindum* (love marriage). Monogamy is the general rule except in sections of population of the Pin Valley and the area around Tabo where fraternal polyandry is practised. Junior sororate marriages are however practised with the consent of the first wife. In the event of wife being unable to give heir to the family, the husband can opt for a second marriage, in which the first preference is given to *sami nomo* (wife's younger sister). There are no symbols of marriage among the Bodhs now, but in earlier times, a *phiroza* (turquoise stone) tied on the forehead of women signified her marital status.

Dowry was prevalent, depending on the economic status of the bride's parents. This was usuallly in kind and consisted of *churu* (a cross between a yak and a cow), horse and *galicha* (carpet). This is no more practised. Nowadays, voluntary gifts are given, but not demanded. The rule of residence is patrilocal, the girl after marriage goes to live in the house of her husband who moves into the big house called *khang chen*. In some families, where there are no male issues in a family, the daughter's husband is invited to look after the in-law's property and stays in the house. He is known as *makpa*. *Che-che* (divorce) is also possible in the community. The common grounds for divorce are adultery and incompatible nature of the husband and wife. It is permitted with social approval. No compensation is paid by any party, and either of the couple can divorce the other. The children, if any, born to the couple, have the option of going to either of the parents. In case the child is an infant, he or she, stays with the mother. Widow, widower or divorcee remarriage is also possible among the community. A person can marry *sami momo* or anyone else. A marriage between a widow and her husband's younger brother can also be solemnized. In that event, the latter have to leave the *gompa* and live a family life. For this the consent of the *rinpochiey* (Avtari Lama) is obtained, who also levies a fine on such persons leaving the *gompa*.

The Bodh family pattern depends on the rule of primogeniture, wherein the eldest son inherits the father's property. The Bodh family is a three tier system. When the eldest son gets married he inherits the father's property and enters the 'big house', locally known as *khang-chen* whereas its occupant, the head of the family, is known as *khangchenpa* and the father withdraws to the smaller house called *khing-chung* and the occupants are known as *khing-chungpa*. The father receives a plot of land from his eldest son's estate for his maintenance. On withdrawing to *khing-chung* the father gives up the maintenance and responsibility of running the *khang-chen*. When the children of the eldest son get married, he moves into the *khang-chen*, the father, who has so far occupied *khang-chen* goes to *khing-chung* and the grandfather shifts from *khing-chung* to a still smaller house called *ying-yung*, and the occupants are called *ying-yungpa*. The younger sons are sent to *gompa* (monastries) in their childhood, and they practise celibacy. In case the younger brother does not go to the *gompa* he is given the produce of the field set aside for the purpose for his maintenance. For this, he is at the mercy of the eldest brother, as he does not have any claim over it. Unmarried daughters are entitled to maintenance from their eldest brother. In the event of their getting married, they forfeit their claim of maintenance. This law of Bodh inheritance is known as Lulan.

Recently, a few responsible and educated persons raised their voice against the inheritance of property by the eldest son, and desired that all should get an equal share, but the people of the 'big house' did not allow this to happen. They threatened that in such an event their share would be withdrawn from them, and those raising the voice of dissent would be severely dealt with. Finding it difficult to get the approval of the community, coupled with the fear that their share will also be lost, these persons abandoned the move.

If the head of the *khang-chen* dies without a son, and his wife happens to be young, one of the younger brothers, who had entered the monastery, is allowed to marry the widow to raise the family and inherit the property. This is known as *khamba zumche.*

Interpersonal relationships within the family are very cordial. The husband and wife have regard for each other. It is obligatory on the part of children to look after the welfare of their parents and grandparents in *khing-chung* and *ying-yung.* The daughter-in-law observes avoidance with her husband's elder male relatives and with all such relations in that line. Joking relationship also exists with the wife's younger sister and all such relations in the line. Conflicting situations arise on issues of maintenance.

The women have an active role to play in the economic activity. They are very agile and industrious and have an equal participation in all spheres. They carry out all the agricultural activity, including ploughing, which in most parts of the country is men's prerogative. They sow seeds and harvest the crops. They also collect fuel and fodder for the animals, fetch water for domestic consumption and prepare food for the family. Women also take part in all social, religious, and recently in political activities as well. Their contribution to the family income in the form of cash, in the strictest sense of the term is minimal, limited to the making of *galicha* and other woollen articles which they seldom sell. Though the entire household activity is managed by her, she has no role in social control and has no decision-making powers. The girl, under normal circumstances, cannot inherit the property. In case the parents have no male heir, they marry the eldest daughter to a person who agrees to be a *makpa* (resident son-in-law), and he is usually the youngest son of some land owning family. The property is transferred to the girl, and if the girl predeceases her husband, he takes another wife from amongst her younger sisters or other female relatives, and their son succeeds to the estate. A widow amongst the Bodh gets *teu* (maintenance) for her lifetime from the person who inherits the property of her deceased husband.

Post–birth pollution lasts up to seven days till which date the mother is not allowed to do any work. *Bingree* (name giving) ceremony is observed on an auspicious day decided by the *lama* (priest). The name is given by the *bama* after consulting the *punthi* (sacred text) and almanac. *Balda* (tonsure) ceremony is observed on the child attaining eight years, and on the date decided by the Lama. On this day, the hair is cut by the mother's brother or the parent, and a feast is given.

Reje (marriage by negotiation) is a simple ceremony. The marriage procession goes to the girl's house. The groom is not allowed to enter the house by the bride's friends. This is known as *gagakache,* wherein the bride's friends demand compensation from groom, for taking away their friend. The *phangama* (bride) and the groom are then made to sit side by side and offered a cup of *arak*, which they exchange after having a first sip, and with this, the marriage is solemnised. The consummation of marriage takes place on the bride coming to the groom's place. Earlier, in some cases, marriage by proxy was also in practice. In this case, the actual marriage ceremony took place when the family was capable of paying the dowry. The boy and the girl would, however, live like husband and wife immediately after *migeur chhang* (betrothal ceremony). In this type of marriage the elders of the community go and bring the girl. and not the boy.

In the event of death, the house remains polluted for seven days and the cooking of non-vegetarian food is avoided during these days. The method to be adopted for the disposal of the dead is decided by the Lama. Ordinarily, the dead are cremated, but in the event of death occurring in between the flowering season and harvesting of the crops, the body is cut into pieces and thrown into the river or on the hill slopes to be eaten by the birds. Infants are put in an earthen pitcher and buried in the ground with some salt. There are three distinct mortuary rites the first known as *chawa* is observed on the fourth day, in which all items belonging to the dead are given to the Lama, *tuzi* observed along with *chawa* (the 39th day ceremony) is held for the peace of the departed soul. Exactly a year after the death, the family members go to the top of the hill and plant a *khotansa* (white flag) in memory of the dead.

The major economic activity of the Lama is the performing of the rites and *pooja* (worship) at the *gompa* and also to act as officant-in-charge of the rituals at the Bodh houses. The Chazangs have agriculture as their main occupation, though some go in for service and the weaving of the carpets which is mostly for self-use. The Zos have ironsmithy and occasionally silversmithy as his primary economic activities, though some take to agriculture. The Betas or Bedas, the musicians are the serving caste and render their services to their clients by music on festive and social occasions.

No one in the valley is landless. Those who had no land or less land have been provided land by the government. The land is independently held by the 'house' to which it belongs. There are certain types of land which are in full ownership of monasteries known as *cha-zhang*. This is considered a common property of the village. Any landlord or resident of the village cultivates them and pays a fixed agreed amount to the *gompa* towards defraying the expenditure of lighting the lamps. Share cropping is also practised, in which the produce is divided between the landlord and the sharecropper.

The Bodhs are dependent on the local market for purchasing things of their need, either in cash or on deferred payment. Barter system is not resorted to except in case of *jau* (barley), where it is exchanged for *matar* (peas) from the residents of the lower altitudes. Occasionaly people even go to regular markets in Manali or Rampur Bushahr, should the demand so arise. To augment their otherwise meagre source of income, men and women go out to work as labourers with the PWD and GREF in road construction and cleaning of roads. Children also render a helping hand. Those who are young look after the young ones in the family, and those not so young work as labourers in PWD. The wages are paid in cash.

For the maintenance of law and order in the community, each village has a traditional council called *armi*, which has a *gadpo* (headman) and *lepha* (village guard), who also acts as a messenger. Both the officials are elected to the post by voice votes. This system exists even today and is only for the Bodhs (Rajput), the Beda and the Zos. The composition of the village council is homogenous and its function is of social control and to prevent any infringement of prescribed social norms. The offences that come up before the *gadpo* usuallly relate to adultery and disrespect for traditional norms. The imposition of penalty on the offender is in cash or kind.

Similar to *gadpo* and *lepha* the Lamas also have a system of social control for the *gompa*. This is headed by a nominated Lama who is the chief, locally called as *rinpochie*, also occasionally referred to as Avtari Lama. He is assisted by a group of 10 to 12 elected Lamas for a period of three years, and are known as *chisowa*. The function of *rinpochie* and *chisowa* is to manage the affairs of the *gompa*. In the event of any Lama leaving the *gompa* to lead a married life, the permission is to be granted by this panchayat, after imposing cash fine. Adulterous relations between a Lama and a Chomo (nun) are frowned upon and result in excommunication from the religious institution. However they may ultimately marry and settle down to a family life.

Buddhism is the prevalent religion in the valley and all the communities living there follow it. In Buddhism, there are four sects, Geylulapa, Nenginapa, Kargyutpa and Dulpa with a number of branches. Among the residents of the Spiti valley a combination of both the red and yellow exists. The most learned of Lamas usually belong to the yellow sect and are called Bara-Lama or *giani* (learned). The persons belonging to this particular sect wear dress of that particular colour, whereas that of the mixed sects wear garments of both the colours. The upper garments are usually yellow in colour, whereas the lower one is red in colour.

The Bodhs have a village deity known as *Yu-la* who is worshipped and propitiated by all for the welfare of the village. Every Buddhist household has a *harsho* (long pole) fixed in its courtyard with cloth tied around it. This is kept to ward off evil eyes from being cast on the families. The sacred centres are the *gompa*, especially the one at Ki and Tabo, which are pilgrim centres for the Buddhists. The Lamas are the sacred specialists for the community. They also do *tana-mana* (exorcism), which is locally called as *kursim*. *Shavans* (amulets) are also prepared and given by the Lamas to ward off the evil eye.

The major fairs observed by the Bodhs are Goetr held in every monastery, on the ninth, tenth and eleventh month of Spiti calendar, and Ladarcha celebrated presently only in village Kibber in the month of August. Till 1962, this was celebrated in Ki Chung village in China, but due to closure of borders this is now being celebrated in the valley. According to the natives, the Chinese come even today, from across the border to participate in Ladarcha. Earlier they used to do trade with their Indian counterparts. The main festival of the valley is the Losar which is celebrated in October-November as their New Year Day. There is yet another important festival known as Da-chang, which is celebrated in February-March by the youth, where feats of archery are performed.

The Rajput Bodhs, Lamas, Kharpans and the Zos are engaged in weaving carpets and woollen *pattu* over which they make exquisite designs to meet their requirements. Certain songs in the Bhoti dialect are sung at special occasions like *yanva* (marriage songs) by the ladies. The Bodhs dance on every occasion of festivals and marriages. Except Lamas, all dance together. *Bukum* is the exclusive dance of the Lamas, in which the music and songs are rendered by the Bedas. *Gar* and *Munkar* are dances done by men and women separately. In the former the music is provided by the Bedas, but in the latter a line of song is provided by the Bedas, which is then repeated by the dancing party. *Jabru* is a mixed dance in which the males sing a line, which is answered by the females, to the accompaniment of dance movements.

As the Bodhs live in isolation in this part of the Himalayan tract, they have imperceptible restrictions as regards commensality. The different segments of the Bodh society do not maintain any sociocultural boundaries. There are a few Zo and Beda families living with the Bodhs in the same village, but no restrictions in commensality are maintained by them, though the latter are a serving caste to the landlord Bodhs. Marriages take place within their respective groups. Ritual kinship is also not resorted to. All communities have access to sharing of water resources, schools, panchayats, *gompa* and cremation grounds.

The Zos, in return for the services rendered by them to the different houses receive a fixed amount of food grain. They receive 12 *patha* (one *patha* = 500 gm) of food grain from *khang chen*, 11 *patha* from *khing chung* and 6 *patha* from *ying-yung* annually. This is in addition to 21 *patha* of barley which they receive for preparing a new *yogshia* (share) and 12 *patha* for repairing an old one. The *darati* (sickle) and *tokchi* (hoe) are provided free of cost to the clients, who patronize them. Similarly, the Bedas or the Hesis receive 12 *patha* of *soaim* (alms) from *khang chen*, 6 from *khing chung* and three from *ying-yung* in addition to one *tong* (bushel) of grass annually.

Modern linkages have been established with other people by these people taking up government and business professions. Though, the indigenous population maintains connubial restriction with outsiders, they have no commensal restrictions. The womenfolk have also started taking part in politics by contesting elections. Besides these, the Bodhs also have symbiotic relationship with other people. They render mutual help to each other in the construction of houses, repairing the old ones, stacking stones to form protective walls around their fields, and also to render help at social functions.

The attitude of the Bodhs towards the various developmental plans being enforced by the Governmental agencies is quite favourable. Though the village is sparsely populated, nevertheless even in this remote area three high schools exist, one each at Kaza, Rangrik and Tabo, which also have free hostel facilities. Besides, there are plenty of primary-level schools and the Bodh now send their boys to schools. However, girls rarely go to schools for want of working hands in the house. Reportedly, none of the Bodh girls have received education beyond matriculation, whereas there are about 20 boys who have attained education up to the graduate level. Education is free, with the facility of free books and stationery and even free dresses to the deserving, besides scholarships to scheduled tribe and scheduled caste students.

In the event of ailments, they first resort to home-made remedies, then to the *tana-mana* of the Lamas, and if still not cured, they go to allopathic dispensaries. The deliveries are conducted at home by experienced women of the community. There are three posts of lady doctors, one at Tabo and two at Kaza. The older generation is averse to the idea of the small family norm, but the younger generation now uses contraceptive devices for regulating the family size.

Drinking water is available in the village through pipeline, which receives its supply from melted ice and *kuhl* (water channels). This supply is maintained only for four to five months in a year. In winter, when all the water sources are frozen (as the temperature goes down to -32° to -40°C), the water is supplied in jerricans at the rate of Rs. 35 to 40 per jerrican. Those who cannot afford melt the ice for water.

The Bodhs have received employment against the reserved quota, and also other posts. A few of the people have also received loans under self-employment schemes. The subdivisional headquarters are connected with Samdo and Keylong by a *kachcha* and *pucca* (metalled and unmetalled) road. It also has a postoffice and wireless office. Most of the villages do not either have post-offices. Only a few villages have electricity, and in that too, the supply is given between 6 p.m. and 9 p.m. Now, with the Rong-tong Hydel project having been commissioned, the electricity situation has improved.

Wood and kerosene are the usual sources of fuel for cooking. *Pangmo thauka* (irrigation), though successful in certain areas, has failed in Kaza. *Tanglang* (local manure) is put in the fields in the month of October.

Chemical fertilizers such as CAN and phosphate are used. Hybrid varieties of seeds have improved the yield of the farmers. Insecticides and pesticides are not much in use. Mid-day meals and nutrition are provided to school-going children and expectant and nursing mothers. Banks, though existing in the valley at the subdivisional headquarters, do not find much favour with the locals. Public distribution system through government depots is present and people avail themselves of the facilities.

The Bodhs are on the threshold of development and their traditional binding ties of the house are loosening with the impact of development activities, availability of education and job opportunities. A change in the dowry system has emerged. Earlier dowry was demanded, but now it is in the form of voluntary gifts. Also, the deferred marriage ceremony, as a result of proxy marriages has been given up due to the abolition of dowry. Another significant change that is visible is the decline of the custom of sending younger children to the *gompa*. Though, in the event of multiplicity of male children, one or two are still sent to the *gompa*, others marry and set up individual houses and earn their livelihood by taking up jobs and businesses. Due to the acceptance of small family norms by the younger generation, the institution of the *gompa* will either become a voluntary institution or may cease to exist.

Rajendra Sarkar

BRAHMAN

The Brahmans form one of the largest social groups in India. According to 1931 Census which gives figures for various castes, the total population of the Brahmans was 15,264,113, i.e., 4.32 per cent of total population of the country. And in Punjab which included Delhi also, their population was 3.81 per cent. According to Baines (1893: 24-25) the original place of the Brahmans was the upper Gangetic region from where they migrated to all parts of the country. According to B.N. Saraswati (1977: 78) "the Brahman settled in the regions North of the Vindhyas are called Gaudas and those in the South the Dravidas. These groups are further sub-divided on a territorial basis. Thus there are *pancha* (five) Gaudas and *pancha* Dravidas. To the former belong (1) the Gauda (whose original home was Haryana). (2) the Kanyakubja (whose original home was Kannauj in the Central Doab), (3) the Saraswat (whose original settlement was on the banks of Saraswati river), (4) the Maithil (who settled in a territory called Mithila in North Bihar), and (5) the Utkala (who lived in Utkal region of Orissa). Among the *pancha* Dravidas are (1) Maharashtra (of the Maharashtra State), (2) Gurjar (of Gujarat), (3) Karnataka (of Karnataka State), Telengana (of Andhra Pradesh), and (5) the Dravida (of Tamil Nadu)". These divisions were further expanded by a number of subgroups in each section on the basis of territories, activities and geographical considerations, etc. Without going into the details of the theories related to the origin of this caste, we can say that in earlier days the Brahmans migrated from one place to the other and thus settled in various parts of the subcontinent. The Brahmans have their *gotra* associated with various *rishi* of ancient times. They consider themselves descendants of seven *rishi* ancestors, namely Gautama, Bharadwaja, Jamdagni, Vasistha, Kashyapa, Atri and Agastya (Saraswati, 1977: 41). In each of *gotra,* there are a number of *gana* and *parivaras.*

In Himachal Pradesh, the Brahmans inhabit all parts of the State, except Kinnaur and Spiti. They are a part of the local tribal community and do not identify themselves as a separate caste. In Lahaul, the Swangla are Brahmans and prefer to retain their identity as such. This tribal group is concentrated mainly in the lower parts of Manchad area of the region. Manchad is known to be the language of the whole of the area and it is noteworthy that a small community of Swangla could dominate the region. At one time Manchad was prevalent in the whole of the region. The Swangla claim to have come from various parts of the Northern regions such as Kishtwar in Jammu and Kashmir, Kullu, Chamba, Mandi, etc. They could not maintain their identity by way of preserving their original language, and priestly work is not undertaken by them. The Bhats, who also belong to this caste conduct priestly work and are considered slightly superior to others. Strangely enough, the Sipis, an outcaste which comprises Koli, Hali and Dumna, etc., speak a dialect which is quite akin to Sanskrit whereas Swangla Brahmans speak only the local form of the dialect known as Manchad (Tobdan, 1984).

Bio-anthropological information on the Brahmans is available on various traits, blood groups, P.T.C. and dermatoglyphics (See bio-anthropological report.).

Among various groups of Brahmans in Himachal Pradesh Gaddi, Purohit, Nagarkotia, Bhateru and Bhojki have been mentioned as major ones by some scholars. But this is not true, as according to various clans, there are a number of prominent Brahman groups in addition to this division. The famous Brahman *gotras* are: Bharadwaj, Saraswat, Gauda, Kaushal, Kashyap, Vashistha, Pathak, Shukla, Awasthi, Upadhyay, Vatsyayan, Sankhyayan, Vatsya, Gautam, Parashar, Garga, Shandilya, Atri, Vatsa, Upamanyu and so on. It is a common belief that Brahmans of this region migrated from the plains from time to time, and as such, sections representing almost all Brahman clans can be found settled in various parts of the State. B.N. Saraswati (1977: 72) says: "In Himachal Pradesh, the Nagarkotia and the Bhateru Brahmans have their separate identity from the immigrant Sarsut (Saraswata) and Gauda. The Nagarkotia Brahmans derive their name from Nagarkot, the ancient name of Kangra district. Originally, Raja Dharam Chand (1528-63) of Kangra settled 13 families, viz. Pandit, Miar, Rehna or Raina (Manth), Panjkarn, Nag, Purohit, Bedibirch, Sotri Bipp, Dichhit, Awasti, Upada and Achari. The Bhateru Brahmans are subdivided into two classes, *pakka* and *kachcha*, each having a number of clans. The *pakka* Bhaterus have the following clans: Dind, Dokru, Sintu, Polialu, Rukki, Pawar, Awasti, Chitu, Kharappa, Nag and Misr Kathu. The *kachcha* Bhaterus on the other hand, have Tugnet, Ghabru, Sughe, Chapal, Chathwan, Awasti Khar Ganji, Awasti Tharknu, Awasti Uprial, Nag Gosalu, Mali, Misr, Achari Pothiar, Pandit Baiswal and Ghogre clans. From the names of the clans and family titles it appears that these two groups have their origins in Kanauji Brahmans, who perhaps subsequently got intermingled with the local population. The titles Misr and Awasti are the surnames of Kanaujiya Brahmans."

In Kangra there are three main types of Brahmans, viz., Nagarkotia, Bhateru and Halbaha. In addition to these categories the fourth one is of the Dogras who are said to be the immigrants from Duggar area of Jammu and Kashmir. In the times prior to the regime of Raja Ram Chand, all Brahman groups were considered of equal status in the society. In order to ward off inauspicious stars of his son Dharam Chand, the ruler invited 13 Brahmans from all over the country who conducted a special *yajna*. The Brahmans who conducted the ritual were later honoured by being placed highest in the hierarchy of caste. He allowed them grants and they settled in Kangra. The Bhaterus were next to the Nagarkotias and the remaining agriculturist Brahmans were lowest in the social hierarchy of this race. The clans of Nagarkotia Brahmans are Bharadwaj, Gautam, Parashar, Vashistha, Kaundinya, etc. These clans are found in Bhaterus and Halbahas also.

The Nagarkotias kept up their superiority for centuries and did not allow their daughters be married to the Bhaterus and the Halbahas, but girls from Bhateru clan were wedded to Nagarkotia boys. With the passage of time, the old traditions are fading and now there are no such considerations. It is interesting to note that like other groups of Nagarkotia, Bhateru and Halbaha Brahmans, there is one clan known as Nag among Nagarkotias and Bhaterus. This clan has three subgroups, namely, Pundrik, Kharapa and Gosalu. It is said that those clans initiated the cult of snake god worship in Kangra. Pundriks were those Brahmans who worship snake god of the same name and Kharapas worship cobra, a dangerous and furious type of snake, whereas Gosalus worship wild and harmless varieties of snakes. The Pundrik clan falls under the Nagarkotias but Kharapa and Gosalu are Bhateru clans. The Awasthi or Aosti clan is found among all the three categories. The Dixits are the *guru* of Katoch family and the Brahman of the Rajanak clan are the *guru* of Guler rulers.

The Nagarkotia Brahmans had the distinction of attending only to religious activities, did nothing excepting reading and writing and to attend to the ritualistic activities mentioned in the scriptures. The Nagarkotias considered agriculture below their dignity and did not possess or use weapons and never preferred service where weapons were to be used. In brief, these Brahmans were required to live the purest form of life and maintained a discipline befitting the highest order.

The Bhateru Brahmans name nine categories. They are of *kachcha* and *pucca* types and belonged to Kangra region since times immemorial. Raja Dharam Chand, for the sake of smooth working, desired that *pucca* Bhaterus could marry their daughters among Nagarkotias. *Pucca* Bhateru clans are (*a*) Ghabroo, (*b*) Chachyal, (*c*) Chhadwan, (*d*) Tugnet, (*e*) Sughe Aosti, (*f*) Garh Gajanoo, (*g*) Awasthi-Chetu, (*h*) Mishr Kathu and (*i*) Nag Gosalu. Bride price is not prevalent among these subgroups also. Nine *kachcha* Bhateru clans are; (*a*) Bhadwan, (*b*) Badaswal, (*c*) Lade, (*d*) Mishra, (*e*) Mali Pandit Bhangaliye, (*f*) Kore, (*g*) Dehkwal, (*h*) Gurhekharwal and (*i*) Drohwal. The *kachcha* and *pucca* Bhateru clans were united during the regime of Raja Bhim Chand and now there are marital relations among them. The word Bhateru is derived from the term Bhat or the Brahmans associated with performing the job of a *purohit*. Those Brahmans who helped Dharam Chand to conduct *brahmyajna* were later designated as Bhaterus. *Kachcha* and *pucca* Bhaterus are from Vats,

Bharadwaj, Parashar, Gautam, Sukyan, Sankhyan, Yatukaran, Neetal and Vyaghraped *gotras*. Among them are Maital, Balmik, Kaushal and Vashistha *gotras* also. There is a legend about the Saroch Padha clan that at the time of Mahabharata when Raja Janmejaya arranged a sacrificial ritual to wipe out snakes and destroyed seven *kula* of Ashtakuli snakes, the last *kula* king Takshak, requested a Brahman of this clan to save his life. The Brahman held the piece of wood on which Takshaka was being put in the *havan kund* and saved his life. Because of the holding the *saroo* (the spoon of wood used for pouring *ghee* in the ritualistic fire), the clan was named as Saroch. The people of this clan do not fear the snakes till this day.

The Halbaha or Halbahu Brahmans are peasant agriculturists and do not know the *karma* of the *jati*. Among the clans of Halbahas are Mohal, Koudin, Atri, Garg, Kaushal, Bharadwaj, Gautam, Upmanyu, Bachhyan, Vashistha, Angiras *gotra* and the subgroups are Kulhal, Suryal, Jail, Patake, Puryane, Sarda, Kashyap, Kuheriye, Kupahate, Tiwari, Nunguyal, Nagehru, Chohlu, Modgil, Dangmar, Harwal, Jangle, Muchale, Joysi, Dinyal, Skohiye, Dhangwal, Tugnet, Bharde, Khiryal, Durochjurohiye, Darohlu, Kusaryal Prashar, Rakre, Reharu, Mehte, Bhagsotre, Panjwal, Basantru, etc. According to an estimate there are about 500 subgroups including various clans of all the three categories of Brahmans out of which 12 categories are of Nagarkotias, about 40 subgroups are Bhaterus and the rest are Halbahas.

Besides these groups there are some other categories of Brahmans in the Kangra region—Mahabrahman or Acharya being one of them. The Acharyas are the progeny of Dronacharya and they conduct last rites of the dead. They also belong to Bharadwaj, Modgil and Parashar clans. They have only four subgroups.

The Gujarati Brahmans are of Garg, Kaushalya and Bharadwaj *gotra*. Garg Brahmans of this category associate themselves with Lord Parashuram and thus they are also called Parshuramiye. The Gujarati Brahman are known as Masku as they take donations in the name of the dead every month. The difference between Masku and Acharya is that the Acharya conducts rites soon after the death of a person and comes to the family till the day of purification but Masku or Gujarati Brahmans start coming to the family one month after death and continue getting eatables and other things from the family for one year or so.

Dakaut is another community of Brahmans. They are also called Bujhroos. They are said to be the progeny of Garg Rishis. The legend goes that Garg Rishi, the son of Brahma, was worried about having a son to continue his clan. In a dream he saw that his wife ate some mysterious fruit and became pregnant. When he enquired from her in the morning, she confirmed that she was given a fruit by some spirit and she took it at night. Later a son was born to her. In his lineage one Varahmihiracharya Rishi gave a blessing to a lady of some other caste, who satisfied her desire to have a son. The son born to her was known as Duk. These days the Duks or the Bujroos get the donations made in the name of Rahu and Ketu, especially at the time of solar and lunar eclipses. The people of this community are called Dakot and are found in various villages of Kangra, Mandi, Hamirpur, Una, Bilaspur and other areas. They consider themselves in the lineage of Brahmans but according to high caste Brahmans, they are inferior to them.

In Kullu Banjar area there are two types of Brahmans, Shukl Varn and Krishna Varn. Shukl means bright and Krishna means black. The Shukl Brahmans conduct social and religious rituals and the Krishna attend to the rites after death. Brahmans are less in number in Kullu and those who are there, are of Gautam, Vashistha, Bharadwaj, Atri and Angira *gotra*. Gaur Brahmans also inhabit the valley.

In Nirmand area there are various types of Brahmans, namely Bhat, Gaur, Bhojaki (Bhojgi) who are also called Shukla. Bhojakis are found in Naina Devi, Chamunda, Jawalamukhi, Chintpurni and in some other areas. They are worshippers of temples. The Pandas, the Brahmans who accept alms and donations are also found in the Nirmand area. The Parshurami Brahmans are those who claim their descent from Lord Parshurama. They are the worshippers of Parshuram temple and conduct various festivals in the temple. In Bhunda (rope sliding) festival, they, along with other sects of Brahmans, conduct a number of rituals. Kriyeshtoo Brahmans are a subgroup of worshipper Brahmans. They perform special *puja* at the time of Bhunda and other ceremonies. The Parshurami Brahmans of Nirmand area are different from the Acharya Brahmans who also claim their descent from Parshuram.

The Brahmans speak dialects of the areas where they reside. The script in earlier days was Tankri and Sanskrit. These days Hindi is the common language and Devanagari is used as the script. A Brahman is expected to know Sanskrit but in villages Sanskrit is the monopoly of the *purohit* and other educated people especially Shastris. The *purohits* prefer to wear *dhoti* as a mark of distinction of their caste, but other members of the group wear *kurta, pyjama, suthan* and cap. There is no special dress for women and they wear what other women of the region wear. In social hierarchy the Brahmans are considered a high class and no concessions are available to them on this basis in the development programmes of the Government.

Most of the members of the caste are vegetarians but according to climatic conditions some are non-vegetarian also. Women usually do not take meat. In areas where the climatic conditions are severe, meat is used as a blessing of the local deity. The staple food of this community is rice, wheat, cereals and maize. Fish is also taken by some members of the community. Some of them are not averse to alcoholic drinks but this is not a common practice. They buy drinks from the market.

The Brahmans believe in the joint family system and preach this pattern of family to their *jajmans*. In *jajmani* they are dependent on the offerings of the *jajmans* who give them foodgrains called *nasrawan* and money when Brahmans visit their houses. They observe almost all the 16 *samskaras* mentioned in the scriptures but the Halbaha Brahmans are not very particular about the *samskara* other than *mundan, yagopavit, vivah, shradh, mrityu* and *asthi parwah* etc. The immersion of the remains of the dead is done at Hardwar, Pehowa and Prayag. The Brahmans of Chamba go to Mattan (Martand) in Kashmir and perform immersion ceremony there. The women observe fasts on pious days like the full-moon day, Shivratri, Ahoi Ashtami, Karwa Chauth, Navratri and during some specific days of the week like Saturday, Tuesday and Friday.

The custom of *batta satta* is prevalent among the Halbaha Brahmans in Chamba and some other areas. Divorce is not very common and very rare instances of it are reported from interior areas. Cases of remarriage of divorced women are found in some areas situated on a higher altitude. Marriages are arranged only through negotiation by the parents of the boy and the girl. Dowry is not demanded but the parents of the girl can give dowry according to their capacity. After childbirth pollution is observed till the ceremony of taking of *panjap* or *guntrala*. It is usually held eight days after the birth of a child. After the death of a member of the family, the house is considered polluted for 16 days, i.e., up to *solia*. Nine days after death, a ceremony to wash clothes is performed and on tenth or eleventh day *kriya* is arranged. On this day, the Acharya or Acharaj takes the offerings made to the departed soul. The Masku gets eatables from the family a month after the death and the custom continues up to one year. After four years *chabarakh* is arranged for the peace of departed soul. The concerned family arranges to light some *jyoti* every night in the courtyard for one full year.

The Brahman caste is an organized one but does not have social control exercised through separate *biradari*. An evil-doer who breaks the tradition is punished by segregation and by others not taking food or water from his family. Even *hukka* is not shared with the men of such a family. Penance is done by taking bath at *tiratha*, inviting neighbourers and members of the *biradari* to a feast and clarifying the position at public functions. Every Brahman has to wear a sacred thread and considers it his duty to fulfil the observances for its sanctity.

The Brahmans are the religious and spiritual guides of the rest of the castes. So some of them recite *katha* and *shloka* on various occasions. In marriage their role is particularly significant and they perform this ceremony by reciting Sanskrit *shloka* and reading from the sacred books written for the purpose. They try to guide the bride and the bridegroom to remain united and consider conjugal relation as a pious duty of life. The Brahmans do not prefer to marry outside their caste, though barriers of hierarchy among clans are fast fading away. Previously they practised untouchability and social stratification but with the passage of time these considerations are getting less importance.

The people of this community, being highly educated and god fearing, are receptive to development programmes. Literacy percentage among the Brahmans is considerably high but no castewise data is available. The members take advantage of the facilities being provided by the government. The Brahmans are good cooks and some of them prepare food at the time of ceremonies arranged by Kshatriyas and Vaishyas. They get *kachcha* food from the other caste people for their religious performances. The members of this caste write Sharma, Pandit and the name of their clans before or after their names. They do not allow shoes to be brought inside their houses. Such is the notion of purity.

B.R. Sharma

BUJRU

The Bujru or Bhujroo/Bojhru/Bojru, is broadly regarded as a community of the Dakaut Brahmans, who traditionally survived on the alms offered to propitiate inauspicious stars in Hindu astrology, the Shani (Saturn), Rahu and Ketu. The name Bujru is sometimes not liked especially by the educated or better-off members of it, who consider themselves of the Agnihotri clan. Another synonym for the community is Panda in certain areas like Bilaspur. In Mandi district they are known by the name Giani. A respectable title as Panditji is often given to them. Some use Sharma or Agnihotri as surnames. According to Rose (1919), the Bujrus were practitioners of black magic and not astrologers. But some Bujrus presently do practise astrology besides warding off the evil effects of the 'harsh stars' (inauspicious stars) by them. The etymology of the term Bujru comes from Hindi word *bujhna* meaning to read one's mind and to make predictions. This also speaks of their astrological or related traditional occupation. The etymology of the broad group Dakaut is from Dak, a saint from whom they trace their origin. Dak Rishi or Garg Rishi gave them a small percussion musical instrument also called *dak*, a mini form of the well-known *damru*—musical instrument of Lord Shiva. They have a belief that if the Dakaut seeks alms and offerings for the evil stars while beating the *dak*, they will not be inflicted with the ills and sufferings caused by these stars. The community sometimes also takes pride in warding off the sufferings of people caused by the evil stars and by the effects of lunar and solar eclipses.

Under different synonyms the community perceives its distribution at inter-regional level in the neighbouring State of Punjab as well. They perceive their spread almost in all districts except in Lahaul and Spiti and Kinnaur. Their major concentrations are, however, in districts of Kangra, Hamirpur, Una, Bilaspur and Mandi. They are usually town or suburb dwellers. Some ethnographic information on the community is available in Rose (1919) and Ibbetson (1916). The community appears to have lived in the area particularly in Kangra for centuries and its members fail to recall their original home or place of migration. They speak the regional dialects of the Himachali or western Pahari such as Kangri, Bilaspuri, etc. and communicate both within and outside the community in Devanagari script. Only priestly or alm-seeking males have some dress markers. They wear a white *kurta* and *dhoti* and put a *parna* on the shoulders or sometimes *safa* on head. They also make a *tilak* on the forehead. Women's dress is like that of the neighbouring communities—a *kurti, salwar* and *chadru/dupatta/chunni.* They wear golden and silver ear and nose studs/rings, necklaces, wristlets and anklets.

Members of the community are occasional non-vegetarians though many of them are vegetarian to the extent of absenttion from consumption of meat, fish and eggs. Liquor consumption is also an occasional habit restricted to some people on festive occasions. Staple food is wheat and maize supplemented by rice. Various kinds of pulses - *urad, masur, moong*, peas, grams, beans, etc., are consumed along with moderate consumption of roots, tubers and green vegetables. Preparations are often cooked in mustard oil and hydrogenated vegetable fat. Non-vegetarian foods and *heeng* (asafoetida) are taboo during death pollution. Festive food preparations are *kheer* and *halwa, seviyan, babru,* etc.

They recall only a few *gotras,* such as Kans, Gautam, Bats or Vats, Nags, etc., and lack any social hierarchy. *Gotra* is used to regulate marriages and suggest ancestry from a particular ancestor. In regional hierarchy the Bujrus are treated below the agriculturist Brahmans and do not have any matrimonial alliance with them. They are at par with the Ard Popo, Masku etc.

They are endogamous and practise *gotra* and village exogamy. Marriages occur through negotiation and occasionally through *batta-satta*, which was a common practice a few decades back. Marriages presently occur after adolescence/puberty and usually after the girl is 16 and the boy is 20. A few decades back pre-puberty child marriages were practised, which was considered an appropriate age for *kanyadan.* A little dowry called *daj dan* is given in the form of domestic articles. Monogamy is now practised. Marriage symbols are *sindur*, ear and nose studs/pins/rings and glass bangles. The bride lives patrilocally.

Divorce is not permitted by the community but presently, either of the spouses can take a judicial course on grounds of maladjustment etc. Usually the woman seeks maintenance and children also become the father's liability. Divorcee remarriage may occur. Widow remarriage is usually not allowed and the women have to live a simple life. The widower can remarry a junior sororate or any other.

The family pattern is mostly nuclear, and vertically extended joint families are breaking up. Avoidance relation exists between *sauhra* and *nuh/bahuti/lari* and betwen *lari* and *jeth* and *nandoi.* Joking relationships are informal and similar to many other Hindu communities of the area. Property is inherited on male lines and equally by all sons on the father's death. The eldest son succeeds the father but the successor has little powers to command the joint family.

The women are mostly confined to the domestic chores of fetching potable water and managing family expenditure, and participate in social and religious ceremonies. But they do not perform their traditional occupational rituals and do not seek alms. A few women are working as schol teachers and contribute to the family income. Political spheres and mechanism of social control is not a woman's domain.

They do not observe specific pre-delivery rituals, but restrictions may exist on the woman before and after delivery. The *sutak* or post-delivery pollution is maintained for 22 days. The purification ceremony called *panjap* or *gunt* is observed by taking water of the Ganges and cow's urine when the woman takes bath. The naming is done as per the Zodiac sign at the birth of the child. The *khirpu* ceremony is observed after the eighth month. *Mundan* or *jamalu* ceremony is observed on odd years by the *mama* of the boy and the hair is offered to Balakrupia or other *kul* deity. *Janeu* ceremony is specifically observed during adolescence or before marriage. Vedic prescriptions are followed while performing this ceremony. A feast is also given to friends and relatives. Ear and nose piercing ceremonies may be observed during puberty or before marriage of the girl.

Detailed Sanatana rituals are observed on marriage which include *mehndi*, *batna* and *tel* ceremonies as the preparatory rituals. *Ved* and *lagan* takes place at bride's place when both *lara* and *lari* circumambulate the sacred fire and bride's parents perform *kanyadan* and give a feast to the bridegroom's party. Consummation of marriage occurs through *muklawa* ceremony on the following day of the marriage.

The dead are cremated and ashes are immersed in the Ganges at Hardwar. *Patak*, the death pollution gets over on the eleventh day when an Acharaj performs ancestor worship and seeks alms. The relatives and friends are feasted on the *solia* (sixteenth day) to open exchange of food with the family. Annual and fourth annual death rites are also observed called *barkhadi* and *chabarkhadi* respectively.

The community is landless and thrives on its traditional occupation of seeking *dan* of the evil stars, lunar and solar eclipses called *grahan dan*, birthday alms and *tola dan* offerred by people afflicted with bad effects of stars or serious diseases. The *tola* is the offerings in the form of iron objects, *urad*, *til*, mustard seeds, salt, oil and some coins or cash. Some also work as *jyotsi* (astrologers) and oracles. They sometimes also seek offerings in the name of the dead. Many also earn by way of petty general merchandize and a few are *rehriwala* or hawkers. A few also run restaurants and sweet shops. Some persons are in Government jobs, in teaching and defence services. Dealings with local market is direct which is of daily nature and is fully regulated. They also sell their offerings to get cash or items of domestic consumption. Child and bonded labour does not exist.

There is no traditional community council but elders of the community resolve their social disputes and also define their clientele. Village or locality disputes are resolved by the Gram Panchayat or ward members of the Town Area Committee. The fear of local deities also helps in solving disputes.

The Bujrus believe in Hindu pantheon trinity Brahma, Vishnu/Narayana/

Thakur, and Shiva. Local/regional deities of prominence are Sitala Mata, Baba Balak Nath and Guga. Some also propitiate Lakhdata and Nahar Singh. Jawalamukhi also evokes special reverence. Various local fairs festivals are celebrated, namely Holi, Baisakhi, Sair, Lohri, Shivratri, Krishan Janmashtami, Diwali, etc. The Holi mela at Sujanpur is famous. Sacred specialists are from within and outside the community for performing all life-cycle rituals. They follow oral traditions of the region; Kangri folksongs and folktales are sources of entertainment besides *bhajan, jagra* or *kirtan* of female deities. Community-specific art or craft are lacking though Bujru women know how to adorn their houses with wall and floor paintings. They also know knitting.

Jal chal (exchange of food and water) is limited to some communities in social gatherings. They may offer a *suchchi rasoi* to certain caste people. Putative Kinship may exist with many caste communities. They have traditional *jajmani* system with a Brahman priest who is offerred *sidha* known as *nasrawan* (rice, sugar and pulses). A *nai* is also sometimes permanently employed who officiates in festivals and festivities and on death rituals. They have emerged as petty shopkeepers and in teaching and defence services.

They have favourably responded to various modern developmental programmes. The literacy level has increased. Boys and girls do receive higher or college education and some receive post-graduate education as well. They use modern health and medicare methods but do have faith in and sometimes also use traditional methods. Family planning is favoured after two or three children in case a couple has a male child. Usually women get sterilized which is the main method of family control. They use/avail themselves of modern mass media (radio, TV, cinema, newspapers, etc.) facilities and all houses are electrified. They are linked with roads and in certain places also have railway links. Tap water is the major source of drinking water and sometimes step-wells are also in use. Energy sources are firewood, cowdung cakes and kerosene oil, and few also use LPG and *gobar* gas.

A.R. Sankhyan

CHAMAR

The Chamar is a well-known and widely spread community of the traditional leather workers listed as a scheduled caste. The word is derived from *charamakar* meaning leather worker. They trace their origin from a legendry ancestor named Chano, who dragged and skinned the dead cow and was therefore, excommunicated by his brother Bano. Chano (Chanoor) a great Tantric and wrestler in the court of Kansa was defeated and killed by Lord Krishna (Chitrav, 1964:209). The Chamar community people worship Siddh Chano as their communty deity in the name of Garha Devta. The Chamars are also variously known as Mochi (usually a Muslim who repairs shoes or leather articles); Ravidasi (a section following Ravidas), and Ramdasis (the followers of Ramdas). In Kangra district, the Ramdasis abstaining from leather work call themselves Arya as they are followers of Arya Samaj sect. The Chamar are both Hindus as well as Sikhs, the latter are also the followers of the Nirankari sect. Some also follow the Radhaswami sect. Most of the Chamars in Himachal Pradesh are probably of local origin and do not recall their history of migration. The Nirankari Sikh section is said to have come from the Punjab plains or the areas neighbouring Himachal Pradesh. The Aryas in Kangra migrated from the erstwhile western Punjab (now in Pakistan) during India's partition. The community is widely spread in the State, but have concentrations in Kangra, Mandi, Bilaspur, Hamirpur, Shimla and Solan districts. Their total population was 224,574 persons according to1971 Census of India (Singh, 1971), which rose to 286668 in 1981.

The Chamars speak the regional/local dialects of the western Pahari, viz., Bilaspuri in Bilaspur and Kangri in Kangra and write in Devanagari script both within and outside the community. Traditionally during the princely regime, a Chamar was not supposed to live in a double-storeyed house, or wear gold ornaments, or enter the village or the courtyard of an upper-caste Hindu without putting off his shoes, and use only percussion instrumental music and not to engage a brass band in marriage. The bridegroom used to walk and not ride on a horse or palaquin. But presently all these social restrictions are not observed. Men wear *kurta* and *pyjama* (trousers) or pants. The women wear *kurta, salwar* and a *chadru*. Traditional ornaments like *chak*, *murki* or *laung* or *tili,* wristlet or rings, anklets and *tandira* (neck-ring) are also worn by their women. These ornaments are usually of silver.

Bio-anthropological information is available on the Chamars (see Bio-anthropological report.). The community is non-vegetarian. Earlier a Chamar used to eat carrion, but presently carrion is largely eaten of a few animals like sheep and goats. Their staple food is maize in winter and wheat in summer.

Rice is eaten occasionally and on festivals or festivities. Various pulses like gram, *urad, moong, masur, kulthi* and peas and beans are taken along with roots and tubers and seasonal vegetables. The cooking medium is mustard oil or vegetable or *desi ghee.* Fruit intake is also seasonal and occasional. There is a trend towards the decrease of non-vegetarian food like fish, egg and meat, which are considered a luxury. Men take country liquor but it is restricted to festive occasions. Women do not consume liquor. Milk or milk products are consumed regularly. Old men usually smoke loose tobacco in an indigenous *jhajri* (a pipeless earthen hubble-bubble) but young men usually smoke *bidi* and occasionally cigarettes. A few persons also chew tobacco. Food taboos exist with regard to non-vegetarian diet and consumption of liquor for the followers of Radhaswami sect.

The Ramdasi Chamars or Aryas in Kangra claim superiority over the Ravidasis. Differentiation occurs at religious level as different sections follow different sects. This is true at occupational levels also as the Ramdasi Aryas have given up leather work whereas the Ravidasis continue to do it. Some Sikh Chamars have also given up leather work and claim superiority over those who are engaged in shoe-making. The clear-cut social divisions are *gots* and *als* (lineages), which are numerous in number and act as exogamous units to regulate marriages and indicate ancestry or descent. These are of totemistic origins and named after place, plant and animal names, etc. Some of the clans recorded during the present study are Janjuhe, Bains, Labube, Janeogal Bhatti, Bilpuj Bhatti, Daroch, Katoch, Kaihal, Heer, Gumre, Kathale, Satralu, Satwal, Badgal, Mahirye, etc. Some of these clans are shared with the Rajputs. The community occupies a low status at local and regional varna level.

The Chamars are endogamous and practise *got* and village exogamy but avoid consanguineous marriages. Junior levirate and sororate are allowed in case of the death of either spouse. Child marriages were prevalent two decades ago but presently the girl is married after puberty and sometimes even at or around 20 years of age. Similarly, the age of the boy at marriage has increased to above 20. Marriages usually occur through negotiation and through *satta batta.* Bride-price existed in the past but presently it is taken only by the poor or in the case of a widower's remarriage. Now the Chamars follow the *kanyadan* pattern and give *daj dakhna* which consists of household articles, ornaments and clothes. Monogamy is practised but bigamy may occur if no issue or no male child is born to the first wife. The marriage symbols are *sindur* or *bindi*, glass bangles and *tili* or *koka.* The bride lives patrilocally. The *Gharjamai* system also exists. There is social approval for divorce on grounds of maladjustment, impotency, chronic illness, cruelty etc. Presently divorce occurs through judicial approval and compensation is given to the wife or aggrieved party and either party can seek divorce. Children are the liability of the father. The divorcee, widow and widower can remarry. *Jhanjrara* (junior levirate) is a common practice in the event of a widow remarriage. But a widower may or may not marry junior sororate. The main changes in the marriage institution are increase in age at marriage, bride-price giving way to dowry, and legalization of divorce.

The family pattern of the Chamars is both nuclear and vertically extended joint family system, but the latter is on the decline. Avoidance relationships of the *lari* exists with *saurah* and *jeth*. Joking relationship exists among the *jija-sali*, *devar-bhabi*, and *jija-sala*. The inheritance is as per male-equigeniture and the eldest son succeeds the father. Conflicts in the family occur mainly on property matters when a father exercises his will against a particular son.

A significant change in the institution of family is that there has been an increase in the number of nuclear families as married sons usually get separated from the parents, especially after the father's death. The status of women is practically equal to that of men. They carry out all domestic duties, collect potable water, fuel and fodder, and work in agricultural fields. They also contribute to family income in kind or cash by rendering menial services to village landlords and by acting as midwives. They also have control over family expenditure and contribute to the decisions regarding domestic affairs. They participate in social and religious ceremonies but have little say in the mechanism of social control and political spheres.

The life-cycle rituals are performed by Chamars' own community priest or *padha* who is also known as *masand*. Pre-delivery restrictions on the expectant mother do occur. Post-delivery pollution called *sutak* is observed for 13 days but usually the mother is not treated as pure before a month is over. She takes cow's urine for purification. A *jatra* is led to the clan or other deity in the case of birth of male, the *jetha* (first) son. Naming and cereal-taking ceremonies are not observed. They used to name the child as per the name of the day, month, place etc. *Mundan* of the boy is the only childhood ritual performed by boy's *mama* on any odd years of birth usually before three years of age. Marriage rituals are similar to those of the other Hindus of the area. They propitiate the clan deity and at bride's place the groom and bride circumambulate the sacred fire and at the groom' place they take rounds of and worship a *bil* or mango or *daran* (pomgranate) tree. The bride's parents give feast to the groom's party and the latter also reciprocate. The *muklawa* now takes place on the next day of the marriage. The death rites are also similar to those of other Hindus of the area. The dead are cremated and their ashes immersed in the Satluj or Beas river. Ancestor worship is observed during the pollution period which lasts for 13 days. Their priest or *masand* performs *havan* and takes offerings or the same may be given to a *dhyan* (married daughter). Annual and fourth annual death anniversaries are also observed to commemorate the dead.

Traditionally, the Chamars subsisted on leather work or shoe-making. But nowadays, many have given up this occupation and started to work in various menial jobs, casual labour, masonry, carpentry, etc. They also possess small landholdings and are engaged in agriculture and animal husbandry. Some cultivate lands in the villages on contract or sharecrop basis as well. A few persons are also in government on regular jobs like teachers and clerks and in army, and also as private workers in industries. Children also help their parents economically by doing some casual menial services in the village and working in agricultural fields and in animal husbandry. Bonded labour however, is absent. The links with the market are direct. Payments are usually made in cash but sometimes in kind also.

The Chamars have their own informal community council. Usually the *sayane* of the village or related elders intervene in solving social disputes, marriage and divorce problems. The members of the statutory Gram Panchayat intervene in resolving village disputes over land and water. Swearing in the name of their patron deity Garha (Siddh Chano), whose place of worship called *than* located in the village, usually resolves many socioeconomic problems. Many people also approach police and civil courts for economic disputes over land and water. Legal course is adopted for cases of theft and violence. The community is mainly Hindu and follows Hinduism. Some Sikhs beong to the Nirankari sect. Siddh Chano is of special reverence. Its worship is known as *dhaja. Churma* (sugar-coated pieces of bread) and sacrifice of a sheep or goat or hen are used to remove the ill effects of its curse on the offender or the guilty. People of all communities in the village are scared of the anger of this deity. This deity is frequently propitiated on childbirth, festivals and festivities.

Besides, they also have reverence for various local deities like Balak Nath, Lakhdata, Nahar Singh, Guga and various female deities like Hari devi, Nabahi devi, Santoshi Mata, Jawalamukhi and Vaishno devi, and visit their shrines on annual fairs or on fulfilment of a desire.

They have a strong belief in diseases caused by supernatural agencies or evil spirits and have oracles in the community or employ the ones from other communities for removing their effects. *Khel* (swaying of head in an induced hypnotic trance by a *chela*) is arranged for such purposes. The birthday of Guru Ravidas is observed. They celebrate various Hindu festivals like Diwali, Lohri, Baisakhi, Krishna Janamashtami. Various regional Pahari folksongs, tales and lores and dances are shared. *Swang* is a comedy play enacted by the members of the community. Percussion musical instrument is commonly used. They also provide instrumental (generally percussion) music on marriage. Leather work is both an occupation and a craft.

They accept *kuchcha* and *pucca* food and water from various communities but can exchange *sidha* or *sukka* with other people. Traditional water sources are seperate. Cremation grounds are also separate but they may visit the same religious shrines. They interact with the upper castes on festive occasions by rendering various services and getting good returns for the same.

A Chamar usually conveys the death news of an upper caste Hindu to his relatives. This is called *sunauni.* Traditional patron-client relationship still exists in some cases supplying shoes to farmers and getting their customary dues in the form of crops. The customary share in the harvest is called *khalothi* and at the time of a festival *tuhar,* whereas during various ceremonies *pariha* is given to them. They also maintain this relationship with a Lohar. Landlord-tenant and, cultivator-labour and other symbiotic relationships exist. Modern intercommunity linkages have emerged in terms of persons in business, white-collar jobs (as teachers) and in defence services. Political leadership has emerged at the regional level.

Modern developmental programmes have made good impact on the Chamars. Nowadays, their children receive education more frequently up to the secondary school level. But children usually do not go for higher education due to lack of interest, and for girls higher education is considered less favourable socially. They favour both modern as well as indigenous health and medicare methods. Attitude towards restricted family has become favourable though there is still desire for at least one male child even at the risk of a number of female children. Usually, men get sterilized. Potable water is available in the villages through taps but traditional springs and *bauri* are also sometimes used. Provisions for intensive rural development exist and they get 50 per cent subsidy on chemical fertilizers, animals and loans for crop threshers and other machines. Their houses are electrified and modern mass media facilities are availed of by or accessible to them. The postal and road communication facilities are also accessible. Energy resources are still fire-wood and cow-dung cakes. ICDS programmes for children are availed of. They receive ration through public distribution system. Many people favour savings but others are still dependent on local money-lenders and shopkeepers.

A.R.Sankhyan

CHANAL

The Chanal is a scheduled caste with a population of 13,134 (1981 Census) that is scattered throughout the State, though concentrated in Kinnaur, Kangra, Kullu, Shimla, and Chamba. The word Chanal is probably derived from the *Chandala* whom all Sanskrit authorities describe as begotten by a Sudra and a Brahman (Rose, 1919). They correspond closely to the Hali of Chamba and Dagi and Koli of Kullu and Shimla.

The Chanals are nevertheless treated to be somewhat lower than the Kolis of Kangra. In Chamba there is a proverb: *Chanal jetha Rathi kanetha,* which means that the elder brother of a Chanal is equivalent to the younger brother of a Rathi. They are broadly a class of the lower social order whose occupation is carrying corpses, executing criminals, and other such public offices (Rose,1914: 152). They speak the local Himachali dialect and can also speak in colloquial Hindi with outsiders. In dress they do not differ from the neighbouring population. Men wear shirt and *pyjama* which are locally known as *suthan.* Men often wear a jacket and a cap specially while going out. Women wear *salwar, kurti* and *chadru* to cover their head.

The Chanals are non-vegetarian in their food habits but desist from eating beef. They normally consume meat of sheep and goat and occasionally that of jungle pond fish. Their staple diet consists of wheat, maize, *kodro* (which is grown in abundance), pulses of *mah* and gram. Seasonal vegetables which are locally grown are also consumed. The media of cooking are mustard oil and hydrogenated fats. Sometimes animal fat is also used while cooking meat. In some areas in the State walnut is available in plenty and people make use of walnut oil in various food preparations. Men are very fond of smoking *hukka* (indigenous pipe) and drinking home brewed liquor which is mostly prepared from rice and barley and is variously referred to as *lugari, chakhati* and *sur.* Even women drink and smoke occasionally.

Socially the Chanals are among the weaker and economically backward sections of the society. They occupy a position almost parallel to that of the Halis so much so that their identity is being merged with the latter. In social rank and status the Chanals occupy almost a position similar to that of communities such as Koli, Dagi, Bansi, Sanhai, Doom and the like. It seems that they belong to one common stock but differ slightly from one another on the basis of occupation. Though it is true that the above-mentioned communities are almost parallel in ranking yet a Chanal of Mandi would not intermarry with a Dagi of Kullu. They maintain endogamy not only at the community level but also at the territorial level. There are no further endogamous sub-divisions of the Chanals but there are exogamous units called *got* which are often the descent groupings and are named either after ancestor or place.

Marriage is arranged through negotiation, mutual consent, *batta-satta* and elopement. The offer of marriage comes from the boy's side and is conveyed to the girl's side by a middleman who may be a common aquaintance or a distant relative. Bride-price is also settled on this ocassion and if it is acceptable to both the sides the marriage finally takes place. In exchange marriages two families exchange brothers and sisters as spouse. This is locally known as *batta.* This kind of marriage is entered into by those who are unable to pay the bride-price but such marriages are not preferred now-a-days. In marriage by elopement the boy and the girl desirous of living as husband and wife decide to meet at a common point from where they elope and stay for a few days at a friend's place. Initially there is resentment from the girl's parents but the boy's parents persuade them to finally give their consent to the marriage. Marriages are monogamous but in case of barrenness of the first wife a second marriage may be contracted. Divorce is granted to both husband and wife. In case the wife deserts the husband and marries another man, the bride-price will have to be returned along with penalty fee by her paramour. The wife on the other hand may also seek compensation through panchayat and law courts from her husband in case he deserts her. The common grounds for divorce are adultery, cruelty, mental or cronic physical sickness, practice of witchcraft, etc. Widow or widower remarriage is known as *gadhoj* and does not entail elaborate marriage rituals. Usually a red *puranda* (hair band) is presented to the woman in the presence of close relatives who act as witness to the union and the marriage is considered to be complete. Levirate and sororate are also socially approved forms of marriages. A woman after the death of the husband usually marries her deceased husband's brother because her interest in the property and that of her children remain unhampered but she is under no obligation to do so. Children however are the liability of the father in the event of divorce and new husband on woman's remarriage after being widow.

Family is extended but in recent years there has been a growing trend towards setting up nuclear homes. The rules of residence are patrilocal and authority is vested in the eldest male member. The inheritance and succession is in the male line. All the sons get equal share and an extra share called as *jiyuk* is kept aside for the parents which is distributed equally among all the sons after the death of both the parents. Daughters do not have any claim on parental property except in the absence of a son. In the above circumstances the father-in-law invites his son-in-law to stay with him and manage his property. This system is known as *ghar javantri.* The intra-family relations are based on cooperation, love and mutual give and take. Both avoidance and joking relationships also exist which depends on age, sex and kinship status. There is no strict purdah system but women are expected to observe some distance and to partly cover their face in the presence of a senior male relatives of the husband's household. On the other hand, joking relationships exist with husband's younger brother and between husband's and wife's younger sisters.

Women enjoy considerable freedom in family management. They are an ecnomic asset. They not only work equally hard in agricultural fields but also tend to cattle, bring fodder, fuel and water in addition to attending to the usual domestic chores. However, despite the hard work, they do not have the right of inheritance and also do not enjoy the right to exercise their economic will in respect of the sale or purchase of any movable and immovable property independently. In religious and political fields also they have very little to offer except for the fact that they take part in rituals and festivals and exercise their right of franchise.

The life-cycle rituals commencing from birth to death are broadly in accordance with Hindu beliefs and practices with considerable dilution at the local level. The birth of a male child is an occasion of joy and celebration. The mother has to observe certain restrictions following the birth of a child. It is believed that both the mother and child are vulnerable to evil influences in the first few weeks following delivery and therefore should be protected. Purificatory rites are observed for both the mother and child on sixth, eleventh and twenty-first day when they are bathed and after that a woman is considered ritually clean to resume her schedule. The child is also taken out of the house. The important ceremony following thereafter is *jattu* which is usually performed for the male child and the maternal uncle first cuts the child's hair followed by other relatives.

Marriage is performed at the bride's residence and consists of simple ceremonies. Before the marriage the boy's side has to approach the girl's father several times and each time they give a few bottles of liquor, and some wheat bread. On the betrothal day the boy brings, in addition, a piece of jewellery, generally bangles for the bride. At this time, the day and date of marriage are also fixed. On an appointed day the bridegroom along with his close relatives comes to the girl's house. They are welcomed by the bride's side. The couple takes four rounds of certain ritual objects and are considered married. *Kanyadan* does not exist. The bride leaves for her husband's home along with her relatives. The maternal uncle acts as priest at the time of the marriage ritual. Similar ritual acts are performed at the bridegroom's place. Usually a he-goat is sacrificed and its meat is distributed among guests. The bride's relatives return after one or two days.

The dead are cremated. Infants and people who die of small-pox and snake bite are buried. Pollution is observed for 13 days. An Acharaj officiates at the time of the death rites. Ashes are immersed in water and the death rites are performed after a month and subsequently every year during the fortnight specially marked to commemorate the ancestors. A funeral feast is given to the members of the *biradari*.

Economically, the Chanal are one among the downtrodden class who are exploited socially and economically. Majority of them work as agricultural labourers for the high caste Rajputs and Brahmans in lieu of a certain share of the produce. They are also asked to perform certain jobs such as carrying fuel, removing dead cattle and other such lowly manual tasks. At the time of death they carry fire in a pot and lead the funeral procession. They are also required to carry the luggage and gift items at the time of marriage. In addition to the above they are also engaged in various kinds of manual labour in road building, forest department, etc., where they are employed on daily wages. Child labour does exist. They have a direct link with the market where cash forms the mode of exchange.

For the maintenance of social law, the community has an informal council of elders who are elected by a voice vote. Marital discords, family feuds, etc., are usually referred to this council whose effort is to bring about mutual reconciliation. Land disputes, loss of property and other criminal cases (which are of rare occurrence) are taken care of by the statutory panchayats which have been functioning since Independence. Their main function is to implement the welfare programmes in the village.

The Chanals' religion is a combination of Hinduism and local beliefs and practices. Shiva is the presiding deity besides other gods and goddesses of the pantheon. There are also clan, village and regional deities which are duly propitiated from time to time. The clan deity is mostly worshipped on important social occasions such as marriage and births. Regional deities have a bigger area under their spiritual jurisdiction. The propitiation of these deities in turn protects the people from the onslaught of natural hazards, epidemics etc. Faith in spirits and supernatural powers is also widespread and protection against the same is sought from exorcists called *chela*. The Chanals do not possess any special artistic attribute. They have a rich heritage of folksongs and dances, folktales and folklore which are different from region to region.

The Chanals maintain connubial and commensal norms with Hali, Bansi and Sanhai who are treated almost at par with each other. Earlier each of these were endogamous but now inter-community marriages are becoming frequent. Despite the fact that the number of such intermarriages has risen considerably, caste restriction with regard to connubial and commensal norms still persist. The Brahmans and Rajputs cannot accept fried food and liquor from them. The Chanals on the other hand accept both *kachcha* and *pucca* food from the high castes.

The developmental programmes have brought in significant infrastructural changes. Electricity, post offices and banks are available at a number of places benefiting even those living in far-flung corners. The number of schools and primary health centres have also risen but still literacy and health standards have not come up to the anticipated level. This may largely be attributed to poverty, ignorance and apathy. Economic programmes like the Integrated Rural Development Programme, employment schemes, vocation guidance centres as also the policy of reservation of posts for scheduled castes and tribes have been widely acclaimed as major steps towards economic uplift of the weaker sections of the society and need to be geared up and implemented on a larger scale.

Vatsala Sarkar

CHANDEL RAJPUT

The Chandel Rajputs, also popularly known as Kehluria Mian, are the descendants of the erstwhile rulers of the Kehlur state, now Bilaspur district. The name Kehlur was given by a Chandel raja, Kahal Chand, sixth in the ruling line, though the state was founded by Raja Bir Chand in A.D. 900 (Mamgain, 1975). Now the common name for Kehlur is Bilaspur which was derived from its ancient name Vyaspur, named after Rishi Ved Vyas, who authored Mahabharata and the 18 Puranas. A cave of Vyas is located on the bank of river Satluj where the township of Bilaspur is built. 'Mian' is a respectable title that was conferred on the Rajput rulers by the Muslim emperors.

Previous to the foundation of the Kehlur state, the territory was under the rule of Rana and Thakurs known as Ruhnds who lost it to the Chandel Rajputs who conquered the area around A.D. 900. It is said that the ruler of Chanderi in Bundelkhand, Harihar Chand, left his ancestral kingdom for his eldest son Govind Chand and undertook a pilgrimage to Jwalamukhi, and arrived at Kangra with his four sons and the army. He had an encounter with the raja of Kangra in which he and his youngest son Sabirchand along with king of Kangra were killed. His other son Bir Chand took the command of Kangra but later went to Bilaspur and established the Bilaspur or Kehlur State, whereas other two sons Kabir Chand and Gambir Chand established themselves in Kumaon and Chamba respectively. Beginning with Raja Bir Chand, about 60 Chandel rajas ruled Kehlur till its merger with the Union of India on October 9, 1948. Anand Chand was the last ruler of the state.

The Chandels are confined mostly to district Bilaspur but are also found in Solan, Shimla, Kangra, Mandi and Chamba districts. They are dispersed over 66 villages in Bilaspur in both Sadar and Ghumarwin tehsils.

The Chandels inhabit hilly and plain places. Geographically, the area has seven main hill ranges (*dhar*), viz., Naina Devi, Kot, Jhanjiar, Tiun, Bandla, Bahadurpur and Ratanpur with varying altitudes of 290 to 1980 metres. The terrain is drained by river Satluj and its six main tributaries, viz., Sir, Sukkar, Sirhali, Gambhar, Gambrola and Ali Khads. With the erection of Bhakra-Nangal Dam, the Satluj has been converted into a huge lake known as Gobind Sagar, which has submerged the old town and capital of Kehlur, and has turned out to be a storehouse of fish and a place of attraction for the tourists. The area is also gifted with three important natural springs—Luhnd, Bassi and Markanda springs, which are of great tourist, religious and medicinal importance. The hill ranges or *dhar* are covered with thick to thin pine, deodar and bamboo forests and scrub forests which supply timber, firewood and other forest produce and enrich the economy. Some of the hill peaks, e.g., Bahadurpur occasionally receive a light snowfall which melts within a few days.

The forests which had plenty of wildlife still contain wild leopard (*lakkar bagha*), wild boar, antelopes, rhesus monkey, hare, porcupine; various kinds of birds, notably hill pigeon, peacock and jungle fowl; reptiles like cobra, krait and boas. The climate of the area is generally warm and temperate with moderate annual rainfall. The humidity is high during monsoon but the rest of the year is comparatively dry.

During the princely regime the language of Bilaspur (Kehlur) known as Kehluri or Bilaspuri had its own script, Tankri. But now Devanagari script is used. Other dialects similar to Bilaspuri are Kangri, Mandiali and Baghati. Presently, the Mians are not distinguished from other communities by dress or ornaments but their traditional male dress was a *kurta* and a *churidar pyjama* and a turban. The women wear *kurti* and *salwar* (earlier a *ghagri*) and *dupatta/chadru*. The gold and silver ornaments worn by women are nose pin or ring called *koka* or *nath*, *kantha*, *teek*, *chak*, *gajra*, *mundri* (bridal ring) and a *jhanjar*. Men used to wear a *nanti* (gold ear-rings) and a ring on the finger.

The Chandels are generally non-vegetarian and meat (of goat), fish, eggs and pork (of wild boar) are frequently consumed both by men and women. Their chief staple food is maize throughout the year supplemented by wheat, and rice. Maize *roti* is eaten with mustard *sag* and butter or *ghee*, during winters. The pulses consumed are *urd, masur, moong, kulth* and gram, beans and peas along with potatoes and *kachalu* tubers. The common vegetables include brinjals, lady fingers, tomato, radish, carrots, gourds and pumpkins. Fruits like plum, banana, guava, peach and mango are taken seasonally. Liquor of better quality is purchased from the market. Wheat products like *putande, babru, halwa, sevyian* are commonly prepared on Baisakhi and Sair festivals. Rice products like *ankloo* and *ankli* are favourite on Diwali and Dussehra. *Kheer* is common on various festivities. *Sag* of mustard leaves is a speciality of Khorhi festival and *khichri* of Lohri and Panch Bhikhmi or Guru Parv. On Sharad Purnima the family priest offers *sag* and *puris*. They also prepare meat on Dussehra, Diwali, Shivratri and Khorhi. On Khorhi day the Mian is entrusted to hunt a wild boar. Food taboos are observed during death pollution. Cucumbers and *chhalli* (maize cob) are not eaten on Sair.

The Chandels belong to the Atrishya Chandrain *gotra*. They broadly classify themselves into the Chandels (true Mian) and the Chandlas. The Chandlas are only distinguished from their village names established by their founders, like Meghpuria, Rajade, Bacholar, Kanhiaru, Raipuria, Doklu, Manjheru, Badhiatu, Naglu, Grewal, Singwal, Chandwal, Darol, Barhial, etc. In fact, the Chandlas are those Chandel Rajput who are remotely connected with the ruling families.

The name Kehluria Mian is sometimes restricted to only those Chandel Rajputs who are the direct or near kins of the rajas and whose genealogies could be correctly traced from a particular raja (ruler). Commonly four such lineages are popular, viz., Sultanchandia (A.D. 1620), Kalianchandia (A.D. 1630), Tarachandia (A.D. 1645) and Ajmerchandia (A.D. 1712-1714). The last lineage ruled Kehlur till its end and claims superiority over others and also sticks to the Rajput social traditions of not touching the plough, observance of purdah by women and non-permission to widow remarriage. The other lineages are accused of being lenient in the upkeep of Rajput traditions and of becoming agriculturists much earlier. Presently, however, most of the Chandels have become farmers and the social distinction between 'Chandel' and 'Chandla' has ended. Their women also do not observe purdah and also work in the fields. During transition fron 'not-ploughing' to 'ploughing' and 'purdah' to 'non-purdah' during the post Independence period, they started working in their fields to save their land going from their hands to the cultivators. Some members of the community however lost much of the *jagir* (revenue-free landholdings) to their *pahu* (the tenants). The Chandels still enjoy a social and economical superiority over other communities and are respectfully wished as 'Jai-Deva' or 'Jai Deya', an expression which conveys respect.

The Chandels are exogamous and marry among the superior Rajput clans, like Katoch, Guleria, Pathania, Jammual, Manhas and Tathwalia. Hypergamy has been a common practice among them but they have occasionally resorted to hypogamy when suitable mates are not available in the desired clans.

They now may also give their daughters to the Patial, Saunkhle, Ranaut, Parmar and Garhwali Rajputs. The marriage is also governed by geo-economic factors. The marriage is almost always negotiated by near relatives and friends and also the family priest and the barber. Marriages occurred before puberty in earlier days, but now marriage age ranges between 15 and 20 years for girls and from 20 and 25 years for boys in most of the cases. There has been no tradition of bride-price among them and dowry was and still is a common feature. Dowry giving is a status symbol but it is not demanded. Cash is not generally demanded. Monogamy is commonly practised. Bigamy or polygyny could be sororal or non-sororal and was considered a sign of royal superiority and richness. The rulers sometimes used to have more than one wife just as keeps (concubines), whose offspring were called as *sartora.* The *sartora* used to marry only among the *sartoras* of other clans. Presently the second marriage is attempted only in case of childlessness or want of a son. The symbol of marriage among women is *sindur,* glass bangles and a ear and nose ornament. The residence of bride is patrilocal. Divorce is against their social tradition as is widow remarriage. *Sati* custom was prevalent among them during the princely regime as a sign of purity of women. Only men have the right to remarry.

The institution of marriage has witnessed changes with increase of marriage age, giving of dowry and acceptance of monogamy. The Biradri Panchayats are trying to premit the remarriage of the young widows and get rid of social evils like dowry.

The Chandel Rajputs predominantly live in vertically joint extended families that are sometimes extended horizontally as well. Brothers do not separate as long as their father is alive. Interpersonal bonds in the family are strong and based on respect and fear of the elders. Sons used to touch the feet of elders who touch head of the young ones to give blessings. The *lari* observes purdah from her *saurah* as well as from *jeth.* Joking relativonship between *devar* and *bhabi* and *jija* and *sali* are generally lacking, but sometimes exhibited at the festival of Khorhi. Other joking relations are seen between the two *kurams* (boy's and girl's parents). Occasions of confrontation among family members are rare and may be on the issues of check on freedom of youngsters or challenge to the authority of the elders and/or on property. The succession pattern among the royal or ruling families had been from father to the eldest son (primogeniture) known as *tikka.* The inheritance is patrilineal and as per the male-equigeniture. Presently, families are breaking down into small nuclear units, and the women are denouncing purdah/*androl.*

The women enjoy a respectable but low status. They generally avoid heavy and rough outdoor activities and traditionally remain confined to indoor activities. But now they have started doing other economic activities like collection of fodder, fetching potable water and some also have joined government service. They participate in all social, ritual and religious ceremonies but lack participation in the mechanism of social control and political spheres. They however regulate family expenditure.

Pre-birth rituals are ignored. Delivery may be performed at home by a midwife of a low caste community. The impure period called *sutak* is observed for 13 days and purification occurs by taking cow's urine known as *guntrala.* Gram seedlings along with sugar are distributed. The *nana* of the baby brings *kangan* for the baby. The ladies sing *badhai* songs. The name of the child is given as per the horoscope by the family priest. *Mundan* (tonsure) is performed by *mama* before the fifth year at the temple of the family deity. The family deity of this community is Saikirthi whose shrine is located near Deoth in Sadar tehsil. Some also perform this ceremony at Naina Devi, Jwalamukhi or even at home. At the birth of the first son, a *yatra* to Guga (at Geharwin) or Nahar Singh (at Dholre) or Deot Sidh (at Chakmoh) is made to ensure happiness and prosperity in the family. Adolescent rituals are *kanchhedan* and *nakchhedan* in young girls, usually done at Khorhi festival. For the boy, the *janeu* ceremony usually occurs at marriage.

After marriage is negotiated, *sagai* and *tikka* ceremonies are performed where rings, sweets and clothes along with cash are exchanged. The marriage rituals are performed as per the Hindu Sanatana Dharam. The first ritual is *samuhat.* The *kuljade* (priest) brings an idol of clan deity Sakirthi on a plate covered with clothes which is propitiated by family members without actually being seen. The second ritual is *sand* (star worship) followed by *bhridi bharna* and the oil ceremony when clothes are offered by the *nankiye* (mother's parents), and *mehndi. Geuchara* ceremony is performed at the bride's place when *purohit* of girl's side visits the camp of the groom which is followed by *milni* (reception) and meals/feast to the *barat* (groom's party). At night *lagan* and *ved* ceremonies are performed by the priest and the bride and bridegroom circumambulate the sacred fire. This ceremony is completed with *kanyadan.* At the bridegroom's place the bride enters his house by the *andrera* ritual. On the third day the bride and groom take rounds of a *banah* shrub and the marriage is then complete. The bride and groom return on the same day to the bride's parents' house. The marriage is consummated with the *muklawa* ceremony on the next day.

The dead are cremated and the ashes are collected on the third day and immersed in the Ganges at Hardwar where *pind dan* is offered to a *panda.* The *patak* lasts for 13 days. The *kirya karam* (ancestor worship) is performed by an Acharaj who is offered clothes, bedding, cot, utensils and cash. This is followed by *solia* on sixteenth day when a family priest performs *havan* and gets offerings in the form of clothes, bedding, cot, utensils and umbrella. A ceremonial feast is then given. After that an annual ritual called *barkhi* is observed and a feast served. Lastly, every year *shradha* is performed by the family *purohit* in the *Pitri Paksha.*

The Mians possess large landholdings. They have inherited these as *jagirs* from the ruling families. But due to post-Independence land reforms, their *pahu* (tenants) became landowners by paying a nominal compensation. In view of this the Mians, who were less industrious, lost some land and started tilling the land themselves. Although they are now agriculturists, many persons joined defence services and other professions like teaching, banking, legal and medicine. They have also taken up business and set up industries, horticulture, petrol pumps, etc. as subsidiary occupations. They also own hotels and general merchandize shops. Child labour does not exist in the community. A significant change is that they have started ploughing and have adopted various other professions.

During the princely regime the social and administrative control was in the hands of the Chandel raja and their kinsmen who used to give severe punishments like *phansi* (hanging), *kath* and *kode* to criminals and *jagir* to the rewardees. Raja Bijay Chand (1908) initiated *qaumi* panchayats of Brahmans,

Rajputs and Thakurs, but these remained functionless. Raja Anand Chand (1932-1942) formed the Education Health Committee, town committees and pargana committees for social reforms and vested these with judicial powers.

Subsequently, the Panjab Panchayat Act (1939) was extended to the Bilaspur State in 1950 and judiciary panchayats were formed. This Act was soon replaced by the Himachal Pradesh Panchayat Act in 1952, finally reshaped as Himachal Pradesh Panchayat Rules 1971. Statutory councils, Gram Sabhas, Panchayat Samitis, Zila Parishads, Naya Panchayats, Samjhauta Samitis and Panchayat Samelans carry out social reforms and developmental activities but some of them are defunct now.

Recently, the elite of the community has initiated Biradari Panchayat (community council), Mahila Mandals and Youth Forums to discourage their traditional rigid attitude towards widow-remarriage, purdah custom, not touching the plough, and to eradicate the social evil of dowry.

The Chandels worship Brahma, Vishnu and Mahesh. There are 16 main Thakurdwaras and seven main Shiva temples in Bilaspur. Village and local deities are Deo Sur, Nahar Singh, Deot Sidh (Baba Balak Nath), Guga Pir and Lakhdata (Bhianu Pir). Deo Sur and Nahar Singh are also regarded as women deities, who control fertility. *Khel* is performed in their temples by a *chela* in which women sway their heads in hypnotic trance and narrate their sufferings. A big loaf of bread is offerred to Deot Sidh on the first Sunday of every month to ensure prosperity. Lakhdata is propitiated by arranging wrestling matches called *chhinj*. Guga is regarded as a controller of snakes.

A Guga Mandali sings Guga folksongs for eight days commencing on Rakshabandhan, and Guga fairs are held at different places. The famous female local deities are Naina Devi, Badoli Devi, Hari Devi, and Jangal Devi. The sacred shrines of the deities are located on the seven hill ranges of the district and yearly fairs are arranged to propitiate them.

The Mian's clan deity is Sakirithi (or Sagirthi) whose shrine is located near Deoth and maintained by a Nai Pujari. In addition they also propitiate family deities called Satis. There are a number of annual fairs, notably the Naina Devi fair, Guga fair, Baisakhi fair, Haridevi fair, Markand fair, Bharnot fair, Bhianu fair, Bhel fair, Nalwari cattle fair (at Bilaspur during the month of Chet), Chakrana fair, Bada Dev fair, Morsinghi fair and Bam fair. The main festivals are Sair (during September, when the maize harvest is ready), Lohri, Khohri, Chiran, Baisakhi (Basoa), Rakhri, Shivratri and Diwali. At Khohri, the Mians have to hunt a wild game animal, especially a wild boar and women collect mustard leaves and cook *sag* eaten with *ghi*. The young girls perform *gidda* dance.

The creation of Kangra/Kehlur paintings is attributed to the Chandel

Rajputs. Certain Pahari folksongs are also supposed to have originated from the deeds of Chandel Rajputs. Pahari folksongs and folktales like *Mohan* (who accepted gallows for the crime committed by his brother), *Ranju-Phulmu, Chenchlo* and *Kunju* love tales, *Chunchu Mian* (more prevalent in Sirmaur), *Gambri, Guga Mandli* and *Chandrauli* are common in the region. The main folk dances of the area are *gidda, nati* and *swang*. In addition religious songs and plays include *bhajan, kirtan, Bhagwad Geeta Katha* and *Ramlila.* The popular pastimes of the Mians had been horsemanship, horse-riding, sword play and mountain treking.

Before Independence due to concentration of political and economical power in their hands, people of other castes were employed as forced labourers, cultivators and cattle rearers by the rulers. Their *jal-chal* commensal norms exist with the *savarna* (inner or clean castes) only in terms of exchange of *kachcha* and *pucca* food. *Jajmani* relationship exists with the Brahman and the Nai. The others (service renderers) are paid in the form of *gadda-gadolu* (bundle of unthreshed and unhusked cereals) in lieu of their services. They get their land cultivated on *theka* (contract) or *adh* (half-crop production), or on daily wages.

The Chandels are affluent and dominate the society economically as well as politically as there are businessmen, scholars, doctors, engineers, advocates, teachers, artists and political leaders in this community.

Under the changing political situation after Independence, initially the Mians disliked road connection to their villages in order to avoid easy access of enemies. But now they have realized its importance. They have responded to a great extent to literacy and higher education. The indigenous health and medical care practices are sometimes still employed. They have favoured family planning measures and sterilization is commonly accepted. Modern mass media (radio, television, cinema and newspaper) facilities are availed of or are accessible to them. Potable water through pipelines is available but *bauri* or springs are also used. The energy sources are fire-wood, cow-dung cakes, coal, sawdust and kerosene. Biogas plants are also used by some and a few also use LPG. Irriagation facilities are also available to some. They make use of chemical fertilizers and pesticides. Banking facilities and public distribution system are also availed of.

A.R. Sankhyan

CHHIMBA/DHOBI

The Chhimba or Chhimbe or Chhippa as the name denotes are the traditional calico printers/stampers or *chhapne wale.* They are regarded equal to the Dhobis (the washermen) as both printing and washing of the clothes was done by them. In the countryside they usually do only the job of washing clothes. Dhobi is as frequently used name as the Chhimba. They are, however, a different community from those of the Lallari or Pharera who are specialists in dyeing of the clothes. The Chhimbas/Dhobis trace their ancestry to a saint Guru Nam Deo. Nam Deo had two sons. One was named Tank from whom the Chhimbas descended and the other named Rhilla who gave rise to the Dhobis. The former consider themselves socially superior to the latter. They have been classified in the scheduled caste category in the State and had a total population of 2,793 persons according to the 1971 Census of India (Singh, 1971) which rose to 12,166 a decade after in 1981. Their main concentration is in districts of Bilaspur, Mandi, Shimla, Solan, Sirmaur and Kangra. They live both in the rural and urban settings, in the Himalayan foothills experiencing in general a warm and temperate climate most of the year.

Like other people of the area the Chhimbas speak the regional dialects of the western Pahari, e.g., Bilaspuri (Kehluri) in Bilaspur, and write in the Devanagari script. Old persons used to write in the Tankri script which is not in vogue at present.

There are no identification markers in dress or ornaments. Older men used to wear a *kurta, dhoti* and a turban but younger ones wear pants, women wear *kurta, salwar* and *chadru.* Traditional ornaments were a conical silver *chak* on head, a golden *laung*, silver *gajra* and *jhanjar.* Their food habits are similar to those of the other people of the area. They are occasional non-vegetarian and eat fish, meat and eggs. Staple foods are maize, wheat and rice. Various pulses like *urad, moong, masur, kulthi*, gram, peas and beans and various roots and tubers and seasonal vegetables are part of their regular diet. Festive food preparations are *anklu/ankli* of rice on Diwali, *khichri* on Lohri, *babroo* on Baisakhi, *sevian* on Sair, plus milk puddings and *halwa.* The cooking medium is usually mustard oil or sometimes vegetable and *desi ghee.* Non-vegetarian food is not taken during death pollution. Men consume country liquor occasionally. They smoke *hukka, bidi* and occasionally cigarettes.

In Bilaspur the Chhimbas claim themselves as the Tank Suryavanshi Kaith. The binary division into Tank and Rhilla is not known to them. They usually split themselves into small exogamous units called *got,* such as Kaith,

Jarial, Panjaru, Kaushal, Indoriye, Dhiare, Chandel, etc., which also denote descent or ancestry. A social hierarchy is lacking in the community. They claim Kshatriya varna status but others' perception about them is low, that of a Sudra.

The community is endogamous but practises clan or *got* and village exogamy. Marriages occur through negotiation, and exchange of sisters called *batta-satta* also occurs quite often. Earlier, child marriages occurred frequently and the bride-price was also taken or exchanges were made. But presently the marriage age has increased to 16 years or above among girls and to 20 years or above in case of boys. The practice of bride-price has given way to dowry which is, however, not in cash but in kind and is called *daj dan* or *dahej*. The symbols of marriage among married women are glass bangles, *sindur* and *tili* or *koka*. Monogamy is the usual form of marriage. A man may acquire another wife in rare circumstances when he gets no issue from the first wife. The wife lives with her husband at his father's home. Widow remarriage is permitted only as a junior levirate if a woman becomes widow at a young age. A widower may marry junior sororate or any other woman. The society approves dissolution of marriage or separation for both the spouses on grounds of maladjustments or cruelty to the wife. Presently, divorce has been legalized through civil courts which also fix compensation or maintenance to be given to the wife. The children become the liability of the father. But if the divorced woman marries again she is not entitled to compensation.

The Chhimbas live in vertically extended joint families, which however, are fast disintegrating giving rise to nuclear families. Usually the married sons get separated. In joint families avoidance and joking relationship exist similar to many Hindu communities of the region. The *lari* keeps *ghoond* (face covered by the shawl) from her *saurah*, *jeth*, *nandoi* and elder males of the village. Joking relationship is seen among *devar-bhabi*, *jija-sali*, *nanad-bhabi* and *jija-sala*. The property is divided on male lines as per the rule of male-equigeniture and the eldest son succeeds father at his death. Conflicts may occur over the division of earnings of different sons and father's property.

The women practically enjoy an equal status. They contribute to the family income by participating in the washing and ironing clothes and by rendering services of midwifery. They also participate in agriculture and animal husbandry collect fuel and fodder, fetch potable water and participate in social and religious ceremonies,etc. They regulate family expenditure and have a say in domestic matters. They, however, have little say or role in the mechanism of social control and political activities.

The life-cycle rituals are performed by the priest of their community. Pre-delivery rituals are not observed but restrictions on the woman exist in the post-delivery period also. The woman is considered impure for 13 days after the delivery and the *sutak* is wiped out by performing *guntrala* ceremony when she has to take cow's urine and holy Ganges water. Naming and cereal-taking are not ceremonised but name to the child may at times be given as per its horoscope by consulting the priest. *Jatlu* or *mundan* of the boys is the only notable childhood ritual performed by the *mama* of the child who gives the first ceremonial cut to the hair. Some *kanya* (small girls) and *bhattu* (boys) are served sweets and given some coins.

The marriage rituals are similar to those of other Hindus as prescribed by the Hindu scriptures. The *sand, samuhat* and oil ceremony precede the major marriage rituals. At bride's place both the groom and bride circumambulate the sacred fire and *kanyadan* is performed by bride's parents who also give a feast to the groom's party and other relatives gathered on the occasion. At the bridegroom's place both the bride and groom worship a *daran* (pomegranate) tree and take rounds of it. This ends the marriage ceremony and is followed by music and dance. The groom's parents serve (meals) *dham* to the gathered kinsmen, friends and villagers. The bride returns to her parents' house the same evening followed by a visit of the bridegroom. The *muklawa* ritual occurs on the folowing day when the girl starts living with her husband.

The death rituals are also like that of other Hindus. The dead are cremated and the ashes are immersed in the Ganges or the Beas and ancestor worship is observed during the *patak* period observed for 13 days. On the thirteenth day the community priest performs a *havan* and seeks offerings in the name of the dead. Prayers are also offered at the gurudwara of Nam Deo at Dehra in Kangra district.

The Chhimbas traditionally thrived on calico printing and washing of clothes. Presently this occupation (except for printing) is continued along with agriculture and animal husbandry as the Chhimbas also possess small landholdings of their own. They have also opened dyers' and dry-cleaners' shops in towns and suburbs. Traditionally a Dhobi used to carry the wedding rolls called *saurh* on marriages in the villages on the back of his donkey or mule. Some people of this community work as daily-wage casual labour. On the other hand there are people in the community who are well employed in government jobs as teachers, doctors, engineers, policemen and defence personnel.

They have a community council for social control whose president is elected by a voice vote for an indefinite period. This *sabha* encourages literacy for children, discourages unnecessary marriage expenditure and solves problems related to marriage and divorce. Socioeconomic or village disputes over land and water are taken up in the statutory Gram Panchayat. Legal course is also taken up in certain serious matters of land and water disputes.

The Chhimbas are Hindus, though Sikh and Muslim Chhimba also occur outside Himachal Pradesh. They propitiate various family, clan, village deities and of the wider Hindu pantheon order. Nabahi Devi and Hari Devi are family *kul* deities. Guru Namdeo is propitiated as patron or community deity. Badoli Devi, Guga Chauhan, Nahar Singh, Lakhdata or Bhianu and Balak Nath (or Deot Sidh) are the other chief deities of the village or the region. Their holy shrines are periodically visited on birth, marriage and other festive occasions and during annual fairs. Various festivals of socio-economic and socio-religious importance are also celebrated, viz., Lohri, Baisakhi, Chiran, Sair, Navratre, Guga Navmi, Rakshabandhan, Dussehra and Diwali. The community hardly practises the traditional art of calico printing at present.

The various folk oral traditions and music and dances of the area or region are shared. Many folktales and proverbs are popular about the Dhobi and his donkey and dog. *Bhajan* (religious songs) and *kirtan* are the main folksongs and percussion instrument like *dholak* and valve music instrument like harmonium are used. Sacred specialists are from the same community. The *chelas* are also consulted for treatment of diseases supposed to be caused by evil spirits *(bhoot, pret* and *masan).*

The traditional linkages of the Chhimbas are primarily with the equal ranking communities. The upper caste Hindus do not accept *kachcha* or *pucca* food and water from them except *sidha* or *sukha* or the Chhimbas arrange a separate *suchchi rasoi* cooked by a Brahman. A Chhimba also does not accept *kachcha* or *pucca* food or water from Chamar, Dumna, Julaha, etc. though the latter accept the same from him, but such restrictions are breaking down.

Traditional water sources and cremation grounds may or may not be shared with certain communities. Religious shrines and other public places are common. They maintain the traditional *jajmani* system with a Nai, Lohar and Chamar and pay their customary dues. They render traditional services to the upper-caste Hindus on festive and marriage occasions. Modern inter-community linkages have developed at various levels which have eroded untouchability of the Chhimbas.

Modern developmental programmes have been favoured and have made an impact on the Chhimbas. Formal education is now favoured for both the boys as well as the girls. Some may drop out on account of shortage of economic means or lack of interest or job opportunities. Modern health and medical care facilities are available and favoured though indigenous methods are also in practice. Attitude towards restricted family size has gradually become favourable, but socially there is still a desire to have at least one son. Sterilization has usually been the method of family planning.

Drinking water is available through taps at their doorsteps but sometimes the water sources like springs and *bauri* are also used. There are provisions of IRDP and they avail themselves of the 50 per cent subsidy for the purchase of animals, fertilizers, seeds, etc. Their houses are electrified and many avail themselves of modern facilities of mass media like radio and television and also go to cinema in the towns. Road communication and postal facilities are within their reach. Traditional energy sources like firewood and cowdung cakes are used in rural areas and coal and kerosene oil in suburbs. Rain water is the only source of irrigation. The nutritional programmes and immunization of children are availed of. They also avail themselves of the public distribution system.

A.R.Sankhyan

CHINESE

The Chinese population in Himachal Pradesh is concentrated exclusively in Shimla proper. They came to this place in search ofbetter avenues for business for this was not only the old summer capital of India but a flourishing hill resort. Some families have been residing here since the pre-Independence period but others have recently migrated from Calcutta. All the families are originally from South China and, therefore, they speak Hakk dialect that is spoken in South China. However, with outsiders, they have learnt to speak Hindi and English. Similarly, the script used by them while writing to each other is Chinese but while communicating with others, Hindi and English are used. Men wear pants and shirt and women also sport baggy pants and shirts with floral designs.

Fond of non-vegetarian food, their staple diet consists of rice, noodles, pulses and beans. Beans are liked by the majority. Similarly, they take mutton, pork, chicken and beef but are very fond of eating chicken which they like to cook on all important social festivals and rituals. Men like smoking and also drink occasionally. Among the non-alcoholic beverages, green tea is widely taken, though they have learnt to drink red tea as well. In fact the younger generation is not only taking to red tea but have adapted themselves to Indian styles of food.

The Chinese are divided into territorial groupings and observe endogamy at this level. There is, however, no hierarchy as such since marriages also can take place with other territorial groups. But for the similarity of speech, dress and food habits, marriages are preferably confined to their own groups. They are further divided into a number of patrilineages which are essentially exogamous. They have an elaborate system of numbering the lineages in chronological order and interpersonal behaviour is regulated in terms of the proximity and distance of a lineage with that of the other. Generation and age are very important criteria of stratification within their society. Marriage is settled through negotiation on attaining adulthood. Marriage cannot be performed in one's own lineage. There is no concept of dowry but bride-price exists. An auspicious amount is fixed, usually Rs. 999, and is given to the bride's parents who in turn give it back to the daughter along with other gifts. It is considered bad if the amount is used by the bride's parents. There are no symbols of marriage. The girl goes to live with her husband's family after her marriage. Parallel and cross-cousins do not marry. However, distant cousins may marry but such marriages are not preferred. Divorce and remarriage in the lifetime of the first wife is exceptional and since most of them have embraced Christianity and profess Catholic faith, divorce is ruled out. Widows and widowers on the other hand can remarry.

Joint family is a common form. It is patripotestal with patrilineal inheritance and succession pattern, and patrilocal system of residence. Property is divided equally among all the sons. Daughters inherit only in the absence of a son. Elders are given great respect. For instance, food is first served to the elders and then to the children. They have to be consulted on all important matters and their decisions are respected. There is no avoidance as such but the young are expected to be courteous in their behaviour towards the elders. Similarly in terms of generation, precedence is one of the major criteria of determining their behaviour towards each other.

Women do not enjoy a status equal to men despite the fact that they contribute towards economy in addition to the household jobs they perform. Women have an active role in social ceremonies, rituals and festivals, but lack initiative in political and religious fields. In economic matters, they find themselves generally dependent on their menfolk.

The majority of the life-cycle rituals are performed according to Christian Catholic faith but in addition to the above, some of their birth, marriage and death customs are the traditional Chinese customs. Pre-birth and post-birth restrictions and pollution on the mother is reported. Mother and the child are given a bath on the twelfth day. An egg coloured in red is given to the near and dear ones who reciprocate by giving gifts to the child. Mother and the child remain confined to the house for 40 days. Baptism (initiation) is a must for every child and should be duly performed in the church. The age at which it is to be performed varies. A month after the birth, they celebrate it by giving gifts. In order to ward off the evil eye, they burn feathers of a hen, cover them with sheet and allow the child to inhale the smoke. By doing so they believe that evil spirits are not able to cast an evil influence on the child. The birth of a male child is celebrated with great enthusiasm. Marriage is performed in the church as per Catholic belief. Before the wedding, they consult the horoscope and fix up the date and time of marriage. After the marriage, a feast is given by both the sides. However, the traditional Chinese wedding is different. The boy first goes to the girl's house and he is served Chinese tea. The relatives of the girl's side see the boy and he is formally introduced to them. Likewise, the girl also goes to the boy's house. A lunch is given to the relatives and friends by the boy's parents. Thereafter, the bride accompanied by her younger sister and her parents, returns. After the third day a feast is given by the girl's parents.

Gifts are given to the bride from both sides and consist of clothes, jewellery, etc. The people celebrate their wedding following both the Christian belief and the traditional Chinese practices. The dead are mostly buried but cremation may also take place depending on the wish of the person. A mourning service is held in the church for the departed ones. Whenever a death occurs, the family members wear a black badge around their arms to mark the mourning period. Food is cooked by the relatives of the bereaved family. They call for the elder man of the community who reads the horoscope and decides about the time of the burial.

The majority of the Chinese are in the shoemaking business. They manufacture shoes and also sell them. An entire family works in collaboration with one other where women may look after the sales and men may actually make shoes. They do not, however, skin or tan leather. A few have also opened stalls serving Chinese food which has become quite popular amongst the urban youth. They do not have any landed property in terms of agricultural land in the State. A very few have been able to acquire houses. They maintain direct link with the market. Goods are bought and sold strictly with cash. Since they manufacture shoes and also sell them, they sometimes run into financial difficulties for procuring raw material. In such financial crisis they depend solely on their community members.

The Chinese abide by the law of the land. Nevertheless, some personal issues and conflicts are amicably solved by the elders of the community. Each lineage has its own council or association. Though conflicts are rare, yet in case of any dispute the elders of both the sides are invited and they invariably bring about mutual agreement among the warring parties. Sometimes, though rarely, they have to call on *khew-teang*, their headman, whose office is at Calcutta. The expenditure involved on his travelling, stay and food is borne by the party concerned. His decision is binding on the people. Fines are levied in cash and are rarely opposed. Efforts are always for peaceful reconciliation. Criminal offences are taken care of by the State machinery for maintaining law and order.

All the Chinese families who are residing in Himachal Pradesh have embraced Christianity and profess the Catholic faith. They celebrate Christmas, Good Friday and All Saints' Day and regularly attend Church services. Besides, they also celebrate their traditional Chinese festivals. The Chinese New Year falling in months of January-February is celebrated with gaiety and enthusiasm. On this day it is customary to visit each others' house where the elders give *fung pao* (gifts) to the young ones. When this gift consists of cash it is also customary to always keep two currency notes of the same denomination. The new year festivities last for three days. Another festival called Oom-ya-che falls in the month of May. On this day it is customary to offer mangoes to the parents. They reciprocate it by giving gifts to their children and young ones. In the month of August on the full-moon day it is customary to eat cake after performing worship. People also believe in evil spirits to some extent. They hang auspicious words written artistically in the

Chinese script in front of the entrance door, the purpose of which is to bring good luck and fortune to the house.

The Chinese have preserved their age-old traditions in the form of folktales. They enjoy western music and dance and their traditional music is almost forgotten. Hindi film music has also influenced the younger generation.

Inter-ethnic interactions take place mostly on account of contact in schools and colleges, business and trade, social occasions and festivals. These people show remarkable adaptability to their surroundings. Commensal norms are greatly relaxed and they do not observe any restriction in exchange of food with others. Majority of them are in the shoe business and the entire family contributes its share in this pursuit. They do not have any role in the State or national politics except for the fact that they enjoy voting rights. They have their own association for maintenance of social norms and for ensuring justice in case of any breach.

There has been an overall growth in the technological communication network, electricity, water, literacy and health and hygiene. The community has received all these changes well and shown a positive attitude towards them. The children are receiving formal education in schools, colleges and universities. As a result of high educational level, they show remarkable adaptability towards the modern technological changes which are taking place. They also enjoy the existing facilities of ICDS, family welfare, banking, post offices, ration shops, etc. However, they have not been able to avail themselves of any economic benefits by way of loans and subsidies from the Government. In case of economic crisis they have to depend on their own community for assistance.

Vatsala Sarkar

CHRISTIAN

The Christian are a religious minority distributed throughout the length and the breadth of the country. In Himachal Pradesh the total population of Christians is 3,954 according to 1981 Census. Though present in almost all the districts they are found mostly in Shimla, Solan, Sirmaur, Chamba, Kullu and Mandi districts.

The dialect and dress of Christain show local variation. They speak the local dialect among themselves but are also conversant with Hindi and English. Similarly, in dress, both the local and Western influences are clearly visible. The urbanized sections have shown greater preference for Western clothes.

Non-vegetarian by food habit, the Christians' staple diet consists of wheat, rice, pulses and seasonal vegetables. There are no food taboos but the Hindu converts desist from eating beef. The Old Testament did list some of the items of food like pig as unclean but the New Testament gives sanction to everything which is edible. However certain sections among the Christians, particularly the Adventists do not even take coffee, tea, liquor, pork, etc. Generally, the use of intoxicants and smoking is prevalent among the men. Women take liquor on various ceremonies.

The Christian community is divided into a number of denominations on the basis of the church to which they belong. The reformist churches in England were thus organized into various branches like Anglicans, Baptist, Evangelist and Adventist. Similarly, the church mission in America grouped itself into Presbyterian, Methodist, Episcopal and other territorial sections. Needless to mention that the growing fission in the Christian community was a painful experience for all who cared for the spread of Christinity. As a consequence the process of unification of the different churches referred to as ecumenism was started, bringing the different churches of South India and North India into a common fold. In 1947 many churches of South India were brought under a common umbrella with the inception of CSI (Church of South India) and similarly at least six different churches formed the Churches of North India (CNI) in 1970.

The Christians are an endogamous community. Endogamy is both preferred and practised at the subgroup level which is based on the membership of an individual in a particular church. Thus the two main groups—the Catholic and the Protestant—remain endogamous to this day. Endogamy persists at yet another level which refers to an individual's affiliations prior to accepting Christianity. For instance, a Christian convert who, before his conversion had a place in the caste hierarchy would base his affiliations on the basis of his caste also. The high caste Hindu who became Christians maintain marriage alliance with their own caste. This is true more in rural situation than in urban. Ideally, the member belonging to a common church likes to select a match from within. Nevertheless, under circumstantial compulsions norms are made flexible to accommodate deviance.

The Christians are monogamous. Marriages are settled both by way of negotiation and mutual consent. They marry when they are adult. There is no bride-price. Dowry in the form of gifts exists, but there is no compulsion. Customarily, there is no marriage symbol for married Christian women except the wedding ring but in practice some of them may continue to use as the prevalent symbols of Hindu married women.

Remarriage of a widow or a widower is premitted but divorce does not have religious sanction. It can only be sought through courts. A divorcee cannot remarry in the church. Such marriages happen only through legal courts. A second marriage in the lifetime of the previous wife is also not allowed. Sororate and levirate may occur and depend entirely on the wish of the person concerned. Consanguineous marriages between cross-cousins and parallel cousins have religious sanction but are not so commonly practised. The Catholic priests and nuns who are dedicated to the service of the Church have to take the vow of chastity and marriage is denied to them. Among the Protestants, the priests and other religious functionaries can marry. Another fact which distinguishes the two sections is that the Catholics strongly condemn divorce, whereas the Protestants have more a liberal and tolerant outlook towards the issue. In case of legal separation, custody of the child is decided by the court.

Families are mostly nuclear. In villages joint household pattern is still prevalent. They believe in the patrilineal pattern of inheritance and succession and follow the law of the land. Under the existing law all the children are co-partners in the ancestral property but in practice only sons are given equal shares. On account of growing awareness daughters have made their claim for their share which has been settled by the courts but the percentage of such cases is very small. Often this results in breaking the cordial relations. There is no avoidance in the sense of purdah. Elders are given their due respect. The young are expected to be courteous and polite and pay respect to age and seniority. Among the younger generation, a light-hearted joking relationship prevails. Besides, related families are under mutual obligation to help each other in need.

Women enjoy parity of status with men in many ways and have considerable influence in the domestic field. They also get equal opportunity to avail themselves of education and professional training and to be independent, earning members. As a result of this outlook there are highly educated and professionally trained women among the Christians. However, despite their high education and earning potentials they still do not enjoy full economic freedom. Though legally women are to receive an equal share from the inherited property yet in practice this is not true. More often than not, they surrender their share. A widow has the right of maintenance. In religious sphere, women actively take part in the Christian festivals and attend church service along with men. They may also take to the life of nun or sister who are dedicated to the service of God and humanity. There are yet other women who may spend all their life in missionary activities serving charitable insitutions and spreading the message of God while attending to their wordly domain. Women are also politically conscious and their awareness of the political issues is fairly enlarged. But they generally avoid any active role in the politics at the district, state or national level.

The life-cycle rituals commencing from birth to death are basically common to all the Christian subdivisions and sections yet the manner in which they are observed varies from church to church. When a child is born, post-birth restriction and pollution is observed by the mother for 40 days. The mother and the child are brought to the church for blessing. Baptism (initiation) is the most important ceremony which symbolises the acceptance of the child into the fold of Christianity. The age at which this ceremony is to be performed varies. Some believe in adult baptism for they argue that the child should rightly be baptised when he/she is able to decide the faith he would like to adopt for himself.

Christian marriage is perfomed in the church. Before the wedding, betrothal or engagement takes place which ceremonially involves the exchange of rings. Every marriage is to be announced three times and three weeks prior to the wedding day so that if there are any objections to it, they should first be resolved before marriage. If there are still objections, such a marriage cannot be perfomed in the church. Under these circumstances marriage through court is the only alternative. After marriage the guests are entertained to a wedding feast.

The dead are buried and a tomb is constructed to commemorate the dead. A mourning service is held in the church for the peace of the departed soul. The mourners wear black badge as symbol of their grief. There is no sense of pollution as such but the priest is often called to sprinkle the holy water for the purification of the house. It should be mentioned that though burial is the most commonly observed form of disposing of the dead but even cremation can be performed if the person has so desired. After the initial ceremony in the church the body can be taken to the burial ground or for cremation.

The Christians as a community are not associated with any one occupation; rather they are found in different pursuits in life as servants, businessmen, teachers and in white-collar professions. In villages they also practise agriculture and horitculture. The traditional linkages like the patron-client or the landlord-sharecropper relationship is practically non-existent as far as the community is concerned. For economic development they depend mainly on the missionary organizations which are also an integral part of the church life. There are various funding agencies both local and foreign, namely World Vision, Bread for the Poor, CASA, Wiping the Tears and several others which are liberal in sanctioning financial assistance to the needy and these also undertake various socio-economic programmes for the upliftment of the community as also for others. They also encourage people to form cooperatives to meet various requirement which would be difficult for an individual to achieve, for instance, the tube wells, making irrigation channels, procuring thrashing machines and tractors for planting orchards. The community maintains a direct link with the market and all transactions are made in cash.

In music and dance, the influence of western music and dance forms is clearly visible. A good number of songs are devotional songs sung by the community in religious congregations and assemblies. Some of these songs are composed after folk tunes and local dialects to give it an ethnic touch.

Criminal activities and infringement of social norms are controlled by the existing law machinery through statutory panchayats and law courts. Among Catholic Christians some moral pressure is brought on the offender by the priest and his decisions are morally binding. The church organization itself brings some checks on the individual member by a system of confession and repentence, thereby relieving the person of carrying the burden of guilt. The church organization with its regular assembly and mass address system exerts an indirect pressure on the people to follow norms.

One important fact is that people have a strong sense of attachment to the church which places special emphasis on service to the community and sharing of love with fellow beings. For Christians, Sunday is an important day and most groups celebrate the symbolic meal together which is also referred to as 'communion service'and this rite is in remembrance of the last supper that Jesus had before he was betrayed. He shared his bread and wine with his trusted disciples and this act is repeated to show the presence of Jesus Christ amongst his believers. The mode of worship from one church to another may differ considerably but the Lord himself through Jesus Christ remains central. The church plays an important role in the life of the community. They celebrate all the important Christian festivals together with fellow Christians though the nature or the mode of worship may differ from church to church. The religious functionaries are from their own community. The church has a highly organized structure. Many local churches spread over a wide geograhical area form a diocese under the authority of a person called Bishop. He is assisted by priests or presbyters and deacons. The Roman Catholics have a world authority in the Bishop of Rome who is called the Pope. The offices of the bishops, priests, ministers, etc., are not hereditary but rather people are elected to them.

Since conversion to Christianity has taken place of people from different strata of society, therefore local customs and past traditions influence commensal and connubial relations. Broadly speaking, endogamy exists boths at community level and subgroup level. The main groups namely the Catholics and the Protestants remain endogamous even to this day. The Hindus accept *pucca* or *kachcha* food from them when it is separately cooked and served by the Hindus. The Christians on the other hand do not observe such restrictions while accepting food from their Hindu neighbours but of late they have also started refusing to take meals from them. In the urban context these caste-based restrictions and taboos have considerably weakened because of wider contact, literacy and wider worldview, through common participation in educational insititutions, business, trade, etc.

The attitude of the people towards various developmental activities is positive. Facilities for education, health, electricity, drinking water, mass media communication and transport have been well received by the people. However, for economic development they have depended heavily on the missionaries who with the help of the funding agencies have launched a nation-wide programme of socioeconomic development. The economic aid comes readily from various local and international funding agencies. Besides, the church organization with its dedicated workers has always worked for the upliftment of the weaker sections of the society. A number of Christian missions are engaged in imparting education through educational institutions run by them. There are other organizations for imparting vocational and technical training. There are a number of hospitals run by the missionaries both in rural and urban areas. Many institutions are run for the destitute, the physically handicapped and the socially deprived sections.

Vatsala Sarkar

CHUHRA/BALMIKI

They are variously called as the Chuhra, Chura, Chuhre, Bhangi, Balmiki, Lalbegi, Watal, Mazhabi and Christian Chuhra or Musalli. In some places they are also known as Khakrobe (meaning sweeper of dust). Change of religion involves adoption of a new title, and a Chuhra on conversion to Sikhism becomes Mazhabi, one who embraces Islam is known as Watal, the Hindus are known as Balmiki or Lalbegi and a Christian is known as a Christian Chuhra. It is said that all were Balmikis, but at various times they adopted different religions, and hence so many different names. As far as faith is concerned, they have only changed religion, otherwise for all practical purposes their pre-conversion practices survive. Balmiki and Lalbegi are identical, as the latter was former's disciple.

Balmiki, the progeniture of the Chuhras is believed to be originally a Bhil, who used to rob and kill travellers passing through the forest. One day, seven *rishis*, while passing through a jungle, were attacked by Balmiki. On being asked by the *rishis* whether the people for whom he commits crime, would share his punishment when he got caught. The reply was in negative, as none of the family members were ready to share the punishment. They then told him to give up his evil ways and chant a god's name (Rama), which alone could come to his rescue in difficult times. It is said that since he was a simple person he could not utter the word 'Rama', so the *rishis* told him to utter the reverse, *mara*, rapidly, which ultimately he did, and that sounded like 'Rama'. His sins were forgiven. He was so moved by this episode that he sat for 12 long years chanting lord's name. His body was covered with the dust and grass, and the flesh decomposed. Once again, the seven *rishis* passed by the jungle and heard a faint voice repeating Rama, Rama under a covering of clay. They removed the clay and having reclothed his bones with flesh called him Balmiki (meaning a person born of *balmi*—a snake hole).

Presently, the Chuhras are distributed in almost all the districts of India. In Himachal Pradesh, barring the high-altitude areas of Chamba, i.e., Pangi and Bharmaur, Lahaul and Spiti and Pooh and Kalpa divisions of Kinnaur, they are found all over the State. In Chamba, the Chuhras are found mostly in the urban centres and *tehsil* headquarters as job opportunities for them exist at only these places. In villages, there are no Chuhras, as the scavenging job is done by other low communities. In the urban areas they live along with persons of other communities but in a separate locality on the outskirts.

According to the 1981 Census the total population of the Chuhras/Balmikis/ Bhangis is 19,764, and that of Mazhabis 221 in Himachal Pradesh. The language spoken by the people among themselves is Chambiali (in Chamba), whereas with others it is Hindi. The scripts used by them are Perso-Arabic and Devanagari. They are included in the list of scheduled castes.

The Chuhras are non-vegetarian, with Hindu, Sikh and Christian all avoiding the meat of buffalo, cow and hare, and taking all other meat, including the flesh of goat, sheep, chicken, ghural and fish. The Watals, however, take beef and meat of buffalo, but avoid pork. Their staple food consists of rice and *rongi* or *mah.* They also eat wheat *chapati* in their diet. Vegetables and fruit are also taken moderately. Mustard oil and animal fat are the usual cooking media. Edible roots and tubers are also consumed as vegetables. The people of this community are very fond of alcoholic drinks, and both the sexes take them. Occasionally these are purchased from the market, but most of the time they prefer home-brewed drinks. They also smoke and chew tobacco.

Non-vegetarian food is usually avoided on inauspicious occasions. There has been a change in their food habits—people are now switching over to chapatis in preference to rice. Similarly, people now also avoid taking meat of dead animals. The Watals also avoid taking alcoholic drink.

The prominent stripes among the Chuhra are Sabotra, Bhatti, Khokhar, Nattu, Ravaru, Kaliana, Ladhar Sindhu, Chapribandh, Agwal, Hesi, Khosar, Borat, Dhariwal etc. The primary function of these is to regulate marriages. The Chuhras also have four territorial divisions: Deswali (of the Gangetic plain), Bagri (of the Indian desert), Sotarwala (of the riverine lands) and Jangalke (of the forest tract). These denote the places which they originally belonged to. Though apparently there is no hierarchy among them, the Balmikis regard themselves higher than the converts. The differentation is purely on a religious basis. There has also been a recent change in surnames—earlier people were not writing anything as their surnames, but now they are using 'Balmiki' and 'Arya' instead. The social position of the Chuhras vis-a-vis other communities of the area is low, and this fact is also acknowledged by others. Though they have the knowledge of the Varna Vayavastha yet they do not place themselves within it. They call themselves 'Harijans'.

The Chuhras marry within their own community, exogamy being practised at the subcaste level. Marriage with wife's sister is permitted after the death of the wife. Cross-cousin and parallel cousin as well as consanguineous marriages are not allowed. Where a man has married in a certain family, all his male relatives leave that family for marriage. Hypergamy and hypogamy are permitted. Both senior and junior levirate are practised. Marriages in the pre-Independence period used to take place in childhood, on attaining the age of five years, but the *gaona* (departure of bride to the groom's house) was deferred, until the girl came of age. In the present times, adult marriages are practised with the girl attaining the age of 18 and boys of 20 to 22 years of age. There are two popular modes of acquiring mates—one by exchange and other by *byah* (negotiation). Monogamy is the general rule, but bigamy is alo resorted to if the first wife has not been able to produce a heir for the family. In this case, the first wife is the head of the family and has all the rights and privileges. A widow of an elder brother may marry the younger brother and a widow of a younger brother may also marry the elder brother. Similarly, the wife's younger sister can also be taken as bride. Traditionally, there were no marriage symbols, but nowadays, vermilion is put on by the Balmiki women in the parting of the hair as a marriage symbol though this is not strictly observed.

Bride-price was prevalent, with the price being paid by the groom's family. The amount of bride-price was settled by the two contracting families. This has now been taken over by dowry system in a more lenient form, in the sense that the gifts are given by the bride's parents as per their economic condition. Among the Muslims, *mehar* amount is to be paid to the bride in case of annulment of marriage. The usual form of residence is patrilocal, but in certain cases *ghar jamai* is arranged, wherein the groom comes to stay with his in-laws.

Divorce with sociojudicial approval is permitted. In case of impotency, leprosy, or lunatic tendency in the husband, the wife can claim separation. Infidelity is the ground for an husband to repudiate his wife. A woman claiming separation has to pay fine and give dinner to the panchayat. Among the Muslims, a *qazi* is called in to annul the marriage, which is done by uttering the word *talaq* three times. In the event of the husband divorcing the wife, a penalty has to be paid to the panchayat, and the marriage expenses have to be paid to the aggrieved party. Either of the party can initiate divorce proceedings. The children are the liability of the father. Widow, widower and divorcee remarriage are also permitted. A widow who remarries within her husband's family has the right to her deceased husband's property, and the one marrying outside does not have any claim.

The usual form of family is of mixed extended type, which is a combination of vertically and horizontally extended types. In such a family, husband, his married, and unmarried brothers, their children, unmarried sisters, father, mother and father's brother stay under one roof. The eldest male member controls and binds the family together. Intra-family relationships are that of mutual respect, love and cordiality. The daughter-in-law observes avoidance with her husband's elder male relatives. Joking relationship is observed with husband's elder and younger brothers, and wife's younger and elder sister. It is obligatory on the part of the parents to see their children well placed in life. On the other hand, it is expected of the children to look after their parents in old age. Though a situation of conflict and confrontation rarely comes up, whenever it does, a decision in family matters are arrived at together, and the decision of the elders is honoured.

Property is inherited according to the Chundaband law of inheritance, with all the male children, irrespective of the mothers, inheriting the property equally. A widow inherits the deceased husband's property on behalf of the children, but in this case, she has either to lead a life of a widow or marry within the family. Adopted children inherit like the biological children. In the event there is no male child, the property passes on to the collaterals, in case a son-in-law is not invited to look after the in-law's property. Succession is always in the male line with the eldest son succeeding the head of the family. Now-a-days the family form is changing from extended to nuclear type, because of deviation from the traditional occupations.

The status of women among all religious groups is regarded as equal in view of the fact that they carry out all economic pursuits along with their menfolk. In the economic spheres, they carry out their traditional occupation of scavenging and lifting the night soil from private houses, besides taking up of jobs for cleaning roads and offices in municipality and other Government departments and contribute directly to the family income. The women also take part in all social, religious and political activities. Their participation in elections is so great that they campaign and canvass for their community candidate, besides casting of votes. Other than this, they also have a full role in family management. They are responsible for the cooking of meals, doing household chores and looking after the young ones. They are virtually the managers of the household and control the family expenditure.

Pre-delivery rituals are observed in the fifth and seventh months of pregnancy in some of the families, for the welfare of the mother and child and safe delivery. Post-natal rituals and observance of pollution are reported. The house is considered polluted for six days after birth, at the end of which the mother and the child are given a bath. This is called *chhati*. The restriction for mother continues for a period of 21 days, during which time she is not allowed to enter the kitchen.

Whatever name comes to the elders is given to the child. *Jattu* for the boys is done, when the child is of 12 months. The head of the child is shaved by an elderly person of the community and a feast is given. This is only done in case of the Balmiki children. No such ceremony is observed by any other Chuhra community. Among the Muslim Chuhras (Watal) circumcision of the boy is performed at the age of one, three or five yeares. Among the Mazhabis, a ceremony is conducted where a turban is tied on a child's head, and he is given *prasad* called *amrit-chhaka.* Though no adolesence rituals are observed, yet an initiation ceremony for admitting a person of any other community to the Chuhra community is carried out.

Biah among the Hindus and *nikah* among Muslim are solemnized at the bride's residence. Among the Balmikis, the marriage is performed by Brahmanical rituals by *phera* (circumambulating) seven times under a thatched canopy. The Muslim families solemnize by *nikah*, but a great many observe the Hindu *phera.* The Mazhabis and the Christians have the option to solemnize marriage either by *phera* (as per the Balmiki custom) or by *anand-karaj* in the Gurudwara, or amongst Christians in a church. The marriage feast is given by the bride's parents. The nuptial ceremony in all cases is performed at the groom's place.

The Balmikis and the Mazhabis cremate their dead, whereas the Watals and the Christians bury their dead. The women of the Mazhabis have a peculiar way of mourning. They beat their breasts and thighs and cry. This is known as *siapa.* Women do not accompany the funeral procession, and at the most they go up to half-way and then return. The Balmikis are carried on a new bier, whereas other community members carry the deceased on the usual bier. Three days after the death, the Balmikis and the Mazhabis visit the cremation ground and pick up the unbrunt bones and ashes and immerse them in the river. Among the Watals, on the fourtieth day, *chehlam* is observed wherein prayers are offered for the peace of the departed soul. In some of the families, pollution is observed for a period of 17 days. Some of the Balmiki families however observe *barsi* wherein offerings are made at the end of an year.

Traditionally the major occupation of the Chuhras was the removal of dead animals, scavenging and removal of night soil. But now they have acquired land, allotted by government or purchased by themselves. A few of them also till the land of big landlords on share cropping. Despite this, even today, the primary occupation of the Chuhras remains scavenging and removal of the dead animals, in addition to agriculture and other skilled and unskilled jobs, which are their subsidiary occupations. They usually receive payments in cash and occasionally in kind for the services rendered by him. Since most of the Chuhras live in or near the urban centres, the remuneration received by them is usually in cash. Their dependence on local, regulated daily market is total, for they have to purchase almost everything that they need. Children below fifteen years both boys and girls assist their parents in doing their traditional jobs, as well as helping them in agricultural and household activities. They receive both in cash and in kind.

They have their traditional Biradari Panchayat. This is headed by a *sarpanch* (chief), the post of which is more often than not hereditary. Both the *sarpanch* and the elected members *panch*—whose number is not fixed and fluctuates from three to five—are elected by voice votes, depending on their ability to render impartial judgements. The *panch* settle disputes relating to breach of community norms, marriage, and divorce. They punish the offenders by *hukka-pani band* (excommunication) and also by imposing fines in cash and kind. Though the modern statutory panchayats have been established for looking after welfare activities, still people have great faith in their traditional panchayat, which holds greater sway.

Each of the different religious groups of the Chuhras profess its own religion. The Mazhabis belong to the Sikh faith and are of the Nanakpanthi sect. The Watals belong to the Sunni sect of the Muslims; whereas the Chuhra Christians belong to the Protestant sect. Nevertheless they have belief in some common deities which are worshipped by them alike.

They worship their dead ancestors, and seek blessings for the prosperity of their families. The Balmikis worship their deity in the form of a small raised mound, where they offer prayers. The Muslims have a faith in Guga Pir. Every believer of the Pir has a *nishan* (flag staff) in the house, which is worshipped in the Bhadaon (August-September) month. The Balmikis have faith in Chamunda Devi and the Mani Mahesh temple in Bharmour, which they regard as their centre of pilgrimage. The Mazhabis regard Amritsar as their sacred centre. The sacred specialists of the Balmikis and Watals officiate at marriages and funerals. The Muslims have Maulvis, Sikhs the Gyanis, and Christian the Father, who officiate and carry out all life-cycle rituals. The person empowered to ward off evil spirits like *bhut* and *churel* is known as *chela.* They observe, if Hindus, the festivals of Holi, Diwali and Basant, if Muslims the festivals of Id and Muharram, if Sikhs the festivals of Gurparab, and if Christians then Easter and Christmas. Besides, they also mingle freely and take part in each others festivals. In Chamba, the members of this community attend to the local fairs like Minjar, and Sui-ka-Mela and Mani Mahesh Yatra.

The Chuhras are proficient in the art of *kirari* (basket-making). The community also has oral traditions in the form of folklore and folktales. Some of them play musical instruments like bagpipe and *shehnai* (clarionet) and drums.

The traditional inter-community linkages of the Chuhras existed with almost every community, for no one could have dispensed with their traditional services. They also receive clothes and belongings of dead persons of their clients' family. They also accept clothes worn by women at the time of birth. At marriage and other social functions, at their clients' house, their presence was very much demanded for they carried the leftovers of food at the *dham* (feast) given on such occasions. These people also had ritual linkages with their clients who belonged to different communities, especially at the time of eclipses—solar or lunar— when they went around the village asking for alms at such occasions. They accept both *kachcha* and *pucca* food from members of their own community, irrespective of the religion practised by them, the only restriction being on the acceptance of prohibited food items, by the various religious groups.

In the urban centres, there is no restriction on these people sharing common water resources, temples, etc., but in rural settings entry of these people into the house of the upper caste communities is not permitted. In the high hills, untouchability is not as rigidly observed as in the plains. The Chuhras have a certain clientele with other castes to whom they render their traditional services, in lieu of which they are paid in kind at the harvest times. They are also paid in kind at social ceremonies in the client's family. The incresed education among them has resulted in the loosening of caste ties.

The attitude of the Chuhras is positive towards education, as both boys and girls are sent for schooling. Since a majority of them stay in urban locales, there is no problem finding educational facilities. Though both are given freeships, free books and stationery and scholarships, yet, in many of the cases the boys go in for college education, whereas, the girls drop out after matriculation. This is simply because the girls grow up and they are married off and if they are highly educated it becomes difficult to find a match for them.

The Chuhras' attitude to modern system of medicine is favourable and they visit the government hospitals and dispensaries. The bulk of the younger generation is in favour of small family norms, and prefer not more than two children. They adopt modern methods of contraception, except sterilization, which they desist.

Being the scheduled caste, the majority of the men and women have got some job or the other in government departments and municipalities. A few of the educated have also got white-collar jobs and are in teaching and other government departments against the reserved quota. A few enthusiasts among them have secured loans under self-employment schemes and are also doing poultry farming. Drinking water and electricity are available. Their settlements are also well connected with roads, telecommunications, post-offices and television. However, certain interior rural areas do not have link roads; the post offices are far-off; electricity and television are not available. They, however, have access to films shown by extension agencies and at video parlours. Firewood and kerosene are the usual fuel resources.

The mid-day meal scheme and nutritional programme under Integrated Child Development Scheme are available and is availed of by school-going children and by children in 0—5 year age group as well as by expectant and nursing mothers. Food, kerosene and cloths are available to the community at subsidized rates through government fair price shops. At the urban centres, they have a favourable attitude towards savings.

Rajendra Sarkar

DAGI

The Dagi in district Lahaul and Spiti are Hindu musicians, originally hailing from the Kullu valley. The term is not relished by the community as in some areas it is used in a derogatory sense also. They are known as Bethus in the Outer Seraj area of the Kullu district. It is a generic term for an "impure" caste in Kullu and are common in Kangra. The name is derived from *dag*, i.e., dead cattle, because they dragged the dead and skinned its carcass. Quite a few have left this work and do not intermarry with those who continue to do so. The community is reportedly without any groupings. They live today in small numbers in the Pattan valley of the district, where the Hindu population belonging to the area is located. The community perceives its distribution at the local level. The community was on the verge of remigration to the Kullu valley, from where they had initially originated, as deriving subsistence from this profession was difficult for them in this sparsely populated arid region, where even alternative pursuits are restricted. Also there existed more prospects in the Kullu valley. The natural environment is characterized by extreme cold with severe winters and heavy snowfall, high mountainous terrain with arid and semi-arid conditions prevailing at a high altitude valley, low humidity, the precipitation being mainly local and hence rainfall is low and forests are sparse. They belong to the scheduled caste category and number only 1548 in the State according to the 1971 Census. The 1981 Census gives only a slightly higher (1625) figure for the community.

The Dagis speak Manchati and Chinali, which are a mixture of Bhoti and Kulvi as well as the vocabulary of the earlier language of the area which is said to be akin to Mundari.

The Dagis are non-vegetarians. They eat all types of meat except beef. Fish is also consumed as it is available from the river. Their staple diet consists of wheat, supplemented by maize, barley or millet and rice. All and every kind of pulses are taken. Vegetables are scarce in these regions and are taken rarely, only when they are sometime given by their patrons from their kitchen gardens or when grown in their own backyards. Their cooking medium is vegetable or animal fat and mustard oil. Butter is consumed often. Roots and tubers available locally are eaten. Potatoes also form their staple diet. The area is noted for commercial growth of good quality and cheap potatoes. Fruit consumption is occasional and limited, consisting of crab-apples, apricots, peaches, etc., which can be taken freely from the local wild growth. Some of them are too poor to purchase fruit. They take *gur-gur* (buttered tea) regularly. Both men and women take *chhang* (millet beer) and *arak* (local whisky) prepared at home. The former is taken regularly. They smoke the hubble-bubble. The younger generation smoke cigarettes and *bidi*. Milk and milk products are rarely consumed. Occasionally, however, they may add to their menu the food items which are popular in the lower regions.

Some of the Dagis have adopted Sanskritic names alongside their traditional first names. The community's self-perception is low and others also similarly perceive them. The high caste Hindus consider them ritually polluted, though not the Buddhists. They consider themselves to be at a low level in the Varna system, though they do not endorse the Sudra status.

Marriages are at the community level. Cross-cousin marriages are permitted, as are junior sororate and levirate. Child marriage does not take place. Mates are acquired by negotiation. However, love marriages, elopement, symbolic capture and service marriages are also accepted. Their marriages are mostly monogamous due to their social and economic background. Symbols of marriage include *bindi* and some ear, nose and wrist jewellery.

There is no dowry and a symbolic bride-price is given, as women are economic assets in these regions. Residence after marriage is patrilocal and inheritance patrilineal. Divorce is permissible and easy, and so is remarriage. Premarital and extramarital affairs are condoned and not considered sin. However, adultery can be taken up as a cause for divorce by either spouse. Divorce is given with social approval, the grounds being barrenness, adultery, incompetence, mental incompatibility, lack of male heir, chronic illness, and witchcraft. The guilty party, as decided upon, compensates the other. In the event of divorce, the children are the liability of the father but may stay with the mother if so decided upon. Remarriage of widow, widower and divorcee of either sex is permissible. Marriage rules and practices have not changed.

Family types are mixed extended or nuclear. There are no social formalities regarding avoidance and joking. One point of conflict is the check on the freedom of youngsters. Inheritance, of whatever little is available, there is invariably in the male line. Sons inherit equally. The daughter is given her share at marriage and on marriage acquires the right to her husband's assets, but on divorce regains her right to her parental property while losing the same with her husband. Absence of male heir entitles the daughter, even if married, to the assets of her parents. Unmarried daughters retain their right to the parental property. Succession is by the eldest son. These family patterns have not changed over time.

Women bear the brunt of all the economic activities and are held in esteem. In social functions and domestic religious rituals, women have a role to play. Women have a high status but are lower than men. They do all the household jobs and control the family expenditure and management.

Decision-making powers also rest with them to a great extent.

Pollution at child birth and ritual cleaning are observed. By the seventh day, the child is named, when purification ceremony is also done. A male child is tonsured between one to three years. Adolescence ceremonies are not much in vogue. Boys and girls get married at a relatively advanced age. Both sides feast on the occasion, while the main rituals are performed at the bride's place. Nuptials are at the groom's and ceremonial consummation of marriage immediately after that. Pre-marital intercourse is not uncommon and acceptable.

Death is treated as a journey to another world. The departed soul has to be appeased and satisfied. Rituals are observed. The dead are cremated and the pollution period lasts for 11 to 13 days. Certain foods are taboo during the period. Ritual function and observance of rites are diminishing due to the growth of a secular philosophy. They are also becoming more expensive and hence the younger generation, already modern-oriented, tries to do away with the elaborateness.

Since they are musicians, their initial economic activity was playing the musical instruments on any occasion. However, since this profession is not so much in demand and cannot help to make them self-sufficient, they have supplemented it with labour jobs, agricultural or otherwise. They were mainly a landless community, never having a really permanent residence. However, later, the landed barons patronizing them gave them some land for permanent residence, part of which was used for kitchen gardening. Some of them even grew crops on them.

Children above the age of 10 years help their parents in earning subsistence. Payment by the well-to do are made in cash and kind. Others pay in kind for the services rendered.

The Dagis have their own council of elders whose decision is binding in all matters. However, if it does not satisfy the party or parties concerned, they can take the matter to secular and State set-ups. There is a village panchayat to settle disputes and punishment is given in the form of compensating the aggrieved party either in cash or in kind or both and or throwing a feast to the community at large, and the accused or the guilty has to apologize publicly. However, crime or dispute rates are very low and hence the occasion for it seldom arises. Disputes regarding land are minimal.

The Dagis belong to the Hindu fold. They believe in ancient spirits belonging to the ancient Loong Pai Chos creed of the region, Buddhist deities of various forms and figures, as well as Hindu deities, gods and goddesses. Worship of Shiva and his consort is something special. Linga (phallic form of Shiva) worship is prevalent with them as it is with all Hindus. Malevolent spirits, like Lhu, are propitiated. Udaipur and Triloknath temples in the Pattan valley of Lahaul are pilgrimage centres. Their sacred specialists are

Brahmans, who officiate at *rites-de-passage*. For removal of evil spirits Bodh clerics are engaged. Witchcraft is similarly treated by witch doctors.

The Dagis are known for their musical talent and singing of songs. They sing songs of yore, of gallant deeds of kings and potentates and feats of gods and demons, of nature's bounty and awe and mercies of the Supreme Being. Some of them have taken up the job of blacksmiths to supplement income and have specialized in the art of shaping iron tools and silver and gold jewellery into traditional and local designs. The musical instruments they use are mainly percussion, wind and valve instruments. They have a traditional dance. Mainly the men dance, with the women sometimes joining them.

Discrimination is not so rigid or marked, as may be found in the plains. Food and water are freely exchanged with their own category of communities. The Bodh population does not treat them in a derogatory manner, as far as exchanging food and water goes. The community shares the same cremation ground, water resources, other facilities and shrines with other communities. They participate with the rest in all the major festivals of the area relating to the local deities and occasions relating to the environment, harvest and calender occurrences, wherein they are traditionally bound to play musical instruments. The higher communities requisition their services for musical performances and playing of musical instruments on all occasions. They are linked with them as well as all other communities, whereever and whenever music is required on the traditional basis—a sort of symbiotic or *jajmani* relationship. However, they are not duty-bound but have a voluntary social obligation to perform these services more on the basis of division of labour. There is no economic bondage as such; only the traditional customs and ties to make the society more cohesive.

The Dagis have been and are too uneducated to have produced any man of letters or to participate in any avenue of advancement and organized service or to participate in any political activity. They supply labour to their clients and patrons on payment in cash and kind, including meals and drinks for the period of deployment, and the relationship is, on the whole, a cordial one.

The Dagis' attitude towards literacy and education as provided by development programmes is very casual, as they do not perceive any utility in them, and of the time involved in it, which they think, could be better utilized in some gainful economic pursuits. Hence, their children go to school erratically and drop out before reaching the middle level. This economic perspective should be taken into account by the authorities to keep the schools open during the snowy winter months when other economic activities come to a standstill and their spare idle hours can be devoted to studies.

Conception of health and medical care is yet to be built up with these people on organized lines, which will come about only with education. Health centres on modern lines are also generally ill-equipped in these far-flung areas, as well as ill-stocked with medicines, and thus do not render the desired welfare services. Hence, they rely more on the *amchi* (the indigenous medicine man). Family planning also does not mean much to this community whose population is dwindling. The terrain and ill-equipped medical services and the life they lead makes them prone to death due to unforseen circumstances and hence some more children are welcome as they would fill the vacuum that may be created by such change in circumstances.

Drinking water is had mainly from springs and hill streams, which is also used for irrigation purposes. Sometime pipelines are used to make the water available nearer to their homes. Employment opportunities are limited and availed of by those who are not very enthusiastic in continuing their traditional profession.

Transistor sets are popular and are the Dagis' only means of communication and contact with the outside world. These also provide entertainment to them. Television network does not exist in the area but video parlours have recently come up by means of which they can watch movies. Dissemination of information is occasionally through extension agencies. Motorable roads are limited and may sometimes be at a distance from their homes. Post offices do exist at places.

Electricity exists at places and is usually generated locally from locally instituted hydro-electric power houses, tapping energy from the local waterfalls for such generation. When the water freezes in winter there is no electricity. Villages which do not have a waterfall nearby are still without electricity. Fuel resources are mainly firewood, available locally, and sometimes cowdung cakes and kerosene. Irrigation is through *kuhl* or channels cut from the water sources. They are biased against the use of chemical manures.

In places where the Dagis stays, no organized nutrition programme was noticeable. Their economic circumstances are such that they are not left with much to save. Banks distribute rural credit, which they do not and cannot avail themselves of, since they are not a farming community. When in need of monetary help they either approach their fellow villagers or their patrons.

A postscript may be important. In the near future probably not a single Dagi will be left in Lahaul by that name, except under the name of Lohars who, it is said, were once Dagis but due to meagre income they took to blacksmithy and in course of time came to be known as Lohars. As already mentioned elsewhere, this community, because of economic constraints, is on flight to the more verdant pastures of the Kullu valley.

Again, the impact of Christian missionary activity has helped the people in Lahaul economically and socially. Education on modern lines was first introduced by the Moravian Missionaries. So were better medical facilities and health care, improved hygiene, better ventilation system for their houses and homes, the iron stove with a chimney for outlet of smoke, vegetable farming and cultivation of potatoes, which has since become the cash crop of Lahaul. But missionaries have since left the district though they have left behind their impact which has done the district a world of good.

T.K. Ghosh

DAGOLI

The Dagoli is considered synonymous with the Kamoh or Kamboh. The name Dagoli is not liked by the people and considered derogatory. They identify themselves with the Koli or even call themselves Jamani Koli or presently use the term or title of Nay Rajput in Bilaspur and Mandi districts. The Jamani Kolis claim their origin from palanquin carriers, as the name *jaman* stands for palanquin, belonging to the Rajput. Some cite a legend that the outcastes who ate and smoked with a Chamar were called as Jamani Kolis or Dagolis. However, the name Dagoli was acquired because they dragged dead cattle and skinned the caracases. Some admit that their ancestors also used the intestines of the animals they skinned as ropes and were therefore named as Dagolis.

Rose (1919: 555) cites a legend of Dagoli and Koli origins from a Kanet who had two sons in Shimla hills. The eldest son killed a bullock with an axe while ploughing in the field and was therefore outcasted. The outcasted had two sons, one of whom started a respectful life and the other was found guilty of having skinned a dead ox and eaten its flesh and was therefore named as Dagoli. Presently, in the area of study (Mandi district), a section of the community calls the other Dagoli and itself Koli but neither section would admit or accept the name Dagoli for itself. In district Bilaspur, during the princely regime of Kehlur (the old name for Bilaspur) Raja Bijai Chand upgraded the so-called Dagolis (of Badoli Devi) and called them Nersu Chandel or new Chandel and therefore as Nay (new) Rajputs. In Mandi, they find it respectable to be identified with the Kolis. In Shimla and Sirmaur district they are also known as Dooms.

The community under the name Dagoli/Kamoh has been placed in the scheduled castes list and in the social and cultural tables of the Census of India, 1971 (Singh, 1971) and is shown to figure more in Bilaspur, Solan and Shimla districts.The people do not endorse the name Kamoh. The census figure of the 1971 Census of India for the community is 362 persons. But, interestingly, the 1981 Census shows a lower population figure of 249 for the Dogoli/Kamoh community in H.P. This may perhaps be attributed to the non-acceptance of this name by these people. They mostly occupy the hilly terrain and valleys of the outer Himalayan ranges experiencing a warm and temperate climate, medium rainfall and low humidity during most part of the year. The hill ranges are covered with thin canopies of pine forests.

The Dagolis speak local dialects - Bilaspuri and Mandiali of the western Pahari and write in the Devanagari script like other people. . Men wear *kurta* and *pyjama* or pants. Women wear a *kurta, salwar* and *chunni* or *dupatta/chadru* in the lower hills and *dhattu* in the middle Himalayas.

They are occasional non-vegetarian in food habits. In the upper hills, the Dagolis are accused of eating the *langur*, monkey, bear, leopard and buffalo like the Dagis (Rose, 1919: 556). They consume home-made liquor prepared from sugar molasses quite frequently. The staple foods are *chini, kangni, kodra, cholai, fafra* (all millets), maize, wheat, rice and barley along with various pulses - *urad, moong, kulthi* and *masur,* and gram, peas, potato and beans. Different types of seasonal vegetables, roots and tubers are consumed quite regularly. Milk and milk products are also consumed. Fruit intake is occasional or seasonal. Food taboos are lacking. Men smoke tobacco in the indigenous *hookah* (hubble-bubble), and *bidi* and sometimes cigarette.

The Dagolis claim Kalyan *gotra* and Chauhan and Chandel clans of the Rajputs and are known as Nay Rajputs (in Bilaspur). In Mandi they distinguish two sections—Masehru Koli claiming social superiority over Jamani Koli. There is little significance of clan and *gotra* for regulating the marriage but marriages are avoided at cross-cousin levels. In the regional social hierarchy the community is placed at a very low position among the Sudra. Rose (1919: 555) stated that the Dagolis ranked socially even below the Dums. However, now the self-perception of the community is not so low and some of them see themselves in an intermediate position among the Sudra, whereas the others claim a Kshatriya descent by the virtue of Nay Rajput status.

The community is endogamous and may or may not marry within the clan/*gotra* and practise both junior sororate and levirate marriages. Marriage used to occur before puberty in the recent past and exchange of sisters was prevalent. Bride-price was also given. But presently, a girl is usually married after 16 years of age and a boy at or around 21 years of age. Bride-price has given way to the custom of dowry and *kanyadan* is performed. Negotiation is the mode of marriage and monogamy is practised but a second wife may be acquired if there is no issue or no male issue from the first wife.. Marriage symbols are *sindur*, nose-ring or nose-stud, pin and glass bangles. The bride lives patrilocally.

There are provisions for dissolution of marriage and remarriage in the community both socially as well as legally. Either of the spouses may seek separation on grounds of maladjustment and cruelty and usually compensation is given to the wife if no bride-price has been taken on marriage. The younger children are the liability of the mother and the grown-up children are to be taken care of by the father. Both male and female divorcees may remarry. Widow and widower marriages are permitted socially and usually junior levirate and sororate are practised. The institution of marriage has witnessed changes in increase in the age of marriage and abandoning of bride-price in favour of dowry.

The Dagolis presently live mainly in nuclear families, and the traditional vertically extended joint family system has declined considerably. Avoidance relationship of the *lari* or *bahuti* exists with her *saurah*, *jeth*, *nandoi* and elderly members of the village. Joking relations exist between *devar-bhabi*, *jija-sali*, *jija-sala* and *nanad-bhabi*. The inheritance of the family property is as per the rule of male-equigeniture and the eldest son succeeds the father. But still conflicts on the distribution of paternal property may at time arise and are settled by the statutory Gram Panchayat.

The status of women is for practical purposes equal to that of men. They sometimes contribute to family income by rendering labour services and midwifery to the big farmers of the village. They also control or regulate the family expenditure and have some say in domestic decision-making matters. They do all types of domestic, agricultural and animal husbandry jobs, collection of fuel and fodder, and bring potable water. They also participate in social, ritual and religious ceremonies but have little say in the political sphere and in the mechanism of social control which still remain as man's domain.

The life-cycle rituals are performed by the priest of their own community. Pre-delivery restrictions on the pregnant women exist. The first delivery generally takes place at the paternal home. Post-delivery pollution lasts for thirteen days when *gunt* ceremony by taking cow's urine and sprinkling Ganga water takes place for purification from the *sutak*. The only childhood ritual is *jatlu* or *jamalu* of the boy which is performed by the *mama* or any other person considered a god-brother of the mother on any odd year before five years of age and the clan deity is propitiated.

Their community priest performs the marriage rituals as per the Hindu Sanatan tenets. Clan deity is worshipped by the groom and his parents. At bride's place, the *lari* and *lara* circumambulate the sacred fire. The parents of the bride feast the groom's party. On the next day the bride and bridegroom worship *khair* tree (*Acacia catechu*) and take its rounds by wrapping a thread around its stem. The kith and kin of the bride are served meals. The bride returns to her parents the same day followed by the groom to his parents-in-laws house along with a *lajoru* (companion). Some rituals are performed there and he brings the bride back with him the next day. This is called *muklawa*, after which the bride resides with him. Earlier, the nuptial ceremony or consummation of marriage used to occur after the girl had attained puberty.

The death rites are also observed as per the Sanatana tenets. The dead are cremated and the ashes are immersed in the Satluj or Ganga river and *pind dan* given to a *panda*. Ancestor worship is observed during the *patak* period for 13 days. On the thirteenth day the community priest performs a *havan* and takes offerings. Some of the offerings in the name of the dead are also given to a *dhyan* of the family or kin group. The annual rite called *barkhi* and fourth annual death rite called *chabarkh* are also observed and meals are served to the gathered relatives to commemorate the dead. No festival or festivity is observed for one year after the death of a family member.

The Dagolis traditionally subsisted on scavenging or disposal of the dead animals or casual labour, and agricultural labour, which is still retained in some cases by these people. Some also take to horticulture or industry. They rear cattle, goats and sheep. Some till the land of village farmers on contract basis on cash terms or on share crop basis. Women also render miscellaneous labour services to the big farmers and get some return in cash and/or kind. A few persons are employed in government departments on lower posts. The links with the market are direct and the market is of daily and weekly nature and fully regulated with dealings in cash. Child labour does exist but bonded labour is absent.

The community lacks any formal community council but usually the *sayane* of the community or village resolve the social and socio-economic disputes. The members of the statutory Gram Panchayat solve the disputes over land and water. But sometimes legal course is also adopted when the matters go beyond the control of the Gram Panchayat. In some areas the traditional non-formal panchayat of respectable elders of the community also settles disputes.

The Dagolis follow Hinduism and propitiate various family, clan, village and regional deities and gods. The Lohakhri Devi and Dharmi (Mahu Nag) in Mandi district and Badoli Devi and Badwari Sidh in Bilaspur are *kul* or clan deities of special reverence on festival/festivities, etc. In Shimla, Sirmaur and Kullu districts the worship of Nag, Asura, Lankura, Koelu and Nahar Singh is prevalent. Nahar Singh is commonly called as Bajia and is the village and women deity in addition to Guga and Balak Nath which are also regional deities. Other regional deities propitiated are Nalakha Mahadev, Mata Bhavani, Koela Mata, Hateshwari Devi, Balakhameshwar, etc. Various fairs of these deities including Sair fair, Nalwari fair, Chiran fair, etc., are visited. They celebrate different Hindu festivals of regional (Budhi Dewali, Bhoonda, Bishu, Sair & Chiran) and national level (Lohri, Holi, Diwali, Baisakhi, Rakhi or Rakshabandan, etc.). They share Pahari folk oral traditions. The common folk songs and tales are *Raja Bhangalia, Gogte da Rana, Khunwal da Rana, Godhawra da Rana, Balo & Mahia, Gangi, Rupu-Mian, Daria Raupi, Thindu-Kamrau, Debku, Kunju-Chenchlo, Ranjhu-Phulmu, Chhinj* songs, etc. *Gidda* and *nati* are the favourite dances. *Hudki, nagara, damru, dhol, khanjri*, etc. are musical instruments.

They traditionally accept *kachcha* and *pucca* food and water from Brahmans, Rajputs and others. A few well-off families of the Dagolis may invite some friends of upper castes to their social gathering and offer *suchchi rasoi* cooked separately by a Brahman/Rajput. Alternatively, they may offer *sukka* or *sidha* to the upper-caste Hindus with whom they have social exchange. Traditional water sources like *bauri* and springs are shared with different communities and generally with upper caste people. The crematoria and religious shrines are common.

Developmental progammes have made little impact on them. Formal education is favoured for boys who usually study up to secondary school level but higher education is still not within their reach. Also there is a lack of zeal for it even though they avail themeselves of freeships. For girls education is partly favoured and they mostly study up to primary or middle standards due to social reasons, e.g. a girl's target is mainly to get married and not to seek a job. Both modern and indigeneous health and medicare facilities are availed of and favoured. The uneducated amongst them still depend upon village *chela* and quacks for treatment of ailments. The attitude towards restricted family size is becoming favourable but no limit for children is considered as at least one son is the first consideration for a family, even at the cost of more daughters.

Drinking water is available in the village through pipes but traditional *bauri* are still used in times of scarcity of water. Provisions for Intensive Rural Development Programme (IRDP) exist and they get 50 per cent subsidy on chemical fertilizers, animals and on other loans. Modern mass media (radio, television) are available in the village and road communication and postal facilities are within their reach. Their houses are electrified. They use old fuel resources like firewood and cowdung cakes. Biogas is getting popular with those having a large number of cattle in the lower hills. Some of the nutritional programmes for children, (ICDS) are available.

A.R. Sankhyan

DARAIN

The Darain, also pronounced as Drai, Drain, or Daryai is a scheduled caste. The community's name has been derived from its association with *darya* or *drya*, meaning river. The Census of 1981 has however shown the community under two separate scheduled castes—the Darai or Daryais whose population was higher (6385) and the Darain who numbered 656. But these appear to be synonyms of the same community. They traditionally used to carry people across the rivers with the aid of inflated skin bags called *khatnahu.* The history of the community's origin is not known, but in Kangra the people tend to associate themselves with the lineage of Satyavati (daughter of a boatman) who was married to Raja Santanu of the Mahabharata. Brief introductory notes on the community are given in Ibbetson (1916) and Rose (1919) but no detailed ethnographic account is available. They are spread mainly in the districts of Kangra, Bilaspur, Mandi and Chamba and their villages are located in the valley of the rivers Beas, Satluj and Ravi. The terrain is mainly hilly with warm and temperate climate with moderate rainfall and low humidity. They speak local dialects like Kangri and Bilaspuri of the western Pahari and write in the Devanagari script both within and outside the community. There are no community-specific patterns as far as dress and ornaments are concerned which are shared with other communities of the region.

The food habits of the community are similar to those of other communities. Their staple food is maize, wheat and rice. Various types of the pulses and vegetables, roots and tubers cooked in mustard oil or vegetable *ghee* are consumed. They are predominantly non-vegetarian but do not eat beef. Fish used to be a common food item, but now only those families who still continue with the traditional occupation of boating and fishing eat fish. A segment of the community, which has recently become Radhaswami avoids non-vegetarian food and liquor. Other men of this community however consume liquor and sometimes the women also have it. Liquor is purchased from the local market. Men smoke indigenous tobacco in a *hukka.*

The Darains in Kangra is a distinct community but in other parts some Julaha, Dumna, Daule and Sansoi have also adopted the profession as that of the Drains and consider their respective identities for marriage purposes. In Kangra they distinguish themselves into Bharadwaj and Kaundal *gotra* and other finer exogamous units known as septs *al* or inner caste (*anderli jat*), such as Rhial, Bhundhial, Pandhial, Seria and Drumgu Manhas. These septs indicate their ancestry or descent and regulate their matrimonial alliances. In social hierarchy, the community is placed in the Sudra category of the varna system— which is also acknowledged by the community. They, however, consider themselves superior to the Dumnas and the Chamars.

The community is largely endogamous in Kangra though sometimes inter-marriage with the Ghais takes place. The village and *gotra* exogamy is adhered to. The age at marriage at present is above 15 years for girls and above 20 years for boys. The mates are acquired through negotiation. The *batta-satta* is quite common in this community. Monogamy is adhered to and only in rare cases of barrenness of a woman may a man marry again. The marriage symbols are *sindur, bindi*, ear and nose rings, and bangles. Traditionally bride price was taken and was a nominal amount (Rs 60). But now dowry in kind, as in household articles is being accepted. The bride lives patrilocally with her husband. Divorce is uncommon but there are social as well as legal sanctions on genuine grounds of maladjustment. They now prefer legal procedures in this matter and the man bears the responsibility to compensate his wife and children. The widow/widower and male/female divorcee remarriage is permitted. Both junior levirate and the sororate are allowed. Junior levirate is called *jhanjrara* and is marked by a small feast.

The families among the Drains are predominantly nuclear and the joint extended families are gradually disappearing. The *lari* keeps avoidance from her *saurah, jeth* and *nandoi*. Joking relations exists between *devar* and *bhabhi*, *jija* and *sali* and *jija* and *sala*. The inheritance occurs as per the rule of male-equigeniture and the eldest son succeeds the father. The women enjoy an almost equal status as men and contribute to the family income besides doing domestic jobs like fetching potable water, collecting fuel and fodder and regulating family expenditure. They generally work as maid-servants, midwives and render labour services to the village landlords. They participate in various social rituals, religious ceremonies, but mechanisms of social control and political activities are not their concern.

The post-delivery pollution (*sutak*) is observed for 13 days and purification occurs by observing *guntrala* ceremony, which also occurs intermittently on the fifth, seventh and twelfth day. The third day of birth is called *ghuardin* when germinated grams and sugar are distributed among the kith and kin to celebrate the birth of a child. There is no observance of a naming ceremony but *annaprashan* is observed by some people. The main childhood ritual observed is *jatalu* ceremony performed at Jawalamukhi or at any other holy shrine or at home by *mama*.

The marriage rituals of the Drains are similar to those of any other low-caste Hindu. These are performed in a simple way as per the Vedic rites by a learned man of the community. The bride and the groom circumambulate the sacred fire and *kanyadan* is performed by giving a rupee to the boy or the girl. A feast is arranged for the bridegroom's party by the bride's parents. The groom and bride worship the *daran* (pomegranate) or *amb* (mango) or *bil* or *bel* (*Aegle marmelos*) tree at the bridegroom's residence. The *muklawa* ceremony takes place on the day following the marriage.

The dead are cremated and their ashes immersed in the Beas at Kaleshwar. Some people may also go to the Ganges at Hardwar for the immersion of ashes. Death pollution is observed for 13 days (*dashang*) when a *havan* is performed to purify the family and a small feast is given to friends and relatives. Intoxicants, garlic, onion and non-vegetarian diet is not consumed during the pollution period. Some utensils and clothes are offered to a *bujru* or to *dhyan* in the name of the dead person. The annual death ritual, *barkhi*, and fourth annual anniversary, *chabarkhari* are observed. The subsequent annual *shradha* is also observed. But the followers of the Radhaswami mission considerably avoid observance of the Vedic rituals of birth, marriage and death.

The traditional major economic resource of the Drains was water and they used to earn their living as boatmen or otherwise by swimming on inflated skins to help people cross the rivers. But due to the construction of bridges, this has become a tradition of the past days. Fishing in the river was also a major source of livelihood, but presently it has been reduced to a secondary occupation for most of them. Besides, the Drains served as forest labourers for transporting wooden logs by floating these in the river. This process known as *ghala bahana* has also become uncommon these days. They were landless in the past but most of them have been allotted some *nautor* land for cultivation. Since this is insufficient for earning a livelihood, so they have started working as labourers in road, and dam construction, forest, quarries, etc. Their children do render labour services to big landlords. Links with the market are direct and the market is fully regulated and of daily nature. The dealings are in cash.

The community has its community council headed by a *pradhan*, elected by a voice vote. This Biradari Sabha serves to control some social evils like early marriage, dowry, divorce and illiteracy. But with the advent of post-Independence statutory Gram Panchayat, the traditional community council has virtually lost hold on the people and it lacks the power of punishing the guilty. Statutory measures are taken for the solution of socioeconomic disputes.

They worship gods and goddesses of the Hindu pantheon. There are family and clan deities along with village and regional deities. The same deities are usually propitiated by some as family deities whereas others worship them as local or regional deities. The special ones are Balaknath, Balakrupia, Lakhdata, Kaleshwar Mahadev, Mahabir Hanuman, Jawalamukhi, Chamunda Devi, Chintpurni Devi, Brajeshwari Mata and Vaishnu Devi. The Khawaja or Jal Devta is propitiated by all the Drains as the community deity. *Dalia* (half-sounded boiled wheat), gram *ghungni* and *roat* (a big loaf of bread) are offered to the river god particularly in the month of Shrawan. The shrines of the deities are visited on annual fairs and festivals. The major festivals are Baisakhi, Chiran, Sair, Shivratri, Ramnavmi, Nag Panchmi, Diwali and Lohri. The sacred specialists are from within as well as from outside the community. Some are involved in the Radhaswami socio-religious movement and about 5 per cent of them have turned up as Radhaswamis.

There is no specific traditional art and craft of the community though some of the old men used to make ropes in their spare time. The regional folksongs and tales, music and dances are shared by the community. *Kirtan* and *bhajan* are more common. *Gidda* among young girls is a popular dance. Other folksongs of the region like *Kunju, Mian Manglotu, Mian Manager, Subhadro-Wazeer, Sipahia Dogria* and *Kangre de fauji* are also popular in the community.

They accept only *sidha* food from the Dumnas and Chamars. The ritual-based friendship, however, occurs with the higher castes as well. There is no restriction for the Drains at public places and religious shrines. Patron-client relationship usually exists with a Lohar. They have some persons in military and police and some Drains are also teachers and also have representation in the statutory Gram Panchayats. There has been some progress in the Drain community in respect of literacy, health and modern medical care, family welfare, drinking water, electricity, road and mass-media facilities during the post-Independence period. They send their children to schools but higher education is still not within their means and is less favoured for girls. Traditional health and medicare methods are still used in some cases. Modern methods of family welfare (sterilization) have been recently adopted for restricting family size. Mass-media, electricity, road communication, postal, telegraph and water supply facilities are availed of or are at their doorsteps. They have also been given land for agriculture though it is hardly sufficient to earn a livelihood. The rural development programmes (IRDP) are availed of but have had a limited impact on the community. Immunization is availed of under the ICDS programme. Facility of public distribution through fair price shops is also availed of.

A. R. Sankhyan

DAULE

The Daule or Daole are a scheduled caste. Traditionally they washed gold from the alluvial soil of the rivers (Rose, 1919). They have, however, been listed as two separate communities and so enumerated separately in the 1971 Census (Singh, 1971). Their respective population according to the 1971 Census is 650 and 597. An enquiry reveals that both the sections form a single community of gold washers and their names are probably synonyms. Their combined population is 2101 (1981 Census). They are chiefly concentrated in the districts of Bilaspur and Mandi. The elymology of the term *Daule* (plural) or *Daula* (singular) is associated with 'Danvin', an area in Bilaspur District. The area was ruled by Danav Sehsrarjun or Sehsrabahu who is worshipped as a local deity named Dano Deo. The capital of Sehrabahu was at Sunni in the present Shimla district. The Daole or Daule belonged to the area and extracted gold from the sand of river Satluj in the past. Later they migrated to various parts of State. The literal meaning of Daule is also suggested to mean a 'tricky person' (*dao wala*) since they are proficient in wrestling, swimming and fishing. A village of the community is also named as Dabla, probably denoting its affiliation with the name of the community.

Their villages are located mainly on the banks of the streams and rivers or near them. Men wear *kurta* and *pyjama*, and women *kurti, salwar* and *chadru*. They speak local dialect, i.e., Kehluri (or Bilaspuri) of western Pahari and write in Devanagari.

They are largely non-vegetarian and eat fish in plenty. Their meat intake is low but vegetables are consumed in plenty; staple food consists of maize and wheat supplemented by rice. Various types of pulses like *urd, moong, masur, arhar*, beans, *kulthi* and peas together with tubers—potato and *arbi/kachalu* are consumed. The fruit intake is low and only seasonal fruits like mango, banana, peach, guava and apple are taken. The men are fond of country liquor purchased from the local market and also smoke tobacco in an indigenous pipe called *kali* or *jhajri* and *hukka*. Milk and milk products are taken quite often. The festive foods are *khichri* on Lohri, *sag* (mustard leaves) on Khori, *ankloo* on Diwali and Dussehra, *seviyan* on Sair and *babru* on Baisakhi. Non-vegetarian food is not eaten during death pollution.

The Daule are divided into several *got* or clans and septs/*al*, like Sansoi, Phalehre, Ludu, Chandel, Mahele, Andrehru, Chalogar, Pahariye, Turaiye, etc. In certain places, the Sansoi section regards itself superior to others and sees itself at par with the Lohars and the Jheewars and also recognised a separate community in Kangra. In the local regional social hierarchy they are placed among the Sudra after the Lohar, whereas the Julaha, Dumna and Chamar follow them.

It is an endogamous community who practises exogamy at *got* and village level. Monogamy is the practice. Child marriage was prevalent about two decades back but presently it has given way to post-puberty marriages at the age of 14 to 17 years for girls and above 18 years for boys. The mode of acquiring mates is through negotiation and by exchange of sisters, called *batta-satta,* which has been a common practice. Alternatively, bride-price ranging between Rs. 500 and Rs. 2000 was paid in the event a sister for exchange was not there in a family. Presently, however, the *punya* or *kanyadan* marriage (without exchange and bride-price) is respected and is becoming popular. Dowry is also given in the form of household articles, clothes and ornaments. *Sindur* is used as a marriage symbol but its observance is not strictly adhered to. Often a *bindi* is put on. Other symbols are glass bangles and nose-pin. The bride lives patrilocally with the husband. Divorce is rare but is allowed socially. The husband has to bear the responsibility of the children and pays a maintenance allowance. Both the divorcees may remarry. Widow/widower remarriage may occur and both junior levirate and sororate are permitted.

The family pattern is predominantly nuclear. The married sons usually establish a separate household. Joint extended families were common in the past. The inheritance is patrilineal as per the rule of male-equigeniture and the eldest son succeeds the father. Avoidance relationship is maintained by the *lari* with her *saurah* and *jeth* and by *kurmani* with *kuram* by covering her face in front of him. Joking relations exist between *jija* and *sali* and between *devar* and *bhabi.* Their families are linked, socially, economically and religiously at various occasions.

Women have almost an equal status to men but lack the right to inheritance. However, they are a great economic assets to the family as they fish and also assist men in gold-washing. They manage the family affairs, collect fuel and fodder and fetch potable water. They also participate in social and religious ceremonies but have no say in the mechanism of social control and political activities. They contribute to the family income as midwives and by rendering household services to the village landlords.

Pre-birth restrictions exist. The post-delivery pollution called *sutak* is observed for 13 days and purification occurs by taking cow's urine in a ritual called *guntrala.* Christening and cereal-taking ceremonies are ignored. The *mundan* ceremony is performed before the child is five years of age. It is performed by the child's mother's brother and a feast is arranged for young children.

The marriage rituals are observed as per the Hindu Sanatan Dharma by a Brahman priest. The various rituals preformed in succession are *samuhat, sand, sehrabandi, geuchara, milni, bhareedi bharna, lagan, agniphere* and *kanyadan.*

In earlier days, a Daula bridegroom used to walk on foot whereas the Brahman priest was carried on a palanquin ahead of the groom. But now this has changed and the groom goes in the palanquin. The bride and the groom also circumambulate a pipal tree at the bridegroom's place. The consummation of marriage takes place on the second day after the marriage. But in the days of child marriage this occurred after the girl attained puberty.

The dead are cremated and their ashes are immersed in the Ganges at Haridwar. Ancestor worship is performed on the thirteenth day marking the end of death pollution, *patak* period, by the Acharaj and Barkhu who are offered some cash and a cot, bedding, utensils, clothes, etc. Subsequently, *barkhi* and *chabarkh* rituals are also observed by holding community feasts.

Water has been the traditional economic resource of the Daule. But, during the post-Independence period every Daule family has been allotted some land. *nautor,* for agriculture and animal husbandry. But this is not sufficient for making a living, rendering them practically landless and they continue to work in their traditional occupation of gold-washing along with fishing. Many Daule also run *gharat* (water-flour mills) to earn their livelihood. Besides, they are also daily-wage labourers in road construction, forests and sandstone quarries. Some have also become carpenters. There are others who till the land of big landlords on contract or sharecrop basis. Child labour sometimes does exist. The market is fully regulated and is daily in nature and the dealings are in cash.

They had an active Biradari Panchayat, but it has become almost defunct. Now, elderly persons resolve social problems, but village disputes are being taken to the statutory Gram Panchayat which performs various social welfare activities also.

The Daule are Hindus and worship various gods and goddesses of the wider pantheon. Some have recently become Radhaswamis and curtailed some of the life cycle rituals. Many propitiate Badoli Devi/Tiamli Devi/ Balak Nath as their family and *kulja.* Balak Nath, Lakhdata and Guga are propitiated as regional deities and their shrines are visited during annual fairs. Balak Nath is also propitiated when a male child is born. The *sehra* (marriage crown) is offered to Lakhdata after the marriage ceremony is over on a Thursday. Khwaja Peer is specially propitiated by offering a *roat* for protection against floods and accidents in water. A snake deity, Guga, is propitiated by offering a *roat* on the eighth day of the Rakshabandhan festival when Guga fairs are held at various places. The major fairs are of Guga, Balak Nath, Lakhdata and of female deities like Badoli Devi, Sohni Devi, Hari Devi, Naina Devi. Festivals like Lohri, Baisakhi, Holi, Guru Parv (Panjbhikhmi), Chiran, Sair, Shivratri, Krishna Janamasthami, Ramnavmi, Dussehra and Diwali are celebrated. They have *chela* who is often consulted for warding off diseases caused by evil spirits in people and cattle. He is also consulted for predictions about future and fortune.

The folklore, folktales and folksongs are region based. The *bhajan, kirtan*, and the *mandli* and *bharath* (ballads of Guga) are commonly attended to.

Their traditional drinking water sources like a *bauri* or springs were separate but recently their villages have been connected with water pipelines. Their *masankhdi* (cremation grounds) are located along the streams or on river beds. They share temples and can enter into the houses of the people (except kitchen) of upper-castes without any caste discrimination. The patron-client relationshsip has existed since the time they became agriculturists and employed Chamar, Lohar, Kumhar, Nai, etc.on *chhamahi* (six-monthly) basis. They have some teachers and persons on non-commissioned ranks in the army. They are politically active.

The community has favourably responded to and accepted modern development programmes but their fruits have reached only a limited section of the community. They send their children (both boys and girls) to school but they usually do not study beoynd the secondary level. The reason is mainly apathy, but social biases against advanced women education do exist. Modern health and medicare facilities are availed of but indigenous methods have also been retained. The modern family planning measures, mainly sterilization, are now accepted by them without any sex considerations. Piped drinking water facility is available in certain areas. Under the Integrated Rural Development Programme they get subsidies upto 50 per cent for purchasing of chemical fertilizers, and animals. Their energy sources are firewood, dung cakes and maize cubs and stems. They have electricity connection but modern media facilities like television are beyond their reach though available in the area. They avail themselves of public distribution facility through fair-price shops. Bank and post offices are also located nearby, but money-lenders still play a great role in the community and many are dependent upon them. Children have benefited from immunization and mid-day meal facilities.

It is worthwhile mentioning about the traditional instrument the Daule use for washing gold. They select a dark coloured alluvial clay bed, which according to them is usually rich in gold contents. A boat-shaped wooden instrument called *rathra* or *sandar* about 3.5 feet long and 1.5 feet broad is first used to collect the soil and is then dipped in water to wash out the gravel. The fine residue left behind consists of particles of gold ore. This residue is put on an elliptical metallic plate known as *phahlu* (1.5 feet long, 1 foot broad) and is heated with mercury. The gold particles stick to mercury and are thus separated. One full day's hard labour put in this washing process may yield up to half a gram of gold for a family. According to them the higher Himalayan rivers are richer in gold content and some of them take to the higher hills during the summer season.

A. R. Sankhyan

ḊHOGRI

The community characterises itself as Dhogri or Siggi but others call them Dhangri. The Dhogris are ironsmiths. The name is probably connected with *dhaukni*, i.e., 'bellows' and *dharna*, to blow the bellows. (Rose, 1919:239). The Dhogris of Chamba district do not use any other title or surname. They suffix 'Ram' with their name. The total population is 2,993 (1981 Census of India). They speak Gadiali and Hindustani. They have no special dress to distinguish them from their neighbours. Constitutionally, they are one of the scheduled castes.

The Dhogris are non-vegetarian and eat egg, fish and meat. Their daily meals consist of maize or wheat with pulses like *tur, rajmah, moong*, gram, etc., and seasonal vegetables like *muli, palak,* brinjal, ladyfinger, tomato, etc. They use mustard oil, groundnut oil and hydrogenated cooking oil. Locally available fruits are consumed by them. There is no restriction imposed on milk and milk products. Tea is a common drink. Both men and women enjoy a puff on the *hukka*. Old people are addicted to tobacco chewing. The younger generation is fond of *bidi* and cigarettes. In the local dialect, wine is called *sur* and is often consumed by them. Mourners, however, observe restriction on foods like egg, fish and meat.

The Dhogris are an endogamous group and have *gotra* such as Kashyap which govern their marital alliances. Each *gotra* is an exogamous unit. For relations, they avoid immediate relations of both the father's and the mother's side. The Dhogris consider themselves of the Vaishya varna, lower than the Brahman and the Kshatriya but higher than the Sipi, Hali, Hesi and Adharmi.

Among the Dhogris, the age for marriage varies from 18 to 25 years for boys and from 13 to 20 years for girls. Marital alliances are negotiated by the parents. Monogamy is the norm of the society. *Laung, puranda* (threaded hair locket/ribbon) for hair and vermilion are the marriage symbols for married women.

Dowry is offered to the bridegroom's father by the bride's father. Dowry received in cash is spent on purchasing jewellery. A *thali* (metal-plate) and *lota* (a metal container) are given to the bridegroom and bride. The Dhogris do not have the practice of giving bride-price. Their marriage residence is patrilocal. Divorce is not accepted by the community. However, if there is any case of divorce, the concerned family is looked down upon by the fellow villagers. A widower can remarry according to his choice including his deceased wife's younger sister. Generally, a widow does not remarry but in some cases she can also live with her husband's brother. In cases of remarriage,

marriage functions are not as elaborate those on the first marriage.

Although the common form of family is the nuclear type, yet patrilineal extended family type also occurs. Within the family, the father and elder brother command respect. The relation between parents and children is informal without avoidance or fear. The relation between husband and wife is of cooperation and of mutual understnading. An elder sibling is affectionate towards the younger ones. The husband's elder brother maintains avoidance relationship with the younger brother's wife. The husband's younger brother and younger sisters have joking relations with the elder brother's wife. Younger sisters and younger brothers of the wife can joke with the elder sister's husband. Both elder sister and brother of the wife get respect from the younger sister's husband.

The property is inherited from father to son. The eldest son is not the owner but a custodian of the paternal property after the death of the father. If paternal property is to be divided, each son gets an equal share. Inter-family linkages are cordial.

The life of the Dhogris would not remain so strong without sincere cooperation of their women. As a wife, a Dhogri woman is a co-worker and a real partner of her husband. She shares her husband's joys and sorrows and as a mother she gets immense respect from her sons, daughters and daughters-in-laws. In economic activities, except ploughing she does all sorts of farming tasks. She is also a good weaver and spinner. The Dhogris have started to send their daughters to school for education. Due to economic hardship most of the girls do not receive higher education. The girls help their mothers in the domestic work.

A corner of a room is provided to an expectant mother. They observe birth pollution for five and seven days for a girl and a boy respectively. All the clothes of the mother and the baby are washed and the house is cleaned. For purifying, they sprinkle a mixture of *gomutra,* milk and *Gangajal* all over the house. During the pollution period the mother and the *dai* cannot touch the food prepared for other members of the house. The mother, midwife and the family members take cow's urine for purification after birth.

When the child becomes six months' old, the christening ceremony is performed. The name of the child is chosen by the parents or the relatives. In the case of a boy people get a horoscope prepared. At the time of christening, a book, a pen, an ink pot, a lump of soil, one coin and a currency note are placed before the child. It is believed that by touching one of these articles the child would indicate his/her future aptitude to work related to these articles. They do not observe any function to mark the adolescence of boys or girls. However, during menstruation girls follow some restrictions in their daily activities.

Among the Dhogris there is no choice in the selection of spouse for either the boy or the girl. The betrothal and the marriage are arranged by their parents or guardians. For selection of mates, the boy should be an earning member and hard working. Similarly, a girl should be industrious so that she can assist her husband. A *lagnotri* is prepared by the *purohit* which serves as a guide to perform the right rituals at the right time. Three, five or seven days earlier, *tel batna* ceremony is held on both the sides. After this *havan* and *navgrahi puja* are performed. The marriage party consisting of relations and friends then proceed to the bride's house.

At the appointed hour, the bridegroom is taken to the *mandap*. The women sing songs befitting the occasion. The *purohit* recites passages from the holy book and the others attend the rituals. The bride is brought to the *vedi* a little later and she is asked to sit close to the groom. They are asked to hold each other's hands. Giving away of the bride is done by the father of the girl. The bride and the groom are required to go round the sacred fire seven times. At each completed round the *purohit* reads verses from the *vivah padhati*. When the bride and the groom reach the groom's house, they are affectionately received by relatives and friends. In case of a remarriage of a woman, these rituals and ceremonies are not performed.

A dying man is placed on the floor. The dead body is washed with warm water and wrapped in cotton clothes. The head is kept towards the north. The Dhogris cremate their dead, but children under five years are buried. The eldest son gives *dag* (flames) to the pyre. He wears white clothes and his head and beard are shaved off. The nearest younger male relatives of the deceased also have to shave their heads. The women do not accompany the cremation party. The ashes of the dead are carried to Hardwar for immersion in the Ganges. The family members observe the pollution period for 10 days. The *daspindi* is held on the tenth day after the death. All family members take bath and wash their clothes and utensils. A mixture of cowdung and urine of the cow is sprinkled all over the house. On the fourteenth day the deceased's relations and those of the wife's side give a feast and thus the mourning period ends. After three months, oblations are again offered in the name of the deceased. Similar ceremonies take place at the end of six months, the *barkhi* and the *chaubarkhi* after death.

As mentioned earlier, the Dhogris are blacksmiths. Some of them also now possess cultivable land. Some even work as agricultural labourers or as quarry labourers. They also breed sheep in limited numbers. Sometimes they take charge of extra sheep for rearing from other owners who have large herds. For this they are paid in cash by the owner. Spinning and weaving form subsidiary occupations for them. This contributes substantially to their economy. Other cultivators pay them in cash for preparing their required implements. Due to the peculiar terrain they have to use traditional implements for agricultural pursuits. It is for this reason that a few of the Dhogris still maintain their traditional occupation.

The Dhogris of Deol village in Chamba do not have a traditional council. When there is any dispute between the two parties, the elders of the community are consulted for arbitration. Earlier, they used to have a territorially organised community council. They had a right to punish who ever broke the social norms. The punishment was *hukka-pani band* or *dham* i.e., having a feast from the guilty. But this type of punishment is now not too frequently seen. At present the statutory panchayat which has come into being after Independence settles disputes and affairs of the village through a *samajhauta* committee. It settles disputes and helps to maintain social harmony in the village. It also implements developmental programmes in the village.

The Dhogris believe in Lord Shiva as their Supreme God and the Chamba area is known as Shivabhumi. They also worship Banni Devi, Sati and Brahama, and Lakshmi Narayana, Krishna, Rama and other gods and goddesses of the Hindu pantheon. Haridwar, Kedarnath, Badrinath, Vaishno Devi, Mani Mahesh, Jawalamukhi are the shrines they visit. Prayer is performed, accompanied by *kartal*, bell and drum during *arti*. The economic hardships of the Dhogris have considerably influenced their social life. They also participate in fairs and festivals. Sui fair, held at Naina Devi temple at Chamba on the first day of Baisakh is attended exclusively by the women. Bharmaur Jatra is celebrated at Bharmaur village and begins on the day following Janamashtami. People of this area assemble there in their traditional dresses, and along with the priest move in a procession and circumambulate *(parikarma)* the temples. During festive days men and women dance in separate groups to the accompaniment of *shehnai* and *dholak*. This creates an atmosphere of fun and gaiety.

Besides these fairs, they also observe the festivals like Sair on the first of Paus, Shivratri in Phalgun (February-March)—generally called Shiv Chaturdashi and Holi in Phalgun. During these festivals there is feasting and dancing. *Sur* is consumed in large quantity on all festivals. On Janamasthami and Shivratri, they abstain from liquor.

A few of them have now acquired the art of drawing and painting in the Chamba style. They know the art of spinning and weaving. Folktales and folklores related with the places and deities are prevalent among the Dhorgis. Fairs and festivals offer opportunities to the Dhogris to sing and dance. Their folksongs are simple in composition and sung with clarity of expression. Their dances are accompanied by singing, and songs are often amorous. Their song and dance patterns are more regional than specific to the community.

The Dhogris live in multi-ethnic villages. They are an artisan community and hence have an occupational expertise. Villagers collect their iron implements for daily and household use and for agriculture from the Dhogris. Brahmans and Rajputs do not take cooked food from the Dhogris. Sipi, Hali and Hesi do accept cooked food from the Dhogris. They enjoy equal treatment for facilities of road, schools, crematorium, etc. They visit religious shrines like all other castes. In winters, they migrate to Kangra and Chamba. During that period they interact with outsiders and share their views with them.

There has been a marginal impact of the proliferation of educational centres on the Dhogris. A small section of the Dhogris is now literate. Previously, due to their hard life-style they were less interested in formal education but, nowadays, some have started sending their children to the village school and also to the middle school and high school which are far from their villages.

Though their attitude is favourable towards the system of modern medicine, they still have a soft corner for traditional and indigenous medicines. A few educated and enlightened persons express a favourable attitude towards family planning methods but are reluctant to undergo sterilization. Drinking water is collected from springs. Employment and self-employment opportunities provided by the Government are still not within easy reach of the Dhogri. Metalled roads are constructed up to the foot of the hills but their settlements at hill tops are connected by narrow irregular paths only. They like listening to the radio. Television transmission has not yet reached the area. Electricity has reached the Dhogri settlements. Their main fuel resource is wood. Besides rainwater, they sometimes channelise spring water up to their fields for irrigational purposes. They mainly use organic manures in their cultivation. Subsidised foodgrains are distributed throughout the hill area. There is a bank and a cooperative society is functioning in the block area. Some of the Dhogris have obtained loans from these organizations in connection with the development programmes. Socioeconomic changes are steadily taking place among the Dhogris.

D.K. Chakraborty

DOSALI

The Dosali, Dashal or Dosal as it is variously referred to, are a community who traditionally make cups and plates of leaves by joining them with small pieces of dried straw, *dusa*, and hence are called Dosali. Rose (1919: 247) speaks of them essentially as a 'hill caste' "a small caste found in Hoshiarpur but not east of Sutlej." The history relating to their origin and migration is obscure, but according to the people some of the families of the Dosalis came to Chamba from the erstwhile princely state of Suket. It is said that when the raja of Chamba married the daughter of raja of Suket, some Dosalis were sent as personal attendants as part of dowry with his daughter.

They live mostly in the districts of Chamba, Mandi and Bilaspur and other areas situated in the Himalayan foothills.In Chamba they speak in Chambiali, which is a dialect largely used by all those inhabiting the Chamba region. During the princely regime their script had been Tankari which is rarely used nowadays. Urdu has been the second most popular language in Perso-Arabic script used by a majority of the people. Moreover, those who have received formal education use Hindi and English while talking to outsiders.

The Dosalis are non-vegetarian and take the meat of goat, sheep, chicken and fish. Eating buffalo's and cow meat is taboo. Their staple diet consists of *makki* (maize), *rajmah*, pulses like *mah,* and *sag*. Liquor is procured from the market and sometimes is locally brewed. Smoking of *hukka* and *bidi* is in vogue among both the sexes, though men do so quite regularly. Among non-alcoholic drinks, tea is consumed by the majority.

In the regional hierarchy the Dosalis are grouped along with Banjara, Doom or Dumna but are held superior to Chuhra/Balmiki and Chamar. A Brahman normally does not officiate their marriages and when he does come, he does not accept any food *pucca* or *kachcha*, but is given *sidha* and cash. They have clear preception of varna order and place themselves among the Sudra.

They are an endogamous community but while settling marriage, *gotra* exogamy is the rule. Marriage in the *gotra* of father, mother, and father's mother is avoided. Marriages are settled by negotiation, but marriage by exchange *batta-satta* is also prevalent. Nowadays the practice of bride-price is fast giving way to dowry. Dowry is however, not demanded but depends entirely on the wishes of the girl's parents. No tangible reasons could be supplied by the informants for the disappearance of the practice of bride-price. They however seemed to attribute it to the growing contact with the outside world, wider communication network and spread of literacy. This can be gauged from the fact that they feel ashamed to admit the presence of bride price and normally try to hide the fact.

Widow remarriage, widower remarriage, *gadhoj*, is permissible. A second marriage after the death of the spouse is performed in a simple way without any elaborate rituals. A widow is offered *paranda*, in the presence of a few close relatives of both sides. Remarriage after divorce is also possible both for men and women after paying the compensation money to the aggrieved party. For instance, if the woman wants to divorce and remarry, her paramour has to first pay the compensation to her former husband before he marries her. In the well-to-do families, men may marry more than once.

The eldest man in the family is the household head and is given due respect. He is normally consulted on important family issues. Joint families are still holding ground, but nuclear households are also coming up largely due to limited space becoming too small for the growing size of the family, lack of adjustment and petty family quarrels.

Property is inherited in the male line but in the absence of a male issue a daughter is entitled to the share. In such cases the son-in-law normally is invited to look after the property of the father- in-law and is known as *ghar javantri*. All the sons are given an equal share. If there are four sons, the property is divided into five equal parts—the fifth part being referred to as *jiyuk*, which is the parents' share and is given after the death of the father to the eldest son who would be responsible for paying all the debts of his father. Among the Dosalis even an illegitimate child is given a share of the parental property under special cirsumstances. For instance, if a woman conceives after the death of her husband and does not leave his house for four consecutive years, the child thus born is called as *chakhandu* and is entitled to a share.

The status of women is deemed low despite the fact that women are equally hardworking and share the major burden of work outside the house. Since the traditional occupation of the people is making leaf plates, it is essentially the job of the women; only the collection of leaves from the jungle is done by men. Women do most of the agricultural work except ploughing, besides doing other odd jobs like bringing fuel and water, tending to the animal, and doing all the household chores. In the domestic sphere women enjoy considerable freedom in running the household, take active part in domestic rituals and functions. In the political sphere their activities are, however, limited to casting of votes in elections.

Post-birth pollution is observed. On the sixth day *chatti* and eleventh day *dashthon* (purificatory bath) is given to the mother and the child. The parturient mother is not expected to cook or do heavy work for 21 days after the birth of the child. When the child attains six months of age, he/she is for the first time given a cereal diet, generally a rice pudding known as *khirpo*.

Thereafter, *jattu* is held either in the first, third or fifth years.

Marriage is settled through negotiations, the boy's side presents a silver *bang* (bangle) to the girl as a symbolic action of their betrothal. Before the actual marriage, another ceremony known as *mehndi* is observed , which is applied on both the bride and the bridegroom by their respective sisters-in-laws. At the time of marriage it is customary on the part of the boy's parents to bring five items, namely, *balu* (nose ring), *tika, paranda, mehndi* and a *bang* which are considered essential symbols of marriage.

The dead are cremated and it is normally the eldest male child who performs the death rites of the parents. The exception to this rule is that when the wife dies then the last rites are performed by the husband. Pollution is observed for 13 days and ends with feeding 13 Brahmans. The house is then deemed fit to resume normal day-do-day activity.

The Dosalis are a community of leaf plate makers; the men go to the jungle and collect the leaf of *trimbal* and *kamal*, while the women make plates out of them. Besides, some of them also have land and those who were landless have been provided with land. The Dosalis do not have the traditional *jajmani*, with other communities. The services they render are paid in cash. There are also those who subsist on agricultural labour and are given a certain share of the produce. Some of them have also entered in Government and semi-Government organizations; some are shopkeepers while others supplement their meagre resources through manual labour. Child labour is reported. As regards their traditional rights on the natural resources, they continue to have customary rights in the forest whereby they can get wood for fuel free of cost and can get trees for house-building purposes at a nominal rate. They are also free to collect leaves for making leaf plates from the demarcated portion of the forest.

For the effective control of social crime like incest, elopement, disregard for community rules and divorce, the traditional Biradari Panchayat has still a role to play. The punishment accorded to the offender is both in cash and kind. Generally the offender is asked to host a feast for the *biradari*. Nevertheless, with the introduction of the statutory panchayat and judicial courts, people sometimes approach them if effective solution does not come forth from the traditional council.

The Dosalis are Hindu and regard Shiva as their patron deity. Whenever there is a long-desired wish to be fulfiled, they promise to make an offering to Lord Shiva through a ritual known as *nawala*. If the wish is fulfiled, then on an auspicious day they invite all the relations and well wishers. A garland made of fresh wool of sheep is offered to Lord Shiva and sometimes a sheep is also sacrificed. For this purpose a member of the Jogi community acts as the sacred specialist who is a *chela* between the devotee and the deity. The ceremony continues for the whole night with singing of songs in praise of

Lord Shiva. These special religious songs are known as *ainchali*. People also take part in the fairs and festivals like Shiv-ka-Mela, Minjar, Lohri and Bisoa. In the month of September there is a famous pilgrimage, *yatra*, to the shrine of Manimahesh in Bharmaur tehsil of Chamba district. They also have their separate clan deities who are propitiated on auspicious occasions. Some of the names of their clan deities are Jalpa and Panjapiri. The faith in the powers of magic and evil spirits is also well ingrained in the Dosalis. In order to ward off the evil spell of the maligned sprits, they take the help of a *chela* who is invariably from the Sippi community. The role of the temple *pujari* and *purohit* is restricted to performing sacred duties at the temple and for performing various rituals at both private and public occasions.

Mutual interdependence of one community on the other is observed in one way or the other and is locally referred to as the *birtandari*. For example when a house is to be constructed, a member of each family in the village voluntarily comes to assist in the work. Similarly people holding land may seek each other's help for agricultural labour during peak agricultural season. Since the Dosalis occupy a middle status in the regional hierarchy, some discrimination is still practised in relation to communities at higher echelon like the Brahmans and the Thakurs who would receive *sidha* or cash for the services rendered. However, if the food is cooked separately by a person of a clean community and served separately, then it may be acceptable to these higher communities. Incidentally, there are no inhibitions with regard to the sharing of water from the same source. The Dosalis can now enter the temples though earlier there were some reservations with regard to their entering the *sanctum sanctorum*. With urbanization and growing culture contacts the worldview is changing and as a result many of the restrictions and inhibitions pertaining to social distance vis-a-vis other communities are gradually fading out.

The Dosali children are attending schools in larger numbers now, but there are no incentives like freeships, free stationery or mid-day meals. The Dosalis avail modern system of health and medicare. They are aware of the family welfare programme and its objectives of small family norm, but their practice this hardly ever conforms to the ideal. Drinking water is available easily through pipes and taps. Integrated Rural Development Programme and Employment Guarantee Scheme have made little impact on the Dosalis but more on the scheduled castes. It is for this reason that some Dosali families are trying hard to obtain the caste certificates of another community, Jogi, so as to derive the benefits being provided to the scheduled castes. The transport and communication, is available and is made use of by the people except in the remote areas.

Since the people have very meagre landholdings, the agricultural facilities by way of chemical fertilizers and irrigation are availed of in a very limited way. Certain other facilities like getting ration through fair price distribution shops, the post offices and banks also exist. With the advancement in the field of literacy and education, health and family welfare, and improvements in certain basic amenities like drinking water, electricity and transport, people feel satisfied when they review their present situation.

Vatsala Sarkar

DUMNA/BHANJRA

The Dumna are a large scheduled caste of traditional craftsmen in bamboo and grass. There are many synonyms for this community, viz., Dom, Doom, Dumne, Domra, Mahasha, Bhanjra or Bhanjre, which, according to Ibbetson (1916) and Rose (1919), are basically of one stock. The Mahasha and the Bhanjra are also identified as two subgroups of the Dumna as the generic community, whereas the others simply call themselves Dumna. The community is spread in various regions of the country though the people in the study areas, the districts of Bilaspur and Kangra, perceive their distribution at the regional level. Sporadic ethnographic descriptions of the community are given in Ibbetson (1916) and Rose (1919) but the history of their origin and migration is not known. The Bhanjra subgroup of the Dumna is found mainly in the districts of Bilaspur, Kangra, Hamirpur, Sirmaur, Shimla, Mandi and Solan. Their population is mentioned under two communities, namely under the Bhanjra (Bhanjhre) 2,736 and 5,120 under Bhanjre (Dumna) whereas the total Dumna population is 39,022 according to the Census of 1971 (Singh, 1971). But the 1981 Census provides a population figure of 4,359 for the Bhanjra/Bhanjre separately and 54,489 for the total Doom/Dumna community. Separate population figures for the Mahasha segment are not known, but they are chiefly restricted to Kangra district. The physical environment is characterized by hilly terrain and valleys of Shivaliks with warm and temperate climate in general, low humidity, medium rainfall, no snowfall and thin forest canopies on the hill ranges.

The Dumna community, including both its segments, the Bhanjra and the Mahasha, are identified through its characteristic traditional occupation of basketry or bamboo work. The name Bhanjra itself is derived from *bhanj* or *banjh* (bamboo). The name Mahasha is, however, given to a section which came into the Arya Samaj fold. They speak local dialects of the western Pahari, Bilaspuri and Kangri and use Devanagari script for writing. The Mahashas in the study area, Indora (Kangra), however, speak Punjabi and Kangri/Pahari. There are no identification marks in dress and ornaments. Like other people of the area the men wear shirt and trousers or pants and *kurta,* and the women *salwar* and *dupatta.* The traditional ornaments of women are a silver funnel-shaped ornament of *chak*, *murki* (coiled nose ring) or large or small *tilli*, *choora* and *paijeb*.

The community is non-vegetarian and eats fish, eggs and meat. The common staple food is maize for most of the winter supplemented by rice on festive occasions. Wheat is consumed more in summers. Various types of pulses—*urd, moong,* grams, peas, beans along with vegetables, roots and tubers are consumed regularly. The cooking medium is mustard oil, vegetable oil or *desi ghee.* Milk and milk products are consumed almost regularly. The intake of fruits like banana, apple, peach, guava and mango, is occasional or seasonal. Festive foods are various products of wheat like *babroo, sevian* and of rice like *ankloo* and *ankli,* the latter are eaten with milk and *desi ghee.* Men smoke loose tobacco in indigenous *hukka* besides *bidi* and cigarette. They occasionally consume country liquor, especially during festive and marriage occasions. There does not seem to be any perceptible change in the dietary habits.

The Mahasha section claims superiority over the Bhanjras or other Dumnas at social and economic levels and usually restricts matrimonial alliances within the Mahashas. However, at the regional level such differentiation is not fully marked and all Dumnas are treated at par. They are segmented into several exogamous units called *got* and *al.* Some of the Dumna/Bhanjra clans noticed in Bilaspur are Chauhan, Manhas, Saini, Kaundal, Mahle, Nariyal, Bhadiar, Gurnwariye, Phallehre, Saluriye, etc. Among the Mahasha such sections are Shamial, Badan, Mor, Madruthiye, Badraliye, Bhagotiye, Gurnwariye, etc. Although the Dumna claim descent from the Kshatriyas, they are placed among the Sudras at the regional and the local level.

The community is endogamous and usually practises village and *got* exogamy. But sometimes village endogamy may also occur when spouses of different *got* and *al* are available. Earlier child marriages were prevalent in the community but at present the girls are usually married in their post-puberty period and the boys in their teenage. Marriage is negotiated through parents and relatives. *Batta-satta* is also a common practice to avoid payment of brideprice. Presently, however, they adhere to the *kanyadan* pattern and do not take bride price, rather give dowry in the form of household articles, clothes and ornaments. Monogamy is practised and junior sororate and levirate are permitted on the death of the spouse. The marriage symbols are *sindur,* glass bangles, nose ring and nose pin/stud. The bride lives patrilocally with the husband's parents. Divorce occurs rarely but has social as well as judicial approval for both the spouses on grounds of maladjustment and cruelty. In such cases the minor children are the liablity of the mother and the grown up ones of the father. The husband pays compensation or maintenance expenditure to the wife. There has been no change in the incidence of divorce but presently there is a trend of seeking divorce through judicial approval. Both the divorcees may remarry. Increase in the age of marriage is a recent development.

The family pattern is both nuclear as well as vertically extended. The joint family ties are on a decline. The *lari* or *nuh* keeps avoidance from her *saurah* and *jeth*. Joking relationship is observed as in many Hindu communities of the region, that of *devar-bhabi*, *jija-sali*, and *jija-sala*. The inheritance of the property is as per the principle of male-equigeniture and the eldest son succeeds the father. The points of conflicts are generally in property matters. The women have nearly an equal status. They do all the domestic duties and fetch potable water, collect fuel and fodder and work in agricultural fields. They also earn and contribute to the family income by doing menial services to the big landlords of the village as well as acting as midwives. They participate in basket-making as well. Women take part in various social and religious ceremonies but their role in the mechanism of social control and political spheres is negligible. They, however, have a say in family matters and a control over household expenditure.

The life cycle rituals of the Dumna are similar to those of many Hindus and are performed by their own priest. Post-delivery pollution called *sutak* is observed for 13 days and after *sutak* period is over, purification is attained by taking *gunt*. However, post-delivery social restrictions on the mother last for over a month. Christening and cereal-taking ceremonies are ignored. *Mundan* or *jatlu* is the main childhood ritual observed in case of a boy on any odd year after birth. The ritual is performed by the *mama*. Marriage rituals are performed by their own community *purohit* as per the Vedic rites. Oil ceremony is observed as among other Hindu castes. At the bride's place the bride and the groom circumambulate the sacred fire four times and at the groom's place they take three rounds of a *pipal* tree. The bride's parents hold a feast for the groom's party. The kith and kin of the bride accompanying the bride to the groom's place also receive a treat from the groom's parents. The *muklawa* or *phera-ghera* occurs on the following day of the marriage. The death rituals are also similar to those of the other Hindus. The dead are cremated and their ashes are immersed in the Ganges or Beas river. The sons shave off their head on father's death. The *patak* lasts for 13 days when purification ceremony is held by performing a *havan* and making offerings to the poor or a *dhyan*. Annual and fourth annual death rites are also performed.

The community subsists mainly on its traditional occupation-cum-craft of basketry. They prepare various objects of bamboo, including baskets of different sizes, winnowing fans called *sup*, and small to large cereal containers called *peru* or *peri* and other articles like mats, chiks, fans, ropes and strings. They also have small landholdings and are engaged in agriculture and animal husbandry to supplement their earnings. Many people work as masons and tailors. They also go for daily-wage casual labour for road and house construction. Some act as musicians or band masters and give instrumental music on marriages. Womenfolk of the community sing in marriages and on other festive occasions of big landlords and high caste Hindus. A few persons of the Dumnas are employed in Government jobs in lower cadres and some in the army. Child labour exists. The economic position of the Mahasha subgroup among the Dumna is comparatively good and there are doctors, engineers, advocates and teachers among them.

The social disputes of the community are solved by the community council which is largely informal, but is formalized at some places. Its *pradhan* is elected by voice vote for an indefinite period. The members of the statutory Gram Panchayat usually intervene in the socio-economic disputes of the village. The Gram Panchayat also imposes cash fines on the guilty, besides performing usual functions of development and welfare. Major disputes involving violence are taken to police and a legal course is adopted.

The Bhanjras follow Sanatan Dharam while the Mahashas follow Arya Samaj and some others follow the Radhaswami sect. The Dumnas have various female and male deities as *kul* and village deities. Nabahi Devi, Godria Sidh, Kamlahiya Sidh (in Bilaspur), Baba Buland Singh and Seetla Mata (in Kangra) are some of the community deities of special reverence who are propitiated particularly on marriage and child birth. The various regional male deities like Nahar Singh, Lakhdata, Guga and Balak Nath are also propitiated. Different female deities like Jawalamukhi, Chintpurni, Vaishno Devi, Naina Devi are worshipped and annual fairs are arranged at their shrines which are well attended. The Sair fair of Baba Buland Singh, held at Mukeri (Punjab) is of special significance to the Mahashas. They share regional Pahari and Punjabi (particularly the Mahasha) folksongs, folktales and folklore. Dussehra, Diwali, Lohri, Baisakhi, Sair, Chiran and Nag Panchmi are the different festivals of socioeconomic and socioreligious importance. *Gidda* is a dance popular among women particularly on marriage occasions.

The traditional water sources like *bauri*, may be shared with the upper castes. Religious shrines and various public places are common. The community is strongly interlinked socioeconomically with various agricultural and other communities. They receive and render economic services and have traditional *jajmani* with the Lohar, Nai and Chamar. The community has some members in business, holding white-collar jobs, as teachers, doctors and engineers and the political leadership has emerged at the local or the Gram Panchayat level (among the Mahasha).

Modern development programmes have made considerable impact on some sections of the community like the Mahashas, where the literacy level has gone up. But the lot of others has not yet been improved and many are still poverty-stricken. Among them the literacy level is low and usually the boys and girls receive school education up to the secondary level only. Very few go in for college education due to poor economic conditions. Higher education for girls is not favoured socially. In the field of health and medicare they follow both the modern as well as indigenous methods. Belief is still prevalent about diseases being caused by supernatural factors. Hence the oracles still earn considerably. The attitude towards the small family norm is becoming favourable and they have adopted sterilization as the method of family planning.

Supply of drinking water through pipelines has recently been provided, although the traditional water sources like *bauri* and springs are also used in case of scarcity of water. Provisions for rural development exist in the Integrated Rural Development Programme but people are not satisfied due to the ineffectiveness of this programme. They also get 50 per cent subsidy on chemical fertilizers and for the purchase of cattle and agricultural appliances. Modern mass media (radio and television) facilities are availed of by them and their houses are electrified. Road communication and postal facilities are also accessible. Fuel resources used are firewood, cowdung cakes and kerosene oil. Rainwater is the only source of irrigation. Nutritional and child health care programmes including immunization are availed of by many.

A. R. Sankhyan

FAQIR

The Faqir or Faquir is a Muslim community whose name is derived from their traditional occupation as ascetics wandering about and seeking alms. Gradually they almost became beggars and some also adopted the methods of earning money by future-telling and curing ailments supposedly caused by supernatural influences. The Faqirs seek alms in the name of a legendry saint called Roda Malang, who is believed to be their ancestor. The legend goes that a childless couple went to the saint. The saint blessed the woman and gave her 101 *jantra* (charms) to eat on successive days. The women, however, forgot the instructions and ate them at one go. As a result she conceived and gave birth to 101 babies. As she was scared of the babies she asked her husband to take them away, who on the advice of the saint were buried under a clay mound in a jungle. After many years, the man happened to pass through the jungle and stopped on hearing a sound of drum beating near that mound. He saw that there was a burrow leading into the mound and the sound was coming from within. On checking he found that his 101 sons, later known as Malangs, were making the sound. The man threw his long turban through the hole to enable them to wrap themselves. On this, the Malangs came out of the mound but ran away in all directions and disappeared. It is said that the Faqir and the Bharai communities originated from these Malangs. Ibbetson (1916) and Rose (1919) have given some ethnographic information on the community.

The earliest mention of the Faqir in Himachal Pradesh is found in the *Shashi Vansh Vinod* by Kavi Ganesh Singh in 1892; when they totalled only 53 in the Kehlur (Bilaspur). Presently they probably number only a few hundreds in district Bilaspur. In addition, they are also found in Mandi and Hamirpur districts. Now a settled community, they live in the Shivalik hills and dales along the tributaries of the river Satluj in Bilaspur. The climate of the area is generally warm and temperate with moderate annual rainfall and low humidity. Thin forests exist on the hill ranges.

They speak local dialects of western Pahari like Bilaspuri or Kehluri and Mandiali. The script used is Devanagari but for their religious communication they use Urdu in Perso-Arabic script. No traditional saintly dress is worn by the Faqirs today and they are now indistinguishable from other local communities by the dress, ornaments or flag emblem.

The Faqirs are non-vegetarian who eat fish, eggs and *halal* meat but refrain from beef and pork. Their staple food comprises maize, wheat and rice; the last item is uncommon and eaten commonly on festivals and festivities. Pulses like *urd, moong*, gram, *masur* and *kulthi* are commonly eaten. The intake of fruits is occasional and generally limited to the seasonal occurrence of local fruits, like mango, banana, guava, *ber*, figs, peach and *jamun*. The consumption of roots is uncommon though tubers like potatoes, *arbi, yam, kachalu etc.* are more frequently consumed. The vegetable intake, notably of mustard leaves, *bathua, kachalu* leaves, lady finger, *tori, lauki, kaddu* and *petha* (gourds) is in plenty in their respective seasons. The rice cooked in *lassi* is called *jhol*. This is seen as the food of the poor. Milk intake is by and large limited to children, whereas the elders take tea. The Faqir adult males are fond of drinking and smoking. Country liquor is purchased from the market. The women do not drink or smoke. Like the Hindu communities of the area, they prepare *khichri* on Lohri, *seviyan* on Sair, *babru* on Baisakhi and *ankloo/ankli* on Diwali, besides mutton on Bakrid festival of the Muslims. Some change in food habits of the Faqirs has taken place, and their eating standard has improved.

The Faqirs have two main clans in Bilaspur and Mandi districts—Chauhan and Bhatti. They claim a Kshatriya descent. By virtue of their saintly traditions and performance of priestly duties they claim superiority over other local Muslim communities, like the Sunhak (Chandel Muslims), Bharai, Teli and Raeen. But these communities do not give them higher or even equal status in view of the begging habits and poor economic position of the Faqirs. Barring the Bharai community, the Faqirs are also not acceptable to other Muslims for marriage.

They are largely endogamous but occasionally also marry among the Bharais. They, however, maintain village and clan exogamy, though the latter is not strictly adhered to. The marriage between close relatives up to the first cousin level is generally avoided, which however is not a rule. The common marriage age was 12-15 years for girls and 16-18 years for boys during the recent past. But this has slightly increased recently. The exchange of sisters called *batta-satta* has been a common marriage practice to economize marital expenses. Monogamy is the common form of marriage and a second marriage is contracted in rare cases of childlessness, death and divorce of the first wife. The marriage is negotiated through parents, friends or relatives. Generally, marriage symbols are lacking but glass bangles are regarded as a marriage symbol. Bride-price is also not taken and presently exchange marriages are also becoming rare, giving way to the *dharam pun* marriage with some dowry. The dowry is, however, in the form of household utensils, beddings, cot, chairs and table, boxes, clothes and ornaments. A wrist watch and a transistor radio are also given by some economically well-off people. The bride is given *mehar* equivalent to the traditional silver coins of Rs. 32.25. Divorce is a rare event but permitted as per the Islamic socioreligious sanctions after the *iddat*. The divorcees and widow/widower can remarry but junior levirate is rarely practised. The bride resides in the patrilocal home, but the cases of the boy residing with the girl's parents, *ghar jamai,* are also observed in the community. The main trends noticed in the marriage institution of the Faqir are, increase in marriage age, decline of exchange marriages, and picking up of the dowry system.

They live in nuclear families. The married sons often get separated from their parents but the unmarried sons live with the parents. The Faqir women do not observe *burka* (veil) but avoid the elders. They cover their face with a *ghoond* while facing *saurah* and *jeth*. The *lari* also touches the feet of her *sas*, *saurah*, *jeth*, *jethani*, *nanad* and *nandoi.* The elders are addressed by the juniors by kinship names as a mark of respect. The occasions for conflicts and confrontation on domestic matters are however, not infrequent in a Faqir family. An informal joking relationship exists between *devar-bhabi* and *jija-sali.* The succession goes to the eldest son and the inheritance is patrilineal as per the rule of male-equigeniture (all sons get an equal share) though there is also some provision for unmarried daughters. The Faqir families interact among themselves at various occasions, like festivals, childbirth, *sunnat*, marriage, death and social gatherings.

The Faqir women enjoy a lower status than the men but often dominate in domestic decisions. They work in agricultural fields, collect fuel and fodder, bring potable water and rear cattle, goats and sheep. They also participate in various social and religious ceremonies but do not contribute to the family income and do not accompany the men in begging or alm seeking expeditions. Their role in local political activities and in mechanism of social control is non-existent.

Birth takes place in the home and delivery is performed by a *dai* of their own community. *Azan* is whispered in the ear of the child. The post-delivery period of pollution called *sutak* is observed for 40 days when a *maulvi* recites the Quran and *sharbat* is taken by the woman to get purified. Sweets or meals are also served to kith and kin and villagers. They consult the *maulvi* to give the child a name. The male *mundan* ceremony is performed within or after a year, and the haircut is given by the *mama* or any other person regarded as the *mama.* The *sunnat* is the major childhood ritual in the Faqir community and is apparently called a 'half-marriage' of the boy. It is done by an Abdal or a *maulvi* or a barber. On this occasion the *maulvi* recites *kalma* from the holy Quran. Sweet rice is served to friends and relatives and to the villagers. *Sunnat* can be performed in the third to the twelfth year.

The marriage is negotiated by the parents/relatives or a friend. All months and dates except the dates 8, 18 and the 28 of a month are open for marriage. No horoscope is consulted. The marriage is fixed by a *karmai* ritual when the boy's father accompanied by a *maulvi* goes to girl's parents along with sweets or *shakkar,* clothes and some ornaments for the girl. The regular marriage ceremony is called *biah* in which the major ritual is *nikah*. The *maulvi*, with a witness, asks the bridegroom and the girl three times about their agreement for each other and then the marriage contract is signed. This is completed by giving of a formal *haq mehar* to the girl. The girl's parents arrange a feast. The bride and bridegroom sit in two separate *palkis* and the procession goes with brass band music. The *jathere* worship is performed by the couple and *gulra prasad* is distributed. The *muklawa* ceremony is observed after some days/months of the marriage depending upon the age of the girl.

The dead body is bathed and *sharbat* is poured into the mouth of the dead and *fatiha* is recited. The body is wrapped in 32 meter long coffin contributed by other communities in the neighbourhood. The dead body is then carried on a cot to the burial ground. A five feet deep trench is dug out and half filled with bamboo *barghes* (sticks) before the body is laid down with the head towards the north. There are seven stages of the death pollution period when ancestor worship is observed, namely, third day (*teyia*), seventh day (*sata*), tenth day (*dasa*), twentieth day (*beeswan*), thirtieth day (*teeswan*) and lastly the fortieth day (*chalia*). Only the economically better off families observe all these stages by serving meals to the gathered relatives, but the last rite is observed by all in which sweet rice and fruits are served. Some, however also serve non-vegetarian diet, *halal* meat of goat or sheep. A *qazi* or *maulvi* (earlier an Abdal) is offered a cot, bedding, *thali*, shoes and clothes in charity. The Abdals used to play on *sarangi* on this occasion and get alms.

Many of the Faqirs, were traditionally vagrants, exorcists and mendicants without landholdings about some decades back. They received some *bhet* (grants) of land from the last ruler of Bilaspur state. Presently, each Faqir family owns about five *bigha* of land and are primarily cultivators. Some however, still continue their ancestral way of seeking alms to supplement their earnings. They have also taken up road, building-construction and agricultural labour work. Some have also adopted tailoring as their subsidiary occupation. Child labour exists to some extent. The dealings are in cash.

A significant change that has occurred in the economic life of the Faqirs since Independence is that they have nearly given up their tradition of begging as the new generation feels ashamed of it. They have become settled agriculturists and adopted manual labour as their supplementary occupation. Some are also employed in Government jobs.

Some elders exercise social control and solve disputes of the community. The local or regional deity 'Guga' is entrusted for punishing a guilty. The statutory Gram Panchayat for various communities in the area performs the functions of revenue collection, social welfare and development, and also solves petty village disputes over land and water. They also take up some matters of interest to all Muslims with the Islamic committee which speaks up for social reforms and advocates Islamic viewpoints.

The Faqirs follow the Sunni sect of Islam. By virtue of their saintly descent, they act as priests to the local Muslim communities. They propitiate Guga Chauhan as their family and clan deity and offer him sweatened *roat* or maize *roti*. Guga is considered the deity who also controls the snake bite. They sing the folklore of Guga in a *Guga mandli*, which commences with the festival of Rakshabandan, and seek alms by paying door-to-door visits to the various villages in the area. While singing the life story of Guga they beat a *damru* (dumbell-shaped percussion musical instrument) and a bronze plate. This continues for eight days and during night halts of such *mandli*, called *dera*, they perform *khel* dance in which persons afflicted by evil spirits sway their heads in a continuous state of shivering and hypnotism. They narrate the story of their sufferings to the *chela*. The Faqirs claim that no deaths due to snake-bites have ever occurred in their community.

The Roda Malang is specially propitiated by performing a special protective ritual by some male persons, who move round the village/house afflicted with evil spirits while beating a *dhol*, *chimta* (tongs), and carrying an earthen pot. They take rounds of the locality or village called *kaar*, which ensures portection to people and cattle against diseases and sufferings caused by the evil spirits, like *bhoot, churail*, etc. This *kaar* of the Malang is usually performed during *kala mahina* (black month) in August-September every year. But they usually perform *dhamal* when they beg in a group. In *dhamal* they move in a circle calling Ali Ali.

The Faqirs also propitiate regional deities, the Panj peers (five Peers) like Khwaja Peer, Bhianu or Lakhdata Peer, etc. who are offered *roat*, to ensure the well-being of a family. Wrestling matches are arranged in propitiation of Lakhdata in Bilaspur. An annual fair is also celebrated at Bhianu and visited by all communities. The Guga fairs are arranged at various places where Guga temples called *Gugheri* are located.

They celebrate major Muslim festivals like Id and Bakrid. They also celebrate local Hindu festivals of Lohri, Baisakhi, Sair, Chiran, Diwali, etc., and prepare special foods like the Hindus. Mosques are uncommon in the region and are visited by them only for *namaz*. Presently there is an increasing trend of re-activation of the Islamic tenets.

The folktales of the Roda Malang and folklore of Guga are common among the Faqirs. The Faqir *dhamal* and *khel* are their socioreligious public rituals in which the musical instruments used are a drum and a tong. Other *pahari* folksongs and tales are also shared.

By virtue of their being a wandering and alm seeking community, their social linkages are very limited. They are largely surrounded by Hindu communities with whom they have little social and occupational interaction, except that they seek alms at the doors of such communities. They have their own water resources or share them with certain Hindu castes. The Muslim communities, however, exchange food and water with them which was not the case earlier. But since they became settled agriculturists and abstained from begging, social interaction has increased in terms inter-dining. Water resources, schools, mosques and panchayat *ghar* are common but the burial place is shared with other Muslims.

Almost all the boys and girls are now receiving school education but higher education is still outside their means. They use modern health, medical care and family welfare facilities available in the nearby Primary Health Centre and civil dispensary. Sterilization has recently been accepted by both men and women after three or four children. Many families have received buffaloes on subsidized cost under the Antyodaya rural development programme, but employment guarantee schemes have had no favourable effect on the community. Mid-day meal or feeding programmes at school for children are available along with immunization facilities. Their houses are electrified and piped water is available. Chemical fertilizers are used for agriculture but no irrigation facility is as yet available. The awareness about conservation of environment is there. Modern mass- media (radio and TV and newspaper) facilities are in the vicinity and road communication is at their doorsteps. They avail themselves of public distribution system.

A. R. Sankhyan

GADDI BRAHMAN

The Gaddi Brahman are one of the four groups included in the generic category called Gaddi, a scheduled tribe. The Gaddis trace their origin to immigration from the plains. It is believed that the Gaddi Brahmans accompanied raja Ajia Varma to Chamba in A.D. 850-870 to serve him as priests (Rose, 1919: 256). They live in the area with the Rajput section of the Gaddis in the inhospitable terrain between the Pir Panjal and Dhauladhar ranges of the Himalayas. It is a high altitude area and experiences heavy snowfall most of the time. The area has thick and dense forest cover with low rainfall and low humidity. The total population of the Gaddis is 76,860 (1981 Census). The language spoken by the community amongst themselves is Bharmauri or Gadiali. Tankri was the script which they used earlier but now is known only to a few. Nowadays, colloquial Hindi in Devanagari script is used for communication with others. Their dress is similar to that of Gaddi Rajputs and consists of *chola* and a long woollen rope worn around the waist *dora*. The use of white turban is also a characteristic of a Gaddi man whereas a flared Scottish skirt *luanchiri* is a characteristic of a Gaddin (a woman of this community) of the area.

Bio-anthropoligcal information is available (see bio-anthropological report).

They are non-vegetarian and are fond of the meat of sheep and *ghural* (hill-goat). Their staple food consists mainly of *makki-ki-roti* (unleavened bread of maize) and pulses of *mah* or *rongi*. Milk is consumed in the form of tea, *lassi* and curd. Their consumption of locally grown vegetables cooked in mustard oil is moderate. *Sarson-da-sag* is their principal leafy vegetable. Fruits like apples, apricots, peaches, plums and walnuts are locally grown and consumed moderately. Like Rajput Gaddi they too are fond of *sur* (home-brewed liquor) and of smoking tobacco. Special dishes like sweet preparations and *madra* form an important food item on festive occasions.

The Gaddi Brahmans are divided into a number of endogamous *gotras* (Rose 1919: 256-57). These *gotra* are sub-divided into countless *als* or *septs* which are exogamous and at times are also styled as *gotras*. Thus, among the Brahmans we find the Bhat from the Bhattiyat, and also Ghungaintu, both *als* of the Kaundal *gotra*. Many of the Gaddi Brahman *als* bear nick-names as mentioned by Rose (*op. cit.*) such as Chadhu (cross-legged), Dundu (one-handed), Tanju (cat-eyed), Bhangretu (squinter), Chuntanhru (debauchee), Ghunain (one who speaks with nasal assent), Jukku (gambler), Marantu (one who escaped to the plains to avoid cholera), Jirgh (dumb), Nansain (adopted by *nani*), Sasi (one who lived with his mother-in-law), Litkar (lame) and Chupetru (reticent). Some names also denote occupations, like Sundheta, Palihan, Bardan, Sahdhrantu, Sipainu, Ranetu, Adhkaru, Saunpolu, Langhe, Jogi, Khuthlu, Thurne, Phangtain, which are by no means Brahmanical, but indicate the occupation, which their ancentors might have carried on.

The community is aware of the Varna-Vayavastha and ranks along with the highest order of the Brahman.

Traditionally child marriages were performed among them, but at present these have given way to adult marriages. Monogamy is the general form of marriage but in the event of the first wife being barren a second marriage is also held. *Byah* is the most common form of acquiring a mate, the other forms being *batta-satta*, *ghar javantri*, *bariana* and *jhind phuk* and *brar phuk* (marriage by burning bushes). Though the community is largely endogamous yet there are no restrictions or social taboos with regard to matrimonial alliances with the Gaddi Rajputs. The symbols of a married woman are a *nath* or *laung* and *lal chura* both of which are not strictly adhered to. *Reet* or *lag* (bride-price) was traditionally practised but this has now given way to dowry which is in the form of material gifts and depends on one's economic status. Divorce is not permissible by the community and is resorted to only in exceptional cases with judicial approval but such instances are very rare. Widow remarriage was traditionally not permissible but nowadays a few cases of widow remarriage can be seen. Widower remarriage is however practised.

The family traditionally was the vertically extended type but due to diversification and migration they are tending to lose their hold and nuclear families are becoming more common now. The relationship within the family is based on love, cordiality, mutual respect, paternal and filial ties. A bride observes avoidance from her father-in-law and her husband's younger brother, wife's younger brother and wife's younger sisters. The property is inherited on the rule of male equigeniture. The eldest male member is the head of the family and his decisions in all family matters are honoured. They are arrived at after mutual consultations, which leaves no room for conflict, but if there are disputes, they usually relate to property matters.

The women have equal status to that of men. They take part in all socio-economic activities within the house, but are not involved in any economic pursuit outside their houses. They carry on all agricultural activities in their fields except ploughing. They also take part in all social and religious functions and in all family rituals. They do all the household work, right from cooking food to looking after the young ones. They do not however contribute to the family income but have control over the expenditure.

In the sphere of the life-cycle rituals, pre-delivery rituals and restrictions are observed by the expectant mother for the safe delivery and welfare of the child. The period of pollution, *sutak,* last for 40 days, until which time the house is regarded as impure. During this period the mother is not allowed to do any household work till the *suddhi* takes place by the observance of *dasthon* on the tenth day in the case of a boy and on the eleventh day in the event of a girl. The *khirpu* ceremony is observed six months after the birth of a child, and this occasion is also utilized for naming the child. *Jattu* is observed in the third or fifth or seventh year after the birth, but sometimes it is deferred till the time of marriage, when instead of the entire head being shaved off the hair are cut in a way where *choti* (cue) is left. *Janeu* for the male children is performed normally at the age of five years, but it is also deferred at times till marriage, mainly for economic reasons.

The girls have to observe pollution during the menstrual period. The woman in her menses is not allowed to go near the hearth for a period of five days, and any food touched by her is not be accepted by other members.

Byah ceremony is performed at the bride's residence by *kanyadan* and *pradikshna* (circumambulation). The marriage feast is also given by the bride's parents. The consummation of marriage however takes place at the groom's residence.

The dead are normally cremated but those who die due to small pox or leprosy and one whose *janeu* has not been performed are buried. The ashes of the cremated dead are immersed in the river. The house remains polluted for a period of eleven days, when the purificatory rites are observed. Rituals connected with the dead are also observed at six months, *barhi* (twelve months) and *chobarhi* (four years). Ancestors are worshipped on each death anniversary during the period of *shradha.*

The majority of the community members since princely times have been landholders. The land was gifted to them free of revenue, but they did not plough the land themselves, as it was a taboo to them. They only indulged in acting as *purohit* or *pandit* and officiated at family rituals and performed sacredotal services. Presently they plough the land themselves, and the especially educated lot have secured white-collar jobs, whereas some are also involved in road construction, maintenance and other jobs as labourers. Priesthood still continues to be their traditional occupation. The other deviation from the normal Gaddi culture is the absence of pastoralism among the Brahmans. They do not keep sheep and goats. Cows are however owned by almost all the families. Children assist their parents in both the household activities and outside, thereby increasing the family income. They receive their wages in cash.

Social control in the community is maintained by their own *bhaichara* panchayat which is homogeneous and has on its council, members who are elected by a voice vote. They dispense justice on issues like adultery, elopement, disrespect for traditional norms, insult to traditional council or petty thefts. The offenders are penalised by cash fines or by the imposition of a punitive feast. When members from the community are not available, elders from the Gaddi Rajput communities are invited with whom they share many of the traits. Though statutory panchayats are a heterogeneous body that implements welfare activities, yet it is their traditional panchayat which holds a greater sway. They profess Hinduism with a strong emphasis on the Shakti and Shiva cults—the latter being the presiding deity of their area. They also have faith in supernatural forces like Kailu Bir, Nag Deota, Khetra Pal and Bhabir—each being the presiding deity over various natural resources. Besides these, they also have faith in other deities of the Hindu pantheon. The sacred specialists are from amongst themselves who perform life-cycle rituals. *Chela* are from the Sippi community. The major fairs of the region are the Sui ka mela, Brahmour Jatra, Minjar fair and Manimahesh fair, each being celebrated on fixed dates according to the Hindu calender. Their important festivals are Dholm, Lohri, Holi, Janmashtami, Baisakhi, Bisoa, Diwali and Shivratri—all of which have social and religious significance.

The community unlike the others is not involved in the craft of weaving, but they are very good in the graphic arts. Generally, women decorate walls and doors with certain geometric patterns. These are of aesthetic and religious value. They also make line drawings. Kamdev is particularly worshipped at times of marriage. Men also make drawings representing Navagrah and Ganesha at the time of worship.

The Brahman *purohit* performs *pooja*, at the house of his clients, no matter whether they are Rajputs, or a low community like Sippi or a Rihara. While a Brahman would accept only *kachcha* food from his own community people, he can accept *pucca* food from a Rajput, Khattri or Rathi, prepared in their house. His acceptance of *pucca* food from the house of a Sippi or Rihara is restricted to the extent of food being prepared by a *savarna.* They can accept *dakshina* from all castes. All other community people can accept both *kachcha* and *pucca* food cooked in the house of a Brahman.

A Brahman also has a system of traditionally sanctioned mutual obligation between individuals and families other than kinship. In Brahman, *bersord* type are prevalent. It is a relationship between a family and its Brahman *purohit* and is similar to *jajmani* relationship. The Brahman receives a certain percentage of food from the *jajman* (employer) mainly at four Sankrantis—festivals celebrated, when the sun enters from one zodiac sign to another. This share is given to them irrespective of the fact whether he has performed any of such rituals in the preceding years or is going to perform it in subsequent years or not. However, when there is a need to this effect, he renders his services to the family, without charging anything extra for them.

The problem of untouchability is not so grave in the Gaddi community as among other communities. There is no restriction on other castes with regard to entering the temple or sharing common water resources. Separate cremation grounds exist for all communities. Restrictions however exist for Rihara and Sippi and other similar castes for entering the houses of Brahmans. If invited to a *dham* they would sit at a distance and eat.

Though the Brahmans are regarded as religious priests, yet it is the Sippi who are considered as the best *chela*, that is why in spite of their being low in the social hierarchy, they enjoy a better status. At the time of a hypnotic trance, even a Brahman consults a *chela* and touches his feet.

They have favourably accepted development programmes which have made an impact on them. Formal education finds favour with the boys who even go out to the town and study up to the post-graduate level, whereas with girls it finds partial favour and as such they study only up to the secondary education level after which there is no arrangement for education in the vicinity. In the sphere of health and medicare, modern medicines also find favour with them which they use in addition to their traditional home-made remedies. They are also now favourable towards family welfare programmes and control the number of children to about four by using modern family planning techniques. But there is no preference for sterilization amongst them.

Drinking water is available through snowfed streams. The communication system is poor, but those near the tehsil headquarters avail themselves of communication and media facilities. The use of electricity is also limited to only a few families. Firewood and cowdung cakes continue to be used as fuel and to keep them warm during the severe winters. They have availed themselves of the assistance provided under the Integrated Rural Development Programme for agriculture. Some have also procured loans for setting up petty shops under various schemes. Irrigation facilities are not available and people have to depend on rainwater for irrigation purposes. Chemical fertilizers are used in combination with organic manure in agriculture but the use of pesticides is limited only to the horticultural produce. Mid-day meal scheme for children, nutrition programme for infants, expectant and nursing mothers and immunization schemes are availed of. Public distribution of essential commodities at controlled prices is available through Government fair price shops. Their attitude towards saving is favourable and they avail themselves of the banking facilities available at the tehsil headquarters.

Rajendra Sarkar

GADDI RAJPUT

The Gaddi is a generic term used for all of the indigenous populations of the Bharmaur area of Chamba district. The Gaddis include the *savarnas*—like Brahman, Rajput, Khatri, Thakur and Rathi—and the non-*savarnas* like Hali, Sippi, Rihare and Dom (Rose 1919). Although all are categorised as scheduled tribe by virtue of their living in a scheduled area, the non-*savarnas* are also included separately as scheduled caste. Though all call themselves Gaddi, yet only the *savarna* Gaddi Rajputs and their allies, who are identical and do not have much differentiation among themselves, are discussed here. All the scheduled caste have beeen described separately. This is also in consonance with the custom prevalent among the *savarna* of calling themselves as Gaddi, whereas calling others by their respective caste names.

The word Gaddi means 'seat', and since Bharmaur was the seat of the Raja of Chamba, all the people of the Gaderan (the area) called themselves Gaddi. History confirms that Gaddi Rajputs migrated from Lahore (now in Pakistan) to this place in order to avoid religious persecution. A saying, "*Ujjra Lahore te basiya Bharmaur*" prevalent in the community further confirms this. Khatris are also believed to have migrated from plains, and have come to acquire status parallel to that of the Rajputs. Presently, the bulk of the population lives in Bharmaur tehsil of Chamba district, but a scattered population of this tribe is also found in the adjoining districts of Kangra and Mandi. The total population of the Gaddis in 1981 is 76860, which also includes a small population of Gaddi Brahmans. The community occupies the inaccessible, inhospitatble terrain in between the Pir-Panjal and Dhauladhar range, between Ravi and Chenab. It is a high altitude area and remains cut off most of the time because of heavy snowfall. The area has thick and dense forest with low rainfall and low humidity.

The language spoken within the community is Bharmauri Gadiali. Tankri was the script used by the old people. With others, however, colloquial Hindi is spoken whereas Devanagari is used as a script. The Gaddi man is identified by typical dress which consists of a *chola* and *dora* whereas the woman by *luanchiri* (a flared Scottish skirt). The women also adorn gold earrings, which are worn by men too. Men also wear white turban, which is a characteristic of the Gaddi dress.

The community is non-vegetarian but they mostly take the meat of sheep, chicken and *ghural*. Families who keep poultry, also take eggs. Their staple food consists of *makki-ki-roti* and occasionally wheat *chapati* with *mah* and/or *rongi*. Children take goat milk, whereas elders use milk in tea.

Occasionally *lassi* is also taken. They also make moderate use of vegetables, including roots and tubers, and fruits. Mustard oil is the usual cooking medium. People are very fond of *sur* which is taken daily. Women consume it only on festive and social occasions. They also smoke tobacco in *hukka*, which forms a part of their daily sittings. Their special *madira* along with a sweet preparation is a must on all social and festive occasions.

Bio-anthropological information is available (see bio-anthropological report).

The Gaddi Rajputs are divided into Thakur and Rathi or Khatri. The Rathis and Khatris are few in number and are regarded on the same level as that of Rajputs. The Rathis are lower than the Rajputs, but, since they are numerically small, they form a part of the Rajput community. Each group is largely an endogamous division, but an exception to this rule is Rajputs who are hypergamous. Each section is further subdivided into a number of exogamous *gotras* which are of two types i.e., the *anderla* (or the rishi *gotra*) and *baherla* (or the territorial *gotra*) denoting the place of origin) *gotras*.

They continue to write 'Singh' as their surname; which indicates their Rajput origin. The community perceives its superiority and are regarded as high in social hierarchy and the fact is acknowledged by all neighbouring communities. They are also aware of the varna order and the Rajput, Rathi and Khatri communities align themselves with the Kshatriyas.

There is no restriction on anyone marrying within the village provided *gotra* exogamy is maintained, and that there is no common relative from the father's or mother's side up to three generations in the family one is marrying into. Restrictions exist in marrying into the families in which a sister or a daughter has been married, with the exception in cases of economically poor families, where marriage by exchange is practised. Hypergamy and consanguineous marriages are not permitted, whereas, levirate and sororate are permitted. Traditionally child marriage followed by *gaona* was practised, but now adult marriages are practised at the age of 16 and 25 for girls and boys respectively. Among the various modes of acquiring mates, *byah* is the most common, the other forms being *batta-satta*, *ghar-javantri*, *bariana* and *jhind-phunk*. Monogamy is the general rule, with polygyny is resorted to in exceptional cases, where the first *lari* is unable to give the family an heir. The usual symbol for a married woman is a nose ring and a *choora*, but this is not being strictly adhered to these days. *Reet* or *lag* was prevalent, which traditionally consisted of giving of at least 60 silver coins, but today it has been replaced by voluntary dowry given in kind, and depends on the economic status of the person. Residence is usually patrilocal, but there is a tendency nowadays to separate soon after marriage due to various reasons.

Divorce is permitted and can be initiated by the aggrieved party on grounds of infidelity and incompatibility of nature, with sociojudicial approval. A divorcee is compensated by way of returning the marriage expenses. Children are normally the liability of the father in divorce cases, but in the event a divorcee woman wants to take them she can do so if the divorcee husband also desires the same. *Khewat* (divorcee remarriage) can however take place. Widow marriage is also permitted with either the husband's elder or younger brother and so is widower remarriage.

The family is of joint type, with father, mother unmarried and married sons and daughters and their children living in the same house. The interpersonal relations in the family are that of love, cordiality and mutual respect. The head of the family is the eldest male member and commands great respect. His decision on all family matters is final, which is usually arrived at after taking all factors into account. Conflict and confrontation never comes up but if it ever occurs, it is due to the checking of freedom of youngsters and on property matters. Avoidance is observed between a woman and her husband's elder male relatives for about a year after marriage, after which it is not strictly observed. Joking relationship exists between a man, his wife and their younger male and female relatives.

The inheritance of property is in the male line according to the locally recognized mode of inheritance known as *chundaband* and *mundaband.* According to the former, the property at the first instance is divided into the number of wives and subsequently each share is further sub- divided according to the number of sons. According to the latter, all sons, legal or illegal, inherit the father's property equally. Children on being taken by the divorced mother lose their right to their biological father's property; but can inherit on returning to their father or can share the their father's peoperty in the event of their mother geting remarried.

Women have no right to inheritance as per the traditional laws. Her social position is regarded as equal to that of the husband. She works equally with her husband in agricultural work except for ploughing. She is also responsible for the collection of fuel and fodder, both for immediate use and for storing them for use in the winter months. She traditionally did not work outside the four walls of the house but recently the educated girls have taken up jobs in various occupations and are working outside the house and adding to their family income. They also take part in all social, religious and ritual activities. Though girls' participation was limited traditionally to the casting of votes in elections, today they have started becoming more active and some have been nominated as members at the Block level. In addition to all her work outside the house, she also attends to all the household chores, which include cooking food and looking after the children. In spite of the tremendous role of women as an indispensable part of the Gaddi economy, they do not have any decision-making powers in family matters, though they do manage the family expenditure.

Restrictions on the movement on the enceinte women exist. The Kailubir is propitiated for the safe delivery of the child. *Sutak* is observed for a period of 11 days till which time all auspicious ceremonies are deferred. The mother is also not allowed to do any household work until *shuddhi* takes place. Six months after the birth of a child *khirpu* or *sugru* is celebrated, which is a ceremony observed jointly for naming and cereal-taking. This is followed by *jattu* ceremony, which is celebrated on the third, fifth or the seventh year. Marriage rituals are performed at the bride's residence, including *kanyadan* or *sanklap* and *pradikshna* or *char lavi* (walking round the fire four times), with the bridal knot having been tied to the bride and the groom. A feast is also arranged by the bride's parents. The nuptial ceremony is performed at the groom's residence. The dead are cremated, with the last rites being performed by the eldest male member. The mortal remains are then collected and either taken to Haridwar or thrown into any river. The house is considered polluted for a period of 13 days; the rituals connected with the dead are observed at *chha-mah* (six months), *barhi* (twelve months) and *chobarhi* (four years) after the death. Ancestors are worshipped annually during the days of *shradh*.

The majority of the Gaddi Rajputs are landowners and practise agriculture as their primary means of livelihood. They are also pastorals and own large flocks of sheep and goats, as a subsidiary occupation. This has also resulted in their *bartandari* (customary) rights on forest land which are Government owned. Today, many of them have also taken up jobs as teachers, in government and private organizations, and other white-collar jobs. Some are also working as unskilled labourers in Public Works Department and forest departments to augment their income.

The community has a total dependence on local market, where at times the people barter their meagre surplus cereal produce with the shopkeeper, who acts as middleman between the people and the market. Horticultural produce is sold to bigger markets through local collecting agents. Barter is rarely resorted to, and cash forms the usual medium of exchange. Though there has been a rise in the daily-wage casual labourers, yet no one is landless or a bonded labourer. The children below 15 years, both boys and girls, assist their parents in and outside the household activities, and also tend the cattle. While working as casual labourers in road maintenance they also receive wages in cash.

For solving family disputes, cases of theft, and for maintenance of traditional norms the people of the community have their traditional *bhaichara* panchayat, which is headed by a set of people who act as the jury, and who are elected by general consensus. The guilty are punished by social boycott, or fine in cash or kind, depending on the gravity of the crime. Though the Gram Panchayat has come up after Independence, for excercising social control, planning and implementing welfare and development activities, yet people have greater faith in their traditional panchayats.

The community professes Hinduism, with emphasis on the worship of Lord Shiva and faith in Shakti cults. This land is called Shiv Bhoomi. They also have faith in Kailu Bir, Nag Deota, Khetra Pal and Bambir, each being a presiding power over natural resources. Ancestors are worshipped and propitiated as family dieties for the welfare of the family. Sacred specialists are invited for performing family rituals. The major fairs of the region are the Sui Mela, Bharmaur Jatra, Minjar fair and Manimahesh fair. The festivals are, Dholru, Lohri, Holi, Janmasthami, Baisakhi/Basoa, Diwali and Shivratri.

The people are experts in weaving *pattu* and *gardu*. They also sing folk songs and dance to amuse themselves. Traditionally the women danced inside their houses but today they take part in dances at public places. A few of them have taken part in National Day celebrations. The folksongs are common to the region. Folklores and folktales about the heroic deeds of their ancestors and about the beauty of the womenfolk are also prevalent.

Traditionally they do not accept food from Hali and Sippi. *Mitr-bhai* (putative) kinship is established with persons who are not related but belong to an equal ranking community. Such a person is obliged to take part in family rites and rituals and is expected to behave as a real kin. They have separate cremation grounds. *Kameen-bartani* (patron-client) relationship exists with various serving communities like Hali, Sippi, Rihara and Lohar, who in lieu of their specialized services, are paid in kind at annual harvest.

Education and employment have brought them in contact with the wider world.Liberalization of the caste considerations have been observed in families which have got educated and moved to urban centres. The Gaddi Rajputs have started taking part in political activities at the regional level.

Their attitude towards the various developmental programmes excepting the family welfare programme is favourable. They are sending their children to schools. The boys receive education up to high school and beyond, the girls rarely continue beyond the primary level for social reasons. They respond to modern medicine at the primary health centres in combination with their indigenous medicine. Facilities like job reservations, Integrated Rural Development Programme loans and Rural Employment Schemes have helped in ameliorating their poverty. Drinking water is available to everyone through natural streams, whereas electricity is available only to a few. The remoteness of the area is a stumbling block in the development of the area.

Rajendra Sarkar

GADERIYA

The word Gaderiya or Gaderia, Gadarie comes from the word 'gadar' meaning sheep. Gaderiya is a caste of shepherds, and blanket weavers (Crooke, 1896). They have a scattered population in Himachal Pradesh, mostly in the foothills and the valleys but they are numerically far more in the adjoining states of Uttar Pradesh, Punjab and Haryana. They are said to have migrated from Khari village also known as Khidrabad in Haryana about a century ago. They left their original home as pastures were getting scarce for their flocks and settled in the foothills of Himachal Pradesh where there was plenty of grass and forests. Their exact population number at present is not known, but according to the Census of 1911 their population was only 16 in Himachal Pradesh. The dialect of the people is Haryanvi mixed with Hindi and words of Sirmauri, but with outsiders they speak in colloquial Hindi. The traditional dress for men is *dhoti, kurta,* and *orhni* but nowadays, the younger generation of men have started wearing *pyjama*-shirt or pant-shirt. The use of turban is limited to old people. Women have almost discarded the traditional *ghagra* in favour of *salwar-kameej.*

They are occasionally non-vegetarian, their staple diet consists of wheat, pulses of *urd, chana, kulth, moong* and *masur*, cooked in *toriya* (similar to mustard) oil. They use seasonal vegetables. The consumption of fruit is very occasional. Men are fond of smoking *bidi* and *hukka*. They also consume alcoholic drinks. Some women also smoke *bidi* but do not consume liquor. Tea is a common beverage among men, women and children. Betel chewing is not prevalent.

The Gaderiyas are divided in two main sections namely, Dhengar and Nikhar. To these two, a third section named Ochre is also sometimes added. They are further subdivided into numerous *gotra*, some of which are famous Rajput clans. The first two sections are endogamous and consider each other superior to the other. In the local hierarchy, they are placed in the lower-middle stratum in the Sudra varna. The community is endogamous but exogamy is maintained at the *gotra* level. Endogamy is also strictly maintained at the sub-group level. Marriage is settled outside the *gotra* of father, mother, mother's mother and father's mother. They are monogamous and a second marriage is only contracted in exceptional cases where the first wife has failed to produce an offspring. There are three forms of marriage: (a) *dan pun*—this is the regular form of marriage which is settled through negotiations and celebrated with full Vedic rituals, officiated by a Brahman; (b) the marriage by exchange (*batta-satta*); and (c) the much less prevalent marriage where bride price is taken as a precondition known as *mole-ki-sadi*. Divorce, *chhutta-chhutti,* is granted in exceptional circumstances on grounds of adultery, impotency or frigidity, cruelty, mental sickness and the like. This is invariably decided by the panchayat. In case the wife is deserted by the husband without sufficient reasons, a compensation is invariably demanded for the maintenance of wife and children and the dowry given at the time of marriage may be returned to the wife. Remarriage of widow, widower and divorcee is allowed and so are junior levirate and sororate. In case of widow remarriage, no regular ceremony takes place. A feast may be hosted for the *biradari* members and the woman may be presented with new clothes or a piece of jewellery. In the event of her remarriage outside her husband's family, she forfeits her claim to her deceased husband's property. Children remain in the custory of the father.

The family type is mostly of the joint type, but breaks up into nuclear family due to frequent domestic quarrels, growing intolerance among family members and unequal division of labour. The eldest male member heads the family and important decision are taken at his behest. The women observe purdah in the presence of the elder male members whereas, light-hearted joking relationship prevails with younger and peer groups. Property is inherited by all the sons equally. Succession is from father to the eldest son. In the absence of a male issue the daughter receives a share. In fact, the son-in-law is invited to manage the property.

Women do not enjoy an equal status with men, especially in terms of economic independence. Their politicoreligious identity is almost non-existent. Participation of women in politics is limited only to the casting of votes. However, in domestic spheres they play a major role. They also play an active role in family rituals and festivals. Women also participate actively in the economy, work in the agricultural field, tend to the flock of sheep and goat, bring fodder, fuel and water for the family, besides scores of other domestic work.

The life-cycle rituals from birth to death are no different from other neighbouring Hindu communities. They are by and large governed by Hindu beliefs and practices. Purificatory rites are observed on the sixth and tenth day following the birth of a child. On the sixth day, the mother and the child are given a bath. Sweets are distributed among fellow caste members. On the tenth day, a ceremony known as *jasuthan* is observed. A feast may be given to the *biradari* members and relatives. Post-birth pollution remains for 40 days after birth. *Mundan* is performed for a boy in the temple of a goddess and the shaving ceremony takes place there. The shaved hair are disposed off in a flowing river.

Marriage is performed as per Vedic rites. *Kanyadan* and *phera* constitute the most important ceremony of marriage which takes place at the bride's residence. When marriages were performed in childhood, consummation of marriage was deferred till the girl attains puberty. This was known as *muklawa.* It was followed by another ceremony known as *tarauja.* But nowadays, since marriages are performed after attaining adulthood, *muklawa* and *tarauja* ceremonies are performed simultaneously after marriage.

The dead are cremated and the ashes and bones are disposed off in water. Pollution is observed for 13 days. Important death rites are observed on the tenth day, i.e., *daswan* and the thirteenth day, i.e., *terahi.* The eldest son performs the death rites. Ancestor worship is done. The dead are commemorated annually in the *shradh* days.

The traditional occupation of the Gaderiya continues to be rearing and herding of sheep and goats which is supplemented substantially through agriculture. A majority of them have land and others have acquired it under land for landless scheme. They have their traditional customary rights in the forest for grazing their flock of sheep and goats. They can procure fuelwood, as also wood for construction of house on subsidized rates. Nowadays, there are increasing restrictions on cutting of wood for their personal use without a permit from the forest officials. A licence has to be obtained for grazing also. They maintain direct links with the local market which is fully regulated. Both barter and cash are the modes of exchange. The weekly market system does not operate in the region. They procure goods of everyday need from local shops or from nearby town markets. The agricultural produce is taken to the nearby grain market and is sold off, either directly or through a middleman. There are some members of this community in government service, and military and police services. Some of them are also teachers in local schools.

For the planning and implementation of welfare activities and maintenance of social order, there exists a statutory panchayat. However for purely domestic matters, petty family quarrels or similar issues are settled at their *biradari* who can impose cash penalty on the guilty. Economic offences such as theft, loss of property, encroachment of land or criminal cases are heard by the statutory council. Cash fine is levied on the offender and the revenue thus collected is spent on the general welfare activity of the village.

Predominantly Hindu by faith, the Gaderiyas worship the deities of the wider pantheon but profess more faith in the local (village) and regional deities. They are principally the worshippers of Shakti. The village deity, Khera Devta, is worshipped by all the communities, both Hindus and Muslims alike. An annual feast is arranged in honour of the village deity involving mass participation. Some of the regional deities worshipped by them are Shakhambari Devi and Jagadari Devi. Haridwar is their sacred centre. They celebrate all the major Hindu festivals and participate in the local regional fairs. Belief in evil spirits, ghosts, magic incantations and the like is quite widespread. They share oral traditions, folktales, folksongs and dances with others of the region.

The community shares rituals and has social and occupational bonds with certain communities. The Brahman acts as a ritual specialist for them for which he is paid both in cash and kind. Traditional *jajmani* relations exist with the Nai and Chamar. They are paid a certain share of the produce at each harvest. A Nai not only cuts and shaves hair, but acts as a messenger of good news at the time of marriage and birth. He also carries ceremonial objects at the time of marriage. A Chamar carries the dead and is remunerated for his services. Connubial norms are maintained strictly with their fellow members. They can accept food both *kachcha* and *pucca* from Brahman. They take *pucca* food from Bahti, Jheevar and Nai. Water resources are common.

Formal education has been only partly favourable for the Gaderiya boys and girls who study respectively up to secondary and primary levels after which they drop out for economic and social reasons. People use modern medicine in addition to traditional health practices. Family welfare programme has found some favour with the people and a few women and men have even opted for sterilization. Electricity is available in the village but few persons have availed themselves of the electricity connections. Drinking water is provided through pipe. But as the pipes are not functioning properly, they procure water from the local Giri river. Through Integrated Rural Development Programme and Employment Guarantee Scheme some people have taken loans to mitigate their economic hardship. People listen to radio, watch television, and see movies shown by extension agencies. Roads exist but post offices are far-off. Wood and cowdung cakes are used as major sources of fuel. Irrigation facility is not available and the people are mostly dependent on rain water. This explains the low use of chemial fertilizers and pesticides. Mid-day meal programmes, Integrated Child Development Scheme and facility of public distribution system are taken benefit of.

Vatsala Sarkar

GAUR BRAHMAN

The Gaur Brahmans claim to be the original Gaur (Adigaur) and trace their origin to the Brahmans residing in Nadia and Shantipur in West Bengal. The entire village of Ranva Nagri (Ranvi) in Rampur is owned by the Gaur Brahmans. Their migration and settlement in the Sarahan area of Shimla district has an interesting story behind it.

Sarahan, whose earlier name was Shorinitpur was the kingdom of a demon Banasur. He had a beautiful daughter Usha. One day she dreamt of a prince and was lost in his thoughts. Her friend, Chitralekha, came to know of it through Usha. She was a good artist. She made portraits of all the princes of India, and asked Usha to identify the portrait which matched the man of her dreams. When the portrait of Anirudh (also known as Pradiyuman), the grandson of Lord Krishna was shown, she at once recognized it. When Banasur came to know of his daughter's love, he brought Anirudh to his kingdom with his *tantaric* rituals. Next day when Anirudh was not seen in Dwarika, there was a commotion and everyone started searching for him but could not locate him anywhere. One day Narad Muni while travelling through Shorinitpur saw Anirudh. He went and told Krishna at Dwarika. Enraged, Krishna with his army—which also included Gaur Brahmans to perform the rites and rituals, advanced towards Shorinitpur, and defeated Banasur and his army. As a treaty, Anirudh was married to Usha and the soldiers and Brahmans who went with Krishna stayed back. Since then, the story goes, Gaur Brahmans have continued to stay there.

Presently they are spread all over Himachal Pradesh, but Sarahan till today enjoys the privilege of being the last Brahman village on the Indian territory. Kinnaur, the adjoining territory, does not have any Brahman and Brahmans from this village are called to perform the rites and rituals.

The language spoken by the people among themselves and with locals is Bushairi, but with outsiders Hindustani is used. Earlier the script used among themselves was Tankri, but now it has been forgotten by many and they are using the Devanagari script. The community was identified in olden times by the presence of a cue and a red *tilak* mark on the forehead, but these are no longer a community marker. Unlike the Brahmans of the plains, the community is non-vegetarian and they only take meat of goat, sheep and fish. Chicken, *ghural*, egg, pork, beef and buffalo meat are prohibited. Their staple food consists of wheat *chapati*, rice, *rongi*, and *mah-ki-dal* accompanied by vegetables, which are moderately used. Mustard oil and *desi ghee* are the ususal cooking media. Roots and tubers of the locally available variety like *bhalku*, *linger, nokhi* are also widely used. Wild fruits like *jami, vaimi, aakhi* and *chuli* in addition to apples, peaches, plums and apricots are also consumed during their season. *Guchhi* (*Morchella esculents*) and *chienv* —a variety of mushrooms are also consumed. *Chhang* (alcoholic drink) is consumed by both the sexes and is taken occasionally. The drink is either homemade or is sometimes purchased from market. Milk and milk products are taken by the community either in their original form or in the derived forms. The people neither chew tobacco nor betal leaves. However, they do smoke tobacco either in cigarettes, *bidi* or *hukka*. There are some restrictions on eating certain kinds of food. *Bhalku* is taken only during the winter months; *linger* is not taken after the month of Asarh (July-August); and *nokhi* is taken only during the summer months.

The Gaur Brahmans are divided into Shukla, Krishna and Bhojki or Pujari subdivisions. The two latter groups are equal but inferior to the first. The Shuklas are further subdivided into two occupational groups: (a) non-agriculturists—those who observe Brahmanical rites prescribed by the Shastras; and the (b) the agriculturist who do agriculture, against the Brahmanical dictates of Shastras. The Krishna Brahmans are also cultivators. They accept alms, and also practise widow remarriage. Bhojki is a term that usually refers to the hereditary temple priests of Jawalamukhi, Bajreshwari and other goddesses. The term appears to be from *bhoj* (to feed) that is, the one who offers food to gods and goddesses.

There is yet another group of Brahmans called Parasrami Brahman, who reside primarily in the villages of Singra, Saneri, Ladra, Darsa and Majali in the Rampur tehsil of the Shimla district. It is said that these villages were once upon a time occupied by castes like Sonar, Lohar and Dom, and Lord Parasuram, while passing through the village purified them and converted them to Brahmans and from then on they are called as Parasrami Brahman. They now have adopted the customs of the Gaur, and have started giving daughter to and taking daughters from them in marriage. The Gaurs are divided into various *gotra*, which are further subdivided into pravara, sikha, sutra, veda, upveda and pada. The function of these subdivisions is to assess the status at the time of entering into matrimonial relations. Nowadays, these have been forgotton, and only *gotra* are recognized for regulating the marriage.The Brahmans regard themselves as socially superior to all other communities. This fact is also confirmed by other neighbouring communities. They recognize the varna *vayavastha* and rank at the top of it.

Though monogamy is the prevalent rule, a few stray cases of polygamy are also known. These have been primarily in cases where the first wife has not been able to give a heir to a family. Endogamy at community level is the rule of marriage with exogamy being practised at *gotra* level. Only the *gotra* which is the same as one's own is avoided for the purposes of marriage.

Hypergamy is also practised. A Shukla can take a bride from Krishna and Bhojki, the Krishna from a Bhojki, but the latter two cannot take brides from the Shukla. Similarly Parasrami Brahmans, till about eight decades ago, married within themselves, with the exclusion of the self-*gotra*. With the changing times and attitudes, marriages between Gaur and Bhojki and Parasrami Brahmans are frequently taking place. Consanguinity is prohibited. Junior levirate and sororate are practised, which at one time were prohibited.

Both in old times and in present times, adult marriages were and are still in practice. The most prevalent form of acquiring mates among the Brahman is *byah* the other form being *ghasit lana* (marriage by symbolic capture), wherein the girl of a community is forcibly lifted and carried away. Yet, another form of marriage is *haar*. In this type, a married woman who does not want to stay with her husband, elopes with her married or unmarried fiancee, and the parmour has to return the *reet* as worked out by the panchayat. Marriage by negotiation is of two types: (a) *gaur vivah*, in which at the time of *phera* a *dharam bhai* (ritual kin) is made, and (b) the *sita vivah*, the marriage which is simply performed by seven *phera*.

There are no symbols of marriage among these hill Brahmans. Vermilion in the parting of the hair is applied at the time of marriage, though this is not strictly observed. Neither the practice of bride-price nor that of dowry are prevalent. The bride's father however gives gifts as per his economic status. The gifts are usually ornaments and other things of daily use and are given in kind. The rule of residence after marriage is patrilocal. In the event when there is no male child in the family, the son-in-law is invited to stay with the family, and is known as *gharjwain*.

Chhut is permissible in the community. The aggrieved party can initiate divorce proceedings by applying to the panchayat. Matrimonial ties are broken by asking the person intending to divorce to break a small twig over the head of the other. The common grounds for divorce are constant bickerings between daughter-in-law and mother-in-law, mental incompatibility between husband and wife, infidelity by either of the spouses, impotency and chronic sickness. *Izzat dena* (compensation) is decided by the panchayat, which is usually double the amount spent on marriage and is given to the aggrieved. Sometimes the formal consent of the panchayat is sought later. This usually happens in cases where a woman is in love and leaves the first husband and starts living with her paramour. In such a case, the annulment occurs later when the panchayat is informed and the *harzana* (fine) is paid by the paramour.The children are the liability of the father in divorce cases, but at times when the child is very small, he/she is taken by the mother, who is given a fixed amount by the panchayat for bringing up the child. Such a child goes back to the father after growing up. Widow, widower, male and female divorcee remarriage is permissible. Widow and widower remarriage can occur within or outside the family. Widow remarriage with husband's younger brother is called as *suhag lagana.* Marriage with wife's younger sister is also practised and is called as *samjhauta.*

A change in marriage rules has recently been observed. Certain Brahman boys have married Rajput girls and such a trend is now picking up. As such the rule of endogamy within the community is on the decline. The rule of junior sororate and levirate is also on the decline and people now prefer to marry outside the family. Persons marrying outside the community were earlier excommunicated but this is not done at present. The only restriction still observed is the abstinence from accepting *kachcha* food prepared by the girl of other community, by the people of the boy's community.

The family is of the vertically extended type, in which all paternal relations live in the same household. But, now-a-days the tendency is to separate and set up a nuclear family. Interfamily relations are that of love and cordiality, with the eldest male member of the house commanding great respect. His decisions in family matters are honoured by all the members. More often than not, the decisions are arrived at after consulting other family members. Rarely does a situation of conflict and confrontation come up, but in case this happens, it is usually related to property disputes or when the freedom of youngsters is checked.For about a year after marriage, avoidance is observed between the bride and her husband's elder male relatives and all others in that line, including the mother-in-law. This is usually discontinued after the first delivery. Joking relationships exist with the husband's younger relatives, both male and female, and also with the wife's younger relatives. Property is equally inherited by all sons. In case there are many wives, the share is first divided according to the wives and then each share is further subdivided according to the number of sons. Besides property, even the father's *jajmani* is equally divided among the sons. In the event there is no son, it passes on to the collaterals. Similarly the property of a childless couple also passes on to the collaterals.

The women's right of inheritance of property is limited. Only when there is no male issue in the family can the women inherit. Otherwise, a woman has no right to her father's property but has rights in her husband's property. The women work practically in all spheres, both in and out of the family. They take part in all agricultural operations except ploughing, and augment the family income by working on the fields of others as agricultural labourers. They are also responsible for bringing grass, fodder for the animals and fuel. The women take part in all social and religious festivals and are an integral part of all rituals. No *yajna* (offerings to the fire) is regarded as complete without the presence of *ardhangini* (wife). Though she has no role in the social control mechanism, her role in political spheres is limited to the casting of votes. The women also do not have any direct role in decision-making, but they are instrumental in guiding their husbands for arriving at certain decisions. They are managers of the house and are responsible for bringing up the children, looking after household chores such as cooking and managing the affairs of the family. They also control and contribute to the family income.

The birth of a son is welcome in the family, for it is supposed to bring salvation to the parents. The post-delivery pollution for the mother exists for 10 days, until which time the mother is not allowed to enter the kitchen or cook food. A child is named by a priest by looking into the horoscope. *Jarolan* (tonsure) ceremony is observed for both boys and girls. The ceremony is usually held at home. A week after the first ceremonial head shave, *nashranva,* is observed at home, where the head of the baby boy is again shaved off, but a *choti* is left on the occiput. The head-shaving ceremony is done preferably in the first year of birth, but sometimes it is deferred for the third year. In case of females, second shaving is not observed.

There is the first ceremonial feeding of the child after six months when *kheer* is fed to the child by the mother on an auspicious day. *Upnayan* (thread-wearing) is prescribed at the age of five years for Brahmans, but among the Gaur Brahmans it is observed just before marriage, and forms almost a part of marriage rituals.

Marriage is celebrated with gaiety. Some marriage rituals for both the boys and the girls are performed at their respective places. The actual ceremony is solemnized at the bride's residence. It is a simple ceremony in which the boy and girl feed each other with *gur* (jaggery) and *ghee.* A red *ghanra* also known as *mauli* (a replica of a crown) is tied to the couple who, then, circumambulate the fire seven times, in the midst of chanting of *mantra* (verses) by the *purohit,* called a *bedi.* A feast is given by both the sides at their respective places, but the feast given by the bride's father constitutes the actual marriage feast, as it is given at the occasion of marriage. Nuptial ceremony is performed at the groom's residence.

As a rule the Brahmans are cremated, but for children below the age of three years either *jal-pravah*(immersion in river) or burial is practised. In both the cases, a wooden box (coffin) is prepared and the deceased child is laid in it before being either immersed or buried. In case of cremation the last rites are performed by the eldest male member of the family. In the event of death of a pregnant woman, the husband or sweeper (Bhangi), more often the former, operates on the dead women's womb, removes the child and buries him, and cremates the former. The mortal remains of the deceased are disposed of in the river. The purificatory rights are observed on the tenth day, when some belongings of the deceased are given to the Kartu or the Acharaj. Alms are also given on the first death anniversary, and regularly thereafter until the *chautha* (fourth year), when again gifts are given to the Kartu or Acharaj and sometimes even to Shukla in the name of the dead.

The major economic resource of the community is land. They received the land as gifts from the feudal lords and rich landlords in lieu of the traditional services rendered by the Brahmans to them. These resources are controlled by the heads of the individual families. The majority of the community members own land. The land is used for the purpose of agriculture and horticulture plantation. The traditional occupation of the community has been the performing of rites and rituals at house, and this continues even today. Besides this they ate in government and private service and business. They sell their agricultural and horticultural produce in cash in most cases. There has been a recent increase in the horticultural plantations, because of the low yields from the agricultural fields.

Children below the age of 15 years also assist their parents in their household activities. Boys tend to the cattle, help their parents in fields and also work in others' field as agricultural labourers. They are remunerated in cash as well as kind. A change has been observed in the economic activity since Independence. People have drifted from their traditional occupation of *purohiti* (sacredotal services) to agriculture and horticulture plantation.

The community has a panchayat of its own, to maintain social norms. The members are elected by general consensus. The number of members who officiate in a panchayat varies, and often includes the relatives of both the parties. The panchayat dispenses justice in matters relating to adultery, disrespect for the traditional panchayat, elopement and divorce, and offenders are penalized by cash fines. Though the statutory panchayats exist for the implementation of welfare schemes and for maintenance of law and order, still the traditional panchayat continues to exercise a greater hold on the community.

The majority of the Gaur Brahmans are Shaivites. They also worship the Shaligram ammonite as an emblem of Vishnu, and a triangular piece of phallic stone representing Devi, the consort of Lord Shiva. There are also a few Vallabhachari and Vaishnav among the Gaurs.They have family gods represented by Bhagwati, Shaligram and Ram, which are worshipped and propitiated on all festive occasions. They are worshipped everyday to invoke their blessing for the welfare of the family. Goddess Bhagwati and Pothi Devta are the village deities, and are worshipped by all the communities of the village. There is also a temple of Bhima Kali Devi in the village, which is represented by Bhagwati, and is worshipped as a village deity for the welfare of the village and also to ward off any calamity in the village. Visharu or Basharu Deota is their regional deity and villagers up to Kinnaur have a great faith in him. The sacred centres and places of pilgrimage of the Brahmans are Naina Devi, Jawalaji, Kangra Devi, Chamunda Devi and Baijnath.

A Brahman's own religious observances are performed by his daughter's father-in-law, or by some relative of the latter. A sister's son is also employed sometimes. It is purely a matter of convenience. The role of a sacred specialist is to officiate at family rituals except at death, when an Acharaj officiates.

The major festivals of the region are Lohri, Maghi, Basant Panchami, Shivratri, Navratri, Ganga Dashmi, Dev Shainjani, Rihali, Janamashthami, Ganga Naumi, Sair, Sharad Poornima and Hari Prabodhni festivals. The important fairs are Lavi, Dussehra, Kungal Bahl, Dhal fair, Tharsu, Fagu and Birshu fair. All the communities take part in them.

The community members are adept in drawing and painting. Whenever any religious performance is to be given or rituals are to be performed, coloured designs are made on the floor with *atta* (flour), *abir* and *gulal* to represent *navgraha* (the house of nine planets). The women are deft in the art of *alpana*, which they make with rice paste with or without turmeric. The women also engage in body painting on festive occasions. During the Shravana months, the women and young girls colour their palms with *mehndi*. The married women must colour their feet and nails as this is regarded auspicious. Folksongs like Jhoori, Malku and Gol are sung mainly by womenfolk on festive occasions within the four walls of the house. Men generally do not take part in dance.

Being Brahmans of a high order, they accept *sidha* food from other communities. The commensal norms are at two levels, one with the ritually pure communities and the other with the unclean communities. From the ritually pure (i.e., the Rajputs), they accept only *pucca* food cooked in their house. A Gaur Brahman may accept *kachcha* or *pucca* food from the Acharaj or Mahacharaj. The former, that is, the Gaur Brahman and their allies, can however accept *pucca* food from their clients, provided the food is cooked by a Brahman in a separate place. The norms for acceptance of the *kachcha* and *pucca* food are so rigid that even in case where a Brahman has married a Rajput girl none other than her own hushand in the family will accept the *kachcha* food prepared by her. Traditionally, the *hukka* was shared among the Brahmans alone, but now it is being shared with the Rajputs also but he will either put his hand over the nipple and then smoke or will remove the nipple. The *hukka* is not shared with any other community.

The custom of making putative kinship *dharam bhai* exists among the Brahmans. In almost all the Gaur *vivah*, a girl at the time of marriage adopts a *dharam bhai*, who is one of the male members of the groom's village, and has come with the marriage party. The girl feeds the *dharam bhai* with *gur* and *ghee* and ties a *mauli* to the boy's wrist. Thereafter, the boy vows to protect the honour of the girl, whom he accepts as a sister.

The traditional *jajmani* relationship existed among the Brahmans and other communities in the performance of rituals by Brahmans at the clients' houses. In return for the specialized services rendered, they were paid in cash and kind which consisted of cereals, *pattu* and clothes. The amount and quantity to be paid depends on the economic status of the family. The modern intercommunity linkages have brought many changes in them. They now actively take part in political activities, canvassing and/or at times even contesting elections. They usually give their lands situated far-off to members of other communities members to cultivate, and share the crop at harvest.

The attitude of the people of this community towards literacy and education has always been more positive for the boys who go for higher education up to post-graduate level. The girls study mainly up to college level, beyond which they discontinue. The attitude of the community towards modern system of medicare is favourable and they are taking both allopathic and ayurvedic medicines along with their traditional homemade remedies. The attitude of the younger generation towards family welfare programmes is also favourable, but they prefer to have two or three children, regulating their families by using modern contraceptive devices.

Drinking water facility is available through piped water. A few have received grants under self-employment schemes for setting up shops. The village is well connected by metalled roads, on which public transport plies. Postal, telegraph and telephone facilities are also available in some of the villages. People listen to radio sets and watch television, either at home or on community sets. People also see movies, shown to them by extension agencies. All the houses of the village have electricity connections. Some places, especially the village lanes, are provided with streetlights for which solar energy is tapped by using solar panels. The major fuel resource for the community is fuelwood, but most of the houses also use kerosene to meet their demand. Irrigation is only through rainwater. They are using chemical fertilisers along with organic manures. Pesticides are primarily being used in horticulture. In Balvadi the expectant and the nursing mothers and children between 0-5 age groups are provided with milk, soya products and immunization facilities. Public distribution system is availed of and the food items are provided to the people at a controlled price. The attitude towards savings and investment is also favourable and they are investing money in a bank in the village. The people are self-sufficient and are not depedent on money-lenders or shopkeepers.

Rajendra Sarkar

GHAI

As the name signified, Ghai, Ghasi or Ghasiara, all synonyms, were traditionally grasscutters (*ghas* or *gha* stands for grass) of the erstwhile rulers employed for the purpose of supplying grass fodder to their horses, mules and elephants. Gradually, they formed a community of their own. There is no historical and ethnographic account of the community except a brief note on the community in Rose (1919) and Ibbetson (1916). Their exact population number is also not known but they are mainly living in Kangra, Bilaspur, Mandi, Solan and Shimla districts. In Bilaspur they live in the town along the Satluj river converted into a big lake called Govind Sagar by the construction of Bhakhra Nangal dam. The terrain is hilly and climate is warm and temperate with medium rainfall and humidity. The hill ranges are covered with thin forests of pine trees and rarely receive snowfall.

They speak regional dialects, e.g., Kehluri or Bilaspuri in Bilaspur, Kangri in Kangra and Mandiali in Mandi districts of the western Pahari and communicate in Devanagari script both within and outside the community. The men wear *kurta* and *pyjama* or pant and *kurta*. The women wear *salwar* and a *dupatta* or *chunni* or *chadru*. The women usually wear a *laung* or *tilli* as an ornament.

The Ghais eat the same food as the other local people of the area. They eat fish, meat and eggs occasionally. The staple food is maize, wheat and rice along with various pulses like *urd, kulthi, masur,* gram, peas and beans and various seasonal vegetables. The cooking medium is mustard oil or vegetable *ghee.* Those who keep buffaloes also consume *desi ghee.* Roots and tubers are eaten frequently. The intake of fruits is seasonal and fruits like apples, peaches, guava, mangoes and bananas are taken. Men consume country liquor occasionally, during marriages or on other festive occasions. Liquor is purchased from the local market. Milk intake is poor among the non-agricultural people of the community but milk and milk products are frequently consumed in rural areas. They also smoke *bidi,* cigarette or indigenous *hukka,* but chewing or snuffing tobacco are not characteristic of the community.

The Ghais may have different groups like the Jogi in Bilaspur. The clans are units which regulate marrriages and which also indicate descent/ancestry. Some of their *gotras* are Kaundal, Kasab, Manhas, etc., and they associate themselves with the Kshatriya varna. However, others usually see them as belonging to the Sudra varna. They desire to be included among the scheduled castes because of their matrimonial alliances with the Drain and

Dumna who are already classified in this category.

Although largely endogamous, marriages also occur outside the community; *got* and village/locality exogamay is adhered to. Their marriages also occur in different towns and districts. The marriages age has presently increased to above 16 years for girls and above 20 for boys, but a few decades back pre-puberty marriages were quite common and bride price too was a common practice or exchange of sisters occurred frequently. But presently they perform *kanyadan* and give some dowry in the form of domestic items to the girl. Marriages occur through negotiation and monogamy is practised. Bigamy occurs in rare circumstances if the first wife is childless. Marriage symbols are *sindur*, glass bangles, *koka* or *tilli* or *laung* or coiled nose ring called *murki* which however is not in practice now. The bride's residence is patrilocal. Widow and widower re-marriages, junior levirate and sororate are socially approved. Junior levirate marriage is without any ritual and simply called *baithana* or *chadar dalna* or *jhanjrara.* Divorce is also permitted on grounds of maladjustment and cruelty to wife, and either of the spouses may seek divorce. Usually compensation or maintenance amount is fixed for the livelihood of the divorced wife, and children remain the liability of the father. Both the divorcees may remarry. Presently, they prefer legal course for divorce to avoid difficulties faced by the community council in resolving such disputes.

The family pattern is predominantly nuclear and married sons usually get separated especially after father's death. In joint families the *lari* maintains avoidance relationship with her *saurah*, *jeth* and *nandoi.* Informal joking relationships also exist between *devar-bhabi*, *jija-sali*, *jija-sala* and *nanad-bhabhi.* Daughters lack the right of inheritance to father's property and property is inherited as per the rule of male equigeniture. The eldest son succeeds the father after his death. The reasons of conflict generally concern distribution of property or earnings of the father.

The status of women is deemed low even though they contribute to the family income by assisting the men in their daily routine and act as mid-wives and render labour services to village farmers or moneylenders to make an economic contribution to the family. They do all types of domestic duties and participate in agricultural and animal husbandry activities, collect fuel and fodder and bring potable water. They also participate in social and religious ceremonies but have little say in the mechanism of social control and political spheres.

The life-cycle rituals are performed by their community priest by observing certain Vedic rites. Pre-delivery rituals are not observed though the woman has to observe certain restrictions, both pre- and post-natal. Birth pollution called *sutak* is observed for 13 days and purification of woman occurs by taking *gunt* and the water of the Ganges. A name may be given to a child by consulting the priest but no ceremony is observed. The only childhood ritual is *jamalu* or *jatlu/mundan* for boys performed by the child's *mama* on an odd year after birth. Some take religious procession, *jatra,* to Nahar Singh, a local deity.

The marriage rituals are similar to those of the other Hindus of the area. Clan deity is propitiated by the family and bridegroom. At the time of marriage, the major rituals are *lagan* and *ved* performed at the bride's residence when the *lari* and *lara* circumambulate the sacred fire and pledge for a peaceful cohabitation. The girl's parents perform *kanyadan* and a feast is arranged for the bridegroom's party. At the groom's place they worship a *pipal* or *banah* or *daran* tree and circumambulate it. The marriage ends with dancing and a feast to the community and the bride's kins by the groom's party. The *muklawa* occurs on the next auspicious day of the marriage at the groom's place.

The death rites are also performed by their community priest. The dead are cremated and their ashes are immersed in the Satluj river (in Bilaspur) or in the Beas (in Kangra) or some people go to Hardwar for immersion in the Ganges and offer *pind dan* to a *panda.* Ancestor worship is observed at the end of *patak* period on the thirteenth day by a purificatory *havan* and taking *heeng* and making offerings to a *dhyan* of the family and finally serving meals to the gathered kinsmen. Annual death rite, *barkhi,* and the fourth annual rite, *chabarkh*, are also observed to commemorate the dead.

The Ghais are an almost a landless community or possesses little landholdings in the rural areas. Most of them are engaged in jobs of general labour in the countryside. They work as agricultural, road, forest or daily-wage casual labourers. They also till land on cash contract or sharecrop basis in the villages. Many persons have adopted different professions or occupations like, tailoring, barbery and masonry. A few run petty general merchant shops. Some persons are employed in government jobs and as school teachers and clerks, and also in the army. Child labour exists. The links with the market are direct and market is fully regulated and dealings are in cash.

There is no formal *biradri* or community council but the *sayane* of the community try to resolve the social disputes. The ward members or members of the statutory Gram Panchayat usually solve village disputes over land and water but serious matters involving violence and property disputes are taken to civil courts.

The Ghais are Hindus and worship gods and goddesses of the pantheon order and different family/clan, village and regional deities. Badoli Devi, Naina Devi, Nahar Singh, Deot Sidh (Balak Nath) and Lakhdata are propitiated as family/clan/village or regional deities. Guga is also propitiated during Rakshabandan, when Guga fairs are held at different places. There are different fairs/festivals of the local deities which are celebrated with great zeal.

Nalwari cattle fair is famous in Bilaspur and is held annually. They celebrate various Hindu festivals like Lohri, Baisakhi, Chiran, Sair, Rakshabandan, Dussehra, Diwali and Holi which are of socioeconomic and socioreligious significance. Sacred specialists are from the community and some like *chela* or *puchh-wala* (fortune teller) from other communities are also consulted to treat certain ailments. They share Pahari folksongs, tales, music and dance. Popular folksongs are *Mohan, Gambri, Ranjhu-Phulmu, Kunju-Chenchlo,* etc.

Traditional intercommunity linkages of the Ghai are mainly confined to the Dumna/Bhanjra and Drain in terms of commensal annd connubial norms.

Modern developmental programmes have made a limited impact on the Ghais. Formal education is favoured for the boys but they usually do not go in for higher/college education due to economic reasons. The girls are usually supposed to remain less educated than the boys due to social reasons. They are not regarded as job seekers but merely liabilities to be got rid off by marriage. Modern system of health and medicare is favoured but ill-afforded by the poor who usually go for indigenous methods of treatment. They do favour small family size and use sterilization as a method for that purpose. But at least one son, who is also a bread earner and support for old age, is considered essential even if they have to have more girls in that attempt.

Drinking water through pipes is available at their doorsteps but sometimes traditional sources may also be used whenever they are available in the rural areas. They deny having availed themselves of any benefits from rural develoment programmes (IRDP) though provisions for these do exist. They are mainly self-employed. Some of them avail themselves of modern facilities of mass media, like radio, television and cinema in the town, and road and postal facilities are available in the vicinity. Their houses have electricity connections. Fuel resources are firewood, cowdung cakes, coal, sawdust and kerosene oil. Some landowners use chemical fertilizers and organic manure. Immunization among ICDS programmes for children is also availed of. Facility of public distribution system is availed of. Most of the people are economically weak and dependent on moneylenders and shopkeepers, especially in the rural areas.

A.R. Sankhyan

GHIRATH

The Ghirath/Ghirth, Ghrit or Chowdhary come next to the Brahman and Rajput as the predominant Hindu community in the north-western part of Himachal Pradesh. Etymologically, Ghirath is derived from *ghrita* or *ghee* as per a legend Shiva made them out of *ghee* (Rose, 1919:288). They are said to be the most indefatiguable people and very industrious and successful cultivators. They have two main subgroups, the Bahti (after *hal bahna,* i.e., ploughing) and the Chahang in Punjab. The Ghirath is a Pahari (hill) name and its etymology from *ghee* reveals their traditional occupation of animal husbandry and agriculture. However, some knowledgeable persons of the community claim their descent from a saint known as Ghrit Rishi and also associate themselves with the Kaurvas of the Mahabharata. According to some researchers, the references to this community are available in the Vedas and Puranic scriptures. They claim Rajput or Kshatriya descent but like many other communities their origin and migration is shrouded in mystery. The community is critical about its name and status, etc. Their *mahasabha* wants to call the community with the name of Ghrit and not Ghirath, as they are known in local parlance. They, however, like the name Chowdhary used for them.

They seem to be very remote inhabitants of the soil alongwith the Khasa. They are predominantly distributed in the district Kangra, Una, Hamirpur and Bilaspur, but are also scattered in all the other regions of Himachal Pradesh. They speak regional dialects like Kangri and Bilaspuri (or Kehluri) among themselves and with the neighbouring people and write in the Devanagari script. Men wear *kurta* and *pyjama* (or pant) and the women wear *kurti*, *salwar* and *chadru*.

Their staple food is maize, wheat and rice. Various types of pulses—*urad, moong, kulthi, masur, arhar*, peas, beans and grams are eaten. They also eat fish, eggs and meat of goat and sheep. But commonly they take vegetarian diet only. Men sometimes are fond of country liquor purchased from the local market. Milk and milk products are consumed in large quantities. Fruit and vegetables are eaten moderately. The festive foods are *khitchri* on Lohri, *ankli/ ankloo* and *kheer* on Diwali/Dussehra, *babru* on Baisakhi and Nauhle, *seviyan* on Sair as special preparations. Food taboos are observed on certain festivals, fasts and during death pollution.

Bio-anthropological information on the community synonymised with the Chowdhary is discussed in the bio-anthropological report.

They have numerous *al* or *septs*. Rose (1919) mentioned eight large subdivisions of Ghirath—namely Kaundal, Bhardwaj, Pathari, Chhabru, Reru, Badial, Chhora and Bhattu. Most of their sections carry the names of animals, plants, colours, different occupations, and are totemistic in origin.

The Ghiraths are endogamous but in some cases, there are cases of intermarriage with some other communities. Village and *got* exogamy is maintained. During pre-Independence period child marriages were very frequent in the community but now post- puberty/adult marriages are performed. Their matrimonial alliances are fixed through negotiation by a negotiator known as *rabara* or *rabaru*. The exchange of sisters called *batta-satta* was a common feature in the recent past and bride-price called *brina* was prevalent in case no sister existed in the family for exchange. The exchange marriages are now mainly limited to the poor and resourceless families or where the boys and the girls are illiterate. In cases where the man marries a second time, called *dhuwaju*, bride-price is also taken but since it is not favoured socially, it is taken secretly. Such cases are however only exceptions. Dowry has become almost a regular feature now and the girl is offered in *dan*. Monogamy is the rule, but a second wife is desired in case of no children, without divorcing the first wife. *Sindur*, glass bangles, *bindi* and nose ring/pin and bridal finger-ring are symbols of a married woman. The residence of the married girl is patrilocal.

Widow remarriage is permitted as junior levirate through a brief ritual called *jhanjrara* or *chadar dalna*. Junior sororate is also permitted. Divorce is permissible in cases of maladjustment, cruelty, insanity and impotency for either of the sexes. Children in such cases may live either with father or mother. Presently, the divorce cases are, however, dragged to the court of law and the woman receives compensation and man is also responsible for the children.

The Ghiraths have nuclear as well as vertically extended families. The inheritance is patrilineal and as per the male equigeniture, and the division of property is by *chundaband* system when man has two wives; succession is patrilineal and the eldest son succeeds the father. Avoidance relationship of *lari* with *saurah*, *jeth* and *nandoi* often exists. Joking relations are seen between *devar* and *bhabi*, *jija* and *sali*, *jija* and *sala* and *nanad* and *bhabi*.

The Ghirath women participate in various economic activities, including casual/daily-wage agricultural labour and as maid-servants, mid-wives, etc. They discharge the usual domestic duties, collect fuel and fodder, fetch potable water and participate in various social, ritual and religious activities. Generally the mechanisms of social control and political spheres are not within their domain.

Post-delivery pollution called *sutak* is observed for 13 days and purification occurs by taking cow's urine, on the seventh and thirteenth day called *gunt* or *guntrala*. Christening ceremony is not observed but a Brahman priest suggests the name after consulting the horoscope. The *mundan* ceremony is performed for boys on odd years after birth by the mother's brother. The hair of the eldest son is cut at the shrine of a regional deity like Balakrupia (in Kangra district) or Deot Sidh (in Hamirpur district) by affluent families/or regular devotees.

The marriage is performed as per the Sanatan Dharma rituals by a Brahman. It commences with *sand* and *samuhat* followed by *mehndi* and oil ceremony called *tel-talwai*. At the bride's place marriage rituals like *lagan, ved* and *kanyadan* are performed and the bride and groom circumambulate the sacred fire. The bride's parents arrange a feast for the groom's party. At the bridegroom's place, both bride and groom worship *pipal* tree and some worship a *daran* tree and circumambulate it. The *muklawa* ceremony occurs on the next day after marriage. The *lari* does not live with her mother-in-law during the first *kala mahina* (Bhadon).

Death rituals are performed by a *purohit* and an Acharaj. The dead are cremated and their ashes are immersed in the Ganges at Hardwar or at Beas in Kangra.On father's death the sons and nephews shave off their heads. Ancestor worship is observed during the *patak*. The Acharaj performs the death rites on the thirteenth day and seeks offerings in the name of the dead. This is followed by a community meal. The annual death rite called *barkhi* is performed by a Barkhu or Masku. The last death rite is known as *chabarkh* performed in the fourth year.

Agriculture and animal hushandry are the major occupations of the Ghiraths and they are also variously employed as agricultural labourers and cultivators for which they are especially noted. This is revealed from the popular saying in the area: '*Ghirath bachcha jam paya, daal basoot kamb paya*' (meaning when a Ghirath is born, all the bushes in the field are scared of being uprooted). They have assimilated all types of labours. There is no landless and bonded labour in the commuity. Child labour is prevalent in the community, besides assistance by children in the agricultural and animal husbandry pursuits of the family. Ghirath children also work in agricultural fields and homes of Brahmans/Rajputs or big landlords. They also find employment in hotels/cooking *dhabas* and canteens in various neighbouring towns and cities. People also till land for big landlords on contract or on sharecropping and/or daily wages. At present, however, the community has also adopted various occupations and sought employment in trade, industries, government jobs, banks, etc.

The Akhilbhartiya Kshatriya Ghrit, Chahang and Bahti Mahasabha is actively engaged in the welfare of the community. The election of the *pradhan* is held through a voice vote and the functions of the council are to eradicate social evils like child marriage and dowry in the community. The punishment for offenders is excommunication called *hukka pani band* and/or cash fine.

The modern statutory Gram Panchayat has also almost taken over such functions besides its social development activities.

The Ghiraths propitiate Hindu pantheon gods and goddesses in various local forms. Almost every family has a separate space inside or outside the house where some stones along with an earthen pot are kept and the *jathere* (ancestors) are worshipped. The village or local male deities are: Balakrupia, Deot Sidh (Hamirpur), Guga and Lakhdata (Bilaspur) Baba Barbhag Singh (Una), Bulha Baba (Kangra), Nahar Sigh (Bilaspur), Kaleshwar Mahadev (Kangra), etc. Among the female deities the commonly propitrated are Jawalamukhi, Brajeshwari Mata and Chamunda Devi in Kangra district, Vaishno Devi (J & K), Naina Devi (Bilaspur) and Chintpurni (Una). Their holy shrines are visited by pilgrims from time to time especially during annual fairs. The Nag Mela, Guga Mela, Peeplu Mela, Chamukha Mela, Baisakhhi Mela and various other fairs visited by the people.

Their sacred specialists are from other communities. A Brahman *purohit* officiates a marriage and death, an Acharaj and a Barkhu or Bedue on death. The *chela* are commonly consulted for warding off *bhoot* and other evil spirits. The *chela* performs a *khel* in which the person afflicted with evil spirit narrates his sufferings. Socioreligious movements have affected the community recently as some people have joined the Radhaswami and Nirankari missions.

They have progressed considerably from the traditional occupation of cultivators and now have industrialists, businessmen, artists, advocates, political leaders, scientists, doctors, engineers, persons holding various white-collar jobs in government and private sectors, etc.

The attitude towards all developmental programmes is favourable and the programmes have given considerable boost to the community. They avail themselves of modern facilities in respect of education, health, family welfare, drinking water, mass media and communications, electricity, irrigation, use of chemical fertilizers and insecticides, banking and public distribution systems. But the rural masses are still conservative about higher education for women and to some extent about the family planning measures.

A. R. Sankhyan

GORKHA

The Gorkha or Gurkha is a term applied to any person of Nepalese origin. "The Aryan Nepali language is often referred to as Gurkhali. The Nepalese serving in the British Indian Army were described as Gurkha..." (*Encyclopaedia Britannica,* 1969:1046). It is in this sense that "the term is applied to all soldiers of Nepalese descent whether or not they differ in caste, language or race from the martial people of Thakuri and Chhetri caste whose ancestors founded the Gurkha Kingdom". These people came mostly as warriors and rose to power in the second half of the eighteenth century under the leadership of Prithvi Narain Shah who captured Kangra. Maharaja Ranjit Singh pushed them beyond Satluj river but they were able to keep their hold on the areas east of Satluj. People were tired of their harsh and tyrannical rule. They united themselves and took stand against them with the help of Britishers and compelled the Gorkhas to leave the country in A.D. 1816. Those who stayed back are found mainly in Sirmaur, Kangra and Chamba districts. The other factor which marks their presence in the districts was the existence of the cantonment during the British Raj, where these people found jobs in the Gurkha regiment. The Gorkhas are identified by their typical mongoloid features, the Gorkhali headgear and the *khukhri* (dagger) as their identity markers. They speak in Gurkhali amongst themselves, whereas the regional dialect is used with others. The script of the older generation is Nepalese but that of the younger generation is Devanagari.

Bio-anthropological information in respect to certain genetical traits and somatometric traits is available (see bio-anthropoligical report). They are non-vegetarian. Their staple diet consists of wheat *chapati*, pulses with moderate consumption of vegetables and roots and tubers, which are cooked in mustard oil. Animal fat is also used occasionally in non-vegetarian preparations. They are also fond of smoking tobacoo and drinking liquor which they purchase from the market.

The Gorkhas are divided into two categories, the high consisting of Brahman, Chhetri, Magar and Gurung, and the low as, formed by Dameng and Damai. These are endogamous divisions. Each of these are further segmented into *gotra* which denote their ancestry. *Sagotra* (same *gotra*) marriages are prohibited. Marriage is negotiated in adolescence (above 15 years of age) nowadays, and initiated by the boy's parents. Dowry is given in kind and depends much on the economic status. Coloured *pote* (bead necklace) and *sindur* constitute their marriage symbols, which are followed rigidly. *Chhut chhurawa* (divorce) is permissible by either of the spouses on grounds of adultery, maladjustment and cruelty. The compensation in the form of return of marriage expenses, gifts and penalty is decreed to the aggrieved party whereas the children of the estranged parents remain a liability of the father. Widow, widower and divorcee remarriage is practised and so is levirate and sororate. Monogamy is the usual rule but in the event of barrenness of the first wife a second marriage is done.

The rule of residence is patrilocal and the family is patrilineally extended, which is now tending to be nuclear. Interpersonal relationship in a family is based on considerations of paternal and filial ties, age and sex. The eldest male member of the household is regarded as the head and his decisions are given due regard. The family is a well-knit social group and the situation of conflict is rare as all decisions are invariably arrived at after mutual consultation, but should such a situation arise it usually relates to property disputes. The property is inherited by the rule of male equigeniture and the succession is in the male line. Avoidance and joking relationship exists. The daughter-in-law observes avoidance from father-in-law and with husband's elder brothers. Joking relationships exist with husband's younger relatives.

The status of women is considered equal to that of men, though normally she does not have any right of inheritance to the parental property but has the right of maintenance her husband's property. In the event of the death of the husband she acts as a custodian of his property till the time her children grow up. She takes part in all the agricultural activities, animal husbandry, bringing water, fuel and fodder besides being engaged in other economic activities. She also takes part in social functions and rituals but her participation in the religious sphere is limited to the observance of rituals. In the political sphere, her role is limited to exercising her franchise. Her most important role is however in the management of domestic affairs and control of family expenditure.

In the sphere of life-cycle rituals, the Gurkhas observe *sukheri* (birth pollution) and pre- and post-natal restrictions. The birth pollution ceases with the observance of *dasuthan* on the eleventh day when a *hom* (offerings are made to the fire) by the *pandit* (priest) and thereafter the child is named. If the child is born under the constellation of *garh mool* then the purificatory rites are deferred for 40 days. *Chewar* (tonsure) is performed at home by the *mama* but if a family wishes it to be done at the *devi's* (goddess) temple then it is performed there. First *bhat kholai* (cereal-feeding) of the child is observed at the age of five months. The child is fed symbolically with pulses, vegetables and cereal along with a sweet dish.

Marriage is solemnized at the bride's residence by taking seven *phera* (circumambulation) in the *lagna mandap* amdist chanting of *mantra* by the priest. The *muklawa* ceremony was earlier deferred for three to four years after marriage till the girl came of age but presently this is being performed at the time of marriage since marriages are now being performed after the girl attains puberty. Menstrual impurity is strictly observed by the Gorkhas. A Gorkha woman lives practically in isolation for four days during menstrual period and after a bath she is considered clean but she is still not allowed to touch water and attend to religious duties until the fifth day.

The dead are cremated but the infants are buried. The ashes are immersed in a river. Death pollution is observed up to *terhvi* (thirteenth day) and ceases with observance of *got khana* when a feast is given to the consanguineous members of the father's lineage and to the priest. During the period of pollution food is cooked only once a day and without any salt. Mortuary rites are observed on *barkhi* and till the observance of *barkhi* no marriage ceremony can take place in the family. Certain rites are performed on each death anniversary to commemorate the dead.

For the maintenance of norms or punishing the offender for the infringement of social norms, the community has its own council. The office of the chief is not hereditary and the members are elected by a voice vote to officiate and dispense justice in matters of adultery, disrespect for traditional norms and insulting the panchayat. The offenders are penalized by cash fines which are utilized for defraying expenditure of the panchayat. Besides their traditional panchayat, the statutory panchayat also exist which is heterogeneous in nature and whose primary duty is to plan and implement welfare activities.

The community is engaged in government and defence jobs, and also as teachers, doctors, scientists and in other white-collar professions. As a subsidiary means of their livelihood they have taken to agriculture. Some are owner-cultivators whereas some hold land of others on tenure. There are some landless families also. In remote areas child labour exists where they are paid in cash. They have direct dependence on daily regulated market where cash forms the medium of exchange.

The Gorkhas are worshippers of Shakti. They also have reverence for family, clan, village and regional deities. The sacred specialists and the exorcists are from other communities who officiate life-cycle rituals and cure a person afflicted by evil spirits. The Gorkhas take part in all the fairs and festivals of the region but the festivals of Dussehra and Diwali are of special socioreligious significance. Dussehra lasts for 10 days. The first six days are known as *shradh*. On the first day barley is sown in a pot and is watered everyday. On the tenth day barley plants are taken out and exchanged as gifts. The last four days known as Phulpati, Ashtami, Naumi and Dashmi are of great importance. The Asthami rite is of significance when buffaloes or goats are sacrificed by means of decapitation with a *khukhri,* and severing of the head by the executioner with one stroke qualifies him for the reward of a white turban by the community.

In matters of art and aesthetics the Gorkhali women are fond of tatooing. They often get their husband's name or some floral design tatooed on their arms. Dancing and singing play an important part in the life of the Gorkha. The Damai section of the Gorkhas are skilled players of flutes and drums. Their songs are always heard on festive occasions such as Dussehra and Holi. The community also has folklore and folktales which are full of the heroic deeds of their ancestors.

The community has commensal relations with all the high caste Gorkhas and non-Gorkhas. They accept water and *kachcha* food from those equivalent in status or superior to them but from those of lower status, only *pucca* food is accepted and that too if it is cooked by a person of high caste. *Jajmani* relations exist with Brahmans, Lohar, Badhi, Nai and Dom who render their traditional specialized services, in return they are paid in cash and kind. Connubial linkages are established with one's own community. All the Gorkhas from the Brahman to the lowest caste may contract *mit* (friend) relationships with anyone they are particularly fond of. Once contracted, the new relationships hold good for commensal and connubial purposes. They share well and water resources and visit religious shrines with other communities. With the diversification of economic pursuits traditional caste rigidity has loosened in urban centres resulting in the formation of new linkages.

Their attitude towards education is favourable for both boys and girls. Boys receive education up to college and post-graduate level, the girls on the other hand study up to secondary level after which they drop out for want of schools in the vicinity. They also favour modern system of medicare along with the traditional one. They also show a favourable response to family welfare programmes and try to restrict their family size to three or four children by using modern methods of family planning.

Drinking water is available in the locality through piped water. Electricity, media and communication facilities are available. Self-employment avenues are available and many have procured loans for setting up their own business. In Sirmaur district, irrigation facilities through the system of canals are availed of. Consequently people are also using chemical fertilizers and pesticides. Mid-day meal and immunization facilities are available and so is the facility of public distribution system through government controlled shops. Banking and investment facilities are also made use of by the people.

Vatsala Sarkar

GOSAIN

The word 'Gosain' is vaguely employed to mean a 'devotee' whether he leads a life of a celibate or resides in a house like others as householders. He may lead an idle existence or work in any trade. The mark, as pointed by Sherring (1879) which distinguishes all who bear this name is that they are all devoted to a religious life. They largely are followers of Shaivite sect. They are drawn from Brahman, Kshatriya, Vaish and Sudra categories but once they joined this fraternity in eating and drinking, they were cut off forever from their own natal groups. The Gosain are a distinct and legitimate caste and not merely a religious order (Sherring, 1879). They are believed to have migrated from Rajasthan during the Muhammaden invasion and took refuge in the hills of Himachal Pradesh. They are sporadically distributed in the State.

The dialect spoken by the people is Rajasthani which they use among their kinfolk but with outsiders they converse in Hindi. The dress pattern of the two sections of the Gosain varies. The mendicants wear an ochre coloured robe, *rudraksha* necklace and distinguishing sacred marks on their forehead, arms and chest. On the other hand, the Grihastha Gosains who lead a domestic life, dress like people of other communities. Men wear shirts and pant or *pyjama,* whereas women wear *salwar* and *kameez* or *sari.*

The Gosains are both vegetarian and non-vegetarian. They can take the meat of goat, chicken, fish, wild boar and deer but not beef, which is tabooed. Their staple diet consists of wheat, pulses of *gram, moong, urd* and seasonal vegetables. They also use mustard oil and oil of *til* as cooking media. Fruits are consumed only occasionally. Men are fond of smoking *bidi* and *hukka.* They also consume alcoholic drinks.

Since the Gosains belong to a religious order and their membership is also through induction, therefore, social divisions are not the same as found among pure caste groups. However, twelve and a half divisions are reported which do not have any sharp differentation; but the differences are based on the mode of worship and the *math* (monastery) to which they belong. Sherring (1879) and Bhattacharya (1968:297) name only 10 divisions which are collectively known as Dasnamis and are derived from the names of ten disciples of Shankaracharya who is said to have founded the sects. These are Saraswati, Bharati, Puri, Tiratha, Asram, Ban, Giri, Aranya, Parvata and Sagara. It should be mentioned that all these sects are not found in Himachal Pradesh as many of these groups are localized.

A Grihastha Gosain leads the life of a householder and marries within the same order though outside one's own *gotra*. The usual age at marriage for a girl and a boy is between 14 and 15, and 17 and 18 years respectively. Marriages are commonly arranged through negotiation at the behest of a middleman. Exchange marriages may take place but are not preferred. The marriage symbols are *chutki* (toe-ring) and *lakh-ki-churi* (lac bangles). The residence is patrilocal as the girl leaves for her husband's home after marriage. Widow and widower remarriage is permissible and so are levirate and sororate. *Istifa* (divorce) is granted on grounds of adultery, chronic mental sickness, impotency and cruelty. A divorcee, male or female, can remarry. The children born of the previous marriage remain in the care of the father. The remarriage of a widow or divorced woman is solemnized in a simple manner without going through the elaborate marriage rituals.

Nuclear families are tending to replace the old system. Truly joint households with married and unmarried sons and daughters living under the common roof sharing a common hearth, are rarely seen. Nevertheless, elders are given respect and are consulted on important issues. Women observe purdah in the presence of the elder male relatives of their husband's household. Joking relationships exists with peer group members and with the husband's younger brothers and sisters. Inheritance is patrilineal and the eldest son succeeds after the father's death. All the sons get equal share from the property, but daughters do not have any claim except in the absence of a son. In such a case the son-in-law is made the custodian of the property.

Women do not enjoy equal status with men for they are economically dependent on their husbands, nor do they enjoy freedom to exercise their will on economic, religious and political issues. However, women play an important role in house management. They also take an active part in economic activities by working in the agricultural fields, besides doing various other jobs such as bringing water, fuel and fodder. Besides, they also actively participate in rituals and religious festivals but do not hold any religious office. They lack political consciousness.

The life-cycle rituals of a Grihastha Gosain are the same as for any other Hindu community. However, the initiation ceremony of the Gosain when he enters the religious fold is both elaborate and distinct. The birth of the son is an occasion of felicitation and celebration for the family. Post-birth pollution is observed and the purificatory rites are observed on the sixth day and then subsequently on the eleventh day. The mother and child are given a purificatory bath, new clothes are worn and a *havan* is performed after washing and plastering the house with cowdung. After this, the house becomes clean ritually, but the woman is not supposed to cook or undertake heavy work till the 40 days are over. *Mundan* is performed for the son. The child is taken to the temple of Gurgaon Mai in Haryana. The hair of the child is shaved off in the temple premises.

The marriage comprises important rituals like *kanyadan* and *phera* and takes place at the bride's residence. Before the actual marriage, *tel* ceremony is performed at both the bride's and the bridegroom's house in which *tel* and turmeric are applied to both the bride and the bridegroom by the female relatives of the respective sides. Marriage songs are sung on this occasion.

The dead are cremated and pollution is observed for 13 days. It was customary to give a feast in case an old man died. *Ladoo* (sweet) preparation each weighing more than a kilogram,are distributed among the members of the *biradari* but this custom is disappearing now. Important death rites are performed on the third, tenth and thirteenth day. Ancestor worship is observed annually, during the *shradha* (a fortnight specially devoted to the dead ancestors) days.

The mendicants chiefly subsist on the alms and charity of others and lead a wandering life going from one pilgrim centre to another. The Grihastha Gosain on the other hand may be found engaged in various pursuits namely, agriculture, business, service and trade. A majority of them living in the rural areas have landed property and therefore, they subsist on culvitation. In addition, some have opened shops while others have taken jobs in factories as also in government and semi-government organizations. There are small shops of daily provision which serve their purpose. If need be, they go to the nearest town market to procure things of their requirement. Both cash and barter are prevalent but the former is more prevalent than the latter.

The mechanism of social control was previously in the hands of the *biradari* or caste councils but it has now been almost totally replaced by the statutory panchayats. The statutory panchayats through their duly elected members decide the cases of commission and omission and also dictate the course of action to be taken against the offender. The punishment is in the form of cash fine. The other function of the panchayat is to implement the welfare activities in the village. Domestic discords and purely family issues are mutually solved by the intervention of the elders of the *biradari*.

It has been pointed out in the beginning that the Gosains are chiefly devoted to a religious life. Some take to ascetic practices but it is recommended that a man must first discharge his domestic and social responsibilities before taking to the life of a monk or a mendicant and therefore the members who are initiated into this fold have to go through certain ceremonies and only after the completion of the *vijaya hom* rite, as described by Sherring (1974), is a Gosain supposed to renounce his material connections to lead the life of a celibate. It is for this that a novitiate does not undergo the complete ceremony and the same is deferred till a person is free from his domestic responsibilities. Lord Shiva is their principal deity. All the Gosain households have a Shivlinga as the principal object of worship. They also worship the clan deity known as Pitra Devta and at every Amavasya (dark fortnight) they offer *kheer* to the deity. This pudding is later distributed as *prasad* among the blood relatives of the father's side. Besides, the village deity known as Khera Devta or Gram Devta is worshipped by all the communities. Some of the minor gods and goddesses and saints are also worshipped. For instance Gurgaon Mai temple in Gurgaon near Delhi is of great importance to the people. They also undertake pilgrimage to Hardwar, Prayag and Ujjan, etc., at the time of Mahakumbha and Ardhakumbha. The journey is performed in the month of July-August. Other important pilgrim centres which are sacred to all devout Hindus such as Amarnath, Vaishno Devi and Badrinath are equally sacred to them.

The Gosains have folk tales which are replete with references to Lord Shiva and his consort Parvati. They also have folktales about Baba Gorakh Nath, his disciple Raja Bhartari Chandra and his pious and learned wife Rani Pingla. Folksongs are the same as sung by other neighbouring communities of the region.

They maintain relationship with the members of their own order and also with those of other neighbouring communities. With other communities certain restrictions with regard to the acceptance and exchange of food are observed. A Brahman *purohit* who comes to officiate at their wedding ceremonies is paid in cash and given *sidha*. But, there is no taboo in either sharing the common water sources as well as entering a temple. A Grihastha Gosain shows special reverence to a fellow Gosain who has become an ascetic. Putative kinship also exists with certain castes. The old *jajmani* relationship involving the obligatory nature of relationship is not evident now. The services rendered by the various specialized service and artisan castes are paid for in cash or kind whenever such need arises.

Education facilities are not availed of adeqauetly. The dropout percentage is very high after the primary and secondary stage. Boys dropout mainly because of economic reasons, whereas girls discontinue on account of social reasons. Likewise, health programmes have also met with little success. The economic programmes run by the State government for providing loans, subsidies and vocational centres have yielded fruitful results and many have been benefited. However, there is also a lack of awareness which is a major stumbling block in the path of economic uplift.

Vatsala Sarkar

GUJARATI BRAHMAN

The Gujarati Brahmans are known by this name in Bhatiat tehsil of Chamba and parts of Kangra district. The Brahmans of this category live in Una, Hamirpur, Mandi, Chamba and Kangra districts. According to an unpublished manuscript Kangra Vanshavali by Shankara they seem to have come from Gujarat to settle down in the hilly region a hundred years ago. In Kangra, the Gujarati Brahmans are found in Suliali, Nurpur, Fatehpur, Damtal and some other villages in the vicinity of Kangra town and Palampur area. In district Chamba they are found in Bhatiat and Chamba tehsils. In Suliali, Ladori, Nurpur, Jassur, Bhadwar, Kotla, etc., their population is scarce but they are seen as a distinct community.

Their various clans are Garg, Kaushalya, Bharadwaj, etc., and they are called Parshurami also. The aforesaid manuscript states that: "These Brahmans came from Gujarat and as such are called Gujarati. They also accept donations given in the name of the dead but till the time the departed soul is called 'Preta', only Mahabrahmans accept the donations and after that Masku is given the alms. Masku gets the donations and meals every month. No one, except the Gujarati Brahman, get these donations including food and other eatables and a pitcher of water up to three years after the death." This account places them with the Masku or Mahku Brahmans but in some areas the Mahkus do not associate themselves with the Gujarati Brahmans. It has also been mentioned in the Kangra Vanshavali , that some Katoch ruler visited eastern parts of the country and brought these Brahmans to Kangra. Afterwards Raja Bhim Chand gave them monthly alms and they performed the duties of Acharya (Acharaj) Brahman; so they are counted among the Acharya Brahmans. It seems that the account given in the manuscript is not based on facts as it mentions Mahabrahman, Dak Brahman and Bujhru Brahman.

The male mambers wear *dhoti* and turban while performing ritualistic functions. They have their clientele in the areas they reside in like other Brahmans of the areas.

They speak local dialects of the respective regions and have working knowledge of Sanskrit to conduct social ceremonies. The script used by them is Devanagari.

They are purely vegetarian and do not take any meat. Green vegetables and staple food like wheat, pulses, maize, rice and fruits are consumed. The younger generation in some cases takes eggs but it is not a practice with most members of the community. No tubers, barks and roots are eaten. But in some areas seasonal local tubers which are used as vegetables are consumed. They are not in the habit of taking alcoholic drinks. Milk is consumed in plenty. They like *lassi*, curd and milk preparations. Special *pakwan*, like *ankali* and *babroo* are prepared on special occasions.

There are divisions among the Gujarati Brahmans in the form of *gotras*, which facilitate matrimonial settlements among themselves. They do not want to have marital relations with other groups of the Brahmans and consider the Acharya, Bujhru and Dak as inferior to them. But some Brahman clans consider themselves superior to the Gujarati Brahman. The basis for differentiation is only occupational. They prefer to write Sharma or clan name as surname but all were called *pandit*. They are endogamous in nature, very ritualistic with pure food habits practising untouchability and thoughts of cleanliness are given utmost importance. In the varna order, they place themselves in upper strata of Brahmans but others do not accept them as such.

Brahmanical marriage rules are observed by the Gujarati Brahman. The age at marriage is about 20 years for boys and about 16 years for girls. But late marriages are also permitted. The marriages are settled with the consent of parents of the boy and the girl. The betrothal is an important ceremony in which an ornament, clothes for the girl, and sweets and other things are given by the boy's parents. The community is conservative and no money is taken as the bride price. The marriage system is traditional and according to the scriptures. *Sindur* and the ornaments are the marriage symbols. The married women put *tika* on their foreheads. Dowry is given according to the wishes of the parents of the girl and is not demanded. It is always in kind. The bride resides with her husband at her in-laws' house. Divorce is rare in the community. In case of disputes, the village panchayat or local courts take decisions in consultation with both the parties. If divorce is inevitable, the decision of both the parties prevails. Remarriage is allowed only in the case of male members. Widow marriages are not allowed.

But changes in marriage institution are being noticed. Now young boys and girls have started putting forth their preferences for life mates and the parents are sometimes ignored while taking decisions. Divorce and remarriage cases are also coming to the fore but their number is minimal.

Joint family is the common rule for the community. Due to service conditions, the in-service sons take their wives to their places of posting but remain in touch with the other members of their families. Brothers divide the family property after the death of their parents. In some cases the old parents divide the property and distribute it among the sons in order to keep the honour of the family and to avoid disputes at a later stage. There is perfect harmony in the joint families and work is shared by all. Avoidance is observed between male elders and younger women who have got wedded in the family. The younger *bhabhi* has avoidance relationship with her father-in-law and the elder brother of the husband. Joking relations exist between *bhabhi* and *devar*. Only sons are entitled to family property. All the sons have equal shares in the family property. The joint family system is fading away due to division of labour and earning habits.

The women of the community are entitled to an equal share in the property of the husband. After the death of the husband, the mother has to depend upon the sons for help and for day-to-day necessities. Their religious and political position is respectable but they do not take part in political activities directly. Their main duties are to look after the household and children. Some women have now started taking up jobs after getting education.

The Gujrati Brahmans have their *jajmani* system under which they inspire others to carry on rituals according to sixteen *sanskara* (ceremonies) meant for Hindus. They themselves also celebrate those *sanskara*. Though all the 16 *sanskara* are not organized, the most important among them are, *mundan, yagopavit*, marriage, celebration of birth anniversaries, *shradh* after death, etc. *Janam* (birth), *namkaran* and sending the children to the school on an auspicious day are also important *sanskara* among the Gujarati Brahmans.

The community seeks employment in private or in Government, does business and receives donations from families one year after the death in a family. The ritual organized after one year after the death is called *barkhi*. On the *barkhi* day, a Gujarati Brahman performs *puja* in the family and gets *dan* given in the name of the departed soul by the family. They also get the *dan* from the *jajman* every month on the day of the death. The ritual is called *mahki* in local parlance and on this day a *pandit* is invited to take meals in the family in the name of the departed soul.

The community, generally, is not interested in agricultural pursuits or labour. They, however, practise astrology and indigenous medicines, and are respected for their specialized approach in these fields. Now only some of the families of this community are living on their ancestral profession of getting donations in the name of the dead and are adopting other, more respectable jobs as government officials, contractors, suppliers and traders.

The Gujarati Brahmans have a *biradari panchayat*. The *panch* and head of the *biradari panchayat* are capable of deciding community disputes. The Biradari Panchayat is constituted locally and verbally and each family has a member in the panchayat. The members elect the head of the panchayat who continues to function in this role for at least a year. Rewards are generally given by way of appreciation, whereas an evil-doer is punished through social criticism, segregation and coercion etc. In the villages where the households of the community are not enough, the people approach the local Gram Panchayat for redressal of their grievances. A change is visible and now the people are not so much dependent on the verdict of the Biradari Panchayat and the statutory panchayat has taken its functions.

The Gaur Brahmans worship Shiva, Rama, Krishana, Durga and other gods and goddesses of the Hindu pantheon. They go to *tirtha* like Hardwar, Prayag and four *dhams* on religious missions. Their festivals are Diwali, Dussehra, Holi and other regional functions. The community is religious-minded and arranges religious ceremonies from time to time. The socio-religious movements of the community do not differ from other Brahman subgroups in the area. Chanting of *mantra* in religious ceremonies and observance of fasts on sacred days by the women is a common practice. Their religious faith is strong and deep-rooted, and there has been no change in these practices.

The women are experts in embroidery, knitting and other household arts, such as stitching, carving, engraving and motif-making on the floors of the houses. The male members excel in pulse-reading and horoscope-making. Some of them know how to make designs on papers to be used for making horoscopes. They share regional folktales and folksongs. They have only local legends about their ancestors and relate the miracles of some of their ancestors.

The community is responsive to formal education. Their children prefer to study Sanskrit as one of the languages. Most of them are educated. They avail themselves of modern health and medical care facilities They know the value of local herbs and some of them practise local medicine for common ailments. They are interested in family planning. They prefer self-employment with bright prospects but in the villages such opportunities are very rare.

B.R. Sharma

GUJJAR (HINDU)

Tradition has it that the Gujjar or the Gujar are a pastoral community with no fixed abode. A large number of Gujjars have now settled down and taken to farming. In some areas, they continue to pursue agricultural activity alongwith animal husbandry. Traditionally, they were cattle breeders and milkmen. During the Turkish, Afghan and Persian invasions, they earned notoriety for preying upon the dead and the wounded left in the battlefields.

The Gujjars are identified by General Cunningham with the Kushan or Yachi or Tochari, a tribe of the Eastern Tartars. About a century before Christ, their chief conquered Kabul and Peshawar, while his son Hema Kadbhises extended his sway over the whole of upper Punjab and the banks of the Jamuna as far down as Mathura and the Vindhayas. His successor, king Kanishka, the first Buddhist Indo-Scythian prince, annexed Kashmir to the kingdom of Tochari (Bingley 1904; Rose, 1919; Negi, 1976). The probability of Gujjars being the descendants of the ancient Yachi or Kushan is suggested by the fact that besides the Jat, they are the only numerous race of foreign origin in the north-western part of the Indian subcontinent who are known to have been powerful during the early centuries of the Christian era.

The origins of the Gujjars are still shrouded in mystery, but the majority of the scholars are of the view that these people migrated to India during the sixth century from Central Asia, from where communication with India was a regular feature along well-established trade routes. It is also said that they inhabited the western part of India, where the province Gujarat exists after their name. The Gujjar rulers founded the city of Gujarat in Akbar's reign. Unforseen circumstances compelled them to migrate towards north to Jammu and Kashmir where they settled in the forests. The Hindu Gujjars entered Himachal Pradesh from the neighbouring areas of the plains in isolated and stray migrations (Rose, 1919).

Most of the historians believe that the Gujjars were a Rajput community. The word 'Gujjar' appears to have been derived from *gurjara*, which means a warrior class of Rajputs. Cunningham (*vide* Rose, 1919), confirming this writes, "the ancient name of Rajputana was Gujar or Gujara (Gujarat)...".

The Hindu Gujjars of Himachal trace their origin from Jasoda, mother of Lord Krishna. The Hindu Gujjars are found mostly in the district of Mandi, Kangra, Sirmaur, Solan and Bilaspur, whereas, the Muslim Gujjars are dispersed in the districts of Chamba, Mandi, Bilaspur, Solan and Sirmaur. The dialect spoken by them is of the region. Devanagari is the script used in writing. The Hindu Gujjars do not have any identity marker.

The Hindu Gujjars are usually vegetarian, and their diet depends upon the availability of cereals. During summer months they take wheat and rice and in winter months they prefer maize to wheat. They are occasional non-vegetarians and take meat of goat and chicken. Their staple diet consists of wheat or maize *chappati*, *dal* of *urd* and gram, vegetables or milk products and curd. Milk and milk products occupy an important position in their normal menu for these are their own produce. They are occasional consumers of alcoholic drinks, which are purchased from the market and are taken on festive or social occasions. But women do not take alcoholic drinks. Smoking of tobacco, *bidi*, and cigarette is very common among the males. Elderly women also smoke *hukka*. On marriage and festive occasions preparations of mutton, sweetened rice and of *dal* of *mah* or *chana* are a must and cooked by all families. In the event of death in a family, non-vegetarian and spicy foods are avoided and so also during the *pitra-paksha*. Mutton is also avoided on festive occasions except Holi.

Bio-anthropological report provides biological information.

The Gujjars have two endogamous religious setions—Hindu and Muslim. Each section is further subdivided into a number of exogamous *gotra* like Khatana, Chohan, Gursi, Didhar, Bhumphal, Kalarya, Parswal, Malehria, Koli, Kautiya, Motte, Chaichi, Bhunch, Bargat, Kalas, Chhore, Ladi, Chai, Bajar and Badhana (Rose, 1919). These *gotra* denote their ancestry and regulate marriage alliances. They are also aware of the *varna* system and place themselves along with the Kshatriyas, though other communities place them a grade lower.

In the selection of spouse, the socioeconomic condition of the negotiating families is seen and four *gotra*, that is, self, father's, mother's and mother's mother, are avoided. The usual age of marriage for boys is 18 to 25 years and 15 to 18 years for girls. Child marriage was in vogue, but now it has given way to adult marriages. The common symbols of marriage for women are *koka*, *choori*, *tika* and *bala*. After marriage, the residence is patrilocal. Dowry in the form of gift and cash exists, but is not asked for.

Both widow and widower remarriages are practised. Junior levirate and sororate are also practised. However, if the husband's elder brother is a widower, he can marry the widowed wife of his younger brother. Likewise, remarriage of divorced man and woman can also take place. Remarriage of widowed women is without any rituals and can take place only after a month of her becoming a widow. Though rare, divorce can be sought on grounds of adultery, cruelty and impotency. The divorcee woman can seek maintenance provided she chooses to remain single. Children of estranged parents remain in the custody of the father. Infants accompany the mother to be returned later to the father after they grow up.

The Hindu Gujjars believe in the superemacy of the traditional joint family system. The head of the family is the eldest male member in the family whose decision in family matters is final and is respected. Nowadays, a change in the family structure is seen where they share the same roof but not the same kitchen. When the differences among the members surface too frequently, the joint setup splits into nuclear types. The elders in the family are given due regard and respect. They are consulted and obeyed by the younger ones. Purdah is observed by a wife with her husband's elder male relatives of the family. Purdah is known as *ghoond* or *ghoongat*. Joking relationship exists with husband's younger brothers and sisters and betwen the husband and his wife's younger sister. The relationship between husband and wife is that of love and respect. They do not take each other's name but address teknonymically.

The family property runs along the male line. A daughter can claim the property of the father in the absence of a son. Normally, if a father dies without making any will, the property is transferred to those of the collaterals. Nowadays, in the absence of a son, the son-in-law is invited to stay and look after the family and the property. Under normal circumstances the property is equally divided among the sons, with the widow having a right to maintenance.

The Hindu Gujjar women are hardworking and besides household chores, do other work like tending the cattle, making cowdung cakes, plastering the walls and floors of the house with cowdung and bringing potable water, fuel and fodder for the cows and buffaloes. The women of well-to-do households may not, however, like to work in the fields, but during the peak harvesting season their assistance is inevitable. A woman's role, both in the domestic as well as in economic sphere is significant, but she does not enjoy the same status as her male counterpart. Her political role is limited to the casting of votes in the local or general election. In the religious sphere women take an active part in domestic rituals, festivals and fairs.

The major life-cycle rituals commencing with the birth of a child to death are broadly in accordance with the Hindu customs. The birth of the male child is an occasion for gaiety and celebration. The first childbirth is welcomed with greater enthusiasm than the subsequent ones. A worship called *matri-havan*, is offered to the family deity, in the seventh or ninth month of pregnancy by the Hindu Gujjars to avoid miscarriage. Post-birth pollution is observed for both the mother and the child, and for this they are given purificatory baths on the sixth, eleventh and fortieth days, after which the child and the mother are considered ritually clean. A child is named on the eleventh day. *Mundan* is performed for the male child. A Nai cuts the hair, and in return is paid in cash and given some *gur* to eat.

Marriage is known as *byah* or *shadi*. After the selection of the spouse on an auspicious day, *sagai* takes place, wherein the boy's parents go to the girl's house and offers the girl a piece of jewellery. The girl's father also gives token cash to the boy. The date for marriage is settled after cosulting the priest. Prior to marriage, another ceremony known as *haldi charhahna* is held in which turmeric and mustard oil is applied to the bride and also to the bridegroom by the womenfolk in the respective houses of the girl and the boy. On an appointed day the *barat* leaves for the bride's house, where the actual marriage ceremony is performed, consisting of *kanyadaan* and *phera* around the sacred fire. The entire marriage ceremony is presided over by the priests from both the sides who recite Vedic *mantra*. This is finally followed by the *doli* ceremony, signifying departure of the bride from her maternal home for her husband's house. When child marriages were performed, another important ceremony known as *muklawa* was performed at a later date when the girl actually attained puberty, and was then allowed to stay with her husband.

The Hindu Gujjars cremate their dead. Only children up to the age of five are buried and also those who die of small pox and leprosy. The eldest son performs the last rites but the last rites of a wife are performed by the husband. On the tenth day, that is, *daswa* they go to Pehowa, a place near Kurukshetra in Haryana, when offerings are made to the Brahman in the name of the dead. On the thirteenth day, *terhaee* is performed and food is served to the Brahman and young girls. Again after 40 days Brahmans are feasted and the house is considered to be free from pollution. During the period of mourning very simple food is cooked without turmeric and *ghee*. It is customary that on first three days, the food is brought from the neighbour's house. Ancestor worship in the form of *sharadh* rites is held annually, during the dark fortnight falling in the months of September-October which is specially devoted to the commemoration of the dead.

The traditional economy of the Hindu Gujjars revolved around cow and buffalo herding and selling milk and milk products. The Hindu Gujjars lead a settled existence and practise agriculture. The majority of them are landowners. Owners of large landholdings may employ agricultural labour and pay them a share from their produce for their labour. Milk and milk products like *ghee*, and curd are directly sold in the market. It is customary for each family to keep a cow, but the milk is only for self-consumption and not for sale, because of the fact that they trace their origin from the famous Yaduvansha to which Lord Krishna belonged, whose fondness for cow herding is all too well known.

Aside from practising agriculture and animal husbandry, some have taken to service in government and semi-government organizations. Some of them are education officers, forest guards, members in police and military services.

They have their traditional rights on the forest, from where they can take wood for fuel. For building houses wood is procured by a permit from the forest department at nominal rates. They have a regular market where they sell their produce directly. A majority have good landholding and have a decent income through buffalo and cow herding.

Enforcement of traditional laws and social control is managed by their own *gharelu* panchayat which is headed by a Chowdhary and four other elderly experienced male members of the community. They listen to all the cases of land disputes, division of property and family, divorce, separation and compensation, petty thefts and the like. People mostly sort out their differences through their own panchayat, whose decisions and judgement are morally binding. If a person feels dissatisfied, he may approach the law courts. Such cases are, however, very few. The offenders are penalized by fines in cash or kind. These ranges from tending a simple apology before the *biradari*, to giving a feast to the *biradari*. In serious breaches of community norms a person may be excommunicated. The fine thus realised are spent for the common welfare of the community. Since the inception of statutory panchayats , the control of the traditional panchayat has declined but nevertheless it still continues.

The Hindu Gujjars trace their mythical ancestry from the famous Nand Vansha, where Lord Krishna was brought up by Mata Jasoda. They have faith in the local gods, goddesses and regional deities also. Amongst the female deities Mata Shitala is worshipped as she is responsible for causing small-pox. Similarly, Budhe-Baba is propitiated for his displeasure and is believed to cause skin eruptions. He is duly worshipped in the month of June and July on Wednesday. A sweet dish made of *gur* (jaggery) and wheat flower known as *gulgula* is prepared and offered to Budhe Baba. This offering can only be eaten by a member of the Khubbar *gotra*, because Budhe Baba belongs to this *gotra*. Likewise, whenever a calf is born, they offer some grains and jaggery at the temple of Baba Garibnath. Besides, they worship Mata Sakhambari, whose temple is situated in Saharanpur district of Uttar Pradesh. All the major Hindu rituals and festivals are celebrated with devotion. The village deity known as Khera Devta is propitiated every six months. Every family of the village, both Hindu and Muslim, contributes ration which is cooked and the entire village community eats. The offerings are made to the Khera Dev for the common welfare of the village.

The womenfolk are deft in making embossed floral patterns on the walls of the house. During Navratra festival (9 days devoted to the worhip of Durga), they make their own clay model of goddess Dugra for worship which is later immersed in the river. Some of them make intricate applique on the straw fans and do embroidary as well. These are not for sale but are kept for their use. They share folksongs or dances of the region.

The Hindu Gujjars maintain their traditional *jajmani* relations with communities like Badhai, Lohar, Nai, Jheewar and Chuhra. Each of them render their traditional services, both social and economic, at their clients' house. The Lohar and Badhai repair their agricultural implements, whereas the Nai cuts hair and acts as messenger on social occasions. The Jheewar carries water for them and the Chuhra collects the cow-dung and takes away the dead animal. All these in return are paid bi-annually, at the harvesting seasons, a fixed share from the produce. A Brahmin who comes to officiate during their rituals at birth and marriage is given cash and raw grains *seedha.* A Brahmin priest also receives *seedha* during certain other festivals such as Sankranti. The sharing of water is through piped supply.

The impact of the various developmental programmes is evident from the overall growth, modernization and industrialization, in terms of electricity, water supply, transport and communication network. Under the Integrated Rural Development Programme, they have been able to secure loans at a nominal interest, and with heavy subsidy for opening their own dairy, buying agricultural implements, tube-wells and for installing *chara* machines. The educated unemployed youth can get a loan up to a limit of Rs. 25,000 for opening any shop, business, small-scale or cottage industry.

Their girls and boys manage to secure primary and secondary level education. Girls drop out to help their mothers in household. Another factor dissuading the boys and girls from studying further is that for college education they have to travel far. Immunization programmes are availed of. For all serious illness they to go to the hospitals which are not far from their village. The attitude of the people towards family planning programme is not very encouraging. People like having large families, especially male children.

Rajendra Sarkar

GUJJAR (MUSLIM)

In Himachal Pradesh the Muslim Gujjars are included in the scheduled tribes and their population is 28121 according to the 1981 Census. They are predominant in Chamba, Mandi, Bilaspur, Sirmaur and Solan (1,174) districts. They inhabit the forest areas of the banks of rivers and live in small makeshift *deras* (shanties), which they keep on changing while migrating from high to low attitude during winter and from low to high altitude (*dhar*) during the summer in search of green pastures.

They speak Gujri dialect amongst themselves, which is a mixture of Gujarati, Urdu and Dogri, but while conversing with others they use broken Hindi. Their script is Perso-Arabic.

A Gujjar male is recognized by his typical beard and dress. They wear a specially embroidered conical headgear called *gujjari topi*, *jawaharcut* coloured embroidered jacket, a loose *kurta* and a *tamba*, while their women wear *chooridar pyjama* and loose *kurta* usually of brown, black or green colour.

Bio-anthropological information with respect to haemoglobin variants, somatometry, serology, genetics and dermatoglyphics in the community is available (see bio-anthropological report).

They are mostly non-vegetarian, but mutton is consumed occasionally and on important occasions only due to lack of availability. Eating pork is taboo. They do not eat beef or buffalo meat. Their staple diet consists of maize *chapati*, pulses of *urd, mah* and gram, roots and tubers and leafy vegetables. Their cooking media are mustard oil and *desi ghee*. Preparations of milk products like *lassi* and *dahi*, also form a part of their daily diet, which are their home products. Taking alcoholic beverages is a taboo as per the tenets of their religion, but a few do consume it. They also consume non-alcoholic beverages like salted tea and *lassi*. Smoking is very much in vogue among the Gujjars and practically every one smokes from their earthen *hukka*.

Special dishes for marriages and festive occasions are cooked. These are preparations of mutton, sweetened rice, and *dal* of *mah* or *chana*.

They have two groups, Bhatariye and Bhanariye. These groups do not intermarry. They are further segmented into exogamous *gotras*, viz., Bhatti, Chandel, Chauhan, Banja, Lodha, Kasana, Bhensi, Chopra, Chechi, Khatana, Padha, which indicate their Rajput clans. Though believing in the reality of blood ties on the patrilineal lines, they neither have any localized clans nor possess any tendency towards local exogamy or endogamy. The prohibition against clan endogamy, a special feature of clan custom, is lacking these days. This may to some degree be attibuted to the Islamization of the Gujjars, which permits marriages between cousins of all levels.

Marriages are performed nowadays in adulthood by negotiation. A distinictive feature of their marriage is that consanguineous marriages take place. A boy can marry his cousin, either on the father's or mother's side provided they have not in their infancy been suckling from the breast of the same mother. The marriages take place by *nikah* in which both the boy and the girl agree to marry each other in consideration of an agreed amount of *mehar* which has to be paid in the event of annulment of the marriage. Both junior levirate and junior sororate are permissible. Dowry is not demanded but is given in kind in the form of a buffalo or cow as per one's economic position.

Chhut is permissble by either of the aggrieved parties with the approval of the panchayat on grounds of adultery, maladjustment, chronic sickness and cruelty. A compensation is decreed by the panchayat to the aggrieved depending upon the person who is responsible for breaking the alliance. The children of estranged parents remain a liability of the father. Widow, widower, male and female divorcee, junior levirate and sororate marriages are permissible.

The family is mostly of the vertically extended type, but occasionally nuclear families also come up on account of bickerings in the family. There is a feeling of mutual love and respect in the family, with age, sex, paternal and filial affliations forming the basis of interfamily relations. Avoidance is not reported in the community but joking relationship does exist between elder brother's wife and husband's younger brother, wife's elder sister and wife's younger sister and with wife's elder brother and wife's younger brother. The eldest male member of the family is the head of the family and commands great respect and honour. His decisions in all family matters are given due regard. Though relationships in families are harmonious and a situation of confrontation rarely comes up, but if it ever does, it is related to property issues.

The inheritance of property is from father to sons, who equally share it, except the eldest who gets the *jethbar*, which is slightly more than the share given to other brothers. But, any debt against the father has to be repaid back equally by all married brothers, irrespective of the fact whether the eldest has received the *jethbar* or not. The unmarried brothers do not have to pay the father's debts. If there is no male child in the family, the property goes to the widow who has only usufructory rights, but in case(s) she remarries outside the family she loses her right to the property. In such an event it is equally shared among the brothers of the deceased. In case where there are no brothers or sons, it passes on to the nearest collaterals. In case where a person has more than one wife, the property is equally shared by them, and their respective shares are divided equally among their sons. In case a woman does not have any issue, it passes on to the son of the next wife.

The status of the women is low. Though they do not have the right to property, the right in the matter of selection of spouse and freedom to change the husband at her will do give her a certain amount of independence, though this is not socially appreciated. She plays a considerable role in the economic activity of their pastoral economy. She milks the cow, makes *ghee*, *panir* (cottage cheese), *khoya* and other milk prepatations and often also takes them to the market. Thus, she also contributes indirectly to the family income. She also carries out all the household duties besides animal husbandry, collection of fuel and bringing potable water. She has no right in the religious and political fields but has rights to family rituals and participation in social functions. She also controls the family expenditure.

Pre-natal restrictions do exist. A pregnant woman is not to visit burial grounds, forests and other desolate places which are believed to be haunted by evil spirits. She also cannot take part in the mourning functions nor look at a dead body. All these precautions are taken for protecting her from the evil spirits and also to prevent any deformity to the child or miscarriage. Soon after the birth and the cutting of the chord, an elderly Gujjar male in the absence of the *maulvi* whispers *azan* in the right ear of the child. The birth pollution lasts for 40 days and ceases with the taking of bath by the parturient mother and the child. After this bath she is fit to resume her normal life which remains suspended until then. No formal name-giving or the first cereal-feeding ceremony is held.

After the birth *aqiqa* is performed for both the male and the female children in which a he-goat is sacrificed and the child's head is shaved off. *Sunnat* for a male child is a very important ceremony in the life of a Muslim, and is performed while the child is young because the younger the child the lesser the pain. The operation is conducted by the family barber.

The marriage is a set of ceremonies conducted both at the bride and the groom's place, with negotiation being started by the boy's side. The actual marriage ceremony takes place at the bride's residence by *nikah*, which is conducted by the *maulvi* in the presence of the relatives and friends of both the parties in consideration of an already agreed amount of *mehar*. After this *khutuba* (explanation of Arabic verses in Quran in Urdu) is recited and *nikahnama* is signed by the bride and the groom which is testified by the *gawah* (witnesses) and the *vakil* (Maulvi as advocate). Gifts in the form of silver ornaments of nose, neck and arms are esentially given by the bride's parents, besides other gifts such as buffaloes, clothes, utensils, etc.

The dead are buried and the mourning lasts for three days, after which members of the family resume their normal work. Congregational prayers are held on Friday following the day of the demise at a graveyard. Rituals connected with the dead are also observed on the *chautha*, *sata* and *chalisa* which correspond to the fourth, seventh and fortieth days after demise. The house remains polluted for 10 days, within which the members of the bereaved family have to observe certain taboos. The last ritual known as *saal-da-drood* is observed at the first anniversary. Offerings are made on the grave of the departed soul on each death anniversary.

A majority of the Gujjars are pastorals and they eke out their livelihood through the sale of milk and milk products. They have herds of buffaloes with which they keep on migrating from low to high and high to low altitudes during summer and winter seasons in search of green pastures. The *ghasaia* (pastoral land) at these altitudes are allotted to them by the Forest Department which are owned by the government. If overgrazing is detected on the pasture land they are then heavily penalized. Due to the constant harassment by the forest officials on various issues, a few of them have left their age-old traditions and have taken to agriculture, for which land has been allotted to them. Since such land is meagre and the produce of which is insufficient for a year, they have taken to other means of livelihood, working as sharecroppers, businessmen and in government and private jobs.

They have direct links as well as through middleman to the regulated daily market to market their produce, where cash forms the medium of exchange. The presence of child labour in a few cases cannot be ruled out.

The Gujjars have their traditional *bhaichara* panchayat. The members of this panchayats are elected by a voice vote on the basis of their age, experience and knowledge. They dispense justice on issues of adultery, divorce, disrespect for traditional norms and insult to the panchayat. The offenders are penalized by cash fines or social boycott, but can be readmitted after they give punitive feast.

In Himachal Pradesh, the Gujjars are members of the Parvatiya Adim Jati Sevak Sangh, which was founded in 1956 to extend welfare activities among the tribes of the area. The welfare programmes undertaken by the Sangh are in the field of education, cottage industry and in all sociocultural fields. The main objective of the Sangh includes development of leadership among the tribals to encourage village crafts, to eradicate untouchability and to eliminate inferiority complex among the tribals. The Sangh has been taking special care to educate the children of Gujjars by starting a number of primary schools, bring the general problems of the Gujjars to the notice of the Government.

The Statutory panchayats exist and are even valid for those who are now leading a sedentary life, but for those who are still leading a nomadic life they do not exist. The nomadic mode of existence, coupled with their own past indifference to their franchise has deprived them of their exercise of the right to vote as an ordinary citizen of the State. In a majority of cases their very names are missing from the voters list, and wherever they do get listed, only very few get to cast their vote.

The Muslim Gujjars observe the doctrine of the Quran and believe in prophet Mohammad. The Gujjars rarely offer *namaz* (prayers) in the mosque except on festive occasions, for they rarely change clothes and take bath, as is prescribed by their religion. Only those persons who are now leading a settled life visit mosques for regular prayers. Their living in the hills and moving through forests have established their belief in the existence of evil spirits, which are believed to inhabit these areas. They also have faith in regional and village deities because of the local influence and they have family affiliation to Pirs. Their sacred specialist is Maulvi who officiates at life-cycle rituals whereas exorcists are from their own community. They take part in all fairs and festivals of the region which are of socioreligious and economic importance.

The Gujjar women are skilled in embroidery with coloured thread on caps and Jawahar jackets. They also decorate the walls of their house by makings floral and animal designs. They sing regional songs and dance on social occasions purely for amusement within the four walls of their houses. The Gujjars have folklore and folktales about the region and their community.

The Muslim Gujjars continue their traditional occupation of selling of milk and milk products to their clients around or in the market.

They establish *dharam bhai* and *dharam bahin* relations with members of other communities. They share water sources with other communities and participate in traditional festivals. As a majority of them are pastoral, they do not have patron-client, landlord-tenant and cultivator-labour rerlationship, but such of them who are now leading a sedentary life have started developing these relationship. With the increased awareness and wider world view, political leadership has emerged among the settled ones at the regional level.

Sufficient effort has been made by the Government to rehabilitate them in colonies in Solan, Sirmaur, Chamba and Kangra, where facilities of electricity, water, schools, medicine and health are available. Education is viewed by them partly favourably. Though both the boys and girls are sent for education, yet they study only up to secondary and primary level, after which they dropout for economic and social reasons. They make moderate use of traditional and modern system of medicare but are not in favour of family welfare programmes. Drinking water is available through streams, springs and taps. Because of lack of awareness and literacy some are unable to procure loans under the Integrated Rural Development Programme or from banks and have to depend on shopkeepers and moneylenders with whom they have frequent economic interaction. A majority of them are self-employed in agriculture.

Roads and other communication media are available in the urban fringes and they avail themselves of communication and mass media facilities.

Firewood and cowdung cakes continue to be their chief fuel. Mid-day meal, immunization and nutritional facilities are availed of under the Integrated Child Development Scheme. Food items at controlled prices are also made available to them through the public distribution system.

R.C. Rojhe

HADI

The Hadi is a vegetable-growing community who also sell petty household articles in Kangra where they are chiefly distributed. The etymology of the word Hadi is derived from *haddi* (bone) as they think that the community was involved in the collection of animal bones. They used to collect gold and silver ornaments from the ashes of the cremated dead bodies. This tradition is presently even looked down upon, but some Hadis still continue with it. They are generally ignorant of the history of their origin and migration but claim Rajput ancestry and call themselves Ranas having affiliation with the Maharana Pratap of Chittor. Sherring (1879) called Hadi a clan of the Rajputs of Ajmer (Rajasthan).

The Hadis are confined to Kangra and a few also live in Kullu valley. Census figures about them are not available yet according to the people's own estimate there are about 2,000 Hadis living in Kangra valley. They wear the dress and ornaments of the area. They speak the local Kangri dialect of the western Pahari and communicate in Devanagari script among themselves and with others.

Their staple food is wheat and maize supplemented by rice. The community consumes meat, fish, eggs but not beef. Intake of non-vegetarian food is occasional. They occasionally also consume country liquor available in the local market. The consumption of vegetables is substantial in the section of the community growing vegetables, but in others it is moderate. Food taboos and festive foods are similar to those of other Hindu community of the area.

Most of them distinguish themselves as Rana, others as Chauhan, and claim Kaundal *gotra*. The finer divisions of the Hadis are in the form of exogamous units called septs or *al*. These septs are Sinnu, Chanauriye, Dande, Bhanghaliye, Panduliye, Chimre, Dhel and Badhi. There is however no social hierarchy among these septs. The community faces an identity crisis in the regional varna hierarchy. They claim to be Rajput of the Rana dynasty. Rana is also used as a synonym for the community and many also use it as a surname. Their Kshatriya varna status is, however, not endorsed by the higher Rajputs, who place them at a low social position at par with the certain Sudras in view of their association with the ashes of the dead and their inferior occupation. In view of such a social position, they wish themselves to be included in the category of scheduled castes for statutory benefits.

The Hadi is an endogamous community but sticks to village and *al* exogamy. The marriage age is above 15 year for girls and above 20 years for boys. The marriage is contracted through negotiations and a Brahman priest may be consulted for matching the horoscope of the boy and the girl. Monogamy is practised and is the common form of marriage. They do not have the custom of bride price and *batta-satta*. The *sindur*, bangles of glass, nose-ring/pin and ear-ring/pin are the symbols of a married woman. Dowry is a usual practice but is confined mostly to giving of household articles. The residence of a married girl is patrilocal. The society rarely approves divorce but now it may occur through a judicial approval. The reasons for divorce could be many and either of the spouse is free to dissolve the marriage but children in such cases are the liability of the father. There is also a provision for compensation to be paid to the divorced woman if the husband divorces her. Remarriage is permissible in case of divorce as well as on the death of the spouse. The usual practice of junior levirate and sororate is presently not approved by them.

The family pattern of the Hadis is nuclear as well as vertically extended joint. The son's wife maintains avoidance relationship with her husband's father and his elder brother by covering her face. The inheritance is patrilineal as per the male equigeniture, and succession is by the eldest son. Joking relationships are similar to those of the other Hindu communities of the region. The women have no inheritance right, but they contribute to the family income by selling petty household articles in different villages. They perforrm all household chores, manage family expenditure and participate in social, religious and ritual activities. Practically,they enjoy a status equal to that of men but they have little role in the political sphere and mechanisms of social control.

Post-delivery pollution called *sutak* is observed and purification occurs by taking cow's urine on the thirteenth day called *gunt* ceremony. No christening and cereal-taking ceremonies are observed but a Brahman may be consulted to give the name as per the constellation of stars at the time of birth. *Mundan* ceremony is performed at around three years of age at Chamunda temple by the *mama* or a Nai. *Janeu* is put on at marriage.

The pre-marriage rituals are *tikka* and *sagai* or *karmai* ceremonies. The marriage rituals are performed as per the Brahmanical procedures by a Brahman priest or by a learned man of their own community. The clan deity or *kulja* is worshipped. The boy and girl circumambulate the sacred fire. A twig of *daran* tree is put in a pitcher and worshipped by taking rounds of the same by the bride and the groom. The bride's parents also hold a feast for the groom's party. The marriage is consummated after *muklawa* ceremony which occurs soon after or day following the day of marriage.

The dead are cremated along the riverside and ashes are immersed in the nearby Chamunda/Beas or Banganga rivers. Death pollution is observed for 13 days when ancestor worship is performed by a Charaj/Bujru whom *dan* is given. Some also give *dan* to their *dhyan* (married daughters). The community is served a ceremonial meal. Annual and fourth annual death rites are also observed.

Earlier they used to collect gold and silver pieces from among the ashes of the dead in the cremation ground and used to sell them to jewellers. Presently this occupation is looked down upon by others, though it stealthily continues in some cases. In addition, they also used to collect gold/silver, copper particles by washing the waste of the jewellers thrown into drains. But, presently these occupations have become secondary. The community has also been noted traditionally as growers of vegetables. They take contracts for growing vegetables in the agricultural farms of big landlords and of selling the same in the market. They are said to be excellent vegetable growers and businessmen in that trade. The Hadi women commonly go out of their homes for selling articles of common consumption as hawkers in nearby villages and earn cash or cereals. The men act as general labourers on road, building construction, forestry, and as coolies at bus stands and railway stations. They also trade in domestic animals—buffaloes, ox, sheep and goats. They have no land of their own. The children help their parents in their economic activities. There is however, no bonded labour in the community. The market is located in the vicinity.

The social control of the community is usually in the hands of the elderly males and also with the statutory Gram Panchayat. The traditional caste council is ineffective, though recently they have revived it and made it a formal body known as Hadi Nav Kalyan Sabha controlled by a *pradhan*, a secretary and some members elected by the people by indirect polling or a voice vote. This Sabha strives for improving the social lot of the community by educating children, controlling marriage expenditure, and also fights for achieving a constitutional status of a Scheduled Caste for the community.

The Hadi worship Hindu gods and goddesses. Some propitiate Ambika Devi as their clan deity. Brajeshwari Mata, Chamunda Devi and Jawalamukhi are propitiated as local and regional deities. The holy shrines of the deities are visited, particularly on annual fairs as well as on occasion of marriage and birth. Their sacred specialists include a Brahman priest for performing marriage rituals, *chela* for removing evil spirits like *bhoot* and for confirmation of theft and guilt, a Bujru/Charaj for performing death rites. The Hadis participate in all Hindu festivals; the main local fairs attended by them are - Nag mela, Draman fair, Navratre fair, Bilbhadra (wrestling) Chhinj fair, Mataur fair, Rait fair, etc. There is no community-specific art, craft. Regional Kangri or Pahari folksongs, folklore, folktales are shared.

In Kangra they live in the locality of the sweepers (Balmiki) from whom they do not accept cooked food and water but only *sidha* food. Balmiki and Julaha are also offered only *sidha* food. The cremation grounds however, are located on the riverside and are not specific to the community.

Modern developmental programmes have made little impact on the community. The boys and the girls get only primary and middle school level education, barring a few boys who entered college at the time of this study. Poverty/poor economic resources are the main reasons for this. Health and medicare facilities are accessible but they can little afford the same and they also use traditional methods of medicare. They avail themselves of electricity, drinking water and railway and road communication facilities at their doorsteps. Mass media (radio, television and cinema) facilities are available in the neighbourhood. Presently some have accepted sterilization as the method of family planning. IRDP has not given them any assistance and they live in slum-like dwellings on the fringe of the Kangra town. Only immunization is availed of under ICDS. They use firewood, coal or kerosene oil as energy sources. Fair price shops are located in the vicinity for public distribution of the essential commodities. People have little to save and most of them remain indebted to the local shopkeepers and moneylenders.

A. R. Sankhyan

HALI

The Hali, Arya or Dhingra is chiefly employed in field labour, either as farm servants or as tenants. They predominantly inhabit Chamba district and other parts of Himachal Pradesh adjoining Punjab where they are classed as a scheduled caste and have a population of 20,485 (the 1981 Census). The word Hali, means a person who earns his livelihood by *hal* (plough). They are believed to have come as servants in gift along with the princess of Delhi in marriage to Chamba sometimes in the past. Rose (1914): stated the names Koli, Dagi, Chanal and Hali all are used almost synonymously with a territorial differentation to denote the low caste in the hills. The term 'Koli' is used in Kullu and Kinnaur, Dagi in upper part of Lahaul-Spiti, Chanal in Kangra and Mandi and Hali in Chamba. All of them traditionally practised the same occupation, of skinning and tanning the dead animals, removing the carcass and doing other low jobs, and were regarded as untouchables. However, this does not hold good today, as each of the communities mentioned earlier maintain its respective identity.

The Halis share their homestead with other communities, but in a separate locality, which is wholly occupied by them. They are basically illiterate people, with very few who have gone in for education. They converse among themselves in the Chambiali dialect whereas with others they converse in Hindustani. Their script among themselves is Perso-Arabic, and a few also know Tankri. With others Perso-Arabic and Devanagari scripts are used.

They are non-vegetarian. Traditionally, they used to eat the flesh of dead animals, but have given up the practice now. Presently, a section of them avoid taking meat of dead buffalo or cow, but others do take it. Their staple food is rice and *rongi* or *mah*, with occasional to moderate consumption of vegetables, roots, tubers and fruits. Mustard oil and animal fat are the usual cooking media. Milk, *lassi*, curd and *ghee* are consumed. They take alcoholic drinks, which are often home-brewed, but occasionally are also purchased from the market. They smoke tabacco and sometimes chew it. Usually non-vegetarian food is avoided at solemn occasions, but their intake increases along with that of liquor in winter months. The use of carrion has been given up, by the followers of Arya Samaj movement.

Some bio-anthropological information on the community is given in the bio-anthropological report.

There are a number of exogamous *septs,* viz., Badhora, Badi, Basiura, Chilkhwan, Dhulkan, Ghahi, Ghelan, Jurgho, Kahan, Kardocha, Kharere, Khawal, Khripar, Kodhe, Marenu, Mahan, Pachran, Ramsan, Rihanu and

Torain. These helps to regulate the marriage alliances.The people have started using 'Arya' as their surnames nowadays, to upgrade their social position. A few also suffix the term Dhingra.The community occupies the lowest place in the social heirarchy and are almost treated as untouchables by the upper caste communities, and this fact is acknowledged almost by all. They are also aware of the varna system and their low position in it.

Endogamy at the community level and exogamy at the septs level are practised for regulating marriages. Hypogamy meets with social approval. Consanguineous marriages are prohibited. While contracting marriages, seven generations on the father's side are avoided whereas four generations are avoided on the mother's side. Junior sororate and levirate are practised.

Till almost Independence, child marriage followed by *gaona* at the time of attaining puberty was prevalent, but now marriages are performed at the age of 18 and 21 for girls and boys respectively. Mates are acquired by *byah* and by service. In the former, marriage is performed by circumambulation, whereas in the latter it is performed by service, wherein a son-in-law serves in the prospective bride's house for sometime and then marries her.

Monogamy is usually practised, but bigamy is resorted to when the first wife is unable to bear a heir to the family. *Dori* and *bala* are the traditional marriage symbols which continue to be strictly adhered to even today. Some women also put vermilion in the parting of their hair. *Malia* (bride-price) was prevalent once upon a time which consisted of 60 silver coins to be paid in cash, but these days it is being replaced by *dahej*, which is usually in kind and includes items such as utensils, clothes, agricultural equipments, *charkha* (spinning wheel), sheep, goat and cow. The girl after marriage comes to stay with her husband, but when there are no sons, a *ghar-jawai* comes to stay with his wife's family.

To leave or *chhad-chhada* (divorce) is prevalent, and either of the parties can divorce with the approval of the panchayat, on grounds of infidelity, maladjustment and cruelty. The compensation is decreed to the aggrieved on the merit of the case, but children normally are the liability of the father. *Gadhoj* (widow marriage) is permitted. It is a simple ceremony and is symbolised by gifting a *choli* and *dori* to the widow. In case a widower remarries an unmarried girl, full marriage rites are observed. A widow, even without performing *gadhoj*, can continue to live in the house and bear children, such children being called *chakhandu*.

The family is of a vertically extended type. The eldest male member is the head of the household, and commands greater respect and authority in the family. The interpersonal relations within the family are that of love, cordiality and respect. The husband and wife refer to each other teknonymically. Avoidance is observed with the husband's elder male relatives and joking relationship exists with the husband's and wife's younger relatives of both the sexes. A situation of conflict or confrontation rarely comes, but if it does, it relates to property matters.

The property is inherited according to the *mundaband* law of inheritance, where all male children inherit parental property equally. Even the *chakhandu*, has the right to inheritance. *Hallad* (illegitimate children) have no right of inheritance.

The position of the women is low. This is in spite of their full-fledged economic participation in and outside the house. They carry out all the agricultural activities except ploughing. They also work as agricultural labourers in others' fields and contribute to the family income. Presently, some of the women who are educated, have taken up white-collar jobs in Government and private organizations. They also arrange fodder and fuel wood for stocking for the winter months, besides managing the entire family affairs right from cooking, to doing all the household chores. They participate in all the religious rituals and social activities, and also take part in political activities which is limited only to casting votes.

Post-natal restriction on the mother and pollution is observed for a period of 20 days. On the completion of 90 days of birth, the child is brought out of the house and shown the sun and moon. This is known as *akraran*. Six months after the birth, *khirpu* ceremony and the christening ceremony are observed. At two and a half years or in the fifth year *jattu* is observed, wherein the boy's head is shaved off.

Marriage is solemnized at the bride's place by circumambulating the sacred fire seven times in a thatched canopy, amidst chanting of *mantra* by a Bitlaha (a degraded Brahman) who conducts the ceremony. Nuptial ceremony is observed at the groom's house, but in earlier days, the bride was first offered to the Laxmi Narayan deity. The dead are cremated with the last rites being performed by the eldest male of the family. The remnants of the bones and ashes are immersed in a river.

The traditional occupations of the community were to skin and tan dead animals, to remove carcasses, and to play music. All the community members have given up these traditional occupations, except the playing of musical instruments. Currently a majority of them depend on agriculture, which is self-owned and is the primary source of their livelihood. Some persons also plough the land of others on *ghar* (sharecropping) in which the entire produce is divided on a 50-50 basis. As a subsidiary occupation, they have taken up jobs in both Government and private organizations as unskilled labourers and farm servants. A few of them have also taken up white-collar jobs. They have direct dependence on the daily market, where cash is the medium of exchange. The children below the age of 15, both boys and girls, also attend to the cattle and work as farm labourers in others' field where they are paid both in cash and kind.

Social control is maintained within the community by their traditional *biradari* panchayat. It is headed by a *mukhiya* who is assisted by a group of three to five nominated *panch* on their ability to impart justice impartially and with prudence. They usually deal with cases of marital discord, breach of community norms and petty thefts. The judgement is pronounced by the *mukhiya* in consultation with the *panch,* which is binding and has to be honoured. On not honouring the decision, the guilty person is excommunicated or is fined usually in kind, but occasionally a cash fine is also imposed in case the crime is severe. The fine thus realized is spent towards defraying the expenditure on panchayat. After Independence statutory panchayats have come into existence for implementation and planning of welfare activities. But their traditional council still has a greater hold among on the people.

The Halis follow Hindu religion, and are basically Shaivite. They have family deities which are their ancestors and propitiated for the welfare of the family members. They have clan deities who are represented by Nag Deota. Their regional deity is Chamunda Devi, Jalpa, Shakti and Sitala who are also worshipped by all. Besides, they also worship other gods and goddesses of the wider Hindu pantheon. Their major sacred centre is Manimahesh, the pilgrimage of which is a must for salvation. Their sacred specialists the Bitlaha officiates at life-cycle rituals and the *chela* is from the Sippi community.The major fairs are Jatra and Minjar and the festivals are Basoa, Lohri, Shivratri, Diwali and Dusherra. All these have socioreligious significance which are recalled in their myths.

They have been the greatest beneficiary of the reformistic movements. Prominent among these are the Arya Samaj and the Nirankari movement, which resulted in their becoming vegetarian, adoption of Sanskritic rituals and adopting the Arya Samaj way of life and Sikhism.

They are skilled in the art of weaving woollen *pattu* or *gardu* essentially for their own use. They are also deft in the art of Chamba embroidery which is made over a *rumal* (piece of cloth). The folktales and folksongs are shared with other communities of the region. The men play drums and provide music at social occasions. Women dance on social occasions purely for amusement.

The traditional intercommunity linkages existed with other communities, to remove dead animals and to tan their skin and as musicians at social ceremonies. No *savarna* accepted *kachcha* or *pucca* food from them. On the other hand they could accept both types of food from others. From a Chuhra or a Sippi, a Hali can accept only *pucca* food. Intercommunity marriages do not take place but putative kinship exists. The community has access to common water sources, temples, panchayats and schools. *Jajmani* relationship existed with different communities from whom they received foodgrains at harvest times in lieu of their services and till land as sharecroppers.

Attainment of education has provided them jobs in the public and private sectors. Awareness has also brought them in the political arena. Consequently political leadership has emerged at the local and regional level. Their interaction with the people of different communities in urban areas has loosened some rigidity, but in the remote villages it is still observed.

The Halis have been greatly benefited by the Government developmental programmes. They send their children to colleges for higher education. But in the villages the girls dropout after primary or secondary school due to lack of educational facilities. People avail themselves of modern medical facilities in addition to their traditional medicines. The younger educated generation prefers having two or three children and use modern contraceptive devices. They are however averse to sterilization because of the prevalent belief that it renders them weak in doing any physical labour. They have availed themselves of the facilities of loans from government agencies for poultry farming, or setting up shops of general merchandise. They also obtained employment as administrators and in police departments, through reserved quota.

In the townships, piped drinking water is available, whereas in villages water is available from streams. The villages which exist near the town are well-connected with metalled roads, public transport, television and post and telegraph offices. Electricity is available in many of the villages through hydroelectric sub-stations. Wood and kerosene are the usual fuels for cooking. Mid-day meal scheme, nutritional programmes and immunization schemes under the Integrated Child Development Scheme is availed of by school-going children, infants, nursing and expectant mothers. The people avail themselves of the public distribution facilities which provide them food items, clothes and kerosene at subsidized rates.

Rajendra Sarkar

HESI

The Hesi were the traditional vagrant minstrels who used to subsist by playing a pipe (*shehnai*) and beating *tambourin* or *dholak* and singing wedding, greeting and folk songs. The community is also pronounced as Hensi in Kangra. The Sanhai community also plays *shehnai*, but it is observed that the people consider the Hesi and the Sanhai belonging to the same community. Usually the community members take pride in calling themselves Sanhai, which is a more respectable term than Hesi. It is said that the name Sanhai is given to the community when they play *shehnai* on auspicious occasions or marriages. The name Hesi is given to them when they play shehnai on deaths. The Hesis are considered an eighteenth caste and an "odd caste" (Ibbetson, 1916; Rose, 1919). They have been given the unauspicious month of Chaitra of the Hindu calendar which falls during March-April called *Hesion ka Mahina* (Hesi's month) for begging. During this month, which is considered a closed month for marriage among Hindus, they wander from place to place and play *shehnai* and sing folksongs and earn cereals. This community is similar to the Beda/Beta in Spiti, Turi in Kullu and Bainsi in Chamba in the traditional occupation of country musicians.

The communities having this occupation are identified in different regions of the country but the Hesis perceive their distribution at the regional level. They inhabit mainly Bilaspur, Hamirpur, Mandi, Kangra and Shimla districts. The population figures have been shown separately for the Hesi (2037) and the Sanhai (1,675) according to the Census of India, 1981. They are classified among the scheduled castes in the State. They live in the hilly terrain and valleys of the sub-Himalayas experiencing generally warm and temperate climate most of the year with medium rainfall and low humidity. The hill ranges are covered with thin canopies of pine forests. They speak the regional dialects of the western Pahari, e.g., Bilaspuri in Bilaspur and Kangri in Kangra district, and write in Devanagari script within and outside the community. The men commonly wear a cap, *kurta* and *pyjama* and the younger men wear trousers. The women traditionally wear a *kurti*, a *ghagri* and a *chadru* or *dupatta*. The women also wear silver ornaments of nose, ear, wrist and ankle, like *murki, bali, choora* and *paijeb*.

The Hesis occasionally consume non-vegetarian diet which includes eggs, fish, meat and sometimes pork. The staple food is shared with other regional communities, which is mainly maize for most of the winter and wheat for most of the summer, supplemented by rice. Various pulses—*urd, moong, masur, moth, arhar/kesari, kulthi*, peas, beans and whatever they acquire through begging/offerings are eaten. Different seasonal vegetables and roots and tubers are regularly eaten. The cooking medium is vegetable *ghee* or mustard oil. There are no food taboos except on death. Milk intake is occasional but milk products like *matha* or *lassi* are frequently consumed. Fruit intake is occasional and seasonal. Men and women occasionally drink countrymade liquor from the sugar molasses prepared by some people. Men smoke tobacco in indigenous *chilam* or *hukka* or *bidi* and cigarettes, if available.

Kaundal, Jaswal, Rattanjot, Vaid, Gial, some are social units which suggest ancestry/descent and regulate marriage alliances. The Hesis claim descent from the Kshatriyas but their claim is never entertained by other people and they are placed among the Sudras at par with the Chamar, Dumna and Julaha in the regional social hierarchy. Their marriages are regulated by the rules of community endogamy and clan/*got* and village exogamy.

Marriages mainly take place through negotiation, and exchange of sisters in common called *batta-satta.* Bride-price was prevalent in the recent past but presently it is looked down upon socially and they adhere to *dharam-punya* marriages or *kanyadan* pattern and also give some dowry, called *daj* or *dahej.* Presently, adult marriages are common but earlier a girl married before the attainment of puberty only was considered *kanyadan.* Marriage symbols strictly observed are *sindur,* glass bangles and a nose pin/stud or ring. The bride lives patrilocally at the husband's parental home. Junior levirate is resorted to for widow remarriage, and a widower may marry junior sororate or somebody else. Divorce is also socially approved for both the spouses on grounds of maladjustment and cruelty to wife. Presently it becomes viable through judicial approval and the man pays compensation or maintenance to his spouse. Children are also his liability. Both the divorcees can remarry.

The family pattern of the Hesis is becoming predominantly nuclear and the vertically extended joint families usually breakup when the sons get married. In the joint families the *lari* maintains a *ghoond* from her *saurah, jeth* and *nandoi.* But in Mandi, Kullu and Shimla hills, the *ghoond* is not observed. Joking relations, as in many Hindu communities of the region, exist between *devar-bhavi, jija-sali, nanad-bhabi* and *jija-sala.* The property is inherited on male lines as per the rule of equigeniture and the eldest son succeeds the father at his death, but usually an earning son commands the family. Conflicts may arise on property matters.

Women's status is at par with that of men for all practical purposes. They contribute to the family income by participating in seeking alms from people by accompanying men for singing. They also earn by rendering various services to village landlords. They participate in agriculture and animal husbandry (wherever the Hesis possess some landholding), collect fuel and fodder and bring potable water. They also participate in social and religious ceremonies but have little say in the mechanism of social control and political activities. They however have freedom in family decision-making and regulate family expenditure.

The life-cycle rituals are performed as per the Hindu scriptures by the priest of their own community. Pre-delivery rituals are lacking, but restrictions both before and after delivery are imposed on the woman. The birth pollution called *sutak* is maintained for 13 days and the woman remains confined to a corner of the lower storey of the house and would not touch the meals of the family. *Gunt* ceremony makes the woman and family pure from *sutak*. Women songs are arranged. The christening and cereal-taking ceremonies are ignored. *Jatlu* or *mundan* among boys is the main childhood ritual performed by the *mama* of the child or *dharam bhai* on any odd year before the child is five years of age.

They follow Vedic rites for marriage. Worship of the *kulja* and oil ceremonies are observed before the major marriage rituals, *lagan* and *vedi* which are observed at the bride's place. The bride and groom circumambulate the sacred fire and in the end the parents of the bride give *sankalap* (*kanyadan*) of the girl. They also arrange a feast for the groom's party. At the bridegroom's place the bride and groom worship a *pipal* tree and circumambulate the tree in a ceremony called *Brahmapuja* (worship of Lord Brahma). Under this tree *dharam bhai* of the *lari* (bride) and *dharam bahin* of the *lara* (bridegroom) are made by tieing a *mauli* (red thread) on each other's wrist and giving some coins or rupees. With this the marriage ends followed by dance and music and a community feast. The bride returns to her parents soon after this, followed by the visit of the groom and his assistant called *lajoru*. Some rituals are performed at the bride's place and on the next day he carries the bride with him which is called *muklawa*. At bridegroom's place the bride performs *dawar puja* and *bauri puja* (well/step-well worship) after which she lives with her husband.

The death rites are similar to those of other Hindus. The dead are cremated and the ashes are immersed in the Satluj river (in Bilaspur) or in the Beas at Kaleshwar or Bhaleth (in Kangra). A few do the same in the Ganges at Hardwar and offer *pind dan* to a Panda. *Patak* lasts for 13 days and ends with a *havan* by the community priest who is also given some cash. The offerings are usually made to a *dhyan* of the family. Annual *barkhi* and *chabarkh* death rites are also observed.

The Hesis are traditionally village musicians who earned their livelihood by this occupation. They still continue with this occupation and move out especially in the month of Chaitra (March-April), to earn cereals and other alms. Some persons have given up *shehnai* and formed a brass-band party which performs instrumental music on marriages. They are mainly landless or possess small landholdings and rear a few cattle or sheep and goats to supplement their earnings. Many persons seek casual labour on daily wages on roads, forest and some are agricultural labourers. A few persons are employed in government jobs as peons and teachers, and a few are also in police and army.

There is no formal community council but the *sayane* of the community usually resolve social disputes and problems of profession, marriages and divorce. Village disputes are solved by the members of the statutory Gram Panchayat or by some influential persons of other neighbouring communities. The local village deities are also helpful in the mechanism of social control and the guilty feel scared of the curse of the deity.

The Hesis are all Hindus and worship various family/clan, village, regional and other deities of the wider Hindu pantheon. Lakhman Sidh is propitiated by some as family/clan deity. Other local/regional deities like Deot Sidh (Balaknath), Lakhdata, Nahar Singh, Bharthri Sidh and Guga are specially propitiated as village deities at different times and *roat*, a big loaf of bread coated with sugar is offered to please them for happiness in the family. Various female deities of greater reverence are Pandwin Devi, Sohni Devi, Naina Devi, Jawalamukhi, Chintpurni, etc., whose shrines are visited on annual fairs or on fulfilment of certain wishes. Various festivals like Lohri, Holi, Baisakhi, Rakhri (Rakshabandhan), Guganavmi, Navratre, Diwali, Shivratri, etc., are celebrated. The sacred specialists are from within and outside the community. The *chela* (oracle) are often consulted for certain diseases considered of supernatural origins caused by evil spirits.

The community plays the *shehnai*, beats *dholak* (drum) and sing folksongs or light classical or Hindustani music. Both men and women usually sing songs of Shiva-Parvati and Rama-Sita *byah*. Other folksongs sung are *Jhanjoti, Kunju-Chenchlo, Phulmu-Ranjhu, Gambri, Mohan* and other popular film songs. In Kullu a dance without the music of the Hesis is regarded incomplete as is reflected in a folk saying: '*Baaj nai dholia dhili nati, jaach ni bandi Hesi ghati*'. *Gidda* among women and *Nati* or simple dance among men are usually performed on occasions of marriage.

They may exchange *kachcha* and *pucca* food and water with the Chamar, Dumna/Bhanjra and Julaha. In some cases, some well-off Hesis may invite some people of upper castes in their social ceremonies—marriage or a *bhati/yagya* (feast) but offer a *suchchi rasoi* cooked by a Bramhan/Rajput *boti* (cook) or may also give *sukka* or *sidha*. Cremation grounds are separate or may overlap and located on the bed of a stream or streamlet. Religious shrines and other public places are common. Their role on festive occasion is to give music. They have some members in teaching and defence services and as members of the statutory Gram Panchayat.

The modern developmental programmes have made some impact on the Hesis and most of the people of the community have given up their vagrant life, have settled and possess some landholding. The rate of literacy has increased but is more favourable for boys. The boys however do not study beyond secondary school level whereas the girls usually get primary school education only. The reasons are both economic and social. The latter is applicable for girls who are considered mere social liabilities to the parents and have to be married off soon. In the arena of health and medicare, modern treatment is favoured but is not easily available or they cannot afford costly medicines and therefore often use indigenous methods. Presently, there is a favourable response to limiting the family size up to three children but a male child is desired very much. They adopt sterilization as a method for family planning.

Drinking water is available in the village through pipes but sometimes traditional sources like springs and *bauri* are also used at the time of inadequate supply of piped water. Provisions under the Intensive Rural Development Programmes (IRDP) have been kept for the community as for other scheduled caste. They get loans and 50 per cent subsidies on the purchase of animals, threshers and on chemical fertilizers. Their houses have electricity and some of them enjoy modern mass media (radio and television) facilities as these are available in the villages. Road, communication and postal facilities are within their reach. Their enery resources are firewood and cowdung cakes. Some of the nutritional (ICDS) programmes are available to their children. Public distribution system is availed of. The people generally live from hand-to-mouth and generally remain indebted to local shopkeepers and landlords.

A.R. Sankhyan

JAIN

Jainism is one of the indigenous religions of India. The term 'Jain' is derived from Jina, or the one who conquers enemies like attachment, passion, jealousy and so on (Shah, 1983: 77). A true Jain should entirely renounce all thoughts of self. The Jains not only reject all spurious additions, but look upon them with absolute horror. Four or five centuries ago the Jains exercised sovereign power in several provinces but nowadays they are powerless. According to Jain faith all beings are divided into two classes, animate and inanimate. Animate beings are composed of a soul and a body, and the souls, being radically distinct from matter, are eternal. *Nirvana* is annihilation of the soul. The way to *nirvana* is naturally revealed by the Jina. The means of reaching it constitute the *triratna*—first, perfect faith; second, perfect knowledge; and third, perfect conduct. Jain religion probably was founded by Parsvanath and reformed by Mahavira who was a contemporary of Buddha. Vaish Agarwals who adopted Jainism, are a religious minority. The Jain, being mostly traders, live in towns. In Himachal Pradesh, there are 1064 Jains (1981 Census). They are not indigenous to the State. According to historical accounts they came to this part of the country in search of livelihood. The climate of the area is cold; during summers it is pleasant. The area has hilly terrain, low humidity and thin forest with medium rainfall. In winters the area gets moderate snowfall. They speak Hindi both in the house and outside. They use Devanagari script while writing.

They are pure vegetarians who do not eat onion and garlic, but nowadays a few have started taking them. They chew betel, take tea and some also smoke cigarettes. Their staple food consists of wheat, rice, pulses like gram, *moong*, *arhar*, beans and all types of seasonal vegetables like spinach, brinjal, lady finger, cauliflower, cabbage, carrot, cucumber, etc. They use mustard oil, groundnut oil and hydrogenated cooking oil for preparing curries. They also take fruits, milk and milk products.

They are divided into two sects the Shvetambar and the Digambar. The former is a 'white-clad' sect, which derives its authority from Parshvanath, while the latter are 'sky-clad' or the nude sect. The holy men among them still maintain nudity, whereas others wear coloured garments. The basic difference between the two sects is of ideology. The Shvetambars feel that one can get *moksha* in family life while the Digambars refute the idea.

They are further subdivided into seventeen and a half exogamous *gotras*, which derive their names from different sages. The community maintains endogamy at the sect level, but marriages with non-Jains or Vaish-Agarwals are commonly practised. The marriages are performed in adulthood by negotiation in which dowry is given both in cash and kind. The marriage symbols of *bindi* and toe-ring are not rigidly observed. Divorce and widow remarriage is socially not permitted, but widower remarriage and sororate are permissible. The residence for the bride is patrilocal, but the families which originally were of mixed extended type are giving way to nuclear families. Avoidance exists with the elder male relatives of the husband, but joking relationships exist with the husband's and wife's younger relatives. The inheritence is as per male equigeniture, and the eldest male member succeeds as head of the family.

The status of woman is equal to that of the men. She takes part in other economic activities and contributes to family income besides having a role in the social and political sphere, but has little role in mechanism of social control. The Shvetambars give women full membership in the monastic order, but the Digambars prohibit them from entering the temples.

In the sphere of life-cycle rituals pre- and post-natal restrictions exist and post-delivery observance of pollution is also reported. *Mundan* ceremony is observed for both males and females. The most important rite is the *parojan* (initiation) when the child is initiated into Jainism. When a novice is initiated, he renounces the world and takes *diksha.* Shaving off the hair under a tree is the most important rite. Marriages are performed at the bride's residence but the consummation takes place at the groom's house. A feast is given by both sides in marriage. When the bride and the bridegroom reach the groom's house they are affectionately received by the relatives of the groom. The dead are cremated and ashes are immersed in river. They reject the *shradha* or rites for the repose of the spirit.

The community is primarily involved in business, trade and industry. A few also work in government and private service. They have direct links with the daily local market which is fully regulated, where cash forms the medium of exchange. The community has councils, Jain Sabhas, which operate at national and regional level. These are basically for regulating their religious activities, controlling social evils and reviving community unity. Statutory panchayats also coexist with these councils. They follow their individual sectarian faith. Their chief objects of worship are the Jina or Trithankara, whom they worship with flowers and incense and candles. Hymns of their praise are sung. Each Tirthankara has a separate sign which is usually placed below his image. Their sacred text, *Agavr,* preaches *ahimsa* (non-violence) which helps in reaching the ultimate salvation *moksha.* Most of the Jains today also have faith in the deities of the wider Hindu pantheon. Their sacred specialists are from outside as well as from within the community, who officiate in their temples and conduct ceremonies of wedding and of funerals. The Jains observe twelve ceremonies for purification. They possess some of the most remarkable places of pilgrimage situated in the midst of mountains in the west, south and east. Their most important festival is the Mahavir Jayanti which is of socioreligious significance. The community has oral traditions which are in the form of folktales and folksongs which are sung by women.

The Shvetambars would seek their food each day from many houses of their own community in small quantities but the Digambar would accept food from only one of the homes. When the sun sets they do not take any food and do not take water without straining it first. Many of them put on cloth over their mouth so that they may not inhale insects or any living thing directly or indirectly. With the clean castes the Shvetambars can accept and exchange *kachcha*, *pucca* and *sidha* food, but with the unclean castes this is not observed. Intercommunity marriages take place, but putative kinship does not exist. They share cremation ground and water with other communities. The Jains observe all Hindu fasts and visit the Hindu places of pilgrimages though they have holy places of their own. They participate in traditional festivals but have no specific role. The community has entrepreneurs, scholars, creative artists, teachers, administratiors, doctors and engineers. The modern linkages have loosened traditional rigidity.

Being traders and businessmen the Jains are economically well-off and they take much interest in the education of their children. Their boys and girls join colleges and universities for higher education. But their daughters drop out from studies due to social reasons. Whenever they feel sick they go for modern medical care. They also use homeopathic medicines for their children and elderly persons. They are aware of the benefit of a small family and they adopt family planning methods at the doctor's advice. Though preference varies from person to person, many of them have two to three children. They collect drinking water from taps. There is no special programme of development specifically for this community only as it is one of the enlightened communities. They are engaged in both employment and self-employment.

D. K. Chakraborty

JAT

The Jat is a well-known community of the traditional cultivators identified at national/interregional level. The meaning of the word 'Jat' is derived from the *jata* (hair) of Lord Shiva. Accordingly there are two main divisions of the Jat, namely, the Shivgotri also called *asli Jat* (true Jat) and the others Kasabgotri. There are further subdivisions of the two categories (Rose 1919; Ibbetson, 1916; Bingley, 1904) but this categorization is of little significance in Himachal Pradesh where they distinguish themselves only by *got*. Historical and ethnographic accounts are available for the community in various old books. Historically, the Jats are regarded as degraded Rajputs who broke away from the Rajputs as they started ploughing, practised widow remarriages and accepted bride price (Rose 1919).

The Jats migrated to the Shivalik hills in Himachal Pradesh from the Punjab plains in the recent past but they are unable to recall the history of their migration. They are concentrated in the districts of Bilaspur, Hamirpur, Mandi, Kangra and Una, occupying a hilly terrain and valleys of the Himalayan foothills experiencing in general a warm and temperate climate, low humidity and moderate annual rainfall. The hill ranges are covered here and there with thin canopies of forests. They have assimilated regional/local cultures and are indistinguishable from other agricultural communities in language, dress and ornaments. They speak the Bilaspuri dialect in Bilaspur and Hamirpur districts and Mandiali and Kangri dialects in Mandi and Kangra respectively of the western Pahari. Written communication within and outside the community is in Devanagari script. Men wear a *kurta* and *pyjama* or trousers and sometimes a *safa*. The women wear *kurti*, *shalwar* and *chadru* or *dupatta*. Common traditional ornaments of women are golden *laung/ tilli* or *murki*, *chak* on head, *bali* or *kante*, *har*, *gajra* or *choora* of silver and *paijeb* or *jhanjar* of silver.

The Jats are occasionally non-vegetarian, eating fish, eggs and meat including pork. But, in recent years many of them have started following the Radhaswami socioreligious movement. As a consequence many of them have given up eating non-vegetarian food and have become pure vegetarians. Their common staple food is wheat and maize supplemented by rice. Barley flour is also eaten sometimes in the form of *sattu*. The pulses frequently consumed are - *urd, moong, masur, moth, kulthi, raungi*, beans, peas and grams. Various types of local vegetables—*lauki, kaddu, tori, karela, bhindi, baingan/ bhathe, phool gobhi, band gobhi, mooli, gajar* and mustard leaves are commonly eaten. Among tubers, *kachalu, arbi/beju, alu* and *zimikand* (yams) are frequently consumed. The cooking medium is mustard oil or sometimes groundnut oils or *desi*/vegetable *ghee*. Common fruits eaten include mango, guava, banana, peach, apple, *jamun*, mulberry and berries and sometimes wild figs like *dangle, tiamlu, akhe, kainth* and *garnu*. Festive food preparations include *babru, bhalle* (cakes of pulses), *halwa* and *kheer, seviyan, ankloo* and *ankli* of rice flour. *Khichri* with *desi ghee* and curd/milk is eaten during Lohri festival and *sag* of mustard leaves is frequently eaten during winters.

The distinction between the Shivgotri and the Kasabgotri Jats is not known to most of them and they simply know the names of their *got*. There is no hierarchical stratification. The various clans noted in the study area are Rai, Gill, Dehal, Bains, Hear, Dhaliwal, Bansre, Panchalad and Malait. The *got* or clans denote descent from a particular lineage and are used to regulate marriage alliances. Some also use these as surnames. The religious differentiation at sect level has not yet given way to social matrimonial differences. The Jat claim their social position in the regional hierarchy among the Kshatriyas but usually they are placed just at par with the Kanet Rajputs.

Their institution of marriage is also quite similar to the Kanet Rajputs. The community is endogamous and follows the rules of *got* and village exogamy. Marriages occur through negotiation by parents and relatives, but *batta-satta* also occurs. Earlier pre-puberty or child marriages were common and bride price was taken. But presently bride-price is not taken any more and post-puberty or adult marriages occur. Bride-price has completely given way to *kanyadan* pattern and dowry is given by the parents in the form of household and agricultural articles, cloths, ornaments and domestic animals. Slowly, costly modern items are also being given or are being demanded and some rich people give cash too.

Monogamy is the common practice but a second wife can be taken if the first wife does not produce any male child. Marriage symbols are *sindur* or *bindi*, glass bangles and nose/ear ornaments. The bride lives patrilocally. Widow remarriage or junior levirate is approved of socially. Such a marriage is almost ritualless and is completed by putting on a *chadar* (cloth) on the widow and an ornament is given to her by her new husband. A small feast is sometimes arranged for friends and neighbours.

At present, however, the younger generation does not favour junior levirate and widows may not even remarry or may live with any other man of their choice. This is called *baithna* (to sit). A man may marry a junior sororate or any other girl. Divorce is also allowed in the community with social approval or with the approval of civil courts, and either of the spouses may dissolve the marriage on grounds of maladjustments and cruelty. Children become the liability of the father and the woman is also compensated. The divorcees have freedom to remarry. The main changes in the institution of marriage that have occured since India's Independence are increase in the age of marriage, bride-price giving way to dowry system, dislike for junior levirate remarriages and legalization of divorce rules, protecting women's interests.

The community has still retained the vertically extended joint family system to a considerable degree. The family does not break as long as the father is alive or dominating. The elders are respected. But clashes on property matters, due to favouritism shown by parents towards a particular son or his wife and unequal division of labour are contributing to the breaking of the joint families. Also, the sons working outside the home force their parents to allow their families to live along with them. *Lari* maintains avoidance relationship with her *saurah*, *jeth*, *nandoi* and other elderly males of the village/community. The *lari* also touches their feet but covers her face from them. Joking occurs between *devar* and *bhabi*, *jija* and *sali*, *jija* and *sala* and *nanad* and *bharjai*. The two *kuram* and *kurmani* at marriage also cut jokes with one another.

Paternal property is inherited by the rule of male equigeniture. The eldest son becomes the successor of his father at his death but the mother's voice also prevails. The status of Jat women is lower than that of men even though they do all domestic, agricultural and animal husbandry work, collect fuel and fodder and bring potable water. They also regulate family expenditure and have a say in domestic decision-making. They participate in all social and religious ceremonies. The mechanism of social control and political activities are however not their domain and they also do not contribute to family income by way of seeking employment. Presently, however, a few women have sought employment in government.

The life-cycle rituals are observed as per the Hindu tenets. Those adhering to the Sanatana Dharma observe fairly elaborate rituals but the followers of the Radhaswami sect observe only a few Sanatana Dharma rituals and mainly arrange a religious gathering called *satsang* and visit the shrine of their Guru at Beas in Amritsar district (Punjab). The post-delivery pollution called *sutak* is observed for 13 days when the woman remains impure and is confined to a room in the house. The purification ceremony is called *guntrala*. Sweetened germinated grams are distributed and the village ladies sing greeting songs called *ranjhunana* on the birth of a boy. The christening and cereal-taking ceremonies are ignored. *Mundan* is the main childhood ritual performed for the son by the child's *mama* or any other person who has a putative kinship. *Janeu* is put on marriage only.

Among the pre-marriage rituals are *sagai/karmai* and *tika* in which the marriage is fixed by exchanging *shakkar* (sugar) or sweets and giving ceremonial clothes and rupees to the boy and the girl by the prospective in-laws. On the marriage day the usual rituals are *sand* and *samuhat* in which a Brahman priest (among non-Radhaswami) performs *puja* and the girl/boy are applied *batna* and *mehndi*. Most of the rituals occur at the bride's place when the bride and groom circumambulate the sacred fire in the *vedi* and the parents of the bride perform her *kanyadan*. They also give a feast to the groom's party. The bride enters the house after the *andrera* ritual. The other major ritual is *pipal* or Brahma worship. The bride and the groom take rounds of the holy tree and tie a white thread around it. Putative kinship-based friends are made on the spot by the bride and groom. The marriage ends with music and dance and finally a feast called *dham* is given by the parents of the groom. The *muklawa* occurs the next day.

The dead are cremated and their ashes are immersed in the Ganges at Hardwar by the Sanatana followers but in the Beas river by the Radhaswami. Death pollution is maintained for 13 days and the Acharaj officiates to perform ancestor worship. But the Radhaswami do not employ an Acharaj and a simple *havan* is performed. Among the followers of the Radhaswami sect, the widows do not stop wearing bangles/ornaments and the sons do not get their head shaved off as is observed by the adherents of the Sanatan Dharam. The latter also perform annual *barkhi* and fourth annual *chabarkh* death anniversaries and annual *shradha* in the *pitra paksha* and serve meals to a Brahman priest and feed the crows, a cow and a dog. The rituals are being curtailed by the Radhaswami and ceremonies are becoming less expensive and simpler to perform, though the services of a Brahman priest are still used.

The community consists mainly of cultivators and they own land and practise agriculture and animal husbandry. Some also practise sericulture as a supplementary occupation. During their spare time the uneducated persons in the village seek casual daily-wage labour in road construction and forests. Many educated persons are employed in Government departments and private enterprises on various posts holding white-collar jobs like teachers, doctors, engineers and surveyors, and some are also in army. A few run chemist and general merchant shops, tea stalls, flour mills, etc. in the suburbs. The links with the market are direct and market is of daily nature and fully regulated. The dealings are in cash. The child labour exists to some extent and children assist their parents in various agricultural, animal husbandry and other activities. Some persons also plough other people's land on contract or sharecrop basis.

There is no organized Jat council and the elders of the community resolve social disputes. In some areas multi-ethnic village council plays some role in resolving socioeconomic disputes. But, at present the statutory Gram Panchayat usually resolves village disputes over land and water besides doing various welfare and developmental activities. Serious matters involving violence are referred to the police and a legal course is adopted.

The Jats worship the Hindu trinity. Besides, they have family/clan deities, like Ton Bharari, village or local deities like Guga, Balak Nath and

Lakhdata, Hari Devi and Santoshi Mata. The affiliation to the deities is family oriented or individualistic. Balak Nath and Guga are offered *roat* on each harvest. The Radhaswamis do not attach much importance to the various deities and from time to time they visit the shrine of their Guru at Beas to seek blessings. They also hold weekly *satsang* (gatherings) at different places in which the teachings of the Gurus are read. They still believe in evil spirits and *chela* are employed to remove their ill-effects. They celebrate various Hindu festivals like Lohri, Baisakhi, Chiran, Sair, Rakhri, Guga Naumi, Ram Naumi, Janamashtami, Shivratri and Diwali. Various local fairs of the deities are visited. Women know the art of knitting. They share various regional *pahari* folk oral traditions, folksongs and folktales. Popular among these are *Gambri, Mohan, Ranjhu-Phulmu, Mahia, Kunju-Chenchlo, Kangre de fauji, Bhala sipahiya dogria, Narsi Seth, Puran Bhagat, Nirgun Bhajan, Mata dian bhetan* and *kirtan*. Percussion music by *dholak* is common. A simple dance by men and *gidda* dance by young girls are performed on festive and marriage occasions.

Modern developmental programmes have made considerable impact on the community. Formal education has increased substantially but the higher/college education is usually not favoured for girls due to social and economic reasons and because colleges are far away. Boys drop out due to general lack of interest and because of the absence of job security for the educated youth.

Modern methods of medicare are adopted but indigenous methods are also sometimes used if modern methods do not yield good and quick results. The attitude towards family planning is becoming favourable and sterilization is the usual method adopted. Usually two or three children are desired in the family but they want one or two of these to be male children. Their houses are electrified and they use modern mass media (radio and TV) along with video facilities.

Drinking water is presently available through taps but during inadequate supply the traditional springs and *bauri* are also used. Road communication is quite near to the village and post and telegraph facilities are also within reach. Their energy sources are firewood, cowdung cakes and sometimes kerosene oil and Gobar Gas as well. Only general provisions exist under IRDP and are of little help to them specifically. Among the ICDS programme immunization facility is availed of. The sources of irrigation are mainly rain water or occasionally small streams. As progressive cultivators they use chemical fertilizers and pesticides plus organic manure.

A. R. Sankhyan

JHEEWAR

The Jheewar, also pronounced as Jhiwar/Jhinwar/Dhimar, are fishermen identified at national level by different names. They are also known as Gharati, the Kahar, the Mallah and the Mehre. The Jheewar or Jheeur or Jheer/Jhir is the more common name for the community. The glorified community name adopted by the community is Kashyap Rajput and local people also sometimes address them as Rana. Brief ethnographic acounts are available for the community in different old texts (Ibbetson, 1916; Rose, 1919; Crooke, 1896). The etymology of the Jheewar or Dhimar is traced from Dhingar, the son of Akis, a Chauhan Rajput of Garh Mukhiala of Salt Range. He was treated by people as a servant and nicknamed Jhiwar. His son Bhat had four sons who founded four *muhins,* each containing several *gots.* (Rose, 1919: 382). But the history of their origin and migration of the community in the State is unknown. They have probably been living in the State since time immemorial and are in considerable size though their exact population figure is not known. A clue about the population size of the community may be taken from their considerbale number (1,765) in Bilaspur district alone at the end of the nineteenth century (Kavi Ganesh Singh, 1892). The community is distributed almost in all districts in varying climates ranging from warm to temperate to cold with low humidity and moderate annual rainfall. Their settlements are usually located along the streams or near springs.

The Jheewars speak various dialects of the western Pahari, e.g., Bilasuri in Bilaspur district and write in Devanagari script both within and outside the community. During pre-Independence India, the script of Bilaspuri or Kehluri language was Tankri but it is not in practice these days. The common dress of older men was a *kurta* and a *kapeen* or *langot* (loin-cloth), but on festivals and festivities they used to wear *pyjama* and a *safa*. Women wear a *kurta* and *salwar* or *suthan* (flared trousers) and a *chadru/odni/chunni*. The older women used to wear a *dhatu* (head gear), *kurti* (short shirt) and *ghagri* (flared petty coat). Traditional ornaments of women were : a silver *chak* (a conical ornament of head) that was later replaced by a golden cup-shaped occipital *chak* called *gut da chak*, *kante* (golden earlets), *laung/tilli* (nose studs) or *murki* (coiled nose rings) now replaced by a *koka* (nose pin) and large studded *nath* (nose ring), silver *mahel* or *tandire* (necklets/rings), silver *gajre/choore* (large wrist rings) and silver *pajeb* or *jhanjar.*

The Jheewars are non-vegetarian. Fish is eaten more as compared to eggs and meat. Pork is also eaten at certain places. The main staple food is maize during most of the winter and wheat during summers. Rice is often cooked during festivites, feasts and for marriages. Various locally available pulses like *urd, moong, masur, kulthi, raungi,* soyabean, grams and sometimes peas are frequently consumed along with various green vegetables, roots and tubers. The cooking medium used is mustard oil or vegetable *ghee* or *desi ghee.* Milk is generally consumed by the children but the grown ups usually consume milk products particularly *chhah* (butter milk) and curd. Tea has also become a common non-alcoholic drink. Liquor is occasionally consumed by men and purchased from the local market. The followers of the Radhaswami sect generally remain vegetarian and also do not take liquor. Men smoke *bidi* or loose tobacco in an earthen hubble-bubble called *jhajri* or in a brass/bronze *hukka.* The rich smoke cigarettes. Fruit intake remains occasional and seasonal, the fruits eaten being the local mangoes, guava, peach, sometimes apples, mulberry, and figs like *dagle* and *tiamlu.* Festive food preparations are puddings like *kheer* and *halwa,* sweetened fried wheat cakes *babru, dhandru* or sweetened and fried wheat *putande* and similar product of rice called *ankli* and cake-like *anklu, seviyan* (vermicelli), *bhaturu* or *baturu* (fermented *roti*), *bhalle, khichri,* etc. Among the food taboos are the consumption of non-vegetarian foods, liquor and *heeng* (*Asafoetida*) and chewing of hard eatables like grams during death pollution. Cucumbers and roasted maize are also not eaten on the Sair festival day.

There are four *muhins* of the Jhiwar: (1) Lungo, (2) Ghul, (3) Dhengi, and (4) Tak, all having 15 clans. According to another legend Rani Kokilan, the guilty heroine of the Raja Rasalu married a Jhiwar and her three sons founded three *got:* siz, Sabir, Gabir and Sir (Rose 1919: 383), which serve to regulate marriages and denote ancestry. Some of the *al,* named after the ancestral villages, are Karlotu, Kasohlu. Malheru, Jangle, Retru, Matliane. Baglu etc. The clans are Chandel, Taak, Behdwal, Sansoi, etc. Most of the Jheewar claim Kashyap *gotra* but other *gotra* like Kaundal and Pundeer are also indicated in the community. Some persons suffix the *gotra*/ clan names and/ or Rana (a glorified title or name given to Jheewar) as surnames. There is some differentation at religious or socioreligious level when some people follow the Radhaswami movement, whereas the others follow Sanatana Dharma. Such differentation however, has not caused hierarchical or matrimonial discriminations. Claiming themselves to be Kashyap Rajputs, the Jheewars place themselves among the Kshatriya varna. However, at the regional level, the Rajput and Brahman conceive the social position of the Jheewar below that of the Rajput and at par with the certain Sudras, and the same is also reflected in the various services rendered by the Jheewar.

The community is endogamous and performs *al/got/gotra/* clan and village exogamy. The age of marriage for the girls at present is about 16 years or above and for the boys at or above 20, but some decades ago pre-puberty marriages were quite frequent and bride price also existed. In the absence of bride price *batta-satta* was practised. But, presently they perform *kanyadan dharam-punne* marriages and give some *daj-dan* in the form of articles of domestic use and sometimes a buffalo/sheep/goat as well. The exchange marriage is also infrequent at present. Monogamy is practised and negotiation is the mode of acquiring mates. A man may also marry another woman in case the first wife has not produced any male child. The marriage symbols are *sindur*, glass bangles and a nose and ear ornament. The bride lives patrilocally. On the death of a spouse both widow as well as widower may remarry. Earlier junior levirate was practised for widow remarriage and junior sororate for a widower. At present, however, junior levirate is not liked by younger persons, and either the widow does not marry or if she is young and childless, she may marry any person of her choice if considered fit by her parents and in-laws. A widower is free to marry any woman. The dissolution of marriage could occur as per the approval of the community council some decades back, but presently, it normally occurs with judicial approval of the civil courts. Either of the spouses can divorce on grounds of maladjustments and cruelty, but the wife seeks maintenance from the husband, and the father is liable to support the children. Both the divorcees are free to remarry.

The family patterns is still considerably of the vertically extended type and the sons usually obey their father. Usually the families do not breakup as long as the father is alive. Nevertheless, at times, the joint families do breakup when there is mismanagement, unequal division of labour, rude behaviour of the *sas* towards the *lari* and similar *jethani-devrani* and *nanad-bhabi* relations. The unfair distribution of the parental property quite often contributes to conflicts and breaking up of the joint families. Another reason is the son moving from his hometown/home place due to employment reasons. Avoidance relationship exists in the joint family and the *lari* avoids by covering her face in the presence of her *saurah*, *jeth*, *nandoi* and other elderly males of the village. There are joking ties between *devar* and *bhabi*, *jija* and *sali*, *jija* and *sala*, and on marriage occasion between the *kuram* and *kurmani*. The paternal property is inherited on male lines as per the rule of male equigeniture. After father's death, the eldest son becomes his successor.

The status of women in the Jheewar community is almost equal to that of men, though they lack a say in political matters and in the mechanisms of social control. They contribute to the family income by rendering services to the village landlords and acting as midwives in the village. They also assist men in attending to the flourmill. They do all domestic jobs, collect fuel and fodder, participate in agriculture and animal husbandry, bring potable water and participate in various social and religious ceremonies. They also regulate family expenditure though decision-making is finally a man's domain.

The Jheewars observe major Hindu life-cycle rituals. Pre-delivery rittuals are not observed but restrictions, both pre-natal and post-natal, exist on the woman. She is confined to an inner room called *obra/obri* on the ground floor of the house for delivery. Post-delivery pollution is observed for 13 days and purification occurs by *guntrala* ceremony in which she takes cow's urine and *Gangajal*. On the birth of a son sugar-coated germinated grams are distributed and the village women sing *ranjhunane*. The mother's father, *nana* of the child brings a *jhagu-topu* (child's dress) and wrist rings. The christening and cereal-taking ceremonies are ignored. The main childhood ritual is *mundan* or *jatlu* of the male child performed on an odd year after birth before five years of age. It is performed by the *mama* of the child or the *dharam bhai* of the child's mother. A feast is given to the young children of the village and a Brahman priest performs *havan*. The sacred thread ritual is performed at marriage only.

The pre-marriage rituals are *sagai* or *karmai* when sweets, clothes and a small ceremonial cash are exchanged by parents of the boys and girl and offered to the prospective mates. The rituals performed on marriage day are *sand* and *samuhat* when *batna* and *mehndi* ceremonies are observed. The family propitiates its *kuldevi*. The *lagan* and *ved* are the major marriage rituals performed by the Brahman *pandit* at the bride's residence. The bride and bridegroom circumambulate the sacred fire and finally the parents of the bride perform the *sankalap* or *kanyadan* and they offer a feast to the bridegroom's party. At the bride-groom's place, the first ritual is entering into the house, *andrera*. The second ritual is *pipal puja* in which the bride and groom take rounds of the *pipal* tree and tie a white thread round its stem. Putative kinship-based friends of the bride and groom are made at this time by tieing a *mauli* on each other's wrist. The marriage ends with music and dance and with a *dham* to the gathered friends and relatives. The *muklawa* is just a formality at present and occurs on the next day of the marriage and the marriage is consummated. The followers of the Radhaswami socioreligious movement have curtailed the rituals and simplified them.

The death rituals of the Jheewars are similar to those of the upper-caste Hindus. The dead are cremated and ashes are immersed in the Ganges at Hardwar but the Radhaswamis immerse them in the Beas river. The immersion and *pind patal* (ancestral worship) is performed by a *panda*. At home an earthen lamp is lighted for 13 days during *patak*. On the thirteenth day ancestor worship is performed by an Acharaj who seeks offerings in the name of the dead. The Brahman priest performs a purification *havan* and also seeks offerings. A ceremonial feast is given to the relatives, and villagers on the *solia*. Annual and fourth annual death anniversaries are also observed to commemorate the dead and ceremonial feasts are given. Annual *shradha* during the *pitri paksha* is observed and the Brahman are served meals, particularly *kheer* and the cows and crows are also offered a piece of the ceremonial meals.

Water has been the traditional natural resource for the Jheewar community but presently they have also acquired small landholdings and are engaged in agriculture and animal husbandry to supplement their income. Most of them run their own or shared *gharat.* They also fish to supplement their earnings. Fishing was quite a profitable occupation of the community, but now due to check by the Government on fishing without licence, only some of them practise this occupation. Some also run meat and fish shops and tea stalls and *dhaba* in suburbs and in the towns. Some persons also till land of others on sharecrop or cash-contract basis. There are many who work as labourers on the riverside as boulder-dressers and sand sievers, and as road and forest labourers. They also render customary services on festive occasions. Their women also earn as midwives and by rendering various services to the village landlords. Child labour exists.

The Jheewars have their community council, Biradari Panchayat, which consists of several members, one or more from each village and headed by a *pradhan.* This panchayat is however not very effective these days, though at times it is helpful in pressing their socioeconomic problems with the local administration or State Government. The Biradari Panchayat tries to create awareness among people for giving education to their children, to avoid unnecessary expenditure on marriages, to discourage early marriages, etc. Its *pradhan* is elected by a voice vote. Every family pays one rupee per month as subscription. The post-Independence statutory Gram panchayat performs the usual social developmental functions and sometimes also takes up certain socioeconomic disputes of the community. Usually statutory procedures are followed to seek economic justice.

The Jheewars, as Hindus worship gods and goddesses. There are different family and clan deities, e.g., Badoli Devi also known as Jalpa Mai or Jal Devi. Deot Sidh, Nahar Singh, Lakhdata and Guga are village as well as regional male deities. Various females deities of special reverence are Naina Devi, Hari Devi, Jawalamukhi, Vaishno Devi and Nabahi Devi, whose sacred shrines are located on the higher elevations of the Himalayan foothills and are visited on annual fairs. The Jheewars also propitiate Khuwaja Peer as a water deity by offering a *roat* on Thursday. It is supposed to protect them and their *gharat* from floods. The Jal Devi also protects against death or accidents in water. Different families also propitiate *hatya,* the stone idols of the women who committed suicide under social pressure and *autar,* the men of the clan who died issueless. They celebrate various local festivals like Sair and Chiran as well as regional/national festivals like Dussehra, Diwali, Baisakhi, Lohri, Holi,

Janmashtami, and Ramnavmi. Certain sacred specialists from within the community and from other communities are consulted for removing diseases caused by evil spirits and for knowing one's fortune. The community has recently become involved in socioreligious movements of the Radhaswami Mission, which discourages their dependence on deities and encourages simple food habits and living.

They practise traditional art and craft of making fishing nets and ropes and share various oral traditions of the region is respect of music and dance.

The Jheewars are traditionally linked socially with higher Hindu castes for serving as *panihare* (water-carriers), for brooming, cleaning utensils, disposing of leaf plates, and for carrying palanquins as *kahar* on marriages. Ritual-based friendships like *dharam bhai/dharam bahin* exist with various communities. They also render social service by helping people to cross streams, as they are good swimmers. They share wells and water and crematoria. The community has produced doctors, engineers, persons holding white-collar jobs, teachers, petty businessmen, etc. Political leadership has also emerged at the district level from this community.

The community has progressed considerably through modern developmental programmes. Their children receive school and college education. They use modern health and medical care facilities, though indigenous methods are still favoured and used. Modern mass media, communication and electricity are at their doorsteps. Some of them have their own irrigation facilities along the river side. They also use chemical fertilizers, insecticides, organic manures and also avail of the public distribution system, banking and postal facilities. Some have also been benefited through subsidies for purchase of animals under various rural employment programmes (IRDP). Immunization is availed of under ICDS. Their fuel resources are like those of other communities, i.e., firewood, cowdung cakes and sawdust. A few people also use coal and kerosene oil. People are generally self-employed and are self-sufficient, and are not dependent on moneylenders or shopkeepers.

A. R. Sankhyan

JOGI

The Jogis or Naths were divided into two main classes, the Aughar and the Gorakh panthi (Crooke 1896:59). It is said that there were 12 disciples of Gorakhnath, each forming his own sect and each having a following. Of these 12 disciples, the name of a legendary raja Bhartari Chandra is of great importance for there are several anecdotes in praise of his great sacrifice and divine powers, viz., an oft repeated saying is: *Jab tak dharti hai, tab tak Bhartari hai* (name of Bhartari would live as long as there is life on earth).

The Jogis of the ascetic branch are usually referred to as Naths. They are also known as Kanphata Jogis. They have been further classified into two sections. One of these sections gets only one ear pierced and wears *kundal* (ring) whereas the other gets both their ears pierced and wear *kundal* in both. The two do not enjoy even commensal relations as the former beg from all castes, whereas the latter would only accept alms from some specific castes. The former groups of the Jogis are included in the scheduled caste list of Himachal Pradesh where their population is 11183 (1981 Census). They are scattered in the adjoining States of Uttar Pradesh, Punjab and Haryana also.

The dialect spoken by them is Himachali, but while talking to outsiders, they make use of Hindi. The script is Devanagari. The ascetic branch of the Jogis whose prime source of livelihood is begging can be distinguished by the large size of *kundal* and they wear generally ochre clothes with a *jholi* (bag) and *ektara* (a single string musical instrument).

The staple food of the people is wheat *chapati*, pulses of *mah, rajmah* and seasonal vegetables. Earlier, meat, egg and liquor were not consumed by the Jogi, and those who were ascetics abstained from these, but on the contrary certain narcotics like *bhang* are consumed because it is said to be associated with Lord Shiva. However, a significant change noticed is that the younger generation has started to eat non-vegetarian food and have also taken to meat, egg, liquor and smoke. Among the non-alcoholic beverages, tea is most common. Milk and milk products are also consumed but since milk is expensive, it is rarely used for drinking.

The Jogis are divided into a number of sects and subsects. Another broad classification divides them into *savarna* and *asavarna* Jogis; the two do not have any connubial or commensal relation with each other. The *savarna* Jogis wear a sacred thread whereas the *asavarna* Jogi (the scheduled caste) are regarded quite low down in the regional caste hierarchy because they accept food and other articles from all castes. The *savarna* Jogis are also invited to play an important role when somebody wishes to make special offerings to Lord

Shiva. The Jogis are aware of the *varna* system, but are uncertain about their place in the scheme.

Within each of the endogamous divisions, there are a number of *gotra* which are exogamous, the function of which is to regulate marriages outside the blood kin on both father's and mother's side. In settling marriages, the *gotra* of self, mother's, mother's mother and father's mother are avoided. The usual age of marriage for girl is 17 or 18 years and for boys it is above 25 years. Usually the marriage of a boy is settled when he starts earning. The socio-economic status of the family is of prime importance in the settlement of marriage. Negotiations are held through middlemen. When all the initial formalities of match-making are over, the boy's parents come to the girl's parents and offer a piece of jewellery, signifying the finalization of the marriage negotiation.

Marriages can also be performed by exchange. This is known as *dora*. The symbols for marriage are toe-ring, bangles, and *bindi* but these symbols are not strictly adhered to. After marriage the residence for the bride is patrilocal. Dowry is not prevalent, but gifts in the shape of utensils, clothes and other items of household utility are given to the daughter at the time of marriage.

Both widow and widower remarriage are recognized, and levirate and sororate are practised. A widow normally marries the younger brother of the deceased husband, as it saves her from the problems arising out of the division of property, her maintenance and the custody of her children. Nevertheless, she is under no obligation to do so, and is free to lead a widowed life in her husband's home, or marry someone else outside the family. In the latter case, she may then have to forgo her rights in the husband's share of property. The children from the previous marriage remain in the custody of their father's family, but very small children or infants are allowed to stay back with the wife and are claimed back when they grow up. If a mother wants to keep them with herself, the children may have to forgo their rights in their father's property. *Faisla* (divorce) or *rajinama* can be sought by either of the spouses, and they are thereafter free to marry a person of their own choice within the community. The most legitimate ground for divorce is adultery. The other causes are impotency, cruelty and mental sickness. If a husband divorces the wife without any reasonable ground and against her wish, the elders of the *biradari* intervene to bring about a reconciliation, failing which she can move the court for maintenance.

Though nuclear families are also coming up, the traditional joint family still continues with the eldest male member being the head of the household. Women observe purdah with the father-in-law and elder brother-in-law, but with younger brother-in-law, sister-in-law and peer group, the relationship is free from inhibitions and restraints. The inheritance of property is patrilineal, with all the sons getting an equal share in their father's property.

Daughters do not have any rights to the same, but nowadays, in the absence of a male issue, a daughter is entitled to a share in her father's property. Normally in such cases the parents arrange the marriage of their daughter with a person who agrees to live with the wife's parents. He is called a *ghar-javantri*.

Though women do not have the traditional rights to inherit, yet socially they enjoy a better status in many ways. Their women are very industrious and hardworking and their contribution to the economy is considerable. They have a right to divorce and marry a person of their choice. A widow too enjoys considerable freedom in exercising her choice of partner in her second marriage. Women, however, lack a role in the religious and political life of the community.

The life-cycle rituals beginning from birth to death are broadly in accordance with Hindu religious practices. There are no pre-birth rites, but post-birth rituals are observed from time to time. On the eleventh day after birth, a purificatory ceremoy is held which is officiated by a Brahman priest. The child and the mother are given a purificatory bath, and they make an offering in the *havan*, that is performed. From then on the woman is considered ritually clean to resume her normal day-to-day life. When the child attains six months of age he or she is taken out of the house. This act is locally known as *sajarna*. Some sweets are prepared and distributed to all the people in the neighbourhood. *Jatolna*, i.e., tonsure is performed in the first, third or fifth year. Some families perform it in the temple of a goddess, whereas some prefer to perform in their homes. The maternal uncle cuts the hair first and then the hair is shaved off by a barber. The barber receives some remuneration in cash or kind. When the boy attains the age of 17 or 18, *janeu sanskar* is performed by the *savarna* Jogis. This is a significant rite, and a Brahman *purohit* officiates on this occasion followed by a big feast given to the village *biradari*, relatives and friends. Sometimes, due to paucity of funds the same can be deferred till the time of marriage and is usually performed on a day prior to marriage.

The important ceremonies associated with marriage are giving of daughter's hand, *kanyadan*, and going round the sacred fire locally known as *lai*. For the first two and a half circles, the girl leads the boy, but for the rest the boy leads the girl. The dead are cremated. However, the *savarna* Jogis who have become ascetics are buried in a *samadhi* instead of being cremated. The pollution lasts for 13 days following death. During this period certain restrictions are observed regarding food. The food is cooked without turmeric, onion and garlic. Besides, meat is not be consumed during this period. The eldest son normally performs the death rites of his father but if a married woman dies, the same is performed by her husband. A widow does not adorn herself with marriage symbols and can put them on only when she remarries.

Traditionally, the Jogis earned their livelihood mainly through begging for alms, but nowadays, they are pursuing different vocations like service, business, labour and agriculture. Most of them have acquired land under the Twenty-Point Economic Programme and are engaged in agriculture. Those who turned to asceticism continue to live on charity. It was observed that one of the male members in the family may turn to begging. These people get their ear pierced and wear large ear-rings made of a bone, put on saffron coloured robes, *rudraksha* necklace and roam around singing songs in praise of Raja Bhartari Chandra and Baba Gorakhnath. They usually carry an *ektara* and live on charity both by way of cash and kind. A major change in the economic attitude of the people is marked by the fact that the Jogis are gradually leaving begging as their profession and taking to Government jobs, service, business, labour and agriculture.

The traditional council or the *jati* panchayat is engaged in solving minor domestic issues. Nowadays, all the cases of theft or criminal assault, loss of property through negligence, divorce and its compensation are referred to the Nyay Panchayats. And if not satisfied, people move to the courts for justice. This change has been noticed ever since the inception of the formal statutory panchayat system which came in force soon after Independence.

The Jogis are Hindu by faith and devout worshipers of Shiva. Their principal deity is Baba Gorakhnath who is said to be an incarnation of Shiva. It is said that Baba Gorakhnath had 12 disciples who later formed separate sects. Besides, they also worship regional deities which are different for different areas and hence worshiped by the people of that area. It is a widely held belief that these deities guard the place they reside at and have a definite area under their surveillance. Some of the names of the regional deities are Jarunal of Shivari Gram, Jakh of Archoli, Baisaru of Baisar and Kajal of village Gosav. They celebrate the festival of Lohri with great enthusiasm. The Lavi fair is held in the month of September and is participated in by all the people of Rampur Bushair. Another fair of Phag is held in the month of March which coincides with the festival of Holi, when all the regional gods and deities are brought in a palanquin with a lot of fanfare.

They have a rich heritage of folktales, folksongs and anecdotes which are replete with instances of glorification of Baba Gorakhnath and his great disciple Raja Bhartari Chandra. The Jogis sing devotional songs about the divine powers and great sacrifices of Raja Bhartari Chandra.

The two sections of the Jogis do not mix with each other. The castes like Brahman, Rajput, Rathi, Mahajan traditionally do not accept *pucca* or *kachcha* food from the hands of the *asavarna* Jogis. However, as regards sharing of water and entry to the temple, it is now commonly open to all.

The Jogis get grants and loans easily. They have also received land under the Twenty-Point Economic Programme. The loans under Integrated Rural

Development Programme and Employment Gaurantee Scheme are also made use of. The post-Independence period has witnessed much faster growth and development in the field of literacy, medicine, transport and communication, electrification and water supply which has considerably changed the life-style of the people on the whole and the Jogis are no exception to this fact. Nevertheless, the expected growth is yet to be achieved. Though children, both boys and girls, are sent to schools, yet the percentage of dropouts after the higher secondary level is alarming, leaving a few who enter colleges and a fewer still who graduate. In places where this facility exists, the low percentage of school-going children is not only due to overall poverty but also due to the apathy of the people. The education for women is still worse. The younger generation seems to be aware of this lacuna and are willing to educate their children. The facilities of health and medical care are adequate for those who are living around urban centres. The State Government has launched an extensive family planning programme but the response to the same is not encouraging. Likewise, there is an immunization programme for the people but they do not avail themselves of it because of lack of awareness and also due to fear and misconceptions. The facilities of post office and ration shops are availed of by the people. Banking facility is utilized by only a limited section of the people living mainly in and around the urban localities.

Vatsala Sarkar

JULAHA

The Julaha/Kabir panthi/Koer are weavers. The word is literally derived from the Persian '*julah*', meaning a ball of thread (Rose, 1919). A similar etymology of the name is suggested from Hindi *jala* or *jali*, which means a network of threads. Common synonyms for the community are Julahe and Kabirpanthi or Kabirvanshi as they often associate themselves with and follow the preachings of a well-known Hindu saint, Kabir. According to traditional belief Kabir was an abandoned child of a Brahman widow and was brought up by a Julaha couple having no child. Koer is referred to as another synonym or a subgroup of the community. The history of their origin is not known but ethnographic description of the community is available in literature. The community has been categorized among the Scheduled Castes. According to the 1981 Census their population is 102,838. The community is also identified at the national level, and in Himachal Pradesh they perceive their distribution at the regional/inter-regional level. The major concentration of the community is in Kangra, Bilaspur, Mandi, Shimla, Solan and Hamirpur districts. They live in different altitudes in the hilly terrain and villages under variable climate.

The community has assimilated the culture of the region it occupies. In Bilaspur they speak within and outside the community the Kehluri or Bilaspuri dialect of the western Pahari, having Devanagari script. In the past the dialect was written in Tankri script. Men wear a *kurta*,and *pyjama*, but young ones wear pants. A turban called *safa* is worn by older men on festive or marriage occasions. The women wear *kurti*, *salwar* or *suthan* and a *chadru* or *dupatta*. Traditional ornaments were *chak*, *bali*, *laung/tilli*, *murki*, *har* of silver, *chura* or *gajra* and *paijeb*. Most of these ornaments are not in use at present.

The Julahas are occasional non-vegetarian in food habits and consume eggs, fish and meat. The staple foods are like that of other people of the area. Maize is commonly eaten, more during winters, and is supplemented by rice. Wheat is eaten more during the summer months and its products like *babru* and *patande* are eaten with milk, *desi ghee* and sugar on festive occasions. *Halwa* and *seviyan* are also other festive preparations. Various types of pulses—*moong*, *urd*, *masur*, *kulthi* and peas and beans—along with roots and tubers are frequently consumed. Various vegetables and mustard leaves are also eaten. The cooking medium is mustard oil or vegetable *ghee* and sometimes *desi ghee*. Food taboos are normally lacking but non-vegetarian foods are not eaten during death pollution. Fruit intake is occasional and seasonal. Milk or milk products like *lassi* or *mattha* and *jhol* are consumed frequently. Some who have entered the Radhaswami sect of Hinduism do not take non-vegetarian food. The men occasionally consume country liquor except the followers of the Radhaswami sect. The women ordinarily do not take alcohol but at times may do so.

The Julahe and the Kabirpanthi or Julaha/Koer may be considered broad social divisions but social hierarchy is not observed. The community usually recognizes small exogamous units called *got* like Tiamlu, Janeogal Bhatti, Jubliani, Dod Jubliani, Gautam, Dhiane, Ralot, Bhoor Chhathwaru, etc. These regulate marriage alliances and indicate descent. The Radhaswami sect tries to create a little religious differentiation but has little impact on other social institutions. The community perceives its low social position in the region among the Sudra varna. But they place themselves higher than the Chamar and the Dumna. Rose (1919) indicated that there were Julaha Chamar or Chamar Julaha who adopted the occupation of weaving. But such a distinction is not known in the study area (Bilaspur District).

The institution of marriage among the Julahas is similar to that among other Hindus. The community is endogamous and practises *got* and village exogamy and no consanguinity is seen. Marriages commonly occur through negotiation by parents and relatives. Earlier, child marriage was prevalent and bride price was also taken. But now the age of girls for marriage has gone up and normally is not below 16 or 17 years. For boys it is usually above 20 years. *Batta-satta* was more common in the past which relieved the family of the burden of the bride price. Presently such marriages do occur but are uncommon and *dharam-punya* marriages are more common in which the parents of the girls perform their *kanyadan* and do not take anything from the boy or his parents, but in turn give some dowry or *daj/dahej* in the form of household articles, clothes and ornaments. Earlier, *daj* was also a common practice along with the bride price and some well-off parents also used to give a buffalo/sheep/goat in *daj*.

The symbols of marriage like *sindur*, glass bangles and *koka/tilli* and sometimes *nath* are observed. The bride lives patrilocally. The community traditioally approves widow and widower remarriage. A widow is usually married as junior levirate and the ceremony is called *jhanjara* or *chadar-dalna* and ends with a *bhati* (small feast). A widower marries either a junior sororate or any other girl. Divorce is usually looked down upon but in certain circumstances of maladjustments and cruelty to the wife, the community approves of divorce. Presently, however, it becomes viable only through legal sanctions in the civil courts and either of the spouse can divorce on these grounds. The man has to pay compensation or maintenance to his spouse and is also responsible for maintaining the children. Divorcees can remarry.

Traditionally the community lives in vertically extended joint families but presently this system has considerably broken down and given rise to nuclear families. Usually sons do not get separated as long as the father is alive or all of them are not married, but a large family may break up on property matters or other domestic quarrels over routine matters like division of domestic work. In joint families avoidance and joking relations similar to those in many Hindus of the region are seen. The *lari* covers her face from her *saurah*, *jeth*, *nandoi* and other elderly male members of the village. Joking relationships exist between *devar* and *bhabi*, *jija* and *sali*, *jija* and *sala* and *nanad* and *bhabi*. The inheritance is as per the rule of male equigeniture and the eldest son succeeds his father. While dividing the parental property the eldest son has the first choice to pick up his share. The daughters lack the right to inherit father's property.

The status of women, however, remains almost equal to that of men. They participate in various economic actitivies and contribute to the family income by weaving and rendering menial services to village landlords. They perform all domestic duties, bring potable water, fuel and fodder, participate in agricultural and animal husbandry duties and in various social and religious ceremonies and also control family expenditure. Their participation in the mechanism of social control and political sphere is, however, little as compared to men.

The life-cycle rituals are performed by their own community priest as per the Hindu scriptures. Pre-delivery rituals are lacking but restrictions on women during pregnancy and after delivery are imposed. *Sutak* is observed for 13 days and the woman remains confined to a corner of the lower storey of the house. The pollution ends with a *guntrala* ceremony. A son's birth is rejoiced by distributing germinated grams and sugar and by women singing *ranjhunana*. The child's mother's father brings *kangnu* and *jhaggu* and *topu*. The christening and cereal taking ceremonies are usually not observed. *Jatlu* or *mundan* of the male child is the only childhood ceremony and is performed by the *mama* of the child on any odd year of the birth. On this day *kulja* is also worshipped. A *jatra* may also be led to the shrine of a local/regional deity on fulfilment of the wish for the birth of a son.

The marriage rituals are also similar to other Hindus. The *jija* acts as a Nai. The *lagan* and *vedi* are the major marriage rituals performed at the bride's place when the bride and groom circumambulate the sacred fire and the bride's parents perform *kanyadan/sankalap*. They also feast the party of the groom. At the bridegroom's place the *lara* and *lari* worship a *pipal* tree and circumambulate it. They also tie a white thread round it and pour water. Kinship-based friendships of the bride and groom are also made under the *pipal* tree. The marriage ends with music and dance, and a feast is given to the gathered relatives and friends. The *muklawa* of the bride occurs on the next day when the spouses start living together.

The death rituals are also similar to those of other Hindus. The dead are cremated and their ashes are immersed in the Ganges or Beas rivers and *patak* is observed for 13 days and various death rituals are performed. On the thirteenth day a purification *havan* is performed by the community priest who also seeks *dan* in the name of the dead. Annual and fourth annual death rites are observed. The followers of the Radhaswami sect do not observe elaborate death rituals and instead arrange a simple *satsang* .

Traditionally the Julahas subsist on weaving but presently most of them have given up this occupation. Some, however, have become modernized and use electrically operated looms. Besides, they have acquired small landholdings and practise agriculture and animal husbandry to supplement their income. Some people till the land of the village landlords on contract or sharecrop basis. Many seek daily-wage casual labour in house construction, roads and forests. A few persons are also in Government services as peons, *chowkidar*, clerks, teachers, junior engineers and electricians, and some are in the army as well. Some persons have also taken up masonary, tailoring and some have petty shops. The links with market are direct which is fully regulated.

The community has its Biradari Panchayat which is however not organized. Generally the elders of the community resolve their social disputes regardings marriage and divorce. Village disputes over land and water are taken up by the members of the statutory Gram Panchayat which also performs the usual activities of welfare and development. Usually legal channels are used for disputes over land.

The Julahas are Hindus by religion, following the Sanatan, Kabirpanth or Radhaswami sects. The followers of the Radhaswamis frequently visit their shrine at Beas in Punjab. The Sanatani propitiate various family or clan deities, village and regional deities. The Ton Bharari, Guga, Gugri, Balak Nath and Asapoori (at Palampur) are family/clan deities. Other regional deities frequently propitiated are Nahar Singh, Lakhdata, Naina Devi, Vaishno Devi, Santoshi Mata and Jawalamukhi. Hindu festivals like Lohri, Baisakhi, Diwali, etc., are celebrated. Various religious shrines are visited on annual fairs. The sacred specialists are within the communities and the *chela* of other communities are also consulted quite often for treatment of certain diseases supposed to be caused by the evil spirits. They share various folk oral traditions of the area. The community is known for performing a comedy play called *swang*. They also sing and play *damru* and bronze plate in Guga Mandli during Guga Navmi festival, and participate at night in the traditional Chandrauli folksong and dance in which one man acts as a woman and dances while other men sing and play on percussion instruments. The community has weaving as its art and craft.

They accept *kachcha* and *pucca* food and water from the many Hindu castes. The Julahas also traditionally do not accept food and water from the Chamar and Dumna except *sidha* or *suchchi rasoi.* Water sources likewise are shared or are separate.

They have members in business, teaching, engineering and defence services. Political leadership has emerged at the local and village panchayat level. Modern development programmes have made an impact on the community. Formal education level has increased. The girls generally study up to primary or secondary school level. Boys in general receive secondary school education a few of them go to colleges. The main reasons for drop outs are economic and social, especially in cases of girls, who are seen more as liabilities and are married off as early as possible.

In respect of health and medicare, both modern as well as traditional methods are favoured. As modern medicare is costlier, therefore, they quite often use indigenous methods and traditional spiritual specialists. Presently, they feel the compulsion of restricting their family size due to economic reasons and favour sterilization, although they want at least one son even at the cost of more daughters. Drinking water is available near their houses through pipes but the traditional sources of water like springs and *bauri* are still used as the pipe-water supply is largely inadequate. The Julahas have provisions for Integrated Rural Development Programme (IRDP) as are applicable for the scheduled castes in general. They get 50 per cent subsidies on purchase of chemical fertilizers, animals and crop threshers under special programmes like Antyodaya. They are self-employed as well as employed in Government. Their houses have electric connections and many also avail themselves of the modern mass media facilities like radio and television. Road communications and postal services are also present in their vicinity. Their energy resources are largely traditional like firewood and cowdung cakes. Some nutritional programmes like mid-day meal and immunization for small children are availed. Mostly people favour savings in banks and post offices and are not dependent on local moneylenders or shopkeepers, though some still depend on these traditional sources.

A.R. Sankhyan

KANGHIGIR

The literal meaning of word *Kanghigir* is maker of comb, derived from compounding the root words, *kanghi* meaning comb and *gir* meaning maker. Ibbetson (1916: 231), writing on the Nai says, they appear to be as Kangera or "comb-man" in the hills. This fact could not be authenticated by the informants. They belong to a group of Multani Lohars, and claim Mughal ancestry and are Islamic by faith. As Multani Lohars, such people who took to the profession of fixing horseshoes were known as Nalband and those who took to comb-making were known as Kanghigir. In Sirmaur district of Himachal Pradesh there were about 50 to 60 families prior to partition in 1947, and in Kachcha Tank, a whole *mohalla* (locality) was named after them. After partition, a majority of them left for Pakistan, and a few went to the adjoining districts of Saharanpur in Uttar Pradesh, leaving only a few families to carry on their traditional occupation. At the time of field investigation, only one family was found continuing their occupation and that too was on the verge of closing the business and taking up some other more profitable business. The language spoken among members of the community and with others is Hindustani. Devanagari and Arabic are the scripts used for communication.

The community is non-vegetarian. They take the meat of goat, sheep and jungle fowl or chicken and prefer *halal* meat. As non-vegetarian food is expensive; the intake of such food is restricted to festive or social occasions. Their staple diet consists of wheat *chapati*, rice and pulses of *moong, masur, urd* and *chana*. Though the usual cooking medium is mustard oil, but occasionally *till-ka-tel* (seasum oil) and *desi ghee* are also used. Edible wild roots and tubers especially *turar* and *sharad* are consumed. *Ber*, plums and peaches locally available during the season are moderately consumed, and so are vegetables. Milk is consumed by infants and invalids, but tea is a drink taken by all. Milk products like *lassi* and curd are consumed. Alcoholic drinks are taboo. Special food preparations like *seviyan* are cooked on Id-ul-fitr and Barawafat, while mutton is a must on Bakrid. Abstinence from food and water is also observed from sunrise to sunset during the period of *roza*.

The community was traditionally endogamous but because of their dwindling population, they have started intermarrying with their Nalband, with whom differentation exists on the occupational level. The community is endogamous at the religious and territorial level, while exogamy is practised at the level of sharing mother's milk. Cross- and parallel-cousin marriages are practised and preferred. Marriage with father's sister's daughter and mother's sister' daughter is preferred. Marriage among the children of siblings are also allowed. Marriages are performed in adulthood, with the girls getting married at the age of about 20 years while the boys getting married around 25 or 26 years. The most prevalent form of marriage is by negotiation which is solemnized by *nikah*.

Monogamy, junior levirate and junior sororate are the usual forms of marriage. Two real sisters cannot be taken as wives simultaneously under any circumstances; however, if the first wife dies, then the second sister can be married. In case of multiple marriages, the consent of the first wife is essential. Where the first wife refuses to consent a second wife cannot be brought. The first wife is termed as *biahta*. If at any time the need for a second marriage is felt, preference is given to the cousins of the wife. The common marriage symbols are *choori* and *chutki*, but these are not strictly observed. Besides, dowry which consists of items in kind, *mehar* is also fixed which is in the form of gold, cash or silver, as agreed upon at the time of *nikah*. The amount of *mehar* fixed cannot be less than Rs. 32.25 as the same amount was fixed for Fatima Bibi, the wife of Hazoor Sahib. This amount is meant for the maintenance of the divorced or widowed woman for the period of her *iddat*. *Talaq* is permissible by the mere utterance of the word *talaq* in the presence of witnesses. It is permitted on grounds of maladjustment or infidelity; and can be initiated by any of the partners. But if a woman seeks divorce from her husband, she forfeits her claim to *mehar*, but if a husband divorces her, then he has to pay the *mehar*, and return her dowry. The *talaq* is recorded in the *nikahnama* (marriage document) and the involved parties sign it. After dissolution, the woman has to observe a period of *iddat* for three months and 10 days, before she is permitted to remarry. Children of estranged parents are the liability of the father, but in case of infants, they are allowed to accompany the mother, subject to the payment of suitable compensation to be decided by the panchayat. In all such cases, the child is returned to the father after he grows up.

The residence for a newly wedded woman is patrilocal. The family is of the extended type. Avoidance is not practised these days. Joking relationship is quite common with relations who are potential mates. The eldest male member of the family holds the supreme status. He is respected, obeyed and held in veneration. Paternal and filial affection and due regard as per status of the person form the basis of mutual relationship. Male equigeniture is the basis of inheritance of property. A widow however has a right to a share for her maintenance for her lifetime, which ultimately devolves down to the son after her death. In the absence of males, the property passes on to the daughter or alternatively to the nearest collaterals.

The social position of the women can be considered to be equal in view of the fact that they are the family managers. They are invariably consulted on all important family issues. Though divorce is very rare but should it occur, the *mehar* and the *dahej* have to be returned. Second, if a man has divorced his wife in a fit of anger, he cannot remarry the wife again, unless the woman marries someone else and divorces him. All this enhances her social position.

The women carry out all the household activities. They bring water, and manage the house. Though they are not involved in any productive economic activity, they indirectly contribute to the family income as occasionally, they may stitch clothes or do embroidery on payment. Normally women are not allowed to work outside the house except under certain circumstances. The political and religious status of the women is considerably low, for they are not allowed to take part in politics, except for casting votes, nor they are allowed to act as religious functionaries or visit mosques.

Among the life-cycle rituals, though no pre-natal rituals are observed, yet restrictions like going out in the open on an eclipse day, or cutting of fruit by enceinte mother are prohibited. Post-natal restrictions exist on the parturient mother. She is confined for a period of six days when *chhathi* is performed and both the mother and the child are given a bath. From this day onwards, she starts doing household work and cooking, but is not allowed to go out of the house for 40 days. Pollution is restrictd to the room of confinement and not to the whole house. On the seventh month after birth, *aqiqa* is performed when the child's head is shaved off by the Nai. On this event, in case of a birth of a male child two *khadu* or *dumba* (he-goats or ram) are sacrificed, whereas in case of a girl only one is sacrificed and a feast is served.

Till almost three decades ago, no *nikahnama* was signed, and it was all verbal, but now *nikahnama* is signed in the presence of a *maulvi,* two *gawah* and the parents of both the boy and the girl. Three copies of it are made, one is retained by the girl's parents, the second by the boy's parent and the third is kept with the *maulvi.* In this document the amount of *mehar* fixed also finds a mention. Though the *nikah* is performed at the bride's house, yet negotiations are initiated by the groom's parents. The bride's parents arrange a marriage feast while the groom's parents give a *dawat-e-walima,* when the bride reaches their house.

The deceased are buried in the family graveyard. Mortuary rites are observed on the third day, which is known as *tehiya* or *sayan,* when the *maulvi* recites *kalma* a lakh and a quarter times, by throwing one grain of black gram out of the lot of five and a quarter kilograms kept for the purpose. It is believed that the required number of *kalma* can be recited from the grains of the assigned lot, and these grains serve the purpose to keep a count. The house is regarded as impure and food is provided by family friends and relatives to the members of the deceased family during this period. *Kool*, a type of *kalma*, is also recited on the *daswa, biswan* and *chaliswan*. On each of these days food is distributed to the needy and the poor. This is believed to bring peace to the departed soul.

Economically the community is dependent on forest for its need of *kaura* and *karaunda* woods, which are needed for the preparation of various kind of combs like *likhra*, *kangha*, *kanghi* and *tel-wali kanghi*. These forests are owned by the government, but the wood is given to the people on permit, which specifies head load to be collected from the forest area, without the use of axe or saw, and within a particular time period. Till recent, there were no such restriction, but nowadays due to the stringent forest laws, permit for *kaura* wood is generally not given. This particular type of wood, because of its hard nature, provides durability to the combs. Owing to the non-availability of this kind of wood, they prepare the combs from substitute wood, *karunda*, which is a soft wood. Considering the demand of these combs in the hills, the Kanghigirs are unable to cope with the demands due to the non-availability of the required wood in sufficient quantity. The deteriorating quality of combs, coupled with high cost in comparison to the machine-made plastic combs, has resulted in low market for the wooden combs. Consequently, a few of the families have left this traditional occupation and have taken to jobs in factories as mechanics, in Government and private institutions. The only family left in this occupation is also almost on the verge of leaving this occupation and settling to the work as ironsmiths. The community is landless and is wholly involved in this industry. It is totally dependent on the market for marketing their produce both directly and through middlemen. They also market their products in fairs in different parts of Himachal Pradesh. The community is self-sufficient, and is not under any hereditary debts or under the influence of moneylenders.

They have a Biradari Panchayat, which is headed by a Chowdhary who is elected by a voice vote. The panchayat dispenses justice in matters of breach of commensality rules, exercises control over marriage expenses, divorces, family disputes and theft. The Chowdhary is assisted by village elders in arriving at a decision. In case of difference of opinion, the matter is referred to the headquarters in Deoband in Saharanpur. Sometimes letters are also sent to the headquarters stating the facts of the case and then a moderate opinion is formed after the reply from the headquarters is received. The offenders are punished through cash fine. This money is then utilized for the upkeep of mosque. The statutory panchayats exist since Independence. They plan and implement welfare activities and maintains law and order. But their traditional council continues to enjoy the sovereignty of the community.

The Kanghigir belong to Sunni sect. Theologically of the 72 *firqa* prevalent among the Muslims, they share the Deobandi *firqa*. The tenets of the *firqa* dictate and regulate their social and religious life. The community also pays obeisance to their departed family members, and other *faquirs* by offering *chadar* and buring incense sticks at their tombs. Their sacred centres are Mecca, Madina and Ajmer Sharif. It is the cherished desire of every devout Muslim to visit these shrines at least once in their lifetime. Their sacred specialists *maulvi* are from amongst the others. The *maulvi*, and the *faquir* who officiate at the *dargah* (tombs) also give charms and amulets to cure the sick person and ward off evil eyes and spirits.

The community shares major fairs of the Muslims. Urs, which are religious fairs held in honour of the revered saints at their tombs, are occasions for community participation in the celebrations by making offerings and singing hymns. Id-ul-Fitr, Id-ul-Zuha and Shabebarat are important festivals.

The women, like the other Muslim women, are skilled in the art of embroidery, making of graphic and floral designs on hand, palm and feet with henna especially during marriages. There are folksongs, folktales or folklore, which are often shared with other Muslim communities. Dance and songs are performed for purely recreational purposes at social occasions and are the exclusive domain of the women.

To both Hindus and Muslims they sell their articles on cash. Most Hindus traditionally would not accept any type of food from them unless cooked by a Brahman, outside their house, in different utensils. The Kanghigirs can accept all types of food from their brethren Nalband and most of the Hindus. Connubial restriction existed within the community, but in the present times they also marry with the Nalband. They have access to all the public places, except to temples.

As a result of the development programmes, especially related to education, the community has been greatly benefited by way of freeship, half-freeship and scholarship provided to deserving students. Both sexes study up to graduate or post-graduate level. They avail themselves of modern medicine, which is coupled with the use of traditional homemade remedies. Family planning also finds favour with the educated younger generation who prefer using modern contraceptive devices. There is however no preference for sterilization. Self-employment schemes for the educated unemployed are availed of. Loans for setting up cottage or small-scale industry are also available through banks and other financial institutions.

The community is largely urban, and avail themselves of various civic facilities.

Rajendra Sarkar

KAYASTHA

The Kayastha or Lala as they are often referred to is a class whose vocation has been to serve as a writer specializing in the art of administration and accountancy. The word 'Kayastha' is derived from the word '*kaya*' meaning body. According to *Padam Purana*, they derived their origin, "like the superior castes from Brahma—the first deity of the Hindu trinity. The Brahmans assent to this, but add that it is from the feet of the Brahma, the Kayasthas have proceeded". They trace their descent from Chitragupta—their legendary ancestor who was created from the body of the Brahma to help Yama, the God of Death in maintaining the records of all the good and evil deeds done by the people in the world (Sinha, *nd*). The community is widely distributed in northern India especially in the States of Uttar Pradesh and Bihar. In Himachal Pradesh they live in small numbers in urban centres of almost all the districts except Lahaul-Spiti and higher reaches of Chamba, Sirmaur, Shimla and Kullu, where they have migrated from the adjoining State to serve as Government servants and businessmen. They still use Perso-Arabic script and speak in Hindustani while communicating with fellow community members, whereas with others, local dialects and Devanagari script are used.

The community is largely non-vegetarian but does not take buffalo meat However, individual families, Mathur and Bhatnagar, which are subcastes of the Kayasthas, are lacto-vegetarians. Presently, they are only occasional non-vegetarians and are shifting to vegetarian diet because of the high cost of meat. Their staple diet consists of wheat *chapati*, rice, pulses, vegetables, roots and tubers. All are cooked in mustard oil. Fruits, milk, milk products are consumed by all, but alcoholic drinks are generally taken by men only. The drinks are purchased from the market. The community avoids taking non-vegetarian food during the death pollution period. Widows generally refrain from taking non-vegetarian food. Fish is also not eaten during rainy seasons. Certain special types of food are also prescribed for certain festivals.

The Kayastha are divided into 12 endogamous groups. They are believed to have sprung from the 12 sons of Chitragupta from two wives Iravati (also known as Sobhamati) and Nandini, who gave birth to eight and four sons respectively. Their hierarchy is based on their relative seniority of age and mother. Thus in the order of precedence they rank as Mathur, Gaur, Bhatnagar, Saxena, Ambhast, Nigam, Karan and Kulshresta from Iravati and Srivastav, Surajdhwaj, Valmiki and Asthana from Nandini. (Sinha, *nd*)

Of the 12 subcastes, only Bhatnagar, Mathur, Srivastava, Nigam and

Saxena are found in Himachal Pradesh. Each of these subcastes are further subdivided into *al* and *gotra*. The former denote their historical ancestors or the place of their migration, whereas the latter reveal the ancestry of persons. These are recognized social orders within which marriage is prohibited. The community usually suffixes their subcaste names as their surnames, but certain titles like Singh, Sarkar, Sarkari, Pandiya, Raizada and Rai are also used by the Kayastha. They are ranked high in the local social hierarchy in terms of their educational and professional status. In the varna order they place themselves along with the Kshatriyas.

As the Kayastha population in Himachal Pradesh is small, endogamy at the subcaste level is not rigidly observed and intra-subcaste marriages are held. Restrictions however exists to the two real sisters marrying two real brothers. Also girls are not taken as bride from the family where a girl has been given in marriage. Levirate is not practised but junior sororate does exist and monogamy is the prevalent form of marriage. The marriages are solemnized nowadays in adulthood through negotiation, though a few cases of elopement, love and civil marriages have also occurred. The common marriage symbols are vermilion, glass bangles and *bichchia* which are rigidly observed. Dowry is given both in cash and kind among the Srivastava, Saxena and Nigam, whereas it is usually in kind among the Mathur and Bhatnagar. Divorce is permitted through judicial courts on grounds of cruelty, impotency, maladjustment and the like, which can be sought by either of the aggrieved. The children are the liability of the father, but a woman can have the custody of the child in case of infants. Divorcee and widower remarriages are allowed. The traditional restriction on widow remarriage has also loosened and is permitted.

The rule of residence after marriage is patrilocal and the families which were of extended type are tending to be nuclear. The eldest male member is the head of the household and all decision concerning the house are arrived at after mutual consultations. There is a feeling of mutual love, affection and respect between members of the family, which are based on factors like age, sex and relationship. Traditional avoidance relationship has loosened. Joking relationship however continus to exist with the sister's husband and the wife's younger sisters. The property is inherited by male equigeniture. The girls give up their share in favour of their brothers as their claim over the family property at the time of division only creates bitterness and tension in the family resulting in unsavoury relationship between brothers and sisters. The succession is patrilineal.

The Kayastha women have no right of inheritance and are placed below men. This status is conferred mainly on ground of the dowry that is to be paid to secure a groom for a woman. The traditional social restriction on widow remarriage and the dissolution of marriage exists. In the economic sphere the traditional role of women was confined to household work, but with the spread of education and literacy they have moved out of the house and have taken up jobs as administrators, scientist, architects, engineers, teachers and are in other white-collar professions, sharing responsibility with men and contributing to family income, besides managing the household. They take part in all the ritual and religious activities also. No *yagya* is considered to be complete without the presence of the *ardhangini*. Their role in the political sphere is however limited to the exercise of their franchise. Even so, they have a considerable influence over family matters.

In the sphere of life-cycle rituals, pre-natal rituals are observed in the fifth and seventh month of pregnancy known as *panchmasa* and *satmasa* when family deities are propitiated and their blessings invoked for the safe delivery of the child. Restrictions exist on the movement of the enceinte mother. She is not allowed to cut fruits, vegetables or go out of the house during eclipse. She is also prevented from viewing a funeral sight or move about alone at the night. On the birth of a male child a *pandit* is invited to prepare a horoscope and to see if the child is born under *mool nakshatra*, after which appropriate rituals are performed by the *pandit* to ward off its evil effect. The post-natal ritual consists of the *chhatti* and *barhi*, the sixth and twelfth day purificatory rites. Six months after the birth, *annaprashan* ceremony is observed in which the child is fed with *kheer,* preferably by the mother's brother. *Mundan* is performed in an odd year after birth either at home or at Devi's temple. On the seventh day *turan* is performed when the child's head is once again shaved off, leaving a cue at the occiput. *Janeu* or *yagopavit* ceremony is usually deferred till marriage when three strands of thread are hung from the right shoulder to the left by the priest.

Marriage consists of a series of rituals consisting of *barikcha, tilak, darwaza-ka-char, kanyadan, phera, bhat, barhar* and *bidai*. Of these the *kanyadan* and *phera* constitute the actual ceremony and are performed at the bride's place. On the fourth day of marriage (*chauth*) or *panv phera* is performed, though in some families it is performed along with *bidai*. The consummation of marriage takes place at the groom's place.

The dead are cremated except infants and those dying of small-pox, who are instead buried or immersed in water (*jal-pravah*). The house remains polluted for 13 days. Mortuary rituals are observed on the tenth and thirteenth day, when a corresponding number of Brahmans are fed and gifts are given to the Maha Brahman. *Barkhi* is observed after a year, thereafter, every year *shradh* is performed on the day according to Hindu calendar during the fortnight devoted to ancestors for the peace of the departed souls in the *Pitri-paksha*.

As the bulk of the community members are in urban centres, they have no direct dependence on natural resources. They are in various occupations, some in business, some in teaching and administration, whereas others are engineers, architects and scientists and in various other white-collar professions.

The various subcastes of the Kayastha have a *sabha* (association) of their own known by their subcaste names. This association works for social causes like curbing of dowry and controlling lavish expenditure on social ceremonies. Aside from these, there are also Chitragupta Sabha and Akhil Bhartiya Kayastha Mahasabha, which cut across the subcaste barriers. These have elected office-bearers. Though the statutory panchayats have come up after Independence, they have in no way let up the activities of the *sabha*, as the *sabha* are more reformistic in nature, whereas the panchayat looks after the welfare and development of all the communities in the village.

A majority of them follow Sanatana Dharma, though a section of them are Shaivites and Arya Samajis also. During the Mughal rule a few of the Kayastha took to Islam and have formed a different community known as Muslim Kayastha with whom the Hindu Kayastha have neither any commensal nor any connubial norms. Every family has a deity who is worshipped on all important occasions along with ancestors. Chitragupta is their community deity who is worshipped on the second day of Kartik Amavasya known as Yamdutiya. Besides they also worship gods and goddesses of the wider Hindu pantheon. Their sacred specialists are from the Brahman community, who officiate and perform all life-cycle rituals. They take part in all the fairs and festivals of the Hindus which have socioreligious or socioeconomic significance.

The women are deft in the art of graphic painting and drawing. They decorate the floor on festive occasions with line and geometric designs by using rice paste. Motifs of human figures are also made on walls and papers representing Parvati and Lakshmi at the time of Karwa Chauth and Diwali festivals. Traditionally, vegetable and natural dyes were used for this purpose, but nowadays chemical colours are also used. Different kind of folksongs such as *Sohar, Chat, Devi geet, Swagat, Biah, Nakta, Bana, Gari, Lava Parchara, Chunri* and *Bidai* are sung with different rhythms. These songs are not community specific but region specific. Besides, befitting songs are also sung to suit the mood of Chait and Sawan months. Folktales are also present which are narrated to signify the importance of a particular observance.

They exchange *pucca roti* with community members, but the acceptance of *kachcha* food is restricted to those who are from their own group. They can accept *kachcha* food from a Brahman, who in return would accept only *pucca* or *sidha* food. Similarly, a Kayastha can accept *pucca* food from a similar caste, but can accept *kachcha* food provided it is cooked by a Brahman. Food is not traditionally accepted from the Chamar and Chuhra are also not allowed to enter the houses of the Kayastha though in the urban centres caste rigidity is not so strong. Connubial norms were once restricted to one's own subgroup, but with the changing times inter-subgroup marriages have received recognition. Putative kinship such as *dharam bhai* and *dharam bahin* is established with a person of a specific class only by taking a holy dip in the Ganges and exchanging sweets or by tying a *rakhi*. Such kin are expected to carry out all rights and obligations as are expected of a real kin.

As the bulk of the Kayasthas in Himachal Pradesh are in white-collar profession, this has resulted in the development of new liberal relationship cutting across the community barriers. The attitude of the people towards the various developmental programmes has been favourable in respect of higher education, health and family welfare. They use both modern as well as traditional home-made medicines.

Rajendra Sarkar

KHAMPA

Kham is the name of a state in Tibet and the people of that state are known as Khampa. Likewise Bod is Tibetan word for Tibet and people of Tibet are Bodpa in their language. According to another view, there is a place in Tibet called Kham, and as such the people who come from Kham, were known as Khampa. It is believed that they came to India about 100 years ago as itinerant traders form Tibet and moved in the upper part of the Himalayas, which they included in their annual nomadic beat. The Khampas, who stayed back in India, are referred to as Gyakhar or Gyagar (a Tibetan term for India) Khampas by their brethren across the Himalayas (Negi, 1976).

In Kullu they are also called as Bauddh and in some other parts they pass as Tibetans. In Uttar Pradesh, they are distributed in Darma and Byans villages of Pithoragarh district, where they are called as Shah Khampa; in Spiti division of Himachal Pradesh as Piti Khampa; in Kinnaur as Khunnu Khampa; in Kullu as Neondi Khampa; in Chamba as Thava Khampa; in Lahul as Gharja Khampa. There is yet another section of Khampas who are nomadic and are known as Nekhor Khampa (*ne* means pilgrim places; *khor* means journey) literally meaning, the people who came for pilgrimage. They are a scheduled tribe and the population figures for the Khampa clubbed together with Jad, Lamba and are 1,221 according to the 1981 Census.

The dialect spoken by the people among themselves is also known as Khampa. With others they converse in Hindi and can also write, read and speak in English. Their traditional script is Tibetan, but nowadays, Devanagari is being used while communicating with outsiders.

The traditional dress of the Khampas consisted of *chhuba* (long gown black in colour for males and brown for females), *banjug* (shirt) and *siring kingar* (cap). The men also wore *along* (ear-ring made of gold, about two inches in diameter, with blue or red beads). At present the young men put on shirt, pants, suits, jeans, whereas the old women still prefer to put on their traditional dress.

The Khampas are non-vegetarian, with people traditionally taking the meat of sheep and goat only, but now they also take chicken, fish and eggs. The meat of yak, pork and beef is still a taboo for them. Older people still do not take eggs. Their staple food is *chapati*, rice, and pulses of *mah, chana* and *malka* alongwith vegetables. *Momo* are cooked on festive occasions. They also take edible roots and tubers like *bhalku, linger, nokhi, chiaru* and *guchhi* (mushrooms). Besides, apples, apricots, plums which are widely grown, they also consume wild fruits like *jami, vami, aarvi,* and *chuli* which are locally available in abundance. The staple diet of the Khampa earlier used to be *thugpa* and *momo*, but now they have changed to wheat *chapati* and rice.

The Khampa is a generic category which includes many territorial groupings as mentioned above like the Piti, Khunu, Neondi, Thava, Garja and Nakora, mainly after the names of the place from where they hail. Though there are no perceptible restrictions on entering into matrimonial ties with any of the section of the Khampa, as all are regarded equal, but economic status of the negotiating families is taken into consideration. In terms of the local social hierarchy the Khampas rank at par with the other Rajput communities, with whom some of them have started entering into matrimonial ties. Among the Rajputs, on the question of social equality of status the opinion is divided. Though in Spiti, Lahaul and Kinnaur people accept them at par, but in Chamba, Kullu and Shimla people do not accept them as equals. The people of areas which have Buddhist dominance accept them on parity because of similar religious belief, but where Hinduism dominates, they are not recognized as equals.

Endogamy is practised at the community level, irrespective of the territorial groupings. Family status is the only consideration. Village endogamy is also practised. The community is divided into a number of exogamous clans or sects which denote origin from a common ancestor. For establishing marriage ties, patriclans should differ. Immediate relations of the mother's side are also avoided. Beyond this, other relations are hardly given any recognition. Of late there have been a few instances of a Khampa entering into matrimonial relationship with local higher caste Rajput families. Marriage with parallel or ortho-cousins are prohibited, but cross-cousin marriage finds prevalence. Junior levirate and sororate are also practised. The age at marriage for boys and girls is 19 and 16 years respectively; the ideal difference between the ages of husband and wife should not be more than three years.

Monogamy is the general rule of marriage, but polygyny is resorted to only in cases where the first wife has not been able to bear a child for the family. Till five decades ago, polyandry of fraternal type was the prevalent form of marriage, with only two brothers sharing a wife in common. But gradually this has given way to monogamy. Marriages are usually fixed by *phaktun* (negotiation). The community does not have any symbols of marriage. Bride-price is not prevalent but parents give gifts to their daughters according to their status. The usual form of residence is patrilocal. *Ja-tsari-jha-dal-va* or *khatal-je or kheje* or *jha-cho-che* (divorce) is permitted when initiated by either of the aggrieved parties with the consent of the community council. The grounds for divorce include maladjustment, adultery and barrenness. The panchayat decides on the payment of compensation, which usually is the return of gifts brought by the girl from her parents' house plus an amount in cash. In the event of divorce the infants remain the mother's responsibility.

But grown up children and children who do not warrant mother's attention stay back with their father. Widow, widower and divorcee remarriage is permissible. A spectacular change has occurred in the institution of marriage from polyandry to monogamy and from intracommunity marriages to intercommunity marriages.

The Khampas have the extended type of family. The parents avoid calling their daughters-in-law by name and vice versa. The daughter-in-law observes avoidance with her husband's elder male relatives, and with all such relations in that line. Joking relationship also exists with wife's younger sister, wife's younger brother and all such relations in the line. The husband and wife use teknonymic terms to address each other. The property is inherited in the male line, with all sons sharing the parental property equally. In the event of no male issue, the property is inherited by the daughter on the condition that the son-in-law agrees to stay with the in-laws. If the daughter also does not have any male issue, the property passes on to the collaterals. A widow also has the right to enjoy the property for her lifetime, after which it devolves to the son, but does not have the right to sell, gift or mortgage the property.

The Khampa women are enterprising, who not only assist their menfolk in economic activities, but also carry on the economic activities independently. They are seen working as hoteliers and shopkeepers, dealing mostly in foreign goods. These shops and restaurants are manned by the women while the menfolk assist by getting them goods). The Garja and Piti Khampa who are agriculturists are assisted by their womenfolk in agricultural operation, in almost all spheres except ploughing. Besides, they also bring fuel and fodder for animals. The social position of the Khampa women is high. They are the incharge of the house, and manage and control the family affairs. Though the authority in the family is vested in the menfolk, but a decision on vital issues is invariably arrived at after consultation with the wife. Though divorce is rare, and the gifts brought by the women at the time of marriage have to be returned alongwith a fine decided by the traditional council. Traditionally they were not allowed to hold any post in the council, but indirectly influenced the decision of the council through their husbands. Nowadays, however, they have their representation in the statutory panchayats, but are seldom able to give an independent decision. In religious spheres the women carry out their family rituals. Old women can be seen rotating turquoise bead in their hand, chanting the *mantra* of Lord Aucokiteshvara.

The child is named by the Dalai Lama or the Avtari Lama, after consulting the sacred text and almanac. *Raldak* (tonsure) ceremony is observed before the child is two years of age, on a date decided by the Lama. The hair is cut by the mother's brother, or in his absence by the parents, and a feast is given.

Phaktun (marriage by negotiation) is a simple ceremony. The bridegroom goes in a procession to the bride's house. Before reaching the bride's house, he is prevented on his way by friends of the girl who block the road by stones. The girls sing *timde-luh* (question-answer songs), whereby some questions are passed to the boy's side, and if they answer correctly they are given the way. They are held back once again, before entering the house, where again a set of questions are posed. The boy's father ties a *thodkar* (white turban) on the head of the girl's relatives. The boy and the girl are then made to sit side by side, and the mere feeding of *desil* (a sweet preparation of rice and curd) to each other, amidst chanting of verses from the scripture by the Lama, solemnizes the marriage. After the ceremony, the bride accompanies the groom and comes to his natal house, where the consummation of marriage takes place.

The disposal of dead is decided in consultation with the Lama. Generally, the dead are cremated. Infants are kept in a wooden box and immersed in the river. Impurity lasts in the house for only a day, the next day a Lama is called, and he performs purificatory rites. Rituals connected with death are also observed on the *chizik* (fourth day), *duzik* (seventh day), *shipchu sherku* (forty ninth day) and *logar* (one year) when alms are given and prayers are offered for the peace of the departed soul.

The traditional occupation of the Khampas, while they were in Tibet, was sheep herding. They kept sheep, and traded in wool. A little later, when they started trade with India, they left their traditional occupation and brought to India *pashmina* wool, sheep, goat, yak and other items laden on *khachchar* (mules) and on return took carpets, *moonga,* etc. With the closure of border in 1961, the traditional trade links with Tibet have ceased to exist. Now they have left the nomadic trading life and have settled themselves as agriculturists and as orchardists. Some have even taken to shopkeeping and running of restaurants. In their shops one mostly finds foreign goods, which they get from across the border.

The others are employed as labourers in road building or in mule teaming. The majority of the Garja and Piti Khampas own land and work on their own fields, but the Thava and the Khunu Khampas are in trade and business. The Khampas have regulated market in the area where they live, and depend on it for all their daily needs. Children below the age of 15 years assist their parents in their occupation after returning from school and also work with their parents in road repairs, or work as servants in hotels, where they are paid in cash.

A complete change of economy has taken place among the Khampas since 1961 as from itinerant traders they have taken to other diversified field of occupation.

The Khampas have a traditional council known as *shuzam chungi* which is headed by a *gova.* The council consists of five old and learned persons of the community who settle divorce and family disputes and penalizes the guilty for breaking traditional norms. Fines in cash are imposed on the offenders and are paid to the aggrieved. The traditional panchayat had only male members on its panel but the modern statutory panchayats which have come up after Independence have also women members on its board. These panchayats have been formed for the planning and development of the village welfare activities and maintenance of law and order in the village.

The Khampas believe in all the four sects of Lamaistic Buddhism, viz., Galukpa, Ningma-Pa, Sakya-Pa and Kargud-Pa. They visit Buddhist monastries, Gompas, which function as religious teaching institutions. They also have a family deity known as Chhad-Na-Dorje, which is a famous Buddlish deity worshipped by all Buddlist people and by every Khampa. Besides, there are many other deities in the shape of boulders, caves, trees and bushes, which are recognized by different names in different areas. In the case of illness, they often consult the Lama, who advises them to make *puja* and read Buddhist *pragya parmita, vajrachhedika*, etc. Almost every house posseses its own family deity represented by a stone slab or pillar, and on each slab or pillar boughs of junipers are placed. They are worshipped with the smoke of juniper leaves every day. The Khampa often go on pilgrimage to Sarnath, Kushinagar, Nepal, Bodh Gaya, Rewalsar and visit monastries in Spiti, Lahaul and Chango which they consider their sacred centres. Lamas, besides acting as sorcerers, also act as sacredotal specialists, and officiate at the rituals connected with life-cycle at a Khampa house.

The major fairs connected with the Khampas is the Losar (their New Year's Day) which is observed on the 24 or 25 of February according to their calendar and Galde Gamche which is observed in the month of May when prayers are offered and the day is devoted to the memory of the Buddha. Besides, prayers are also offered on the *panchami* (fifth day) and *dashmi* (tenth day) of each fortnight. In Spiti and Kinnaur the Goetr and Ladarcha fairs are held, in which the Khunu and the Piti Khampas take part.

The art forms of the Khampas are visible from their craft, especially in the weaving of carpets, on which they make exquisite designs. The most popular design with the people is that of a dragon, which is made in dominant shades of red and black. This weaving is done by both the sexes, though there are more women involved in it. They are also skilled knitters and knit beautiful designs on sweaters and pullovers. Besides, they also weave *suktu*—a woollen shawl wrapped around the body, and *sukdan*—a woollen bed sheet mainly for self-use, whereas carpets are made for commercial purposes.

The Khampas have oral traditions. Certain songs in their local dialect sung on the occasion of marriage are called as *yanva* or *timde luh*. The women also dance on festive or marriage occasions.

The Khampas living in the valley have strict commensal norms. They exchange both the *kachcha* and the *pucca* food from the Brahmin and Rajput, but do not accept *kachcha* food from other communities except when it is cooked by a person of either a Brahman or Rajput status. Other community people can however, accept both types of food from the Khampas. The Khampas do not suffer from any sense of untouchability among their various territorial groupings. Previously, the Brahman used to observe social distance by refraining from taking cooked food from them, but now this stigma has disappeared. In the urban situation no discrimination is observed even from amongst the communities such as Sippi and Lohar and water and food are freely accepted from them. Marital ties traditionally existed only amongst themselves, but now the Khampas have started entering into matrimonial relationship with other Rajput communities. The Khampas can enter temples with out any discrimination and have access to common water resources and panchayat *ghar.*

Jajmani relationship exists with the communities who are in rural setting, like the Lohar and Beta, who render their traditional services, for which they receive a fixed amount of foodgrain at the harvest time. The modern linkages have brought the Khampa in contact with other communities, with whom they interact regularly in their business and hotel deals. The educated among them have also entered into professional or Government offices. The illiterates come in contact with the other communities by working as labourers. Besides these, the Khampas also have symbiotic relationship with other people. They render mutual help to each other in the construction of new houses, repairing of old ones, stacking of stones to form a protective wall around their fields, and also render help at social functions.

The Khampas' attitude towards the developmental plans is positive. Their children avail themselves of educational facilities. Among the modern generation about 80 per cent are admitted to schools, of which 40 per cent drop out after primary, 20 per cent drop out after high school and 5 per cent after college. Girls do not study beyond matric level because there are no school in the places where they live, and the people do not send their daughters outside the villages. The Khampas share the benefits of health and medicare and have no prejudice against family planning and welfare programmes which have reached them through health centres. Their faith in the traditional system of medicare continues but they also visit Government hospitals and dispensaries. Some of them have been benefitted from village employment and self-employment schemes, and have also received loans and other facilities for starting small business and for horticulture development.

Many of the community members own television sets and radio, and also see cinema, at the cinema halls or in the village, shown by extension agencies. They have electricity, but use wood and kerosene as fuel. A few of the economically better-off members also have telephone facilities and automobiles. Most of the Khampa villages are connected by *pucca* motorable roads. Drinking water is made available through piped water. They mostly depend on rainwater or at places thay are provided with irrigation facilities through *kuhl*. They use both organic and chemical fertilizers and also use insecticides and pesticides for preventing their crops from being damaged. School-going chilldren are provided with mid-day meal in the school, given to them through Block departments. The infants and nursing and expectant mothers avail themselves of the Integrated Child Development Scheme.

Rajendra Sarkar/V.S. Negi

KHASA

The Khas, Khasa or Khasha is distributed in Shimla, Sirmaur, parts of Kullu and Kinnaur districts of Himachal Pradesh and Tehri, Kumaon and Garhwal areas of Uttar Pradesh. In Kinnaur, they call themselves Khosia or Khashyia and associate themselves with the Rajput. In Jaunsar Bawar area of Uttar Pradesh as well as in Chopal and Shillai areas of Himachal Pradesh, Khas Brahmans are those Brahman who entered into matrimonial alliances with the Khasas. The term Khasa is found in *Pauranic* and epic literature. Khasira of *Vayu Purana*, Khasa of *Markandeya Purana*, Khasa of Nepal, Khasya of Kumaon and Garhwal, Khasa of *Bhagvata Purana* and *Vayu Purana* are the people of the same ethnic stock. The ancient *Khasdesh* belonged to these people which is situated between the North-western Provinces and Nepal. In *Brihat-Samhita* of Varahmihira, the Khasas are mentioned with Kulutas (the residents of Kullu region), Tanganas and Kashmiras. At the time of Rajsuya yajna (coronation ceremony) of Yudhishthira, the Khasas and the Tanganas brought heaps of gold raised from underneath the earth, Yak tails (*chanvara*) and sweet honey extracted from the flowers found in the Himavat region. Grierson (1916:8) observes that "the great mass of the Aryan speaking population of the lower Himalaya from Kashmir to Darjeeling is inhabited by tribes descended from the ancient Khasas of Mahabharata".

The Khasas have the village god system. Almost every remarkable hill is considered the abode of some spirit. The village gods are the heads and protectors of the habitat. The *gur* (oracles) represent the spirits and village gods are made to dance in wooden palanquins. Sacrifice of goats and rams are made to village gods and other spirits.

The Khasas have *khoond* (warrior groups). These khoonds act as distinct clans. Mainly two types of *khoond* or groups of the community form the basis of subgroups. These are Shatha (sixty, i.e., Kaurava group) and Pasha (five, i.e., Pandava group). Shatha and Pasha are further divided into subgroups of Chhabishi (i.e., 6 x 20) Charbishi (i.e., 4 x 20), Barabishi (i.e., 12 x 20), Pandrabishi (i.e., the 15 x 20) and so on. These subgroups show that availability of warrior young men for battle was the main criterion for those subgroups. In ancient times the clans were to supply warriors to the Ranas or the heads of the region on demand, so the *khoonds* were required to supply a particular number of soldiers which could be counted up to twenty only.

The Khasas are accompained by Doms or outcastes who have settled near their habitats almost everywhere. The subgroups include 15 to 20 area— Kedarta, Parshetka, Sadani, Kambi, Kastaimu, Jishtu, Richu, Dhirta, Khanna,

Baradu, Kayath, Damta, Jant, Chopta, Chant, Kanet, Thankoo, Sanail, etc., and in Sirmaur these include Chauhan, Tomar, Negi, Shingtan, Gupau, Agran, Bhons, Lehta, Samanta, Namsau, Bargwan, etc. *Bhauy* is the common name for the habitat of the community in Sirmaur. In Chopal, their subgroups include Shilhi, Paralu, Gochi, Chinghan, Dharan, Jhagta, Badhan, Thundu, etc. It seems that these *khoonds* do not include or indicate the original clans to which they belonged but these are based on the names of their ancestors or places to which they belonged in the remote past. In some cases, these are occupational and chivalorous names. The community has also various *gotras* but the most common among these is Kashyap *gotra*.

There is no particular type of dress of the community but there are variations according to local conditions. In Kinnaur, the men and women use *gachi* (waist string) and *chhuba* (long coat) as well as *dohru* (warm *sari*), but in other areas *thipu* (head scraf) is used by the women and men wear *achkan* with folds inside. *Thoda* (martial bow and arrow game) is their common interest and they arrange this sport in open courtyards or grounds from time to time. The participants in *thoda* wear typical type of dress with rough and high heeled shoes and *suthan* made of very coarse and rough cloth.

The script of the community in the past was Takri or Tankri but they use Devanagari now.

The community is non-vegetarian consuming meat fish, pork and eggs, etc. It has a tendency towards local and non-local alchoholic drinks. Their staple food is cereals like wheat, rice, barley and maize and they use pulses such as, *rajmah, mah, moong, arhar, channa* and green vegetables such as cabbage, tomato, potatoe, *sag,* etc. Apple, peanuts, chestnuts, grapes, etc. are relished. The Khasas live in difficult areas and the climate is cold in these places. Buffaloes cannot be reared in snowbound areas and as such cow milk is used. Curd is rarely used and worshippers of Pawasi Mahasu didn't use even milk in earlier days but now there is no such restriction. The Mahasu cult is very prominent among the people of the community and other gods like Hatkoti Devi, Nag deities, Chureshwar, Dom, Chikhreshwar, Koteshwar, etc., are also worshipped. Special dishes like *poltu, siddu,* etc. are popular. Meat of goat, sheep and wild birds and animals is specially prepared and liked.

The Khasha is, by and large, a pastoral and peasant community. There are warriors and hunters as well in the community. Among the *khoonds,* head-hunting had also been a practice in cases of mutual animosity. In Thoda sport the subgroups divide themselves in Shatha (60) and Pasha (5) groups denoting competition among the sixty Kauravas and five Pandavas. Contrary to the belief that Kauravas were one hundred in number the term 'Shatha' indicates that according to a popular belief they were only sixty.

The Khasas have *biyah, praino* and *gadar* types of marriages. The marriage is dissolvable by mutual consent at any time. In some cases, the practice of marriage by force is also found. In *byah* system, the marital relations are settled by the parents. *Praino* is a type of love marriage from the ancient term of '*pranay*' or love. In *gadar* type of marriage, the bride goes to the house of the bride-groom and the wedding ceremony is conducted there. The ancestoral property is divided among all the sons of the family but the eldest, and in some cases, the youngest son get the additional share of a field and an ancestral house. This is called *jethong* for the eldest brother and *kanishong* for the youngest brother. There is no *tekwa* or *niyog* system among the Khasas of Himachal Pradesh but it was found among the Khasas of Jaunsar Bawar, Tehri and Garhwal. According to it, the dead or an ailing and incapacitated husband could be replaced by some other man to act as a hired husband to procreate a male child in the family.

The oracle system is also a peculiarity of the Khasas of Himachal Pradesh and some parts of Uttar Pradesh. According to this practice a man represents the village god and speaks for him. The sermons are considered to be the wishes of the spirit.

The *sanskara* of birth, marriage and death are very important. The dead are cremated. Biradari Panchayats exists and village gods act as heads of the habitats. Untouchability is practised even by village gods. The society is changing in every sphere and the people are receptive to the schemes initiated by the government or other agencies for social welfare.

The Khasas are now very well-off as in every part of their habitat, apple orchards and potato crops are coming up. Some of them are herdsmen and rear goats and sheep. Their habitats are protected by domestic dogs and their dwellings are closely built and well knit. Each *khoond* worships a *thari* goddess and sacrifices a goat to it.

The customs are changing with the passage of time and people are conscious of the pace of change towards the betterment of their lot.

B. R. Sharma

KHATIK

The Khatik a scheduled caste is spread all over the State, except the high altitude areas like Bharmaur, Pangi, Kinnaur, Kullu and Lahaul-Spiti. The word 'Khatik' seems to be a derivative of Sanskrit *khattika*, which means a 'butcher' or 'hunter'. The Khatiks are believed to be migrants from Punjab and also from Uttar Pradesh, who came to the hills in search of livelihood and started selling meat and acting as butchers. According to a myth, "Brahma assigned to them a goat's skin, the bark of trees and lac so they graze cattle, dye the skin of goats and deer, and tan hides with bark and lac" (Rose 1914: 500). The total population of the Khatiks is 449 according to the 1981 Census. They speak Punjabi and Chambiali among themselves, whereas with others they converse in Hindustani. Among themselves, they use Persian as the script and with others they use Devanagari.

The Khatiks are non-vegetarian. They take almost all kinds of meat like that of sheep, goat, fish, chicken and ghurral, but do not take meat of cow or buffalo. Since pork is not available in the higher hills, it is not taken but there is no social taboo for taking it. Their staple food consists of *chapati*, *dal* of *mah* or *masur*, vegetables and meat. Rice is occasionally taken. Vegetables and fruits are used in moderate quantity. Edible roots and tubers are also moderately taken. Milk is taken by adults in tea, but children, old and invalid persons, however, do take milk. They also use milk products like *ghee* and *dahi*. Alcoholic drinks are also taken by menfolk occasionally. They smoke cigarette and bidi, loose tobacco is also taken in the indigenous pipe called *hookah*. *Pan* are also chewed by some.Special foods like *madra* and other sweet dishes are cooked on festive occasions, whereas non-vegetarian food and other delicacies of meat and fish are avoided on solemn occasions. On days of religious festivals also, non-vegetarian food is avoided.

The Khatiks are divided into two religious groupings, the Hindu Khatik and the Muslim Khatik (who are also known as Kasai). There is no social interaction between the two groups. It is believed that at one time they might have been one and the same community, but at some point of time some of them got converted to Islam. The Hindu Khatiks are divided into three subcastes: Chik, Buchar and Sunkhar. The Chiks make *sup* (winnowing fans) and the Buchars sell mutton but not beef and the Sunkhars sell fruits and vegetables. The Buchars are further sub-divided into two endogamous subdivisions—Mehra and Badi. Each of these has a number of exogamous *gots*, the function of which is to regulate marriage. The basis of differentiation of the major groups is religious, whereas that of the sub-groups is occupational, and that of the sub-sub-groups is social.

The Khatiks, of late have started using 'Singh' as their surname. This is being used to uplift their social position, and is a step in the direction of Rajputization in order to identify themselves with the Rajputs. Though the community perceives its superiority in the social hierarchy and ranks itself along with the Kshatriyas, the locals place them low down in the order, because of their association with the unclean occupation of butchery. A Khatik can enter into matrimonial alliances with a Hali or other such communities of the area. Though in terms of varna, the community places itself at the second highest level, i.e., Kshatriya; other communities see them along with Panchma and rank them only superior to Chamar and Chuhra. Crook (1896) however mentions numerous sub-divisions of the Hindu and 7 sub-divisions of the Muslim branch of Khatiks.

Marriages are performed normally within the community and among one's own religious groupings. Endogamy also exists at the sub-caste level, but at the *got* level exogamy prevails. Hypergamy is prevalent and the boys of the community are allowed to marry girls of other castes. Hypogamous union results in excommunication. Consanguineous marriages are prohibited, but junior levirate and sororate are allowed. At one time child marriages were performed at the age of 10 or 12 years, with the consummation of marriage taking place on the girl attaining puberty. But now-a-days, marriages are performed with girls gettting married at 17 or 18 and boys at 22 years or so.

Marriages are performed by *byah*, *batta-satta*, or at times when the boy is unable to pay the bride price, by serving in his prospective in-laws' house for seven years, and thus compensating for the bride price. They also had a custom of paying *mamla* (bride price) in cash to the bride's parents, but today this has been replaced by dowry. Dowry is not demanded and depends on the economic status of the family, and is usually in kind.

Monogamy is the rule but in the event of the first wife being unable to bear a male child, polygamy, not necessarily of the sororal type, is resorted to. The usual form of residence is patrilocal, but in exceptional cases, when the family has no male child the *jamai* is invited to stay with the bride's parents. Earlier, the women had only marriage symbol of putting vermilion in the parting of the hair, but this is not strictly adhered to these days. Divorce is permissible with sociojudicial approval; and the proceedings can be initiated by either of the aggrieved parties. The common grounds of divorce are infidelity, impotency or maladjustment. Divorce compensation is paid to the aggrieved party, which normally is the return of bride price or actual marriage expenses. This is known as *mamla de-dena*, and the amount is decided by the panchayat of the community. The children of divorced parents are the liability of the father, but should a child accompany the mother, he loses the right in the father's property.

Widow remarriage can take place both in and outside the family. But in the event of her marrying outside, she loses her right in the property and has to return the expenses. So as a first preference usually a deceased husband's younger brother whether married or unmarried is preferred. Even if she does not marry the husband's younger brother, the widow can continue to live in the family and have illicit relations. Children of such relations are called *chakhandu* or *hallad* and have a right of inheritance to the property, and such children are regarded as children of the deceased husband. Widower and divorcee remarriage are also permissible.

The family is of vertically extended type in which all the married sons along with their children and unmarried sons and daughters share the same hearth. As a result of this, there is a feeling of mutual love, dependence and respect within the family. The eldest male member who is also the head of the family commands greater respect and his decision in family matters is final. A situation of conflict or confrontation rarely comes up, since due importance is given to all members of the family. If a situation of confrontation comes up, it usually relates to restraining the freedom of youngsters. Avoidance is observed between a daughter-in-law and with all her husband's elder relatives and all such relations in that line. The daughter invariably covers her head or face when she is face to face with the elders and also avoids talking. Similarly joking relationships exist between a man and his wife's younger sisters and brothers and that between a wife and her husband's younger brother and sisters. Traditionally, the husband and wife were forbidden to take each other's name, but nowadays they freely address each other by name.

The property is equally inherited by all the male children. Girls do not have any share in their father's property as they are believed to have taken their share at the time of their marriage. However, at times when there is no male issue, *ghar jamai* is invited to live with the girl's parents, that the girl inherits the property of the father. But in the event of her also having no sons, the property returns and passes on to the collaterals. A widow has the right to enjoy her deceased husband's property for her lifetime, provided she stays back in the family. However, if she remarries outside the family she loses her right. If a widow takes her children along with her, they also loose their share in the ancestral property; but in the event of her remarriage, if the new husband accepts the child, he can inherit the stepfather's property.

The women continue to enjoy equal status with their menfolk. They contribute to family income indirectly, doing all the household chores and managing the affairs of the family. Since all the Khatik families live in urban locales they do not have to go for collection of fuel. The educated womenfolk also join Government service and private organization, work as teachers, and contribute to the family income. They also take part in social and religious festivals. They also take part in political activities, which is limited to the casting of votes. Khatik women do not have any role in social control.

The enceinte mother worships the *kuldevta* to invoke his blessings for the welfare and safe delivery of the child. Pre-delivery restrictions also exist on the mother, and she is not allowed to go out alone at night, or watch a dreadful scene, or see a sun or moon in eclipse, as these sights are believed to harm the foetus. Post-natal pollution exists for 12 days. Six months after the birth, the ceremony for first cereal-feeding and naming of the child is observed. A *pandit* suggests the name after consulting the horoscope and almanac. *Jattu* or *mundan* ceremony is observed for boys at 2 $^1/_2$, 3 or 5 years after the birth. The child's head is ceremonially shaved off keeping a *pagga* (cue) on the occiput. Marriage ceremony is observed at the bride's residence with a feast being served by the bride's parents. The marriage is solemnized by circumambulating five times a pitcher under a canopy, with the apparels of the boy and the girl tied by *jaul* (bridal knot). Prior to this, *pai-pujji* is performed by the bride's parents where they touch and wash the feet of both the bride and the groom.

The dead are cremated, but those whose *jattu* ceremony has not been performed are buried. The pyre is lit by the eldest male member. Pollution continues for nine days, after which purificatory ceremony is observed. Every year in honour of the dead person, food and delicacies to the liking of the deceased are offered in *pitri-paksha*.

The Khatiks are engaged in the business of slaughtering sheep and goat and selling their meat. Some are however also involved in tanning skins. As a subsidiary means of occupation, they have taken up jobs in Government and private organizations; some have also qualified for the teaching profession. The Khatiks are totally dependent on the market for their daily needs. Sheep and goat are purchased from the locals against deferred cash payment.

The Khatiks have their own Biradari-panchayat, which is headed by a Chaudhary . The office of Chaudhary is not hereditary; he is elected by general consensus along with the *panch*, who assist the Chaudhary, in dispensing justice. The cases that come up before the panchayat relate to family disputes, adultery, elopement and disrespect for traditional norms. In earlier times, the orders of the Chaudhary used to be enforced but this practise has now ceased, and a fine in cash is imposed which is utilized for defraying the expenses of panchayat. Sometimes excommunication is resorted to but the excommunicated are readmitted on paying a fine. The statutory panchayats have come up after Independence for maintaining social control and planning and implementing welfare activities. For intercommunity disputes people still rely on their traditional panchayats more than on the statutory ones.

The Hindu Khatiks are followers of Nanakpanthi Sikh sect, yet they observe none of the Sikh tenets. The community worships Bhairon,

Maldeota and Sidh Masani also known as Mata Masani. Every family has a family deity known as Kuldeota who is worshipped and propitiated for the welfare of the family. Village and regional deities do not exist, but gods and goddesses of the Hindu pantheon like Rama, Hanuman, Krishna, Durga and Chamunda are worshipped. Their sacred centres are Hardwar, Manimahesh and Mata Vaishno Devi. Gaur Brahmans are their *purohit* who perform *puja* and all life-cycle rituals. For warding off evil spirits, the exorcists are invited. The Khatik's major fairs are Minjar, Sui Mela and Bharmaur Jatra the festivals being Baisakhi, Lohri, Holi and Diwali. All of these fairs and festivals have socioreligious significance, which is recalled by reciting stories at the time of performing the rituals attached to them.

Change of religion has taken place among the Khatiks, as a result of which a section of the community got converted to Islam. Socioreligious movements also did take place among the Hindu Khatiks, whereby they got converted and started believing in the Nanakpanthi sect. However, the pre-change practices still survive.

The Khatik women make colourful diagrams on floors at festivities. They also do embroidery on cloth with silk and gold threads which they have learnt in recent times. They sing songs prevalent in the region at social occasions and also dance within the four walls of their houses purely for amusement. Folklore and tales are same as those of the region.

No *savarna* caste would traditionally accept water or *kachcha* or *pucca* food from a Khatik. But a Khatik would accept all kinds of food from the *savarna*. The Khatiks would also not accept *kachcha* food prepared by a Chamar, Dum, Pasi or Dhobi, but can exchange *pucca* food with these castes. Traditionally intercommunity marriages were prohibited, but the Khatik could take a girl from the Panchams like Hali. Putative kinship can be established with a person of equal social status, but who is not related, and such relations are expected to perform duties as a real kin.

In the hill communities since the caste ties are not that rigid as in the plains, these communities did not have any restriction on the sharing of water from common water resources. But restrictions did exist on their entry in the houses of the *savarna* or temples. *Jajmani* relationship also never existed in this community.

Their education, and consequently better employment has resulted in the emergence of political leadership at the local level, and a couple of them are now holding elected posts in the Chamba municipality. They are also taking part in all social and religious functions. Employer-worker relationships have also come up as a result of their taking up varied occupations in addition to their traditional ones. Since the people are economically well-off, they have been able to secure brides and grooms from other castes.

The impact of various developmental programmes, especially literacy drive and free education, on the Khatik community has been substantial. Almost the entire Khatik community of Chamba is literate. The boys and girls both study up to the post-graduate level. Their interest in sending their children to school is further activated by the fact that they are provided with free schooling and scholarships.

Though for small ailments the Khatiks still rely on their traditional home-made remedies, but in case of disease not getting cured they resort to allopathic medicine, which is readily available to them since they are living in townships. Attitude of the community people towards family planning is also favourable, and they now have smaller families with two or three children. As for the modern methods of family planning they use all other methods other than sterilization.

Drinking water is available through pipes. The people of the community have also been provided with employment under Integrated Rural Development Schemes and also under reserved quota for scheduled castes. A few of them have also secured loans from blocks and banks under self-employment schemes and have started poultry farming. The localities of the Khatiks are well connected with media and communication system. Electricity is available and is availed of. Firewood and kerosene oil are the usual fuel resources. Irrigation and use of chemical fertilizers and pesticides is not applicable to the people, as the community is not involved in agriculture. Under the nutrition programmes, the mid-day meal scheme is availed of by school-going children. Mother-infant care and immunization facility are provided through Integrated Child Development Scheme. These services are availed of by expectant and nursing mothers and children between 0-5 age groups. Facilities of ration, kerosene and cloth at subsidized rates are available through Government fair price shops. Savings and investment facilities are available and are also availed of as the people are economically well-off.

Rajendra Sarkar

KHATRI

The Khatri is a well-known mercantile community distributed over various districts. They are migrants from the adjoining areas of Punjab and have entered into the State at different times. Many people have also come at the time of India's partition in 1947 and are also known as "refugees". But many of them have lived in the State for over hundreds of years and some of them have become agriculturists. Generally the Khatri is thought of as a community of traders, businessmen and shopkeepers. Many also act as moneylenders and are popularly addressed respectfully as 'Shah' or 'Shahji'. In this way they are similar to the Mahajans and a section of the Khatri actually calls itself Mahajan. However, Mahajan is nearly a distinct community of the traditional money-lenders and traders who did not practise agriculture and includes sections of the Baniya, Kayastha and Khatri communities. Main concentrations of the Khatris are seen in the towns of districts Bilaspur, Solan, Kangra, Hamirpur, Una, Mandi, Kullu, Chamba, Shimla, etc., but their exact population is not known. They live in different terrains ranging from the sub-montaneous valleys to high hills and in warm and temperate to cold climate with medium annual rainfall and low humidity.

They have assimilated the regional cultures. They speak the local dialects, like Bilaspuri and Kangri of the western Pahari and write in the Devanagari script. Many of them living in the towns speak Punjabi as well as Hindi. They converse in English with some of their customers. Older persons also know Urdu. The ones who do agriculture and animal husbandry in villages are almost indistinguishable from the other natives but the town-dwelling traders do give an impression of being outsiders. However, much distinction cannot be made in dress and ornaments of the community and that of other neighbouring communities. *Cholu, paswaj, suthan,* etc. have been the traditional dress of the women in Mandi, Chamba and Kangra. The men wear a shirt and *pyjama* or trousers whereas the women dress in *kurta* and *salwar* with a *chunni/dupatta* as in Punjab. The common ornaments worn by the women are: golden *bali, koka/tili* or *nath*. A chain with a locket in the neck and a finger-ring are also adorned. Some wear golden bangles as well but glass bangles of different hues are quite commonly worn.

The Khatris' major staple food is wheat and rice but in rural areas the first place is given to maize in terms of consumption followed by wheat and then rice. Various types of pulses: *urad, moong, masur, kulthi, moth, arhar,* peas and beans *rajmah,* and grams are frequently consumed. The vegetables cauli-flower, gourds, lady finger, brinjal, *karela,* etc., along with roots and tubers and leaves of *palak*, mustard and *methi* are consumed in routine. The cooking media are mustard or groundnut oils or vegetable *ghee.* Milk and milk products, curd, *panir, lassi/chhah, kheer*, etc., are frequently eaten. Fruit intake is moderate to high in towns but low or seasonal in rural areas. Mango, banana, guava, apple, peach, plums, etc., are the common fruits. *Toot* (mulberry), *tiamlu* and *dagle* (figs) and *jamun* are also eaten in the villages. They are generally non-vegetarian in food habit and quite frequently eat eggs, fish and mutton and sometimes pork as well. Men consume liquor purchased from the market on festive occasions, though some are also regular drinkers. They smoke cigarette/*bidi* and loose tobacco (in rural areas) in an indigenous pipe called *hukka* or *kali.* Festive food preparations are *halwa* and *kheer, kachauri* (fried sweetened cakes), *dahi-bade, puri/bhature* with *chhole, bhalle* of pulses, *seviyan*, and *ankli* of rice flour (in rural areas). Non-vegetarian foods are not eaten during death pollution. Certain foods are also taboo on certain fasts. Recently some followers of the Radhaswami mission have started avoiding non-vegetarian foods.

Bio-anthropological Report provides some biological information on the Khatri community.

In the old ethnographic literature (Ibbetson, 1916; Rose 1919) three main sub-divisions of the Khatris are mentioned, viz., Bari, Bunjahi and Sarin. The first sub-division consists of 12 and the second as many as 52 sections. But in rural areas the people are generally not aware of these main divisions and distinguish themselves only by the *got* or clan names. Sarin is also commonly used as a clan rather than a sub-division. The Khatris also assimmilate the Aroras within its broader design and are generally endogamous. Social hierarchy does not exist or may be apparent only in terms of one's economic position. Usually the mercantile Khatris dominate over the cultivators and are also economically well-off in comparison to the latter. There is little differentiation in terms of sectarian divisions though some follow a Radhaswami sect. In the regional social hierarchy the Khatris find a third place in the Vaishya varna after the Brahman and the Rajput even though they are generally richer than the former. The *got* or clans are frequently used as surnames and distinctly indicate descent or ancestry. They serve as exogamous units to regulate marriage alliances. There are several clans. Some of the common clans noted during the study (in Bilaspur district) are Chadda, Sethi, Ratwan, Chopra, Kaure, Mehta, Mehra, Varma, Jagota, Vaidya, Bohra, etc.

The Khatris are endogamous or broadly endogamous with the Aroras. Recently they have also become inclined to extend marriage alliances to other socioeconomically equal ranking communities like Baniya, Mahajan and Sood. The main rule observed is *got* exogamy. But in towns the rule of *mohalla* (locality) exogamy does not apply. Marriage occurs through negotiation and in adult age. There was and is no tradition of bride-price. However, dowry has become a custom. The dowry may be given in cash or kind or in both, and is also considered a status symbol among the economically well-off people of the community. There is an increasing trend towards giving and taking of dowry. Monogamy is the prevalent form of marriage and only rarely may a man also marry another woman in case the first is unable to produce any child. Symbols of marriage are *sindur*, glass and/or golden bangles, finger ring, nose and ear-ring/pins. The residence of the bride is patrilocal. Widow remarriage is not practised by the community though it is not a rule but junior levirate does not exist. A widower may marry a junior sororate or any other girl. Divorce is also not approved of by the society but it may happen on judicial approval in the civil courts and either of the spouse has the freedom to divorce on grounds of maladjustments. But the man bears the liability of the children and pays compensation to the wife. Both the divorcees may remarry. There is no marked increase in the incidence of divorce but there is increasing liberty for women to divorce or dissolve an unhappy matrimonial alliance.

The Khatris live in both nuclear and vertically extended joint families. Usually the sons do not get separated until all the sons are married and/or settled. But presently nuclear families are on the increase. In joint families the junior members are supposed to respect their elders. But points of conflicts may be regarding irregularities in distribution of parental property or unequal division of labour. Avoidance relationship is more strictly seen in the rural areas where the *lari/nuh/bahuti* keeps a *ghoond* from her *saurah, jeth, nandoi* and the elder males of the village. But in urban families the avoidance relationship has almost died out. Joking relationships are informal and may occur between *jija* and *sali, devar* and *bhabi, jija* and *sali, jija* and *sala* and *nanad* and *bhabi.* But for all practical purposes the elder brother's wife is respected next to mother. The inheritance of the paternal property occurs as per the rule of male equigeniture but brotherless sisters inherit father's property. The succession goes to the eldest son. Khatri families are very much intertwined on festive and sad occasions and are very helpful to each other.

The status of women in Khatri society is nearly equal to that of men. The women are respected and addressed as 'Shahni' (as men are addressed as 'Shah') and they keep the family command in their hands even though they have little role in political activities and in the mechanism of social control. They are not confined to domestic chores but also assist men in their business or shop work. Some women are also employed in Government and other services. In rural areas they also participate in agricultural and animal husbandry duties at present, but earlier they remained confined to the household activities only. They also collect fuel and fodder and fetch potable water in villages. They take parts in various social and religious ceremonies.

The life-cycle rituals are performed by a Brahman priest. Among birth rituals, restrictions on women exist pre- and post-natally. The birth pollution called *sutak* is observed for 16 days and purification occurs by a *gunt* ceremony in which the woman takes cow's urine and *Ganga jal* and takes bath. Sweets are distributed in the neighbourhood and among relatives. At the male child's birth the ladies of the locality/village sing folksongs. A feast may be given and a *pandit* performs a *havan.* Naming ceremony is also observed by some and generally the name is given as per the horoscope of the child by consulting a *pandit. Annaprashan* ceremony may be ignored. The major childhood ritual is *mundan* among male children and performed by the *mama* of the child or by a barber. A small feast is arranged for young children. Adolescent rituals are not observed. *Janeu* is worn on the occasion of marriage.

Marriage rituals are performed as per the Hindu tenets. Pre-marriage rituals are *sagai, tika* and *thahaka* (betrothal) when the boy and girl are offered some ceremonial clothes/ornament and some rupees. Ring ceremony also comes within these rituals when a golden ring is offered to the girl by the boy, but this occurs mainly among the Punjabi Khatris. On the marriage day *sand, samuhat, haldi* and *mehndi* ceremonies are observed in preparation of the marriage. Major marriage rituals called *lagan* and *vedi* occur at the bride's place when the Brahman recites vedic hymns and the bride and groom circumambulate the sacred fire. Finally the parents of the bride perform *kanyadan* or *sankalpa.* They also offer a feast to the groom's party. At the groom's place, the first ritual is *andrera* and the other is *pipal* worship. In *pipal* worship the bride and groom circumambulate the sacred tree and tie a white thread around it. Putative kinship-based friendships are also made at this time. Finally the groom's parents give a marriage feast to the gathered kin and friends. The *muklawa* occurs on the following day or soon after the marriage and nuptial ceremony occurs at the groom's place.

The dead are cremated and ashes are collected on the third day and immersed in the Ganges at Hardwar and *pind dan* is given to a Panda. The pollution called *patak* lasts for 13 days when the *uthala* occurs and an Acharaj officiates to perform ancestor worship. Presently, in towns some observe *uthala* on the fourth day and observe *rasham pagri* (succession of the eldest son) at the father's death. But feast and *dan* are given to Brahmans and the poor on the thirteenth day. The family priest also performs the purificatory *havan.* A ceremonial meal is given to the community on the sixteenth day called *solia* which makes the family pure and fit for exchange of food and water. Annual and fourth annual death rites are also observed and ceremonial feasts are given to commemorate the dead. Every year in the *pitri paksha* of the Hindu lunar calendar, *shradha* of the dead and other ancestors is observed and a sweet meal usually *kheer* is offered to the family priest and food is thrown to the crows. The followers of the Radhaswami sect do not observe the detailed Sanatana rituals but observe a simple *satsang* (religious gatherings) and visit the shrine of their Guru at Beas in Punjab.

The Khatris thrive mainly on their mercantile profession or business entrepreneurship. Most of them run general merchant shops in towns or do various types of business. Some living in the villages have also adopted agriculture and animal husbandry as major sources of livelihood and supplement their earnings by running petty shops of essential commodities for the routine comsumption of the villagers. Many people are also in various jobs in Government, banks and other private enterprises. They hold white-collar jobs, and are in teaching, medical, engineering, defence services, etc. Child labour does occur sometimes in the rural areas or the children assist their parents in their occupations. Dealings with the customers are both in cash and credit but they also accept cereals and other agricultural produce from the farmers for selling their goods.

There is no organized community council but the Khatris solve their social disputes with the involvement of the *bajurag* or *sayane* (respected elders) of the community or village or locality. Some socioeconomic or village dispute over land and water are solved by the members of the statutory Gram Panchayat. Conflicts of a serious nature involving violence, etc., are taken to the civil courts. There is not much role of the caste or village council in the mechanism of social control at present and generally legal course is taken by the people.

The Khatris are Hindu in Himachal Pradesh and worship gods and goddesses of the Hindu pantheon. They have special reverence to Naraina/ Vishnu and Laxmi (the goddess of wealth and happiness). On Diwali night, Laxmi is specially propitiated to ensure prosperity in the family. They also propitiate various local and regional deities as family, clan and village deities. Among these the chief ones are Balak Nath, Nahar Singh, Guga, Bharthri Sidh and Lakhdata or Pir Bhianu. Family or individual affiliations are seen to the Pirs or Sidh. In addition, various local female deities revered are Nabahi Devi, Hari Devi, Ton Bharari, Vaishnu Devi, Santoshi Mata, etc. The shrines of the deities are visited during their annual fairs and/or at festive occasions and childbirth. Lakhdata is visited by every newly-wed couple and *sehra* (wedding crown) is offered to the deity on the first Thursday after marriage. Their sacred specialists are from other communities employed for performing life-cycle rituals and other acts like confirming thefts and curing ailments, etc. They celebrate various Hindu festivals like Lohri, Baisakhi, Sair, Rakhi, Navratre, Ramnavmi, Janamashtami, Dussehra and Diwali. Women celebrate Karua Chouth festival and keep a fast. They lack any community specific art and craft and share regional Pahari and Punjabi folklore, songs, tales, music and dances. *Gidda* is a popular dance among women performed on festive occasions like marriages. *Bhajan* and *kirtan* during nights called *jagrata* and *Bhagpat* (Geeta Path) are popular folk traditions.

The Khatris are in business, agriculture and in various white-collar jobs, teaching, medical, engineering, defence services etc. They have a regional level political leadership as well.

Modern developmental programmes have made considerable favourable impact on the Khatris. The formal education has spread without any discrimination of the sexes. They now receive higher post-graduate education. But many having their own business enterprises do not prefer higher education and study only up to the secondary school or graduate level. Modern methods of health and medicare are used and favoured. But at times they also use indigenous methods in case the modern system of medicare is not effective. Attitude towards the small-sized family norm has become more favourable and modern methods of contraceptives including sterilization are used. But socially at least one male child is very much demanded in the family even at the risk of having more female children.

A. R. Sankhyan

KINNAURA

The inhabitants of Kinnaur district are known as Kinnaura, Kinara, Kanawara, Kanaura or Kinnaurese. According to Bhagvatpurana, they trace their origin from the shadow of Lord Brahma. Yet another legend says that they have sprung from the toe of Brahma along with the Yakshas. But according to the Bhavricopanishda, Devi created the Kinnaurese along with Brahma, Vishnu, Rudra, Maruta, Gandharva and Apsara. In the Mahabharat, they have been grouped with the Gandharva, while in Matsyapurana their kinship with Kirata and the Yakshsa has been focused (Sharma, 1976; Bajpai, 1987).

The Kinnaura are a scheduled tribe with a population of 47,913 according to the 1981 census. It may be pointed out that while the Kinnaura have been declared as a scheduled tribe, the Chamang, (Lohar), Domang (Koli), Badhi and Nagalu are scheduled castes. The community occupies the high altitude area of Himachal Pradesh inhabiting the Kinnaur valley which has mountainous topography, cold climate, dense forests, low rainfall and heavy snowfall.

The Kinnaura are very colourful in attire. While the *thepang* (cap) and *gachhang* (waistband) is common to both sexes, the male dress consists of *chhuba* (coat), *suthan*, *chamukurti* (jacket) and *kameez*. The female dress consists of *choli* (blouse), *kameez*, *dohru* (woollen sari) and *chhauli* (shawl).

The Kinnaura speak the Kinnauri dialect which, according to G.A. Grierson (1909-III:1430-40) comes under the Himalayan Group of Tibeto-Burman family of languages. At present, the Kinnaura have Hindi as the second language. Besides, Bhoti is also spoken in upper Kinnaur. English is known only to those who have school or higher education.

The Kinnaura are non-vegetarian. They are also fond of *chhang*, and smoking tobacco. The staple food consists of *chappati* of buck-wheat and barley or maize, with *rongi* or *mah*. *Chapati* of *ogla* and *phafra* (millets) are also prepared. Potato is the staple vegetable. Fruits like apple, apricot, pear, grape, peach and nuts are grown, and are also taken during the season.

Bio-anthropological Report provides biological information on the community.

The Kinnaura belong to different ethinic groups. Among them the Rajputs (also known as Kanet, Khas, Khosia or Khasa) are the dominant group. Next comes, Koli—who are weavers and artisans, leather workers and ploughmen (Hali), followed by the Lohar, Badhi and Nagalu who are ironsmiths and silversmiths, carpenters and masons, and basket makers, respectively. In general the Kinnaura have two broad categories, i.e., Khosia and Beru. Beru is further sub-divided into three sub-categories (a) the Domang which includes the Lohar and the Badhi or Ores; (b) the Chamang, which includes Nagalu; and the ethnic Rajputs inhabiting the upper part of Pooh sub-division, being Buddhists, are called Jad or Zad. (Rose, 1914; Negi, 1976).

The Khosias or the Rajputs have three *khel* or status groups, viz., Orang, Morang or Maorang and the Waza (Raha and Mahato, 1985; Raha, 1987). These are endogamous status groups and are based on their hierarchical positions, and are found only in the Hinduism-dominated areas. The *khels* are further sub-divided into a number of lineages or *khandans* which are original and immigrants. The latter are the families who came and settled in villages as wives or as *makpa* (son-in-law) or came on migration. The functional difference between them is that while the former can directly take part in social, economical, political and religious functions, the latter cannot. Some of the *khandans* are further sub-divided into sub-*khandans*. The reasons for their sub-divison are not known.

Each *khel* follows *khel* endogamy. In earlier days, all these three status groups were strictly endogamous. The member of one status group was not allowed to marry into other status groups. But with the march of time rules restricting inter-*khel* marriage have started showing slackness, as a result of which marriages have started taking place between the Orang and Morang *khels*. *Khandans* are marriage regulating units. They are exogamous. Marriages between members of two sub-*khandans* is also prohibited. The members of superior *khandan* prefer to marry a superior *khandan* and inferior into inferior. Marriages within seven generations of father and three generations of mother's *khandan* are prohibited whereas with that of father's mother's *khandan* is preferred. The marriage age for the boy ranges between 16 and 30, and, 15 and 25 for girls, but in pre-Independence era child marriages were prevalent. *Izaat* or *dhori* (bride-price) is prevalent among the Rajputs as well as among other castes.

Though polyandry of the fraternal type is practised as a norm, monogamy is no less common. Monogamy is practised by those who are the only sons in the household, and those who left Kinnaur and settled outside. The same rules of marriages are also applicable to the scheduled caste population of the district. Polygyny is not popular among the Kinnaura. Very few cases of polygyny have been observed. This usually results in divorce, if the wife is barren, but while going in for the second marriage, the consent of the first wife is sought. The different forms of marriage prevalent among the Kinnaura are *byah*, which is regular marriage performed in accordance with the Vedic rites, marriage by exchange, sororate marriage, marriage by elopement (locally known as *dab-dab* or *khukichimo)*, *damchaltshis* (love marriage), and *haari* (it is a combination of both divorce and remarriage). In this, one set of brothers divorce their wife in lieu of *haari* (compensation). *Dolangchim* (offering money at the feet of the mother-in-law by the bridegroom) is an important ritual. The bridegroom, on his first arrival after the marriage has to bow at the feet of the mother-in-law and offer some money according to this ritual (Sharma, 1976).

The symbols of a married woman among the Hindu Kinnaurese are ornaments, red mark on forehead and vermilion on the parting of the hair. Descent is reckoned in the male line. Unmarried children belong to their father's *khandan*. After marriage the sons retain their father's *khandan* but daughters accept their husband's *khandan*. An adopted child usually get the *khandan* of a person who adopts him.

Divorce is locally known as *shingtickashimig* or *thagchocha*, and is permitted by both the husband and wife. The divorce is usually demanded by the husband because the wife is quarrelsome, adulterous, or does not like to work or suffers from a contagious or incurable disease. And divorce is sought by the wife if the husband is unable to feed the wife or tortures her, is debauched or suffers from incurable contagious disease. The divorce proceedings are initiated by the aggrieved party in the Biradari or Gram panchayat, who after hearing them, makes them stand face to face, holding the two ends of a *dingi* (small stick) and asking them to break it. The break of *dingi* signifies breaking of marital relations. There is no restriction on widow remarriage, provided the widow stays in the deceased husband's house for one year and none of the kin marry her during that time. If, however, she is pregnant at the time of her husband's death, she cannot remarry till she is breastfeeding the child.

Among the Kinnaura, virilocal residence is a common practice, wherein a wife after marriage moves to her husband or husband's house and shares the house with his relatives. Though in this polyandrous society husbands who are brothers, normally lead a peaceful life with their common wife, at times, the inability of the wife to distribute her love equally to all husbands results in conflict. Also sometimes, when some brother brings a young wife, she by custom becomes the wife of all, the first wife gets jealous and starts conflicts. The cordial relationships in family are breaking up due to the tendency towards monogamous marriages and setting up of nuclear households.

The father acts as a guide, teacher and friend of his children and he showers love on them, whereas the mother disciplines them and bring them up. The children also respect their parent's elder brothers and sisters. Partial avoidance is present between father-in-law and daughter-in-law and between son-in-law and mother-in-law. Name taking is taboo. Son-in-law and daughter-in-law do not take the name of their parents-in-law. Similarly the husband and wife do not take each other's name; instead they refer to each other as father and mother of so and so. Joking relationship is present among different relatives, especially between man and his wife's younger sister.

Among the Kinnaura, the property is inherited according to the *jathong* and *kanchhong* rules. Under this rule, before the partition actually takes place, a good part of agricultural land is given to the *jathong* (eldest) brother and the ancestral house to the *kanchhong* (youngest) brother, and thereafter the property is equally divided. The last wish of the dying man known as *tonglong* is usually honoured. A widow in the absence of children can inherit the property but cannot sell it. After her death the property passes to the collaterals. Children of all the wives of a husband and with those whom he could have married share the property equally. Children born to a woman whom he cannot marry do not inherit the property. If a man has no son, property can be transferred to the daughters by making *hibba* (will) while he is living. After the daughter inherits the father's property but fails to have any issue, the property in that event will not be inherited by nearest kin of the son-in-law, but will be vested back with the nearest kin of the man.

The women are the chief economic asset of the family. They practically do all the agricultural activity except ploughing, and collect fodder for the milking cattle, cook food and bring up children. Being the common wife of the brothers, she is greatly pampered and loved by all. She also has an equal right in the religious activities. In the political field their participation is limited only to the casting of votes.

Among the Kinnaura, though there is a liking for a son but there is no apathy towards a daughter. The first pregnancy is a very significant event and an event of joy for the father and relatives. The birth takes place in the house in a separate room. The expectant mother is helped by an elderly experienced woman of the community who acts as *aapi* or *pangrokhna* (midwife) and cuts *naing* (umbilical cord) with *chaku* (iron knife) and buries it in the field. The mother is kept secluded from the rest of the family members and *sekhor* (birth pollution) is observed from 7 to 15 days, when the house is cleared and a bath is taken. In Buddhist-dominated area, a Lama is called on the third day for *sang* or purification. On the seventh day the Lama is again called and *newang* ceremony is held when verses from sacred scriptures are recited and a feast is given. The naming ceremony is performed by the Lama when the child is 15 days old. He prepares at the same time, some *taweez* (charm) designed to secure the child a long life. When the boy is a year old his head is shaved and the Lama performs sacrifice such as *hom, puja* or *math*.

The marriage ceremony is very elaborate and is known as *byah, zanekang* or *zanchang*. The most important marriage ritual is the turban tying ceremony, which symbolizes the polyandrous marriage. All brothers sit in a row and the bride sits before them. The groom and the bride are garlanded with *obal* (garland), made of locally available dry fruits. The maternal uncle of the groom then takes a piece of white cloth, and ties *pagri* on the head of each brother. This indicates the marriage of all brothers with a common wife. The marriage ceremony in Buddhist-dominated areas is almost similar, excepting that it is presided by a Lama.

The dead are disposed of by *agang* (cremation). Burial is taken into account only in case of a minor child (below 3 years) and persons suffering from contagious diseases like leprosy, small pox, etc. Sometimes in case of stillbirth or infant death up to six months, the body is kept in a wooden box and immersed in water. If a woman dies during her pregnancy, the child is taken out of the womb and first buried and then the mother is cremated.

The traditional occupation of the Kinnaura had been agriculture, trade and sheep rearing but nowadays different kinds of occupations like cultivation, sheep and goat rearing, spinning and mule-tethering are combined together. The other important point is that while most of the male workers of all ethnic groups have more than one occupation, their females have only two occupations—agricultural work and preparing woollen cloths. Very few inhabitants of Kinnaur are landless. Most of them own land though the acreage varies. The average landholding among the Rajputs is higher than among the Kolis. Under the *shingmo* or *hala* system, the Koli cultivates the land and does all agricultural work of Rajput families, in lieu of which he gets a fixed amount of cereals. The *jajmani* system among the Kinnaura is known as *binana* system. It is the system of mutual cooperation between the Rajput and Koli, Lohar, Badhi and Nagalu. With the Kolis, they have *bonu* and *sui binana*. Under the former, the Kolis are given wool to weave cloth, and in the latter cloth is given for stitching. In lieu of the services rendered, they get cereals and sometimes cash. Similar relations also exist with Ores, Domang and Chinal where they are paid in cash or in cereals in lieu of the various services rendered by them.Besides, *binana*, *bhoara* and *mokomokheyasimig* systems also coexist, in which under the former, all related persons are invited for economic pursuits and social affairs, and under the latter one's neighbour (related or unrelated persons) are invited, and in lieu of the work they are served food. It is socially obligatory on the part of a person to render mutual help whenever called upon to do so.

Prior to the closure of the border, trade was carried on with Tibet, which has since been stopped. Now the Kinnaura market their produce through Lavi fair and middlemen to Shimla and other places in the country.

For maintaining law and order in the community, the Kinnaura have a traditional council called *char-bhai*. It consists of *char, halmandi* and *tokniya,* besides a *mukhiya*. The posts of the *mukhiya* and *char* always belong to Rajput whereas that of *halmandi* and *tokniya* are filled by Koli. Usually when a conflict occurs between two persons concerning any economic, social, religious or other affairs, the case is referred to *charbhai*. In the caste council the village deity also performs a major role as a judge through *grokch*. The verdict of the deity is final and supreme. The guilty persons are punished with excommunication or are fined according to the severity of the crime. The penalty imposed is utilized in drinking and eating. The term of office of *charbhai* is not defined. The termination of the incumbent from the office depends mostly on the necessity felt by the village deity. The Kinnaura follow an unwritten code of conduct. Women never become a member of *charbhai*. Though nowadays statutory panchayats have come up but still the traditional council holds a greater sway.

Kinnaur is a place of curious coexistence of Hinduism and Mahayanaist Buddhism. People embracing Buddhism belong to Nyingmapa, Dukpa, Kargyutpa, and Gelukpa sects. On entering a Buddhist village, one finds a tomb and *chorten* or *chosten* in various direction of the village and also in individual houses, which are meant to ward off evil spirits. The centre for their religious activity is the *gompa* or *labrang* which is headed by a Lama.

The central feature of Kinnauri Hinduism is its numerous *devta* or *devi*. In this district each household has a deity which is called *Kinshu* and the village deity is called *ghori*. The principal deity, the *ghori*, exercises his or her control over all the deities under that *ghori*. Similarly, *khunt* which is formed of some *ghoris*, has a *khunt devta* or *devi*. The major deities are Maheshwar, Chandika, Badrinarayan and Dabla. The function of these deities is to ensure the welfare of their clientele and redressal of their sufferings. While *Kinshu* is worshipped in the corner of a room of every household, the other deities have their abode in *santhong* (temple premises). There are 18 major deities of the Kinnaura who are said to be the progeny of Banasur and Hidimba.

The Kinnaura believe in spirits. Bakharshuna, Banshi's, Chou's, Khunkch are the spirits who reside in high altitude forests, *deodar* and *kail* trees, particular stones on a highway, and in cowsheds respectively. While the Khunkch does not harm unless put in trouble, the others harm anyone coming their way. Churail, the spirit of pregnant woman is warded off by wearing amulets and charms. *Thatha* ceremony is held every two to five years to ward off evil spirits. If a person is overpowered by a spirit, a *shaman* (oracle) is called. Buddhist erect village gate to ward off evil spirits.

Bishu Dakhraim, Bees, Bhadon, Ookhayang, Phulaich, Diwali, Sazo, Songya, Faguli, Lossar, Dazu, Rokfo, Namgin, Chuan and Chhija are the important festivals of the region and are celebrated by Hindus and Buddhists alike. With the advent of better communicational facilities in the region and their contact with Hindu civilization, many Hindu deities have secured place in their pantheon. Besides, their visit to other parts of the country and religious places have infused a feeling of the other gods and goddesses of the "Greater Tradition".

The Kinnaura are deft in the art of knitting, weaving and basketmaking. They, however, do not sell their woollen or basket products.

In the Himalayan set up, intercommunity linkages are very important. The traditional economic linkages between the Kanet and Koli had been that of landlord and tenant. The *savarna* do not allow outcasts to enter the *sanctum-sanctorum* of the temple premises. The Rajputs accept food and water only from their own community, but they can accept tobacco, *bidi*, cigarette, fruits from Badhi, Lohar and Koli. Badhi can accept food, drinks and dry things from Kanet and Lohar and only dry things from Koli. The Lohar can accept food and drink from Rajput and Badhi and dry things from Koli. A Koli can however accept food from all except from the Nagalu, whereas Nagalu accept everything from other castes. Intercommunity marriages are not socially recognized. However, these restirctions are breaking down.

In Kinnaur, when ceremonial friendship occurs betwen a man and a woman, it is called *jokheya*, and when it occurs between two women it is called *konech*. The friendship is established by exchanging garlands of fruit called *jokheya un* or *konech un*, on an auspicious day, and by exchanging food and home brewed wine. It is expected of a ceremonial friend to help each other in the hour of need.

Similarly, ceremonial brotherhood and sisterhood is also established within the same ethnic group and same status group, but not with the same *khandan*. This is known as *kokheya* or *dharambhai* and *rinkchje* or *dharam-bahin*. During one's distress, one's *kokheya* or *rinkchje* comes forward to help.

In such an interior district, it will be worth while evaluating the attitude of the people towards the various developmental programmes launched by the government. During the 1951 Census, the percentage of literacy recorded was 5.5 per cent in Kinnaur. But gradually with the opening of schools and provision of other facilities the literacy in the district had gone up to 26.23 per cent in 1971 and 34.8 per cent in 1981. This indicates the awareness and attitude of the people towards education. Communitywise, the Rajputs have the highest literacy percentage and the Kolis follow them. Sexwise, more males are literate than females. The low level of education is because of the absence of high and middle schools near the villages and for the female literacy is also because of their isolation and conservatism.

In every tehsil there are primary health centres. Diseases are usually attributed to be the overpowering of some spirit; which can be cured by the *shaman*. The Kinnaura also depend upon indigenous herbs and roots. However, in serious cases they go to the district hospitals. For family planning vasectomy and tubectomy are accepted. As a result of mass communication the people are aware of the utility of the small family norms and are regulating their family size. Drinking water is available from the snowfed streams as there is no other source of water. Electricity is present in *tehsil* headquarters and in most of the villages. Villages on the highway have given job opportunities to the residents in road building. Under the self-employment scheme of the Government loans are being given for setting up poultry units. Loans have also been advanced for boosting horticulture and planting temperate fruits. Irrigation is dependent on melting of snow, which is channelized through *kuhl* in the middle and high altitudes. In lower parts rains meet the requirements of irrigation. People are so much aware of the benefits of irrigation that they keep awake the whole night to channelize water in their field when their turn comes. Despite awareness and use of improved seeds, fertilizers and spraying of insecticides, the yield has not increased considerably. This is because of soil erosion, i.e., washing away of top fertile soil due to steep nature of the terrain. That is why more attention is being diverted to horticulture.

Recently there is some impact of the programme of Anganwadi, where free milk and nutrition is given to nursing and expectant mothers and children up to five years because of the difficult terrain. People at the district headquarters put their savings in banks.

Rajendra Sarkar

KOLI

The Koli or Kori is a scheduled caste numbering 3,01,925 according to the 1981 Census. Broadly the word Koli means the remote inhabitants of Kolarian region but the term indicates some different meaning when it is also used in practically the same sense as Dagi or Sippi in the hills. In some Shivalik areas, the Kolis call themselves Kshatriya or new Rajput. Regarding the origin of the Koli several legends are prevalent. As per one popular version, they are believed to have sprung from abandoned Kanets who volunteered to remove carcasses in the absence of Chamar when disease claimed the lives of large number of cattle (Rose,1919). They are widely distributed throughout the State. Their dialect and the dress differs from region to region. They speak the wide variety of dialects which are broadly classed as western Pahari or Himachali. In Kullu their women wear *suthan* which is narrow at the ankle, *choli* (top) and a large shawl which is wrapped around. They also sport *thippu* (scarf) to cover the head. Men wear the traditional *suthan* and *jora* (a flared shirt) but nowadays they have taken to *pyjama*/pant and shirt. They are known as Sippi in Lahaul and speak a dialect akin to Sanskrit, and in other parts their speech is of Indo-Aryan family with admixture of vocabulary from Mundari and Tibeto-Burman. In Shimla and Solan areas they have a distinct community dialect.

Though non-vegetarian, the Kolis' staple diet consists of wheat, maize, pulses of *mah* and *channa*, seasonal vegetables and moderate use of locally grown fruits. Men are fond of smoking and drinking locally brewed liquor namely, *lugari* and *sur* (made of rice and barley). Some women also consume alcoholic drinks occasionally. In some parts of Kullu valley the use of tobacco is forbidden as according to popular belief, its practice angers the local deities. But now this belief is fading away and the Kolis are free to take to smoking like people of other communities of the region.

Bio-anthropological report provides biological information on the community.

The Kolis, though numerically dominant, rank comparatively low in the regional caste hierarchy occupying a position lower than that of the Lohar, Bajgi, Barhai but slightly above that of the Chanal and Dumna. Their relative position, however, differs from place to place. In Shimla according to one account, "there are clean Koli with whom Rajputs may even drink and there are others who remove dead kine and eat beef" (Rose, 1919). In the traditional varna *vyavastha*, they occupy a place at par with the Sudra.

Marriages are settled through negotiation outside the *got* of the father and mother side. Marriages by mutual consent and elopement are also given social sanction. In the past cross-cousin marriage with the father's sister's children was allowed but is now considered improper. The usual age at marriage for girls and boys is between 18 and 20, and 20 and 24 years respectively. The common symbols of marriage are nose stud-pin and red *puranda*. The bride lives patrilocally. Bride price exists which is locally known as *randh*. Both divorce and remarriage of widow or widower are allowed and so are the practices of levirate and sororate. In the case of divorce and remarriage of a woman, her paramour has to first pay back *randh* or *reet* to her former husband.

Both nuclear and extended types of families exist among the Kolis. The inheritance and succession is patrilineal. All the sons inherit father's property equally. Daughters, however, do not get any share unless there is an absence of a son in the family. The interpersonal relationship with the members of the family is cordial and of avoidance and joking nature depend on the age, sex and kinship status of the respective members.

Women have an important role in both domestic and economic spheres. They take part in all the agricultural activities except ploughing. Gradually they are also finding a place in the statutory panchayats. In religious spheres, they actively take part in the rituals and festivals but certain religious objects are tabooed for them and they also cannot hold any religious office.

The life-cycle rituals observed from time to time are similar to those of other communities in the region. The birth of a son is especially felicitated. Purificatory rites are observed for the child and the mother. Pollution lasts for 12 days and on this day they worship the clan deity and the woman is deemed fit to resume normal activities. Parents may distribute sweets and close relatives bring some gift to the child. *Jattu* is usually performed for the boy. The maternal uncle cuts the hair, and a priest officiates on the occasion. A sheep may also be sacrificed to mark the occasion.

Marriage consists of a number of rituals. After the *mangni* the actual marriage ceremony takes place at the bride's house. The practices of *kanyadan* and *phera* do not exist. The binding part of marriage ritual is the ceremony in which the *goru* (priest) takes the sacred lamp five times around the couple-in the name of water, cereal, deity, *dharach* (metal plate), *gugul* and lastly *sur* (liquor). Another important ceremony takes place when the bridegroom returns to his place along with the bride—as soon as the couple reaches the place, a sheep is thrown from the balcony and instantly sacrificed. The following day, another sheep is sacrificed, but before that, the *goru* sprinkles some water over its body and ear and asks whether the marriage would be a success or not. If the sheep flutters its ears, it is considered to be a good omen meaning thereby that the deity has given his blessings.

The dead are cremated. The bone-collecting rites are performed on the third day. A death feast is given to all the *biradari* members. The *dholi* who beats the drum in the funeral march is given clothes and some personal belongings of the dead. The bones are immersed either in a nearby river or at Hardwar. A *thar* (raised platform) is constructed for those who die an unnatural death. Ancestor worship exists and pollution is observed for three days. Family members plant a tree or construct a *chabutra* by the wayside in memory of the departed soul.

Economically, the Kolis are among the backward lot. They are landless, and a majority of them work as agricultural labourers or as sharecroppers. Under the Twenty-point Programme they have been given land, with incentives on seeds and manure and the purchase of cattle. They also get saplings for orchard plantation. A number of them find chance in PWD and state forest department for doing various jobs including road construction. Besides, they perform jobs as masons, carpenters, basket-makers, weavers, wool cleaners, etc. Bonded labour does not exist but child labour is prevalent. Payment of wages is in cash. Mode of exchange is also cash, though barter system is also present to some extent. A few shops in the vicinity of the village help them to meet their basic requirements.

For the mechanism of social control, the Kolis have their council of elders to punish the guilty by either imposing cash fine or through social boycott. Statutory panchayats also exist. Criminal cases are mostly dealt with by statutory panchayats. Divorce and domestic quarrels are settled by their own Biradari Panchayats. The role of the traditional Biradari Panchayat is getting gradually restricted since its functions have largely been taken over by the statutory councils.

Hindu by faith, the Kolis worship major gods and goddesses of the pantheon order, but have great reverence for the local gods and goddesses, and their village and clan deities. They do not undertake any auspicious work without the consent of a deity. Each region has its own deity which is held in great respect by every individual. The editors (BRS) add that the Kolis do not take palanquins of major village gods on their shoulders but in Kinnaur they are allowed to do so in case of junior deity when he is going on a long journey. Further, Kishnu is considered to be their local deity and Narain is the regional deity which is worshipped by all the community members. In some areas Garha Devta is worshipped as their community god.

The Kolis share the regional folksongs and dances, folktales and folklore with others of the region. Both men and women participate in dances and folksongs.

The Kolis maintain their socioeconomic relationships with other neighbouring communities. They have the traditional patron-client relationship locally known as *puli* with certain artisan communities, namely, Lohar and Bard who make and repair iron implements and baskets respectively. People of certain castes employ the Koli as agricultural labourers and give them a share from the produce on each harvest and also on festive occasions. Socially, they are avoided for acceptance of water and food. Many castes who come to attend their feasts are served food prepared separately by one of their own members. They also do not go inside the *sanctum sanctorum* of the temples. In the past the Kolis were not allowed to enter the houses of Rajputs, but such practices have gradually diminished over the years. The interactional level of the Kolis has enlarged considerably owing to better and quicker means of transport and communication network. It is also due to the spread of literacy and migration of people from rural areas to urban areas, where new economic linkages have been established. With growing awareness and political awakening, political affiliation have also come into being. As a result, Koli political leadership has emerged at village, district and state levels.

Through developmental programmes providing transport and communication facilities, drinking water and electricity, significant improvement has come about in the civic condition of the Kolis.However, poverty has prevented some of them from sending their children to school. Primary health care centres have come up in the Koli area. Mass propoganda has been launched to propogate family planning measures and it has helped the community to have small families. Integrated Rural Development Programme employment schemes have proved beneficial for the people. Many Kolis have taken loans, grants and subsidies to improve their economic conditions. A few of them have utilized these economic aids to set up cottage industries. They also receive incentives for improving agricultural production by way of getting improved manure and seeds. Irrigation facilities are also availed of. People have been encouraged to plant apple orchards. Facilities of public distribution system, postal and banking services are also availed by the members of the community.

Vatsala Sarkar

KUMHAR

The Kumhar are the traditional potters of the country who make earthen pots. The name Kumhar is derived from the Sanskrit, word *kumbhakar* meaning earthen pot or pitcher maker. They are variously pronounced as Ghumhar, Ghamiar, etc., and bear a common title 'Prajapati' meaning the lord of the people of the world (Rose, 1919; Ibbetson, 1916; Crooke 1896, etc.). This title has a link with the legendary origin of the community according to which one of Brahma's sons succeeded in preserving a fresh sugarcane in an earthen pitcher and as a mark of respect to him, his descendents were titled as Prajapati or Kumhar. The Kumhar's are widely distributed in the State in almost all districts in the hills and dales in different climates, but prefer warm and temperate climate suitable for their work relating to making earthen pots. The community is identified namly from its traditional occupation. They speak regional dialects of western Pahari or Himachali. Men wear *kurta* and *pyjama* or trousers and elderly persons prefer *safa* as their head-dress. Women wear *kurta* and *salwar* and put on a *dupatta* or *chunni*. They wear golden *tili* or *murki* now replaced by *nath*. Ear-rings and necklace are also worn.

The Kumhars share the dietary habits of the area. The common staple food during winter is maize supplemented by rice, and during most of the summer season wheat is consumed. Various types of pulses like *urad, moong, kulthi, masur,* grams, peas and beans are taken along with seasonal vegetables, roots and tubers. The cooking medium is mustard oil or vegetable or *desi ghee*. Milk and milk products are consumed frequently. Fruit intake is occasional and seasonal. Festive foods are *halwa, kheer, seviyan* and other wheat and rice products like *babru* and *ankali* of rice. They are occasional non-vegetarians except those who follow the Radhaswami sect. Men consume country liquor occasionally. They smoke *bidi* or cigarettes and loose tabacco in an indigenous pipe called *hukka* or *kali* or *jhajri*.

The Kumhars are segmented into small units called *got* and *al*. These social units serve to regulate matrimonial alliances and denote ancestry or descent. Some of their *gots* are Sandil, Kashab and Bharapdariye. Although some people follow the Radhaswami sect, yet this differentiation has not emerged to the extent to creating a social hierarchy. They perceive a middle position in the Hindu varna hierarchy and are considered *savarna* and treated at par with the Lohar and Nai.

The institution of marriage is similar to that in many other Hindu castes. Marriages occur within the community as per the rules of *got* and village exogamy. They take place at present on attaining maturity but earlier pre-puberty child marriages were common and bride-price also existed. *Batta-satta* was also a common practice. But presently they follow *dharam punya* marriages and perform *kanyadan* and give some *daj dan* to daughters. Monogamy is practised. Bigamy is socially permitted in case the first wife is barren or bears no male child. Marriage symbols observed strictly are *sindur* or a *bindi*, glass bangles and a nose and ear ornament. The bride lives patrilocally with the husband's parents. Widow remarriages occur only in cases of young and childless widows. Junior levirate is accepted. But, presently this old custom is disliked by younger persons. A widower can remarry a junior sororate or otherwise. Divorce usually does not occur nor is liked socially but either of the spouses can dissolve marriage through judicial approval on grounds of maladjustment, cruelty and impotency. The husband in such cases bears the maintenance cost of the divorced wife and is also liable to support the children. Both the divorcees may remarry. The marriage institution is witnessing changes in respect of the age of marriage, rejection of bride price and acceptance of dowry.

The family pattern of the Kumhars was predominantly vertically extended type till the recent past. But now joint families normally break up after the marriage of all the sons or when the father dies. Avoidance relationships are strong in the joint families. The *lari* covers her face from and touches the feet of her *saurah*, *jeth*, *nandoi* and other elderly male members of the village. Joking relationships are similar to many other Hindu communities of the region. These may occur between *devar* and *bhabi* and *jija* and *sali*. The family members are obliged to respect their elders. The inheritance is on male lines as per the rule of male equigeniture and the eldest son succeeds the father. However, conflicts in the family may arise on matters related to property and disobedience of elders by juniors.

The status of women in the Kumhar community is practically equal to that of men. They participate in economic activities i.e., pottery work, where the work involves bringing clay, making pots as well as selling the products door to door in the villages. Women do all domestic jobs, including fetching potable water, collecting fuel and fodder, participating in animal husbandry and working in the agricultural fields. They also render various services to village *zamidars* and contribute to family income. They participate in social and religious ceremonies but have little role in the mechanisms of social control and political activities. But they contribute towards domestic decision-making and regulation of family expenditure.

The life-cycle rituals of the Kumhars are like those of other Hindu communities of the area. Pre-delivery rituals have lost significance and are not observed, but restrictions on mother before and after delivery are prevalent. Post-delivery pollution is maintained for 13 days when a purification ceremony called *guntrala* is observed. A male child's birth is rejoiced by singing *ranjhunana* by village women who are given seeetened germinated grams. The child's *nana* brings *jhagu-topu* and *kangnu*. Name-giving and cereal-taking ceremonies are usually ignored but some arrange a meal for small children called *kanya* or *kanjkan* (girls) and *bhatu bulana* (boys). *Jatlu* or *mundan* of the boy is the major childhood ritual. It is performed by the *mama* of the child and *kulja* is propitiated and a feast is arranged.

The marriage rituals are performed by a Brahman priest as per the Vedic tenets. Various rituals like *sand, samuhat, mehndi* and oil ceremony are observed before the actual marriage rituals, called *ved* and *lagan*. These rituals are performed at the bride's place when the *lara* and *lari* circumambulate the sacred fire. The parents of the bride perform *sankalap* or *kanyadan* and offer some *daj dan* and give a feast. At the bridegroom's place a major ritual is *andrera* and *pipal* or *Brahma puja*. In tree worship both the bride and groom circumambulate the sacred tree and tie a white thread around it. Putative kinship-based friends of the bride and groom are also made at this time who tie a *mauli,* red thread on each other's wrist and embrace each other. The marriage ends with music and dance. *Muklawa* occurs on the following auspicious day when door worship, pitcher worship and *bauri* worship is observed by the young couple and they touch the feet of elders and seek blessings. The wedding crown or *sehra* is offered to Lakhdata, a local deity visited on Thursday. *Lari* does not stay with her mother-in-law during the month of first *kala mahina* (Bhadrapada) falling during July-August and the first delivery takes palce at maternal home.

Death rituals are also observed as per the Hindu tenets. The sons shave off their head hair on the death of their father. The dead are cremated and ashes are immersed in the Ganges at Hardwar by the eldest son who performs *pind dan*. An Acharaj performs ancestor worship and seeks alms and the family priest performs purification *havan* and gets his dues. Gathered relatives are offered a meal. Annual *barkhi* and fourth annual *chabarkh* death rites are also observed and *pitr* are commemorated every year.

The Kumhars mainly thrive on their traditional occupation of pottery. They also possess small landholdings and do agricultural work and animal husbandry. Some persons seek casual labour as well as agricultural labour or till land on contract or sharecrop basis. Many persons are in government jobs on various cadres including teaching, engineering, medical profession, police and army services. Some are in private jobs also. Many have abandoned the pot-making occupation. The links with market are direct and the market is of daily nature and is fully regulated. Child labour exists. Dealings are generally in cash but they also sell their produce for cereals.

The community has its Biradari Panchayat but it is usually less functional though it occasionally deals with social problems related to marriage and divorce. This council also raises the voice of the community for seeking aid from Government for the purchase of latest equipment for pot-making and allotment of suitable pieces of land for digging clay as they face difficulties in getting suitable clay for pot-making. Economic disputes are resolved by the village *sayane* or members of the statutory Gram Panchayat, which also does the usual acts of social welfare and development. Serious disputes are taken to civil courts.

The Kumhars are Hindus and propitiate gods and goddesses of the wider pantheon order. Godria Sidh, Balak Nath and other local deities are propitiated from time to time. Other local and regional deities of special reverence are Lakhdata, Nahar Singh and Guga. To propitiate Lakhdata, *chhinj* are arranged and Guga is specially propitiated for eight days following the Rakshabandan festival and Guga fairs are arranged at various places. Nahar Singh, the whistling deity stays on *pipal* trees and can be invited through various excorcist media. The spirit is considered to be a great benefector of the worshipper and a benevolent god for all. The followers of the Radhaswami sect have little belief in deities and visit the shrine of their *guru* at Beas in Punjab quite frequently. Various Hindu festivals of socioeconomic and socioreligious importance that are celebrated are Lohri, Baisakhi, Holi, Chiran, Sair, Rakhri, Ramnavmi, Guganavmi and Diwali. On the Barlaj day following Diwali they propitiate Vishwakarma by worshipping *chak* and observe fast and do not make pots for three days. Their sacred specialists are from other communities like Brahmans as priests, Nai for performing certain marriage rituals and *chela* for curing diseases of supernatural origins. The folksongs, tales, lore and music and dances of the region are shared. Among the famous traditional regional folksongs are *Mohan, Gambri, Ranjhu-Phulmu, Balo-Mahia* and *Kunju-Chenchlo.* Generally, a *dholak* is used for *bhajan* and other folksongs. Usually young girls participate in folk dances like *gidda.* Pottery is both an occupation and a craft of the community in addition the women know knitting.

The Kumhars are considered *savarna* or *anderke* for having exchange of *kachcha* and *pucca* food and water with the certain Hindus. They traditionally have no exchange of *kachcha* and *pucca* food and water with the Chamar, Julaha, Dumna, Hesi, etc., but many sometimes accept a *suchchi rasoi* cooked by a Brahman or Rajput cook. Water sources are likewise shared with only certain Hindus. Their cremation grounds are on the bank of a stream or *choe* and may be overlapping with those of other communities. Temples and other public places are common. Putative kinship-based friendship may occur with other communities. The community has traditional *jajmani* links with many communities and the members seek their customary dues on each crop for providing services of pottery to their clients. The share to the Kumhar given at the time of harvest is called *khalothi.* They have this relationship with a

Brahman priest, Nai, Lohar and Chamar, besides others, mostly on exchange basis. Ceremonial visits are also paid by the Kumhar to their clients on festive and marriage occasions to give earthen pots, especially during Diwali to collect *tyohar* or festival share from them. They have members in business, teaching, engineering and medical professions and in police and army services. Political leadership has emerged at the local Gram Panchayat level.

The modern developmental programmes have made considerable impact on the community. Formal education is favoured for both the sexes up to the secondary school level. In the sphere of health and medicare, they favour both modern as well as indigenous methods as the case may be. The family planning method usually adopted is sterilization, mainly tubectomy. But the desire for at least one or two sons is still strong in the community even at the cost of many daughters. Their houses are electrified and they avail themselves of modern mass media, communication and postal facilities. Drinking water is available through taps but the traditional sources like springs and *bauri* are still used as the water supply through taps is inadequate. Energy sources are firewood, cowdung cakes and sometimes coal and kerosene oil. They have facilities under Integrated Rural Development Programme (IRDP) and take benefits according to their requirements. Immunization is the main facility availed of under ICDS programmes for children. Facility of public distribution system is availed of like others.

A. R. Sankhyan

LABANA

The Labana, Lobana or Lavana is said to be an offshoot of the Banjaras of Mewar (Rajasthan) who probably entered Himachal Pradesh around two centuries ago. According to a popular legend, a Banjara known as Lakhi Banjara, who had one lakh cattle used to trade in *sendha namak* (Indus salt) and so received the name of Labana. Obviously, the name Labana appears to have been derived from *lavan* which means salt. The name Labana is also supposed to have been derived from the term *ladna* (to load) (Rose, 1919) as these people used ox as the means of carrying the Indus salt and slates. The characteristic *boli* (dialect) the Labanas speak among themselves is similar to the Marwari spoken in Rajasthan, which also indicates their migration from that region in the past. They, however, know and speak the Bilaspuri (Kehluri) dialect of western Pahari and write in Devanagari script within as well as with the local people. The community has an interregional distribution. But they conceived their distribution in Himachal Pradesh in Bilaspur, Hamirpur, Mandi and Kangra districts. The earliest figures for Labana in the erstwhile Kehlur State (Bilaspur) was 304 (Kavi Ganesh Singh, 1892). But their present population is not recorded in the Census of India. They generally inhabit the dales surounded by the hilly terrain of the Himalayan foothills covered with thin pine forests which are drained by the tributaries of the river Satluj (in district Bilaspur). The climate is generally warm and temperate with low humidity and moderate rainfall. Presently, no dress identification of the community is observable, but traditionally a black *kurta* with a *chooridar pyjama* and white turban was worn by males; a *kurti* and a *ghagri* and colourful *dupatta* was worn by women.

They are non-vegetarian in food habits and eat eggs, fish, goat and sheep meat and pork, but not beef. Their staple food is wheat and maize *roti* supplemented by rice. They consume all types of local roots and tubers, pulses and fruits depending upon their seasonal availability. The cooking medium is mustard oil or vegetable or *desi ghee*. They keep cows and buffaloes for milk. They are fond of liquor and of self-made alcoholic beverages made of *gur*. They also purchase country liquor. Women also sometimes consume alcohol and some old women smoke tobacco/*bidi* as well. Special foods are prepared on festivals, like *khichri* on Lohri, wheat and rice products like *ankloo* on Diwali, *babru* on Baisakhi, *seviyan* on Sair, etc.

The Labanas have 11 *got* as listed by Ibbetson (1916) and Rose (1919), viz., Ajrawat, Ghotra, Datla, Pilia (Peliye), Parwal, Khabriya, Gojalia, Gujar, Tatra (Tadra), Wamial (Mathaun) and Narowal. In Bilaspur they recalled some of these, but also added two other *gots*, like Nalhajalha and Kalia. These indicate descent and are used for avoiding *got* endogamy. Their social position in the Hindu varna system is not certain but they are taken as *savarna* and are placed below the Lohar in the local social hierarchy even though they claim an equal ranking with them. The Labanas in general face a caste crisis and are not comfortable with their Sudra varna status sometimes attached to them by others. In view of their characteristic dialect, traditional occupation and certain social and religious ceremonies, they are currently aspiring for a scheduled tribe status like the Gujjar.

The Labanas are endogamous and practise both village exogamy and endogamy but *got* exogamy. Marriages among the next-door neighbours are also observed when they find suitable mates of different *got* in the same village. They also practise second cousin-level consanguinity. Child marriage was prevalent over a generation ago, but presently a girl is usually married when she is above 15 years of age and a boy between 20 and 25. The marriage is negotiated by parents, friends and relatives, and monogamy is followed. Bigamy is a rare phenomenon and occurs in case of childlessness. *Batta-satta* marriages have been a common feature and still persist. Earlier, purchase of bride was common in the absence of any sister to exchange. But, presently they have borrowed the tradition of dowry, generally given in kind in the form of household articles, clothes and ornaments. The symbols of marriage are *sindur,* glass bangles and nose and ear ornaments, but these are not strictly adhered to. The bride resides patrilocally. The tradition of *chhoot* is quite common and both men and women are considerably free to leave each other on grounds of maladjustment, cruelty or any other reasons with the approval of the Labana community council. Presently, however, they are also adopting judicial sanction for marriage in which case the woman gets compensation and the man is liable to the children. Either of the divorcees can remarry. Widow remarriage is permissible with a junior levirate as well as with another man.

The Labanas generally live in vertically joint extended families with an approximate family size of 7–8 persons. The elder members are respected but confrontation and quarrels over domestic and property matters are not uncommon. *Lari* maintains *ghungat* from her *saurah* and *jeth*. But this is declining. Joking relationship exists between parents of the boy and girl on the occasion of marriage and between *jija* and *sali,* and *devar* and *bhabi.* The eldest son succeeds the father and inheritance is patrilineal as per the male equigeniture.

The Labana women enjoy a great deal of liberty in domestic, social and political matters and therefore have an almost equal status. They manage family expenditure, collect fuel and fodder, fetch potable water and bring flour from *gharat.* They participate in social and religious functions and are also members of their Biradari Panchayat and therefore have a say in the mechanism of social control. They may also contribute to family income by rendering various household, agricultural and animal husbandry services to big village landlords.

On delivery day the oldest woman in the family used to observe a fast for two or three days and break it by eating *seviyan* (Rose,1919). But this ritual is not observed now. Post-delivery pollution is maintained and presently cow's urine is taken for purification. The *mundan* ceremony is observed among boys before the third year and the hair cut is given by the *mama,* and young children are given a feast.

The marriage is performed as per Hindu *Sanathan Vidhan* by a Brahman priest. A peculiar tradition (presently not in vogue) called *panj padauni* or *panj propi* was observed. Rose (1919) has also made a mention of this custom. In this five persons from the bridegroom's party sit in the courtyard with faces covered with a black blanket and are offered *shakkar* (sugar) to eat. While eating, women from the bride's side throw ashes, cow-dung and dirt on them and also beat them with a *kalag* (stick).

There is another interesting ritual performed before *lagan phere.* A man loads salt on the ox and beats the *goon* (rug-sack) with a long stick and strikes at the *prauli* (the over-projection of the ceiling). This is symbolic of their traditional occupation of ox-loading which has almost disappeared at present. No *purohit* was called in marriage over a generation ago, and only one Bharai used to beat a drum and a Nai voiced the *ransinga* (trumpet). But now a Brahman *purohit* performs the marriage rituals as per the Vedic rites and the marriage music is given by a brass-band party. The consummation of marriage occurs on the day following the marriage.

The Labanas cremate their dead and immerse their ashes in the nearby river. The pollution period of 13 days is maintained and an Acharaj and a Brahman priest perform ancestor worship at present.

The Labanas traditionally traded in salt, slates, potatoes, ginger, etc., which they used to carry on ox back. But now this occupation has almost disappeared, though some of the Labana now keep mules for transporting sand and *bajri* from rivers. Recently, they have taken to agriculture and animal husbandry. But the land allotted to them is insufficient and of poor quality and is suited to keep cattle herds. As such, they have taken to different occupations, like casual labour in road and dam construction, forest and also as agricultural labourers. A few are in petty business or general merchandise. The Labanas lack persons holding white-collar jobs in Government. Market is located at some distance and is of daily nature. Child labour exists.

The Labanas have their traditional community council, now designated as the Labana Hitkarni Sabha. It has recently been raised to a State-level body with 51 executive members, a *pradhan*, a *uppradhan* and a cashier. The elections are held annually by voice or ballot votes. At the local level, the Sabha has 13 members including women members. It functions to uproot social evils of dowry and child marriage and to encourage literacy and for putting a demand for a scheduled tribe status. The Sabha used to punish social offenders in the past by socially boycotting or by fine in cash or kind. Reinstating occurred by a liquor party and feast. The statutory Gram Panchayat performs the usual welfare activities.

The Labanas are influenced by Brahmanical socio-religious traditions and now follow Hinduism and believe in Hindu pantheon gods and goddesses. Jawalamukhi is propitiated as *kulja.* Other local deities, Jangal Devi or Neersa Devi are worshipped at marriage and every married couple visits the devi temple for blessings. They also propitiate the *sati* stones as family deities. After marriage, the newly wedded couple takes rounds of the *sati sthana.* Guga, like others is propitiated as a village and regional deity besides Balaknath, and Lakhdata. The shrines of these deities are located on hill tops and are visited during annual fairs. Guga Navmi is celebrated with great pleasure besides almost all other festivals like Diwali, Lohri, Baisakhi, Navratre, Sair and Chiran. The sacred specialists are from other communities.

The folk music, dances, folksongs, tales, etc., of the region are shared. The folktales and couplets of Lakhi Banjara, whom they consider the first Labana, are narrated by old men.

The Labanas are treated as *savarna* by other Hindus and have commensal norms, but not connubial norms. They also establish putative kinship, like *dharm bhai* and *dharm bahin* with other Hindus at marriage and *mundan* ceremonies. They share water sources, temple and cremation grounds with other communities. They serve as *panihare* (water carriers) on marriage occasions of certain Hindus.

The Labanas now send their children to school but higher education is beyond their means. Both modern and indigeneous medicare is favoured and also have favourable attitude towards family planning, and have recently adopted sterilization. Their houses are electrified and potable piped water is available. The modern mass media have reached their homes. They avail themselves of the facility of public distribution through fair price shops. They make some use of chemical fertilizers and organic manures but irrigation is through rains only. Employment opportunities under IRDP have not yet been exploited . They burn firewood, cowdung cakes and straw of maize. They are generally self-employed. ICDS programmes provide them the facility of immunization. In general, their attitude towards savings is not favourable and they remain dependent on local shopkeepers and money-lenders.

A. R. Sankhyan

LOHAR

The Lohar is the traditional village blacksmith or ironsmith as the name suggests. Blacksmithy and carpentry are usually performed by the same person in the lower hill region, such as Bilaspur, Kangra, Hamirpur, etc., but Lohar is a popular name for the community and a distinction from the Tarkhan (carpenter) is normally not made. But in the upper hills of Kullu, Shimla and Sirmaur, the Tarkhan/Badhi is a separate community of the woodcutters/ carpenters whereas the Lohars are ironsmiths. The State list has included the Lohar among the scheduled castes but not the Tarkhan/Badhai. The history of origin of the Lohar community is not known but there is some ethnographic information available in Rose (1919), Ibbetson (1916), Crooke (1896), etc. The community perceives its distribution at interregional level in almost all districts of the State, inhabiting different climatic zones, hills and dales. The climate in the study area (Bilaspur district) is warm and temperate with low humidity and medium annual rainfall. The terrain is hilly and thin forest cover exists on the hill ranges, which also contains some wild fauna. The population of the Lohar is112,389 according to the 1981 Census of India and their major concentrations are shown in Mandi, Shimla, Bilaspur, Sirmaur and Kangra districts.

They speak local dialects of Pahari like Bilaspuri in Bilaspur and write in Devanagari script both within and outside the community. Bilaspuri *boli* had its own script called Tankri during the pre-Independence period but is no more in practice now. Men wear a *kurta* and a *pajama* or pant and women wear *kurti, salwar* and a *chadru.* Traditional ornaments were conical silver *chak* on the head which subsequently was replaced by a golden *gut ka chak,* a golden *murki* or *laung/tili, kante/bali, har, gajra* and *jhanjar.* A studded large nose-ring of gold called *nath* is a more important ornament at present and considered a status symbol among women. In upper areas such ornaments as *chak, kach, kanthi, chanderhar, phulli, murki, hansli, dhajula,* etc., are used by the womenfolk, with *chapkan, gachi* and *dhathi* as the distinctive features in dress. Men wear *loia, suthan* and a round Himachali *topi.* A Lohar's home settlement is identified from a short distance by the presence of a small shed called *nihali* where iron implements are prepared, reshaped and repaired.

The Lohars share the food habits of the area. They are occasional non-vegetarian and eat eggs, fish and meat. But their major routine food habit is vegetarian. The common staple food of winter months is maize supplemented by rice. In summer months wheat is commonly consumed. Various types of pulses—*urad, moong, masur, kulthi, moth,* peas, beans, grams, etc., along with seasonal vegetables, mainly lady finger, brinjal, gourds, cauliflowers and cabbage, roots and tubers are consumed. Certain special vegetables— of the raw figs called *bharuni*, buds of *kachnar* or *karyal*, *manu* (a bush stalk), spinach of mustard and other leaves are also eaten. The cooking medium is mustard oil or *desi ghee* or vegetable *ghee*. Milk and its products are eaten frequently. *Chhah* is a common milk product and rice cooked in it called *jhol* is frequently consumed by the poor. Likewise, *mahani* (cooked juice of raw mangoes) and *khatyai* or *kurhi* (fried raw mangoes) are consumed in summer season but are a more frequent part of the diet of poor people. Festive foods are *kheer, karah/halwa, babru, bhalle* and products of rice flour called *ankli* and *anklu*. *Seviyan* are eaten on Sair festival. *Sag* of mustard leaves and *khichri* are eaten during Lohri. Fruit intake is seasonal (plenty of local mangoes) but otherwise occasional (banana, apple, peach, guava and papaya). Other fruits are *akhe, dagle* and *tiamlu* and *toot* and wild berries (*ber* and *garnu)* mainly eaten by children while grazing sheep and goats. Food taboos are observed during death pollution when members of the family cannot eat non-vegetarian items and *heeng*. They do not enter into kitchen and the man offering *pind dan* does not take milk. Menstruating woman cannot enter the kitchen and do not touch drinking water pots of the family. Country liquor is consumed occasionally but some men are regular drinkers. They are also regular smokers of loose tobacco in an indigenous pipe called *hukka* or *kali* at home or smoke *bidi*, and sometimes cigarettes also. Change in food habits has been seen in some followers of Radhaswami mission who avoid non-vegetarian diet.

The community has *got* and *al* which serve to regulate matrimony and suggest ancestry or descent. Some of the common *got* noted are Kaundal, Kashab, Gial, Sandil and Ludu, and the smaller units, *al*, are Changru, Tattar, Telru, etc. which lack hierarchical stratification or distinction at the social level. Some people following Radhaswami sect show sectarian distinction but it does not create much social distinction. In the regional social hierarchy the position of the Lohar is different in different regions. In the lower region, they are treated as *savarna* Sudra like the Kumhar and are synonymous with the Tarkhan or Badhai. They enjoy this status in Sirmaur and Shimla districts also. But in Kullu district, the Lohar are considered *asvarna* Sudra equivalent to Dagi who have taken up ironsmithy, whereas the Tarkhan or Badhai is at par with the Kanet. In Spiti the community performing ironsmithy is known as Zon or Zobo and occupies an intermediate social position between a Chazang and Hensi/Hesi/Betu.

The institution of marriage is governed by the rule of community endogamy and *got* and village exogamy. Monogamy is practised and marriage occurs through negotiation. *Batta-satta* is still practised but was quite common during the pre-Independence period along with bride price. Also, child marriage was practised in the past. But presently adult or post-puberty marriages are practised and bride price is not taken. Instead *dharam punya* marriage is performed through *kanyadan*. Dowry is given in the form of household articles, clothes and ornaments and some agricultural implements along with a buffalo, sheep or goat. Now, radio and watches are also given. Some also give television and other costlier items. Monogamy is the rule, but men may marry twice in case the first wife has not produced any child or a son . Marriage symbols are *sindur* or *bindi*, glass bangles and ear and nose ornament, ring or studpin. The bride lives patrilocally. Social and/or judicial approval is sought for divorce. But divorce has been rare and presently judicial approval has gained significance on grounds of maladjustment and cruelty. Compensation is paid to the aggrieved party; normally children are the liability of the father. Widow remarriage is allowed and junior levirate was a socially approved custom in the past. But now younger and educated men do not like it. Junior sororate is also allowed for a young widower. The divorcees can remarry.

The family pattern is both nuclear and vertically extended type. Usually, as long as the father is alive, the sons do not get separated but make an *ad hoc* arrangement of cooking if some trouble arises in the joint family. But, presently there is a growing trend of the breaking up of the large joint families. Interpersonal relationships in the family are normally based on respect for elders. Avoidance relationship exists between *lari* with her *saurah, jeth, nandoi* and elderly male members of the village. Joking relationships are not very formal but exist in general as in many Hindu communities of the area. The popular ones are between *devar* and *bhabi, jija* and *sali* and *nanad* and *bhabi*. The major point of conflict is unfair distribution of paternal property. But other situations also create difficulties in the smooth running of the family, like unequal division of labour and the traditional dry or curt attitude of the *sas* towards the *lari/ bahu*. Division of property occurs by the rule of male equigeniture and the eldest son becomes the successor to his father.

The status of women is deemed low even though they do much more work than the men in the sphere of agriculture (except ploughing) and animal husbandry. They do all domestic jobs, bring potable water, collect fuel and fodder, help men in collecting the customary dues on each harvest from the landlords and participate in social and religious ceremonies. The mechanism of social control and political activities, however, is not their concern. They also lack decision-making powers in vital matters. They usually do not seek regular jobs but control family expenditure.

The Lohars observe Vedic rites in their life-cycle rituals. Pre-delivery rituals are ignored but pre- and post-delivery restrictions are imposed on the woman. *Sutak* lasts for 13 days after which the woman takes a bath and the purification ceremony is called *gunt* or *guntrala* in which water of the Ganges and cow's urine is sipped and sprinkled. The birth of a son is rejoiced over by distributing *shakkar-chhole* (sugar-mixed germinated grams) and by singing *ranjhunana* by the women of the village. Men take drinks and offer the same to their friends. Some consult a Brahman to give a name to this child. Cereal-taking ceremony is observed by a few who invite *kanya* and *bhattu* (small children) for a meal. *Jatlu utarna* is the major childhood ritual performed by the *mama* of the boy. Clan deity and village deities are propitiated and a small feast may be given to young children. The *janeu* is put on at the time of marriage only.

The marriage rituals are performed by a Brahman priest and a Nai. Proper dressing and adornment of the bridegroom and bride is the job of the Nai and his wife. Pre-marriage rituals called *kurmai* or *sagai* are simple. The *sand, samuhat* and oil ceremony precede the marriage rituals. The major marriage rituals are *lagan* and *vedi* at the bride's place when the *lari* and *lara* circumambulate the sacred fire and the priest gives them advice for an ideal married life. Finally the parents of the bride perform *kanyadan.* They give a feast to the groom's party. The rituals that occur at the bridegroom's place are called *andrera* and *pipal pujan.* The bride and groom take rounds of the holy tree and tie a white thread on its stem. Putative kinship-based friends of the bride and groom are made. The marriage ends by music and dance followed by a feast called *dham. Muklawa* occurs on the next/third auspicious day.

The death rites are similar to those of other Hindus of the area. The dead are cremated and the ashes are immersed at Hardwar in the Ganges and *pind dan* is given to a Panda. At home the death pollution, *sutak,* lasts for 13 days. For nine nights the Brahman priest recites Garud Purana by lighting an earthen pot. On the tenth day the family members take bath and wash clothes. On the thirteenth day *kirya karam* rites are performed by an Acharaj who is given offerings. The family priest performs the purification *havan* and gets his dues. The community is given a ceremonial meal on the *solia* (sixteenth day) by which the family becomes pure to exchange meals with others. Annual and fourth annual death rites are also observed and ceremonial feasts are given. Before the completion of the annual death rite, no festivity or marriage can be celebrated in the family. The followers of the Radhaswami sect do not observe elaborate rituals of the Sanatana but observe a simple *satsang* in the name of their *guru* at Beas in Punjab.

The Lohars thrive on their traditional occupation of blacksmithy together with carpentry. They get their dues in each crop of the farmers whose agricultural and other implements they prepare and repair. They make *vedi* on the occasions of marriage of their clients. They also cut the funeral wood on death of their client. They also possess small landholdings and are engaged in agriculture and animal husbandry. Many Lohars work on contract for doing carpentry work and thatching of houses. Many persons are employed in Government services in various professions like teaching, engineers, doctors, and in the army in the low hills. Some persons have established their small-scale saw industries. Some run general merchant shops as well. The Lohars sets up a marry-go-round in village fairs and earn cash. In upper areas of Shimla, the Lohars used to get their share of food grains known as *khaltha* at the time of both harvests in return for their services.

There is no formal community council but the *sayanas* of the Lohar usually resolve social disputes. The economic or village disputes over land and water are solved by the statutory Gram Panchayat which also deals with the welfare and development of the village. The fear of the local deities is also helpful created by swearing of them to control certain disputes, like theft. Police intervenes in violent quarrels and legal course is adopted.

The Lohars follow Hinduism. Most believe in and propitiate various family, clan, village and regional deities and gods and goddesses of the wider pantheon order . Balaknath, Guga, Bharthri Sidh, Nabahi Devi, Hari Devi, Jangal Devi (Badoli Devi) are family/clan deities of many, besides being village and regional deites. Other deities of special reverence are Nahar Singh, Lakhdata, Naina Devi and Santoshi Mata. The shrines of the deities are visited during annual fairs or on fulfilment of a wish. They celebrate various festivals, viz., Lohri, Baishakhi, Chiran, Sair, Guganavmi, Rakhri, Navratre, Diwali, etc. On the Barlaj day, following Diwali, they specially propitiate Vishwakarma by worshipping their tools and do not work on that day. Various Pahari folksongs and tales are shared, e.g., *Gambri, Mohan, Ranju-Phulmu, Kunju-Chenchlo*, etc. Other folksongs prevalent in the area are *Narsi Seth, Puran Bhagat, Mai Heera*, excerpts from Ramayana, religious songs or *bhajans* of Jawalamukhi, *Nirguna* songs, etc. *Gidda* and *Nati* are popular dances among young girl and boys. The musical instrument is usually *dholak* and *dantara* (a single string instrument).

The Lohars have members holding white-collar jobs, teaching, medical and engineering, and military services and some having business entrepreneurship. The political leadership has emerged at local/village panchayat level.

The modern developmental programmes have made a favourable impact on the Lohars. Formal education has increased but higher education is favourable for the boys and only partly so for the girls, who usualy study up to the secondary school level. The children may drop out from studies due to economic reasons at times but mostly due to lack of interest in higher studies. The girls are generally regarded as social liabilities to be married as soon as possible and are not supposed to earn money for parents. Both modern and traditional system of health and medical care are favoured. The traditional *chela* still plays some role in treating ailments of supernatural origin due to the *khot* (unhappiness) of a local deity. Modern methods of family planning like sterilization are used. They, presently favour small family due to economic compulsions, but at least one son is socially demanded for the family to achieve salvation even at the cost of more daughters.

Their houses are electrified and many enjoy modern mass media (radio, television) facilities. Postal facilities are also accessible in the neighbourhood. Presently, drinking water is availbale through taps in the village but quite often due to inadequate /irregular water supply, the traditional springs and *bauri* are also used. They enjoy special concessions under IRDP and also get loans as admissible to the Scheduled Caste communities. They are mostly self-employed. A few persons have some landholdings along a river/stream and have provisions for irrigation but most depend upon rainwater as a ususal source of irrigation. Fuel sources are wood, sawdust, coal and cowdung cakes. They use organic manures and chemical fertilizers. ICDS programmes generally provide immunization and mid-day meals to children. The public distribution system is availed of. Most of them favour savings.

A.R. Sankhyan

A view of the Minjar fair, Chamba

A Bangali couple exhibiting a tortoise—their favourite delicacy

A Koli girl in traditional attire

A Beda (Bodh) old woman in traditional dress

Faces of a village deity, Mandi district

A view of the Manimahesh festival, Chamba

Village gods assembled for the Shivratri festival at Mandi

A view of the Chandratal lake

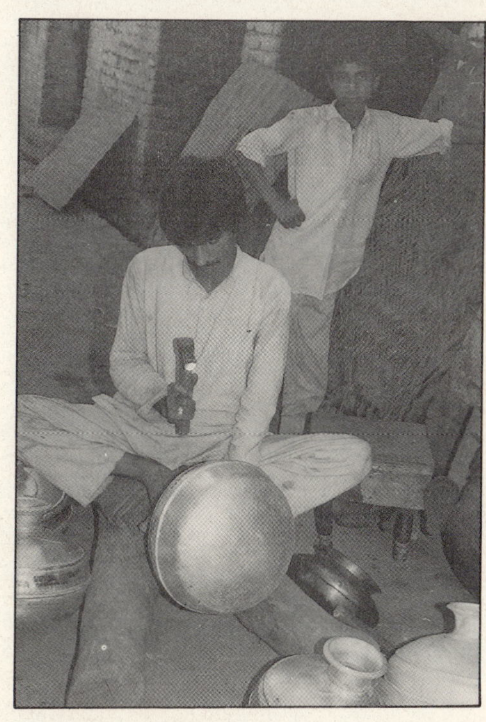

A Thathiar at work

A Bodh woman in festive dress, Spiti

A Kinnaura mother and daughter in festive dress

A Swangla old woman in leisure time: smoking indigenous pipe

A Malaneese man spinning wool

A Malaneese old woman in traditional dress

Eleven juries of the Malaneese village council

A Penja at work

A Lohar at work

Gaddi women in traditional attire

A Bodh from Spiti

Jathera—the place of ancestor worship, Kangra

A Buddhist chorten, Lahaul

A Masterpiece of wooden engravings: ceiling of the Myrculla Temple, Lahaul

Colourful dolls: a handicraft of Kullu

MAHAJAN

The Mahajan, literally "the great folk" is a community of the money-lenders. They are also titled as Shah or Sahukar, a rich person who lends money. It is not a caste and is normally not recognized as a community in all parts of Himachal Pradesh except in some areas, particularly Kangra district. Three main caste constituents (groups) form the Mahajan community, viz. Baniya, Kayastha and Khatri. Among the Baniyas, it is the Bohra group and not the Aggarwal, which comes in the fold of the Mahajan community in Kangra. The Bohras and the Kayasthas or Kayath were collectively known as Karar or Kirar (Rose, 1919) and the same is also used as a synonym for the community by the outsiders. Locally, "Karar" stands for a "unbendable person", as is also noted from a popular saying *karar di jangh uppar hi rahindi* (the Karar always keeps his leg up). But this name is not respectable among the Mahajans. 'Mahajan' is also suffixed as a surname by many persons. The history of their origins is obscure but they conceive their distribution at interregional level in Punjab and Himachal Pradesh. In Himachal Pradesh they are mainly concentrated in Kangra, Hamirpur and Bilaspur districts but are also found in the urban centres of Mandi, Kullu, Solan and Shimla districts. Their population is not recorded in the Census reports. The community is almost confined to the towns/urban conglomerates and is engaged in business entrepreneurship. They are one of the prosperous communities of the State. They live in varied climates, warm and temperate to cold, and in hilly terrain with low humidity and medium annual rainfall.

The Mahajans lack any specific community markers except their typical mercantile profession. They speak local dialects of the western Pahari, viz., Kangri and Bilaspuri, and write in Devanagari script among themselves or with their neighbours. With outsiders they may also speak in Hindi, Punjabi and English. Some old persons know Urdu which was their official language for maintaining credit accounts of the people. Generally the men now wear shirt and trousers and the women wear *kurta* and *salwar* along with a Punjabi *chunni/dupatta*. Older men used to wear a *kurta, dhoti* and a *safa*.

Presently the ornaments worn by women are *koka, nath, bali, gut da chak,* and a chain and pendulum of gold. Some women also wear golden bangles. Some bio-anthropological information is available on the community. The Mahajans have higher (62.55 per cent) frequency of 'r' followed by that of 'q' (23.42 per cent) and 'p' (14.03 per cent) among ABO blood group (vide Singh *et al.*, 1994). See also the Bio-anthropological Report.

The Mahajans share food and food habits of the region. Quite a few persons are non-vegetarian and eat eggs, fish and meat frequently and also consume liquor purchased from the market. But many of them being the followers of the Arya Samaj movement abstain from non-vegetarian diet and liquor. A few are also pure vegetarians and may even avoid onion and garlic.

Their staple food is wheat, maize and rice. Various types of pulses are consumed, viz., *urad, moong, kulthi, masur*, peas, gram and beans along with different seasonal vegetables. They cook their meals in mustard oil, groundnut oil or in hydrogenated vegetable *ghee*. Roots and tubers are eaten frequently. Fruit intake is moderate but quite frequent among the rich ones. Festive foods are *kheer, halwa, seviyan, babru, bhalle, ankli*, etc. Maize *roti* and *sag* is also popular during winter. Food taboos are observed on death occasions. Certain foods are also not eaten during fasts. Milk and milk products are consumed frequently. Other drinks include fruit juices, tea and coffee. Men smoke cigarette, *bidi* and loose tobacco in an indigenous pipe called *hukka* or *kali*.

Among the Mahajans certain sections, viz., Gupta and Bohra (Baniya), Diwan (Khatri) and Kayasth are regarded somewhat socially superior, but there is no clearcut social hierarchy. Probably it was so because they were richer than the other sections. The community generally conceives further divisions into several sections equivalent to clans,or *al* many of which are of totemistic origins. The sections noted during the study are: Kathyale, Drabre, Dhankan, Suan, Phally, Malwan, Mehte, Chhapre, Puwari, Guleriye, etc. These sections denote descent or ancestry from a particular ancestor or place, and are used as exogamous units to regulate marriages.

The Mahajans also have a few *gotra* divisions, two of which known to the informants are, Kashyap and Wahil *gotra*. The Mahajan place themselves in the Vaishya varna, but economically they are a very dominant class in the region. There is another community in the region which is often remembered and rated with the Mahajan. It is the Soods who are also mercantile in their occupation and are quite frequently seen in the areas where the Mahajans live. But the Mahajans consider the Soods as socially inferior to them even though at times the latter excel in business enterprises. Presently, however, the Soods are coming at par with the Mahajans socially because of their economic status and some marriages between the two communities are seen taking place, particularly with the Khatri group of the Mahajans.

The Mahajans are not strictly endogamous. The Baniya group marries in itself, so do the Kayasth and the Khatri. But sometimes they may intermarry and also marry outside the community with the Soods and with the other Khatris not falling in the Mahajan fold. Village and *got/gotra* exogamy is however adhered to.

Normally adult marriages are practised by the community, and these take place through negotiation. They do not practise exchange marriages that are quite common among many Hindu communities of the region. Bride price does not exist in the community but dowry is quite prevalent. It is given in cash, kind and in the form of gold or silver ornaments. Taking dowry is considered a status symbol and may be demanded from the girl's parents. Gradually this has become a social evil.

Monogamy is practised, though the man may marry again in case the first wife is unable to produce any or a male child. Marriage symbol is *sindur* which may be substituted in routine by a *bindi,* a nose and ear ornament of gold. The bride lives patrilocally. Widow remarriage usually does not occur but is allowed socially in case of young widows. Usually junior levirate is not practised in such cases, but is also not ruled out. A widower may remarry a junior sororate or any other woman. Divorce is socially disrespected and disallowed but it may occur among the educated ones as per judicial approval on ground of maladjustments. In such cases the man has the liability to give maintenance to the woman and children. Either of the divorcees may remarry. The main changes in the marriage institution that have occurred over time are: trends towards community exogamous marriages; increase in age at marriage and dowry system.

The family pattern is predominantly nuclear at present and the married sons, when running their separate enterprises may establish separate households. But the elders command respect. Older women observe avoidance relationship but with women's education this is disappearing. Avoidance may be seen between *nuh/lari* and the *saurah* and *jeth.* Joking may occur between *jija-sali, devar-bhabi, nanad-bhabi* and *jija-sala.* Points of conflict in the family are mainly on property matters, but sometimes in more conservative families the same may be on account of traditional mother-in-law—daughter-in-law relationships and unequal division oflabour or of household workload.

The rule of male equigeniture is followed for inheriting paternal property and the eldest son succeeds the father. Women enjoy almost an equal status as men and some also contribute to the family income as they are employed in Government and private concerns. In rural areas they also fetch potable water. They participate in social and religious ceremonies and also assist men in general merchandise. They regulate family expenditure and also have a say in domestic decision-making. But barring some women usually the activities of social control and political activities are not of much interest to them.

The Mahajans observe the Sanatana rituals but the followers of Arya Samaj curtail these rituals. Pre-delivery rituals are ignored but restrictions, post-natal and pre-natal, are observed. Birth pollution called *sutak* is observed for 16 days and purification occurs by a *guntrala* ceremony. Sweets are distributed and ladies' songs are sung in rural areas or a feast is given to friends and relatives on the birth of a son. Name is given by consulting a Brahman priest who prepares the horoscope of the child.

Similarly, some people also observe *annaprashan* ceremony but many ignor it. *Mundan* is the major ritual during childhood performed by the *mama* of the child. It is observed only in case of male children on any odd year of birth before the fifth year. *Janeu* among boys and *karan bedhan* among girls are ceremonies observed at the marriage time. The pre-marriage rituals are *sagai, tika* and *thahaka*. The marriage rituals are observed as per the elaborate Sanatana or short Arya Samaj rituals. Accordingly the rituals occur at bride's place or in a temple. The boy and girl circumambulate the sacred fire and the parents of the bride perform *kanyadan*. They also give a feast to the *barati* (groom's party). At the groom's place, the first ritual is *andrera*. The other major ritual is a *pipal puja*. The bride and groom circumambulate a *pipal* tree or its branch by tying a white thread. The marriage ends with music and dance and a *dham* is given by bridegroom's parents. The *muklawa* ceremony occurs on the following day.

The dead are cremated and the ashes are collected on the same or third day and immersed in the Ganges at Hardwar or at Beas river. The *patak* lasts for 13 days when the *kirya* is performed by the Acharaj and ancestor worship is observed. *Dan* and food are offered to the Brahmans. The family priest performs purification *havan* and the relatives and friends are offered a ceremonial meal. Annual death rite, *barkhi*, is performed by a Mahku who seeks the alms. Fourth annual, *chabarkh*, death rite is also observed to commemorate the dead.

The Mahajans are essentially a non-agricultural community. They thrive traditionally on business entrepreneurship and money-lending. They run general merchant shops and are self-employed. However, many persons are also in various employments in Government departments and banks on respectable jobs. Labour is lacking in the community. Money-lending or *shahukari* tradition has recently faded away and their major source of income remains general merchandise and different employments.

The Mahajans had their caste council during the pre-Independent India which, however, became subsequently defunct. But, recently in Kangra they are reviving the activities of the community council. It has been made a formal body with a president, secretary and office bearers elected by voice vote for an indefinite period till they enjoy the confidence of the community. Each family contributes five rupees per month as a subscription to carry out the activities of the *sabha*. The *sabha* aims at discouraging taking dowry and advocates simple and less expensive marriages. It also raises funds for poor children for their studies. Various social disputes are also solved by the *sabha.* Statutory Gram Panchayat functions in the rural areas and performs various developmental and welfare activities.

The Mahajans are Hindus and propitiate Hindu pantheon gods and goddesses along with various family/clan, village/ local and regional deities. The *jathere* (ancestors or men of reverence from the lineage) are propitiated as family deities on birth, marriage and other festive occasions. Balak Nath is a family, clan as well as local/village and regional deity. Lakhdata, Guga and Nahar Singh are also propitiated as regional deities. Their sacred specialists are from other communities. They visit various local regional fairs of the various deities. Various festivals celebrated by the community are: Lohri, Baisakhi, Sair, Rakhi, Ramnavmi, Nag Panchami, Janamashtami, Dussehra, Diwali, etc. Diwali festival is of great socioeconomic significance to them and goddess Laxmi, the goddess of wealth is especially propitiated.

Most of the Mahajans are followers of the Sanatan dharma but some also follow Arya Samaj and Radhaswami movements. The community shares the regional folklore. The notable traditional folksongs are *Ranjhu-Phulmu, Gambri* and *Mohan* (in Bilaspur), *Subhadro-Bajir, Kunju-Chenchlo, Bhala Sipahiya dogria* and *Kangre de fauji* (in Kangra). Percussion instrument like *dholak* is the more common musical instrument. *Gidda* is popular among young girls as a folk dance. People commonly enjoy Hindi film music.

Traditional *jajmani* relationship is retained to some extent with Brahman priests and barbers. Modern intercommunity linkages exist in terms of persons in business entrepreneurships, in teaching, medical, and engineering professions, as advocates and in defence services. Political leadership has emerged at the regional level.

Modern developmental programmes have made a considerable impact on the Mahajans in various spheres. The formal education has been favourably received by both the sexes including higher post-graduate education. But in view of their traditional mercantile occupation, many may opt out of higher studies.

Modern health and medicare is favoured and used frequently, but indigenous system of medicare may also be used if they are effective and desired. They also have faith in faith healers and use their services for curing certain diseases. Modern family planning measures including sterilization are used and the small family size of two or three children is favoured. But still the attitude towards a son is more favourable than for a daughter and the former is regarded as an asset and the latter as a liability.

Potable water is available through taps but in suburbs or rural areas the springs and step-wells are also used. Electricity is available to all and they enjoy modern mass media (radio and TV) facilities, and visit cinema. Road and, in some areas, railway exist. Post and telegraph facilities are available in the vicinity. People are generally self-employed in general merchandise and there are also schemes for the youths under IRDP. Fuel resources are kerosene oil, coal, LPG in urban areas and in rural areas fuelwood. Immunization is availed of under ICDS.

A.R. Sankhyan

MALANEESE

The Malaneese are the inhabitants of Malana village in Kullu district. Though backward and living in isolation, they are not included in any of the scheduled categories. The origin and history of these people is obscure and shrouded in mystery. From local narratives and other corroborative evidence it appears that the community was very much in existence during the period of emperor Akbar in the sixteenth century. This view is substantiated by the fact that statues of horses and elephants presented by emperor Akbar to propitiate the local deity Jamlu are lying preserved to this day, in the treasury of the deity in Malana. According to the elderly people of Malana, their ancestors had migrated from different places in the Parvati and Kullu valleys. The names of five out of eight existing clans in Malana village lend support to this contention. Ibbetson (1883) and Maclagan (1892) trace the ancestry of Nagwaning clan to Nagoni village in Kothi Naggar of Kullu district, while those of Themaning, Puchaning and Dharaning clans are said to have migrated from Thale village in Baragarch Kothi, Pos village in Kanawar Kothi and Dhara village in Kais Kothi of Parvati and Kullu valleys, respectively. Shillu of Dhara-Behr came from Shilla village in Kanwar Kothi or Parvati Valley (Sharma, 1985).

Owing to scarcity of land in and around the village, the Malaneese do not allow outsiders to settle down permanently in the village. However, in the past, it is said to have provided shelter to criminals who crossed over to Parvati valley in search of a safe hideouts.

Malana village is situated at an altitude of 2,633 metres (between 70° 15' 30") north latitude and 30° 04' 04" east longitude). The village is territorially divided into two parts, the upper part called Dhara-Behr and lower part known as Sara Behr. The two portions are placed about fifty metres apart from each other. The village is bounded by a hilly terrain with scanty forest. The climate is cold with heavy snowfall in winters, and plentiful rain almost round the year. The population of Malana, estimated from the demographic data collected during 1979-80 (Sharma, 1985) was recorded as 744. The Malaneese speak a unique dialect called Kanashi, which is known only to these handful of people. Kanashi, according to Grierson (1909), belongs to the western sub-group of Tibeto-Burmese languages. There is no script as such of Kanashi dialect. The Malaneese generally use Kulvi to converse with people from neighbouring valleys and outsiders. Some can also speak in Hindi.

It is easy to recognize a Malaneese from his dress, especially the womenfolk, as they always wear a round brown cap with a fine lining of dark brown or black border. They clad themselves with a grey or dark brown woollen fabric which is wrapped around the body. It is held tight at the waist by tying *gacchi* (long soft cloth) or multiple folds of a brownish woollen cord. Menfolk dress similarly as the peasantry in Kullu valley with grey or brown woollen coat, and a *pyjama*. Wearing a cap by males is not uncommon in Malana. The Malaneese themselves knit and weave the fabric used for making clothes. *Poolas* (strand shoes) are generally used by both men and women. Socks are also made from rough pure wool. People wear warm clothes almost round the year due to cold climate.

The Malaneese have a fair complexion with scanty hair on the body. The face is long with a prominent but narrow nose and medium to narrow bizygomatic breadth. While they have retained their linguistic uniqueness to this day, their physical features bear imprint of some intermixture with local populations. Information in somatometry, genetics, population structure and nutritional status of the community is also available (see bio-anthropoligical report).

The Malaneese take both vegetarian and non-vegetarian food. Their staple diet consists of wheat, maize, rice and *kathu*. Maize and rice are not grown in the village. These are bought from Jari and Parvati valley. Pulses form an important part of their daily diet. Fresh vegetables such as *sag* and potatoes are also consumed besides some locally available roots and tubers. *Mash* and beans form the principal dishes. Mustard oil and *desi ghee* are generally used as cooking media. *Gur* is commonly used for preparing milk tea. Mutton is taken occasionally by both men and women. Milk is seldom taken as such, but is used in making *ghee* and the rest for preparing tea.

Alcoholic drinks made from *gur* are commonly taken by menfolk. Smoking of *bidi*, cigarette and tobacco is quite common among the Malaneese. Women do not smoke openly. A few people use snuff but chewing of *khaini* (tobacco) has not been reported.

Malana is predominantly inhabited by Kanet also known as Rajputs. Out of 141 families of Rajputs, there are only three families of scheduled castes (one weaver, two blacksmiths) living in Malana. The latter are not the original inhabitants of Malana. They were brought from the Parvati and Kullu valleys about 3-4 generations ago on the request of Malaneese. Occupational differentiation forms the basis of caste hierarchy in the village. The Rajputs occupy the highest rung in the social hierarchy, followed by weavers and blacksmiths in that order.

The entire Rajput population of Malana is further divided into eight patrilineal clans, namely, Birigij, Dharaning, Punchaning, Shillu and Themaning who occupy Dhar-Behr, and Nagwaning, Thochbahru and Yochbahru who live in Sara-Behr. The offices of *kardar* (deity's manager) and *pujara* (priest) are a prerogative of Themaning and Nagwaning clans. The remaining six clans enjoy equal status vis-a-vis each other with no further hierarchical stratification. The Malaneese regard themselves as superior to the Rajputs of neighbouring valleys. This impression seems to have taken root because the Malaneese cannot communicate freely with other people of this region due to linguistic barriers.

The Malaneese are an endogamous community. But they observe exogamy at the clan level. In recent years a few cases of village exogamy and clan endogamy have been reported. Avoidance of marriage with close consanguineal relations is a desired rule of marriage in Malana, but cannot be adhered to very strictly due to the small size of the population, limited choice of mates in the compatible age groups and economic constraints. While marriage between cross-cousins is permitted, marriage with parallel cousins is prohibited. Marriages between the children of siblings of opposite sex are not uncommon, but no cases of marriage with father's brother's daughter and mother's sister's daughter have been reported to take place. Consanguineal relationships like first cousin once removed, and second cousin once removed are the more prevalent types of marital unions in Malana. The mean age at first marriage among the males of this community works out to 21.39 years, whereas in the case of females it is found to be 17.90 years (Sharma, 1977).

The common mode of acquiring mates among the Malaneese is marriage by mutual consent. Other forms reported are marriage by factual or symbolic capture, marriage by elopment and trial or service. Monogamy is the general rule, although occasionally polygamous unions have also been reported. Maclagan (1892) and Kangra District Gazetteer (1917) report the presence of polyandry in Malana, but Peter (1963) strongly refutes the presence of this type of marriage in the Malaneese. There is no special symbol of marriage. On the occasion of marriage both the bride and groom dress themselves in new clothes and the bride covers her face with a black veil, a ceremonial wear.

In Malana, girls are regarded as an asset to the family. The demand of *barni* (bride price) is a common practice in this community. The amount of bride price which is settled before marriage depends upon factors like age of the bride, social and economic status of the groom's family. Half of it is paid to the girl or her parents soon after the marriage ceremony is over. The remaining half is paid after the bride has completed one year of successful stay with her husband.

The residence after marriage is patrilocal. In exceptional cases other rules of residence, like neolocal, matrilocal and avunculocal, etc., have also been observed.

Divorce is permissible by either partner at any time, for reasons like maladjustment, cruelty, barrenness, adultery, impotency and insanity. For a petty consideration of Rs. 20 and six metres of cloth a man yields the right to his wife, and seeks a fresh mate from the village. The newly united couple have to sacrifice a lamb or a goat for legitimizing the consummation of alliance. In case of divorce, children generally stay with the father. Widow, widower and divorcee remarriages are permitted. From Behr exogamy was reported in the past; the level of exogamous unit has come down to a patrilineal clan. To maintain solidarity of the village, sanctions against marrying within the clan also seem to have been waived in certain cases. An upward trend is seen in the amount of bride price payable.

A majority (75 per cent) of the families belong to the nuclear type; however, mixed extended families are also found. Male equigeniture is the general rule of inheritance but at times it is also the main cause of conflict and confrontation. The eldest son is always given the right of succession in this community. In case there is no son, this right goes to the adopted son or the nephew. Due to the small size of the population, almost all families in the village are closely linked to each other. Although extended family system is continuing, there is a growing preference for nuclear families under the impact of modernization. There is, however, no change in the inheritance as well as succession rules.

Their women do not have the right to inherit family property. As compared to the males, they are more hard working. They have an important role in agriculture, animal husbandry, collection of fuel and fodder and other economic activities. Political and religious activities of the village are the domains of men only. Females are treated as inferior to males. Decision-making powers generally rest with men inspite of the fact that the women contribute equally towards the family income, besides attending to the usual household chores and other day-to-day activities.

The concept of post-delivery pollution is evident from a variety of post-natal restrictions imposed on the mother for a certain period after the child birth. *Mundan* ceremony is performed only in the case of a male child.

In arranged marriages rituals are performed at the bride's as well as groom's place. It is generally the groom's parents who give a feast to celebrate the marriage of their son. Wedding ceremony is normally performed at the groom's residence.

The Malaneese cremate their dead and also observe pollution for a week on the death of a member of the family. The ashes of dead persons are disposed off by immersing in the nearby stream. They also strongly believe in ancestor worship. There has been no significant change in the life-cycle rituals and restrictions of the present-day Malaneese in comparison to their ancestors.

The Malaneese are essentially an agrarian community. Land forms their major economic resource which is supplemented with forest produce. The entire cultivable land of the Malaneese is treated as the property of their tutelary deity Jamlu. They consider themselves to be the tenants of their esteemed deity. For all practical purposes, land is controlled by the rights of lineage proprietorship. There is barely any family in the village which does not hold land. Other natural resources like forest, river water, etc., are under the control of the State Government. The Malaneese's subsidiary or non-agricultural occupations include collection of medicinal herbs, rearing sheep goats and cattle, weaving, non-skilled labour, beekeeping, business and moneylending. Metal work is exclusively the job of the blacksmiths. A wide variety of exotic and costly herbs of medicinal importance grow wild in forests of Malana glen. These are not only used in curing ailments in the local system of medicines but are also collected and marketed in large quantities. Some of the important herbs include *banafsha* (*Viola cinera*), *ban-ajwain* (*Thymum serphylum*), *chora* (*Angelica glauca*), and *guchhi* (*Morchella esculenta*).

The Malaneese are partially dependent for their basic requirements on the nearest market in Jari, which is situated at a distance of about 12 kms from the Malana village. There are two little shops in the village run by the local inhabitants which fulfil the auxiliary requirements of these people. They often come down, fortnightly or monthly, to Jari to sell their local produce like medicinal herbs, *desi ghee*, honey, etc., and in return, purchase wheat, maize, rice, *gur*, salt and other items of daily use. The intra-village transactions are based on the Malaneese's own barter system which operates on a different scale. The price of various items like *desi ghee*, honey, etc., are fixed much below the price they normally charge when they sell their produce to outsiders. In this special exchange system, nobody is permitted to resell the goods, which have been purchased for personal consumption to an outsider.

Because of poverty, limited land resources and increasing price of daily needs, the villagers are increasingly taking to work as labourers on a daily-wage basis. For jobs undertaken in the village, wages are given either in cash or in kind, but outside the village they prefer cash payments. The scarcity of cultivable land in their native village, together with the effect of modernization have impelled the Malaneese to come out of their refuge in search of skilled jobs.

The most interesting and outstanding feature of this isolated community is its parliamentary form of government that exists in the form of *jayasthang* (village council), which has been functioning since time immemorial. The *jayasthang* comprises 11 officials. Out of these, three members are permanent appointees while the remaining eight members are elected periodically by the villagers following certain well-defined procedures. The permanent councillors include the *gur* (mouthpiece of deity) or *chela*; the *pujara* and the *karmist* (manager) or *kardar*. These three are collectively known as *jestha* (jurymen). All kinds of offences like adultery, elopement, disputes over land and theft are settled by the council. The offenders of the traditional norms are purnished by cash fine and social boycott.

In addition to the traditional village council there is also a Gram Panchayat which has been in existence for over three decades. Its main function is to plan and implement various developmental and welfare programmes of Government for the upliftment of the people. The people of this village are reluctant to avail themselves of the services of Gram Panchayat.

The Malaneese claim themselves to be Hindus, but it cannot be said with certainity who these people originally were. Jamlu alias Jamadagini or Jamadaggan (a *rishi* in *Vishnu Purana*) is the principal deity of the community. All the social religious and political activites of this small village are directly under the supreme leadership of Jamlu, the powerful tutelary deity of the Malaneese who reigns over the whole village. The worship of Jamlu is not confined to Malana but people of adjoining areas also pay homage to him. There is also a temple of Renuka (locally known as Naroi), the wife of Jamlu, which is located in Sara-Behr. There is no Brahman family in Malana. They are generally invited on special social and religious occasions from the nearby localities to worship their deity.

Fairs and festivals are a common feature in Malana. Invariably all festivals have some socioreligious significance. The most important festival relates to the famous Akbar-Jamlu legend. It is celebrated every year on the twelfth Phagun (sometime in the month of March). The Malaneese have their own peculiar traditions (folksongs, folklore and folktales) which are transmitted orally from one generation to the next. The traditional musical instruments (*narsingha, nagara, dhol, shehnai*, etc.) of the Malaneese symbolize their local deity Jamlu and are considered to be sacred. These instruments are taken out of Jamlu's *bhandar* (godown) in a procession with great fanfare only on the occasion of certain fairs and festivals. The traditional Malaneese folkdance closely resembles the Kullu folkdance in which both men and women participate equally.

During the pre-Independence days, the Malaneese were virtually confined to Malana village with hardly any links with the outer world. It is only after independence that these people have come out of their refuge and started interacting with the neighbouring people. They accept both cooked and non-cooked food from persons of equal or higher caste groups, such as Brahman and Rajput. In recent years there have been a few cases of intercommunity marriages, which are on the increase. The number of out-migrating females is higher as compared to those brought to village from outside (Sharma, 1985). A relationship like *dharm bhai* is not uncommon in Malana. Kinship ties of this type are generally established with people of neighbouring valleys, who are frequent visitors to Malana and who participate regularly in their fairs and festivals.

Malana being an isolated village does not share its water sources, roads, schools, crematorium, houses and panchayat *ghar*, etc., with any other community. It is only recently that they have started participating in the main festivals held in the neighbouring valleys. Their interaction with Brahmans of Parvati valley is slowly developing into *jajmani* relationship.

On account of their prolonged isolation and lack of education the Malaneese have remained backward and illiterate. As a result, there is little intercommunity linkage at the political level. The socioreligious and political activities of these people are more or less restricted to their internal affairs. Their involvement in the political activities at the district or State level is meagre.

The concept of symbiotic relationship like landlord-tenant, cultivator-labour and employer-worker does not exist in this community. However, the Malaneese do render services on a reciprocal basis to one another for various economic, social and religious activities. This does not involve any monetary considerations.

There is a general apathy among the people of this village to accept any change in their life-style. This probably is the main reason why the developmental programmes introduced in Malana have not made any marked impact. There is a primary school in Malana functioning since 1951, but the villagers are reluctant to send their children, especially the girls, to the school. In the entire village there is not one person who has passed the middle standard examination.

There is one Ayurvedic dispensary in the village, but people prefer their indigenous methods for treating disease. Due to the small size of the population and high rate of infant mortality, the general attitude of these people is not favourable towards family planning.

The village gets ample supply of drinking water from four natural springs located in the village. The rural development programmes introduced by the State Government have not made any impact on the life-style of these people.

Listening to radio, besides being a source of entertainment, is the only means of receiving information from the outer world. There are two precipitous hilly tracks leading to the village, one across the Chandrakhani Pass, and the other along the Malana torrent. Both these approaches are difficult and ill-maintained.

There is no electricity in the village at present. It is, however, likely that, on the completion of Malana hydroelectric project, which is being constructed on the Malana stream, the village will get electricity. The main energy source of these people is firewood and cowdung cakes. They seldom use kerosene oil. They are mainly dependent on rainwater for irrigational purpose. Cowdung is commonly used as a manure in the fields. They are not familiar with the use of chemical fertilizers and insecticides to improve their crops.

The impact of various nutritional programmes introduced by the

Government agencies has remained ineffective, primarily due to the belief of the Malaneese in "untouchability". The facility of public distribution system through fair price shop is only available at Jari. The villagers have to traverse a long distance to avail themselves of these facilities. The people of Malana depend to a large extent, on local money-lenders as there is no banking, saving or investment facility in the village.

V. Bhalla and P.C. Sharma

MASKU

Kangra is an old historical district inhabited by many communities and their segments. Within the Brahmans itself there are three main classes: Nagarkotiye, Bhatedu and Halwaha. There are others like Charaj, Masku, Naul, etc. in the class of the Brahman. But at the social level this fourth class is supposed to be inferior to the others. The basic reason for this is that they perform death rites and live by the food received in return.

The Charaj, Mahacharaj, Masku and Naul, all four communities are associated with death rites, but the rites are divided among them and they perform it within these limitations. The current name of this caste is 'Masku', but its old name 'Mahku' is also quite common. They are called Sanyasi or Sanyasi Brahman too, because the name Sanyasi is more acceptable to this class than other names.

As far as the history of the Masku is concerned, like the Chaplain community this community too was attached with royal families. From such families they got their livelihood as alms and donations relating to death rites. Originally they held themselves to be Brahmans only, and that consequent to the division of work, they got their present name and job. The historical tradition of their original residence too lead us to the conclusion that their residences are found in the royal cities like Haripur, Guler, Kangra, Nurpur, Sujanpur and Kathaur. With the passage of time, this community dispersed to other cities and towns, and started living in one or two families and earning a livelihood. It is worth mentioning here that the tradition of death rites was common mostly among Brahman, Kshatriya, and Sudra communities. Therefore their habitations are found only in such cities and towns where these communities reside. The Masku families inhabiting most of the towns of Kangra have migrated from the prosperous estate of Haripur in Kangra. This community scattered mainly in search of livelihood, and due to helplessness.

The spread of the Masku is said to have been slow. They generally believe that the communities performing of funeral rites do not grow because they thrive on others alms, and do not donate out of it. Consequently examples are found even of the vanishing away of the whole community.

The natural background of Kangra district is quite attractive. An English administrator has written:

> In my view such a natural sight is rare elsewhere. The open inclined fields-*khaliyan*, rivers, rivulets, steep hills, forests, trees, silkcotton, are its greenery beauty. The gurgling streams flowing through the villages and

towns of the district, waterfall from mountains, lakes, temples of the gods and goddesses, circular roads, serpentine paths, seasonal rain, snowfall, clouds, fog, thunderbolts, festival, etc., are its natural features.

The Masku population is sparse. There are approximately 60-76 houses of this community in the whole of Kangra. As per the record of Kangra municipality, there were only two families of this community here, whereas all other communities were in dense population.

From the business point of view there has been among the Maskus the practice of reading and speaking Sanskrit. All the rites are performed in Sanskrit only. But there has been no tradition of Sanskrit learning and language understanding among women. Only the local dialect, Kangri or Pahari, is spoken in houses. Both men and women have a practical knowledge of this language (dialect). Their folksongs and stories are also recited and told in this language only. Urdu and Persian were used before Independence. But now, like other communities, they use Hindi. Correspondence with others is in both Devanagari and Perso-Arabic.

The Maskus dress is almost priestly. *Dhoti, kurta,* waistcoat, jacket, tight or loose trousers, turban and cap form their traditional dress. After independence some changes have occurred in these too. But on the occasion of rituals, they wear their traditional dresses only. They also like to put on woollen blankets and shawls, but their clothes are not so clean as those of the rite-performing Brahmans. Probably they feel that if they wear clean clothes, people will think them to be economically prosperous and will reduce their alms. Their women wear all the ornaments that the wives of Brahmans wear. In widowhood also all the myths and traditions are complied with. Widows do not wear jewellery. Men while performing funeral rites wear a gold ring, so that the *jajman* will offer them a gold ring. As far as possible the host fulfils their demands. On this very occasion clothes and jewellery are presented to the women too, especially at the time of yearly woman- rites.

Only men have the right to hold property, purchase, sell and transfer the succession. In case of no other heir they are the sole owner. Birth and death rites in them are the same as usual. As per some myths generation growth among them is rather low and in some places they have almost vanished.

On the occasion of performing funeral rites, the host serves them with delicious food cooked and fried in pure *ghee*. However, their daily dishes are quite ordinary.

The Maskus were vegetarian. As expected, they used to worship in the evenings. In this respect they had also to be idealistic and virtuous in activities. But some who were well-versed in music, took intoxicants also. The chaplains are invited on funeral rituals and other auspicious occasions. On invitations of these families, they offer them utensils as death gifts. At present their earlier attitudes have changed. Now they consume meat and wine as well. The host also has no objection to this. They eat mutton, chicken and fish. Like other communities they also like the meat of wild pigs. They like lentils, kidney-bean, gram, etc. Their favourite vegetables are spinach, radish, mustard leaves and carrot. They also like to eat fruits and sweets which they are served on performing funeral rites. The Maskus drink milk, for which they keep cows and buffaloes. Special dishes like, *bhaturu, polu, batkhadu, paratha, daal-pakodu* and *dahee* cooked in pure *ghee*, are favourite of the Maskus. These special dishes are served to them on the occasion of ceremonies. The Maskus put their hosts in a spot by making demands of all kinds. For which they are not looked upon by the hosts with such respect. They have also become addicted to *bhang, ganja,* wine, cigarette, *bidi* and tobacco.

As stated earlier on the basis of social classification this community has been placed in Brahman classes. But due to the nature of their work this community is regarded as inferior Brahmans. At the start of auspicious acts and journeys, their coming across the way is thought to be a bad omen. Even uttering their names in the morning is supposed to be inauspicious.

At the time of *barsi,* the Masku stays in the house of the deceased, and as long as he stays, no cooking is done in the family, and until the rites are perfomed, nobody in the family goes to anyone's house, as it is thought to be inauspicious. Death messages are also not conveyed by the deceased's family. Conveying such information is thought as bad as to invite death in the family again.

Only a Masku is entitled to receive gifts and alms from annual to triennial *shradha.* A Brahman's turn comes in the fourth yearly (*chabarkh*) *shradha.* Till then the departed soul remains a ghost. In the Garud Purana it is mentioned that before the fourth *shradha,* only Charaja or Masku is entitled to receive the *pind dan.* For performing the rites they are offered all articles needed for a man such as grains, money, utensils and clothes.

The funeral rites have been divided as *pind dan*, cremation, *kirya, masak, barkhi* and biannual and triennial *shradha.* Similarly, Charaj and Masku have mutually divided these rites among themselves.

The earlier names and surnames of the Maskus continue to exist. But their social status has changed. Now they do not depend wholly on their traditional occupation. This community is said to have originated from the families of *rishi.* Likewise, they desacribe their *gotra* to be Bharadwaj and Vashishta. Usually they write Pandit or Sharma after their names. They say that they are original Brahmans and they have been given their names for performing funeral rites. The other classes of society think them to be inferior for these very acts.

Some of the customs regarding marriages are: inspecting the bride and groom, negotiations through mediator, tallying the horoscope, and fixing up engagements. Interview between the bride and groom was never a fashion of the community. They depended on the parents for final decision. The marriages are solemnized on mutual agreement of both the parties. For marriage, the groom rides on a horse and a *barat* moves along with music of *shahnai, nagada*, trumpet and drum. Neighbours and relatives are invited. The bride's parents offer her to the groom under the *mandap*. There is no custom of giving dowry in cash. After marriage the married couple is given a separate room in the house of boy's parents which is called *obari*. But in some cases grooms lives at his in-law's house.

There have only been a few examples of husband and wife deserting or divorcing each other because of the limited population of this community, far-spread habitations, faith in rituals, etc. There is usually a mutual compromise between them. In a few families, bigamy has also been noticed due to the desire for sons. In case of divorce, Hindu laws are complied with and panchayats of communities are also consulted.

Remarriage is not practised. But the society does not object to keeping a widow or resettling her. There are some instances of this, in which case court marriage is resorted to.

At present the all-round social and economic development due to extension of education and consciousness towards other's occupations, has changed the thinking and the life-styles of the Maskus. Therefore, certain changes have occurred in age and, sanctity of marriage, choice of bride and groom, dowry, residential accommodation for the new family, divorce and remarriage. Now this community wants to be recognized as Brahman only. It detests being called Sanyasi or Sanyasi Brahman. They now contract marriages with other Brahmans such as Bhateru. The new generation has no concern with their parental profession, except the awareness that the society recognized their importance. Now the Maskus even hesitate to go to the families of the desceased. The affected families carry the alms to their house or donate them to institutions as a matter of their duty.

The Masku families are father-dominated. The law of inheritance is similar to that in other communities. In case there is no issue, wife is the heir of the property and thereafter a close relative or whosoever serves her. There is always love and sweetness in relations, honour and respect and gratefulness for each other.

Before Independence the status of women was not respectable. Poor economic condition of the community might have been the reason. The temperament of the Maskus was also not normal due to the consumption of intoxicants and therefore there were conflicts in families on petty matters. Women were not educated. They had to depend on husbands for every requirement. The women had also to tolerate their husbands. They had to keep quiet because of the fear that the husband might bring another wife.

The Masku women contribute equally in the economic improvement and fulfilment of the family requirements. Sweeping, cleaning, and decorating the house, cleaning the buffaloes and cowdung, arranging the grass for the cattle, sewing, knitting, spinning, cooking food for the family and arranging beds etc are their duties in which they are efficient. On social-cultural occasions and festivals they create a festive atmosphere by putting on new dresses and jewellery. They prepare the articles required for these. In other words, in the economic management of the family they contribute a major share. The condition of the women has also improved. They are now in Government services also; some of them are teachers, and they equally share the prosperity of the family. Women's rights are similar to those in other communities.

All traditional Brahmanical ceremonies, are common to the Maskus. During pregnancy the tradition of *athwan nahan* is just for namesake. At the birth of a baby in the family a *sootak-shudhi* rite is performed. The study of birth-moment, determination of the auspicious moment, naming-ceremony, *annaprashan, kheerpu, mundan/jamalu, yagopaveet* and so many of the rites relating to marriage and death are performed just as in a Brahman community.

The birth of a male baby is celebrated with greater happiness than that of the female baby. Lamps are lightened and songs are sung. These days the mother and the baby are looked after by some *dai* (nurse). Apart from remuneration the *dai* is presented clothes as gift. *Awaranda* is performed on seeing the face of the baby. The maternal uncle also presents the baby *cholu-topu* and new clothes to his sister. To keep the child safe from the evil eye a mark of black ink is put on his forehead.

Negotiations for marriage are conducted through a mediator. *Lagna* is tallied after seeing the bride and groom. *Thahka* or tea ceremony, *shanti, parsahi, tamol,* riding on horse etc., are performed at the goom's place. Similarly *samuhat, ubtan, lagna, mukh-dishta, vedika, saptapadi, dadam, vidayee,* etc., are performed at the bride's place. Some other popular folk customs are also observed. On return, *androl* is performed at the groom's place. Some sweet dishes are prepared and served to the gods and goddesses. A feast is also given.

In funeral rites, a lamp is lighted at the head-side of the dead body. Offerings of grains and cow are made. Various other rituals are performed as per one's capacity. *Sutak* is observed during the mourning days. No auspicious ceremonies are performed during such days.

The Masku community does not depend merely on agriculture. Hardly 2 per cent of families have got land given to them by some *jajman* and that too not more than one or two *bigha.* Such land is cultivated for vegetables. Shopkeeping and playing instrumental music have been their complementary occupations. The most important for them are Government jobs. This has changed their living condition, way of eating and drinking and conversation. Thus for nearly one-fourth families *jajmani* has now become a supplementary occupation.

There are no associations for deciding disputes. Such problems are solved in village panchayats or courts in the city and town. The disputes regarding parental *jajmani* are decided in their community. In comparison to Charn communities the disputes of *bontesri* are in large numbers. But they settle such dusputes on their own. Such disputes are not forwarded to courts. Disputes with other castes are settled only in the village panchayat, and this is acceptable to them.

The Maskus are orthodox followers of the Hindu religion. They are noted for devotion to mythical gods and goddesses. In Kangra district Vaidyanath, Aghanjan Mahadeo, Nandikeshwar, Kaleshwar Mahadev, Triloknath, Kedareshwar, Mahadeo, Shobhanath, etc., are the Shiva temples. Chamunda, Mahamaya, Brajeshwari, Bhondawali, Jawalamukhi, Chintpurni, Ashapuri, etc., are goddess temples and their devotion centres.Ram temple (Damtal and Jarsinghpur), Krishna temple (Nurpur), Vishnu temple (Alampur), Mata Nagni (Bhadwar), Shibo da Thaan, Bharmad Naag, Tripal, Guga, (Saloh), Balaknath, Peere Veer, Pariyan, Achchhara Kund (Kangra), Machhendra Naldu, etc., are the regional gods and goddesses worshipped by them. Besides these, they have faith in the worship of the sun, the moon, the stars, the planets, the earth, the sky, sea, water, etc.

Women do Ralee Puja and Navratea Puja, and also observe popular fasts and festivals. They also go on pilgrimages to places like Hardwar, Triloknath, Badrinarayana, Chardham. The methods of celebrating festivals are like those of the Brahman community. No change is found in such religious activities.

There has been a tradition of folkart among the Maskus. For ritual purposes *mandap* writing is done on the ground and *mandap-lekhani* on *masak*, *kriya*, etc., is also generally done. On the dung-coated floor designs are made with wheat flour and rice representing gods, goddesses and the planets. In some families music is also a tradition. Like women of other communities, the Masku women are also good at dung-coating and designing on events like marriage, festivals and other auspicious occasions. They are good at sewing and embroidery also.

Folksongs such as *sohag, bhajan, vida-geet, badhayee*, etc. are sung on marriages, birth and other auspicious occasions. The folksongs have a nasal tone that makes it unique. Men are associated with the story-telling tradition; their tales are full of the descriptions of kind, helpful and generous characters. Male dances are not in tradition. On the occasions of marriage, etc.,women participate in dances.

Before Independence though the Maskus moved with other communities, there were restrictions on dining with them, not because of untouchability, but because they cooked grains received from their clients for performing funeral ceremonies. The Maskus had to face difficulties in getting mates due to the limited population of these community. Consequently, they searched for mates in other states.

The Maskus now take active part in elections in villages and towns. This community is fully desirous of its betterment and progress. The Maskus have a healthy attitude towards literacy and education. The present generation is holding posts in Government offices, schools, colleges, hospitals, transport, and army. Children are receiving higher education. In earlier days they looked distinct in dress and manners, etc. but there is no such distinction at present. They are conscious about health and family planning. They avail themselves of employment schemes and have benefited from them.

Gautam Sharma 'Vyathit'

MEGH

The name Megh or Meg or Mihngh stands for 'weaving'. The etymology is also derived from *megh* (cloud) as it is said these people had mystical power to stop or call clouds (rains). According to Ibbetson (1916) and Rose (1919), the Meghs were considered Chamars, but were placed higher in social ranking than leather workers. The people, however, claim a Brahmanical descent and like Brahmans perform the *kiryakaram* on the eleventh day. But the history of origin and migration of the community is not known. The community has been classified among the.scheduled castes. It perceives its distribution at regional level especially in the bordering areas of Punjab. They are almost confined to the Kangra and Chamba districts in Himachal Pradesh. The population according to 1981 Census of India is 1,485. They live in a valley of the Himalayan foothills experiencing a warm and temperate climate. The area is covered with orchards of a variety of the orange bushes known as *kenu*. They speak Punjabi and Kangri or a mixture of the two, and write in Devanagari as well as Gurumukhi scripts. Devanagari is presently more in practice than Gurumukhi. Some older men also read and write Urdu (Perso-Arabic script). Their dress is similar to that of other neighbouring people. Men wear a *kurta* and *pyjama* or pant and women a *kurta, salwar* and *chunni/dupatta*. Common ornaments of women are *tili/koka* or *nath*, ear-rings or studs, golden chain with a locket, finger ring and golden/ glass bangles.

The Meghs are occasionally non-vegetarian in food habits eating eggs, fish and meat. But in daily routine vegetables and pulses predominate in their food intake. Their staple food is mainly wheat. Rice is eaten about twice a week, and so is maize. Pulses of different types like *urad, moong, masur, kulthi*, peas, beans and gram are frequently consumed. Various types of seasonal vegetables, roots and tubers are also consumed. The cooking medium is mustard oil or vegetable or *desi ghee*. Milk and milk products are frequently in use. Fruit intake is moderate, and fruits like *kenu*, banana, papaya, guava, mango, apple, peach, *toot*, berry, etc., are commonly eaten during the season. Food taboos do exist. The followers of Radhaswami mission do not consume non-vegetarian food and liquor. Similarly such foods are also not eaten during death pollution and on certain socioreligious festivals. Alcoholic drinks are occasionally consumed by some. Men smoke *bidi*, cigarette or loose tabacco in *hukka*. Festive food preparations are *kheer* and *halwa, bhalle, kachauri, puri* and *bhature* of wheat flour, *sag* with butter and maize *roti*, etc.

Rose (1919) has mentioned Basith as a group of the Meghs but having a higher social position with respect to other Meghs. But during the present study the community did not speak about any social hierarchical patterns and indicated its groupings into different *gots* such as, Khokkar, Bogle, Sipahiye, Panjghotre, Mianmandle, etc. though Rose (1919: 79) has listed 31 names as the *gots* of the Megh. These *gots* are used as exogamous units to regulate marriages and also suggest ancestry/descent from a particular lineage. The Brahmanical descent of the Megh is not accepted by their neighbours and most of them also do not assert such a status but safely put themselves in the Sudra varna of the Hindus. Locally, they are regarded as at par with the neighbouring Labana, the Arya and the Lohar with whom they exchange food and water.

The Meghs are endogamous and follow the rules of *got* and village exogamy. Mates are acquired through negotiation and with or without exchange of sisters. Marriages occur in adulthood or in the post-puberty age but some decades ago pre-puberty or child marriages were quite frequent. Bride price also existed to some extent in the past but presently they perform *kanyadan* and also give some dowry in the form of articles of domestic use, clothes and ornaments. Monogamy is practised but man may acquire another wife in case of childlessness or no male issue from the first wife. The symbols of marriage are *sindur*, bangles and nose and ear ornaments. The bride lives patrilocally. Dissolution of marriages is usually not permitted in the community and is considered bad. But it may occur as per the judicial approval if either of the spouses proceeds to court on grounds of maladjustment, cruelty, etc. In such cases, the father is liable to support the children and pays compensation/maintenance amount to the woman. The divorcee remarriage may occur. Widow remarriages may also occur in the community and junior levirate is allowed but seldom occurs. Men may marry a junior sororate or any other woman. The main changes in marriage institution are increase in age at marriage and the practice of dowry. Incidence of divorce does not show any trend but a liberal attitude for judicial approval has developed.

The family pattern is vertically extended joint system but presently the joint families are breaking down and giving way to the nuclear types. Usually the sons do not get separated as long as father is alive or all family members are married. The elder are respected and obeyed by the junior members as a tradition. But conflicts do arise at times on matters related to property and due to social conservatism towards the son's wife by her mother-in-law and *nanad* and due to unfair or unequal division of labour. The avoidance relationship of the *nuh/bahuti* exists with her *saurah, jeth, nandoi* and elderly males of the village community. Joking relationship exists between *devar* and *bhabi*, *jija* and *sali*, *nanad-bharjai*. Parental property is inherited on male lines as per the rule of male equigeniture. At the father's death the eldest sons becomes the successor, though for all practical purposes the mother plays a dominant role.

The status of women remains lower than that of men and women do not seek any employment or do not participate in money-earning activity and also have no role in the mechanism of social control or in political matters. However, recently the some women have made Mahila Mandal which aims to discuss problems of women and provide facilities of common interest to the village. They do all domestic jobs, fetch potable water, participate in agricultural and animal husbandry and collect fuel and fodder. They control family expenditure and have some say in domestic decision-making. They also participate in social and religious ceremonies.

The life-cycle rituals are performed as per the Hindu tenets by their own community priest. Many birth rituals have lost significance or are being ignored. Pre-birth rituals are not observed but the woman is asked not to visit certain places before delivery. She is confined to an inner room of the ground floor of the house for delivery. The birth pollution called *sutak* is observed for 21 days and purification occurs by *guntrala* or *gunt* ceremony on fifth, thirteenth and twenty-first day by taking cow's urine and water of various rivers. Sweets are distributed on a son's birth and the child's *nana* brings clothes and *kangan*. Naming ceremony is not observed but the name may be given by consulting a priest. *Annaprashan* ceremony may also be ignored. The main childhood ritual is *mundan* of the boy performed by the *mama* of the child on any odd year of birth before five years of age. A feast may be given to young children of the neighbourhood. Adolescent rituals like nose and ear-piercing are not ceremonized but may be done by the girls at any time or before marriage.

Pre-marriage rituals are *sagai, tika* and *thahka*. When the marriage is fixed, the boy and the girl are given ceremonial clothes and some rupees. On marriage day *haldi* and *mehndi* are the preparatory ceremonies. The *kuldevi* is propitiated. Marriage rituals called *lagan* and *ved* are performed at the bride's residence. The bride and groom circumambulate the sacred fire and the parents of the bride perform *kanyadan* and give a feast to the groom's party. At the groom's place the first ritual is door worship and then worship of a tree. The bride and bridegroom tie a thread round a berry or *amla* tree and circumambulate it. The marriage ends with a meal to the friends and relatives. The *muklawa/gaona* occurs on the following day, though earlier it used to occur after the girl attained puberty.

The dead are cremated and ashes are immersed in the Ganges by the followers of the Sanatana. The Radhaswamis however immerse these in the Beas river and do not observe the detailed death rites and also do not weep on the death of a family member. Others observe pollution period for 11 days and on the last day the Acharaj officiates to perform ancestor worship called *kirya karam* and seeks offerings. The family priest also performs a *havan* to purify the family and a ceremonial feast is given to the gathered relatives.

Annual *barsi* and fourth annual *chabarsi* death rites are also observed.

Traditionally the Meghs were weavers but presently this occupation is virtually non-existent and they are involved in agriculture and animal husbandry. They are landowners with individual proprietorship. Horticulture has also developed considerably in the area and the people normally take a good *kenu* crop. Some persons have also adopted different occupations like petty shopkeeping and auto-rickshaw repair and some also seek daily-wage casual labour to supplement their income. Some persons are in Government civil service on lower cadres and in the army. The links with the market are direct and the market is fully regulated and is of daily nature. The dealings are in cash. Child labour does exist. The children assist their parents in agriculture, horticulture, animal husbandry and other activities.

The *sayane* of the community solve their social and village disputes. The statutory Gram Panchayats usually resolves the socioeconomic disputes and generally all communities agree to its decisions. But some also go to civil courts in certain serious cases, and the police maintains the law and order if the need arises.

They are Hindus but in the neighbouring areas of Punjab the Meghs are also Sikhs. They worship pantheon gods and goddesses and various family, *kul*, village and local deities. Sajyoti Devi is propitiated as a *kul* deity and her shrine located at Rias in Jammu is visited on childbirth and marriage. Sidh Gauriya, Pir Maradia and Lakhdata are deities of special reverence and affiliations. Vaishno Devi is also propitiated by many. The Radhaswamis have more faith in their *guru* whose shrine is located at Beas in Amritsar district (Punjab) and visited from time to time. They also arrange *satsang* at different places. The Meghs revere Kabir, as all weavers do. The sacred specialists are both from within and outside the community. People also have faith in supernatural objects or spirits and the *chela* treat various diseases that are attributed to evil spirits. Various festivals of socioeconomic and socioreligious importance celebrated by the Meghs are Baisakhi, Diwali, Nag Panchmi, Ramnavmi, Shivratri, Rakhri and Lohri. The fairs are also held during the festivals and at the shrines of the deities.

Weaving was the traditional craft of the community and the womenfolk practise art of decoration on floors and walls. They share various regional Himachali and Punjabi folk oral traditions, songs, music and dances. Some Punjabi folktales of the community are *Heer-Ranjha, Laila-Majnu* and *Sohani-Mehwal*. The Pahari folksongs like *Nagni de Mele, Nurpure dia ghatia, Kangre de fauji, Kunju-Chenchlo, Bhala sipahiya dogria* and *Mata dian bhetan* are popular. *Gidda* among women and *Bhangra* among boys are popular dances and *dolak* is a common musical instrument. *Bhajan* and *kirtan* are popular among the aged.

The traditional commensal intercommunity linkages in terms of exchange of *kachcha* and *pucca* food and water exist with the neighbouring Jat, Labana and Arya but not with the Chamar from whom the Meghs may accept only uncooked cereals. The Brahman, Rajput and Khatri traditionally do not accept a *kachchi rasoi* from the hands of the Megh. A *suchchi rasoi* is offered to them. Putative kinship may exist with any community but connubial norms are restricted within the community. Traditional water resources are shared except with the Chamar, but presently drinking water is available through taps in the village.

Crematoria, religious shrines and public places are common. Traditional *jajmani* or *lagi sahbi* relationship exists with a Chamar, Lohar, Kumhar, Soi (tailors) and Nai. Various other relationships like cultivator-labour and landlord-tenant also exist. There are persons holding white-collar jobs, teachers, doctors, engineers, etc., but have a few persons working as petty shopkeepers and joined in defence services. Political leadership has also not developed beyond the Gram Panchayat level. Modern developmental programmes have made some impact on the Meghs. Formal education is favoured but has not increased beyond secondary school level and their attitude is only partly favourable for the education of girls. Restricted economic resources and lack of interest are the main reasons for dropout from higher studies. For girls social reasons also play a part and they are considered social liabilities. Modern health and medicare is favoured but indigenous methods are also used due to old beliefs and also when modern facilities are not available or are costly. The attitude towards family planning is slowly becoming favourable and they are adopting modern methods, especially tubectomy. But socially, the son is considered essential to continue the *khandan* and so in case no male child is born among the first three children they may go on trying it.

Drinking water is available in the vicinity through taps but step-wells or ring-wells are also used. Facilities for modern mass media (radio and TV) are availed of by some and are accessible in the neighbourhood. Cinema facility is also available in the town at an easily accessible distance. Roads exist near the villages and the railway line is also not very far. Postal and telegraph facilities are also available in the vicinity. All houses of the community are electrified. People are generally self-employed but provisions do exist under IRDP and they get 50 per cent subsidies on chemical fertilizers, purchase of animals and other agricultural appliances like crop threshers, etc. Children also get mid-day meals and avail themselves of immunization facility under ICDS. Rain water is the source of irrigation. The energy sources used are firewood and cowdung cakes. The facility of public distribution system is availed of and the savings are favoured.

A.R. Sankhyan

MEHRA (KASHYAP RAJPUTS)

Mehra is also known as Kusha or Kashyap Rajput. They are a community of traditional water carriers and are also at times referred to as Jheewar or Dul. Jheewars also exist as a separate community. According to Ibbetson (1916:306) the Jheewars are called Kahar in the east and Mehra in the centre of the Province. Mehra is a synonym for chief in the service of a prince and seems to be a title of respect. They are carriers, watermen, fishermen and basket makers. They carry water on their shoulders. They receive customary payment for their services. Kusha Rajputs trace their ancestory from Kush, son of Lord Rama who belonged to the Surajbanshi clan of the Rajput.

The Mehras are widely scattered in the lower regions of Himachal Pradesh, in the districts of Sirmaur, Solan, Bilaspur, Una, Hamirpur, Shimla, Mandi and Kangra. The community is believed to have migrated to Himachal Pradesh from Punjab and Haryana in the unremembered past.

The dialect spoken by the Mehras within their own community is Punjabi with a touch of Sirmauri but with others Sirmauri and Hindustani. The younger generation write in Devanagari.

The Mehras are occasionally non-vegetarian and take mutton, fish, jungle-fowl and chicken. Their staple food consists of wheat or maize, *chapati*, rice, *dal* of *urad*, *chana* or *masur* and vegetables which are locally available. They also consume edible roots. Apricots, peaches, mangoes when available during the season are consumed from the home produce, and are rarely bought from the market. Milk is consumed in tea only or as a butter milk by the elders, but children of some well-to-do families regularly have milk. Mustard oil is their main cooking medium, though *vanaspati* and *desi ghee* are also used occasionally. The menfolk are fond of alcoholic drinks which are purchased from the market. Women are fond of smoking tobacco, which they share with their menfolk. The intake of non-vegetarian food and liquor increases in winters and decreases in summers because of climatic factor.

The Mehras have a number of *gots* such as Chauhan, Tomar, Manhans, etc. These are the names of their ancestors from whom they trace their ancestry. *Gots* regulate marriage alliances. Recently, they have started preferring the name Kusha Rajputs over Mehra. As a step further in Rajputization they affix their *got* name as surname.

The Mehras are aware of the varna system and place themselves along with the Kshatriya, but the people of the region consider them at par with the Jheewars and place them at a lower level.

The Mehras are endogamous. Exogamy is practised at the *got* and village level. Only the *got* of own-self is avoided while negotiating marriage. Daughters are not taken from the village where one has given one's own daughter. Marriage of a widow with the deceased's younger brother is also practised, and the marital ties with the wife's younger sister are permissible. Though monogamy is the general rule, the first wife usually gives her consent to the second marriage in the event of her being barren. The normal age of marriage is over 20 years for boys for girls the age has gone up to 15 years.

The present prevalent mode of acquiring mates is by *dan punya.* But payment of *reet* (bride price) prevalent earlier has now been given up but a few cases can be seen at times. In such cases the boy's father gives some money in cash to the girl's parents for defraying marriage expenditure. However, in recent years no such case has occurred. Bride price has been replaced by dowry which is usually in kind and consists of gifts like utensils, jewellery and clothes.

The symbols of the married women are glass bangles and *nak-ki-tilli,* which are taken off on becoming a widow. The residence after marriage is patrilocal. Divorce is permitted with the approval of the elders of the panchayat and has to be given in writing. This is known as *be-dawa.* The common grounds for divorce are adultery, barrenness and maladjustment. Though either of the aggrieved parties can seek divorce, in the event of divorce occuring on grounds of barrenness, no compensation is paid to the girl. If a married woman leaves her house and starts living with some other person of her choice, the boy's parents ask for the payment of actual marriage expenses from the girl's parents who pay these to the former by collecting the expenses from her paramour. Children of the estranged parents are the liability of the father. If the woman is pregnant at the time of the dissolution of marriage the child born goes to the first husband unless he waives his claim over the child. In such a case the new husband is deemed to be the father of the child. Nevertheless, when a claim to a child in the womb is waived, its value is taken into consideration while fixing the *reet* money.

Widow, widower and divorcee remarriages are permissible. In the event of a widow marrying the deceased younger brother, a simple ceremony is performed in which a nose-pin is presented to the widow by the prospective husband. She is also free to marry outside the house (*karewa*), in which case the girl's parents have to pay compensation ranging between Rs. 200 and 1000. Contrary to this, full marriage rituals are observed in case of the marriage of a widower or divorcee with a virgin girl.

Family is of joint type with all the vertically extended relations of the male line living under the same roof. Recently nuclear families have also started coming up. This is primarily because of mutual bickering within the family. The common kitchen if not run and managed on the principles of equality and fairness also tends to pave for division.

The eldest male member of the house is the head of the family and his decisions, which are arrived at in consultation with the male members of the family are final. He is held in great respect. Age is given due respect and the elders are held in veneration. Paternal and filial affection and due regard as per status of the person is the basis of mutual relationships. Purdah is observed between a wife and her husband's elder male relatives for a few months after marriage and thereafter it is limited only to the covering of head with a part of the *chunni*. Joking relationships also exist between a man and his wife's younger relatives and between a wife and her husband's younger relatives.

Property is inherited in the male line with all the sons sharing the parental property equally. A father or a brother can give a part of landed property to a daughter or a sister by way of a written gift deed. Daughters, however, receive equal share in the absence of a male issue. If a person is issueless, the property is passed on to the nearest collateral. With the enactment of the Hindu Succession Act, a daughter is also entitled to an equal share in the property along with the brother but more often than not, this share is given by them to their brothers. A widow has no right to transfer the property. The property gets divided amongst the sons only after her death, and if it is divided during her lifetime a share is kept aside for her which she enjoys for her lifetime. This share is again equally divided among the sons after her death. The different kin, both consanguineal and affinal, have definite roles to perform which bind the families together and these are best seen at social ceremonies.

The economic and social status of a woman is considerably high and a Mehra woman is fully conscious of her value as a fieldworker and a domestic worker. If she does not like the husband, there is nothing to prevent her from eloping with a person of her fancy. There are many instances of such marriages and divorces have been sought on flimsy grounds. Such a happening destroys the entire domestic and agricultural management. A woman plays a pivotal role in the Mehra economy. She tends the cattle, brings fodder, works in the fields and attends to all subsidiary agricultural and domestic activities. Besides, women work in the fields of others as agricultural labourers for which they are paid in cash and thus supplement the family income. She can take part in all the family rituals, visit temples but she cannot act as a functionary. In the political field her role is limited to the casting of votes and cannot take part directly in the panchayat, but quite often is able to influence the judgement through her husband.

No pre-delivery rituals or restrictions on the mother exists and she is allowed to do the work till the last moment for it is believed to facilitate the delivery. The house remains polluted for a period of 11 days when a ritual bath is given to the mother and child. *Dasuthan*, a purificatory ceremony perhaps so named after the tenth day, is however, held on the ninth day among the Mehras. On this day Brahmans are feasted and a name is also given to the child by the priest. The child is named after considering astrological aspects. *Mundan* is done within a year by the eldest male member of the family. This is followed by *up-nayan* ceremony which is observed for the boy and if for some reason it cannot be observed in the first five years it is deferred till the time of marriage, before which it must be performed.

Marriage is performed at the bride's residence by circumambulating the sacred fire four times amidst the chanting of *mantra* by a Brahman priest. This is done under a *mandap* erected over a *vedi.* The three other *phera* are taken around the *khera* who is represented by the *pipal* tree. This completes the marriage. After marriage, the bride accompanied by the groom goes to her husband's house where after staying for a day or two she returns to her parents' house for *paon pherna.* In the days when child marriages were performed *maklawa* was deferred till the time the girl attained puberty.

As a general rule the dead are cremated but infants and children dying of small-pox are buried. In the event of the death of a pregnant woman, the child is taken out of the womb and is buried whereas the mother is then cremated. The last rites are performed by the eldest male member of the house, but in the event of the death of the wife it is performed by the husband. The period of pollution differs according to age. If a young girl or a boy dies the pollution is only for nine days whereas in case of a youth it is 11 days and on attaining full age it is 16 days. Mortuary rites are observed on these days when the Brahmans are fed. Six months after the death, another ritual is observed when the Brahman is invited and is given alms. It is believed that on this day the dead meet their *pitr.* Nowadays death anniversary is observed and Brahmans are feasted on the *shradha* day.

The traditional economic activity of the Mehras which had been to carry the *dola* (palanquin) and fetch water has given way to agriculture owing to the decreasing demand of their professional expertise. They also thatch roofs on payment basis. Today, though a majority of them are landowning, a few are also landless. Because of low landholdings and low yield they also have to work as *batai* on the land of the big owners on sharing the 50 per cent of the produce or they contract the field for a fixed sum of money in cash, known as *jhela.* Traditionally, they also held *hakuk* for grazing their cattle and collecting grass. The members of the family who are landless also work as labourers in road building with PWD and in factories. They also continue their traditional occupation of supply of water to their clients' house. The Mehras are dependent on the local market for the sale of their produce and purchase of their requirment in cash. Children, both boys and girls, work as agricultural labourers and are paid in cash or cereals.

The Mehras have a traditional council of their own for dispensing justice within the community. This consists of the elders (male) of the community who are elected by voice vote. The panchyat deals with cases relating to *be-dawa,* elopement, adultery and breach of traditional norms. It also decides the compensation to be paid by the offender. The fines imposed are usually in cash and are given to the aggrieved party. Mehras have their representation in statutory panchayats which plan and implement welfare activities in the village and also have social control in their jurisdiction. As such, the Biradari Panchayat is now not as strong as it once used to be.

The Mehras believe in all gods and goddesses of the Hindu pantheon. They also have their own deities which are worshipped on all important social and religious festivals. Parshuram, son of Jamdagni, is remembered and held in veneration by all the people of the region. They also have a village deity which is represented by a *pipal* tree and is known as *khera dev* believed to protect the village against any calamity. The Mehras' sacred centres of pilgrimage are Hardwar and Poanta Sahib, where temples of Parshuram and Sita-Ram exist.

The major fair of the region is the fair at Renuka held in the month of November in honour of Renuka, mother of Parashuram. Other fairs of the region are Bisu fair which falls on the first day of Baishakh, Maghi held on the twenty-eighth day of Pusa, and Salono held on the *purnamasi* of Savan. The major festivals are Lohri, Ramnavmi, Navratra, Dussehra, Janmashthmi and Diwali.

The Mehras are deft in the art of thatching roofs. The womenfolk also make beautiful floral designs on the walls of the houses for decoration. They also make floral designs on their palms with grounded henna especially during the month of Savan. Women are also fond of tattooing and get their hand arms and face tattooed with floral designs. The young girls learn the art of embroidery in schools and at training centres opened by the Government. The Mehras have folklore and folktales relating to the community and sing regional songs and dance purely for amusement within the house at social and festive occasions. The men do not dance but occasionally sing.

Traditional intercommunity linkages of water carriers are with most of the communities and in lieu of which they are paid a fixed amount of foodgrains at harvest time. The rendering of the services of thatching the roof is purely occupational against payment in cash or kind. In terms of commensal norms they exchange both *kachcha* and *pucca* food with the Bahti and Jheewars. With Brahman and Rajput the community can exchange *sidha* food. Though the Mehras can accept both *pucca* and *kachcha* food from a Brahman, the latter accept *pucca* food if only it is cooked separately by a Brahman.

Ritual kinship is established by the exchange of turbans among men and women. This exchange makes them *dharam-bhai* and *dharam-bahin.* Yet another practice of exchanging handful of water at a sacred place enables a person to enter into putative kinships and people entering into such relationships are expected to behave as is expected of a real kin. They do not have any matrimonial ties with each other's families.

Political leadership at the regional level has also emerged among the Mehras and they are now contesting elections for the legislative assembly. They are alsoo members of the statutory panchayat.

Their attitude towards development programmes has been positive but these programmes have not made much impact on the Mehras' lives. In the field of literacy and education, though the majority of the elders continue to be illiterate, the younger generation of boys and girls are sent to school. They receive education mostly up to fourth or fifth standard, after which they usually drop out. The boys dropout for economic reasons whereas the girls do so because of social reasons.

Health, medicare and family welfare schemes have been able to make some impact on the Mehras and they avail themselves of the facility from primary health centres. There is also a consciousness about the need of a small family but the preference is for at least three children. They resort to modern methods of contraception but are averse to the sterilization programme as it is believed to affect their health adversely. Along with modern medicine, they also make use of the traditional system of medicare including homemade remedies.

They are also aware of IRDP schemes and some have availed themselves of the facility of loans for purchase of bullocks, manure and hybrid seeds. Drinking water is provided to the people from the Giri river. Electricity, facilities like postal services, transport, radio and television and cinema are available to them. Cinema is also made available through extension agencies. Firewood continues to be the main cooking fuel. Organic manure is freely used while the use of chemical fertilizers is limited. Insecticides are also used. The mid-day meal programme for the school-going children is available and so are ICDS facilities wherein children in 0-5 age group, expectant and nursing mother are given nourishing diet and are also given free immunization. Public distribution is available through fair price shops at controlled rates. Banking and saving find favour with some who have taken up paid employment at factories and in other Government departments.

Vatsala Sarkar

MIRASI

The Mirasi is numerically a small Muslim community. The Arabic meaning of the word *miras* is 'inheritance', and the Mirasi as a 'genealogist' corresponds to the Hindu Bhat. According to the Mirasis the name Mirasi is derived from the servant of the Prophet Mohammad named Mir Asa (Rose, 1919). Traditionally, the Mirasis were considered "tenants-at-will" and attendants of the rulers who used to accompany their masters on marriage and death occasions and bring their daughters from the father-in-law's house and/or accompany the son's wife to her parental home, etc. The Mirasis would recite the genealogies of the rulers, sing and dance and play on *tabla* and *sarangi*. Rose (1919) has made mention of 10 Mirasi groups, viz., the Rai Mirasi, the Mir Mirasi, the Dhadhi Mirasi, the Kalawant, the Karhala or Khariala, the Kumachi, the Mir Mang, the Kannas, the Naqarchi and the Rababi (the Sikh Mirasi). However, no such differentiation was noticed in the community in this study. They are either the Naqarchi or the Dhadhi as they were tradtitional drumbeaters, but presently provide brass-band music in marriages.

The Mirasis perceive their distribution in Bilaspur, Una and Hamirpur districts but their exact population is not known. They live in the Shivalik Hill region receiving moderately heavy monsoon rains and experiencing moderately cold climate in the winters and largely warm and temperate climate for the rest of the year. Thin pine forests exist in the vicinity of their habitat. They speak local Bilaspuri (or Kehluri) dialect of Western Pahari and communicate mostly in the Devanagari script, but Urdu language in Perso-Arabic script is also used, especially in their socioreligious communications within the Muslim communities. There is no typical dress pattern of their own. Men generally wear a *kurta* and *pyjama* and the women *kurta, salwar* and a *chadru*.

They are predominantly vegetarian in their food habit, but both men and women also eat fish, eggs and mutton (only *halal* and not *jhatka*), but not beef. The meat of goat and sheep is a speciality of their Bakrid festival. All types of locally available vegetables and fruits are consumed. The milk intake is however poor, though milk products, like *chhah* or *lassi* are common drinks and are also used for preparing a common dish called *jhol* eaten with *chhali-di-roti* (maize) or wheat *chapati*. Many men take country liquor but women do not consume liquor. The religious-minded persons however do not consume liquor. Pork is a tabooed food item. Men also smoke tobacco or *bidi*. There is no apparent change in their food habits.

The Mirasis have some sort of social hierarchy, the Rai Mirasi and the

Mir Mirasi being superior to other groups. But, no such group differentiation as well as social hierarchy were noticed in the course of this study. In the local Muslim hierarchy, the Mirasis of the area are however treated at the lowest level. But generally the Mirasi, Faqir and the Bharai are seen at par in the area. The Islamic committee constituted by all Muslim communities of the area however discourages social hierarchical differentiation and encourages inter-community endogamy. The Mirasis distinguish themselves into some *gots* or clans, namely Bhatti, Padhe, Quireshi, Bral and Ghorwahe, which indicate their ancestry and also serve as exogamous marriage units.

The Mirasis are generally endogamous and prefer village exogamy. But they may go in for marriages among the Faqir or Bharai or Teli. Consanguineous marriages are preferred at cross-cousin levels. Junior sororate is permitted. The marriage of the girl generally occurs after the attainment of puberty or more commonly between 15 and 20 years of age and that of the boy after 18 years of age. Marriage occurs through negotiation. There is no specific marriage symbol, though a golden nose pin may signify marriage. Monogamy is the chief form of marriage even though polygyny is permissible. Man goes for another wife in case of childlessness or want of a son from the first wife. There is no bride price. *Mehar* is promised in the form of a contract or *sharatnama* in the presence of a *maulvi.* It is traditionally an amount of thirty-two silver rupees and 25 paise, but presently its equivalent or an amount of Rs. 5,000 to Rs. 10,000 may be promised. Dowry is given in the form of household articles, clothes and ornaments. The bride lives patrilocally. Divorce is permissible for men through religious sacrament, but a woman can also seek divorce through the social approval of the community Islamic committee in the event of maltreatment, cruelty and impotency and may receive the full amount of the *mehar* promised in the *sharatnama.* Minor children live with the mother. Widow remarriage is not permitted ordinarily, but may occur in case the widow is young. Man can marry his deceased wife's younger sister (junior sororate) but levirate is generally not practised though it is allowed. Only a few changes have occurred in the institution of marriage i.e., increase in the age at marriage, the practice of dowry and increase in the amount of *mehar.*

The Mirasis have a predominantly nuclear family pattern and a few have vertically extended joint families. Married sons usually get separated from the parents. The *lari* keeps avoidance from her *saurah* and *jeth.* Joking relationship exists between *devar* and *bhabi* and *jija* and *sali.* The parent-children relationships are based on mutual love and fear of elders, but parent-children conflicts and confrontations are also not uncommon. Generally all sons equally (male equigeniture) inherit the father's property, but the daughter can get up to one-eighth of the father's property, which, however is claimed only under exceptional circumstances of divorce. The eldest son succeeds the father. The

Mirasi families are strongly interlinked—economically, socially and religiously. The only significant change in the family structure of the Mirasis is the breaking up of the joint extended pattern.

The status of woman is generally low. They usually lack the right of inheritance and also usually do not seek employment. Their lives are centred around the bringing up of children, doing household jobs, animal husbandry, collection of fuel and fodder and working in agricultural fields. They also participate in social and religious gatherings but lack a role in political activities. Their decisions are however respected and carried out by men particularly on the domestic front. They also regulate family expenditure.

On birth of a child a ceremony known as *azan* may be performed in which a *maulvi*/aged person utters the name of Allah in the ear of the baby. Birth pollution is observed and *chhati* may be performed for purification and people distribute gram seedlings coated with sugar. For naming a *maulvi* is consulted. On *aqiqa* some affluent persons may sacrifice a goat/ ram. The *sunnat* or *khatna* of boys is the main childhood ritual for which many people spend a lot and consider this occasion equivalent to "half marriage". In the recent past circumcision was performed by an Abdal but presently many people prefer it to be performed by a doctor to avoid sepsis. A *maulvi* recites hymns from the Quran and is offered clothes by the parents of the child. A goat is sacrificed to feast the kith and kin. It may be performed at any time between two and eight years.

The marriage is negotiated by relatives and friends. On engagement, called *sagai* or *karmai*, the girl and boy are offered clothes and a few rupees by their prospective fathers-in-law and sweets are exchanged and distributed. The *nikah* is performed by a *maulvi*, usually a Faqir. The *maulvi* writes the *sharatnama* and takes the consent of both the boy and the girl for each other three times. This is called *kaul karar*. The *mehar* is also fixed at this time. The bride's parents feast the groom's party. The *muklawa* ceremony occurs immediately after the marriage.

Death rituals are performed as per the Islamic tenets. The dead are buried and *fatiha* recited. The pollution period lasts for 40 days. Feast is given on the *chalia* and usually a goat or a ram is sacrificed. A Faqir or *maulvi* is offered some utensils and cloths as alms. Earlier, an Abdal was given alms to commemorate the dead.

The Mirasis were non-agricultural and subsisted on the traditional occupation of a genealogist of the local rulers, entertaining them by reciting poems in their praise and by giving instrumental music on *sarangi* and *been* and by giving dance performances. They also used to beat a drum, the *nagara/dhad* and *tabla* on ceremonial occasions. They were the "attendents-at-will" of the local rulers. Presently they have become agriculturists and also rear cattle, sheep and goats. Their landholdings are, however, insufficient for their livelihood. As such they supplement their income as daily-wage casual labourers in quarries, and as carpenters and agricultural labourers. Some of them have maintained their traditional occupation of musicians but with the difference that they now constitute brass-band parties to give instrumental music on marriages of various communities. Child labour does exist. Market is within their reach and is of daily nature. Dealings are in cash.

Community councils in the form of Islamic committee exists for all Muslim communities of the area. The committee is headed by a *pradhan* elected by voice vote for an indefinite period, till he enjoys the confidence of the people. There is no specific subscription for membership, and they donate voluntarily and collection is usually made on the festival of Id or Bakrid when people assemble. This committee strives for uplifting the lot of Muslims, eradicating certain social ills like early marriages, restricting expenditure on various ceremonies of marriage and death, encouraging literacy and inculcating habits of following the Islamic ways of life. It has opened Urdu teaching *madarsas* and also tries to construct *masjids* at various places for the benefit of the community. Many learned *maulvis* are also at times invited from outside state for religious preachings and social awareness and integration among the Muslim communities of the region. This committee is however not yet effective to give punishment or reward to the people. The post-independent statutory Gram Panchayat is heterogeneous for all communities, and resolves certain economic disputes and deals with developmental programmes.

They belong to the Sunni sect. Though Muslims they also have faith in regional and local Hindu deities, like Lakhdata, Guga, Saimlehar, Nahar Singh and Devi Sohni. Khawaja, regarded as a water deity, is also propitiated by offering a *roat*. Lakhdata is especially propitiated on a child's birth and at fulfilment of a desire and wrestling matches called *chhinj* are arranged on a Thursday. There are some individual family but not *silsila* affiliations to the regional deities. The shrines of the deities are located on hill tops and are visited during annual fairs. There are *chelas* within the community who perform *khel* to remove the ill effects of *bhoot, pret* and *churel* and also treat sterility in women. The *maulvi* is from among the Faqir. The Mirasis celebrate the Id and the Bakrid but the Hindu festivals like Diwali, Lohri, Baisakhi (or Basoa) and Chiran (a local festival of pet animals) are also celebrated with equal zeal.

They are experts in dance, drum-beating and using musical instruments. They sing the regional Pahari folksongs, like *Gambri, Mohan, Kunju-Chenchlo* and *Phulmu-Ranjhu* as well as Hindi film music. Both men and women participate in dances on festive occasions like a *gidda* dance by women and *nati* by both men and women. Instrumental music is given by brass band, clarionet, *dhol* and *nagara, been, khanjri* and *khartal.*

The Mirasis are interlinked with other Muslim communities socially, religiously and occupationally. Usually all Muslim communities share *jal chal* with the Mirasis. The Mirasis, accept *kachcha* and *pucca* food from the Hindus. Generally, the Mirasis serve *sidha* (cereals) to the neighbouring Hindus or engage a Brahman/Rajput *boti* in the social gatherings for Hindus. They have their own burial grounds. They may visit the temples and other holy shrines of the Hindus. They may share water sources with a Hindu but may not touch their water pot. The Mirasis have access to all public places. The patron-client reltionship exists with a Lohar on *gadda-gadolu* basis on every crop. They do have Faqir as a family priest, and offer him cereals and pulses.

Modern intercommunity linkages have not evolved much as there are no persons holding white-collar jobs baring a few persons in police and in the military. Some are working in hydel projects as welders and foremen. The political leadership has also not evolved.

The Mirasis lag behind in literacy and their children seldom receive college education because they are unable to meet educational expenses. They favour traditional as well as modern systems of medical care but the latter is much more costly for them to afford, except in emergency cases. They also have a positive attitude towards family planning and have accepted sterilization, but generally desire at least one son in the family. Usually women get themselves sterilized. Drinking water facility is available through piped water. They do not get special benefits of any rural employment programmes. They burn cowdung cakes, sawdust and firewood and other agricultural byproducts as energy sources. For children immunization is availed of. The facility of public distribution system is also availed. Most of them lead a hand-to-mouth existence and are indebted to local shopkeepers.

A.R. Sankhyan

NAGALU

The Nagalus, similar to the Badhi, and the Tarkhan or the carpenter caste, derive their name from the word *nagal* which in the hills means bamboo. Since they make pots and baskets of *nagal* they are known as the Nagalu. The community was studied in Shimla Janapada where they are in the scheduled caste list numbering 16,601 according to 1981 Census. They are distributed in the districts of Shimla, Sirmaur, Kullu, and Chamba. They speak the dialect of the region and wear the same dress locally worn. As a result of interaction with the urban population younger men have taken to wearing trousers, coat and shirt but the women continue to wear their traditional attire.

The Nagalu's staple diet consists of maize, wheat, *kodro, chana, mah* and beans. They are occasionally non-vegetarian and can take goat, sheep, chicken and fish. They are also fond of liquor which is procured from the local market and is also brewed at home. Women take alcoholic drinks only during festivals. Men smoke *hukka* and older women may also indulge in *hukka* smoking. Tea as a non-alcoholic beverage is the most popular of all.

The Nagalus have a number of exogamous *gots* which regulate marriage alliance and denote descent. The people are aware of the varna system vaguely but are not clear about their own placement in the hierarchical scheme. They are akin to the Badhi and the Lohar. Certain castes percieve them to be amongst the artisan castes.

The Nagalus are an endogamous group though they can marry from among the Lohar and the Tarkhan castes. Marriages are generally settled through negotiation, but some with mutual consent and elopement, are also recognized. The common age at marriage for boys and girls is between 20-25 and between 15 and 18 years respectively. Consanguineal marriages do not take place except that a person can marry his maternal uncle's daughter. They practise bride-price, which ranges from Rs. 250 to 1000. The expenses of the marriage and even for the food are sometimes borne by the boy's side.

Though monogamy is the commonest prevailing form of marriage, yet instances of polyandry and sometime of polygyny are also reported. Polyandry has also been practised in some pockets of the Rampur Bushaihr since long. But now this has largely given way to monogamy. Polygyny is not too common, as it can only be indulged in only by those who are economically well-off. A woman goes to her husband's house after marriage. The common symbols of marriage are *tili, polali* (toe-ring), *bang* and nose-stud.

Remarriage of widow, widower and divorcees is permissible. A woman on being widowed can get married to one of the brothers or cousins of her deceased husband but this is not obligatory and she can get married to anyone outside her family but within her *biradari*. A woman, if she likes, can marry any one of her choice from her community, if he pays her husband compensation that is locally known as *har*. The payment of *har* which includes marriage expenses and the bride-price incurred by her husband is a must. The subsequent marriage of a widow is by the *karewa* which does not involve any marriage rituals except that a man goes with one or two of his close relatives and may present the woman with new clothes or a piece of ornament and bring her back as wife. Some may choose to distribute sweets but there is no obligation. In case of divorce and remarriage, the children remain under the custody of the father. A woman may be allowed to carry her infants with her but only to be returned later when they grow up.

The family is mostly of joint type, but nowadays after marriage the couple after living for a few years may like to move into a separate residence or within the same household they may choose to have a separate kitchen within the same household. The property goes equally to all the sons. A widow also gets a share which she enjoys for her lifetime, after which it can be equally distributed among all the sons or can be given to the son who serves her. Daughters do not have a customary claim to their father's property except in the absence of a male issue. In such circumstances, the father arranges the marriage of his daughter to a person who stays with him and is known as *ghar javantry*.

The relationship among the various members within a family are based on mutual cooperation. The eldest male member not only heads the household but is held in high esteem by the younger members. He can intervene in any domestic conflict and bring about a reconciliation. He is also normally consulted on important issues. There is no purdah system in the strict sense of the term as women do have to work equally hard along with their menfolk; they may however cover their heads partly in the presence of father-in-law and senior male members of their husband's household. Joking relationship exists between wife and husband's younger brothers and sisters and similarly between husband and wife's younger brothers and sisters.

Women occupy a fairly powerful position in the household for not only do they carry out household work like bringing water, fuel and fodder but also help substantially in the economic activity. On the domestic front, their position is hardly at stake but economically they do not find the same favour as is accorded to their male counterparts. They do not get any share from their father's property nor are they at liberty to plan their own economic expenditure. In the religious sphere, although the women do take part in all the rituals, fairs and festivals they can, however, never become a religious functionary. Their political role is also constrained. They however exercise their franchise in the local and general election and by-elections.

The life-cycle rituals starting with birth, marriage and death are broadly guided by Hindu beliefs and practices but the actual enactment and the manner in which they are performed may differ from region to region and from one community to the other.

The birth of the son is always an occasion to rejoice. The child and the mother are segregated for 15 days after which she can take up her household work. *Halwa* is made on this day and distributed amongst the brotherhood. *Jattu* is performed for the male child at the temple of a goddess.

Marriages are initiated through the boy's side. The boy goes to the girl's house with a bottle of liquor and some sweets. When the marriage is fixed and the conditions settled, the boy along with a few of his close kins again visits the girl's house carrying some ornament usually a *bang* (bangle) for the girl which confirms the marriage deal. The actual marriage ceremony takes place at the bride's residence. On the appointed day, the boy along with his parents, relatives and friends goes to the girl's house where he is welcomed by the girl's parents. The main marriage ritual consists of seven *phere* which the couple performs by taking a *diya* (earthen lamp) in their hands. The priest who officiates at their marriage is from their own *biradari*. The maternal uncle usually officiates at the time of the marriage rituals. Among the poorer section, the marriage proceedings are highly simplfied. The boy along with few of his kin goes to the girl's house and simply brings her along. The former type of marriage is known as *byah* or *shadi* or *vedi-lagan*. This is a socially recognized form of marriage, but other types of marriages through elopement and mutual consent are also given social recognition after initial resistance.

Whenever a death occurs in the family, the kin are informed. A child below five years of age is buried and the rest are cremated. The eldest son performs the death rites of his father, whereas the youngest son is required to perform the death rites of his mother. The house remains polluted for 15 days during which cooking of meat, onion and garlic is tabooed. They also do not use some of the spices like turmeric and *heeng* during the period of mourning. The blood kin get their heads and moustaches shaved off as a mark of mourning for the departed. At the end of the funeral rites, the *biradari* assembles in the house of the bereaved family where they are given food and they in turn give some money in the name of the dead. After this, the family members can resume their normal activity.

The Nagalu's chief economic activity had been making baskets of bamboo locally known as *nagal*. The local terms for baskets is *kirari* or *kilte*, which in the hills are very useful for carrying fuel-wood, water and fodder. They are also careful for carrying stalks of grain. Each big basket can be sold for between Rs. 10 to Rs. 12. They also manufacture big pots of bamboo for storing grain etc. However, this alone does not fulfil their requirements and therefore many of them are doing agriculture to supplement their meagre economic resources. Some are engaged in manual labour in the road construction work.

Since the villages in the hills do not have the facility of weekly or fortnightly market system, the majority of the villages have one or two shops which cater to the daily requirements of the inhabitants. If any special item is required, they go down to the nearby places where such facilities are available. Children even below the age of 15 start assisting their parents in the discharge of domestic as well as economic duties.

For the maintenance of the social order, the statautory panchayats have taken the major brunt. However, purely domestic issues are settled first by the elders of their own *biradari*. If the settlement does not come forth, the same is then referred to the Gram Panchayat. Cases rearely go to the law courts. However, most of the disputes of social and economic nature are effectively settled by the Gram Panchayat. The fine levied is only in cash, which is spent for the general welfare of the village community.

The major shrines for the Nagalu are goddess Durga's temple at Sharaikoti and Bhimakali temple at Sarahan (tehsil Rampur - Shimla). They are Hindu by faith and worship all the major gods and goddesses of the Hindu pantheon. Besides, the worship of the regional and village deities is the most important of all. As for the villagers, these deities are to be properly propitiated from time to time to ensure the welfare of individual as also of the village community in general. The deities have their jurisdiction. There are lesser gods and goddesses, but hold a key place in the psyche of the people. They are specially brought in a palanquin in a procession accompanied by music and dancing. This is usually done at the beginning of the harvesting season. People also have faith in the supernatural powers, spirits, ghosts and also in charms and amulets. The services of the *chela* or the exorcists are sought, whenever they suspect the hands of some supernatural power causing miseries to the individual or the family. The community takes part in the fairs and festivals of their area. The major fair of the Rampur Bushair area is Phag and Lavi fair in which most of the communities of the village also participate.

The Nagalu men and women are deft in making baskets which they make in different shapes and sizes. They also make pots of bamboo for storing grains. As far as song and dances are concerned, the community sings the folk songs prevalent in the region. During fairs and festivals men dance collectively. Folk tales and folklore are also commonly shared with others.

As regards intercommunity linkages, the Nagalus share a lot in common with the Badhi and the Lohar. In some cases the Nagalu and the Badhi are used as synonym as mentioned by Vidyasagar Sharma in his book *Himachal Pradesh Ki Anusuchit (Harijan) Jatiyan* (Salogra). In the local heirarchy they are decidedly above the Chamar with whom traditionally they do not share food. The Nagalu, Lohar and the Badhi share *kuchcha* and *pucca* food and even smoke from the same *hukka*. Brahmans do not normally come to perform their domestic rituals of birth and marriage. The Brahman and Rajput whenever invited to a *dham* (feast) are served the food cooked by a member of a high caste. As far as the sharing of the water is concerned, all the communities share from the same source. The entry to the temple is also open to them. The discrimination practiced with regard to commensality and untouchability are not so sharp but are still carried on to some extent.

The developemental activities have made their impact in the areas of literacy, medical aid, electricity, transportation and communication, availability of drinking water through pipes, etc. Balwaris and primary schools exist. Children normally attend schools upto primary level after which there is a shortfall in the percentage attending schools. The economic condition, the apathy of the people, distance of the school from the place of stay, lack of hostel facilities and incentives in the form of scholarships, dress and stationery are some of deterrents in the way of literacy.

Medical facilities exist by way of dispensaries. In times of illness, both indigeneous and modern medicare is made use of.

The economic programmes launched by the state government provide loan facilities on a big scale for the rural as well for the unemployed educated youth. Some training and vocational guidance centres have also been opened by the government to provide basic knowhow to the people to become self-reliant. Loans can be procured for various purposes like buying tools, cattle, opening a dairy etc. Seeds and manures are also made available to the people at subsidized rates from the Block.

Vatsala Sarkar

NAI

The Nai is a well-known community of barbers. They are also known as Hajam among Muslims and regard themselves as Kuleen Brahman among Hindus. The name may have been derived from the Sanskrit word *napika*, one who cleans the nails, or from the word *nakhun* (nails). Its etymology is also suggested from the word *nahna* meaning "not to refuse" or the persons-at-will who would not refuse to act (Rose,1919). The Nai used to carry the messages of their *jajman* so they came to be regarded as a "persons-at-will". Some also suggest that the community' name has been derived from the Hindi word *nyai* or *nyaee*, meaning justice or judge, as the barber was considered to be a good judge in solving a dispute. The Nai is honoured on ceremonial occasions of marriage and death as Raja (a king) and his wife (Nain) as Rani (queen). He is also addressed on these occasions as Daroga. He plays an important role in negotiating marriages for his patrons, acts their messenger to invite people to assemble on ceremonies. He acts as a personal advisor and/or attendent to the bridegroom and also decorates him on marriage and the Nain does the same to the bride. He plays on a large curbed (S-shaped) brass/bronze pipe called *ransinga* (war trumpet) producing a loud musical sound considered auspicious while the marriage procession proceeds. For rendering all these services and shaving off the facial, head and armpit hair of his patrons he gets his *lag* (dues) on the ceremonial occasions as well as a share in each crop. Some ethnographic accounts are available on the community in old literature (for example, Ibbetson, 1881; Rose, 1919; Crooke, 1896).

The community perceives a wider interregional distribution and is found all over the country. In the State they are distributed in almost all districts but their areawise population is not known. They live in varied ecological zones. In the study area (Bilaspur district) they occupy the hills and dales of the Himalayan foothills with a warm and temperate climate, low humidity and medium annual rainfall. Thin patches of forests exist on hill ranges.

The Nais share the language, dress and ornaments of the area. Usually a country Nai may be identified from a short distance by his tool kit of scissors, razers, combs, soap, brushes, a mirror and cup. Older men used to wear a cap, a *kurta* and a *janghia* (half trousers) but the younger men wear a *pyjama* or pants but no cap. Women's dress is *kurta, salwar,* or *suthan* and a *chadru* or *dhattu* in the higher hills of Shimla and Mandi. The traditional ornaments of the women were a cup-shaped or conical golden/silver *chak* on head or occiput, ear and nose-stud, pins, rings, *har* or *besar* (neclace) *gajra* or *choora* of silver and *pajeb* or *jhanjar*. They speak the local dialects, e.g., Bilaspuri, of the Pahari and write in Devanagari script both within and outside the community.

The Nais share the food habits of the region. The major staple food is maize, followed by wheat and rice. Various types of pulses—*urad, moong, masur, kulthi*, peas and beans, grams, etc., are frequently consumed. Roots and tubers and various other green vegetables are also consumed frequently. Fruit intake is moderate and seasonal. Local fruits—mango, banana, guava, papaya, peach, apple, mulberry, berries, figs, etc.—are also consumed. Milk and milk products find place in their daily diet. The cooking medium is mustard oil or *desi ghee*, but these days vegetable *ghee* is also used. Non-vegetarian foods like fish, eggs and meat are also consumed, but only occasionally. Festive food preparations are *kheer* and *halwa, bhalle, babru, seviyan, khichri, ankli* and *ankloo*. Food tabooes exist. Non-vegetarian foods are not consumed during festivals of socioreligious significance and during the death pollution. Men occasionally take country liquor and sometimes some women may also drink. Men smoke *bidi*/cigarette and loose tobacco in an indigenous pipe called *hukka/hukkri/kali* and *jhajri*. But the followers of Radhaswami sect avoid non-vegetarian foods.

The Nais have several *got/gotra* and clans. Among the *gotra*, the common ones are Kasab/Kashyap, Bhardwaj and Kaundal. Several Rajput clans are distinguished which are also used as surnames by younger, educated persons, viz., Jaswal, Jammual, Patial, Chandel, Katoch and others like Kapoor and Gangotiya. The *gotra* and clans are used as the indicators of descent or ancestry from a particular lineage and are used as exogamous units to regulate matrimonial alliances. The Nai claim Kshatriya descent and also a status of this varna in the regional social hierarchy.

For marriage the Nais observe community endogamy and village and *gotra* exogamy. Marriages are settled through negotiation and exchange of sisters also occurs. Presently the age at marriage is above 16 years for girls and around 20 years for boys. Earlier child marriages were common and some also used to take bride price called *take lena*. But presently this custom has totally changed or reversed and has given way to dowry given in form of household articles, clothes and ornaments. Currently some also demand cash or costly items. Monogamy is practised but a man is allowed to acquire another wife in case he gets no male issue from the first one. Symbols of marriage are *sindur* or a *bindi*, glass bangles and nose and ear ornaments. The bride lives patrilocally. Widow remarriages are not practised but a widower can remarry any girl or a junior sororate. Divorce also has no social sanction, but recently, men and women have sought divorce on grounds of maladjustment or on another legal grounds as per the judicial approval. In such cases, the father is liable to support the children and he pays compensation to the woman. Either of the divorcees may remarry. The main changes in the institution of marriage are an increase in age at marriage and dowry and a liberal attitude towards the remarriage of young widows and dissolution of marriage.

The family pattern is vertically joint extended. The sons usually do not separate as long as the father is alive. But families may break up if there are more sons having more children as the differences usually come up on various family matters; unequal distribution of labour; troubling of the daughter-in-law by her mother-in-law and *nanad* and a similar attitude of *jethani* towards *devrani*. Also, sometimes the parents are more inclined towards a particular son and property may not be distributed fairly. All these factors plus sons employed outside hometown who take their families with them have contributed to the breaking of joint families. The juniors are supposed to obey and respect their elders. Avoidance relationships exist in the joint families. The *lari* covers her face in the presence of her *saurah, jeth, nandoi* and elderly male members of the village. Joking relations are not very formal but exist between *devar-bhabi, jija-ṣali* and *nanan-bharjai*. The property is normally distributed as per the rule of male equigeniture. The eldest son succeeds the father.

The status of women remains low and they do not seek employment or do not contribute to family income except that they seek their ceremonial dues from their patrons at the time of marriage. They also lack powers of social control and participation in political activities. But they do all household chores and participate in agricultural and animal husbandry work, collect fuel and fodder and fetch potable water. They take part in social and religious ceremonies. They do not have decision-making powers in vital matters but regulate family expenditure.

The Nais follow Sanatana rituals in their life-cycle but some rituals have lost significance or are ignored, viz., pre-delivery rituals, *annaprashan* ceremony and adolescent rituals. Pre-delivery and post natal restrictions exist on the mother and post-delivery pollution called *sutak* lasts for 40 days, though purification occurs on the thirteenth day by taking *gunt*. Delivery at home is performed on the ground floor and in an inner room of the house. On the thirteenth day a feast may be given if a son is born and sugar and germinated grams are distributed. The village ladies sing *ranjhunana* songs. The *nankiye* (mother's parents) bring *jhaggu-topu* and *kangnu* for the child. Name is given by consulting a Brahman priest but the poors ignore this ceremony. The main childhood ritual is *mundan* or *jatlu* of the son performed by the *mama* of the child on any odd year of birth before five years of age. A feast may be given to young children of the neighbourhood. *Janeu* is put on at the time of marriage.

The pre-marriage rituals are *sagai/mangni* in which some ceremonial rupees/ornaments and clothes are given to the boy and the girl by the opposite parties and sweets are exchanged and marriage is fixed. On the marriage day *sand* and *samuhat* ceremonies occur in which *batna* of turmeric and *ghee* are massaged on the body of the boy and girl and *mehndi* is applied on hands and feet. The eder daughter's husband acts as their Nai. The family propitiates its *kul devi*. The marriage rituals are performed by a Brahman priest at the bride's place as per the Vedic rites. Major rituals are *lagan* and *ved* in which the bride and bridegroom circumambulate the sacred fire. Finally, the parents and uncles and aunts of the bride perform the *kanyadan* ritual. A feast is given by the bride's parents to the groom's party. At the groom's place, the first ritual is *andrera* which occurs at an auspicious hour when the bride enters the house of the groom. The other major ritual is a tree worship. The bride and groom circumambulate a *pipal* tree. The bride's brother helps her to take rounds of the tree and a white thread is tied round it. Putative kinship-based friendships of the bride and groom are also made at this time. The marriage ends with music and dance and a *dham* to the gathered relatives and friends. *Muklawa* occurs on the next day.

The dead are cremated and their ashes are immersed in the Ganges at Hardwar and *pind dan* is given to a Panda. The death pollution lasts for 13 days and the story of the Garud Purana is read by the family priest on every night during the pollution period and an earthen pot is kept lighted day and night. The Acharaj officiates to perform ancestor worship and seeks offerings. The family priest performs a purification *havan*. Gathered relatives are given a ceremonial feast. The married daughters bring caps or napkins and cover the heads of their brothers. On the sixteenth day called *solia*, a ceremonial feast is given to the community. *Barkhi* and *chabarkh* are observed and ceremonial feasts are given and offerings are made to the priest. The Radhaswamis, however, avoid these Vedic rituals and arrange a simple religious gathering, *satsang* and pay a visit to the Beas shrine in Amritsar and make offerings there.

The Nais traditionally thrived on their customary dues from their patrons on ceremonies and at each harvest. They also run barber shops and modernized saloons and beauty parlours in the towns and suburbs. They supplement their income by practising agriculture and animal husbandry as they also own some land. Many persons in the community are presently employed in Government departments on various posts holding white-collar jobs, teachers, junior engineers, military personnel, etc. The links with the market are direct and the market is of daily nature and is fully regulated and dealings are in cash. There is child labour in the community. Young boys usually start assisting their father in barbery.

The Nais have their formal community council still active at present and has its regional headquarters in Hamirpur district. It is officiated by a president and a secretary and annual subscription of Rs. 12 per household is charged. The office-bearers are elected by voice vote for an indefinite period till they enjoy the confidence of the community. Only men are members of this council. The council works for improving the social and economical conditions of the community, encourages literacy and discourages unwanted marriage and death expenditure. It also solves social disputes and problems of marriage and divorce. The council also aspires for attaining a Backward Class or Scheduled Caste status for the Nais. The statutory Gram Panchayat takes up the usual village problems and solves disputes over land and water. But serious disputes involving violence are dealt by the police and legal course is adopted.

The Nai worship Hindu gods and goddesses. The family/ clan deities are different at different places and are usually the same as they are also village, local and regional deities. Of special reverence are Bharthri Sidh, Baba Balak Nath, Guga, Lakhdata, Mahasu, and Nar Singh among the male deities, and Hari Devi, Naina Devi, Nabahi Devi, Jawalamukhi, Chintpurni, Hateshwari, Vaishno Devi, Santoshi Mata, etc. among the female deities. Their shrines are visited from time to time on fulfilment of a wish and/or during annual fairs and festivities and especially during the Navratras. Sacred specialists are from within and outside the community and they believe that troubles or diseases are caused by local deities called *khot* or *dosh* and by evil spirits like *bhoot, pret, churel, jogni, betal, masan* and *bansheera* etc. These are treated by the *chela.* Various Hindu festivals of socioeconomic and socioreligious importance are celebrated like Lohri, Basoa (Baisakhi), Nauhle, Sair, Chiran, Rakhri, Guga Navmi, Ram Navmi, Shivratri, Diwali, Jagre, etc. The festival of Sair is of special significance to the Nai community. They make an idol of Saraswati goddess from fruits and flowers and carry it in a basket to show to their clients at night and seek alms.

Specific art and crafts are lacking but the Nain makes a wall painting called *Kamdev* worshipped by the bride and groom at the marriage of their clients. Regional Pahari folksongs and tales shared are *Puran Bhagat, Narsi Seth,* excerpts from Ramayana and Mahabharta, *Kunju-Chenchlo, Ranjhu-Phulmu, Gambri, Mohan* and *bhajan, kirtan* and *bhetan* of female deities particularly of Jawalamukhi. Popular musical instruments used are *dholak*, harmonium, *dantar, khartal, khanjar*, tongs and bells. Simple dances and *gidda* by young girls are popular. The Nai is noted for his good humour and wits.

They traditionally share and exchange *kachcha* and *pucca* food and water with the *savarna* but not with the Chamar, Julaha, Dumna and Hesi, as well as the Faqir, Teli, Sunhak, Bharyai, Mirasi, etc. From the latter they may only accept a *sukha bartan* or a *suchchi rasoi.* Traditional water sources are shared with different communities. The Nais have ceremonial roles in marriage, death and other festivals as mentioned earlier. Receiving and rendering of economic and social services exist. There are persons in business, holding white-collar jobs, in teaching, engineering and defence services. Political leadership has developed at the Gram Panchayat level. Modern developmental programmes have made considerable impact in different spheres. The literacy level of the Nai has gone up and both boys and girls receive at least secondary school education, though higher/ college education is not much favoured for the girls due to social reasons and sometimes due to economic reasons, as well as due to the fact that colleges are far-off. Their self-employment as barbers does not encourage more education for boys as well. The modern health and medical care facilities are availed of but indigenous methods are also used. Family planning is favoured and modern methods especially sterilization are adopted. But desire for at least one son is still socially felt even at the cost of a large family.

Electricity is available in every household and modern mass media (radio and TV) facilities are either availed of or are accessible in the neighbourhood. Road communication has also reached most of the villages and postal and telegraph facilities are available at a short distance. Drinking water is available through pipelines but traditional water resources like springs and step-wells are also in use during scarcity/inadequacy of piped water supply. Fuel resources are firewood, cowdung cakes and sometimes kerosene oil. General provisions exist under IRDP but seldom availed of.

A. R. Sankhyan

NALBAND

The Nalband derive their name from the occupation they follow of fixing of *nal* (horseshoe) on the hoofs of horses, bullocks, buffaloes and mules. They trace their ancestry from Hazrat Mohammad Daud, and they believe that he was the first Nalband. According to the legend, one day Hazrat Daud's sister's son was sitting by his side and was boiling a pot of water holding it by his hand. Seeing his hands getting burnt he felt helpless and asked God to help him. Near the fireplace a dog was also sitting with its legs crossed. As Hazrat Daud looked at the dog, he was greatly fascinated by the shape of a *sansi* (caliper) that the dog's leg had formed and immediately he twisted two iron pieces by heating them and made the first pair of *sansi.* From that day onwards, he said, his descendants would henceforth live by working on fire and iron. Even today, as a mark of respect, obeisances are offered to Hazrat Daud by every Nalband in the month of Jeth (May-June) (Ibbetson, 1916).

They are also known as Multani Lohar. They claim Mughal ancestry and are Islamic by faith. Their name Multani testifies that they emigrated from Multan some 300 years back and settled in Haryana and the adjoining parts of erstwhile Sirmaur State which today forms the Sirmaur district of Himachal Pradesh. In Sirmaur they mostly inhabit the Paonta tehsil, especially the tract adjoining the present Haryana. The script used at home and outside by the elderly persons is mainly Perso-Arabic and Devanagari by the younger generation. Similarly a combination of both Hindi and Urdu language is spoken with outsiders, but amongst themselves they speak a mixture of Haryanvi and Himachali/Pahari.

The Nalbands are non-vegetarian. They take mutton, fish, beef and buffalo meat, but pork is prohibited. Their staple food consists of wheat *chapati*, rice and pulses of *moong, urad* and *chana.* The usual cooking medium is mustard oil, but occasionally *tilli-ka-tel* and *desi ghee* are also used. Roots and tubers are also consumed especially *turar. Ber* and plums are occasionally taken. Milk is used in tea or as curd, *lassi,* etc. Though alcoholic drinks are taboo, those who are away from their villages, sometimes take them. The women are very fond of chewing betel leaves. Though men also join them, they are more fond of smoking tobacco. Special food preparations like *seviyan* are cooked on Id-ul-Fitr, whereas mutton is a must on Bakrid.

The Nalbands have two major territorial groups, i.e., Deshwali and Multani. The Deshwalis are the original residents, whereas the Multanis are the ones who migrated to settle here. Both consider themselves superior to the other. The basis of differentiation among them is basically territorial and to some extent economic. The people are of the opinion that the Deshwalis are Lohars but have taken to the specialized occupation of fixing of horseshoes. This explains the differentiation between the two sections. They do not consider themselves superior or inferior to other Muslims professing different occupations. Ali, Mohammad and Khan are commonly used as surnames.

The Nalbands are endogamous at the religious, occupational and territorial level. A Multani Lohar will always marry a Multani. In recent times a laxity has been observed in their attitude, as they have started accepting daughters from the Deshwalis, but do not give daughters to them. Thus they maintain a sort of hypogamy, considering themselves of superior stock. Cross- and parallel-cousin marriages are practised and are preferred. The age at marriage among these people is 20 years for girls and 25-26 years for boys. The most prevalent form of acquiring mate is by negotiation, which is performed by *nikah*. In some cases marriage by exchange, i.e., *batta-satta* is also practised.

In practice only monogamy is allowed. Polygyny is only resorted to when the first wife is unable to give a male child for the family. Junior levirate and sororate are also practised in the event of the death of husband or wife.

The common marriage symbols are *choori* and *chutki*, but these are not strictly observed. *Dahej* is given as per the economic status of the family, but it cannot be more than 3 $^{1}/_{4}$ tolas of silver among other things. The *mehar* amount fixed at the time of *nikah* also cannot be more than Rs. 5000 as has been fixed by their traditional panchayat. According to the Hadi the amount of *mehar* is to be given the day immediately after marriage, otherwise it is "*havan*", but sometimes the wife foregoes it. *Durud-ayad,* if offered 7 or 11 times, absolves a person from paying *mehar.* Patrilocal is the usual form of residence after marriage.

Widow, widower and divorcee remarriage are permissible. A widow can be permitted to marry only after the expiry of the *iddat.* Restrictions also exist on a person wanting to remarry his divorced wife. The common grounds for divorce are maladjustment or adultery by either of the spouse. The liability for the children in divorce cases rests with the father. *Talaq* is effected with the consent of the Biradari Panchayat, which may impose a cash penalty on the guilty along with the payment of the *mehar,* as the case may be. Major change reported in the institution of marriage is that a person marrying outside the community is dispensed with and fined either in cash or in kind.

A majority of the Nalbands have joint family with all the vertically extended relations sharing the same roof and hearth. Traditionally, avoidance was practised between the father-in-law and daughter-in-law and between a man and his younger brother's wife, but this is not observed strictly today.

But still some amount of avoidance is observed in the initial years of marriage. Joking relationship is quite common between cross- and parallel-cousins and so also between a person and his elder brother's wife. The eldest male member of the house is the head of the family and commands great respect. His decision in family matters, which is arrived at in consultation with the family members, is accepted and it is rarely that a situation of conflict comes up.

Male equigeniture is the usual rule of inheritance of property. After the death of the eldest male member of the family the property is inherited by the widow, who acts as its custodian, and supports the family on the interest of property. After her death the property is divided equally among all sons or passes on to the nearest collaterals.

The social position of the Nalband woman is high. She is the manager and controller of family affairs. Though the authority in the family is vested in the menfolk yet the womenfolk are invariably consulted on all important family issues. Though divorce is very rare, should it occur the *mehar* and the *dahej* brought by the wife has to be returned along with the fine.

The economic status of the womenfolk is equal to that of the menfolk. They assist their men in all spheres of agriculture and also work as agricultural labour in others' field and supplement the family income. Only daughters' in-laws are prevented from working in others' field. They also bring fodder, arranging fuel and potable water.

The political and religious status of the Nalband women can be said to be low, because they are only allowed to exercise their franchise at elections. They can offer *namaz* and read the Quran but are not permitted to visit a mosque or attend any religious congregation.

On the birth of a child ritualistic baths are taken by the mother and child on the third, sixth, tenth, twentieth, and fortieth day. *Aqiqa* is held at the age of five years or afterwards, at the convenience of the parents. In the case of the birth of a son two goats are sacrificed and in the case of a daughter only one goat is sacrificed. The child's hair is also shaved by the Nai on the occasion. Before the age of five, *khatna* is performed for the boy by the Nai or *jarrah*. A feast is also given. Occasionally, the *aqiqa* and the *khatna* ceremonies are performed jointly to cut down expenditure. At the age of 6 or 7 years, children are sent to the *madarsa* (religious institution) for receiving lessons from holy scriptures.

Marriage proceedings are initiated nowadays from the girl's side, but in earlier times they were from the boy's side. Rituals are held at the bride's house where *nikah* is performed in the presence of *gawah* and *maulvi* in consideration of a definite amount of *mehar*. Consummation of marriage, however, takes place at the groom's house.

The dead are buried and a *mazar* is built over the grave. The house remains polluted for a period of 10 days, whereupon the food is cooked and distributed to the poor. The death rituals vary from family to family according to the *firqa* to which one belongs, which are 72 in number. The *sunnat jamati* do not observe any rituals, but on the day of burial and reciting of *fateha*, they collect in a mosque, and after keeping five kilogram of black gram in front, about 40-50 members gather and utter the *kalma* 1 $^1/_4$ lakh times. With this, the deceased is believed to have received salvation and no further rituals are required. Restrictions, however, apply to the widow, as she is not permitted to go out of the house or visit the water source during the 3 $^1/_4$ month period of *iddat*.

The Nalband community traditionally was not directly dependent upon economic resources such as land, water, forest, etc., and did not exercise any control over these resources. They were ironsmiths working as ferriers by fixing horseshoes on the hoof of the animals, but today they have diversified their field of activity and have taken up jobs in factories and are also working as blacksmiths. Some have taken up jobs of labourer, whereas others have taken to agriculture, on the *nautor* land allotted to the landless by the Government. Owing to the meagre landholdings, they have also started working on *batai* or *theka* on others' fields. Under the former system, the produce is shared on a 50 per cent basis between the landowner and the sharecroppers whereas in the latter, a fixed amount of money is paid to the landlord, which has to be paid in any eventuality in lieu of the land given for tilling. Though they have diversified their occupation, at least one member of the family continues the traditional occupation, in addition to the other ironsmithy work, in view of the low demands or their traditional occupation.

For the sale of their produce and purchase of items of their need they are totally dependent on the market . Cash is the usual form of exchange, but in villages barter is also resorted to. The children below the age of 15 years also assist their parents. The boys work with them in the fields or in their shops while the girls assist their mothers in household activities. Occasionally they also work as agricultural labourers, where they are paid in cash. After Independence, with the mechanization of transport, the traditional demand for the Nalbands is decreasing resulting in their taking up other occupations.

The traditional council exists among the Nalbands which is known as the Biradari Panchayat. It is headed by a chief who is known as the Chowdhary. He is elected by a voice vote. The panchayat not only dispenses justice in matters of breach of commensality rules but also exercises control over marriage expenses, divorce, family disputes and theft. The Chowdhary is assisted in arriving at a decision by the village elders. With the changing times and breaking down of barriers, the attitude of the community members has also softened and they take a mild attitude towards dealing with offences. Intercommunity marriages earlier resulted in ostracization but now only cash fines are imposed. The fines realized are sent for use by the *masjid* management.

With the introduction of statutory panchayats the stronghold of the Biradari Panchayat has loosened, but nevertheless it still exists and commands respect. This can be viewed as a significant change that has come about in the mechanism of social control of the community.

The Nalbands are Islamic by faith, but some Hindu communities have also opted for this occupation after Independence, and as such some Hindu Nalbands are also found. As among other Muslim communities, the Nalbands are also divided into Kadri or Deobandi *firqa*, which are believed to be 72 in number. They also pay their obeisance to their departed family members and other Faqirs by offering *chadar* and incense at their tomb. Prayers and offerings are made in the name of Hazrat Daud in the month of Jeth (May-June). The Nalbands' sacred centres are Mecca and Ajmer Sharif. It is the cherished desire of every Nalband to visit these sacred centres at least once during their lifetime. Their sacred specialists are from amongst the Muslim order, who officiate at family rituals. Their fairs are known as *urs* which are held at Ajmer. Id-ul fitr, Bakrid, and Shaberat are the important festivals of the community which have socioreligious significance. The importance of Shaberat is so much that it is said that prayers offered for one night on Shaberat are equivalent to the prayers offered for a year.

The Nalbands are skilled in their traditional art of fixing horseshoes. The community does not have art forms and any handicrafts, but recently due to opening of training centres, young girls have learnt the art of embroidery, knitting, stitching, etc.

Folksongs and folkdances are common for the region. However, folktales do exists. Women sing and dance within the house on social occasions especially at marriages and births purely for recreational purposes.

The traditional intercommunity linkage existed with other communities, especially those who owned cloven-footed animals and those who were engaged in muleteering or transportation of goods. They exchange both *kachcha* and *pucca* food with all the Muslims, irrespective of the occupation they profess. From the Hindus they would accept both *kachcha* and *pucca* food except from the scheduled castes, from whom they would not accept *pucca* food. Nalband share *hukkah* with other Muslims. Putative kinship is established with other members of the Muslim community.

After Independence, with the allotment of *nautor* land, under land-to-the-landless scheme, the families have started on agriculture, and this has resulted in the development of ties with other people. Owing to the meagre landholdings, they have started working as sharecroppers and on contract with the big farmers. A few of them, especially the womenfolk, have also taken to agricultural labour, thereby developing cultivator-labour relationship with any neighbouring community. With the opening of factories, a few have obtained jobs and some have also found jobs in other Government, semi-Government and private organizations, where a new employer-employed relationship has developed.

The attitude of the Nalbands in general has been favourable towards the developmental schemes launched after Independence. Though the older generation is mostly illiterate, the younger generation, both boys and girls, are attending schools. The girls usually study up to primary level, and drop out for reasons of no schools nearby, but the boys study up to middle or high school, after which they usually start earning to support their family.

Nalbands' attitude to the modern system of medicare is also favourable, and they avail themselves of various facilities. Family planning programme, does not find much favour with them. They consider children to be the gifts of God and prefer to have as many children as they can have. A few of them have procured loans from the Government under the Integrated Rural Development Programme scheme for improving their agriculture. Their villages are electrified and drinking water is provided by piped-water supply. The villages are also connected by metalled roads, and are also well connected by Government transport.

Under Integrated Child Development Scheme nursing and expectant mothers and children between 0-5 years of age are immunized and provided with nutritional food. Those who have started working in factories have a favourable attitude towards savings and they then invest in banks and post offices. On the whole, the Nalband community has drifted from its traditional occupation and are in the phase of transition, searching for new modes of livelihood.

Rajendra Sarkar

NAR

The Nar or Naur is a small community known for performing a unique ceremony called *kahika.* The Nars believe that they were brought from heaven by Hurang Narain, claimed to be a Nag Deota (Justa, 1986), which is propitiated by the Nar as a local reincarnation of Krishna. The legend goes that in Satyuga, a boy of five or six years old called Narain suddenly appeared in different villages of the Chuhar valley in the Mandi district on different days and performed miraculous deeds. He eventually lived at Hurang village and then disappeared. The Nars narrate a story that once Hurang Narain suffered from leprosy under the curse of Shiva when he annoyed the latter by protecting Parvati (Shiva's consort) from Shiva's sex rampage. The salvation from this sin was only in the hands of the Narmedhi pandits or Nar dwelling in heaven. Hurang Narain brought two pairs of the Nars named as Chitru-Chakorni and Bichitru-Chanhi who performed the *kahika* or *narkhana yajna* and salvaged Narain. This ceremony was to be repeated periodically. Consequently, the Nars did not return to heaven. One pair of the Nars went to Kullu and the other remained in Mandi and performed *kahika* from time to time. The *kahika* eventually became a popular public ceremony and a fair in which the Nars performed the *chhidra* or *moksa* (salvation) not only of the Deota but also of the people and treated the bewitched persons.

The Nars are localized in the districts of Kullu and Mandi. They live in the hilly terrains and valleys of the river Beas and its tributaries. The climate is cold as the hills remain snowclad in winters. The rainfall is moderate to heavey.

The Nars speak Mandiali and Kulvi dialects of the western Pahari or Himachali. Their dress includes a *pattu, thippu/ghundu* (head gear) for women and a Kullu *topi* for men alongwith *kurta* and *pyjama.*

The dietary habit of the Nars is mainly non-vegetarian. It includes meat of ram and goat, besides fish and eggs. The liquor manufactured locally from molasses of barley called *daru,* and from rice called *dhruwali* is consumed frequently by both men and women. Wheat, rice and maize are common staple foods eaten with *urad, moong, kulthi,* and *masur* pulses and peas, beans cooked in mustard oil or *desi ghee.* Cow's milk is consumed regularly and fruit consumption is mainly seasonal. Food taboos are observed on death only. The *bhaturu, siddu* (baked cakes) and *halwa* of wheat flour are the festive foods along with meat and liquor.

The Nars claim themselves to be of the Bharadwaj *gotra* and call themselves Dhurugan Nar. A few others claim to be of the Kasab *gotra*, but a majority are not aware of their *gotra*. They do not place themselves in the four-fold varna system, though they claim themselves at par with the Brahman as Narmedhi pandits. Other communities treat them equivalent to the Acharaj Brahman or as the *pandit* of the Rakshasha (devils). The Dhurugan Nars of Harabagh near Joginder Nagar treat them at par with the Rajput.

The Nars are endogamous, and usually adhere to village exogamy. *Gotra* exogamy is practised if the *gotra* is known. Consanguinity at cross-cousin levels is preferred. The age of the girl at marriage is about 16 years, and of the boy it is higher. The chief mode of acquiring mates is through negotiation by parents and relatives but *har* marriage with mutual consent is also quite common. The main symbol of marriage is a golden *phulli* (nosepin) besides *sindur* borrowed from the neighbouring Hindus. The Nars practise monogamy but a second wife may be acquired in case of childlessness or death of the first wife. In order to perform the ceremony of *kahika* a Nar has to be married. In case of the death of the first wife the consent of village god is sought to get the person married for the second time. The community has no custom of bride price. Presently Brahmanical marriage rituals are followed and are performed by a Brahman priest by *kanyadan*. Dowry is given in the form of household articles. The residence of the bride is patrilocal. Divorce is permitted by the decision of elderly members of the village. The infants live with the mother but the grown-ups live with their father. The post-divorce maintenance is also decided by the members. Divorcee and widow remarriages are permissible. Junior levirate and sororate are allowed.

The Nars used to live in vertically extended joint families in the recent past, but now the family pattern is largely of nuclear type. The *bahu* touches the feet of her *sasur*, but keeps no avoidance. The joking relationship exists between *devar* and *bhabi*, *jija* and *sali*, and between *mami* and *bhanja*. The male equigeniture is the mode of inheritance and the eldest son succeeds the father. Interfamily bonds are markedly exhibited on the occasion of *kahika*.

The Nar women perform all types of household, agricultural, animal husbandry and domestic duties and seek occasional labour as well. They participate in all social and religious ceremonies but have little say in political activities. They lack the right of inheritance to the property and are considered lower than men in social status.

The birth pollution lasts for fifteen days and purification occurs by taking and sprinkling cow's urine and *ganga jal*. Name is given to the new born child by the *gur* of the Deota on any day. The *dudh-lugru* (cereal taking) ceremony is performed by the *mama* who also does the *jattu* or *mundan* ceremony and presents a *topu* and *cholu* and a rupee to the child. The *jattu* ceremony may be performed on any odd year after the birth and is also performed in case of the first-born daughter whose hair is offered to the Deota. No circumcision, *janeu* and puberty rites exist among the Nars.

A few decades ago, the marriage among the Nars used to be almost ritualless. It used to be performed at the temple of the Deota with the bride presented four *praurh roti* (big loaves of bread) by her parents. Presently the Nars follow rituals typical of the Sanatana *biah*, viz., *samuhat, sand*, oil ceremony, *milni*, four *agniphere* in *vedi* and *kanyadan* which is performed by a Brahman priest. The bride and groom also take three rounds of *pipal* tree leaves and some wild flowers called *kura.* The *kulja*, which is Hurang Narain, is propitiated. The girl's parents arrange one and the boy's parents two *dham* or feats. The *phera ghera* (consummation of marriage) takes place on fifth, seventh, nineth or fifteenth day after marriage.

Panjratna (five gems), namely, honey, Ganges' water, cow's urine, tulsi leaves and gold washings are put in the mouth of a dying person. The deceased is cremated with his *sehra* (wedding crown) on his head. They immerse the ashes of the dead in the Ganges or in some other nearby river. Death pollution lasts for 13 days. Ancestor worship is observed. They themselves perform the *havan* (ritualistic fire-worship) on the tenth day. During the pollution period, the family members do not eat potatoes, onion, garlic and lentil. A crow is given a piece of the daily meal before eating. A *dan* in the name of the dead is given to *dhyan* or *bhanja.* The community is given a meal for which a goat is sacrificed on the fifteenth day.

Presently, land is the major resource of the Nar community. Land is individually owned. The agriculture, is supplemented by horticulture and animal husbandry. Traditionally the Nars used to earn only by taking alms in lieu of providing services of *chhidra* or *moksha* of sins of the Deota and people, and by performing death rites and treating bewitched persons. This occupation is still quite paying. A few Nars have also joined Government service.

They also seek occasional employment on daily wages as road, agricultural and horticultural labourers. Children help their parents in various economic activities. The village market possesses essential commodities. The dealings are in cash.

There is no organized community council or *sabha* of the Nars. However, a few *sayanas* of the village may settle the disputes. If they fail, then *gur* of the Deota is finally entrusted to solve the disputes. The *gur* is instituted by the *pradhan* of the various statutory Gram Panchayats of the area to fulfil the wishes of the people and solve problems through the power of Deota. He may be replaced if he does not meet the demands. Devi Fungni is entrusted if there is mismanagement in the temple of Hurang Narain, and the latter is entrusted in case of such an event in Devi's temple. The punishment is in terms of cash and/or kind.

The Nars propitiate the Hindu trinity gods—Brahma, Vishnu and Mahesh—as well as Shakti in various local forms. Hurang Narain is the chief Deota of the Chuhar valley along with seven other Deotas considered as supporters of the Narain, viz., Pashakot, Pekhre Gahri, Drooni Gahri, Tyala Gahri, Chhawar Gahri, Shilh Gahri and Batheri Gahri. There also are five female deities which are regarded as sisters of Narain and who are revered in the *kahika* ceremony. Devi Fungni is the chief and the others are Kahni Fungni, Ghugsosni, Mahajani and Nauni.

The *kahika* is the major relegious ceremony of the Nars and is arranged as a big *mela* by all the Nars and held after every three years at Bhekhli in Kullu in the month of Jeth, and after every fourth year at Padhar and every fifth year at Hurang in Mandi during the month of Sawan and Bhadon (August-September) on a Wednesday, Thursday and Friday respectively. This ritual is held at Hurang, Paddhar, Kataula and Panjani in Mandi district and at Rohlagi, Dyar, Shirar, Dhara, Bharain and a number of other villages in Kullu district after scheduled intervals.

On the first two days people sing and dance. The third day is for the *kahika yajna* in which *gurs* of all eight male and five female deities participate. They are offered a special drink called *thathu vangu ka pani* prepared from over hundred types of herbs/plants. A Nar chosen by the *deota* to perform *kahika* remains on fast. He is revered as Mahadev (Shiva) and his wife as Shakti (Parvati or Sita).

Four slick-like pieces of wood from *kushtika* tree are brought by persons known as Jamam for making a small *vedi,* and for constructing a bigger *vedi,* four sticks, about 7 or 8 feet long, of the *deodar* tree are used. The bigger *vedi* is called *kahika.* The ritual takes place within the periphery of the altar. Four *khadu* (rams) are slaughtered on the four corners of the *kahika mandap.* The Nar recites *mantras*, pours *dhruwali* into the *havan kund* and throws barley, rice and leaves of *bekhal*, *shami* and *bhang* on *deota's* idol to perform his *chhidra* or *moksha*. Then *chhidra* of the people is also performed. With this, all sins of the god and the people go to the Nar. During the ritual a musical instrument called *dhapli* is played by the Nar. Then the *gur* of the *deota* pours water and *bekhal* leaves on the Nar and the idol of the *deota* is put on his chest. Consequently, the Nar becomes unconscious and is laid down on a wooden plank like a corpse. All the gathered Nars and the wife of the Nar utter obscene and sexual abuses and exhibit objects prepared out of wood (*linga*) and gourd (*yoni*) depicting sex act. By doing so, it is believed that the *yogni* (fairies), who can keep the Nar unconscious for long, do not land on the *kahika* site. Then the *arthi* (funeral procession) of the unconscious Nar is taken round the temple. He recovers within three hours. But a Nar not serious about observing *kahika* rules, recovers late and may even die, though this is a rare event. In such cases, all offerings of the *deota* are given to his wife in compensation. At this time, two *gurs* who are called *Jogni-re-gur* and two other persons called Dummach are appointed by the *deota* to keep the expenditure under control.

Besides *Kahkia* here are many annual fairs and festivals of social, socioeconomic and socioreligious importance in which the Nars participate like other people. The community is not involved in any socioreligious movement.

The Nars lack any specific tradition of plastic and graphic arts specific to them but know folksongs, folklore and music and dance. The folktale of Hurang Narain is told during *kahika*. They share regional folksongs and dances, notably, *Nati* and *Lalri*. The commonly used musical instrument are *khanjar, taee* (bell), *thali*, *nagara*, *damru* and *karnal* (a long brass pipe).

The Nar community is traditionally linked with other communities on ritual basis in removing their sins and treating bewitched persons. They accept only *sidha* or *sukka* food from the Jogi/Nath, Batehra, Chamar, Lohar, etc. The Rajput and the Brahman accept only *sidha* food from the Nar, but the latter accepts *kachcha* as well as *pucca* food from a Rajput and a Brahman. The connubial norms are limited to the community, barring a few exceptions of *har* (elopement) marriage with Rajput. Putative kinship exists with other communities. The Nars have an access to the house of a Rajput and a Brahman except to the kitchen. They have also an access to temples, schools, Gram Panchayat and may even share cremation grounds with some. The *jajmani* system exists only with the Brahman priest and the Lohar. Modern intercommunity linkages have not developed much as the Nar community does not have elite, teachers, doctors, engineers, scholars and persons holding white-collar jobs among them, except for a few persons in jobs.

The Nars favour and have received modern facilities of roads, drinking water, electricity, mass media, health and medical care, immunization of children, public distribution system and banking, etc. They use chemical fertilizers and insecticides as well. Family control measures, however, have not been welcomed by the older generation of the Nar, which wanted more children especially a male child because they believed that their population was not growing. Some younger men have, however, got vasectomized. Their children usually do not go for college education due to economic reasons although they are receiving secondary school education. Integrated Rural Development Programmes (IRDP) have not made much impact on the Nar. The community still thrives well on its traditional ritualistic pattern. They use traditional energy resources like firewood, cowdung cakes and agricultural straw. They have a special reverence for *deodar* tree which is indirectly helpful in the preservation of forests.

A.R. Sankhyan

NICHAR

The Nichar or Nachar is a community of traditional singers, dancers and folk dramatists. The word 'Nichar' appears to be derived from *nat* or *nrit, nritya* or *nach* in Hindi. They are considered an offshoot of the Chamar, but do not carry on the traditional job of removing carcass, skinning, etc., and as such differ from them in this sense. The Nichars are distributed in the lower hills, but primarily inhabit Una district. The community identifies itself at the regional level. No ethnographic account exists, but historical accounts are there, according to which they are indigenous to the State. An exact population figure for them is not available but according to the estimate of the people they would be around a few thousands in the State. They speak Pahari amongst themselves and with others, and use Devanagari script. They are characterised by their long, flowing hair and pink-coloured turbans. The men do not keep moustaches or beard. Long hair and clean shaven face help them to dress like a woman or a saint of their folk theatre. Their dress consists of *safa, kurta* and *chooridar pyjama* whereas that of their women consists of *chooridar suthan, kurti* and an *orhni*.

The Nichar had a place of religious importance in their community and that is why they abstained from alcohol and non-vegetarian food, but gradually with the passage of time they have turned occasional non-vegetarians. The use of buffalo meat and beef is prohibited for them. Their staple diet consists of *roti* of *makki, bajra, chari* or *chola* with pulses of *mah, moong, chana* or *moth*. Occasionally they also consume vegetables, roots and tubers, but are especially fond of *redu* and *palada* (curd preparations). Milk is taken in tea but *lassi* is often taken. The food is cooked usually in the oil of *til* but occasionally mustard and *toriya* oils are also used. They are also fond of smoking tobacco and drinking liquor which is purchased from the market.

Monogamy is the usual form of marriage which is performed in adulthood by negotiation. Only nearest remembered relatives are avoided for contracting matrimonial alliances. The marriage symbols of bangles, finger ring, ear-rings and nose-ring are rigidly observed. Marriage is solemnized by *kanyadan*. Dowry is nominal and is given as per one's economic status in kind. Divorce is permitted with social approval by either party on grounds of maladjustment. The children in a divorce case are the liability of the father. In the event of divorce compensation is paid to the wife by way of return of marriage expenses. Widow, widower, divorcee remarriage are permissible and so are levirate and sororate.

The rule of residence after marriage is patrilocal and the family is vertically extended. Paternal and filial affiliations form the basis of mutual love and respect, which are based on factors like age and sex. Avoidance is observed between daughter-in-law and father-in-law and between younger brother's wife and husband's elder brother. This is observed more in the initial years of marriage than in the subsequent years. Joking relationship also exists between potential mates, e.g., between elder brother's wife and husband's younger brother, with wife's elder sister and younger sister, and with wife's elder brother and younger brothers. Though the atmosphere in the family is cordial, sometimes conflicts do come up on property issues. Inheritance is as per male equigeniture and succession is patrilineal. Besides the division of property, even the *chauka* (a territorial unit in which they operate) is also divided equally among the sons.

The Nichar women have equal status with men. They take part in agricultural operation, animal husbandry, they collect fuel, fetch water and have roles in other economic activities, social functions, rituals and in religious spheres but have no role in politics or mechanism of social control and have no decision-making power. They contribute to family income but do not control expenditure.

In the sphere of life-cycle rituals pre-delivery rituals are observed in the ninth month of pregnancy, invoking blessings of the divine powers for the safe delivery of the child. Certain restrictions are also imposed on the mother with respect to her movements. She is not allowed to move alone in the night, or witness a sight of a dreadful object or see a funeral or move about during the eclipse. These precautions are taken for preventing abortions or for avoiding any deformity in the child. Certain restrictions are also imposed on the movement of the mother for a period of nine days, until which time she is not allowed to enter the kitchen. Only after taking the purificatory bath is she allowed to take over the charge of the household duties and move out of the house. The child is named by the father or an elderly person of the community. When the child attains the age of five to six months, on an auspicious day the child is fed with a sweet preparation of rice and milk by the mother, and the lips are touched to all the types of food ordinarily taken by the community.

Marriage is performed at the bride's residence. The boy proceeds, heading the procession, to the girl's house dressed in an attire which consists of a *sehra*, *pata* and a *baint*. Marriage is performed as per Vedic rites by a priest of their own community. Thereafter, the bride is brought home on a *peedi* which is given the shape of a *doli* by tying it with a rope and suspending it from a bamboo pole. The groom follows the bride on foot. A marriage feast is given by the bride's parents. The consummation of marriage takes place at the groom's residence.

The dead are cremated. Their mortal remains are immersed in the river or a flowing stream. Pollution is observed for a period of ten days when purificatory rites are performed. Thereafter mortuary rituals are observed every month and on each death anniversary when alms are given to the Acharaj for the peace of the departed soul.

A significant change which has been observed in the life-cycle rituals is that traditionally the use of *nagara, shehnai* and band was prohibited and so was the use of *sukpal* or *palki*. But over the passage of time these restrictions have gradually vanished.

The Nichars continue their traditional occupation of singing, dancing, working as labourer, working on *adha-batai* (half share-cropping) agriculture, *banbatue* (rope makers) and preparation of shoes from tanned and processed leather. But due to the efforts under the Scheduled Castes and Scheduled Tribes Special Component Plan they are being imparted training and assistance to set up shops to work as cobblers, for dairy and poultry farming. They have also taken up other occupations like animal husbandry, business and Government and private service, where payment is made in cash and kind. They have direct links with the local market which is fully regulated, where barter and cash form the mode of exchange. Child labour is reported.

Social control is maintained by their own Biradari Panchayat which is homogeneous in character and members of which are elected by voice votes on consideration of age, status and knowledge. They dispense justice on issues arising out of infringement of social norms, disputes over land and water, adultery and rape. They also penalize the offender by cash fine or social boycott. Statutory panchayats do exist after Independence which are heterogeneous in composition. They plan and implement welfare and developmental activities.

The Nichars are Hindu by faith and have reverence for family, clan, village and regional deities and for deities of the wider Hindu order. They have reverence for Guga Pir. Their sacred specialists are from the same community who officiate at *rites-de-passage* and also cure ailments and remove effects of evil spirits. The Nichars take part in all local fairs and festivals which are of social and religious significance.

The Nichars are famous for their *dahaja* ceremony which is an exorcist ritual and is celebrated either once a year or once in a couple of years as per their convenience. The basis for this celebration is Chamarad (locality of the Chamar). Every Chamarad has a *kunn* (a place of saints) which is known for the protection of the cattle. The jurisdiction of a *kunn* may extend well beyond the limits of the village. Whenever an epidemic afflicts the cattle, the presiding deity is propitiated by burning incense in the cowshed and beating the *nad* (drum). The *garha* deity acts as a protector. Such is the sanctity of *garha* that no evil can cross the *garha* and enter in their locality. The Nichars do not have *kunn* or *garha* in their locality but they are found in the locality of the Chamars which they share. It is believed that the sacred saints have 360 *sirkis* (sections), but before these are propitiated, the *garha* is propitiated by the *chela* who is from the Nichar community and performs the *dahaja*. It would therefore be appropriate to explain *dahaja* as a ceremony of nightlong tantric ritual, in which various kinds of songs, dances, folktheatre and tantric rituals are performed. The ceremony starts with the acting of Krishanalila which is followed by Lala Faqir and Baura Agri dances. Other associated rituals are acting of Gwar Jat, Gaddi, Bangali, Panch Malang, Dau, Hanuman, Bhairon, Kali Ma, acting of horse and of vehicle of goddess Shakti. The ritual concludes in the morning at four o'clock with the acting of the vehicle of Basa Sidh and offerings of prayers.

The women folk of the community are deft in the art of floor and wall painting as also in basket and cloth embroidery. They also have oral traditions which are in the form of folklores and folktales, relating to Baba Bhathari, Prithvi Singh Rathore, Hir-Ranjha, Sohni-Mahiwal, Mirza-Sahiba, and Hari-Chand. Regional folksongs like *shabad* or *pad, gawah* and *panch malang* are sung and *nati* is played. They also play *dholak*, but men only participate in dance.

As regards intercommunity linkages, though traditionally, a Nichar can accept water, *kachcha*, *pucca* and *sidha* food from all the *savarna* communities, the latter would not accept the same from them. *Jal* and *kachcha* food is exchanged with communities of similar ritual status. Connubial relations are restricted to one's own community. Putative kinship exists. They share wells, crematoria and religious shrines with other communities. They participate in traditional festivals where they dance and sing, for which they are remunerated. Symbiotic relationship does exist. With their wider worldview, the community now has creative artists and members in defence services.

In the sphere of development programme, their attitude towards formal education has been favourable for boys, but only partly favourable for girls. Both drop out after primary or secondary schools, as they have to earn to support their parents. Their attitude is favourable towards modern system of medicare, which they fully use in addition to traditional medicare, but their attitude is not favourable for family welfare programmes. Drinking water is available within the locality through pipes. Integrated Rural Development Programme, Rural Employment Guarantee Scheme and Self-Employment Scheme have helped them to improve their lot. They listen to radio and visit cinema and also see movies shown by extension agencies. Roads and post offices exist, but railways do not reach their area. Electricity, mid-day meal, Integrated Child Development Scheme and facility of public distribution system are availed of but due to the non-availability of irrigational facilities only organic manure is used. Attitude towards savings is favourable and the people are not as much dependent on moneylenders.

O.P. Shant

NOONGAR

The Noongar, Nungar, Teli-Julaha, or Teli, as they are often referred to, according to a historical myth, are an offshoot of the Julaha, and now a separate community. Initially the Noongars were Julaha, but at some point of time in their unremembered past they married Teli woman, from whom the progeny of Noongars came up. Thus, the original section of the Julaha are known as Deswala and the other as Teli-Julaha (Rose 1919:414). Rose further states: "...the eastern Julaha are said to be divided into two great sections, Deswale or those of the country and Tel, the latter being supposed to be descended from a Julaha who married a Teli woman are socially inferior to the former."

The Noongars are confined to Punjab, Haryana and the union territory of Chandigarh. In Himachal Pradesh they are settled in various parts of Paonta tehsil in Sirmaur district, occupying the cis-Giri tract. A few families are also in Kullu district. The Noongar of Himachal Pradesh have emigrated from Marwa village in Haryana since the time of their great grandparents. They are included and enumerated along with the Muslims. No current population figures are available, but according to the 1911 Census their total population in the State was only 40. In Paonta they are chiefly found in Bangram and Misrawala villages. Ever since their emigration they have left their traditional calling and have taken to agriculture.

The dialect spoken by the people is Haryanavi mixed with Sirmauri, both among themselves and with others, though at times they also speak Urdu with outsiders. They write in Devanagari.

The community is non-vegetarian, but also takes meat of sheep, goat, chicken and fish. Pork, beef or buffalo meat is prohibited. Their staple diet consists of wheat or *makki* bread, rice and pulses or *moong*, *urad* and *chana*. The usual cooking medium is mustard oil, but occasionally *til-ka-tel* and *desi ghee* are also used. Roots and tubers, especially of *turar* and *sarar,* are also consumed. *Khumb* (wild mushroom) is also consumed during the rainy season. Berries and plums are occasionally consumed as fruits. Vegetables are also occasionally taken. Milk is taken only by the young and the invalid. Others take it in tea and make *lassi* out of it.

The Noongars smoke tobacco in *hukka.* Liquor is prohibited, but those who have left the village and have gone to urban centres have started taking it. A special food preparation *seviyan* is cooked on Id-ul-fitr, whereas mutton is a must on Bakrid. Similarly, restrictions also exist on the taking of food during the 40 days period of mourning in Muharram, or in the event of death.

During the period of *roza*, food and water is also taken only before sunrise and after sunset.

The Noongars are divided into a member of exogamous groupings called *gots*, which is atypical of a Muslim community. Their *got* names, Badgujar and Chauhan, indicate their being Hindu Rajput converts. The traditional parallel cousin marriage have now been given up. Only one's self *got* is excluded for entering into matrimonial ties. Cross-cousin marriages are however practised. These *gots* indicate ancestry and regulate marriages. Among the Julahas they perceive themselves superior to the Deswalis.

The Noongars are endogamous. Exogamy at the *got* level is observed. Hypergamy is also practised. They can accept daughters as bride from the Deswalis but would not give their daughters to them. Marriages with mother's brother's daughter and father's sister's daughter are practised. Junior levirate and sororate are also practised. They are monogamous, but in the event of the first wife being unable to give family a heir, polygyny is resorted to with the consent of the first wife.

The usual age of marriage is 15 years for girls and 17 years for boys. Marriage is performed by *nikah*, in the presence of a *maulvi* and two *gawah*. If the boy and the girl agree to live together as husband and wife, in consideration of a fixed amount of *mehar*. Till about two years back this was decided verbally, but now the *nikahnama* is signed by the boy, *maulvi* and the two *gawah*, and a copy of it is given to the girl.

Batta-satta is another form of marriage, where two families exchange their daughters as brides. The symbol of marriage amongst the womenfolk is nose-pin and glass bangles. The *mehar* amount is fixed and it consists of Rs. 32.25 of silver coins or its equivalent money in the present-day currency. It is promised for payment on demand but is paid on the annulment of *nikah*. At times, the woman foregoes her *mehar* voluntarily or picks up any item of the house and accepts it as equivalent in value to her *mehar*. The rule of residence is patrilocal, but soon the newly married sons separate out and set up their individual family. In the event of there being no son in the family, a *gharjamai* (resident son-in-law) is invited to look after the family.

Talaq is permissible on grounds of infidelity and maladjustment. The proceedings can be initiated by either of the aggrieved parties in the Biradari Panchayat. The utterance of the word *talaq* thrice in the presence of the panchayat nullifies the marriage. If the boy divorces the girl, he has to return the *daj* and the *mehar*, but if the girl divorces then nothing is given; both the *mehar* and the *daj* are forfeited. In the event of the wife eloping with her paramour, her paramour has to pay the compensation to her earlier husband which is decided by the panchayat. Widow, widower and divorcee remarriage is permissible. Widow remarriage is known as *karewa*, and if she marries the deceased husband's younger brother, it is known as *baithana*. In all these cases, *nikah* is performed again.

The family is of nuclear type, but the household is joint. Interpersonal relations within the family are those of love and cordiality. The eldest male member commands great respect and his decision on all family matters is final. A situation of conflict and confrontation usually comes up when there is a check on the freedom of youngsters. Purdah is observed with husband's elder relatives, and joking relationship exists with all younger relatives of the husband and wife. A bride, no matter how old she may be, will cover her face with a veil, while coming in front of elders. The property is inherited in the male line with all sons inheriting the parental property along with the mother. The mother's share passes on to the son who serves her during her old age.

The status of women is equal to that of the men. The married women have a right of inheritance to their husband's property for her lifetime. The women have a major role in agricultural operations, for, besides ploughing they do everything, in their own fields as well as on others' field as agricultural labourer and get cash. They collect fuel and fodder and bring water from river. They take part in all social and religious functions, and offer *namaz* at home. They have no role in political spheres, and in the mechanism of social control except in family management. They contribute and control the family expenditure.

Post-natal restriction and *chila* (period of pollution) is observed for 40 days. When the child is 40 days' old, the *maulvi*, gives a name to the child. The first head-shaving of the male child is also done when the child is of 1 $^{1}/_{4}$ months by the Nai. This is known as *aqiqa*. When the child is of two to four years of age, *khatna* is performed for the boy to mark his initiation. This is also known as *musalmani*.

Marriage rituals are performed at the bride's residence. *Dawat-e-walima* (marriage feast) is given by the bride's parents. Later on when the bride reaches the groom's residence, another feast is given by some well-to-do families. Consummation of marriage takes place at the groom's residence.

The dead are buried, and a *mazar* is made over the grave. The house remains polluted for a period of 40 days. On the third, tenth, twentieth, and after 1 $^{1}/_{4}$ months, *tehiai, daswa, biswan,* and *kul* are observed, when rice is cooked and the *maulvi* and the family members eat for the peace of the departed soul. After the observance of fortieth day ceremony the house becomes free of pollution.

Land is the major resource of the Noongars, which is individually owned by the family till such time that partition occurs. Though the traditional occupation of the Noongars had been weaving, it has been given up as the primary source of livelihood since the last 50 years. Traditionally the indigenous population living near the forest had certain *hakuks* by virtue of which they received wood for house construction at nominal rates, free fuel and fodder, but now are without these *hakuks*. Now the primary occupation is agriculture, and the secondary is labour in road building or house construction. Some also cultivate the land of big farmers on *batai*, sharing the 50 per cent of the produce or by *theka* on cash contract.

The Noongars have direct links with the market, which is fully regulated. Cash is the standard form of exchange. They depend on the market for selling their produce and buying things. There is an increasing tendency in the rise of casual labourers. Children below 15 years, especially boys, tend the cattle and assist their parents in agricultural operations. Girls help their mothers in household and agricultural operations of their own and of others' for which they are paid in cash.

The Noongars have a traditional Biradari Panchayat. It is headed by a chief called *mukhiya* who is elected by voice vote, and is at times also assisted by elderly members in arriving at the decisions. The judgement pronounced by the *mukhiya* is final and is to be honoured. The Biradari Panchayat maintains social control and punish for the offences related to elopement, divorce, adultery and disrespect of traditional norms. The punishment is in form of cash fine, which is given to the aggrieved party. Traditional social excommunication is no longer practised. Though statutory panchayats have come up, it is the traditional ones which have a greater hold among the Noongars.

The Noongars belong to the Sunni sect. They have faith in Khera Dev, the village deity who is represented by a *pipal* tree. They also have family affiliation to pirs like Baba Bule Shah, Baba Garib Nath, and Dorian Wala Peer. They also take part in the Urs of Makdoor Shah, Nau Gaza Pir and Sabir Mian, which fall on specific days of lunar calendar.

Their major festivals are Id, Bakrid, Muharram and Shaberat. On Muharram *tazia* is collectively built by the village. It is buried on the banks of river Giri as there is no *karbala*. Their sacred specialists are *maulvis*, who are engaged in religious teaching, performing birth, marriage and death rites and protecting people from evil spirits.

The Noongars specialize in the art of weaving *durri* which they sell to supplement their income. Women also do embroidery for domestic purposes. They share oral traditions of the region in the form of folklore and folktales. Folksongs are sung by both men and women separately.

They exchange both *kachcha* and *pucca* food with all Muslim communities, irrespective of their occupation. They even share bell-metal receptacles with them. They would accept both *kachcha* and *pucca* food from the Hindu. The Noongars are traditionally offered food by the Hindus in separate utensils of stoneware crockery, enamel or aluminium which are kept aside. Similar restrictions occur regarding the sharing of *hukka* and on entering the house. There is no restriction on sharing of the burial grounds with other Muslims.

Cultivator-labour relationships exist between the Noongars and the scheduled castes, especially sweepers, who are paid at the harvesting time in lieu of the services rendered by them. Other forms of symbiotic relationship and exchange of labour also exist. Political leadership has emerged at the local panchayat level. A few of the community people are members of the statutory panchayat. They also take part in all elections.

The impact of formal education both for boys and girls among the Noongars is unsatisfactory. The grown-ups are illiterates, whereas many middle-aged people are without formal education. Only a few younger boys and girls are sent to school, but they also drop out after primary schooling for lack of interest and guidance, economic and social reasons. Of late just two Noongar boys have studied up to matriculation in the Sirmaur district.

Though their attitude towards traditional and modern system of medicare is favourable; it is not towards the small family norm. Couples prefer any number of children as children are regarded as gift of God.

Drinking water is brought from the river. A few houses have received a loan of Rs. 6,000 for establishing shops under the Integrated Rural Development Programme. Under Rural Employment Guarantee Scheme, people have got jobs in road building. A few others have also got jobs in the Balvadi Kendras being run by Parvatiya Adim Jati Sewak Sangh.

The village is connected by *pucca* and *kachcha* road. The people listen to radio, transistors and also watch television on the community sets. Cinema is also seen occasionally in towns and in the village shown by the extension agencies. Post offices exist at a distance. All the houses are electrified. The fuel resource is firewood, but also occasionally kerosene.

The attitude of the people towards organic and chemical fertilizers is favourable. Integrated Child Development Scheme is available which provides nutrition and immunization to the expectant and nursing mothers, and to children between 0-5 years. Public distribution system is availed of. Their attitude towards savings and investments is less favourable. Whatever little they save is kept at home and not in the banks.

Rajendra Sarkar

OD

The Od is a small and little-known scheduled caste. The name is also pronounced as Oud or Ud and is synonymous with the Beldar of Uttar Pradesh . In Kullu (the study area) they are confined to the Outer Seraj area in Ani tehsil and are not aware of their origins and/or migration history. Rose (1919) reported that the Ods were vagrant people wandering for employment in earth work and claimed Rajput ancestry from Marwar. A legend goes that Bhagirath, their ancestor, vowed never to drink twice out of the same well and used to dig a fresh well each time for water. Once he continued digging but water did not turn up, and so he never returned. As such his descendants continued the earth work. This is probably why the Ods bury their dead despite being Hindus (Rose, 1919). The Od in Kullu district, however, cremate their dead and claim ancestry from the Chauhan clan of the Rajputs. They derive the etymology of the word Od from *oda* meaning boundary stone. They occupy a very difficult hilly terrain in Ani (Kullu), Kumarsain (Shimla) and Karsog (Mandi). These are more than 5000 feet high and are covered with thin to thick pine, *deodar* and *kail* forests. The hill tops receive moderate snowfall in winter. Their total population is only 639 in Himachal Pradesh according to the 1981 Census. They wear a Pahari dress. The women almost always wear a woollen jacket as a community trait. Men wear a popular Kullu *topi*. They speak regional dialects like Saraji (a variation of the Kulvi) and Mandiali of the western Pahari and communicate in the Devanagari script.

The Ods are non-vegetarian people and eat meat of *khadu* (ram) more commonly than of goat. Their staple food is maize and rice in winter and wheat and barley in most of the summer season, along with pulses of *urad, moong, kulthi,* peas and beans cooked in mustard oil, *til*, *desi ghee* or *shari gutti ka tel* (apricot oil). Potatoes are consumed frequently and other green vegetables are consumed to a moderate degree. Fruits like plum, apricot and apples are consumed in plenty and seasonally. The home-made *daru* (liquor) is quite often consumed by both men and women, especially on festive occasions. *Bhaturu, siddu* and *halwa* of wheat are the festive preparations along with meat and liquor. Cow's milk is taken by children. Food taboos are observed on the death of a family member. The food habits have changed slightly from non-vegetarian to vegetarian as meat has become a costly item and the intake of vegetables and fruits has increased.

All Ods claim to be of the Chauhan clan, besides two finer social units, viz., the Chhin and the Bithu, claimed as their *gots*. These denote their descent and may regulate marriages, though matrimony is unavoidable within a *got*. They claim themselves to be Kshatriya in the fourfold varna hierarchy. They usually do not like to be called as Od but proclaim themselves to be Thavi, who have a well-known Rajput status. This has resulted mainly due to their recent adoption of masonry as an occupation (Thavi are also in the same profession). But their social status is considered low by the Rajput of the area.

The Ods are an endogamous community, and permit village endogamy. Marriages may occur at the cross-cousin level. To salvage them from the sin of marrying within the *got*, the priest performs a *got chhidra* ritual at marriage. The age of the girl at marriage is usually above 15 years and that of the boy above 18 years. The chief mode of acquiring mates is through negotiation by a *kharodi* (middleman) but *har* (elopement) marriage also occurs, marriage also occurs through exchange of sisters and through purchases, monogamy is the general practice but a second wife may be acquired in case of childlessness and /or due to want of a son from the first wife. A golden *phulli* and *sindur* are symbols of a married woman. Bride price was prevalent a few decades back but now it is taken in cases of the marriage of an aged man, or a widower remarriage and in case of a man who has married twice. Now the Ods have also adopted the practice of giving dowry. It is given in the form of household articles and agricultural implements.

The *lari* lives patrilocally, but the practice of *ghar jamai* also exists. Divorce is uncommon but is permitted socially in cases of maladjustment, cruelty, impotency and insanity. If a girl divorces and remarries another man, the new husband has to pay the *reet* to the previous husband. Widow remarriage is called *chadar dalna* or *jhanjrara*. Divorce compensation is decided by the Biradari Panchayat and is paid to the aggrieved spouse or to the parents. The children are the liability of the father. Significant changes have occurred in the marriage institution. Bride price has given way to dowry and the age of girl at marriage has increased. For divorce, legal procedures may also be followed.

The family pattern is predominantly nuclear, but vertically extended families also exist. The *lari* keeps no avoidance from her *saurah* and /or *jeth*. The father's elder brother is addressed as *bara bapu* and the younger brother as *chhota bapu*. The elder sister is addressed as *daee*. Joking relations exist between *devar* and *bhabi*, *jija* and *sali*, *jija* and *sala*, and between *nanad/nanan* and *bhabi*. The inheritance is patrilineal as per male equigeniture and the eldest son succeeds the father. Their families are well interlinked on all occasions of joys and help each other during harvesting. They also attend to each other's guests and render hospitality. The conflicts and confrontations are however not uncommon and can occur on account of children's issues, encroachment into other's agricultural house territories, damage to crop by cattle, etc. The fall of the joint family system is the main change in the family institution.

The Od women lack the right of inheritance to parental property. Though they are kept in lower social status than men, but for all practical purposes they enjoy great freedom and command in household, social and religious activities. They manage the household, collect firewood and fodder, fetch potable water, work in fields and occasionally or seasonally also earn money by working as horticultural labourers. They however have little or no role in political activities.

The delivery is performed at home by an experienced woman of the village. The woman becomes pure by taking cow's urine and the water of the Ganges after 13 days of the *sutak*. The birth of a son is rejoiced by slaughtering a goat and serving to the community. The *bajantri*, a musical band party from the Koli/Lohar sends *badhaee* (greetings) to the parents of the new born. Name may be given on any day by consulting a Brahman priest. *Dudh lugru* (cereal-taking ceremony) is observed. The main childhood ritual is *jattu* or *jaru* (tonsure)which may be performed at a Devi's temple by the *pujari*. The Od girls get their ear and nose pierced but no ceremony is observed for this purpose.

A *kharodi* (negotiator) along with the boy's father goes to the girl's place for *barni* (engagement). The marriage rituals are performed by a *pandit* in accordance with Sanatana prescriptions. A *vedi* is erected and *lagan* and *ved* rituals are performed along with *vedic mantra* when the *lara* and *lari* take seven *pheras* of the sacred fire. The ladies sing songs in which Lord Rama and Sita figure prominently, and the *bajantris* gives instrumental music. The bride's parents give a feast to the groom's party. The dowry articles are exhibited and the *barat* returns when the *lara* and *lari* are carried in a *palki* by the *kahar*. The bride enters her in-laws' house after *deori pujan*. The *daroja* or *pheru gheru*, or *muklawa* occurs immediately after the marriage in case of *ghar byah* but on the following day in case of *dohra byah* when a part of the rituals is performed at the boy's village. The nuptial ceremony occurs at the boy's place. Earlier, the Ods used to observe only a few marriage rituals but due to an outside contact, they now observe elaborate marriage rituals as per the Sanatana Dharam Byah Paddhati.

The Ods cremate their dead. The *astu* are immersed in the Ganges at Hardwar or in the Satluj. The sons get their head shaved off, called *chhilbhadran,* at the death of their father. Ancestor worship is observed on the thirteenth day marking the end of the pollution period. A *kartu* (Charaj/ Acharaj) performs death rites and takes offerings. *Khadu* used to be sacrificed earlier. Men who die of leprosy are not cremated but buried and their death is not lamented but enjoyed and no ancestor worship is observed in such cases.

The Ods is traditionally a mason community but presently being a landowning community it also practises agriculture, animal husbandry and horticulture. They take contracts for building/house construction and are also employed as bridge and dam *mistri* (masons). Many of them are both masons as well as carpenters. Child labour exists. The mode of giving wages is in cash. The local market is fully regulated and is of daily nature but located at distance.

The changes noticed in the Ods' economic life are mainly that they have also adopted agriculture, horticulture and animal husbandry as subsidiary or supplementary occupations though, these are in some cases the main source of livelihood. Some have also adopted carpentry along with traditional masonry.

There is a heterogeneous or multi-community sabha in which mutual disputes are solved by *sayane* of the village. But presently this institution has lost hold on the people and a *pradhan* of the statutory Gram Panchayat may perform this role either in his personal capacity or through the panchayat. The decision of the Gram Panchayat is generally acceptable and/or binding on the people. The Gram Pancha*yat* also performs the usual welfare and developmental activities.

The Ods are Hindus and propitiate the pantheon gods and goddesses in various local forms. Pachhla Devi is their *kulja.* The shrines of a village deity may or may not exist in all the villages. The Thanedar is propitiated as a village male deity. There are six main male local deities whose shrines are located in different villages and propitiated by the Ods as well as by other community people, namely Shamshari Mahadev (Shamshar), Kulchhetra, Mahadev (Olva), Jigeshwar Mahadev (Dalash) and Kuikanda Nag (Shirogi). Two main female deities of the area are: Pachhla Devi (Javan) and Kushumba Mata (Khekhsu). These local deities are propitiated during the annual fairs.

Four fairs are famous in the Od area of Outer Saraj. These are : (a) The Ani Fair during 7th to 9th May in which three deities , Shamshari Mahadev, Pachhla Devi and Panevi Nag participate; (b) The Vashta Fair (8-9 June), in which Pachhla Devi, Kuikanda Nag and Kulchhetra Mahadev are revered; (c) the Dalash Fair (August) in which two deities, Jigeshwar Mahadev and Kuikanda Nag are propitiated; and (d) The Ranikot Fair (6-7 September), in which Panevi Nag and Kuinwari Mahadev are propitiated. The Shamshar Mahadev of the area participates in the famous Kullu Dussehra.

Five festivals are celebrated with more fun and frolic by the Ods, namely, Shivratri, Krishan Janamashtmi, Diwali, Budhi Diwali and Dussehra, which are of great socioreligious importance to them. The sacred specialists are from within or from other communities, viz., a oracle, may be from the Koli/Lohar or other communities, and their priest is a Brahman. Recently the Ods are involved in socioreligious movements of the Radhaswami and Nirankari missions in Kotgarh area.

There is traditional weaving by women as a craft, but for their own family use. They share regional folksongs (*Natisong, Nahni, Bamnu, Lari Shanta*, etc.) and folktales (*Bala Dhyalu, Minyo Ranjha, Raja Bhoj, Kajhera, Alibaba Chali Chor, Sekh Chilu*, etc.). Two main dances are the *Nati* dance and *Thambru Nach* in which both men and women participate. The common instrumental music is given by *karnal* and *nagara* by the *Bajantari*.

All public places, temples, schools, etc., are shared but they have their own cremation grounds. The Isai (Christian) collects cremation wood when an Od dies, and the latter digs graves for the Isai. Political leadership has emerged at village panchayat level only and they have no members holding white-collar jobs, and administrators, engineers, doctors, teachers and persons in defence services, etc.

Their attitude towards modern developmental programmes in respect of literacy and education, family planning, health and medical care is favourable and these activities have also made some impact on the community. Their children receive school education but higher education is beyond their reach and means due to economic and geographical constraints. Their houses are electrified but modern mass media (T.V. and newspapers) are yet awaited. Some men have got vasectomized and the attitude towards small family size is slowly becoming more positive. Modern medical facilities are available in the town but due to difficult terrain are not availed of except in serious cases. Indigenous herbs prescribed by local medicine men and treatment by oracles to remove malevolent spirits are still favoured. The public distribution system through ration cards, banking facilities and immunization of children are available to them. Under IRDP, special training in carpentry is available, and they also get 50 per cent subsidies on purchase of chemical fertilizers. The Ods live in wood and stone built houses. The firewood, cowdung cakes and agricultural products are used as fuel. Most of the people depend upon the local landlords or moneylenders for financial assistance.

A.R. Sankhyan

PAJIARA

The Pajiara or Paziara is a traditional community of worshippers residing in parts of Shimla and Sirmaur districts. Locally this community is called Pajiara but some address it as Pajiala, Paziala, Pryehru and Pijara. In Shimla, they are called Pijara or Pizara. The worshippers of the goddess temples in Shivalik region are called Bhojki but the Pajiara community of Shimla, Sirmaur and other areas are not Bhojki. They live in village Pujarli near Hatkoti, Dharaich, Tiali, Chikkar, Janog and Jais in Shimla district and Rajgarh, Shillai as well as Renuka tehsils of Sirmaur distinct. They are a branch of Brahman community and even in Rajputs this subgroup is distinct in nature. There are Bharadwaj and Kashyap clans among Brahman Pajiara, whereas the Rajput Pajiaras have Chouhan, Kashyap and other clans. The Brahman Pajiara community is generally attached to *upneore deothiye* (gods who sprang naturally and have no parents) whereas the Rajput Pajara or Pajiara community is associated with *manchh deothiye* (gods who were in human form some time).

The Pajiaras are attached to the village temples in the areas where the village god system is prevalent. Now they are landed property holders as the lands of gods which they cultivated and maintained in the name of a particular deity have since been transferred to them according to the land reforms and ownership provisions and they have been declared the owners of the property. They are the custodian of the village god and none from other communities is allowed to decorate the palanquin of god or lift it. The Pajiaras migrated to various villages with the local gods and as such the history of their migration to the present areas is based on legends only. The community is devoted to the village god institution and is not of *karamkand* nature. The habitats is surrounded by high hills and cold zones where snowfall occurs and the winter season is quite severe. In lower region of Sirmaur, the climate is pleasant, tolerable and attractive. The community is located in the apple belt.

In the past they used local Tankri /Bhatakshri for communication and for maintaining temple records. Now they use Devanagari script. Their dialect is Mahasu in Shimla, Sirmauri in Sirmaur and other local dialects in other areas. In some cases the male worshipper of the *gur* (oracle) keeps long hair. They belong to *savarna* caste.

They are, by and large, vegetarian but in case of non-vegetarian habits, the person who performs *puja* or is the oracle of the village god, has to desist from wine. They do not eat fish as it is considered to be the *matsya avatara* of Lord Vishnu. Their staple diet is cereals, pulses and oil seeds used in various forms, which are locally available. Their staple food includes wheat, maize, barley, rice, etc., and pulses of *chana, arhar, masoor, rongi, rajmah, kulath,* etc., are used. They prepare *moori* after parching wheat, maize, *chana* and barley for their consumption. During these days roots, tubers and barks are not eaten but there is no taboo attached to them . Local vegetables like cabbage, *sag, palak, sarson* are consumed in plenty. Apple is the most widely eaten fruit grown locally. Milk is taken in plenty. *Sattu* prepared out of barley flour, and breads prepared from local foodgrains are eaten. *Siddu*, a special dish is taken on festive occasions. *Afeemdana* (opium seed) is put in *siddu* to have special taste. *Ankali* is another special dish made of rice paste.

Barshoh, the history of the deity is recited by the oracles of the community on special occasions. The community is considered respectable and endowed with mysterious powers. They have the right to maintain the assets of the deity and are allowed to go inside the temples to the places where others are not allowed to enter. They wear *dhoti* at the time of entering the *sanctum sanctorum* of the temples.

Marriages in the families of the Pajiara are celebrated according to the local customs of particular areas. In Shimla *gadar* type of marriages are celebrated. In this system of marriage, the bride goes to the house of the bridegroom with a small marriage party and marriage rituals are conducted there. *Preno* type of marriages are love marriages but these are also celebrated with the consent of the parents of the boy and the girl. In Sirmaur, *jahjra* type marriage is arranged. The marriage party members are called *jahjroo*. The married women can seek divorce and the first husband gets compensation from the second husband. The divorce is decided by the Biradari Panchayat. Putting water in or around the hearth indicates unwillingness to pull on with the husband and in-laws. The marriage age for boys is around 20 years and for girls, around 16 years. *Sindur* and ornaments of head and face are the marriage symbols.

The polyandrous system of marriage is still in vogue in parts of Sirmaur district. *Gadar* is also called *gandharva vivah* and it is said that during earlier days the girls had more say than the boys in the field of marriages and it was the prerogative of the girls to select their husbands and to solemnize the marriage in the house of their in-laws. *Ganesh pujan* and the worship of threshold, *dewal* or *deval pujan* are still in vogue. *Moon* (parched grams) and *poldu* (special type of bread) are taken by the marriage party, *gadaru,* to the house of the bride in case the function is to take place at the residence of the bride in the *byah* type marriage, which has since gained ground. The *byah* is arranged after the consent of the parents of the boy and the girl. In such type of adjustment the father of the girl is offered a sum of Rs. 51 or more and this offer is called *sota*. If *sota* is accepted, the deed or alliance is settled. Now the boys and girls have started selecting their life mates and letting their parents know about their selection. *Teeka, bindi* or *sindur* are some marks of identification of married women. Now dowry system is gaining popularity and bride price is out of fashion. Divorce is called *faisla* and can be settled by Biradari or village panchayat. The marriage system is experiencing tremendous changes. Love marriages are taking place where the parents do not have to spend much. On the other hand, the marriages are being celebrated with greater pomp and show and the system of *byah* is becoming more and more expensive.

Joint family is prevalent in the region and the brothers prefer to stay together. But young people prefer to stay alone and nuclear families are emerging. Women keep no purdah but avoidance relationship exists between *jeth-jethani* and *sas-sasur.* Joking relationship exists between *devar-bhabhi, jija-sali* and with people of other castes.

On the division of the family property, all the brothers get an equal share in the ancestral property. The eldest brother gets one additional field which is called *jethong*, and in some areas the youngest brother is given the ancestral house in addition to his share. This special privilege is called *kamshong* share. The Pajiaras are the social and spiritual guides of the village community in which they live. Horticulture and advent of modern facilities of life have helped the people to develop a healthier outlook towards family life.

The women in the Pajiara have a say in household affairs, gather food and fuel, work hard in orchards and fields and look after the family. They attend to the property of their life mates, but in case of any dispute, have the liberty to go in for divorce and seek somebody else as their life companion. The sisters, according to prevalent laws, have got shares in the ancestral property but generally they leave their shares to their brothers and get their due in their in-laws' houses. Ritualistic and religious functions are attended to by the women but they hardly take any interest in political activities. The status of the women is changing fast and with the spread of education, they are becoming more awakened to their rights and duties.

The life-cycle rituals are very important aspects of their social life. The delivery is performed in a separate room called *paomd* and the birth of a son is rejoiced over more as compared to the birth of a daughter. On the birth of a son the relatives offer *joob* or *doob* (*durva*—green sacred grass, considered auspicious and offered on sacred occasions) to the parents of the newborn baby. On the third day, cow-urine (*gonch*) is offered to the child and the mother to purify them. After 9 or 11 days the mother and the child are taken to the upper storey, called *baur. Sutak* is observed for 11 days at the time of birth and *patak* is observed for 9 to 11 days after the death. During the pollution days the family members are not allowed to touch others, go to the temple or do any sacred activity. During *patak* days it is a practice that the family should not chew *moori* (parched grams), use no *heeng, haldi* or *ghee* or oil. The male members are not to shave their beards or heads and should not wash their clothes. A feast is served to the relatives on both the occasions, i.e., on *guntrala* after the birth of a baby in the family and on *shudhi* day after the death in the family. The concerned families remain in mourning for 6 to 12 months during which no auspicious function takes place in the family.

The resources of the Pajiaras are in plenty. The offerings of the temples are the prerogative of the respective families and the Pajiaras get some fixed donations in cash and kind from the followers of the deities after six months or so. The foodgrains received as offerings to the oracles and other worshippers are called *bishtee,* and the ceremonies on which these are given are called *kheer.* The community has orchards and farms which provide them with regular income.

There are Jati councils and regional sabha of the community but the word of the oracle is considered final. Gram Panchayats also exercise control and in many cases the Pajiaras have control over the village panchayats. Many Pajiaras are nominated or elected as presidents of their Gram Panchayat.

The community believes in village gods but worships all the gods of the Hindu pantheon. The functions of various villages are arranged under the guidance and direction of the deities. The members of the community play a major role in the arrangement of such functions. Beeshu (Baisakhi), Jata, Barlaj, Shivratri, Bhunda, Shant, Jagra, Boodhi Diwali, Dakhnod and many other functions are celebrated by the community.

Decoration of palanquins is their greatest art. *Dev Khaul,* a ritualist dance, is arranged by them on special occasions. Intercommunity languages of the community are very cordial. Intercaste marriages are also taking place.

The attitude of the community towards all schemes relating to development in various spheres is very positive. The people of the community help Government officials to implement Governmental schemes by telling people to cooperate.

The community is god-fearing and the people are always polite and respectful to others.

B.R. Sharma

PANGWAL BRAHMAN

The Pangwals are the residents of Pangi valley of the Chamba district. It is a generic term assigned to the natives of the Pangi Valley which include Brahman, Rajput, Hali and Lohar. The origin of the Pangwals is shrouded in mystery. However, three unconfirmed versions are available which give only a faint idea of the origin of Pangwals. According to Census of India 1961, Village Census monograph on Kupha, Paramas, Tamoh and Malet (Singh, 1961) because of the difficult terrain of the area, the authorities considered it the best place for sending those criminals who were condemned to lifelong sentences. It is presumed that these criminals settled here permanently. As years rolled by, their children and grandchildren established different settlements and came to be collectively called Pangwal. To substantiate this version it is said that even today the traditional Pangwal *tope* which is widely worn in this region, bears a close resemblance to the one generally provided to prisoners.

According to the second version, it is said that in time immemorial the settlers of Lahaul and Lower Chinab were faced with great difficulties because of heavy pressure on land and pastures. They were desperately in search of more good lands and green pastures to feed themselves and their cattle. These people finally migrated to Pangi which then had plenty of both. The Pangwal are said to be their descendants.

A third version which appears plausible is of historical background. It is said that in the days of Muslim domination in India, certain Rajput nobles apprehending persecution at the hands of Mughals decided to send their families to a safer place, which was beyond the reach of the attacking army of the Mughal Empire. Because of the difficult terrain, it is said, Pangi was selected as the best place for this purpose. The entire caravan of Rajput women, together with their children, left for Pangi escorted by soldiers and servants. After several days of hazardous journey, the caravan finally reached here. In the meantime most of the Rajput nobles who remained back, died in battles and many were seriously injured and could not join their families at Pangi. When all hopes of their warriors returning vanished, the Rajput women ultimately married servants and soldiers. The Pangwals today are said to be their direct descendants (Singh, 1961).

The Brahman and the Rajput constitute the bulk of scheduled tribe population of the Pangwals. Of the two, the Rajputs are more in number than the Brahmans, but they collectively account for 11,202 people in Himachal Pradesh according to the 1981 Census. They mainly reside in Pangi tehsil of

Chamba district but a scattered population is also found in adjoining Lahaul and Kullu. (Study area is Kullu). Here only those Pangwal Brahmans have been discussed who are mostly Gaur and according to informants came from Kashi during the reign of Akbar to avoid forcible conversion to Islam.

Pangi valley, the area of their concentration, is mountainous. The area is subject to severe winters, heavy snowfalls, strong winds and frequent avalanches, all of which are responsible for many landslides throughout the valley.

The language spoken by the people among themselves is Pangwali, but with others they speak in Himachali. They do not have any script of their own, but nowadays Devanagari script is commonly used with outsiders.

The people of the valley, irrespective of the community to which they belong, have their peculiar characteristic dress by which they are easily recognized. The men's dress consists of *topi, kameej* or *chola, lekhar* (a long buttoned coat up to knee length), *majhir* (a black woollen cord which is wrapped around the waist), *chalar* or *suthan* (a cotton/woollen trousers loose up to the knees but tight below) and *pul* (locally prepared grass or straw shoes), while the women's dress consist of *kameri* or *choli, joji* (a head dress colourfully embroidered with silk and cotton threads with a tail attached to it which is tuck to the hair plait), *chadru, kamarband, chalan* or *suthan* and a shoe made of grass or straw (Singh, 1961).

The Pangwals are non-vegetarians, and take the meat of sheep, goat, *moual* (Impeyar Pheasant), *tarmol* (jungle goat), *kasturia* (musk deer), pigeon, *chaktir* (meisner) and hen.

The Pangwals' staple food consists of barley and *alu*, but in the lower region of Kullu and Chamba, *makki-ki-roti* and *kadhi*, and on every second or third day wheat *chapati* and *chilra* (bread made of *phullan*) form their staple diet. They are very fond of pulses like *mah* and *rardengal*, which are mostly purchased from the market. For vegetables, wild herbs like *chhatrian, bichubuti* and *guchhies* (mushrooms) are plucked from the jungle.

These days every household has started growing vegetables like cabbage, cauliflower, carrot, potato, onion, capsicum, and spinach during summer months taken everyday. During winter months, every household slays one or two goats and after skinning them, they hang them to be gradually consumed everyday. The Pangwals also have moderate consumption of fruits like *chihri* (apricot), *chur* (apple), *miri* (hazelnut), *than* or *khor* (walnut) and *thangi* (carylus colurne). Walnut oil and *ghalil* oil (extracted from seeds of apricot) form the cooking medium, along with *desi ghee* which is also used in every house. The Pangwals take tea during the winter months. Some households purchase tea leaves from the market, but most of them use *choga*—a local spice—and prepare salted buttered tea from it. Every household possesses a *choori* (a cross between a cow and a yak), the milk yield of which is very little and is mainly used for preparation of *lassi* and curd. *Arack* is consumed universally by both the sexes and is brewed from wheat or barley in every house. Some of the important dishes prepared on ceremonial occasions are *maudaj, unes, luchi, beer, bakru* and *kuron.*

The Pangwals are divided into three sections, viz., Gaur, Sungria and Kalia. The Gaur Brahmans traditionally earned their livelihood by collecting alms. They rank superior to the other two groups. Next in the hierarchy rank are the Sungria Brahman who perform sacredotal services and officiate at birth and marriage ceremonies. The Kalia Brahmans are the lowest among the hierarchy and officiate only at *murtua* rites. The main basis of the differentiation among the various sections is occupational. Each of these sections are futher divided into exogamous sections called *gotra.* The chief function of these *gotras* is to denote ancestry.

The Brahmans, especially Gaur and Sungria, perceive their superiority over all other communities of the area, and the fact is also acknowledged by others. The Kalia Brahmans are considered a low community and rank at par with other scheduled castes, though they themselves are not a scheduled caste. The community is aware of the varna system and places itself at the top of the varna order which is acknowledged by others too.

The Pangwals are endogamous in the sense that a Pangwal will always marry a Pangwal. The two communities, i.e., the Brahman and Rajput intermarry among themselves. Exogamy is maintained at the village and the *gotra* level. Junior levirate and sororate are also practised. Traditionally marriage was prohibited between kin up to ten degrees on the father's side and five degrees on the mother's side; but today only seven generation on father's side and three on mother's side are avoided.

The age at marriage traditionally ranged from 16 to 18 years for girls and from 17 to 18 years for boys, but now adult marriages are performed between the ages of 21 and 22 for girls and 25 and 26 for boys. Among the various forms of acquiring mates, the most popular form is *bari-shadi* (marriage by negotiation), other forms being *pith-chuk* or *chori* (marriage by capture), *do-ghri* (marriage by exchange) and *topi-lana* (widow remarriage).

Monogamy is the prevalent form of marriage. However, a second marriage is resorted to only when the first wife is unable to give heir to the family. The traditional marriage symbol among the Pangwal of Kullu and Chamba are *lal chippir* (red shawl) and nasal ornaments like *laung, phulli* and *tikki.*

Retti (bride price) is not prevalent, but dowry exists, which usually includes a *choori* (a cross between a yak and cow), sheep, goat and household utensils, the quantity of which varies as per the economic status of the bride's family.

The residence is patrilocal, but in cases where there are no male issues in the family, the daughter's husband is invited to stay with the in-laws, and the girl continues to stay at her parent's home. Such a resident son-in-law is called *gharjawai*.

Among the Pangwals, women have every freedom and *chorde* (divorce) is recognized. There are two forms of divorce. In the first a paramour pays a certain sum *izzat* to the woman for seeking release from her husband. In the second form the husband gives his consent for the divorce before two respectable men of the village and then breaks a dry stick in two pieces over his wife's head, as a token of having broken the marriage alliances with her. The amount of compensation to be paid is decided by the *panchayat* (traditional council) which is usually double the amount incurred on marriage. The money thus realized is retained either by the boy or his parents. The common grounds of divorce are infidelity, barrenness and maladjustment.

The children in divorce cases are the liability of the father, but in cases where the child is below six years, it is the duty of the mother to bring up the children, and invariably such children accompany the mother, though all expenses towards their upbringing are borne by the father. This amount is decided by the *panchayat*. After six years the boy's parent bring back the children.

Remarriage of widow, widower and divorcee are permitted. *Topi-lana* is the common term for widow remarriage and is permissible a year after the death of the husband. The first right to claim the widow's hand rests with the deceased husband's brother, nephew or cousin who presents her a *joji* in the presence of two respectable men of the community. Her taking of *joji* signifies acceptance. If another man wishes to marry the widow, he must obtain her parent's and *panchayat's* consent, and return the ornaments given to her by the deceased husband.

The family is of the extended type. The eldest male member of the family holds supreme status. He is respected, obeyed and held in veneration. Paternal and filial affection and due regard as per status of the persons is the basis of mutual relationship within the family. Purdah is not observed, but joking relationship exists between husband and wife's younger relatives, both male and female. Husband, wife, father-in-law and daughter-in-law do not take each other's name, but refer to each other teknonymically.

Inheritance is as per *pag-vand* and *chundavand*—their customary law of inheritance. In the former case, all the male offsprings of a wife share the property equally, whereas in the latter case the property in the first instance is divided according to the number of wives and then their respective share is divided equally among their male children. In the event of there being no male issue in the family, the property passes on to the girls, but in such cases the son-in-law has to be resident at his in-laws' house. A widow can also enjoy the husband's property for her lifetime only. After the death of the father, the eldest male son succeeds to the authority of the family.

The women are an economic asset to the family. Earlier the Gaur Brahman women traditionally were not involved in agriculture, but now they assist their menfolk in all agricultural activity excepting ploughing. They also collect fuel and fodder. The social position of the women is also high in view of the fact that they have the freedom of leaving the husband whenever they desire, and start living with the person of their choice, who ultimately will have to pay the *mudda* or *izzat* to her husband. They take active part in all socioreligious and family rituals. However, they cannot officiate as priest in temples or perform sacredotal services at client's house. Still in the traditional community council, they do not have any reperesentation. They do all the household chores and control the family expenditure.

Pre-natal restrictions are placed on the encieinte mother. She is forbidden to take up any heavy work. The house remains *asudh* or *jooth* (polluted) for nine days in case of birth of a male child and 12 days in the event of the birth of a female child. Purification ceremony takes place on the third, nineth or twelfth day of birth, when the entire house is cleaned.

The *naamsanskar* (name-giving ceremony) is held after the first, third, seventh or ninth month of the birth of a child. A small feast is given and the child is named by the father after looking into the almanac.

Shik-vade (tonsure) ceremony is held along with the naming ceremony or sometimes it is held spearately. In any case it is generally done before the first year, and can only be deferred for the third year if a *sukhna* (a wish kept in the name of deity for fulfilment) is kept for the tonsure to be done at the temple of a deity. The first hair is cut by the mother's brother, followeed by father's brother and five other relatives. A goat is sacrificed, and its blood is sprinkled on the hair and on the child's shaved head. After this the tonsured hair is buried in the ground after keeping them in a *kilta* (basket). On the third day, the child's head is again shaved off by the child's father leaving a *chot* (cue) on the occiput. *Janeu* (investiture) ceremony is held at the age of 12 or 14 years. The sacred thread is brought from Hardwar and kept by all families. The child with the sacred thread is expected to observe certain taboos throughout his lifetime viz., he is not allowed to eat chicken or egg, eat from the hand of a women who is unclean (during her menses), eat together with members of other community, and not to let *janeu* to be touched to body when going for the call of nature. Restrictions are imposed on the girl in her menses on cooking food for four days.

Marriage is performed in three stages, viz., *pillan* (engagement), *fakki* (betrothal) and *chakki* (marriage). Negotiations are started from the boy's side who send the proposal. Vaisakha, Asadha, Kartika, Pausa, Magh and Phalgun are considered auspicious months for marriage. The practice is that the boy goes to the girl's house on a Sunday, Tuesday or Thusday and brings the bride home on Monday, Wednesday or Friday. A Sungaria Brahman officiates at the marriage and makes five or seven *pinds* (dough) of *sattu* (roasted barley flour) with *ghee* and worships these. The bridegroom first picks up a portion from the *pind* and feeds the bride, and she reciprocates the same. This exchange of *pind prasad* solemnizes the marriage. This is known as *panihan* ceremony. The *phironi* ceremony (first return of the bride) is observed on an auspicious date set aside after marriage.

In the *pith-chuk* or *chori* type of marriage, if after the betrothal ceremony the marriage is deferred for two to three years for some reason, then the boy assisted by his trusted friends goes to the girl's house and after picking her up brings to his house. In the earlier times even unmarried girls, not accepting the proposal were captured in the similar manner and then married. The consummation of marriage takes place at the boy's house. This is not a very important event, for a Pangwal boy can flirt around with his fiancee after engagement, and her getting pregnant, is not regarded as a matter of shame. The child is brought up and the boy fathers the child. Remarriage is permitted provided the wife does not have any issue for at least seven years, or on the death of the first wife if the husband is young.

The dead are cremated as a rule, with the Kalia Brahman officiating at the mortuary rites. Children below the age of eight years are buried. The last rites are normally performed by the eldest male member of the family. The house remains polluted for seven days in the event of the death of a female and nine days in the event of the death of a male. The ashes and the bones are collected and immersed in Chander Bhaga. On the third, ninth, thirteenth of a month after the death, a *kathi* or *kirya* ceremony is observed in which a feast is given to the villagers. A year later a *badi kathi* is observed. Among the Pangwals a stone slab called *dhaj* is put up in the memory of the dead in the courtyard of the house. These bear an inscription and are usually prepared by the shepherds.

The major economic activity of the Pangwal Brahmans nowadays is agriculture, which is supplemented by what was once their primary occupation, viz., living on alms, performing sacredotal services, and officiating at death rites. Many of them have also taken to animal husbandry, horticulture, bee-keeping, business and jobs. Traditionally, the natives of the Pangi valley had *hak-bardhan* (subsidiary rights) in forest which have now been restricted but nevertheless are still practised on where they can collect dry and fallen branches of trees for their fuel needs, on free pastures in demarcated portions and for free wood for house construction.

Traditional rights over natural water, over which the locals can construct water mills by channelizing the water still exist. Permission is not given to individuals but collectively to nine or ten households, which has to be obtained from the *patwari* (revenue assistant).

The land for agriculture is owned individually by the family heads. The Sungria and the Kalia Brahmans do agriculture themselves but Gaur Brahmans prefer not to do so themselves, and give the land on *adhi* (half). Often agricultural labour is employed for tilling, sowing, reaping, etc. They are paid in kind, in the form of meals and some quantity of coarse grains.

Bee-keeping is also practised by most of the households. Besides, they also collect forest produce and herbs like *zira* (*Carum carvi*), *pateesh* (*Acoritom chasmanthum*), *shilajeet*, *banafsha* (*Viola odorata*), *ban kakri* (*Podophyllum emodii*), *chora*, *guchhies* (*Morchella esulenta*) and *mitha tilla* (Singh, 1961).

Baring a few shops in the valley, which deal mainly in grocery articles and general merchandize, no regulated market exists. They have to depend on the nearest Tarela market which is 60 kms. away, from where they buy things in bulk for the year and also sell their products. Earlier, barter was the medium of exchange but now it has been replaced by cash. Manpower is much needed in this difficult terrain; three or four persons are needed, one for looking after the sheep, the other for the *choru* and *chori*, and children for tending the lambs and kids. Children from the poor family work as labourers in road building and house construction, where they are paid wages in cash.

The traditional council looks after the welfare and maintenance of traditional norms. This is headed by a *mukaddam* (chief) who is helped by nominated members. Cases relating to divorce and breach of traditional norms are decided by the council. The statutory council has started functioning since 1960, as a result of which Gram and Nyay Panchayats have come up, which look after the planning and development of welfare activities and for the maintenance of law and order. The fines imposed by the panchayat are usually in cash and are given to the aggrieved party.

The Pangwal Brahmans belong to the Vaishnava and Shaivite sects. Every family has a deity. The village deities, Nag and Nagini, are propitiated by all members for warding off the evil influences on the family and the village. Their regional diety is goddess Durga, who is worshipped and propitiated by sacrificing a goat. Their *pujaras* (sacred specialists) are Brahman or Rajput who officiate at life-cycle rituals, and whose office is hereditary. They are also entitled to take away eatables, and the left leg and the liver of the sacrificed animal. Durga or Singhasni Mata are offered goats and brass bells as their *sukhna*. The *jatras* are very common among the Pangwals. Some important ones are Iwaan (celebrated in Magh or Phalgun), Unoni and Sainch (held in Chaitra), Darkhan and Baria (held in Sharavan) and Phool Jatra (held in the month of Kartika). The important festivals are Sankranti, Puranmashi, Shivratri, Sheel (observed on the *amavasya* of Phalgun or Chaitra), Hishoo (new year's day) and Miniach. The sacred centre of the community is the temple of Lord Avlaketeshwar at

Triloknath in Lahaul which was earlier a part of Pangi.

The community is well versed in the art of *kilta* making, weaving, manufacture of *kanse-ki-katori* (a dish of bronze), weaving of *thobi* (mat of goat hair), spinning and preparing *phulley* (straw shoes). The Pangwals have great love for their folksongs, which are mainly based on the beauty of Pangi or love affairs and are sung on social occasions. They are also fond of dancing. Men and women dance in separate groups except in *ghorai* in which both dance together but in separate groups. The dancing is accompanied by singing of songs of old myths, legends or traditions to the accompaniment of *nagara* and flute played by the Aryas.

The Pangwals accept both *kachcha* and *pucca* food from the Rajput. From, Chanal and Lohar, a Brahman would accept *ghee*, *sattu*, roasted potato, *sidha* and liquor if served in a *kanse ka bartan*. They would however not sit on the same mat or wooden plank while eating, and would even not eat if their mat touched the mat of the Chanal or Lohar. However, there are no restriction on the Chanal or Lohar entering the temple but if they bring a *rota* cooked in his house, the Brahman would not touch nor offer it to the deity. This will have to be prepared by the person himself, but if he offers the flour and *ghee* to the *pujara*, he then prepares the *rota* and offers it to the deity. There are separate water sources for the Lohar, Chanal, Brahman and the Rajput.

Intercommunity marital exchanges do take place among the Brahmans and the Rajputs, but not with other communities. The Brahmans continue to have traditional ritual linkages with other communities. They render sacredotal services at the house of their client for which they are paid a fixed quantity of coarse grains annually. *Baswai* (putative kinship) is established with persons who are not related, but are expected to carry out all obligations as is expected of real kin. *Jajmani* relationship exists with the serving communities who are paid foodgrains at harvesting and festival times.

New linkages have developed with the taking up of other occupations like business, sharecropping and cultivator-labour relationship. People who have moved out of the valley have found job in Government departments. A few have opened hotels, etc., which have put them in contact with other communities, as a result of which the traditional commensal rigidity has loosened nowadays.

The modern developmental programmes have made a big impact on the people. Schools have started functioning in the area after 1959, but with little impact. Fewer girls go for education than boys. Boys do not study beyond the higher secondary school level. While the girls drop out for social reasons, the boys drop out for supporting the family because of poor economic conditions.

The attitude of the Pangwal Brahmans towards traditional as well as modern systems of medicare is favourable but not towards the family welfare schemes. Drinking water is available through *kuhl.* The community has been benefited by the employment schemes and self-employment schemes, as a result of which people have procured jobs and opened shops due to financial assistance.

Communication is poor, for there are no roads. People have access only to radio and movies are shown to them through field publicity agencies. There is no television. Post offices exist far away and there is only one wireless telegraph office in the area. There is no electricity and to light the rooms, kerosene oil or *jagru* (oiled wood) is used. Dry wood is the fuel for cooking.

Irrigation is through streams or *kuhl* at a few places. Mainly organic manure is used, but a few have also started using chemical fertilizers and insecticides. The children avail themselves of the nutrition programme and Integrated Child Development Scheme. Kerosene and other essential commodities are made available through Government fair price shops at subsidized rates.

Rajendra Sarkar

PANGWAL RAJPUT

The Pangwal is a scheduled tribe. It is a generic name given to all those who inhabit the Pangi valley of Chamba district. There are Brahman, Rajput, Lohar, Badi and Chanal but the Rajput population outnumbers all the rest. In practice, the term Pangwal includes mainly the Rajput and the Brahman who may also freely intermarry. (See Pangwal Brahman).

Bio-anthropological information with respect to blood group and genetics of the people is available (see Bio-anthropological Report).

Fond of non-vegetarian food, their staple food consists of barley, wheat, maize, pulses and *tenegal* (beans), locally grown vegetables, green leaves like *bichubuti, guchhies* (mushrooms), fruits and dry fruits such as *chiri*, *chun*, *miri*, *than* and *thangi*. Though greatly fond of non-vegetarian food, they would totally desist from eating the meat of *choori* (cross breed of cow and yak), yak and buffalo.

The medium of cooking is mostly walnut oil, clarified butter and *ghalel* (made from the apricot nuts). They drink locally brewed liquor, known as *arack* and smoke pipe. Women also consume *arack* occasionally. Green tea locally available is mostly consumed during winter months with a pinch of salt. Red tea is also used which is available from the market.

The Rajput Pangwals have three main subdivisions, namely, Rana, Thakur and Rathi. Intermarriages among them is fairly common, though the Rathi are regarded inferior than the former two groups. They are further subdivided into a number of exogamous *gotra* and claim descent from Surajbanshi and Chandrabanshi Rajput and place themselves among the Kshatriyas in the classical varna order.

In the local hierarchy they are both numerically and socially a powerful group placed only ritually lower in status than the Brahmans. However, for all practical purposes the Rajput and the Brahman Pangwals have both connubial and commensal relations with each other. Marriages are settled through negotiation and the proposal for marriage comes from the groom's side. Marriage by capture and by elopement locally known as *chori* are also recognized. *Diyodari* (exchange) marriages are still practised but are not much preferred now.

Marriage among the *gotra* of father's and mother's side is avoided up to three generations. The average age at marriage for boys and girls is 22 to 24 and 18 to 20 years respectively. The common symbols of marriage are *bulak* (nose-ring) and *fararu* (ear-ring). The bride lives patrilocally. Bride-price exists and consists of cash and kind which is decided at the time of settlement of marriage. Dowry is not demanded but gifts to the daughter are made at the time of her marriage which may consist of common agricultural implements, utensils, sheep and goats. Divorcee, widow and widower remarriage known as *topi lane* are recognized and so are levirate and sororate. Divorce is granted easily.

A married woman wanting to remarry a man of her choice may do so, provided her paramour pays back the bride-price along with the penalty as decided by the panchayat to her former husband. The children born remain in the custody of the father. It is customary that if the girl refuses to marry the person she is engaged to, the boy's side may demand not only the return of gifts but all the expenses incurred by them in addition to the penalty. However, in case the boy refuses to marry there would be no return of gifts from either side. In case divorce is from the wife's side the penalty to be paid to the husband by her paramour may be four times the expenses incurred by the groom's side. The common grounds of divorce are adultery, maladjustment and impotency/frigidity.

Joint families are more prevalent than nuclear families which are usually the result of conflict and friction. The elder male member heads the family and is given due respect. There is no strict observance of purdah and women have considerable freedom of movement and speech in the presence of the elder male members of the husband's family. Joking relationship exists with younger brothers and sisters.

Inheritance and succession is patrilineal. The property is equally divided among all the sons. However, a father wanting to give more to a particular son may do so in writing and the same would be respected. Earlier in the absence of sons the property used to pass on to the nearest collateral but nowadays married daughters and the son-in-law are given this property. Regarding the interfamily linkages the filial bonds are strong and the sense of cooperation is best seen in times of need.

Women enjoy considerable freedom in social sphere. They are virtually incharge of the domestic affairs. Women are hardworking, performing domestic chores as well as taking an equal part in agricultural operations in addition to bringing potable water, fodder and tending the animals. Their economic potentialities as such are socially recognized.

In the religious spheres, however, they do not have any say. The fact that women cannot worship their clan deity with the traditional family lamp is indicative of their low profile. In political sphere women do not have major representation in the local or regional politics as such but senior women are invited when Biradari Panchayat is convened to discuss a certain pending issue.

The major life-cycle rituals are by and large in accordance with Hindu religious sanctions. The birth of the son is an occasion for great rejoicing. Just before the delivery the women is segregated in a ground floor room which is otherwise meant for the cattle and she remains there till the period of pollution, which lasts up to 12 days after birth. Purificatory rites are observed by giving bath to the child subsequently on the third, sixth, ninth and twelfth day. A sweet dish may be prepared on this day and distributed to friends and relatives. House is cleaned and plastered with cowdung and purified after performing *havan* and sprinkling holy water. A child is usually named on this day. *Shik-vade* (tonsure) is performed for both male and female children within a year either on third, fifth, seventh, ninth or eleventh month of birth. The hair of the child is first cut by the maternal uncle followed by other relatives. The hair is put on the bread and covered with a leaf, and is then thrown upto a great height.

Marriage is first negotiated from the boy's side. The boy's father or uncle visits the prospective bride's house with a bottle of liquor and *sattu* and asks for the girls's hand. If the proposal is acceptable to them they accept the gifts brought from the boy's side. This is followed by engagement known as *magnali* and again the boy accompanied by a few of his relatives comes and brings some more bottles of liquor and *sattu* and then asks for the time and the date for marriage which is convenient to the girl's side. At this time he may also bring some jewellery like *bange* for the girl. At the appointed day, the groom's party comes to the bride's place. The bride and the groom are made to sit at a place where *puna* (sacred marking with flour) is made. Some *totus* (made of flour) are also placed around it. Two of these *totus* are given the shape of a cup and filled with honey and *ghee*. The maternal uncle covers them with his hand and asks the bride and groom to eat them. The one who finishes it first is considered to be having an upper hand. The guests are entertained with wine and food. The groom accompanied by the bride and a few of her relatives leave for his home. A lamb is sacrificed and meat is given to all. The same ceremonies are repeated at the groom's place also. After staying for one or two days, the bride's relatives return and the date of her visit to her parental home is also decided.

The dead are cremated and the pollution is observed for seven days. On the seventh day all the agnates get their heads shaved off. A lamb or goat is sacrificed and its blood is sprinkled on all. At the time of the funeral procession, the bier is prepared by a Chanal known as *dwaru* and he also carries an axe. Another person from the Lohar community carries fire in a pot. Ancestor worship is observed. A *thar* (platform) is constructed for those who die an unnatural death.

The mainstay of the Pangwal Rajputs is agriculture supplemented by herding of sheep and goat. The wool sheared from the sheep is usually kept for self-consumption. Every family has a loom. Weaving of woollen cloth for coat and *pyjama* is done by family members. Blankets are also woven. The surplus, if any, is usually exchanged for other items of requirement.

Each family has a customary right in the forest not only for grazing their herd of sheep and goat, but also for procuring wood for the construction of house and agricultural implements. They also get wood for fuel, free of cost. Some trees which get uprooted every year during snow avalanches are also distributed among the villagers. However, the forest department has prohibited the cutting of certain types of trees. Some people have also received the *nautar* land under the scheme of land for the landless but the forest department asks for heavy compensation for dry fruit trees which may be on the land. Since they are unable to pay it they are not able to get possession of the land.

People have a direct link with market. Few shops in each village usually suffice for the everyday requirement of the people. Both barter and cash form the mode of exchange. In the past, butter and the walnut oil were exchanged for wool, salt and the grains, but nowadays, barter is less prevalent. The children are seen assisting their parents in light agricultural activities.

For mechanism of social control they have their own Biradari Panchayat as well as statutory panchayats. The Biradari Panchayat takes up domestic issues like family quarrels, divorce, separation and elopement, and levies cash fine on the offenders. The economic and criminal offences are mostly dealt by the statutory panchayat. The election to the Biradari Panchayat is through a voice vote and consists of senior and knowledgeable persons of the community.

Hindu by faith, the people are deeply religious by nature. Besides worshipping the deities of the wider pantheon, they have more regard for the regional, village and clan deities. The major sacred centre are the Kandwa Nag Temple at Mindhal, Sheetla Devi shrine at Luj and Trilokinath temple and Masan Devi at Purthi. Some of the major festivals of the region are Tyane held in Asadh (August), Dhikhren in Savan and Parvach in Bhadon, all of which have socioreligious significance. The fair of Masan Devi at Purthi is of special significance to the people and is celebrated by all the communities with a lot of enthusiasm, fun and frolic. Men and women dance in groups for the whole night. Besides, people have belief in evil spirits, ghosts, magic, charms and amulets, and take recourse to *chela* whenever afflicted by any of these. Charms are worn on the neck to ward off the evil influences.

The Pangwal Rajputs are deft in the art of weaving woollen cloth. Besides, there is a rich heritage of folksongs, dances, folktales and folklore which they share with others of the region as a whole.

The Pangwal Rajputs and Brahmans share water and food and have free marital exchange. However with certain castes like Chanal and Lohar they traditionally refrain from eating boiled food. Taking liquor, and fried meat and roasted food items is acceptable. Brahmans and Rajputs would also accept the same pipe while smoking *hukka.* Crematorium is different for each community.

The traditional patron-client relationship exists with Chanal and Lohar. The Chanals not only act as agricultural labourers in their fields but also remove the dead cattle and act as a carriers of marriage gifts at the time of marriage. They also carry an axe while leading the funeral procession. The Lohar and Badhi, on the other hand, repair and make the agricultural implement of common use. They are paid their dues in the harvesting season as also on ceremonial and festive occasions. New modern linkages have also developed owing to contact with outsiders, due to spread of literacy and due to people going out in search of employment opportunities. As a result a few have been successful in securing jobs in Government offices and in white-collar professions. Political leadership has emerged at village and regional level.

The area has been declared a scheduled area and as such receives sufficient grants. But the pace of development is hampered on account of natural hazards and harsh terrain. The impact of various developmental programmes and attitude of the Pangwal Rajput towards them is the same as that of the Pangwal Brahmans living together.

Vatsala Sarkar

PATHAN

There is a conflict of opinion concerning the origin and constitution of the Pathan. According to some scholars Afghans and allied races are synonyms, but according to Ibbetson, the Pathan and Afghan were two separate races: "the original Afghans are a race of probably Jewish or Arab extraction; and they, together with a tribe of Indian origin with which they have long been blended, still distinguish themselves as the true Afghans..." (1916:61). Before India's partition some sections of the Pathans lived in Dera Ismail Khan and called themselves Ghilzai, Lodi and Sarwani Pathans. "The Ghilzai were the most famous of all the Afghan tribes till the rise of the Durrani power, while the Lodi section gave to Delhi the Lodi and Sur dynasties" (Ibbetson, 1916: 65). According to Ibbeston again Pashto word "*powal*" (to graze) denotes the warrior traders who carried on trade between India and Afghanistan and the northern states of Central Asia. Ibbetson futher (pp. 62) places them among people of Indian origin by saying that, "the true Pathans are apparently of Indian origin. Their language is called Pashto or Pakhto and they call themselves Pukhtana or Pakhto speakers; and it is this word, of which Pathan is the Indian corruption." He finally says (pp. 62) that "the Afghans and Ghilzais are Pathans by virtue of their language, though not of Pathan origin; the Tajiks and Hazaras, who have retained their Persian speech, are not Pathans while all five are Afghans by virtue of location, though only one of them is of Afghan race."

The Pathans have been coming to various parts of Himachal Pradesh with their merchandise and were conspicuous by their typical dress. These traders were expert in making friendship with local people in the villages and sold their articles even on credit. They were known for their cruelty at the time of getting back the loan offered by them during the past years but local inhabitants had respect for their honesty, friendliness and sharp memory.

These Pathan traders stayed in villages for sometime and used to go back to come again during the following year. But after Independence few number of these people visited villages in the hills. However, some Pathan families have stayed on in various parts of the State. In Una district they are at Gharbasra, Barnoh and Thara Panjoa villages. In Hamirpur district, one family of the Pathans is residing in Mehal Morian village. In an adjoining village near Nangal in Punjab, four families of Pathans are residing. These Pathan families migrated from Afghanistan in the remote past. They say that according to a legend their ancestors worked as defenders of forts in the hills during the regime of Maharaja Ranjit Singh and preferred to stay in the area. The climate of their habitat is moderate with high humidity and medium rainfall and the terrain is hilly with thin to dense forests.

The Pathans now speak Pahari dialect as is spoken by other communities. They know Urdu and Persian but cannot speak Pashto so fluently. Their scripts are Devanagari and Arabic.

Men wear a loose tunic with baggy drawers and round embroidered caps, and carry an Afghan knife and *Jazail.* Women wear a loose and wide gear to their ankles.

The Pathans are non-vegetarian. They take only *halal* meat. Like other communities of the area, their staple food is wheat, rice, maize, *jowar, bajra* and pulses of all kinds and they prepare oil out of mustard seeds for use at home. Drinks are not common but young boys of the community do not hesitate to take occasional drinks which are purchased from the market. The Pathan families are mainly farmers and buffalo breeders, so they take milk, butter and *ghee* according to availability. The menfolk are interested in smoking *hukka* and chewing tobacco and betel.

The Pathans divide themselves into various exogamous groupings which are equal in status. They place themselves in the middle order of the regional social hierarchy, which is also endorsed by other communities.

Marriages are performed within the community usually at the age of 14-15 years for girls and 20-22 years for boys, but outside the exogamous groupings. Consanguineous marriages are allowed at the cross-cousin level. Though their religion permits them to have four wives, in practice monogamy is the rule. Bride-price existed in the past but it has now been given up, excepting in case of poor families when the groom's parents give some money to the bride's parents for defraying the marriage expenditure. *Mehar* is fixed by the negotiating parties, at the time of marriage but is rarely demanded. Dowry is also given in kind which usually consists of animals, clothes, jewellery, utensils, etc.

Divorce is permissible. The desirous husband or wife has to file an application for divorce before the village *maulvi.* Reasons for divorce can be dispute between the parties on some account, maladjustment of husband and wife, disputes of women about the division of property, etc., or attraction of husband or wife towards somebody else. On divorce, no compensation is given but the separating wife can take articles of dowry back if allowed by the *maulvi* and village panchayat. Both husband and wife can seek divorce. After divorce, the minor children are the liability of the mother but elder ones are taken care of by the father.

The families are organized on a nuclear basis. After the marriage, the family of the son is considered a separate *kabila* (family) but the son and daughter-in-law can stay with the parents if they like. The horizontally and vertically extended families which existed once are now breaking up. The eldest member of the family holds supreme status, and land and other property is held in his name. The elders are feared, obeyed and held in veneration, and the paternal and filial affection and due regard as per the status of the person is the basis of mutual relationship within the family. Avoidance is observed between father-in-law and daughter-in-law in the initial years of marriage, after which it is not rigidly observed. After the death of father, the eldest son becomes the head of the family. Inheritance is based on the principle of male equigeniture. The widow has no right of inheritance but has only the right to maintenance from her husband's estate. Though the relationship in family is generally harmonious, yet at times conflicts do arise on account of property matters.

The Pathan women help men in every sphere of agricultural activity except ploughing, which is the male prerogative. They are also involved in animal husbandry, collection of fuel and bringing of potable water from the rivers or streams where piped water is not available. They also work in the fields of others and contribute to the family income. They take part in social functions and family rituals, but their role in the religious sphere like visiting the mosque for prayers or becoming a priest is restricted and their role in political activities is limited to the extent of exercising their franchise. The women are not the controlling authority in the family but have their say in household affairs.

In the sphere of life-cycle rituals *kanji* (pre-delivery ritual) is observed on the eighth month of pregnancy. Though no pre-natal restrictions exists, all precautions are taken for the safe delivery of the child. After birth the child is given a charm written on a paper which prevents him from all eventualities. Restrictions are imposed on the movement of the parturient mother for seven days when *weham* (purificatory bath) is given to the child and the mother. After the expiry the forty days' period of *chilla* (birth pollution) she purifies herself by taking bath and visiting pirs. In some of the families *aqiqa* is performed when goats are sacrificed and the child's head is shaved off. No name is given to the child for three days after which a *mullah* suggests a name.

No age is fixed for the *sunnat* ceremony, which is performed by the barber. But the earlier it is performed the better it is, as it is considered less painful at that time. It should be performed before the boy attains the age of 6 or 7 years and not beyond 10 to 15 years.

In marriages the songs which are popular among other castes residing in the neighbouring villages are sung. The ceremonies are arranged at the bride's as well as at the bridegroom's house simultaneously. But the actual ceremony takes place at the bride's house. It is solemnized by *nikah* in consideration of an amount of *mehar.* The marriage is thereafter registered by the signing of *nikahnama.* Marriage feasts are arranged for relatives and near and dear ones. Hindus also take part in these ceremonies and provided with separate cooking arrangements.

The dead are buried and ancestors are remembered from time to time but there is no particular ceremony to worship them. Pollution is observed for 10 days after death. Life-cycle rituals are being curtailed as the families have meagre income and have to attend to earning their livelihood all the time.

The Pathans are are basically businessmen, yet those who reside permanently in Himachal Pradesh do not have to attend to merchandise and the sale of medicinal herbs as these are not easily available to them for marketing. Such families were tenants of big farmers in the beginning but now have become landowners. They also work as buffalo breeders. They engaged themselves in trading in the past which they continue doing so till date. They have direct links with the market, visited occasionally. Cash forms the usual medium of exchange.

For breach of community rules, the elders of community come together and solve the issue. The offender is penalized in cash or by directing him to give a feast. Statutory panchayats have come up after independence, the members of which are heterogeneous and are elected through ballot. These panchayats are responsible for social control and for planning and implementation of welfare activities.

The community is Islamic by faith. Pirs are worshipped as pious saints who have the powers to fulfil the desires of human beings. The Pathans and other people of the area have great respect for Pirnagah, a shrine nearby and offerings of milk, *chunni* and mustard oil are considered beneficial. Pirnagah is famous for acceding to the prayers of worshippers for buffalo ailments, prosperity, increase in milk yield, and for keeping peace in the family. If a *chhinj* is arranged by the worshippers at that place, it is believed that immediate fulfilment of one's wish is assured. A number of other shrines of Pirs are also visited by these people. *Maulvis* are the sacred, social and spiritual specialists of Pathans. Pathan families do not have their own *maulvi* but consult any of them at the time of requirement. The *maulvis* are considered to be gifted with the powers of driving away all ailments and evil spirits, so the villagers go to them for removal of all sorts of troubles. They observe Id'ul Fitr and Id'ul Zuha like other Muslim communities. The Pathans, like other communities of Mohammadan stock, stick to *namaz* and *roza. Jumma* is considered to be the most auspicious day of the week. A visit to Mecca on Haj pilgrimage is a cherished wish of the members of this community. Hajis (who have been to Haj) are respected persons in the whole community.

The Pathan had both social and economic ties with the neighbouring Hindu and Muslim communities, with whom they had transactions as merchants and moneylenders. They exchange water with all the Muslims. Traditionally, a Hindu on being invited by a Pathan at a social gathering is given *sidha,* or separate cooking arrangements are made for him, only then can he accept *pucca* food.

Marriages are restricted to the community but occasionally people do marry outside amongst the other Muslims. People from all communities get water from water taps. They also share the common burial ground and mosque with other Muslims.

They take part in all the traditional festivals. As they are agriculturists and sheep breeders, patron-client, landlord-tenant and cultivator-labour relationships exist along with other forms of symbiotic relationships.

In the sphere of development programmes, their attitude is favourable for the formal education of boys and girls, who study up to primary level. But a majority of them drop-out due to economic and social reasons. Their attitude towards the modern allopathic medicine system is favourable, but this is rarely available to them in the village. But whenever it is available, they make full use of it in combination with their traditional system of medicare. They are also favourable to family welfare programmes and are receptive to modern methods of family planning.

Drinking water is available in the locality through piped water. Whenever these do not exist, it is procured from rivers and streams. Radio is available in the villages but people yet to have television sets. Electricity and fuel resources are abundant in the locality. Communication facilities are also availed of by them. Information is also disseminated among them through voluntary and extension agencies. People have availed themselves of the facilities of the Integrated Rural Development Programmes to the benefit of their agriculture. Irrigational facilities have been made by the people themselves by channelizing rainwater. The community uses mostly organic manure, but occasionally chemical fertilizers and insecticides are also used.

Their children along with children of other communities avail themselves of the mid-day meal programme at school where they are provided with biscuits and skimmed milk free of cost. Infant and mother care is also provided by government Balwadis which provide nutritional food to children in the 0-5 age groups and to expectant and nursing mothers, besides giving them immunization. They also avail themselves of the facility of food items at controlled rates through Government fair price shops. Their attitude towards banking is favourable as such they are not dependent on moneylenders or shopkeepers.

The Pathans in Himachal Pradesh are a very small community and they have since adjusted themselves with other Mohammadan and Hindu inhabitants and are socially recognized as a viable component of the native social structure.

B.R. Sharma

PENJA

The Penja also known as Pinja, Pinjara, Panjora, Panjuora, Punji or Pinjia is a community of cotton carders. They are also referred to as Naddaf, Dhuna, Dhuniya, Panbakob, Kalaf and Punba elsewhere (Crooke, 1896; Rose, 1914). They live mostly in the Paonta tehsil of Sirmaur district which is adjacent to Haryana from where they have migrated. They are more in number in adjoining states of Punjab, Haryana and Uttar Pradesh. The dialect of the people is Haryanavi mixed with Hindi. They use Devanagari and Perso-Arabic scripts. No current population figures for the community are available but according to the 1911 Census, there were only seven people of this community.

Though non-vegetarian by food habit, their staple diet consists of wheat, maize, rice, pulses of *urad, moong, chana* and *masur*. The cooking media are the oils of *toria* and *til*. Drinking of alcohol is a religious taboo, but is resorted to clandestinely by men. Pork is also a religious taboo which is strictly adhered to. Beef is not consumed. Smoking is common among menfolk but betel-chewing is not prevalent. Tea is the most popular non-alcoholic beverage. Fruit consumption is very occasional and only seasonal fruits which are cheaply available are consumed.

The Penja is an endogamous Muslim community belonging to the Sunni sect. Marriages are now settled after attaining adulthood. The normal age at marriage for girls and boys is between 15 and 16 years and 17 and 18 years respectively. Engagement is done one or two years in advance of the actual marriage. Earlier, child marriages were common. In such cases *muklawa* ceremony used to take place after the girl attained maturity. Marriages are allowed between cross-cousins but parallel cousins do not marry, though under the Islamic provisions they are potential mates. Marriage is negotiated through a middleman called *bicholia*. Marriage by exchange is also prevalent. At the time of settlement of marriage the amount of *mehar* is also decided. It can range from Rs. 500 to 1000 which is either to be paid on demand or at the time of the dissolution of the marriage. However, if the wife leaves the husband, *mehar* is forfeited. Both divorcee and remarriage of widow and widower are allowed. Levirate, both junior and senior, as also sororate, are practised but a man cannot marry his wife's sister while his wife is alive. In the event of divorce, the husband not only has to pay back the *mehar*, but also return the jewellery and valuables which she had brought from her parents' home, at the time of marriage. The panchayat tries the cases of divorce and the *maulvi* is called in to get the formalities completed. In the event of divorce and the woman's subsequent marriage, the children remain in the custody of the father or his family. Sometimes very young children and infants are allowed to go with the mother. A widow can remarry only after observing the period of *iddat.*

Family of the Penja is mostly of the extended type, but nuclear families are also coming up. The eldest male member heads the household. Inheritance and succession are patrilineal. Property is equally divided among the sons, but even daughters have a share as per the Islamic Law but is forsaken in favour of brothers. The parents keep a share for themselves, which is later given to the son who has looked after them. Women observe purdah in the presence of the senior members of the husband's household. They also put on *burqa* while going out of the village. With younger relatives, no such restrictions exist.

Women do not enjoy equal status in relation to men despite the fact that they contribute towards the economic well-being of the family. Women discharges all the household chores as well and have considerable freedom in domestic affairs. They also take an active part in rituals and festivals. However, their activities mostly remain confined to their homes. They do not visit the mosque to attend holy congregations or addresses in such gatherings. Instead, they perform their religious duties within the confines of their home. In politics they play a very little role which ends with the casting of vote in the general and state elections. Economically they find themselves dependent on their husbands.

The life-cycle rituals as observed from time to time are common with other Muslims. The birth of the son is a matter of great rejoicing. As soon as the child is born a *maulvi* is called who recites verses from the holy Quran and whispers hymns into the child's ears. Post-purificatory bath is given to the child and the mother on sixth, tenth, twentieth and thereafter a month and finally on the fortieth day. The pollution following birth ends after this. The house is plastered with cow-dung and the *maulvi* is called. A sweet preparation is distributed among the relatives and neighbours. *Sunnat* can be performed any time, but the earlier it is done the better it is. *Aqiqa* is also performed, and at that time they sacrifice two goats and simultaneously the hair of the child are also shaved off. This is usually performed in the fifth year.

The actual marriage ceremony is performed at the bride's house. Before marriage, betrothel known as *sagai* is done. The girl's parents send sweets and cloths for the boy and his near relatives. Before marriage, another important ceremony known as *mehndi ki rasam* is performed in both the households. *Mehndi* is applied to both the bride and the bridegroom by the female relatives of the respective households. Besides, turmeric and mustard oil is also applied to both bride and bridegroom for three to five consecutive days before marriage. *Nikah* is performed by a *maulvi* in the presence of the relatives and friends of both sides. The conditions of the marriage are documented in *nikahnama* which is read and signed in the presence of the *biradari*. A marriage feast is given to all the guests by the bride's side. If married young, the girl is sent to her husband's house a few years later when she attains maturity.

The dead are buried. Pollution is observed for 40 days. For three days there is no cooking in the house and food is brought by neighbours or relatives. On the third day, sweet bread is prepared and distributed among children. This is known as *tija* which is followed by *daswan* on the tenth day when a *maulvi* is called who recites verses from the holy text. Sweetened rice and gram are distributed among the children. Thereafter, on the fortieth day, known as *chaliswa* the entire *biradari* is called; even their Hindu friends are also invited and food is served to all. In case the husband dies, the widow has to observe *iddat*. She remains confined to her home and also does not cook. After three months have passed, some sweet preparation is cooked and distributed among children. After that, she resumes her normal activities. Ancestor worship is also observed.

The traditional economic activity of the Penjas revolves around cotton carding by subjecting the cotton to the vibration produced by a bow string. The string is usually hung from the ceiling over a pile of cotton. The string is twanged with a wooden scatch and the cotton is turned into a soft fluff. This is used for padding the quilts. They also do the quilting. However, with the introduction of the mechanized cotton carding machines, their age-old profession has suffered a great deal. A majority of the Penja families find it difficult to replace the old system of cotton carding with machines because of insufficient finance. This has resulted in pushing their traditional economic activities into the secondary position. Many of them have acquired land under *nautor* and are practising agriculture. Service, contractorship and labour are the other secondary occupations pursued by some of them to supplement their economic resources. The weekly market system does not operate. A few shops in each village serve the requirements of the people. They also avail themselves of the market facility from the nearby town market. Transactions are mostly in cash.

As a mechanism of social control the Biradari Panchayat as well as statutory panchayats exists. The former settles cases purely of domestic nature, whereas the latter tries cases of social and economic offences and levies cash fine on the offenders. The *biradari* council consists of elders of the *biradari* who are informally elected by voice vote, whereas the statutory panchayats are formally elected bodies. The role of the Biradari Panchayat is gradually diminishing as people have access to law courts.

There are also Hindu Penja but they are not found in Himachal Pradesh.

Muslim festivals namely Id, Bakrid, Saberat are celebrated and the famous mosques and *mazar* are visited. They have great reverence for the Mazar of Baba Bhure Shah where they pay visits on Fridays. Belief in evil spirits and magic is quite widespread. In order to ward off the evil influence, they avail themselves of the services of the specialists known as *sayana*. Often a charm, in black thread is worn around the neck as a protection against the evil spirits. Besides, they worship the village deity known as Khera Devta, like their Hindu brethren.

Their women are deft in making embossed decorative designs on the walls of their houses. They also do embroidery. The folksongs sung on the occasion of birth and marriage are common with other communities of the region. Only wmen participate in the dances.

The Penjas rank along with other occupational castes like Teli, Julahe, Muslim Banjara and the like, with whom they share commensal norms. However, the Hindu communities do not accept anything cooked from their hands. When invited to a feast, the food is separately cooked by a Rajput/Brahman. They, on the other hand, traditionally avoid accepting food or water from Chamar, Chuhre and Mehre. Patron-client relationship exists with certain castes but to a minimal level. Cultivator-labour relationship also exists. New modern linkages have developed because of contact with outsiders and due to improved network of communication system, rise in literacy level and consequently their taking up occupations in urban areas.

With the introduction of electricity, water supply, trasnsport and communication system, the quality of life of the Penja has improved substantially. Literacy percentage has shown an upward swing but the attitude of the people towards female education has remained unfavourable. The children are sent to *madarsa* for religious teaching. Because of poverty and lack of incentives and interest, the drop out percentage for boys is very high after higher secondary level. Health and family welfare programmes have met with some success. Modern, as well as, indigenous medicines are used. In an endeavour to bring about economic uplift, the Integrated Rural Development Programme and Employment Guarantee Schemes have benefited the people by providing loans and subsidies to young entrepreneurs. Seeds and chemical fertilizers are also made available to them from the Block Development Office. Some training and vocational guidance centres for women are also functioning, but their services have not been fully utilized. Irrigation is available through rainwater, and hence they mostly use organic manures. The sources of fuel energy are wood and kerosene oil. Public distribution system by way of fair price shops is available.

Vatsala Sarkar

PHARERA

The Pharera, also pronounced as Pharere or Pharehre, is a scheduled caste, a small community of the traditional country dyers. In view of their occupation as dyers they are also identified as Rangrez or Rangsaz. Literally name Pharera has been derived from *phulehra,* meaning flowery or colourful, and gradually became Pharehra or Pharera. Among Muslims, these dyers are known as Lallari. The history and ethnographic accounts of the community are lacking barring a mention in Rose (1919). They are distributed chiefly in Kangra and Hamirpur districts. Population figures in Census of India 1971 (Singh, 1971) are given under two synonyms, viz., for Pharera 375 persons and for Phrera 89 persons. The latter are shown to occur in the old Mahasu district that covered most of the present-day Shimla district. But the 1981 Census provides the population figure of 1109 for them.

The community lives in the hills and dales of the sub-Himalayas which receive, in general, a warm and temperate climate, low humidity and medium rainfall. They distributed mainly in the suburban or urban settings as the occupation of dying (taken up along with dry cleaning at present) flourishes mainly in urban dwellings. They are indistinguishable from others in respect of language, dress and ornaments and dietary habits. They speak local dialects, e.g., Kangri dialect of western Pahari and write in Devanagari script within and outside the community. Older people also read and write Urdu (in Perso-Arabic script). Men wear *kurta* and *pyjama* or pants and women wear *kurta* and *salwar* and a *chunni* or *dupatta.* Ornaments worn by women are nose stud/pin or *nath,* ear-rings, a neclace, finger ring and *payal* or *pajeb.*

Rice, wheat and maize are common staple foods eaten with various pulses like *urd, moong, masur, kulthi,* peas and beans and various seasonal vegetables, roots and tubers. The cooking medium is vegetable *ghee* or mustard oil. They are occasionally non-vegetarian in food habit except some followers of the Arya Samaj sect, who abstain from meat, fish and eggs as well as liquor. Only the men consume country liquor on festive occasions. Milk and milk products are consumed regularly. Fruit intake is moderate and seasonal. Non-vegetarian food is not consumed during death pollution. Men smoke *bidi* and cigarette and loose tabacco in *hukka.*

The Phareras distinguish a few *gots* or clans, like Manhas, Kaushal, etc., used as indicators of ancestry and for regulating matrimonial alliances. They claim Kshatriya varna status and place themselves in a middle position in the regional hierarchy. But other people perceive Pharera's Sudra status in the varna hierarchy.

The Phareras are endogamous and practise *got* and village exogamy (except in towns). Mates are acquired through negotiation. *Batta-satta* may also occur. Adult marriages occur but some decades back pre-puberty marriages were not uncommon. Bride-price is not taken but *kanyadan* is performed and dowry is given in kind in the form of household articles, clothes, ornaments, etc. Marriage symbols are *sindur, koka/tili* or *laung* or a nose ring of gold and glass bangles. The bride lives patrilocally. Monogamy is practised and a second wife is acquired in rare cases where there is no issue from the first wife. There is social approval for widow and widower marriages which may be junior levirate and sororate. Junior levirate is not ceremonized and is called *chadar dalna*. Either of the spouses may also seek divorce on grounds on maladjustment. Presently, however, divorce has to be through law courts and compensation is given to the wife, and children become the father's liability. The divorcees may remarry. Main changes in marriage rules are seen in the increase in age at marriage, prevalence of dowry and legalization of divorce.

The family pattern of the Pharera is mainly of the nuclear type. Usually the married sons get separated and the joint families are fast breaking up. In the joint families the *nuh* or *bahuti* avoids *saurah* and *jeth*. Similarly, joking relationships like many Hindu communities of the region occur between *devar-bhabi, jija-sali, nanad-bhabi* and *jija-sala*. Paternal property is inherited on male lines and as per the rule of male equigeniture. The eldest son succeeds the father. The status of women is nearly equal to men for all practical purposes. The women also contribute to family income as some are employed as nurses and teachers. In rural areas they participate in the collection of fuel and fetch potable water. They participate in social and religious ceremonies and in political activities as well. They regulate family expenditure and also have a say in domestic decisions.

Hindu Sanatana rituals are observed. pre-delivery rituals have lost significance and are not observed but pre- and post-delivery restrictions are observed. Post-delivery birth pollution called *sutak* is observed and purification occurs by taking *gunt*. Naming ceremony is observed by some and name is given as per the horoscope of the child. *Kheerpu* or *annaprashan* is observed by some in the eighth month. *Jamalu* or *mundan* of boys is performed by the *mama* of the child on any odd year before five years of age. Thread-wearing ceremony occurs at marriage.

The marriage rituals are performed by a Brahman *purohit* as per the Vedic rites. The family propitiates clan deity. Major marriage rituals occur at the bride's residence when in the *vedi* the bride and groom circumambulate the sacred fire and *kanyadan* is performed by her parents and they give feast. The bride and groom also worship a mango or *daran* tree and take its rounds at the groom's place. *Muklawa* ceremony occurs on the next day of the marriage.

The death rituals are performed as per the tenets of the Hindus. The dead are cremated and ashes are immersed in the Beas river at Kaleshwar or in the Ganges at Hardwar and immersion worship is performed by the Panda. Death pollution is maintained for 13 days and a *havan* and ancestor worship performed by the Charaj or Acharaj who seeks offerings in the name of the departed soul. The Brahman priest performs purification *havan* and seeks offerings. *Barkhi* and *chabarkh* death rites are performed by the family priest.

The Phareras are landless and subsist on non-agricultural pursuits. The traditional occupation of dyeing clothes is presently practised by only a few, together with dry cleaning of clothes. Some others have also taken up tailoring as their way of livelihood. Many people run petty general merchant shops and are businessmen, whereas some others have taken up various jobs in Government departments as clerks, teachers, engineers, etc. There are persons in bank and railway services and some are advocates. There are drivers, mechanics, electricians and persons seeking casual daily-wage labourers as well.

Social disputes are solved by the elders of the community or village/ locality or members of the ward or statutory Gram Panchayat as per the nature of disputes. Legal course is also taken up in major disputes.

The Phareras are Hindus and propitiate various family, clan, village and regional deities and pantheon gods. A few follow the Arya Samaj sect but a majority follows Sanatana. Bankhandi Devi is propitiated as a *kul* or clan deity. Guga, Balak Nath, Kaleshwar Mahadev, Jawalamukhi, etc., are village and regional deities of special reverence. The annual fairs of their holy shrines are also visited. Their sacred specialists are from other communities. They also have faith in the local oracles and *vaid* for treatment of certain ailments and for conformation of guilt and theft. Major festivals of socio-economic and socio-religious significance celebrated by the community are Holi, Baisakhi, Nag Panchami, Sair, Dussehra/Navratre, Diwali and Lohri.

They share the regional Pahari, Kangri and Punjabi songs, tales and music and dance. Some of the famous folk oral traditions are *Kunju-Chenchlo, Nurpure da thana, Kangre de fauji, Subhadro-Bajeer, Jhanjhoti, Bhala sipahiya dogria*, etc. *Gidda* and *Nati* are the main dances. A few wall and floor paintings with wheat flour or lime are made to decorate the house on festivals and festivities by women. Embroidery as a craft is also maintained by some, and the women know knitting.

The Brahman and Rajput are traditionally served with *suchchi rasoi* cooked by a Brahman/Rajput *boti* in their social gatherings. Presently, however, there is some relaxation about this norm in the towns. Putative kinship— *dharam bhai* and *dharam bahin*—may occur with other community. The traditional water sources are shared except with certain castes but presently separate taps are used. The cremation grounds are also common, so are the religious shrines and other public places. There is no specific role of the community on festivals or festivities. The receiving and rendering of the economic services exist. Modern intercommunity linkages have emerged strongly as they have people in business entrepreneurship, persons holding white-collar jobs, engineers, teachers, advocates, etc., and political leadership has emerged at the regional level.

The Phareras have responded favourably to modern developmental programmes. They favour education for both boys and girls though higher education for boys is considered more favourably. Higher education for girls is not much desired socially. Modern system of health and medicare is favoured and generally availed of but the attitude towards indigenous medicare is also favourable because it is easily accessible to the poor. They favour small families but desire at least one son. Usually sterilization is adopted as a method for family planning. Drinking water through pipes is available but the traditional springs and *bauri* are still used at times of inadequate supply of potable water. They avail themselves of various facilities of the Integrated Rural Development Programmes of the State and get subsidies on various things, as are in general applicable to the scheduled castes. Modern mass media (radio/television) facilities are availed of and cinemas are also visited. Road and postal facilities are in their neighbourhood or vicinity. Their houses are electrified. They use firewood, cowdung cakes, coal, sawdust, kerosene oil, etc., as the main fuel sources. A few in towns also use liquid petroleum gas for cooking. The nutritional programmes for children (ICDS) are availed of, including immunization. Facility of public distributin system is also availed of.

A.R. Sankhyan

PUNJABI

The term Punjabi has been derived from Punjab, recalled as the ancestral home of Lord Rama's mother Kaushalya. The word 'Punjabi' is made up of two Persian words: *punj* meaning 'five' and *ab* meaning 'water'. Hence, this name was given to this land of five rivers possibly in an era when this region came into close contacts with Persia. In the Vedic period this region was known as *Sapta Sindhu*, the land of seven rivers. During the Greek occupation, the territory shrunk to the five rivers of Satluj, Beas, Ravi, Chenab and Jhelam. In the medieval period and especially under Maharaja Ranjit Singh the region was known as the Lahore Province after the name of its capital city. During the British time Haryana (including Hissar) and Delhi were added to the existing territory and it was renamed the Province of Punjab. In 1947, after independence and partition, India got the area lying to the east of the river Ravi under the name East Punjab while the area left with Pakistan was called West Punjab.

The communities/castes living at that time in the Punjab region were known as Punjabis to the outsiders and after partition a large section of the Punjab population which settled in East Punjab and other States of India were identified as Punjabis, irrespective of caste, creed and religion. It is a mixture of many groups. The Punjabi is recognized by the others because of having its own culture, language, dress pattern and forms of religion.

In Himachal Pradesh all the communities of Punjab who speak the Punjabi language and have settled there after partition or before partition are identified as Punjabi whether they are Hindu, Sikh, Muslim or Christian, particularly the first two as they are numerically preponderant. There are a number of Jat Sikhs with various clans, viz. Gil, Sondhi, Lail, Mann, Garewal, Dhaliwal, Bains, Solita, Pandher, etc., and Soni Sikh which includes Giddhl, Grin, Paple, etc. The concentration of Mona (non-Sikh) Punjabi too is high in the State. Besides these there are castes like Khatri, Sood, Banjara, Labana, Sanyara, Tarkhan, Dangotra, Bhatia, Arora, and Punjabi Brahman (Sharma) who are identified as Punjabi in Himachal Pradesh. Sikh and non-Sikh both equally exist in the region and also have their seperate identities. The total population of the community is not known. They are spread in Paonta Sahib, Shimla, Solan, Nahan, Kullu, Manali, Chamba, Mandi, Dharmshala and other parts of the State. Their concentration in Shimla, Solan and Sirmaur districts is higher than in other parts, some of them migrated from Hoshiarpur, Jalandhar and Patiala (East Punjab) and Lahore, Rawalpindi, Mianwali (West Punjab) about 150 years back particularly to Sirmaur district.

Other Punjabis also came and settled after partition in Himachal Pradesh.

They speak Punjabi language among themselves and use Gurumukhi script. While communicating with others they use Hindi and English and use Devanagri script. *Kesh, kripan, kanghi, kada* and *kachcha* are the main identification markers of Punjabi Sikh community bearing Pagri while the Mona Punjabi use the common dress as worn by the others. Pants and shirt among the men and *salwar, kurta* and *dupatta* among women is the common dress and very much popular among the community. The scheduled caste Punjabis, have also the same status in Himachal Pradesh.

They are mostly non-vegetarian and take almost all kinds of edible meat except beef. They also take fish and eggs. Some groups who are Vaishnava do not take non-vegetarian food. Their staple food consists of wheat *chapati*, rice, maize, vegetables and pulses normally of *urad, moong* and *rajmah*, roots and tubers. Fruit consumption is high. Vegetable oil and rapeseed oil are used as cooking medium, though mustard oil is gradually being used more often. The use of alcoholic drinks is common among the men and on certain jovial occasions like *sagai* and marriage. Women may also take them. The drinks are purchased from the market. They do smoke *bidi*, cigarette or hubble-bubble. Among the Sikh the use of tobacco in any form is religiously prohibited. Consumption of milk and milk products is high among them. The frequency of intake of non-vegetarian foods and alcoholic drinks is more in winter months than in summer.

The Punjabi which comprises many castes/communities and religious groups also has differentiation on the basis of clans, occupations, economic and educational and social status. The Punjabis hold themselves in higher esteem than the other communities of the region. They place themselves in the varna order according to their caste and subgroup status.

The community is endogamous but clan exogamy is always observed. Among the exogamous sections marriage with the near cognates is prohibited. Hypergamy exists in sporadic cases but no consanguinity is followed. Junior levirate and sororate are practised. Adult marriage is the norm and age of marriage is usually between 20 and 25 years for both boys and girls. Negotiated marriage is the prominent feature while some cases of love marriage have also occurred in urban and rural situations. The girl's father takes the initiative for marriage and contacts a suitable family. Sometimes the services of a matchmaker, who is generally the common friend or relative of both the families, are used. Monogamy is the general practice but in some castes bigamy is also allowed if the first wife is barren. Nowadays, the symbols of married women are vermillion, bangles, *bindi* and toe-ring, though in the past it was not necessary to put on vermilion.

Because of the Punjabis' involvement in trade and business entrepreneurs, there is a more of dowry in the community. The bride goes to live with her husband after marriage. Divorce is permissible with social and judicial approval, though in some lower castes it is sought through their Biradari Panchayat. The common grounds for divorce are inability of the husband to support his family, bigamy, adultery, barrenness, impotency and cruelty. Compensation is given to the wife and either of the parties can seek divorce. Children are the liability of the father after divorce. Widow, widower and divorcee remarriages are permissible in the community, but in case of widow remarriage no rituals are performed and only *sindur*, bangles and *chadar* are offered by the man to the widow in simple, common gathering, sometimes in a Gurudwara (among Sikhs). The marriage of a widow with the deceased husband's younger brother is solemnized with the consent of panchayat and is known as *chadar dalna*.

The joint family particularly of the vertically extended type was the usual pattern of family in the past and also exist today. But, it is now being gradually replaced by nuclear families, owing to the constraints of modern living. Generally the new couples establish new households after marriage, particularly in urban areas but in rural areas the mixed extended families are still in common. The interpersonal relationship in the family is that of respect, love and cordiality. Elders in the family are respected and are also looked after in their old age or when incapacitated. It is the duty of the parents to see that their children are well placed in life. It is the joint responsibility of the parents for bringing up their children. Avoidance relationship is maintained between *jeth* and younger brother's wife and between the son's wife and *sasur,* in rural areas and villages where married women put veil by *dupatta* on their faces before *jeth* and *sasur*. Joking relationship exists between husband's younger brother and sister-in-law and between husband and wife's elder and younger sisters.

After the death of the father, property is equally divided among the sons. In the event of there being no son in the family, the son-in-law is invited to the house and the girl instead of going to her husband's house stays with her father, and the son-in-law inherits the property of the in-laws. Succession pattern is followed on the male line, with the eldest son succeeding the father.

Punjabi women have equal status and work shoulder to shoulder with men in farms, fields, cattle sheds and other walks of life. They have an intense love for work. Their role in economic affairs is tremendous, for they carry out practically all the agricultural activities except ploughing. They collect wood and give fodder to the animals, milk the animals and prepare items out of it. They have a pivotal role in all the spheres of life and participate in all social functions, rituals and control the family expenditure. They are good managers of the family for they carry out all the household activities right from cooking of food, looking after the children to managing the affairs of the family.

The life-cycle rituals among the Punjabi community vary from caste to caste, group to group, religion to religion and territory to territory. The birth of a male child, especially if it happens to be the first issue, is greatly rejoiced over in the family. Pre-delivery ritual is observed in seventh or ninth month of the pregnancy called *godbharai* in which certain articles like dry fruits, clothes, ornaments, sweets/sweet rice are sent by the gril's father. Birth pollution is observed for 13 to 40 days depending upon the tradition of the family, and on these days a purificatory bath is taken by the parturient mother and the child, which is called *dhaman uthana* (end of pollution). In the Sikh community *namkaran sanskar* is observed after 40 days or six months. *Mundan* ceremony is observed in Punjabi Hindus while in Sikh it is religiously prohibited and in place of *mundan* the ritual of *kanghi* is observed.

Marriage is solemnized with the consent of the parents, after being satisfied about the suitability of the match. A go-between is employed to negotiate, and he is normally a relative. The marriage is solemnized by circumambulating the sacred fire seven times in Punjabi Hindus, while in Punjabi Sikh the couple have to go around the Guru Granth Sahib four times. The circumambulation is known as *lavan phera.* In a marriage ceremony the important rituals which are observed both by the Punjabi Hindu and Sikh are *sagai, kudmai, akhand path, mehndi reet, gana, ghudchadi, kwardhoti, lavan phera, phera milni* or *dukao doli. Kanyadan* is performed only by Punjabi Hindus, and the Sikh observe *mundri* ritual. After marriage the bride goes to live with her husband.

The dead are cremated but the infants are buried. The last rites are performed by the husband in case of wife and by the eldest son in case of father. The pollution is observed for 10 days in Sikh community while in Punjabi Hindus it lasts for 13 days. Ashes are collected on fourth day and disposed of in the Ganges or any other holy river. In Punjabi Sikh, in the event of death *akhand path, bhog* and *rasm pagri* rituals are performed on 10th day, and after one year, *salana* is observed.

The Punjabi is a community of cultivators and businessmen both, depending upon the geographical region in which they live. Most of the members of the community who are settled in rural areas depend on agriculture and animal husbandry and utilize land as the main resource. But in urban areas most of the families do their own business, run industry, shops, transport, textile business, jewellery-making, etc. They are big landowners and control their resources by individual proprietorship. In most of the families now, people are educated and are holding different government jobs such as doctors, engineers, teachers, administrators, etc. Being economically well-off, only a few of them work as labourers and industrial workers. They have a direct link with the daily market which is fully regulated. The entire trade is in cash only. There is total dependence of the community on the market, where they market their produce and also purchase commodities of their daily need. Cash is the prevalent currency of exchange in a regular market, sometimes deferred payments are also accepted.

Earlier the community had Biradari Panchayats to solve their problems and disputes but now these are restricted only to villages. Only Punjabi Sikhs have their panchayat consisting the aged persons, respectable members of the community and office bearers of the Gurudwara committee in the urban areas. This works to bring about compromise or to seek peaceful solution of problems. But the committee does not have any strong say or strict hold on the society. Though chieftainship is not present, yet a person is nominated by voice vote to head the panel of *panch* (jury) and is known as *chowdhary*. The statutory panchayat maintains law and order and plans and implements welfare and developmental activities. Beside these panchayats, Punjabis also have their own associations, unions and committees to regulate the norms of the society. These associations hold monthly, biannual and annual meetings at regional, State and national levels respectively.

The Punjabi community being a mixture of many castes, and groups, follow different religions. Their family, clan and regional deities differ from caste to caste and from region to region. For Punjabi Sikhs Guru Nanak Dev and Guru Govind Singh are especially propitiated besides other Sikh gurus. On the other hand, Punjabi Hindus believe in and worship the pantheon gods and goddesses Rama, Krishna, Shiva, Durga, etc. The major sacred centres are Amritsar, Paonta Sahib, Bangla Sahib, Vaishno Devi, Haridwar, Badrinath etc. Their sacred specialists are from the same community for religious teachings and to perform bith, marriage and death rites. Holi, Diwali, Dussehra, Raksha Bandhan, Janamashtami, Baisakhi, Guru Parabs and different birthdays of their prophets are celebrated with great gaeity and enthusiasm and all the festivals and fairs are considered of great socioreligious and socioeconomic significance.

Many groups of the Punjabi community like Sunar, Tarkhan and other artisan castes have their own arts and crafts. The art of embroidery has continued to flourish in Punjab and other regions. Embroidered shawls and *phulkari* of Punjab are known throughout the country. Making of silver and gold ornaments has always been the tradition of the Sunar community. The community has oral traditions, folklore, folktales and folksongs of their own. *Bhangra* and *Gidda* dances are famous throughout the country and the community has their own musical instruments like *gubgubi, damru, ghara, iktara, toomba, sarangi, chimta, dholak, tabla, nagara, tasha* and *rabab*, and these are used in folkdances and folksongs. Both women and men participate seperately in their traditional folksongs and dance with enthusiasm.

Traditional intercommunity linkages existed with other members of the Punjabi and non-Punjabi communities, with many castes and communities involved in trade, service and agricultural practices. For cultivation, they employ labourers from various castes residing in their region and *jajmani* system is still prevalent in rural areas. On the occasions of marriage, birth, death and festivals, the services of carpenter, goldsmith, ironsmith, Brahman, sweeper, etc., are required for their specialized services. They are paid both in cash and kind after harvesting and on other occasions. The community shares crematorium and religious shrines. Because of being involved in trade, business and service, they always maintain cordial relations with their clients irrespective of caste, creed or religion. Being well-off and well educated, the community has many scholars, doctors, engineers, administrators, etc. among its members. Political leadership has emerged and they contest elections.

Developmental programmes have left a good impact on the community in all walks of life. Their attitude towards formal education is very favourable and they are paying greater attention towards the education of boys and girls. The children of the Punjabis study up to the highest level available in their region. The Punjabis are very conscious of their health and they eat nutritious diet and work hard to keep themselves physically fit. They believe in the saying *dab ke wah te raj ke khab*, i.e., work hard and eat well. But if ever they fall sick, they use allopathic medicines, having favourable attitude towards modern medicines. Family planning programmes have been very popular among them and now they prefer only two or three children using modern methods of family planning. It is generally women who get sterilized. Drinking water facilities are available in their locality through piped water, though some areas still lack piped water. Agriculture and business are the primary occupations of the community and also a source of self-employment. In rural areas firewood, kerosene oil and cowdung cakes are used as fuel. Most of the areas still lack irrigation facilities and the entire cultivation depends on rainwater, though chemical fertilizers are now being used to boost up the crop production. The facilities of public distribution system are availed of by the community.

Anand Saran

PUNJABI REFUGEE

By the term "Refugee" we mean all those people who came from the North West Frontier Province and from the western part of Punjab which now forms part of Pakistan following India's partition in 1947, and are still called as such. The circumstances which led to their exodus were almost catastrophic in nature; they were uprooted from their homeland and faced the problem of finding their roots again. The fury of communal tension which engulfed the whole nation led to loss of life unprecendented in history. The task of the rehablitation was challenging and often painfully slow. Initially they were housed in camps and later distributed to different States. In Himachal pradesh they were rehabilitated in Sirmaur, Chamba, Bilaspur and Shimla. Ethnically, the majority belongs to the Khatri stock. They have, however, territorial groupings differing to certain extent in dialect, dress and food habits from one another. Amongst their own people they still converse in the dialects of their respective places of origin, but have also learnt Hindi, Punjabi and the local Himachali to facilitate communication with outsiders. They use Perso-Arabic and Devanagari scripts. The traditional dress for men used to be loose trousers, a long shirt down the knee and a *pagri*, but this has been practically restricted to a few among the older generation. The young men have started wearing western-style pants and shirt. Women wear *salwar* and *kurta* with a *chadar* to cover their head, and also wear *sari*.

Their staple diet consists of wheat, maize, rice and pulses of *mah*, gram, beans and some seasonal vegetables. They also take non-vegetarian food which normally consists of mutton. Beef is strictly prohibited. The medium of cooking is mustard oil, hydrogenated fats and also clarified butter. They also like to smoke and drink, which are locally purchased from the market. Tea is liked and consumed by all.

The Refugees have territorial groupings since they hailed from different districts comprising the North West Frontier and also parts of Western Punjab, such as Bannu, Dera Ghazikhan, Dera Ismail Khan, Hoti Mardan and Peshawar. Each of the territorial groupings tended to be endogamous earlier but ever since migration there have been frequent intermarriages. Since ethnically they mostly belong to the Khatri caste there are subdivisions, sections and subsections among them. Besides there are also Hindu and Sikh amongst the Refugees, intermarriages between whom were fairly common but of late a trend towards segregation is seen. The major Khatri subdivisions are Bari, Bunjahi and Sarin. A kind of hypergamous relationship existed among the first two groups whereas it is said that Sarin are endogamous. Each of these subgroups has *gotra* and is exogamous. Some of the usual *gotra* names are Bhasin, Jolly, Chug, Seth, Mehra and Arora. The Aroara is also a separate community among the Punjabis like the Khatri. In the regional caste hierarchy they have a high-middle status.

Marriage is settled through negotiation, avoiding the *gotra* of father, and mother's side. The proposal for marriage is initiated by the groom's parents. Adult marriage is the general practice. It is usually contemplated when the boy starts earning and girls cross at least 16 years of age. Bride price is not reported. Dowry in the form of gifts and items of day-to-day use are given to the daughter at the time of her marriage but there is no compulsion for giving the same. They are monogamous but a second marriage may take place in case the first wife is barren.

Remarriage of widow, widower and divorcee is permitted and so are levirate and sororate. A widow remarriage generally takes place when the woman is young and issueless, otherwise they themselves do not go in for a second marriage. Divorce is socially disapproved and is rare, but in cases where rapproachment is impossible, divorce may be affected through courts. The custody of the children in divorce cases is also decided by the court.

The traditional joint family system is undergoing change and nuclear families are encountered more often. The family has a strong patriarchial base, the residence being patrilocal and authority patripaternal. The inheritance and succession are patrilineal. All the sons receive equal share in the father's property. The daughters do not have the rights on property except in situations when there is no son to inherit the same. Under present-day law the daughters are to receive equal share in the father's property but in practise this is not adhered to in a majority of the cases.

The interpersonal relationships amongst the members of the family are based on love and cooperation especially in times of need. Both avoidance and joking relationships exist as per age, sex and kinship status. Women observe some distance in the presence of the elder relatives from the husband's side whereas with younger brothers and sisters, relations are fairly relaxed and of joking nature. This is not to suggest that conflicts are unknown; rather some petty quarrels do occur on division of labour, over property issues, check on the freedom of the youngsters, but these are viewed as part of the system.

The women do not enjoy parity with men. Customarily a daughter does not have a share in the ancestral property nor does she have complete economic freedom or the liberty to exercise independent socio-economic decisions. For all this she must seek the prior consent of her husband or father, brother or son, as the case may be. In the discharge of domestic management she decidedly enjoys an indispensable position. She also helps in the family business and thus contributes indirectly to the economy. In religious fields she has very little role except for the fact that she participates in rituals and festivals. Politically she is not actively conscious and her participation ceases with the casting of votes. Of late some refugee women have emerged as political entities at the district level.

The life-cycle rituals commencing from birth to death show a queer admixture of Hindu and Sikh religious practices for it was fairly common among the Refugee Khatri families to have one or two Sikh members within the house. The influence of Sikh practices is therefore quite firmly interwoven with their customs and beliefs. The birth of the male child is an occasion for rejoicing and celebration. Pre- and post-birth rituals, restrictions and pollution are observed. The mother and the newborn are given their first purificatory bath on sixth, eleventh and twenty-first day after delivery. Thereafter the mother along with the child visits the Gurudwara or the temple and the child is named after consulting the family priest who suggests the name after studying the child's horoscope. It is a fairly common practice to hold the recital of Guru Granth Sahib in the house on important social ceremonies. Among the Hindus the first shaving of the head is mostly observed before the child crosses the fifth year. This is followed by investiture of the *janeu* ceremony which is invariably deferred till marriage.

Marriage is performed in accordance with either Hindu or Sikh rites. After the betrothal or *sagai* the date and the time of the marriage are fixed after consulting the priest who suggests an auspicious day for the occasion. A number of colourful ceremonies precede before the actual marriage which takes place at the bride's house. Those performing the marriage according to Sikh rites hold rituals inside the Gurudwara. *Kanyadan* and *phera* are the most important ceremonies that are conducted at the time of marriage.

They cremate their dead but infants are immersed in the water. The ashes and bones of the dead after cremation are also immersed in the Ganges at Hardwar. Death pollution is normally observed for 13 days. For the first three days food for the bereaved family is brought by relatives or neighbours. On the fourth day a *shanti path* congregation at the hall or temple premises is arranged to offer a prayer for the peace of the departed soul. A *pagri* rite is also performed on this day. The turban cloth is brought by the maternal uncle and is tied to the next eldest male member in the family. On this day the maternal relatives also give some cash. Some of the money is given as charity to the temples and to other charitable institutions as may be wished by the family.

Speaking on the economic potentialities of the community it would be wise to quote from Sir George Campbell's *Ethnology of India* that "they had the whole trade of the Punjab and of most of Afghanistan. No village can get on without the Khatri who keeps accounts, does the banking business and buys and sells the grain. They seem to get on with the people better than most traders and usurers of this kind". They still continue to be so even after the partition and going through the ordeal of reestablishing themselves afresh. With their industrious nature and keen business sense they were able to soon take over the trade from the local businessmen. Of the 968 refugees rehabilitated in Sirmaur alone, 898 are non-agriculturists engaged in trade and commerce.

Besides they have found jobs in Government and private organizations and have also taken up other white-collar professions as teachers, lawyers and doctors. Some have successfully established their own cottage industry, manufacturing shops, hosiery items and have proved their metal in running shops and dealing with different items of trade. They maintain their link with local market either directly or through a middleman for making business transactions. Economically they are now among the well-to-do communities and leading businessmen of the area.

They have formed their regional association which in fact looks after the larger interests of the community. The funds collected are utilized for building community halls, temples, charitable hospitals, and for providing means of support to the widows and destitute women of their community. For all practical purposes, disputes are settled informally by the intervention of the elders of the *biradari*. If the parties are not satisfied, the matter is referred to the courts for legal settlement.

There are both Hindu and Sikh among the Refugees residing in the same house. It is said that Sikh Gurus travelled extensively in the North West Provinces and Western Punjab preaching Sikhism, therefore the impact of Sikh religion was profound even on the Hindus inhabiting those region.

Both the Hindus and Sikhs visit each other's shrine. The Hindus pay great respect to the Guru Granth Sahab besides worshipping the Hindu temples and the gods and goddesses of the Hindu pantheon. There are also regional and village deities which are held in great esteem. The major Hindu and Sikh festivals celebrated are Lohri, Dussehra, Diwali and Shivratri as also the birth anniversaries of the famous Sikh Gurus. The Baisakhi fair is of great importance to them.

The different territorial groups among the Refugee Khatris share a close cultural similarity in terms of customs, folk traditions, namely folktales, folklore and folksongs.

The people maintain cordial relations with the neighbouring communities but share a special bond of love and mutual concern among their own Refugee population. Connubial relation were normally restricted within the Refugee Khatris but nowadays marriages with non-Refugee Khatri are also taking place. Commensality is maintained with certain castes and they would not dine with castes like Doom, Chamar, Chuhra, Mehra and the like. The traditional patron-client relationship is no longer in operation except in some families who may have their own Brahman *purohit* for performing various life-cycle rituals. Besides, modern linkages have developed with neighbouring local population due to common business interests and day-to-day contact in social, political and religious gatherings.

The attitude of the people towards development has been positive and progressive. They have utilized the facilities of education, communication, health, family welfare, transport, public distribution centres, water and electricity. As regards economic assistance, except for the initial rehabilitation process, they have not looked forward to the Government for economic relief. With their great mercantile energy, business sense, industry and cooperation, they were able not only to surpass the traumatic experience of the partition but also were able to establish an edge over the local businessmen by proving their superiority in different business ventures and other fields.

Vatsala Sarkar

RAEEN

The Raeen, also spelled as Arain, and synonymous with the Kunjra, is a small community of traditional cultivators and grocers . They are regarded as converts from the Hindu Saini or Kamboh who got converted to Islam in the twelfth century. They were originally confined to the lower Indus valley. Subsequently they spread up to the five rivers of Punjab (Rose, 1919). They appear to have entered the sub-Himalayan region of Himachal Pradesh from the Punjab plains as is apparent from some of their clan names in the district Mandi (study area) which are similar to the clans found in districts Jalandhar and Kapurthala, viz., Hasi, Mandu, Rame, Rai, Sindhi or Sindhu and Butta (cf. Rose, 1919: 14-15).

They are concentrated in the Balh area of district Mandi and are sparsely settled elsewhere. It is a wide valley in the sub-Himalayan hills with warm to temperate climate in general, low humidity and thin forest cover on the hill and receives medium rainfall but does not experience snowfall. The community perceives its distribution at regional level but the population figures for the community are not available.

The men wear *kurta* and trousers or pants and the women wear *kurta* and *salwar* but no *burka* or veil. The men also wear white *topi*. They usually speak the local Mandiali dialect of the western Pahari among themselves and converse in Hindi with outsiders. Written communicaton is in the Devanagari script. Perso-Arabic is also used in their religious gatherings and communications.

The Raeens are non-vegetarian. They eat fish, eggs and *halal* meat of sheep and goat but beef is not taken. The consumption of vegetables and fruits is moderate and seasonal. Fruits like banana, apple, peach, guava and mango are consumed. The common staple food is wheat, maize, rice and barley which are eaten with pulses of various types—*urd, moong, masur* (lentil), gram, peas, *kulthi* and beans along with tubers like potatoes, *arbi* and vegetables of different types. The cooking medium is generally mustard oil or vegetable or *desi ghee.*

Some men take country liquor locally prepared from sugar molasses, especially on festive or marriage occasions. The women do not take alcoholic beverages. Milk and milk products are part of their daily diet. The men smoke *bidi* and sometimes cigarettes. Usually tobacco in an indigenous pipe called *hukka* is smoked. Betel-chewing and snuf are not seen in the community. There does not seem to be any change in the food habits.

The Raeens distinguish *gots* which are the smallest social units to denote ancestry and are used for deciding marriages. There is no internal social hierarchy. Some of the clans of the area are Hasi, Mandu, Rame and Sindi in Balh area of Mandi district and Bhutto in Bilaspur district. They usually do not affix clan names (barring a few like Bhutto) as surnames. Among the Muslim communities in the region the community perceives itself at the middle level. Other Muslim communities also endorse their middle position in the regional social hierarchy.

Marriage rules are community endogamy, and village and *got* exogamy. Sometimes the rule of community endogamy is relaxed to entertain economically better-off spouses from other Muslim communities. Marriage among the cross-cousins like father's sister's daughter and mother's brother's son are preferred. Monogamy is practised and bigamy is considered a luxury or contracted in case of childlessness or no male issue from the first wife. Marriages usually occur in adulthood and through negotiation. The marriage symbols are glass bangles and nose rings. *Mehar* is promised for future payment in case of divorce and ranges between Rs. 2000 and 4000. Dowry in the form of ornaments, clothes and utensils is given.

Dissolution of marriage is allowed on religious sacrament/social approval for men only and the *mehar* is to be paid back to the spouse. The minor children are the liability of the mother but grown up children are the responsibility of the father. The ground for divorce is usually maladjustment or adultery. Both the divorcees may remarry but generally the women have difficulty in doing so. Widow and widower remarriages are permissible. The men may marry junior sororate but levirate is not practised for women. The increase in marriage age is the apparent change in the marriage institution. Also there has been some increase in the amount of *mehar*.

The family pattern is both nuclear as well as vertically extended joint. But joint families are on the decline. Avoidance relationships exist as in most of the Hindu communities of the area. The *lari* or *bahu* keeps a *ghoond* from *saurah* and *jeth* and other elderly male members of the village. Joking relations are not formal but may exist between *devar* and *bhabi* and *jija* and *sali*. The two *kurams* also cut jokes on each other during the marriage. The junior members of the family are obliged to respect the seniors though conflicts may occur on property matters.

The status of the Raeen women is considered low. They perform all domestic duties, participate in agriculture and animal husbandry, bring potable water and collect fuel and fodder. They participate in all social and ritual gatherings but lack a role in political activities and in the mechanism of social control. They do not seek employment but control family expenditure and have freedom in domestic decisions but not in the external affairs.

The life-cycle rituals are similar to those of other Muslim communities of the region. Pre-delivery and post-delivery restrictions on mother are present. The post-delivery pollution lasts for 40 days. There is no ceremony observed for the christening of the child but a *maulvi* may be consulted on any day to give a name. Some people may observe *aqiqa* ceremony. *Khatna* or *sunnat* of the male child is the major childhood/boyhood ritual performed by an Abdal. But presently some persons prefer to perform circumcision by a doctor to avoid sepsis. The *maulvi* recites *kalma* from the Quran and a feast (usually non-vegetarian) is given to the community.

The marriage rituals are observed as per the Islamic tenets. The oil and *mehndi* ceremony is observed for both the bride and the groom. *Nikah* is performed at the bride's residence. The *maulvi* takes *kaul karar* (consent) of the boy and the girl three times with two witnesses to contract the marriage. He also signs the *sharatnama* for the *mehar.* The bride's parents arrange a feast for the groom's party. The groom's parents also reciprocate the same to the bride's kith and kin on the next day at the bridegroom's place.The *muklawa* of the bride occurs on the following day of the marriage.

The death rituals are also typical of the Muslims of the region. They bury the dead outside the village and observe *chilla* for 40 days. Ancestor worship is observed on the seventh, tenth, twentieth, thirteth and fortieth day. On the last day called *chalia*, a Faqir is offered clothes and some money, and a non-vegetarian meal is served to the gathered relatives and villagers.

The Raeens are landowners with individual proprietorship and have continued this traditional occupation of agriculture and animal husbandry. They also practise weaving in the family. Horticulture has also become a supplementary occupation. With the increase of the family size and limited landholdings some also seek daily wages as casual labourers. Some are also in Government or private employment to add to the family income. Child labour also exists to some extent for agriculture and animal husbandry work.

The market is at a small distance and is of daily nature and is fully regulated. The transactions are usually in cash. The social control is generally in the hands of the *sayane* of the village and the Islamic committee solves socioreligious problems. Generally the problems related to divorce and general social uplift are taken up by this committee which is elected by a voice vote. The multi-ethnic village economic disputes are solved by the members of the statutory Gram Panchayat, which usually deals with the development and welfare of the village. The guilty may be penalized by the imposition of a cash fine by the Gram Panchayat.

The Raeen have faith in Allah but also give importance to family, village and regional deities but have no *silsila* affiliation with the Pirs and Paigambars. They do propitiate regional deities like Lakhdata and Khwaja on fulfilment of their wishes. They also have faith in spirits or ghosts and their exorcists treat diseases of supernatural origins. The *maulvi* is their main sacred specialist and performs all life-cycle rituals and also has knowledge of removal of evil spirits.

The *maulvi* may be from the community itself or from the Faqir community or any other well trained person from outside the district or State. Their major festivals of socioreligious importance are Id and Bakrid. But they also participate and prepare festive food on local Hindu festivals like Lohri, Baisakhi, Chiran. They also visit shrines and fairs of the deities in the area. There are no specific community folksongs, tales or folklore but the various regional traditions are shared with communities. The weaving of woollen garments is a domestic craft and some women are skilled in knitting and embroidery.

Modern intercommunity linkages have strongly emerged as they have persons in business entrepreneurship, in white-collar jobs, teachers, in defence services and in private undertakings. Many persons are working in Saudi Arabia. Political leadership has emerged at the district level.

The community is favourably inclined towards modern development programmes. Formal education is usually favoured for the boys but only partly favoured for the girls for social reasons. Both boys and girls generally receive only secondary school education. There is little interest in higher education and usually teachnical education or training is favoured due to more job opportunities in the latter. The usual goals for the girl is only marriage and no employment.

The Raeens favour and utilize both modern and indigenous systems of medicare. Their attitude towards family planning is becoming favourable and couples usually do not prefer more than three children. but at least one son is desired even at the risk of having more daughters. Their family control measure is only sterilization and generally the women get sterilized. Drinking water is available in the vicinity either through tube-wells, handpumps or thorugh traditional *bauri*.

The provisions for intensive rural development programme (IRDP) also exist. They get general subsidy on chemical fertilizers. Old persons receive old-age pension and there are aids for the blind and other physically handicapped persons. The community is almost self-sufficient and self-employed in agriculture, animal husbandry, small-scale industries, etc.

They enjoy modern mass media (radio and television) facilities and sometimes also visit cinema in the adjoining town. Post, telegraph and road facilities are accessible. All houses are electrified. The fuel/energy resources are firewood, cowdung cakes and some also use *gobar* gas. Rain water is the usual source of irrigation and only a few use streams for the purpose.

A. R. Sankhyan

RAJPUT

The Rajput, one of the erstwhile principal warrior and ruling communities of Himachal Pradesh, "are said to be Brahman by original stock" according to Rose (1914). This community has an exceedingly complicated organization based on the two principles of natural descent and social status independent of that descent. In Vedic literature the term *raja-putra* meant 'son of king'. Later on the original meaning was lost, and the term came to mean "a land owner" (Bahadur 1978:41). The Rajputs in fact look upon Rajputana as their place of origin, but the various legends are vague and do not confirm as to who the earliest Rajput was.

According to an account given in the Phulkian States Gazetteer, "the Rajputs are divided into three *bans* (races), i.e., *Suraj-bansi* (solar), *Chandra-bansi* (lunar) and *Agni-kul* or *Baragh-bansi* (fire). Each *bans* is divided into *khanps*, each *khanp* into *nakhs* and each *nakh*, it is said, into *gots*" (Bahadur, *op.cit*). These three divisions of solar, lunar and *agni* Rajputs were subsequently changed to sections and sub-divisions and further into numerous clans and septs, of which 36 were called royal and singled out for special distinction on account of their power and number.

In Kangra, the Katoch Rajputs are the most ancient ruling class. According to the references available in Kangra District Gazetteer (1924-25), Kangra District was originally a part of the kingdom of ancient Jalandhara or Trigarta. The names Jalandhara and Trigarta are used synonymously in Sanskrit literature. In the works of Ptolemy, the Greek geographer, Kangra has been referred to as Kulindrin or Khulindrine also, which indicates that it might have been inhabited by the people of 'Kulinda' group at one time. Katoch, the rulers of the region in the past, according to the gazetteer referred to above, might have taken their clan name from the name of the district or a state around Kangra, which probably was the nucleus of the State. The earlier name of Kangra town was Susharampura which reminds us of the ruler who fought as an ally of the Kaurvas in the Mahabharata war. The Katoch rulers of the area with their offshoots and independent principalities, such as, Jaswan, Guler, Siba and Datarpur, etc. amply testify to the antiquity of the royal line. According to Sir Alexander Cunningham, "The royal family of Jalandhar and Kangra is one of the oldest in India and their genealogy, from the time of the founder Susharma Chandra, appears to me to have a much stronger claim to our belief that any of the long strings of names shown by the more powerful families of Rajputana." Sir Lepel Griffin, while referring to the Rajput dynasties of

Kangra hills is of the opinion that the Katoch dynasty is the oldest one "having genealogies more ancient and unbroken that can be shown by any other royal families in the world".

Bhumi Chand, the founder of the lineage, was the first ruler and in his 234th place, according to succession, was born Susharma Chandra, the hero of Mahabharata war. The original seat of the family is believed to be at Multan which was afterwards shifted to Jalandhara and during the later years to Kangra region. The Chinese pilgrim, Hiuen Tsiang visited Jalandhara during AD 635 and AD 643 twice and stayed as the guest of the ruler named Raja Utito. This ruler has been identified by Cunningham as Adita of Kangra Vanshavali. Jalandhara during those days was a subject of Harshavardhana of Kanauj.

In 1876-77 Col. Gordon Young, Deputy Commissioner Kangra attested to a classification of Rajput septs in five categories, namely, (i) Katoch, Guleria, etc. (ii) Jarial, Manhas, Samkla, Laddu, Dod Ghorewal, Pathiarch and Harbrol, (iii) Patial, Kanthwal, Changra, Guhaina, Bhabauria, Malhoter, Bhandari, Jaggi, Kharwal, Garl, Sangotra, Bagsotra and Gomra, (iv) Superior Rathis such as Nanwarak, Mungla, etc. and (v) Inferior Rathis, such as Saudimia, Lasai, Barwal, Aheria, Saklahia, Samania, Dhanwal, Thandole, Darbial, Bhalania, Bhotia, etc. This classification however, is not applicable now and the various subgroups can rarely be differentiated.

The Pathanias are also an important group of Rajput of Kangra and other places. The descendants of all the royal or noble houses amongst Katoch, Pathania, Dadwal, Datarpur, Balaurias and all other principalities and subgroups were called Mian. Mian, thus, is an honourable title to distinguish the noble houses.

The Kanet, like Rathi, is other group of Rajput in Kangra and other parts of Himachal Pradesh.

The Katoch clans claim to have emerged from the sweat of the forehead of the goddess while fighting against the demons. The first Katoch ruler was coronated by Saint Kashyapa and as such, claiming their descent from the *chandra* (moon). This group has its clan as Kashyap. It is not out of place to mention that the Nagvanshis also associate themselves with Kashyap clan. It is probable that the rulers might have got something to do with Nagvanshis but their early history is lost in obscurity and futher research is required to reach some definite conclusion. The Nagvanshis have their origin from *Kashyap Gotra.* Kadru, the wife of Kashyap was the mother of Nag people. The Parmar Chauhan, Guhila, Rathod, Chandel, Bhati, Kalachuri, Thakur, Rana and numerous others found in Rajasthan are the clans of the Rajputs inhabiting various parts of Himachal Pradesh. The Khasa clans also form a part of this group (see Khasa).

The community is distributed widely over the whole of Himachal

Pradesh, inhabiting the high altitude mountains to the foothills. Their separate population figure is not available. They speak the dialect of the area which they inhabit, but with the outsiders they speak in Hindustani. Their traditional script was Tankri, which is only known nowadays to a handful of persons, and they use either Persio-Arabic script or Devanagari.

The members of the community do not have any distinctive mark or dress other than the dress prevalent in the area. The special feature of their dress is the turban which is put on during ceremonial occasions. Long mustaches which were once a characteristic feature of Rajputs have now disappeared and the people have now adopted dresses on the western pattern.

The community is non-vegetarian. They take the meat of goats, sheep, monal, and jungle goat. Fish and chicken are rarely consumed. Their staple diet consists of wheat, *makki*, rice, pulses of *mah, moong, rajmah* and vegetables. Milk is generally consumed depending on its availability. *Lassi*, curd and butter are also consumed. The consumption of vegetables is moderate, and so is that of the fruits.

Alcoholic drinks are used by men whereas women generally avoid these. Drinks are normally purchased from the local market, but at times homemade liquor is also taken in remote areas.

Restrictions exist relating the intake of certain food during the period of death in a family. During such an event no spices, especially turmeric and asafoetida are used and mutton is also not taken. During festive occasions, especially, Dussehra, Shivratri and Magh *ka-saja*, meat preparations are a must. In winter months, sheep or goat are slaughtered and then meat is kept by every household to be consumed daily in colder areas.

Bio-anthropological report contains biological information on Rajputs.

The Rajput are divided into six status groups, including Mian, Rajput and Thakur which include first grade and second grade Ranas and Rathis. 'Mian' literally means 'prince', Thakur (baron) and Rana (chief) are simple titles denoting status or rank. However, Rathi is a term which implies loss of status and so is merely used by the Rathis. The status depends mainly on the strictness with which certain social rules are observed, e.g., a Mian should not plough, their women should observe strict purdah, should not practise hypogamy and widow remarriage and accept bride-price and should not smoke except among themselves. A Thakur may plough and may also take a wife from a Rathi. The Rathis practise widow remarriage and that distinguishes them from the Rajput. They also accept bride-price and are in this respect only on the level with the Thakurs of the second grade. Each of these status groups are divided into septs, which also have a degree of social status based on proximity to their original home which are at times hypergamous and their status varies with the locality in which it is settled. These septs are territorial designations to denote from where they hail, e.g., Kahluria of Kahlur or Bilaspur, Kotlehria of Kotlehr, Hinduria of Hindur or Nalagarh, Sirmauria of Sirmaur (Nahan), Mankotia of Mankot, Mandial of Mandi, Dadhwal of Dadh, Chambial of Chamba, Sibia of Siba in Dera, and so on.

Although the status of the different groups was well defined, it could be improved upon or degenerated by marriage, royal favour or through some service rendered. About this, the following saying finds place in Rose (1914) "*Chauthi pirhi Raathni ki raani ban jai*" (literally, a Rathi woman becomes a queen in the fourth generation). This is explained as meaning that a Rathi's daughter, may marry a Thakur in the second generation. In the third generation her daughter may marry a Rajput and her daughter again may marry a Mian or a ruling chief. Thus we arrive at a conclusion that there are no endogamous groups in the Rajput community and no subcastes but a series of status group each more or less hypergamous.

The Rajput claim superiority over all other communities of the region and place itself in the Kshatriya order of the varna system, a fact which is acknowledged by all.

The community is endogamous, but village and *al* exogamy is practised. The girls are also excluded from the villages where a daughter has been given in marriage. Hypergamous unions are permitted and so is junior sororate, but levirate and consanguineous marriages are prohibited.

Though monogamy is the prevalent rule, polygamy is also practised by a few well-off families, who sometime keep two or three wives simultaneously; this signifies their prestige. The prevalent form of acquiring a partner is by negotiation. The normal symbols of marrriage for a married woman are vermilion in the parting of the hair and a *laung* (nose-stud). Among the Rajputs dowry is not demanded but is voluntarily given considerably and consists of gifts in kind. The residence of the bride is patrilocal, but in the event of there being no male issue, sometimes the son-in-law is invited to stay with the girl's parents and looks after the property, though such cases are very rare.

Divorce was traditionally not permitted, but now the husband can divorce his wife on grounds of infidelity or maladjustment by judicial approval. The divorcee can, however, remarry. Widow marriage was prohibited but widower remarriage was practised. Due to changing times, and with the greater awareness and spread of education, widow remarriage has received some social consideration, but such instances are very few.

The Rajput family is patrilineal and is vertically extended. The eldest male member is the head of the household and commands great respect in the family. His decision in family matters, which is invariably arrived at after consensus, is final and honoured. The elders are respected and obeyed. Age and relationship are given due consideration and regard.

Avoidance is observed between a wife and her husband's elder male relatives, though with elderly women avoidance is not observed, but as a mark of respect the forehead is covered. Joking relationship is also prevalent with the wife's younger brothers and sisters and with the husband's younger relatives. The relationship between husband and wife is generally that of mutual love and respect and they avoid taking each others' name, rather they refer to each other teknonymically.

The property is inherited according to the rule of male equigeniture. In the event of a number of wives the property is at first equally divided among the wives and then their respective share is equally divided among their sons. In case of no son in the family the property passes on to the collaterals rarely to the daughter. Though after the death of the husband the eldest son heads the family, the widow continues to enjoy usufructuary rights in the property for her lifetime.

Interfamily ties are best observed between various relatives on occasions of joy and sorrow when all join together. Though traditionally women had no right to inheritance or a share in the parental property, today the modern statutory provisions provide for equal share to the girls in the parental property. But this is rarely demanded and is often bequeathed in favour of the brothers.

The women hold an honourable status in the community. Their social status is comparatively lower than that of males, owing the fact that they do not enjoy freedom outside the house. Similarly, though a widower could remarry, a widow is not allowed to remarry except in lower status groups. Same is the case with inheritance. The widow has usufructuary rights only in property. Though the first legally wedded wife has an honourable status, the subsequent wives or concubines do not enjoy a similar status. On the economic front the women of well-off families are not allowed to go outside the house and take part in economic activities, but women of poor families or those with meagre landholdings have to help by working in their own fields and also by working on the fields of economically well-off Rajputs. Besides, they also carry out all household activities, like bringing fuel, fodder and water, cooking food and looking after the young ones. In the sphere of religion and family rituals they have complete freedom and are at par with their menfolk except that they cannnot become temple priests. In politics, though Rajput women exercise their franchise in all elections, they do not usually contest in elections or take part in the Biradari Panchayat.

With the spread of literacy and education women have moved out of houses and have taken to teaching or Government or private jobs. This has led to their contribution to the family income, and a better say in family affairs. Now a few of the women have also entered in the field of politics and are members of the Block Panchayats.

Thus, it is evident that the community is undergoing change and the spread of literacy has widened their worldview and has also given fillip to the increase of the status of women.

As among other communities of the region, the childbirth, especially that of the first child, is an event of the great rejoicing. *Athmasa* rite is observed at the commencement of the eighth month of pregnancy, when clothes are received from the woman's parents. She must not go near a dead body, nor cross a stream in the evening, for these are believed to bring evil influences on the child. The period of birth pollution is for 13 days and is called *sutak* or *chhoot*. In some cases the mother is separately purified on the fifth day when the mother, child and the midwife partake a mixture of clarified butter curd, milk, Ganges water and *guntar* cow's urine. During the period of *sutak*, she is not allowed to move out of her room of confinement. After the birth of the child, a Brahman priest is called to prepare a horoscope of the child and to foresee the effect of the constellation of stars in which the child is born, and to advise the parents accordingly.

The first feeding of cereal, *khirpu or annaprasana* is observed at the sixth month after the birth of the child, when the child is first fed with preparation of milk and rice *kheer*. Naming ceremony is performed on the child's attaining the age of nine months. A Brahman priest is invited who after looking into the almanac and the constellation of stars under whose influence the child is born, names the child. Tonsure ceremony is observed only for boys between the age of three and five years depending upon the convenience of the parents. The child's head is shaved off by the Nai, and a cue is left on the occiput. This is followed by the thread wearing ceremony, held only in case of boys, when they attain the age of fifteen or sixteen years. Usually, however, it is deferred until marriage, so that the two ceremonies are combined to save the expenses. It is an elaborate ceremony and varies from region to region. The boy dresses like a mendicant and begs for alms from the mother and other relatives. Thereafter *janeu* is worn over the left shoulder, across the back and chest, and under the right shoulder. The ceremony is conducted by the family *purohit*.

Marriage is performed by negotiation and the proposal is initiated by the girl's parents or a *ghataka* (a go-between). It consists of a seies of rituals both on the bride as well as on the groom's side. The conclusive function which seals the marriage bond is the *agni-puja* in which the couple circumambulate the sacred fire five times making each circuit in seven steps, amidst chanting of the *mantra* by the priest. The *gaona* or *muklawa* is observed when the girl attains puberty. She then finally goes to her husband's house. But now, it is performed symbolically along with the marriage.

The dead are cremated with the last rites being performed by the eldest male member of the house or by the husband in the event of a young and issuless woman. The children below the age of five years are either buried or *jal-pravah* is performed. Restrictions exist for the person who performs the last rites, like moving barefoot and sleeping over *kusha* (mat) for a period of 10 days. During this period each day he performs a *pinda* and the members of the dead man's family are not allowed to shave, wear shoes and eat cooked food. On the fourth day *asthi-sanchaya* and the *chaturthik shradh* is performed. On the tenth day, the heads of all the affines are shaved. On the eleventh day *kirya karam* is performed in which the belongings of the deceased are given to the Mahabrahman, and *pind* are offered for the salvation of the deceased. The *barah* is performed on the twelfth day whereas *brahma-bhoj* is given on the thirteenth day, when *dakshina* (food and alms) are given to thirteen Brahmans.

Monthly death anniversary *shradh* and *barsi* ceremonies are also performed, when a Brahman (in case of men) and a Brahmani (in case of women) are fed. The recurring anniversary *khiabi* and *chaubarsi* are also performed on the fourth anniversary, when the poor are fed.

A deviation from the normal rule in the upper hills is the disposal of a deceased pregnant lady. In such an event, the Nath is invited who cuts open the stomach and takes out the child. Whereafter, the child is buried as per the normal procedure and the mother is cremated. For the act performed by the Nath he takes the funeral shroud with him.

The major economic resource of the Rajput was land, as a majority of them were the owners of small principalities and held sole rights over the natural resources of the area whether it be water, forest and land. They did not till the land themselves but got it tilled on *begar* or by agricultural labourers. After independence, with the abolition of principalities and feudatories, the traditional sole rights were taken away from them in respect of the natural resources like water and forest by the Government, but they along with the other native residents of the villages were given customary rights for water and forests by virtue of which they could take fuelwood timber wood from the forests and avail themselves of pasture land in the demarcated area. Due to agrarian reforms their large chunks of lands have also been reduced due to land ceiling, which keeping in view of the topography of the area, is just sufficient for a moderate family.

Most of the individuals particularly the younger generation have taken to other professions like service, horticulture, trade, cottage industries, poultry farming and other self-employment schemes. For some families agriculture still continues to be the primary source of livelihood, whereas for others it has slipped to the second place.

The community is dependent on the market for the sale of their produce or for purchase of articles of their need. In case of cereal products they prefer to take them to the nearest marketplace directly, but those who do not have enough produce employ a midddle man who collects the small produce and sells it in some bigger market. For horticultural produce, middlemen are generally involved since bigger market centres are outside the State. The mode of economic exchange is in cash. The children of the community generally do not work to earn, except those belonging to poor families who work to supplement the income of the family and are paid by their employers in cash and kind.

For control and management of the social problems of the community they have their own traditional council Biradari Panchayat. In the pre-Independence era they were the sole authority for the maintenance of social order, and the offenders were fined and penalized even with corporal punishment. Their territory of adjudication was determined by the area which was in their control. In certain areas the authority of the Biradari Panchayat was not limited to their own community but extended to the entire village. Now, Gram Panchayats look after the planning and development, welfare activities and maintenance of law and order.

The Rajputs follow the Sanatan Dharma. They worship the Vedic gods like Surya, Agni and Indra and also the trinity Brahma, Vishnu and Mahesh. The worship of goddess Kali, Bhawani or Durga and other forms of Shakti also find place in their religion. They also have family and village deities who are worshipped and propitiated. Along with them supernatural powers like Kailu Bir are also worshipped. Guga worship is another form of the Nag cult. Mahasu (Mahashiv), the regional deity is also worshipped.

Their sacred centres are Hardwar and the shrines of Devi Dirga in Himachal like, Naina Devi, Chamunda Devi, Chintpurni, Jawala and the Bhima Kali. At Bhimakali temple at one time the *narmedh yagya* (human-sacrifice) was performed by the ruling Rajput families, but now the practice has been discontinued; instead a goat or a sheep is sacrificed to propitiate the deities and spirits. They also believe in evil spirits, and seek the services of *chela* for the solution of their problems. The Brahman priest who has traditional *jajmani* relations performs all social and religious rites and officiates at rituals connected with life-cycle.

The Rajputs take part in all the fairs of the region, especially the Tarab Fair, held in October on Durga Ashtami. Sair fair is held on the first day of the *Jeth* and *Zat* fair is held on the twenty-ninth day of *Jeth*. On Dussehra fair they worship their arms and ammunition. Other important festivals are Holi, Diwali, Navratra and Bissu which are celebrated with great zeal and fervour and in which the entire community takes part.

Being traditional landlords, the community had intercommunity linkages with other neighbouring communities of the area, in respect of ritual, social and occupational ties. The serving communities like Nai, Lohar, Badhi, Chamar and Barwala had their traditionally defined services which they rendered to their clients on different occasions, in lieu of which they were paid in kind a fixed quantity of foodgrains at harvest time. A Rajput would accept all types of food from a Brahmin and from their own brethren, but with other Hindu communities they will accept only *pucca* food except from certain communities like Chamar, Chuhra, Barwala, etc. from whom they accept only*sidha*. All communities can accept all types of food from the Rajputs.

Ritual kins (*dharam bhai*) are very common in the hills and such relationships are established with people of similar status and rank who are otherwise not related. *Jajmani* relationship still exists with the serving communities, though with the diversification of their economic pursuits, in view of low productivity and fragmentation of landholdings, this system is now not as strong as it once used to be. With the development of horticulture and practising of various occupations like Government service, business, teaching, military and paramilitary forces, the traditional rigidity of community ties in respect of commensality have loosened, especially in the urban centres. In the rural areas, however, such rigidities can still be observed. The community also takes part in politics at all levels, including national, State and regional levels.

The impact of the development programmes, is visible on the Rajput communities also. Education finds favour for both the sexes and they study up to graduation. The girls however drop out after middle or high school for want of educational facilities in the upper hill areas.

The Rajputs share the benefits of health and medicare and has no prejudice against family planning and welfare programmes which have reached them through primary health centres. They prefer three children and use modern and indigenous method of contraception, but have no preference for sterilization. The community has availed itself of the facilities of loans from banks for horticulture, small-scale or cottage industry and a few have even procured loans meant for educated unemployed for self-employment.

They enjoy the facility of radio, transistor and television and also have access to cinema in the village which are shown by extension agencies or are shown in privte video parlours, which exist throughout Himachal Pradesh. Their houses are electrified. Metalled roads connect most of the villages. Besides traditional fuels they avail themselves of the facilities of coal and liquified petroleum gas for cooking.

Most of the Rajput-dominated areas have irrigational facilities through canals and where these do not exist they are dependent on rainwater. They use both organic and chemical fertilizers, insecticides, and high yielding varieties of seeds. Some of them have also resorted to mechanized farming.

B.R. Sharma
Rajendra Sarkar

RANA

The Rana is one of the status groups of the Gaddi community. The word Rana means warrior. Being a warrior caste they differ from the Thakur and the Rathi. They believe that their ancestors fled from Rajasthan to save their culture, religion and chastity of their women from Muslim invaders. They are distributed throughout Chamba, Kangra and Shimla districts. At village Ulansa (study area) in Chandra district the Ranas have greater concentration. This village lies about 8000 feet above sea level at the top of the hills. The village is fairly open with long terraced fields reaching far up to the top of the ridge overshading the village. The land is fertile and productive. Natural water supply is plentiful and small snowfed streams flow throughout the year to unload their water into river Ravi at Kharamukh.

The inhabitants of the area speak in Gadiali dialect and in broken Hindi with outsiders. The women who had their education in schools can speak Hindi but most of the elderly women and the non-school-going girls cannot speak Hindi. The Rana's dress is like other Gaddis which is also similar to the Rajasthani attire. Constitutionally the inhabitants of the areas come under the scheduled tribe category.

The Ranas are non-vegetarian. Their staple diet is wheat, maize and rice. They take *rajma* and *malka* (pulses). They prepare vegetables of potato, cabbage, lady finger, brinjal, onion, beans, green peas, tomato, radish, gourd and *palang*. Tea is a common drink nowadays which is taken in almost every house. Milk is given mainly to the babies.

Alcoholic drinks are common among the men. But they purchase alcohol, either countrymade or English wine, from the local shops. The young ones are allowed to take drinks with their peers. Endowed by nature with an excellent climate and soil for the production of fruit a large number of fruit orchards are grown and the people enjoy fruits like apple, pear, walnut, peach, apricot, *chilgoza* and mango.

The *gotras* are the non-hierarchial social groupings among the Rana. For marriage negotiation, they have to look at *gotra* to avoid marriage within the same *gotra* and they also use this *gotra* name for fulfilment of the offerings of agnates. But due to their small number and hard living conditions, the Ranas sometimes neglect the *gotra* as an exogamous unit. When they marry into their own *gotra* they see to it that there is no blood relation. In the varna order Ranas are second from the top after Rajput and Khatri.

The boys and the girls are not consulted at the time of marriage. Marriage is arranged by their parents or guardians. The Ranas are monogamous. The marriage age of a boys is generally 20-25 years and that of girls 18-22 years. A difference of 2 to 5 years in the age of the boy and girl is maintained. For selection of a mate they look for an eligible youth belonging to a good *kul* and one who possesses a good moral character. He should be an earning member and a hard worker. Similarly, the girl should be beautiful, industrious and adjustable to the new atmosphere. Efforts are made to arrange marriages within a short distance so that they can visit each other on foot when there is a need. The Ranas of Ulansa and few other places marry only with the Ranas, though in some areas the Ranas marry with other Rajputs. The Ranas do not favour polygamy but if circumstances force them to marry a second time in that case they have to take the consent of the first wife. A widower can marry the younger sister of the wife or any other girl. A widow or a divorced woman cannot marry the second time. The Ranas do not allow divorce. Marriage by *batta-satta* is very common in the area. The Ranas do not have the practice of giving bride price nor do they demand dowry. The married women use *sindur* in the parting of the hair on the head. They also wear *nath* and toe-ring on the second finger of the foot.

After completion of the marriage function the bride starts living with the groom's family. If any problem comes up they split and start cooking food in a separate hearth. Gradually the family breaks up and starts to live separately. The family is based on the patrilineal and patriarchal pattern. Though there are many joint families, both horizontal and vertical, nuclear families are more in numbers. The elder members of the family are given respect by the younger ones. Behaviour and relationship between siblings and cousins is usually sweet and harmonious. On ceremonial occason, the *bhanja* (sister's son) is considered a sacred and respected person. Joking relationship is established with sister-in-law, brother-in-law, brother's wife and son's mother-in-law. Property is distributed equally only among the sons. The brothers are responsible for the sister's marriage in the absence of the parents. The eldest male member in a joint family succeeds the social responsibility of the family. The Rana families cooperate during festivals and also in the family functions such as marriage, *upanayan* and death.

The Rana women have no right of inheritance either to the paternal property or to the husband's property. The woman is, as a girl, dependent upon the parents, after marriage on her husband, and in widowhood upon her in-laws or parents. A married woman commands respect in her family according to her intellectual power or on common sense. As a wife, she shares her husband's sorrows and troubes and as a mother, she gets immense respect from her sons and daughters-in-law. In domestic affairs and in economic matters for the management of the house she plays a major role. For the finalization of children's marriage her opinion is considered important.

A corner of a room is provided to the expectant mother. An old woman or a local *dai* attends to her. When the child is born the family priest or a *pandit* is summoned to prepare *janmapatri* (astrological chart) of the newborn. Ranas obseve *sutak* period for 22 days. During this period the mother is not allowed to prepare food for others. Also the lady who works as *dai* is not permitted to touch the food of others. For purification after the pollution period, the mother and the child are given a bath. All utensils of the house are cleaned on that day. After the purification ceremony, all members of the family are free to move about in the house.

When the child is six months' old, a special food is prepared and touched with the lips of the child. On this occasion name of the child is also confirmed by the priest, based on the *janampatri*. On this day another function is observed. A *darat, kodal,* book, pen, coin and *kheer* are placed before the child and he is allowed to touch them in the belief that it will indicate the child's future. On completion of a year they put a knot in a red thread which is repeated every year till the death of the person. They perform *janeu* ceremony at the time of marriage.

With the starting of menstruation adolescence starts for girls but they do not have any special ceremony for this. Marriage is the most important function among the Ranas. After the betrothal, an auspicious day is fixed for the wedding in consultation with the priest. At the wedding ceremony, the *sumuhat* rite is performed by worshipping Ganapati, an earthen pitcher and the *navgrah*. Turmeric, barley flour with mustard oil is rubbed on the body of the boy. Black woollen threads are tied around his right wrist to protect him from the evil eye. After this he is taken out for bath. This is followed by the *janeu* ceremony. During this ceremony Brahma, Vishnu and Kumbh are also worshipped. The boy's maternal uncle presents him *sehra* which is worn by the boy. A *thali* with lighted earthen lamp is waved over his head thrice from right to left. This is known as *arti*. Then the bridegroom, with his relations and friends, leaves for the bride's house. On arrival at the bride's house the mother-in-law of the bridegroom receives him at the entrance and performs *arti*. The bridegroom and bride stand face to face and a *purohit* helps them to touch each other's shoulders thrice. The boy and the girl thereafter sit and the father of the girl offers *sankalap* and performs the *kanyadan* ceremony. *Havan* is performed and the bride and the groom circumambulate the sacred fire seven times. Amidst the chanting of *mantra*, the bridegroom's shawl and the bride's *dupatta* are tied together.

After completion of the ceremonies at the bride's house the bride is taken to the home of the bridegroom where the bridegroom's mother receives the bride and the bridegroom. The first night the bride and the bridegroom live together is called *suhagrat.*

The Ranas cremate their dead. The dead body of the children below 5 years is buried. After giving a bath to the dead, the body is placed on the funeral pyre with head towards north. The eldest son lights the funeral pyre. If the eldest son cannot attend the rite then the younger son performs the task. On second or third day those male members of the family who are younger the dead have to shave off their head. On the same day the wife of the dead person removes her *shringar.* She starts to wear plain white clothes. The ashes collected from the pyre are carried to Hardwar and immersed in the Ganges. On the tenth day *daspindi* ceremony is held. After this the family members wash their clothes and take purificatory bath. On the eleventh day, Acharya, the priest of death rituals, is given clothes, beddings, utensil etc. A goat is sacrificed on the twelfth day. *Pinds* made of barley are offered in the name of dead. After this function the relatives of the wife of deceased come to the deceased's house and give a feast to friends, relatives and well-wishers and with this function the mourning period is over. On every month of the first year, on the *tithi* of the death, *pinds* are given in memory of the deceased. An annual *shradh* and one also four years after death are observed.

Ulansa is mainly an agricultural village and the Ranas hold the maximum portion of land. As the village is on the hill, they practise terrace cultivation. Due to early snowfall they cannot produce two crops from a single field. The land which they cannot use for agricultural purposes is used as grazing fields and in few areas, they have started plantation of fruits like apple and walnut. The land of the family is controlled by the head of the family. The land ownership is individual. The Ranas themselves cultivate their land. At times they also engage labourers for their cultivation work. Next to agriculure, sheep rearing is an important source of their livelihood.

Their women play an important part at the time of harvesting and also sheep rearing. They are also good weavers. They weave blankets called *pattu* and also weave shawls both for their own use and for sale. The excess production either of agricultural or of woven cloth is sold in the market against cash payment.

Many of the Ranas are in the defence services also. In fact in the hills, except for leather work, all other works like carpentry, weaving, washing, tailoring, etc. are done by the community members themselves. With the change in family pattern from joint family to nuclear family, land has also been divided into smaller portions. It is therefore very difficult for them to live on it and many of them have been forced to look for alternative jobs. When they engage any person to work in their fields they make the payment in cash.

Whenever there is a dispute between two parties, the elders of the community are consulted for arbitration who solve their ordinary cases at the village level. The statutory Gram Panchayats look after development works. Since the State Government has vested the panchayats with powers to sanction loans to the farmers and artisans as well as control developmental work in their respective rural areas, these panchayats have become arenas for village-level politics. Elections to the office of *pradhan* are very keenly contested by the Ranas.

The Ranas worship Hindu gods and goddess. Their *kul devi* is Santari. They also worship Nag Deota. The Himalayan land is considered the abode of Lord Shiva, so the people of this area also worship Lord Shiva. The famous sacred place associated with Lord Shiva is Manimahesh. The Ranas also visit places like Hardwar, Kedarnath and Kashi. The *pujari* is the sacred specialist. He performs *puja* and is entitled to receive whatever offerings are made to the deity in cash and kind during their *pari* (duty period). *Pujari* conducts marriage ceremonies also.

On the first of *Baisakh,* a fair is held at Naina Devi. A six-day long fair is celebrated at Chaura areas of Bharmaur during Janamashtami. People do a *parikrama* and perform *puja* on this occasion. Local people attend the fair as spectators or as traders. A week after the Bharmaur *yatra*, a fair is held in the Manimahesh area. The men and women dance in groups to the accompaniment of *dholak* and *shehnai.*

Some of the Ranas get training in clay-modelling, carving, engraving, drawing and painting. They are good spinners and weavers. Both men as well as women know weaving.

Certain castes like Brahman and Rathi visit the houses of the Ranas and the latter also, in turn, visits their houses during marriage, birth and death. The Ranas and Rathis take their meal together. They also accept food from Brahman but not from Sipi, Rehra and certain other castes. At the time of a feast the Sipi, Rihara and certain other castes are served separately in the courtyards. The Ranas of Ulansa do not take any gifts from other communities. They normally do marry their daughters in other communities. But in some places the Ranas and other Rajputs have marital relations.

The children of the Ranas attend school up to primary level in the village itself. For higher education they go to Chamba. Medical facilities are available at the civil hospital at Bharmaur. The younger generation is in favour of planned family. They use various methods for birth control.

The villagers collect their drinking water from the springs or streams.

The Ranas use wood as fuel for cooking their food. They mainly use organic manure in their field. The shopkeepers sell foodgrains at the Government subsidised rates.

D.K. Chakraborty

RANGAR

The Rangar or Ranghar are generally Muslim Rajputs, though a few Hindu Rangars also exist. According to Col. Tod the word is derived from Rana. Rose (1916:322) says that "the term is somewhat contemptuous and is applied in the eastern and south-eastern Punjab to any Muhammedan Rajput—at least by the Hindus. If a Hindu Chauhan Rajput turns Muhammedan, he would still be a Chauhan Rajput, but his Hindu kinsmen would also dub him as Rangar". According to yet another account of dubious authority, "the original issues of the Rajput mothers and Muhammedan fathers were styled Ranghars and they intermarry".

According to Crooke (1896), "the Bhatti or Jaiswar Rajputs of Bulandshahr claim descent from Raja Dilip, son of Jaswant Rao of Nanamau near Bithur in the Kanpur district. He is said to have had two sons named Bhatti and Ranghar. The descendants of the latter were converted at the time of Sultan Qutub-ud-din and Ala-ud-din Khilji, and were called Ranghars after their eponymous ancestor".

Further, according to Sir H.M. Elliot, many of the Kankauiya and Naigauiya Ahirs were converted to Islam and are known as Ranghars (Crooke, 1896:228).

But one thing is certain that the Rangars were originally Hindu Rajputs, who got converted to Islam as is further testified by Blunt (1931:203) who writes: "The Ranghars were Bhatti Rajputs, converted in the reign of Qutub-ud-din (1206-1210) and Ala-ud-din Khilji (1295-1315)". The Ranghar of Himachal Pradesh claim that they emigrated from Haryana and settled in the adjoining parts of Himachal after clearing forest patches.

The language spoken by the people amongst themselves is Haryanvi whereas with others it is Hindustani. Their script is Perso-Arabic while communicating within their community, and Devanagari when communicating with others.

They are non-vegetarians but do not eat beef, buffalo meat and pork. They take the meat of pigeon, rabbit, chicken and goat. Due to the high cost of non-vegetarian food, they are switching over to vegetarian food. Their staple diet consists of maize, wheat and rice and pulses of gram and *masur.* Vegetables, roots and tubers are included in their regular diet which are cooked in the mustard oil, *til* oil and *toriya.* Animal fat is also used occasionally. Milk and milk products are consumed by all. Alcoholic drinks from the market are occasionally taken by men. The men and women are very fond of betel, betel nuts, tobacco and also smoke *hukka.* The men smoke cigarettes and *bidis.*

Special food like *seviyan* and goat meat are cooked on festive occasions, but the cooking of non-vegetarian food is prohibited during the 40-day period of mourning.

The community has two broad sections, viz., the Hindu Rangar and the Muslim Rangar, on the basis of religion. Each of the two divisions are further sub-divided into a number of exogamous *gotras,* which indicate that the Muslim Rangars were Hindu Rajputs once. Though the Muslim Rangars could recall only four *gotras* viz., Chauhan, Tomar, Pundir and Tauni, they think of many more. These *gotras* denote their descent and have no social hierarchy. Among the Muslims they consider their superiority over other neighbouring communities and rank in the order: Rangar, Rawat, Teli, Julaha, Raeen, Bharai, Banjara and Pinja, and this is acknowledged by other Muslims too. Though aware of the varna system, they do not place themselves in it. Their Hindu brethren, however, place themselves along with the Kshatriyas. As a result of the change of their religion, they have dropped the surname 'Singh', but prefer to use Chowdhury as a prefix to their names.

The Rangars are endogamous at the community and religious levels. Exogamy is practised by the Hindu Rangars at the *gotra* level, but among the Muslims only village exogamy is observed. Preference is given to parallel and cross-cousins. Junior sororate and junior and senior levirate are also practised. Earlier child marriages were performed at the age of eight to ten years, but the return of the bride to the groom's place was deferred till the girl came of age. Presently, adult marriages are performed and the *muklawa* is symbolically performed at the time of marriage.

The most prevalent form of marriage is monogamy but if the first wife is unable to give an heir to the family, a second marriage is resorted to with the consent of the first wife. Two real sisters cannot be married simultaneously, but can be married after the death of the first wife. Marriage is performed by negotiation and is called *nikah. Mehar* of Rs. 32.25, originally in silver coins is fixed by their *Anjuman,* which has to be formally accepted by the bride at the time of *nikah* and paid on demand or on the annulment of marriage. Dowry in kind is also given by the bride's parents. The residence after marriage is patrilocal.

Talaq takes place by uttering the word thrice in the presence of two witnesses, thereafter it is documented. The common grounds for divorce are adultery or maladjustment. In the event of divorce the *mehar* amount is to be repaid and the return of the dowry depends on the merit of the case. Only the husband has the right to divorce. The children are also the liability of the husband, but in case of infants, they are allowed to accompany the mother, who is compensated for the upbringing of the child but has to return the child to his/her father when he/she grows up.

Widow, widower and divorcee remarriages are permissible and are solemnized in the same manner as regular marriages. The widow and divorcee wife can, however, remarry only after the expiry of *iddat*.

The Rangar family is of the vertically extended type with all the male relative of the father's side living under the same roof and sharing the same hearth. Now with the diversification of occupation and the people moving out of their village, there is an increase in nuclear families. The interpersonal relations within the family are that of love and respect for the elders and love for the younger. The eldest male member of the family is the head and is obeyed and held in veneration. Paternal and filial affection and due regard as per status is the basis of mutual relationship. Avoidance is observed between the wife and the husband's elder relatives for the initial one year, after which it is not observed. Joking relationship exists between husband and wife's younger relatives. The husband and wife address each other teknonymically.

The property is inherited by the sons. In the event of multiplicity of wives, the property is divided first among wives and then their respective share is equally divided among their sons. The property, however, remains undivided in the lifetime of the wife who has usufructuary rights. In the event of no son, some families prefer to transfer the property in their daughter's name, whereas in some cases it passes on to the collaterals. The succession is in the male line. The interfamily linkages are best seen at the time of joy and sorrow within the family when they come to help each other.

The economic status of a Rangar woman is equal to that of a man, as she shares the agricultural activities. Some also work as agricultural labourers in others' fields to supplement the family income. They also carry out all the household activities, right from bringing fuel and fodder to cooking food and looking after the young ones besides scores of other household chores. However, their social status is lower than that of the men, and they do not enjoy the same freedom as males. Only the man has a right to divorce. Similarly in case of a widow or divorcee, women have to observe a three month thirteen day period of *iddat* before she can remarry. The women also do not have any right to the inheritance of property but a widow only has a usufructuary rights. Restrictions on the movement also exist during the period of *iddat*.

The political and religious status of women is comparatively lower than that of the men. Though a woman has the right to perform all family rituals and observe festivals and at home; she has no right to visit a mosque or a religious congregation. In the political field she has only the right to exercise her franchise but not to contest the elections. She also cannot take part in the *Anjuman* affairs.

Post-natal restrictions and pollution are observed. A purificatory bath is given to the child and mother on the sixth, tenth, twentieth and fortieth days. On the birth of the child a *maulvi* whispers *azan* in the child's ear. The child is named on the *aqiqa* which is performed on the sixth day. At this time two goats are sacrificed and the child's head is shaved off. The maternal relatives have an important role to play as they bring clothes, cash and milk for the occasion. *Sunnat* is performed before the age of ten years by a Muslim Nai. Before the ceremony the child is taken to the mosque and the tomb of a Pir. In recognition of his services the Nai is given a *chadar* or a blanket and cash ranging between Rs. 20-30. This is an elaborate ceremony and is celebrated on the same scale as marriage.

For *nikah* a fixed amount of *mehar* is agreed upon by the bride in the presence of a *maulvi* and two *gawahs* after which the *nikahnama* is signed and a copy each of it is given to the girl's parents, boy and the *maulvi*. More often, the *nikah* is performed at the bride's residence or at the mosque. *Nikah* is preceded by a series of rituals from betrothal to *mehndi*.

The dead are buried and the pollution lasts up to the third day of death. On this day sayings from the holy scripture are recited by the *maulvi* and 15 kg. of black gram and sweets are distributed among the funeral processionists, *kabrkuninde* (grave digger) and the Faqir who bathes the corpse. *Daswa* and *chhaliswan* rites are also performed when *fateha* are recited at the grave of the deceased and also on each death annivarsary.

The traditional occupation of the community has been agriculture, and a majority of them are landowning families. They continue this till date. A few families have also taken to animal husbandry. Those who have less land have taken to sharecropping. The landless families work as agricultural labourers or other kinds of labour. The educated among them have taken to teaching, medical profession, military and paramilitary forces and other white-collar jobs in Government and private organizations.

The community is dependent on the local regulated daily market. In the village, barter also forms a medium of exchange with the vendors and local shopkeepers at times. Children below the age of 15 render a helping hand in agricultural activities in their free hours. They also work as agricultural labourers and earn cash wages. A substantial change in their economic activity can be seen since independence. Due to fragmentation of landholdings, people have taken to other occupations, so what was once their primary source of livelihood has stepped down to the secondary position.

The community has an *Anjuman* for the prevention of any infringement of traditional norms. This is adjudicated by the elders of the communnity, who are elected by a voice vote. The cases that come up before the *Anjuman* are related to adultery, divorce, maladjustment or disrespect of traditional norms. The offender is penalized in cash or kind. The fines thus realised are utilized for defraying the expenditure of the *Anjuman*, maintenance and running of mosque or religious institutions. Along with the *Anjuman*, the statutory council also exists viz., the Gram Panchayats, which look after the planning and development of welfare activities and maintenance of law and order respectively.

Most of the Rangars belong to the Sunni sect. They venerate their Pirs like Sheikh, Mais, and Sabir Shah, for invoking their blessings and for fulfilment of wishes. They also have faith in Khera, the village deity who is propitiated for the welfare of the village. They also pray to the Bure Shah and Marn Sidh for fulfilment of their wish and Lakhdata and Salmat Ali for the welfare of their cattle. Their major sacred centres are the Sindaura, Kaliar and Ajmer. Their sacred specialists are from other communities who officiate at all life-cycle rituals.

The major fairs are Urs at the tomb of their revered Pir at Sindaura and Kaliar in Haryana. Their festivals are Id, Bakrid, Shaberat and Sasaid. All these fairs and festivals have socioreligious significance and all take part in them with great zeal and fervour. Though a change of religion has occurred in the community, no pre-change practices survive among them.

The Ranghar women are well versed in the art of painting. They make floral and geometric patterns with *mehndi* on the inside and outside of palm as well as on the upper part of the feet. This is a must for the bride at the time of *nikah* and is also applied by other young girls. The bride and the young ladies of the family also anoint their feet with *alta* (red colour). Besides, they are also skilled in cloth embroidery, which is done only for domestic purposes. The women of the community also sing and dance within the four walls of the house on social occasions.

The community has free exchange of all types of food with Muslims, irrespective of occupation. From the Chuhra and Chamar, they accept *sidha* food. The Muslims can eat in a Hindu house but not in the same receptacles. The Hindu accept *pucca* food if cooked by a Brahman or a Rajput outside the house. Ritual kinship can be established with a person of other Muslim community, who is expected to carry out all rights and obligations as are expected of a real kin.

The traditional patron-client relationship exists with serving communities like the Muslim Nai, Muslim Lohar, Muslim Badhi, *maulvi* and Faqir, who receive a fixed quantity of grains at harvest. They also receive gifts in cash and kinds from their clients on festive and social events.

The people who have meagre landholdings have entered into economic relations with other landlords as share-croppers or as cultivator-labourer. Others who have entered into business, teachings and other white-collar professions, and have left the villages, have witnessed loosening in the rigidity of traditional commensal ties with other communities.

The attitude of the community towards the various development programmes on the whole has been favourable. Education and literacy do not find favour with girls as they are not sent to regular schools other than religious institutions, but with boys they are favourable as they are sent for college and higher education. The family welfare programme finds favour with the younger generations. They use modern method of contraception and prefer to have at least three children. They also avail themselves of the medical facilities provided by the Government, but they also use their homemade remedies simultaneously.

The Ranghars have been benefited by the Government employment scheme under Integrated Rural Development Programme, and have also availed themselves of the loan facilities under the Educated Employment Scheme and set up shops. Drinking water is available through wells and tube-wells. Electricity is available and so are media and communication facilities. The villages are connected by metalled roads, public transport facilities and people avail themselves of the mass media facilities like radio, television and cinema, which are shown to them through extension agencies. Firewood is the main fuel, though kerosene is also used. Irrigation facilities in the study area are available through Giri Sinchai Pariyojna, and people use both organic, inorganic manure and insecticides. Mid-day meal is availed of by the school-going children and immunization and nutrition are also available to the expectant and nursing mothers and also to the infants.

Rajendra Sarkar

RATHI

The word may be derived from the Sanskrit word *rashtra*, but, according to the people it is derived from 'Rathor' as they are believed to have fled from Rajputana during the time of Aurangzeb. They are essentially an agricultural class and are distributed throughout the Chamba, Shimla, Sirmaur and Kangra districts. The study area (Chamba) is cold during winter months and most of the villagers migrate towards the foothills. The summer season is pleasant but the weather remains generally dry. There are many legends about the name and the origin of the area. They speak among themselves and also with outsiders in the Gaddiali (Pahari) dialect. Their traditional script is known as Tankri but their children can read and write Devanagari script. As they share the dress with the other Gaddis it is difficult to identify them. Constitutionally, the Rathis of the Bharmaur Valley are included among the Gaddis who are a scheduled tribe. The Rathi is treated as Rajput.

The Rathis are non-vegetarian. They take fish, meat and egg. Their staple food is maize, wheat and rice. They consume pulses like gram, *tur, moong*, kulthi and beans. They also consume vegetables like *gogti* or *arbi, cholai-ka-sag*, pumpkin, *tur, lauki, tori, kadu,* brinjal and tomato. For cooking they use groundnut oil and hydrogenated oil. Fruits like pears, plums, peaches, apples and apricots are taken almost in all the houses. Men and women enjoy *hukka.* While the old people confine themselves to smoking tobacco, the younger generation is fond of *bidi* and cigarettes. Alcoholic drinks are common to the male members which they purchase from the local market and sometimes distill it on their own.

The community has numerous *gotras* which are non-hierarchial. Often they are named after the villages they inhabit. Though the Rathis claim themselves to be Rajputs but the other neighbouring communities do not give them full Rajput status. Other Rajputs do not give their daughters to the Rathis but can accept their daughters as brides. This gives them an opportunity of status mobility. There is a popular saying that *Chaauthi pirhi Rathni ki Rani ban jai* i.e., in the fourth generation a Rathi woman becomes a *rani* (Rajput). This speaks of the upward mobilization of the community. In the varna order, Rathis put themselves in second position to the Kshatriya.

The Rathis are an endogamous group. *Gotra* exogamy regulates their marriage alliances. They always avoid marriage alliances between close relatives from father's and mother's side. *Batta-satta* is prevalent among the Rathis. Polygamy is allowed when the first wife does not have any child or she is ill and is unable to bear a child. Generally the boys get married at the age of 20-25 years. The negotiations are started by the boy's side. Relatives of both the party plays a significant role in negotiating the marriage alliance. Before betrothal the parents of both sides verify the character, youthfulness and beauty of the boy and girl. The boy's earning potential is also taken into consideration. Preference is given to a girl of a nearby village. When both parties have agreed to the marriage, an auspicious day is fixed for betrothal. *Laung,* red ribbon or hair-band and vermilion are the symbols of the married women. They do not have bride price and dowry but they have a practise of giving presents to the new couple so that they can be independent. After the marriage, the boy takes his new bride to his paternal house where they live together with other members of the family till they shift to a new residence. The family in which divorce occurs is socially looked down upon. Widow remarriage used to be practised earlier and this practice separates them from the other Rajputs. A widower can also marry the younger sister of his deceased wife.

Most of the Rathi families are nuclear. There are a few joint families which are both vertically and horizontally extended. The inter-personal relations are cordial. The younger brother's wife shows respect to the elder brother of the husband and their relation is of avoidance. Joking relations exist between *kuram* and *kurmani* and one can also joke with his elder brother's wife. The property is inherited by the sons only. In case of any dispute among the sons of the family members, the matter is settled by elder relatives and sometimes by elders of the village.

To the Rathi the daughters are others' wealth and not entitled to inherit the father's property. However, the life of the Rathis is not strong without the active cooperation of the woman. As a wife she is a co-worker of her husband. Her status is the same as that of her husband. She accompanies her husband over a large area from Lahaul to Kangra and other foothills during their seasonal movement. The women also play an important role in the economy. Though they do not touch plough, they do all sorts of work related to farming. They are good spinners and weavers as well. They are hard workers and collect drinking water from springs, prepare food for family members and also collect fuel for family use. The mothers also guide their daughters in matters of social etiquette. As a voter, the Rathi women take part during the polls, but they do not play any part in other political activities.

A pregnant women is not permitted to go near the cremation ground and she is not supposed to carry heavy loads. Delivery takes place in a room on the ground floor and is helped by an elderly woman who is well versed in such work. There is rejoicing when the first son is born. They offer prayers to their family *devta.* The time of birth is noted for preparing the horoscope by the family *purohit.* *Sutak* or pollution period is observed for five days in case of boy and three days in case of the girl. The mother and the women who help in the delivery are not allowed to touch food prepared for others. For purification, they use cowdung and urine and sprinkle it over the articles which are not washable.

In case of a son, the christening ceremony is observed. Food is given to the child after five or six months. Rice cooked in milk is usually given to the child for the first time. On this day the boy is given new clothes. Before feeding the child with rice, a *havan* is performed. Before him, on a *thali* they keep a pen, book, coin and soil and the boy is allowed to touch these items on his own. This, they feel, indicates the boy's future. Puberty rites are not performed and they do not allow the girl during menstruation to prepare food and offer *puja.* A boy wears the *janeu* at the time of marriage.

Marriage by negotiation and marriage by *batta-satta* are accepted by the Rathis. A marriage proposal is initiated by the boy's parents. A middle man who is usually a relative, carries the proposal to the parents of the girl. Apart from the family status and economic factors, the beauty of the girl and her behaviour are kept in view and are the deciding factors for negotiation. Neither the boy nor the girl has any say regarding their marriage. After an argreement between both the parties, an engagement ceremony is held at the girl's parents house. *Tel-batna* ceremony is held on both the sides. Oil is put on the head of the bridegroom with *druba. Batna* is applied on the body of the groom before he takes bath. On the marriage day the groom with his friends and relatives goes to the bride's house there, he is received by the elders of the bride's family. The groom is received by the mother of the bride who performs an *arti* and touches his forehead. At the appointed hour, the bridegroom is taken to the *mandap* by the *purohit* and the bridegroom and the bride sit close to each other. A *havan kund* is pitched in the centre of the *vedi.* The boy's priest place a *duna* containing some rice, a walnut, *druba* and flowers in his hands. The bride is brought to the *vedi* a little later and sits close to groom with her face veiled. One corner of the veil is tied with one end of the *swal chadar* of the bridegroom. The rituals continue for a couple of hours. The bride and groom's hands are placed over each other and tied with a new napkin. The bride's father then performs the *kanyadan* rite. The bride and the groom go round the sacred fire seven times. At each step the *purohit* reads verses from the *vivah paddhati.* Thereafter, the groom puts vermilion in the parting of the hair of the bride which is called *mangbharna.* At the time of *bidai* the near ones of the bride are seen standing around her. When she proceeds towards *dola* the women relations start sobbing. A few persons from the bride's side acompany the *barat.* When the groom reaches his house with the bride, the mother and the elderly women relatives receive them. *Arti* is waved over their head. The women gathered around the bride have a close look at the bride's face and present something in cash or kind. On the third day of the *vadhu praveshtne*, the bride accompanied by the groom visits her parents' house. This is called *phera*. For consummation of marriage they perform *madhuchandrima* at the groom's residence.

Children below the age of 5 years are and persons dying of leprosy and small-pox are buried, while others are cremated. After death the limbs of the deceased are stretched and the mouth and the eyes are closed. *Panchratna* is given. At the time of carrying the dead body to the cremation ground, the people chant *Ram Ram* and *Ram nam sat hai*. After giving a bath to the corpse, the body is placed on the funeral pyre. The eldest son lights the pyre. While doing so he does not face the pyre.

Relatives carry the *astu* (ashes) for Hardwar, for immersion in the Ganges. After completion of the funeral rites, they have a bath and wash their clothes. The mourners sleep on the floor. Villagers and distant relatives do not have water or food from their hands till the period of mourning is over. The *daspindi* is held on the tenth day after the death. The male relatives who are younger in relation to the dead peson have to shave off their head. Next day, *pinds* made of barley or rice flour and one *supindi* are offered in the name of the dead. On the thirteenth day called *sog*, the deceased's relations on the wife's side come to the house. A goat is killed and a feast is given to the relatives and friends which marks the end of the pollution. *Pinds* are offered in the memory of the deceased after three months, six months, nine months and after an year and then after four years. The widow of the deceased need not change her food habits but adornment. She observes fast in the memory of her deceased husband on every *sankranti*.

The Rathis earn their livelihood by agriculture and by rearing sheep and goat. The men plough their fields and the women perform hoeing, weeding, harvesting and thrashing. Due to the ecological set up they can grow only one crop in a year. Maize is their staple diet so they pay more attention to its cultivation. During winters, they leave their villages and move towards the low hills for grazing their flock. The *kharif* crops are paddy and maize and the *rabi* crops are wheat and barley. Vegetables such as brinjal, onion, pumpkins and gourds are grown extensively.

The fields are scattered and terrace cultivation is common. Fields are prepared after levelling. Terraces are supported by the protective walls. Campost manure is used. There is very little irrigation and they have to depend on rains. The head of the family controls land and other property. Horticulture, which was earlier considered unprofitable, is now being given attention for growing apples, plums, peaches, pears and apricots, which helps them to earn money. There are no differences in wage based on sex. Sheep and goats are their wealth and key to prosperity. If a man has got many heads in the flock he takes one or more hired shepherds with him. The hired shepherds are provided with free food, free clothing, two to four sheep or goats and Rs. 50 per month as salary.

They keep migrating between the low hills and the inner mountains of Pangi, Lahaul and other neighbouring regions. During winters they come down to lower hills of Kangra, Nurpur, Pathankot and Jammu. They have to pay grazing tax to the forest department. They also weave woollen cloth locally called *patti.* Women and children do the weaving. They keep the woollen items for self use but the surplus is sold. A few of those who have completed education have joined different Government and non-Government services. Some of them have started small grocer and stationary shops. A few of them have also started transport business.

The Rathis, if they face any dispute, settle it with the help of some old relatives and friends amicably. The Gram Panchayat exists in the village. The villagers take part in polling for electing the *pradhan, up-pradhan* and other members. A secretary is appointed who looks after the administrative set-up of the Gram Panchayat. The panchayat deals with matters like the village road construction, relief for the poor or the needy families through grants from the Government. They also collect land revenue from the villagers.

The Rathis are Hindus. Local deities like Brahmani Devi, Diggu and Murari are worshipped. They believe that Shiva is the supreme God who created this world. There are various folktales about him and the area they inhabit is also known as Shiva Bhumi. They also worship Kailung and goddess Kali. Hardwar, Varanasi, Kedarnath and Manimahesh are regarded as pilgrimage centres by the Rathis and also visit these places. A Brahman *pujari* performs *puja.* The priest carries a *chhari* and a *thali* with articles of *puja.* The people follow the priest in performing *puja* which is accompanied by a *kartal, bell* and *paunl* which are played while reciting *arti.* Folkdance and drama bring enjoyment to their lives. A fair is celebrated for a week at the lake of Brahmani Devi during Janmashtami and on the eighth day of the bright half of the moon in the months of Bhadon or Asoj. A big fair is held at Manimahesh and is attended by them. Holi, Dussehra and Diwali are celebrated with great enthusiasm.

Some of them know the traditional art of famous Chamba paintings. They are good spinners and weavers. Folktales related to the origin of the community and about their homeland can be heard from them. They also sing folksongs of the area. Marriage ceremony, fairs and festivals are the occasions when they enjoy music, dance and songs which reflects their inner gay mood and their way of life.

The Rathis live in multi-ethnic villages, forming part of a composite rural society. On various social, economic, religious and political matters they often come in contact with communities like Brahman, Rajput (Rana, Mian, etc.), Sippi, Hali and Heri, with whom socioeconomic linkages are well established. Though Rathis are nowadays allowed to take food with Rajput and Brahman but they are still not allowed to smoke the same *hukka.* In earlier days, whenever a Rathi took food in a Brahman's house, he had to clear his *thali* himself after the meals and similarly a Sippi, a Hali and a Rihara on being invited to a meal at the Rathi's house, were obliged to clean their dishes after meals. The modern linkages are based on political inclinations and affiliations through the exercise of Gram Panchayat activites.

There are two schools at Bharmaur—one for boys which is a high school and the other for girls which is a middle school. Open-air classes are also conducted due to lack of accommodation. Children of poor families avail themselves of freeship. There is growing awareness to educate their children.

There is a primary health centre and a small hospital. People do not show interest in family planning schemes. However with the effort of the motivators, some of them have undergone sterilization. Water comes down from the glaciers and is brought through suitable pipes to the places of their habitation. Those who can afford take electricity connections. Employment and self-employment opportunities are within their easy reach. Few young entrepreneurs have taken loan from the bank and purchased jeeps for transport business. Communication in general has improved in recent years. All-weather roads, both metalled and unmetalled, have been constructed. For cooking food and to keep the house warm during winters they use firewood and for lighting they use kerosene oil.

D. K. Chakraborty

RAWAT

The Rawat, Rawant, Raut, Rataut, Raut or Rao, according to Rose (1919:331), "appear to be patronymic like many others ending in awat and -ot. It may thus mean 'son of a Rao'. They are admittedly a clan of Chandel Rajputs; but they are the lowest clan who are recognised as of Rajput stock and barely if at all admitted to communion with other Rajputs, while under no circumstances would even a Rathi marry a Rawat woman" (Rose, *op. cit.*). It appears that they were originally Hindu Rajputs, but at some point in the past, Mehandi Hasan, a Sayyad by sect, converted them to Islam and since then they are also called Muslim Rajputs.

Their distribution according to the available literature and as further testified by the informants is in the sub-montaneous region in the Jamuna valley. In Himachal Pradesh they are found in Sirmur district in sizeable numbers. The language spoken amongst the people themselves is Sirmauri, but with others they converse in Hindustani. They commonly use Perso-Arabic but nowadays Devanagari is also being used.

The community is non-vegetarian. They take the meat of goat, chicken and buffalo, but abstain from taking beef, pork and fish. There is a preference for the way the animal is slaughtered. They only accept *halal* and not *jhatka*. Owing to the high cost of non-vegetarian food, the community eats non-vegetarian food only about twice a month. Their staple food is wheat *chapati*, rice, pulses like *masur*, *urad* or beans and vegetables which occasionally also include roots and tubers. Their cooking media are oils of *til* and mustard. Consumption of fruits is occasional and limited to seasonal availability. *Chir*, plum, *nakh* and mangoes are taken during season.

Milk is consumed in its original form by the children, but the adults take it generally in tea and also in various forms like *lassi*, curd and *ghee*. Although drinking of alcohol is prohibited, but the men occasionally purchase it from the local market.

Eating cereal food and even swallowing of saliva is prohibited on the days of *roza* but sweet preparations like *seviyan* are a must on Id-ul-Fitr and cooking of meat is a must on Id-ul-Zuha day. Sweet preparations are also prepared on the Shabebarat day. The major change in their food habits has been a shift from non-vegetarian to vegetarian food.

Though converts, they nevertheless retain their traditional *gotra*, which still speak of their being Hindus at one time. Since there are two sections of the Rawats, i.e., the Hindu and Muslim, each maintains its own endogamy at the sectarian level. The *gotras* are exogamous and denote their ancestry.

Among themselves, they have no sense of superiority and all are treated as equals. In the local social hierarchy, whether Hindus or Muslim, they rank in the order of Rangar, Rawat, Teli, Julaha, Rain, Bharai, Banjara and Pinja, and this fact is accepted by all. They are aware of the varna system. Though the Hindus place themselves along with the Kshatriya order, the Muslim Rawats do not recognize this order.

The community practises endogamy with each of its sections, viz, the Hindus and Muslims marrying within their own sections. The Hindu Rawats maintain avoidance in matrimonial ties up to four *gotras*, i.e., the *gotra* of self, *gotra* of father's mother, mother and mother's mother. Among the Muslims. a few families avoid two *gotras*, i.e., that of self and mother's *gotra,* whereas others do not avoid *gotra* and have preference for cross- and parallel-cousin marriage, as is the general practice among the Muslims. Junior and senior levirate and junior sororate are practised.

Till about two decades ago, child marriages were performed at the age of 8 or 10 years, followed by a *gaona/muklawa* when the girl came of age. Today, adult marriages are practised with the girls getting married between 16 and 18 and boys between 20 and 22.

The usual mode of acquiring mates among the Rawats is by negotiation. Nikah is performed in consideration of a fixed amount of *mehar.* The other form of marriage which is performed among them is *batta-satta.* Monogamy is generally practised, but in exceptional cases when the first wife is unable to bear an heir for the family, a second marriage is resorted to with the consent of the first wife. The marriage symbols among the women are the *nak-ki-tili* and glass or rubber or plastic bangles, though these are not strictly observed. The Rawats give a fixed amount of *mehar* which is decided by their *panchayat.* None of the negotiating parties can enter into matrimony with *mehar* less than the fixed one. *Dan-dahej* is also given to the girl at the time of marriage, which consists of gifts in kind, and varies from family to family depending on their economic status. The residence after marriage is patrilocal. The exception to the rule is when the family does not have any male child and the son-in-law is invited to stay with the girl's parent's.

Divorce is permissible for both the sexes with the socio-judicial approval. It is effected by either of the parties uttering the word *talaq* thrice, in the presence of some witnesses. The common grounds for divorce are adultery and maladjustment. Both partners can divorce but in practice it is the males who go in for divorce. In all such cases, the *mehar* amount is to be paid to the wife, but the *dan-dahej* is either returned or forfeited by the husband, as per the decision of the panchayat, which decides on the merit of the case. Children of the divorcee parents are the liability of the father but infants accompany the mother and return to their father on growing up. The divorcee wife is given a compensation for bringing up the child.

Remarriage of widow and widower or divorcee is permissible, and a wife can also marry her deceased husband's elder or younger brother after the expiry of three and a quarter month period of *iddat*. This restriction exists only for the widows and female divorcees. It is thus obvious that a significant change has come in the institution of marriage especially in matters relating to the rules of marriage and age at marriage.

The Rawat family is of the vertically extended type, with all the relatives on the male side living and sharing the same roof and hearth. But with the people entering into diversified fields of occupation, they are migrating from the villages to urban centres and this is leading to the decline of extended family system and a rise in the formation of nuclear families. The eldest male member of the family holds supreme status and is the head of the family. The elders are feared, obeyed and held in veneration, and due regard as per the status of the person is the basis of mutual relationship. Avoidance is observed between the wife and his husband's elder male relatives whereas joking relationship exists between the wife and her husband's younger relatives and the wife's sisters. Avoidance is observed between the relatives in the first year of marriage after which it declines and with the passage of time it completely vanishes.

After the death of the eldest male member of the family, all the sons inherit the paternal property equally. In the event of more than one wife the property is first divided equally among the wives and then their respective shares are further subdivided equally among their children. The succession is in the male line. Interfamily relations are cordial and they share each other's joys and sorrows. These are best observed at the time of family rituals. The widow enjoys usufructuary rights in the property. A daughter can only inherit the parental property if there is no son in the family. The social and economic status of the women is equal in view of their position. They take part in all economic activity in and outside the house and within their fields. Women of well-to-do families do not go to work on others' field but those of poor background may do so to contribute to the family income. They do all the household work right from cooking to bringing up the young ones. They also bring fuel, water and fodder for the animals. They take part in all the family rituals. They cannot go to the mosque and take part in festivities outside the house. On the political front their participation is limited to casting votes only. They cannot hold any post in the Biradari Panchayat.

As soon as the child is born, a *maulvi* is called who whispers *azan* in the child's ears, and gives a name to the newborn. Though no formal christening ceremony is observed, the naming of the child is very important, so much so that even the child who is born dead is first named and then buried.

Aqiqa is observed normally on the sixth day but can be deferred for subsequent years for economic reasons. In the event of the birth of a boy, two goats are sacrificed whereas in case of a female only one is sacrificed. *Khatna* is performed on male children before the age of six years by the *jarrah*.

Marriage proposals are initiated by the boy's side either by the parents or friends, and solemnized at the girl's house by performing *nikah*, in the presence of a *maulvi* and two *gawah* besides friends and relatives, in recognition of an agreed-upon sum of *mehar*. The *barat-ka-khana* (marriage party feast) is given by the bride's parent whereas after the girl reaches the groom's house *dawat-e-walima* (marriage feast) is given by the groom's father. Earlier when child marriages were performed *muklawa/gauna* was deferred till the girl came of age, but today, it is merely symbolic and is done along with the marriage. The consumation of marriage takes place at the groom's residence.

The dead are buried and a mound is raised at the burial site. *Matam* is observed for a period of three days. The death rituals vary from family to family according to the *firqa* to which they belong. Among the Rawats of Sirmaur the mortuary rites are observed on the third, tenth, twentieth and fortieth day. Every year after the death, the family members offers prayers at the *mazar* and offer incense and *chadar*.

The Rawats are traditional agriculturists and still continue with this profession. Though the majority of them own land, some of them are also landless or have very meagre land, the produce of which is insufficient to last them for a year. Those who have land have forest rights as well, through which they can get and collect dried twigs for fuel, grass for the cattle and wood for house construction at a very nominal rate.

Those with small landholding work as sharecroppers on the fields of the bigger landlords for a half share of the produce or on *theka* at a mutually agreed sum. In the former case the landlord and the tiller both share the profit or the loss. Due to low yield and uncertainty of weather, the people have taken to other occupations like teaching, jobs in Government and in private organization, or are working as agricultural or casual labourers. The people are dependent on the local regulated market for selling their produce and buying things of necessity. Cash is the usual medium of exchange but in the villages barter also takes place at times.

Children both boys and girls work in the agricultural fields in their leisure hours after school. Some of the children, especially boys of poor families, work as agricultural labourers or as casual labourers and earn cash wages to supplement the family income.

A change is seen in the economic activities of the community after Independence. The Rawats have diversified their occupations and for some the primary occupation has assumed the status of a secondary occupation.

For the maintenance of social control the community has its *Anjuman* which looks into the cases of breach of traditional norms, divorce, elopement and maladjustment. The *Anjuman* is managed by an elected secretary who is assisted by elected members. The decision of the *Anjuman* is final and is binding on the members. The offenders are penalized by a cash fine which is utilized towards maintenance or defraying expenses for running of the mosque or the *madarsa.*

Inspite of the coming up of the statutory panchayats like Gram and Nyay Panchayats after Independence, which look after planning and implementation of welfare activities and maintenance of law and order, the *anjumans* have not let loose their hold and still continue to be strong among the Rawats.

The community belongs to the Sunni sect. Besides Allah—the Almighty—whom they hold in reverence, there are other Pirs like Bure Shah and Maru Sidh who are paid obeisance and are held in reverence. Lakhdata and Sahmat Ali are presiding Pirs for cattle who are also held in reverence. They also believe in the village deity locally called as Khera Dev, who is represented by a tree usually on the outskirts of the village. He is venerated by all villagers alike for the welfare of the village.

Their sacred shrines are the *dargah* of Ajmer Sharif and at Sirhind. Their sacred specialists are not from the community. A *maulvi* is invited to officiate at the rites of the life cycle rituals. The major festivals of the community are Id, Bakrid and Shabebarat. Sasa Id is another festival that comes after five days of Id. Those who do not observe *roza* for 40 days, can keep *roza* for five days and celebrate Sasa Id. All these festivals have socioreligious significance. Their important fairs are held at the *mazar* of Makdoor Shah, Nau Gaza Pir and Sabir Mian at Paonta, where prayers are offered for the fulfilment of wishes.

The women of the Rawats are skilled workers in the art of embroidery. The women also paint their palms and feet with *mehndi* and make exquisite designs. *Alta* is also applied by the women on their feet, especially at marriage or on other social occasions. The women also sing and dance purely for amusement and recreational purposes at home.

The Rawats are liberal as far as commensal norms are concerned. They can accept all type of food and can exchange any type of food with other Muslims even though they may be of a different occupation. From the Chuhra, Chamar and Bangali they can accept *sidha* or a *pucca* food cooked by a Brahman or Rajput. The upper caste Hindus accept only *pucca* food from Rawats provided it is cooked by a Brahman outside their house. Ritual kinship is established with any person of a Muslim community, who is expected to perform all obligations as that of a real kin.

Though they have separate water resources, there is no restriction on the sharing of public taps. *Jajmani* exists between the serving and the served communities who render their traditional specialized services in lieu of which they receive a fixed amount of foodgrains at the harvest time from the house of their clients.

With the diversification of their economic activities, new relations of sharecropping and cultivator-labour relations have emerged. Those of the Rawats who have entered Government service or private organization or have taken to teaching profession have developed new employer-employee relationships, and this has loosened the community taboos.

The attitude of the Rawats towards various development activities has been positive and they have been greatly benefited by them. The younger generation, both boys and girls, are sent to schools. Of these, the girls study up to school level after which they drop out for want of educational facilities for higher education in the village. The boys however study up to college and beyond, and drop out to take up some jobs to support the family.

The Rawats still practise their indigenous system of medicare, but due to the opening of primary health centres and Government hospitals, allopathic medicine has found favour with them. The young generation living near urban centres and working in offices prefer to have three children. They use modern contraceptives but have no preference for sterilization.

Under the Integrated Rural Development Programme they have taken loans for purchasing buffaloes and to start dairy farming. Loans have also been provided under self-employment schemes to educated unemployed, who have been able to set up general merchandise shops. Drinking water is available through pipes. Electricity is also available and so are media and communication facilities. The villages are connected by metalled roads, public transport facilities and with post offices. Firewood and kerosene oil are the commonly used fuels. Irrigation facilities are available to the people through Giri Sinchai Pariyojna. People use both organic and inorganic manure and also use insecticides. The infants, expectant and nursing mothers are provided with immunization and nutritional food under the Integrated Child Development Scheme.

Rajendra Sarkar

RIHARA

The Rihara, Rehar or Ruhara are a scheduled caste. They are regarded as one of the groups included under the generic term Gaddi. Often Rihara and Rehar are confused as one. Ibbetson (1916:336) writing on them states: "the Rehar or Rihara appears to be closely allied to the Dumna. He is found in the hills. Like the Dumna, he works in bamboo, but like the Hesi he travels about as a strolling ministrel. He is said to make the trinkets worn by the Gaddi women, and to furnish the music at the Gaddi weddings."

In fact the people distinguish Rehar and Rihara as two different communities. In Shimla district, the Rehars earn their livelihood by making *kirri* and removing cowdung, and are regarded as equal in ritual status to Doom whereas the Rehars are primarily engaged in silversmithy and tinsmithy. No historical or ethnographic account of the community is available but the people consider themselves to be an indigenous population.

The Riharas inhabit the high altitude hill terrain of Bharmaur tehsil of Chamba district, where the climate is extremely cold for most parts of the year, with heavy snowfall, dense forest and scanty rainfall. They share their homestead with other communities in the village but in a separate locality. Their population is 2,383 according to the 1981 Census. They speak the Gadiali dialect among themselves and with locals but with outsiders converse in Hindustani. The literate among them use Devanagari and Perso-Arabic scripts. Their dress resembles that of the Gaddi.

The Riharas are non-vegetarian, but beef and buffalo meat are taboo for them. Their staple food consists of wheat or maize *chapati*, rice, *rongi*, beans, pulses like *masur* and *mah* with occasional consumption of vegetables, edible roots and tubers, which are cooked in mustard oil. Fruits like apples, plums and walnut are taken during the season. Milk is taken by infants. Adults take tea, curd and *lassi*. They are also fond of alcoholic drinks which are brewed locally and are regularly taken by the men. The women also take them on festive occasions. *Bidi*, cigarette and tobacco are also consumed through their indigenous pipe.

Special foods like sweet dishes and *madra* are part of the festivities. There is also a shift from the traditional *roti* to rice, and the consequent increase in the use of vegetables and pulses due to decrease in the consumption of non-vegetarian items on account of their high cost.

The Riharas perceive their position at the low level and ranks along with the Sippi, Koli, Badhi and Hali, and this fact is acknowledged by people of other castes. But they do not recognise the varna system.

The Riharas practise endogamy at the community level. Hypergamy is practised from amongst the Panchamas. Junior levirate and sororate are also permissible. Mates are acquired in adulthood by negotiation, exchange of sisters, service or elopement. Some decades ago child marriages were practised, but these have been given up today. *Reet* was also paid in the past in the form of silver coins but these are being replaced by dowry which is paid in kind and depends upon the economic status of the family. The symbols of marriage are *nath* or *laung* and *paranda.*

Chhad-chhada (divorce) is permissible by either party on grounds of adultery and maladjustment with social approval which also decrees compensation to the aggrieved. In the event of the wife leaving the husband, her paramour has to return the *reet* or the marriage expenses to the former husband. Children of such estranged parents however continue to be the liability of the father. Widow, widower and divorcee remarriage is permissible. In the sphere of matrimony a gradual change is evident as the age of marriage has increased and also dowry has replaced bride price.

The residence after marriage is patrilocal, excepting in cases where the bride's family has no sons. In such a case, the son-in-law is invited to stay with the wife's parents. Families which were traditionally of vertically extended type are tending to be nuclear with the diversification of occupations. Interpersonal relations are based on paternal and filial ties. The inheritance is as per male equigeniture following the *chundaband* and *mundaband* law of inheritance, and the succession is patrilineal.

The women have the right of maintenance. They could inherit only in the absence of male children. Their status was reckoned as low, but nevertheless, they are an economic asset for they do all the agricultural work in addition to their household chores. They also contribute to the family income and control the expenditure.

The enceinte woman worships the goddess Kali for the well-being of the child. Her movements are also restricted after dusk. *Sutak* is observed for 13 days. *Suru* (first cereal-feeding), and christening is done together in the sixth month, which is followed by *jattu* before one year. The marriage is a simple ceremony and is performed by circumambulation and *kanyadan* at the bride's house where a marriage feast is given by the bride's parents. The nuptial ceremony is performed at the groom's residence.

The dead are cremated and the mortal remains are immersed in water. The infants and those dying of contagious diseases are usually buried. Pollution is observed for 14 days and mortuary rituals are performed on the tenth, twelfth and fourteenth day; after the third month and sixth months. Annual rites are also performed on each anniversary, and on the fourth *chaubarkhi* anniversary special rites are performed.

The major economic resource of the Riharas had traditionally been land along with the business of gold, silver and tinsmithy. The majority are landowners and agriculturists. Some who do not have enough land, work as sharecroppers, with gold, silver and tinsmithy taking the second position. A few are also working as casual and unskilled labourers. They have a daily regulated market for selling their agricultural produce and the gold and silver ornaments, against cash payment and at times on deferred payments.

Children below 15 years assist their parents both in and outside the household. The boys also assist their parents in agricultural work and in tending the cattle. Some of the children who work in road clearance and road-making jobs, receive good rates in cash and thus supplement their family income.

The law and order in the community is maintained by their own traditional Bhaichara Panchayat. The number of members differs in each panchayat; and the nomination of the members depends on their ability and general consensus. The offenders of the traditional norms, and those found guilty of adultery and theft are punished by excommunication or by cash fines. The statutory Gram Panchayats maintain law and order and also decide petty cases of social and economic offences. These panchayats coexist, but in no way have the statutory panchayats loosened the hold of the Bhaichara Panchayats.

The community professes Hinduism. They have family, clan and village deities, who are worshipped by every family, community and the village. They also have belief in the other deities of the wider pantheon order. Their sacred specialists are from the Brahman community who act as *purohit* and officiate at life-cycle rituals and the exorcists are from the Sippi community who deal in protection from evil spirits. They take part in the major fairs, viz., Sui Mela, Bharmaur Jatra, Minjar and festivals like Biswa, Baisakhi, Chhinj which are of socioreligious significance and are shared with the other communities of the region.

The community continues its of traditional art forms. The men make gold and silver ornaments and also make amulets by engraving the picture of their deities on gold and silver plaque. They also make tassel, of gold and silver threads. The women are very fond of tattooing and they get their chin and innerside of the arm tattooed. This is done only for aesthetic purpose. The images of Shiva, Parvati, and flowers and/or name are tattooed, they philosophize while describing the necessity of it—that a person may die, but these things will remain even after his or her death. Rihara women, like other women of other communities, also do weaving, which is almost done by every family in the area.

Both the men and women sing and dance at festive social occasions. The males also play on fire. The women dance traditionally within the four walls of the house, but now they also have started participating in public performances also.

The Sippi are regarded as superior to the Riharas. The Rihara can accept both *kachcha* and *pucca* food from the Brahman, Rajput, etc. whereas the latter would accept only the *pucca* food if cooked by a person of the latter community. The latter share their *hukka* with a Rihara, outside the house, but he would remove the *nalki* (nipple) from the pipe. The Sippis accept both *kachcha* and *pucca* food from the Riharas. Though intercommunity marriages within the community are strictly restricted, occasional marriages amongst the Panchama is resorted to because of the loosening of community ties. Putative kinship is established with persons from amongst the community. Such kins are expected to perform all rites and obligations as expected of a real kin. Traditionally, the Riharas have had access to the sharing of common water resources. They share the crematorium with the Sippi only. They may enter into the house except the hearth. They visit the precinct of the temples. *Jajmani* system existed between the Riharas and other people. They render traditional services of making gold and silver ornaments. In addition they also work as sharecroppers and receive half the crop. Those who work as agricultural labourers, receive a fixed quantity of food grains in lieu of their services.The recent entry of the community people in the diversified fields of occupations, has resulted in their establishing new modes of relationship and commensality and has also influenced their behavioural pattern. Consequently a new pattern of relationship like employer-worker, landlord-tenant, sharecropping and mutual exchange of labour *batlami* has emerged. Though none of them are themselves taking part in political activities, yet they very actively canvass for other community members of similar ritual status and cast their votes.

Though small in number, the community is aware of the various development activities being implemented by the Government. This is also because of the areas of their habitation have been identified as a backward region and have been included under the special component plan called the integrated tribal development programmes, which caters to the need of overall development of the region.

Children, both boys and girls, are being sent to school, but only a few study beyond the high school, for economic reasons and their need in family enterprises. In spite of this the literacy has improved over the years. The people are not in favour of the small family norm, as more children are an asset in their day-to-day activities. Their attitude to health programmes is favourable and people make use of modern medicine in addition to the traditional system.

Drinking water is available from the perennial snowfed streams, which is made available through pipes. Roads (metalled) do not exist, and *kachcha* roads connect only some of the villages. Post offices exist at far-off places, railways do not exist. Though cinema halls are not there, but people do see movies shown through extension agencies, and also in video parlours. Electricity is available only in a few villages. Employment avenues are available, which are availed of through Integrated Rural Development Programme schemes. Organic manure is freely used with some chemical fertilizers and pesticides.

Mid-day meals to school-going children are availed of and so are facilities of nutrition and immunization under the Integrated Child Development Schemes. Ration, kerosene and cloth at subsidized rates are availed of through the pulic distribution system. Banking facilities, are available, but the people do not have enough to save for investment purposes.

Rajendra Sarkar

SAINI

The Sainis are "the market gardener caste of the Hindus in the eastern districts, corresponding to the Mali of Jamuna zone and Arains or Baghwan of the rest of the provinces" (Rose 1914:346). Rose further states that though they appear to be the subdivision of the Mali, some of the higher tribes of the same caste would not intermarry with them. In Jalandhar district of Punjab they even claim a Rajput status which is probably doubtful. About the etymology of the Saini, the word is derived from the word *rasaini* or *rasai* meaning skill and since the people did such wonders with land that they are surpassed by none in industry and ability and hence the word Saini (Rose *op. cit.*).

The community is distributed principally in the districts of Hamirpur, Bilaspur, Kangra, Shimla and Sirmaur. According to the informants, they came during the reign of Maharaja Ranjit Singh from the Chanjowal village in Hoshiarpur district of Punjab. It seems quite probable that during the reshufling and reorganization of the undivided State of Punjab into Himachal Pradesh they shifted to this part and were incorporated in the population of Himachal Pradesh.

The dialect of the people is Punjabi mixed with Hindi and Urdu. Many of the members of the old generation also know Persian. The scripts used by the people are Devanagari, Perso-Arabic and Gurmukhi. Those who have attained formal education make use of English as well. With outsiders they use a dialect which is a mixture of Punjabi, Hindi and Urdu. There is no distinct dress, adornment, or head gear which can distinguish them from the rest of the people of the region. The older generation of men wear *pyjama* and shirt. The women wear *salwar* and *kameez* along with *chadar* to cover their head. Young married women observe *purdah* in the presence of elder male member of their husband's family.

The staple diet of the people consists of maize and wheat *chapati* and pulses. Rice consumption is considerably less. They are non-vegetarian and occasionally take meat of goat, rabbit and chicken. The men are fond of smoking and drinking. The drinks are purchased from the market. The women do not smoke or drink. Betel-chewing is not a common habit.

Among the non-alcoholic beverages, tea is most popular and is made use of extensively by all men, women and children. Milk just for drinking becomes quite expensive and is consumed by those who have their own dairies. Roots and tubers, seasonal vegetables and fruits are also consumed to a moderate extent. There has been no significant change in the daily food habits of the people, except for the intake of non-vegetarian items which has considerably reduced owing to its high cost.

The Sainis are similar if not identical to the Malis and the Arains. It appears, and as has been mentioned by Rose (1914), that they are perhaps a subdivision or an offshoot of the Mali. Among the Sainis, there are Sikh also. Both Hindu and Sikh sections may intermarry. The Sainis have been divided into number of *gotras* like Mehra, Masute, Chere, Ghugani, Tambar, Badwal. Rose (*op. cit.*) cites many more names such as Salahri, Bhanga, Bhela, Bhundi, Boli, Cheran, Daule, Cheri, Ghalar, Giddhe, Kolote, Mulana and Sugge. The functional utility of this exogamous unit is to regulate marriage between the kin of paternal and maternal sides.

The community can be placed in the middle stratum of the social hierarchy. The exact placement in the classical varna order is not clear, but judging by the people's self-perception and by the perception of others, they seem to be a part of the wide variety which comprises the Sudra. In Jalandhar, the community claims a much higher status and they rank themselves close to the Rajputs.

Marriages are settled through negotiation and the proposal of the marriage can be initiated from either of the sides, which is purely a matter of convenience. Marriage would be settled leaving the *gotra* of father, mother and mother's mother. Previously, a match could be selected from within the village itself, but nowadays village exogamy is the rule owing to the simple fact that members of the community inhabiting the village are mostly related to each other and also because there is a strong sentiment of fraternity which binds all the girls and boys of the village in common bond of a brother and sister relationship.

The usual age of marriage for girls and boys is between 20-23 and 24-25 respectively. A decade or so earlier, even child marriages in the age group of five to ten were also performed, in which case a second ceremony known as *muklawa* was performed at a later date when the girl actually came of age. With the enforcement of legislation banning child marriages and also partly due to social awakening, child marriages have been largely replaced by adult marriages.

The residence after marriage is patrilocal. The common symbols for married women are vermilion mark in the parting of the hair, glass bangles and toe-rings. The practice of bride price and dowry is not present but gifts in the form of utensils, clothes and jewellery are voluntarily given to the daughter by the parents and no demand in the form of either cash or kind is made as a pre-condition to marriage.

Both divorce and remarriage of widow and widower are permitted. Junior and senior levirate and junior sororate are also practised. Divorce, though infrequent, can be granted on exceptional grounds of adultery, impotency, frigidity, mental sickness or due to the practice of witchcraft. If the wife is barren, a second marriage is possible with the consent of the first wife but this does not call for divorce. A woman on being widowed or divorced can remarry a person of her choice from within the community and in such cases the children born from previous wedlock are the responsibility of the father. In the event the wife is divorced by the husband, the community panchayat can levy penalty of post-divorce maintenance on the husband.

The traditional structure of the joint family still finds a lot of social support despite the fact that nuclear families are also coming up. The relations within the joint household are by and large based on mutual co-operation and interdependence, especially in times of need countering the bitterness caused by petty quarrels and differences arising out of domestic issues. The women observe purdah in the presence of the father-in-law, husband's elder brothers and with all those men who are elder to the husband in age and relation, whereas relations with peer group members and those with husband's younger brother and that of the husband with wife's younger sister and brother are of joking type.

Women do not enjoy the same socioeconomic freedom as has been accorded to men. The women contribute to the family income besides doing household chores, but ironically they do not wield any significant control on the economy of the house. In household affairs, they do have considerable autonomy. Women take active part in family rituals and festivals. But their political will is highly constrained for they hardly know their surroundings to express any independent view.

The *rites-de-passage* as observed from time to time and are broadly in tune with Hindu religious beliefs. The post-birth pollution is observed and a woman who has delivered the child is not allowed to cook or touch the utensils or draw water unless she has undergone the purificatory bath on the eleventh day and subsequently, after a month. Thereafter, she is reckoned physically and ritually clean to undertake normal routine work. *Annaprashan* is observed by giving sweet pudding to the child, which formally initiates the child into a cereal diet. At this time, the child's paternal aunt brings some clothes and sweets for the child. The *mundan* ceremony is performed only for the male child. It is done within the first year of birth or can be deferred till the third, fifth or seventh year.

Marriage involves a series of rites performed from time to time, starting with betrothal locally known as *sagai*. On this occasion the groom's father, brother or uncle visits the girl's house and offers her some clothes or a piece of jewellery. Thereafter, on a pre-decided day, the groom's party, consisting of his near and dear ones, relatives and friends, leave for the bride's house. On reaching, there, they are welcomed by the girl's parents. All the important marriage rituals consisting of *kanyadan* and *phera* are performed amidst the chanting of Vedic *mantras* by the priests of both the sides. This is followed by a ceremony known as *doli* which marks the departure of the bride from her home to that of her husband.

The Sainis cremate their dead. However, children below 10 years of age and also those who die of small pox are buried. The death pollution lasts for 13 days, followed by community feeding on the sixteenth day when another important death rite known as *pagri ki rasam* is performed. On this day, a white cloth for *pagri* is brought customarily by the maternal uncle and is tied to the eldest son of the deceased signifying both transfer of authority and responsibility. It is customary that the eldest son performs the last rites of his father. Earlier all the agnates of the deceased used to get their head and moustaches shaved off as a mark of respect to the dead and also signifying solidarity of the blood kinship, but nowadays the practice of shaving off the head is being dropped. Ancestor worship known as *shradha* is also observed annually during the fortnight especially dedicated to the commemoration of the dead, which falls in the month of September-October. This is known as *pitr paksha* and these days are considered solemn and in a way inauspicious as no marriage or tonsure or similar auspicious activities can take place during this period. People refrain from purchasing new clothes or utensils during *pitr-paksha*.

Traditionally the Sainis have been practising market gardening in addition to farming. Presently, a majority of them are landowner, and cultivate their own fields. Those families which did not have any land have now received land under *nautor* scheme (distributing land for the landless) under the Twenty Point Economic Programme. They also receive subsidy from the Block office for manure and seeds. In addition to agriculture, many of them have opened their own shops, and business. Some have secured job in military and Government.

There are some shops of general merchandise in the village. The fully developed town market is also within the reach of the people. Commodities are purchased against cash, but barter is also practised to some extent. The children up to the age of 15 are held back from their studies to assist their parents.

As a mechanism of social control the Sainis have the formal statutory panchayats. All cases of social disputes are brought to the notice of the Gram Panchayat which can levy fines in cash as compensation for the loss. The fine money thus realized is put to the welfare of the village, for instance in building the village roads. There is no *biradari* council of the Sainis but some purely domestic issues like family quarrels and cases of marital discord are discussed by the senior members of the Saini *biradari* and reconciliation is mostly reached. In case the matters are not sorted out at this level, they are then referred to Gram Panchayat, and if it also fails to reach any amicable solution, then the same are taken to the courts of law for final settlement.

The Sainis are Hindu by faith. Besides the major gods and goddesses of the larger pantheon, they worship the regional deities, such as Nag Devta and Baba Gorakhnath. Sunday is the day which is allocated to the worship of Nag Devta. They also worship the *pipal* tree on the first Tuesday in the month of Jaistha (May-June). Incidentally, Nag Devta and *pipal* are closely linked with Lord Shiva. Baba Gorakhnath and his great disciple Raja Bhartari Chandra are also held in high esteem. A fair is held on Makar Sankranti day in the village Chanjowal (a place of their original habitation) in Hoshiarpur district of Punjab. They go every year to participate in the fair and glorify the saintly and divine qualities of their mythological heroes namely, Baba Gorakhnath and Bhartari Chandra. Besides, they visit the famous shrine of Deot Sidh which is situated on way from Una to Kangra. People also profess faith in magic spells and evil spirits and in the event of a person being afflicted by some chronic disease they seek the help of *sayana* and *bhagat* who are specialists in warding off the evil designs of the maligned spirits.

They share their songs, folklore and folktales and dances with other communities of the region.

The traditional *jajmani* system which is locally being referred to as *seppi* exists only with Tarkhan and Lohars who repair their agricultural implements, and in lieu of the service rendered, they give them one mound of grain on each harvest viz., *rabi* and *kharif.* Earlier, *seppi* existed with other communities such as Dhobi, Chamar and Nai. A Brahman who comes to perform marriage rituals or any family ritual is paid either in cash or kind (usually grains). A Brahman accepts *sidha* or if the food is cooked by a Brahman and also served by a Brahman then it may be acceptable to the Brahman. The Rajputs accept *pucca* food and that too if prepared separately. Communities like Tarkhan, Lohar, Jat, Bazigar and Chimbe accept *pucca* food from them. The Sainis, on the other hand, do not accept anything, either *pucca* or *kachcha,* from the Chamar, Chuhra and Dumna. On social occasions demanding cooperation, all the communities inhabiting the village show exemplary sense of comradeship and brotherhood.

Under the Government-launched schemes of Integrated Rural Development Programme and Employment Guarantee Scheme, many of them have received loans and subsidies. Under the Employment Guarantee Scheme, an educated youth can procure a loan up to Rs. 25,000 with subsidy and at 4 per cent rate of interest. Some of the beneficiaries under this scheme have been able to open their own shops which have substantially increased their income resources. Besides, they can get loan for agricultural purpose, for buying bullocks and agricultural implements. There is a 40 per cent subsidy on manures.

In the field of education and literacy, the Sainis show favourable and positive attitude. The younger generation is more keen to pursue education even at high levels. Young girls are also sent to schools and at least they view education as the most effective means of upward mobility.

Regarding health and family welfare, the facility through primary health centre and also by way of hospitals (at the district headquarters) is available to them. The family planning programmes launched by the Government has done extensive propaganda and advertising and arranged family planning camps from village to village, as a result people have accepted the small family norm of two children. Besides, the scheme for immunization of the mother and child is availed of.

Vatsala Sarkar

SANHAI

The word Sanhai means the one who plays a piped instrument *shehnai* (clarionet) played during ceremonies, religious festivals and in temples. Regarding the migration and history of the community nothing concrete is available. They have been inhabiting the region since times immemorial. The Sanhai is a scheduled caste. According to the 1981 Census there are 1,675 Sanhais.

The people speak Chambiali which is also a common dialect spoken throughout the Chamba district with little variation and modification. With outsiders they can converse in broken Hindi, and those who are literate can read or write in Devanagari. The old script of the people of Chamba in general used to be Tankari, but the script is hardly in use now and has been replaced by Perso-Arabic and Devanagari. They wear a narrow *pyjama*, shirt, waist coat and Himachali cap or may alternatively use a turban. The women wear *salwar* and *kameez*.

The staple diet of the Sanhais consists of maize, wheat and *mah*. They are non-vegetarian and take the meat of goat, fish and chicken. Eating the meat of buffalo and cow is considered taboo. The men are fond of smoking *hukka* and *bidi*. Drinking is quite common among the men, both old and young, and is almost a regular feature, but women may take it only on certain festive occasions or on ceremonies like marriage. Among the non-alcoholic beverages, tea is quite popular and is taken by persons of all age groups. Milk is given to the infants. Seasonal vegetables and locally available varieties of fruits such as apple, apricot and plum are consumed moderately.

The Sanhais have a number of exogamous *gotras,* each claiming its descent from a common ancestor. The function of the *gotra* is to regulate and prohibit marriage within close kins, related either through blood or through marriage.

The community ranks low in the hierarchical grading of the castes and they admit that they occupy a similar position as being occupied by the Hali, Koli, Bainsi and Chanal. In fact, recently there has been a growing tendency to merge their ranks with a numerically stronger group, the Halis who have gained support in local politics and in the region. Very minor differentiations exist only with regard to the occupational specialization of the respective groups. The Bainsis for instance, play the flute while the Sanhais play the *shehnai*, a pipe instrument. There have now also been marriage exchanges among these groups and nowadays, the social discrimination they were being subjected to, at the hands of the castes like Brahman, Rana, Rathi and

Mahajan is far less than was the case some two decades ago. The Sanhais rank themselves higher than castes like Chuhre, Chamar and Dumna.

Among the Sanhai marriage is strictly avoided among consanguineal kin i.e., avoiding marriages within the *gotra* of self, mother's and preferably mother's mother. Marriages are settled through negotiation but exchange marriages are also quite in vogue. The other form of marriage which is less practised is marriage by service and is known by the term *ghar javantri*. In this system the prospective bridegroom has to serve in the house of his in-laws for a specific number of years, before he can finally claim the hands of his daughter. The usual marriage age for boys and girls is between 19 and 20 and 16 and 18 years respectively. Bride price is slowly giving way to dowry. Dowry consists of some gifts of utensils or clothes for the bride and the bridegroom, and it should not be confused with the system as it is normally taken to be. Bride price is still practised by the poorer sections of the community.

Remarriage of widow and widower is allowed and a widow normally marries her deceased husband's younger brother by *ghadoj*, a form of marriage which does not entail any elaborate rituals. Marriage is solemnized in the presence of close relatives of both sides. The woman is offered a red ribbon, *puranda*. Both levirate and sororate are practised but this is not imposed on the widow/widower.

Divorce can be resorted to by both men as well as women. If a woman wants to marry outside the family she may do so, provided her new husband pays compensation money to her former husband. Children may stay with either mother or father. In the former cases, they lose all share in their father's property but, on the other hand, if they condinue to live with their father they enjoy all the benefits. Normally children are the responsibility of the father but in case of very small children the mother takes them along but the children may be claimed back by the father once they grow up. A second marriage in the lifetime of the first wife can be resorted to on the grounds of barrenness of the first wife but this does not necessitate divorcing her. On the contrary the second marriage takes place with the consent of the first wife.

Joint family system still finds its place in their social structure but nuclear families are also increasing side by side. Inter-personal relation among the members fall largely within the normative framework of the joint family system. Purdah which is observed by the women in the presence of the father-in-law and elder brother-in-law, is limited to partly covering their heads. Relation with the younger members of the family and peer-group members are of joking type.

The inheritance of property is on the patrilineal line with the sons receiving an equal share. However, the eldest son is given an additional share for paying the debt of his father. If a person has four sons then the property would be divided into five parts, the fifth part being termed as *jiyuk* and belongs to the parents. This share is given to the eldest son after the death of the father. A son born to a widow after the death of the husband is called a *chakhandu* and is entitled to a share provided the widow continues to live with the family of her deceased husband. A daughter may be entitled to property only in the absence of a son.

The women do not enjoy socioeconomic status at par with that of their men counterparts. Their economic potential and substantial contribution to the domestic income is recognized. They are not allowed to exercise their independent control on property and economic issues despite working hard. They not only look after the house but also bring potable water and fuel, attend to the animals and have a major role in agricultural operations. Except ploughing, the women take the major burden of the agricultural task. Despite all this, she is not given any representation in the local Jati Panchayat and has no freedom to exercise her economic will. Her political role is limited to the casting of votes.

The life-cycle rituals connected with birth, marriage and death are observed much in the same fashion as is prevalent in the rest of Chamba region. Immediately prior to the birth of the child the woman is separated to a room. Post-birth pollution is observed for 21 days and purificatory rites are observed on the sixth and eleventh day. *Jattu* ceremony is observed in either the first, third or fifth year whenever it is convenient for the family. The maternal uncle first cuts the hair followed by other relatives. The barbar also receives his due share on this occasion.

Marriage consists of a number of rituals which are observed at the bride's and bridegroom's house but the binding part of the marriage is the giving of the daughter's hand to the boy amidst the chanting of *mantra* and circumambulating around the sacred fire by the couple four times. This is known as *lavan lai*. This happens in the regular marriage ceremony which is known as *byah* or *lagan*. There are other forms of marriages which are prevalent and involve considerably fewer rituals. A divorce remarriage is known as *jhanjrara* and consists of a simple ceremony. The bridegroom presents the bride with a pair of new clothes and an ornament in the presence of some close relatives of both sides. Similarly, marriage by elopement and a widow's remarriage, namely *gadhoj* or *sarguddi,* are also a simple affair.

The dead are cremated but infants are buried. The important death rites are observed on the seventh, tenth and thirteenth day. A funeral feast is given to the relatives and members of *biradari*. An Acharaj is called to perform death rites. Ancestor worship is observed.

Traditionally the Sanhais play the musical instrument at the temple and during marriages as well as on festivals such as Minjar and Bishu. When they play the instrument during funeral processions, they are known as Hesi. They were better off during the times of princely states and got the protection from the Raja of Chamba. Some were provided land as an additional source of livelihood. The economic condition of the people was also good since there were more opportunities for them, where they could easily get more money and could demand extra renumeration on festive occasions from their patrons. Nowadays, with the growing popularity of the modern musical band and other instruments, the importance of their traditional instrument is fast decreasing, giving them less and less work opportunities.

In order to eke out a living, the Sanhais now resort to other occupations such as labour, both in agriculture and otherwise. They are also petty shopkeepers. As a renumeration for their services at the temple, they are given a room to stay together with a paltry sum of Rs.45 per month as salary. This is far from sufficient and people lament that they should be provided with a reasonable salary from the temple trust for their services. Since they are to play at many temples twice during the day, both in the morning and evening, they cannot take up a full-time occupation elsewhere. Child labour in the family is also present owing to their poverty and deprivation.

The Sanhais have their own caste council for the proper maintenance of the customary laws. All matters relating to elopement, abduction, divorce, intercaste alliances and even theft, are referred to their own Jati Panchayats for effective solution. If the accused is found guilty, he is reprimanded for it. The punishment can vary from giving a simple public apology to a cash fine and even excommunication depending on the gravity of the offence. Since the inception of the Panchayati Raj system and the courts of laws, people now have an alternative course of seeking justice. However, such instances are very few and most of the time matters are amicably sorted out at their own *biradari* level.

The Sanhais are devout Hindus and Lord Shiva is their principal deity. Since they have been mostly associated with temple service, they are more religiously inclined and consider it their utmost duty to offer their regular service to the deities at the temples. Besides they have great faith in the regional deities which they propitiate from time to time. They take an active part in all the major fairs and festivals of the area, namely Minjhar and Sui-ka-mela, which are the major annual features of Chamba's cultural life. Besides, Lohri and Bihu are also very important festivals.

The practice of untouchability and caste-based distinctions are not as visible as they are among the castes groups living in the plains. Restrictions are seen with regard to commensality, and castes like Brahman, Rana and Rajput traditionally do not dine with the Sanhais. They can, in special circumstances, accept *pucca* food only if prepared by members of certain castes and served in separate utensils. The Sanhais are otherwise free to enter the same temple premises or to draw water from common resources. The

Sanhais, on the whole, maintain socioeconomic ties with castes like Bainsi, Hali and Chanal, and nowadays marriages are also taking place amongst them.

The development aspects and its impact are common to the region as a whole. Since they are included in the scheduled castes, they are provided subsidy and loan facilities like other scheduled castes of the area. Nevertheless, these special provisions and allocations are limited to the few who can exert some pressure and pursue the matter. The loan seekers often get disappointed because of the cumbersome procedure involved in procuring the loan.

Vatsala Sarkar

SANSI

The Sansi is a scheduled caste, almost localized, in distribution to the Punjab border of the State. They are concentrated in the Damtal area of Kangra, Barsar area of district Hamirpur, and parts of Una. According to the 1981 Census of India there were 464 Sansis. Almost all are Hindus in Himachal Pradesh but there are also a few Sikhs in this community in Punjab. In Punjab they were known for their criminal tendencies and claim migration from the Marwar and Ajmer regions of Rajasthan. Rose (1919:362) states that they trace their origins from Sans Mal, known as Malang Sahib. In Kangra, they claim a Chauhan Rajput ancestry and suggest the etymology of the word Sansi from Hindi *sahsi*, meaning courageous. During India's partition they migrated from the Shakkaragarh area of Sialkot in Pakistan.

They speak a dialect of their own called Sansi Boli, which is a combination of Punjabi and Urdu. They communicate in Gurmukhi, Perso-Arabic as well as in Devanagari scripts within the community and with other people. In dress/ornaments of the Sansi are similar to other people. Men wear *kurta* and *pyjama* or pants and women wear *kurta* and *salwar* and a *chunni* or *dupatta*.

The Sansis are traditionally known for their peculiar and uncommon non-vegetarian food habits. They eat inferior types of meat of *giddar* (fox), *naul* (mongoose), *kachhua* (tortoise) in addition to pig, sheep and goat. Fish and eggs are consumed in plenty. But they do not eat *halal* meat and beef. Both men and women are regular non-vegetarians and also take their homemade liquor prepared from *seera* (molasses) and *gur* (jaggery) almost regularly. Their staple food is wheat, rice, maize, pulses, roots and tubers. Vegetable and fruits (particularly orange and apple) are eaten frequently. The milk intake is also almost regular. The cooking medium is mustard oil/ vegetable or *desi ghee*.

The Sansis have two broad social groups, viz., the Malka and the Kalka (Rose, 1919; Sher,1965). In the study area, however, they recognize two broad divisions, Mahla and Biddu or Baindu. They acknowledge Bhekut as one of the Sansi groups but not the Manesh who are listed as synonymous with Sansi in Singh (1971). Rose (1919) listed 23 Sansi *gots* of the Baindu and Mahla divisions in Sialkot from where the Sansis of Kangra trace their ancestry. The Mahlas are treated at a slightly higher (or hypergamous) social position than the Baindus and the latter give their daughters to the Mahlas. There are several *gots* which serve as exogamous units to regulate marriages and also indicate their ancestry from a particular lineage or place. These are:

Thulha, Myraso, Lodi, Golewal, Nandowal, Biduwal, Balewal, Bhanewal, Nahuwal and Kamalawal, as were recorded during this field study. These generally bear village names of their ancestors. In the regional hierarchy, the Sansis claim a Chauhan Rajput and Kshatriya status but other people see them at a lower position.

They are endogamous and practise village endogamy or exogamy, and also clan/*got* exogamy. The age of the girl at marriage is above 18 years and of the boy more than 20 years. Marriages takes place through negotiation but exchange of sisters also occurs. Monogamy is the usual practice, and a second marriage is contracted only in case of childlessness. *Sindur*, glass bangles, ear rings and finger ring are the marriage symbols. No bride price is taken but dowry is given in the form of household articles. The residence is patrilocal. Divorce is a rare event but is socially sanctioned in cases of cruelty, insanity and impotency of the spouse. A man divorcing a woman has to pay a fine and return the dowry to the woman. The children are the liability of the father. Widow/widower and man/woman divorcee remarriages are permissible. Widow remarriage is not ceremonized and is known as *chadar dalna*. Both junior levirate and sororate are permitted.

Nuclear families are presently more frequent, than the vertically extended joint families. The *nuh* avoids *saurah* and *jeth*. Joking is allowed between *devar* and *bhabi*, *jija* and *sala*, and *nanand* and *bhabi*. The junior members respect and obey the seniors. The Sansi families are occupationally very cohesive. The inheritance is as per the rule of male equigeniture. The eldest son becomes the successor of his father.

The Sansi women have a respectable and almost an equal status as men. They are not engaged in employment or other economic activities and perform only household jobs, collect fuel and fodder, fetch potable water and rear cattle. They also participate in various social, ritual, religious and political activities as members of the panchayat. They, however, do not have a right of inheritance to the property.

The birth pollution is observed for 40 days. *Gunt* ceremony purifies. There is no naming ceremony for the child but names may be given by consulting a Brahman priest. The *mundan* of the boys is done at a temple but there is no fixed time as to when the *mundan* should be done. The Sansis do not wear *janeu*.

The marriage is contracted by *thahaka* (engagement) in which clothes, ornaments, *lal chura, sindur* and some cash are given to the girl. The marriage rituals are performed at the bride's place by a priest of lower castes employed on cash terms. A *vedi* purchased from a Tarkhan (Badhai) is fixed in the courtyard and four rounds of sacred fire are taken by the bride and groom like other Hindus. The rituals are completed by performing *kanyadan*. The bride's parents give a feast. At the bridegroom's place the *jathere* (ancestors) are propitiated. There is no custom of making putative kinship-based friendship like *dharam bhai* and *dharam bahin.* The *muklawa* occurs on the next day of the marriage.

The dead are cremated and ashes are immersed in the Ganges at Hardwar by Sanatana followers or in the Beas river at Parmandal by the Radhaswamis. Death pollution is observed for 17 days which gets over after a community meal. No Acharaj is employed for performing death rites but a priest from lower castes may be employed to perform ancestor worship. The *dan* is given to the poor.

Presently land is the major economic resource of the Sansi community. It is tilled through tractor or plough. Their secondary occupation is preparing and selling liquor which is sold in the adjoining areas of the Punjab. Child labour exists only inasmuch as they assist the parents in agricultural and liquor-distilling activities. The traditional way of living by thieving and crimes is no longer practised by them. The market is of daily nature and is at a short distance. The dealings occur in cash.

The Sansis have a Biradari Panchayat, the *pradhan/panch* of which is elected unanimously through a voice vote for five years. This panchayat solves disputes of thefts, murder, elopement and marriage within the community. Punishments in the form of cash fines are imposed on the guilty and in case of non-payment the guilty is outcasted. He is readmitted in the community on his paying the desired amount of fine. The Sansis are also governed by the post-Independence statutory Gram Panchayat which performs the social welfare and development activities.

The Sansis are Hindus, Sikhs as well as Muslims (Rose, 1919), but in Kangra they are Hindus. The Hindu Sansis are also involved in various socioreligious movements and segmented into Sanatani, Radhaswami and Nirankari sects. They have family deities. Clan and village deities (Devis and Sidhs) are also worshipped. Lakhdata and Baba Fateh Sahib are their regional deities. The Radhaswami Sansis mainly believe in the preachings of their Baba at Beas in Amritsar district (Punjab). Others propitiate Hindu pantheon trinity and various goddesses, particularly Jawalamukhi. The affiliation to Peers is individual or family-based. The sacred shrines of Lakhdata, Baba Fateh Sahib and other deities are visited frequently. Sacred specialists are employed for ritual performance at marriage, death and for removing ill effects of evil spirit from other communities. The Sansis participate in various local fairs like Chhinj and Sitla Mela, as also in regional fairs and festivals particularly Dussehra, Baisakhi and Shivratri. They share regional Punjabi folksongs, folktales and folklore. *Bhangra* amongst men and *gidda* amongst women are the common dances.

The Sansis are almost cut-off from other communities in terms of exchange of water and food. They generally have little social exchange with other communities, though a few may exchange uncooked *sidha* food with neighbouring people on marriage occasions or may offer clean food, *suchchi rasoi.* They lack any ritual-based friendship with other communities. They have their own water sources (taps and tube-wells) and crematoria, but schools, panchayat ghar, temples and roads are shared with other people. There is no traditional patron-client relationship. The socio-economic relationship with the Lohar, Kumhar, Chamar and Nai are based on cash payment. Political leadership has emerged at the Gram Panchayat and tehsil levels with their own representatives. They are generally self-employed as businessmen and only a few of them have recently joined the army.

The impact of education on the Sansi community is not as much discernible. Only a few study up to matric level but girls generally do not study due to social reasons. Modern health and medical care and family planning measures are however availed of, but traditional system of medicare are also in vogue. They avail themselves of modern facilities of mass media communication (radio, television), have irrigation facility and use tractors for ploughing their fields. They use organic manure, chemical fertilizers and pesticides. They also avail themselves of the public distribution and banking facilities. Their energy sources are wood, coal, sawdust, cowdung cakes, gobar gas, kerosene and electricity. The Integrated Rural Development Programmes have provided them widow pensions and children seek immunization facilities. They are self-employed in agriculture and liquor manufacturing and do not depend on local shopkeepers/moneylenders. Above all the Sansis have abandoned their traditional life styles and are joining the mainstream.

A. R. Sankhyan

SANSOI

The Sansoi or Sansoe is a scheduled caste, similar to the Daula or Daule, who use to wash the river sands to extract gold particles. Rose (1919) treats the Sansoi as synonymous with the Daule, and sees it as a community which sprang from among the Dumna and specialized in the occupation of gold washing. This occupation is also suggested by the name of the community, which is derived from the word *sona* (gold). The name Daule is in common use in Bilaspur and Mandi districts for the gold washers, fishermen and the runners of *gharat*, whereas the name Sansoe is popular in Kangra district. They are also said to be akin to or go together with the Drai or Drain in Kangra. They are almost confined to Kangra district and only sporadically distributed in the adjoining districts of Hamirpur and Mandi, with a total population of 1,052 (Census of India 1981). They dwell in the hilly terrain or valleys of the river Beas and its tributaries in warm and temperate climate of moderate annual rainfall and low humidity. Their settlements are usually along or near the rivers.

The Sansoi appear to be the original inhabitants of the region. They may perceive their distribution at interregional level in the neighbouring State of Punjab as well. They are almost inseparable from other regional communities in the language they speak, the dress they wear and in the food they eat. The Kangri dialect of western Pahari is their language spoken both within and outside the community. But in writing they use Devanagari script and can speak in Hindi. Only a few older men have some knowledge of Urdu. The traditional male dress was a *kurta* and *langot* or *kapin* substituted in public by *pyjama* and a *safa* on head. Women usually wear a *kurti* and *salwar* or *suthan* and put on a cotton shawl called *chadru*, now replaced among young women by Punjabi *dupatta* or *chunni*. Traditional ornaments were usually of silver—a *chak* on head, *bali* or *kanta, har, gajre* or *choora* and *pajeb*. Some jewellers in the community also wear gold ornaments.

Having been also fishermen in the recent past, fish was common in their routine diet but now is taken occasionally. They are occasional non-vegetarian and eat sheep/goat meat and eggs. Vegetables and pulses of various kinds are part of daily food with common staple grains as wheat and maize supplemented by rice. Fruits are occasionally eaten. Tubers like potatoes and *kachalu* and *zimikand* are also eaten. Festival preparations are *halwa* and *kheer, seviyan, babru, ankli/anklu* of rice, etc. Non-vegetarian foods are taboo during death pollution. Men occasionally consume country liquor purchased from the local market. They smoke *bidi* and cigarettes and loose tobacco in *hukka*.

Clans/*gotras* and smaller *al/septs* are recognized as social divisions. Some of these are Phallehre, Chandle, Machhelu, Jasau, Jasal, Jounriye, Takhi Bhadiar, etc. Kaundal is a common *gotra* of many. These sections of the community are also used as exogamous units to regulate matrimonial alliances and also denote descent. Surname is usually not suffixed with name and no title is owned/used by the community. In certain areas the Sansoes conceive hierarchical superiority over the Daule but this is not known to all. In regional varna hierarchy they are treated as Sudra, slightly above the Drai and at par with the Dumna, but above the Chamar.

The community is endogamous and practises village and clan/*gotra* exogamy. Child marriages were common a few decades ago when bride price or exchange marriage called *batta-satta* were also common. But presently marriage age for girl has increased beyond puberty, usually above 18 and for boys above 20 years. Bride price is also no longer taken and *kanyadan* is performed. Some dowry in the form of household articles, clothes and some special items like watch and radio, are also given along with furniture. Marriages are negotiated by the parents/friends/relatives and monogamy is followed. The married women put on *sindur,* glass bangles, *bindi,* nose ring and ear ornaments as symbols of marriage. The bride lives patrilocally. Widow remarriage is permitted. Usually junior levirate is practised and is called *chadar dalna* or *jhanjrara.* But presently it is rare and is disliked by young men. Dissolution of marriage is also a rare phenomenon and usually the society discourages it , but a judicial course may be taken in certain extreme cases of maladjustment and cruelty to wife. The husband becomes liable to compensate the wife and maintain children if any. Divorcee remarriage is allowed.

Vertically extended joint families were a predominant feature a few decades back, but now family structure has changed to an almost nuclear pattern. Two married sons hardly live together for long after father's death or even when he is still alive. Petty family quarrels, social conservatism and rigid attitude of *sas* towards *lari*, and unequal distribution of labour leads to separation of families. Property is inherited on male lines and all sons get an equal share. Avoidance relationship is seen between *lari* and *sasur, jeth, nandoi,* and between *sas* and *jamai.* Joking is permitted between *devar* and *bhabi*, *jija* and *sali*, etc., as in most of other Hindu communities. The eldest son becomes successor of his father.

The status of the Sansoi women is generally low and they do not have powers of decision-making and do not participate in matters of social control and political spheres. They usually perform all household chores, agricultural and animal husbandry duties, collect fuel and fodder, fetch potable water and a few may also seek employment. They participate in social, ritual and religious ceremonies and manage family expenses.

Life-cycle rituals are performed as per the Sanatana tenets. Pre-delivery rituals are ignored but restrictions before and after delivery are imposed and *sutak* is observed. Purification occurs through *panjap* ceremony on the eleventh day. Naming ceremony is not observed but the midwife or sometimes a Brahman priest suggests name to the child. A few observe *khirpu* ceremony. *Jamalu* or *mundan* is performed for the boys on odd years after birth. The haircut is given by the *mama* of the child and the hair is offered to Balakrupia, a clan/regional deity. The *janeu* is put on at the time of marriage as a part of marriage rituals. Ear and nose piercing are not ceremonised but the job is done before marriage. *Sagai* is the betrothal ritual when sweets and a little ceremonial cash may be exchanged. Marriage rituals are performed by a Brahman priest as per Vedic rites at the bride's residence. The bride and groom circumambulate the sacred fire and the bride's parents perform *kanyadan*. They also give a feast/marriage meal called *dham* to the bridegroom's party, relatives and villagers. *Muklawa* ceremony is nowadays observed on the following auspicious day of the marriage.

Their death rituals are like that of other Hindus following Sanatana prescriptions. The dead are cremated and ashes are immersed in the river Beas at Kaleshwar or at the Ganges at Hardwar and they offer *pind dan* to a Panda. Death pollution called *patak* lasts for 16 days. On the thirteenth day an Acharaj performs *pitri puja* and seek alms. On the sixteenth day called *solia*, a Brahman priest performs purificatory *havan* and seeks alms. A feast is given to the gathered relatives and friends. Annual and fourth annual rites called *barkhadi* and *chabarkhadi*, respectively are also observed. A Masku may seek alms every month up to a year.

The community traditionally thrived on gold-washing, fishing and labour. Gold-washing is now a practice of bygone days and fishing is practised by a few. Many are now riverside labourers and sieve sand and *bajri* for building purposes as casual labourers or on contract. They have also been allotted some land and are petty cultivators and also do animal husbandry as a mock of self-employment. A few work as masons, carpenters, basket makers and mat and cloth weavers. Also a few are jewellers. Some are industrial workers and a few others have joined Government service as well. Children assist elders in various activities and occupations.

Traditional Jati Sabha and village councils are now defunct. Normally, the elderly and respected persons of the village sort out social problems mutually. Village disputes over land and water are taken up in the statutory

Gram Panchayat which also performs developmental activities.

The Sansoes are almost all Hindus and believe in gods and goddesses of the pantheon. In addition, many regional deities some of which are also village and clan deities, are propitiated on child birth, marriage and festive occasions. The main deities are Balak Rupi, Guga, Baba Balak Nath, Lakhdata, Nahar Singh — also called as Sindu Paharia or Dalan wala Devta, and female deities like Jawalamukhi, Chintpurni and Brajeshwari Mata or Kangre Wali Mata, are specially propitiated and their annual fairs are attended. *Jathere* (ancestors) are family deities for which a space is kept in the courtyard. Major festivals celebrated are Lohri, Basoa (Baisakhi), Nauhle Sakranti, Chiran, Sair, Rakhi, Karwa Chauth (by women), Shivratri, Diwali, etc. Priests are from among the Brahmans, but they may have medicine men, fortune tellers and *chela* within or outside the community to consult in different cases and to ward off evil spirits.

Basketry, weaving, mat-making and silver/gold smithy are their traditional craft-cum-occupations. Wall painting and floor painting with common colours is done by many women. The community shares Pahari/ Kangri folksongs and tales, music and dances. Some persons in the community are band masters and provide music on marriages. They enjoy Hindi film and religious songs.

Commensal norms are extended to other communities. The Brahman and Bania traditionally do not accept *kachcha/pucca* food and water from them but may accept *sidha* or a *suchchi rasoi*. They also abstain from taking water and *kachcha/pucca* food from the Chamar. Water resources and cremation places on riverside may be shared with other caste people. Religious shrines are common. Putative kinship may exist even with upper caste people. Many people have emerged as jewellers, band masters, junior engineers and persons holding white-collar jobs and in defence service. They also have members in the statutory Gram Panchayat, beyond local level.

The community has partially assimilated the benefits of modern developmental programmes. Children receive secondary school education to a considerable extent but only a few receive college education which is socially less favoured for girls. Both modern and indigenous methods of health and medicare are followed. The attitude towards family planning after three children is favourable and usually women get sterilized as men have to do more strenuous jobs. They avail themselves of electricity and modern mass media (radio and TV) facilities at their doorsteps and are also linked by roads. Drinking water is inadequately available through taps and indigenous sources of springs and step-wells are still used. Their energy sources are traditional firewood and cowdung cakes. They have provisions under IRDP, get subsidy on chemical fertilizers, crop threshers, cattle, etc., and some also get widow pensions. Immunization is availed of under ICDS and foodgrains and sugar are available on subsidized rates through fair price shops.

A. R. Sankhyan

SAREHDE

The Sarehde/Sarere/Siryare/Sarde or more sophisticatedly Surehra as it is called is a scheduled caste. The etymology of the word Surehra is not known, but one local version suggests that during the persecution of the Kshatriyas by Parasuram some people were hiding in the bushes of *surar*, a kind of grass, and when they were spotted they indentified themselves as Surehra and denied their Kshatriya status; literally, therefore they are *'Surar* bush dwellers'. Sondhi (1916), however, cited the 1891 Census about the etymology of the Sarera from Sir-hara, meaning "share of the sons of a certain Dhund Sirdar by a low caste woman having been less than that of his other sons". Dhund is a Rajput clan. The etymology is also derived from Salehria (Rajput): Salehria literally stands, for 'low lander' or 'Salehr'—sub-montane tract (Rose 1914: 273).

The traditional occupation of the Surehra is to scutch cotton similar to the Penja or the Dhunia of the plains (Rose, 1919), but they also undertake miscellaneous occupations or jobs, such as labourers, makers of pestle and mortar, workers of the sandstone quarries, masons, tailors and some even run *gharat*. It is said that the first man of the community who started scutching cotton was Dadu Pinja from whom the community inherited the traditional occupation.

The Surehras are distributed in districts of Kangra, Hamirpur and Una but are also found in Bilaspur and Chamba. The 1971 Census of India gives their population figures under two community names, viz., Sarera/Sarare/Sarde and Surehra as 6,173 and 155 respectively (Singh 1971). Their population during 1981 has grown to 9,663. Their settlements are seen in the valley as well as on the slopes of the Shivalik hills experiencing generally a warm an temperate climate. They speak local dialects like Bilaspuri (Kahluri) and Kangri within and outside their kin groups and the script used is Devanagari. They share local dress and ornaments.

Their staple food is maize and wheat supplemented by rice along with various types of pulses—*urd, masur, moong, kulth*, grams, peas and beans. They are largely vegetarians, but also take meat, fish and eggs occasionally. The men are fond of of liquor but those who are followers of Radhaswami sect abstain from non-vegetarian diet and liquor. Non-vegetarian foods taboo are during death pollution. The special festival foods are similar to those of other local communities like *khichri* on Lohri, mustard leaves on Khori, *seviyan* on Sair, *babru* on Baisakhi and *ankli/ankloo* on Diwali.

The Surehra recognise several *gots* (clans) and *als*, viz., Ranaut, Chandel,

Chauhan, Kalamotia, Kaundal and Pundir (as were recorded in Bilaspur District), and Powariye, Pathgariye, Sardhial, Malhotre, Mankotiye, Heer, Chambial, Ganthial, Puniye, Janjuhe, Narial and Dabhal (in Kangra). No social hierarchy is observed among these and the *got/al/* clans regulate marriage. In view of many Rajput *gots* they claim the Kshtriyas varna status. But because they have been put in the Scheduled Caste list, they do not sick to such a status and are constantly reminded of their Sudra status in the varna hierarchy. They place themselves slightly lower than the Jheewar.

They are endogamous, and adhere to clan/*got/al* exogamy. Village endogamy may occur when appropriate matches of different *gots* exist in the village and marriage of both boys and girls occurs at present at adulthood though child marriage existed in the recent past. The mates are acquired through negotiation but exchange of sisters can also occur.

The symbols of marriage are *sindur*, nose-ring and glass bangles. At present there is no practice of bride price, and dowry is given in the form of household articles. But some poor people used to take bride price in the recent past. The residence after marriage is patrilocal. Divorce is rare but has social and judicial sanctions on grounds of malajustment and the man bears the liability to support and compensate the woman and children. Widow remarriage is permissible. Junior levirate/junior sororate are also permitted. the divorcees can also remarry.

The family pattern is predominantly of joint extended type. Avoidance relationship exists between *lari* and *saurah* and *jeth*. Rule of inheritance is male equigeniture, the succession pattern is through the elderst son. Nuclear families are on the increase due to conflicts among brothers after father's death on property matters. Joking relations are same as in many other communities.

The status of women is almost at par with that of men as they also contribute to the family income by rendering service in the village. They are not limited to the domestic chores but also participate in agricultural and animal husbandry duties, and social ritual an religious ceremonies. They also regulate family expenditure. But they have little role in the mechanism of social control and political spheres.

Post-delivery pollution is observed for 13 days and purification occurs by taking cow's urine called *gunt*. The *mundan* ceremony is performed among boys in the similar way as in many other Hindu communities of the region.

The marriage rituals are performed by the Sanatana Vidhan by the community's own priest. The bride and groom circumambulate the sacred fire at the bride's place and also a *daran* or mango tree at the groom's place and circumambulate it four times to complete the marriage. A feast is given by the bride's parents. The marriage is consummanted through a *muklawa* ritual which occurs the day following marriage.

The dead are cremated and the ashes immersed in the Ganges at Hardwar or in a nearby river and ancestor worship is observed. Some families of the Surehra in Bilaspur district are the Ramaupashki, who immerse the ashes in water at Nalagarh-Bela in Solan disrict. The Radhaswamis immerse ashes in the Beas river. Death pollution lasts for 13 days and the community priest perform ancestor worship and seeks offerings. The community is served a meal to open exchange of food and water.

The Surehras traditionally were cotton scutchers and general labourers. But a few became agriculturists and rear cattle, sheep and goats. However, the land is not a sufficient economic resource, and therefore,they retain different types of occupations as road and forest labour, masonry, tailoring, cotton scutching and general merchandise. Child labour is present in the community. Presently some persons are aslo employed in Government service on white-collar jobs, as engineers, doctors, administrators and officers in the defence services. The market is located in their reach and is fully regulated. The dealings are in cash but sometimes in kind as well.

At present the Surehra have no traditional caste council but the elders of the community usually solve social disputes. The statutory Gram Panchayat of all communities presently takes up most problems of an economic nature. Other statutory legal measures are also taken in serious economic disputes over land and water.

The Surehras are mainly Hindus by religion though some are Sikhs as well. The Hindu Surehras worship the gods of the pantheon order and various family/clan, village and regional deities. Some families worship *sati* stones and Godri Sidh (Bilaspur) and Panjpiri and Mal Devi (Kangra) as family/clan deities. The other village and regional deities are the same as for other communities like Nar Singh, Lakhadata, Deot Sidh, etc.

The major fairs and festivals are common with other communities of the area like Baisakhi, Sair, Chiran, Rakhi, Guga Navmi and Diwali. Their sacred specialists are from other communities. The Surehra community is involved in socioreligious movements of the Radhaswami, Nirankari and Ramaupashki missions. The community has no tradition of plastic and graphic art though a few persons do make objects of stones like *sil-batta* and *kundi* (pestle-mortars) usually for domestic consumption. The oral traditions and music/dance are shared with others.

They share wells and other public facilities with the other caste communities. They participate in various public functions and political activities and also have teachers, inspectors, engineers, scientists, doctors and other elites in the community.

Modern development programmes have made a considerable impact on the community. Their children receive higher (college) education though the majority still study up to the secondary school level due to social or/and economic reasons and lack of interest. The girls are not supposed to seek employment, so most of them do not seek higher education.

Modern health and medicare facilities are availed of though traditional methods are still employed. Their houses are electrified and most of them avail themselves of modern mass media (radio, television) facilities and also have road connections in the vicinity.

The Sarehde presently respond to the modern family planning measures especially sterilization. But at least one male child is regarded as a social need even at the risk of more girls. Potable water is presently available through pipelines but traditional sources like step-wells or springs are also used to supplement their needs. They make use of chemical fertilizers.

They get 50 per cent subsidy under the Integrated Rural Development Programme. The children are given immunization under ICDS. People are both self-employed and in employment. Facilities of public distribution system are available and many people favour savings in banks and post offices, though some lead a hand-to-mouth existence and are indebted to local shopkeepers.

A.R.Sankhyan

SAYYAD

The Sayyads occupy the foremost position among the four major classes of Muslims, viz., Sayyad, Sheikh, Mughal and Pathan. Though all are equal, yet in practice there has been a hierarchical grading among them. The claim of the Sayyad to the prime position is uncontested by virtue of their descent from Prophet Muhammad. The population of the Sayyads and their distribution in Himachal Pradesh is not known but they are mainly distributed in the sub-montane region. They have been inhabiting this track since long and the informants do not remember the history of their settlement in detail but claim that their forefathers came from Afghanistan (Ahmad, 1978; Mushio-ul-Haq, 1983).

The local influence is apparent in their dress and dialect. They frequently use the local dialects and commonly wear the same dress as worn by others. The use of Urdu and Persian is limited to the literates. The men wear *pyjama*, shirt and jacket, whereas women wear *salwar* and *kameez*. Ceremonially women wear a special flared *pyjama, gharara* and *kurta* along with *odhni*. In some families it is customary for women to wear *burqa* while going out, but the use of the *burqa* is gradually being discarded by women especially in urban areas.

They are fond of non-vegetarian food. The staple diet of the Sayyads consists of wheat, maize, pulses of *chana, mah, rajmah, masur* and seasonal vegetables. Mustard oil and hydrogenated fats are used as a cooking medium. Pork is a religiously tabooed item of food for Muslims. Beef, though not tabooed, is also not consumed because it is not available, and more so because open acceptance of beef would badly hurt the religious sentiments of the Hindus who regard the cow as sacred. The use of intoxicants is also tabooed for the Muslims. However, their use is present among men though it is not openly admitted. Smoking is common among men but chewing of pan and tobacco is not prevalent.

Unlike the Hindu caste structure, the Muslim society does not presuppose any gradation as high or low and clean or unclean but stratification has come about dividing the Muslim, into the divisions like Ashraf and non-Ashraf. The four major classes, as mentioned earlier, are Sayyad, Sheikh, Mughal and Pathan and among these the Sayyads are placed on the upper pedestal holding some kind of superiority over the others. These divisions are further divided along sects, the most important being the Shia and the Sunni, both being strictly endogamous.

Under the Islamic prescription there is no taboo on any Muslim group to contract marriage alliance from other groups but in practice equality in status and rank became the prime consideration in the selection of the spouse. The Sayyads who occupy the highest position remain endogamous in so far that they do not give their daughters to other Muslims, but on the other hand, they may take bride from others. The rule of hypergamy prevails. Marriage is settled through negotiation. The offer of marriage comes from the boy's side. The age of marriage for boys and girls is 22-25 and 18-20 years respectively. Early marriages were prevalent in the past but due to legislation and emphasis on education, it is customary for boys to get married when they are ready to support themselves. In the selection of the spouse cross-cousins and parallel-cousins get the first preference.

In fact marriages are usually arranged within the same *khandan* which is an extended descent grouping or lineage. This checks the flow of property from going outside the family. Marriage between real siblings and between the step brothers and sisters is however tabooed. Theoretically a man can acquire more than one wife (to a maximum of four) at a time but practically monogamy prevails. The *mehar* amount which is settled at the time of marriage and is payable to the wife either on demand or at the time of the dissolution of marriage is one of the most important features of the Muslim marriage system. A husband is obliged to pay this amount to his wife any time she desires. Ideally a man cannot attain salvation if he has not paid this amount to his wife. The wife can forgive him for non-payment of *mehar* only on consideration of his economic condition or physical health.

Talaq is granted on grounds of infidelity, maladjustment, chronic sickness and mental ill-health. It is generally a one-way process by which a man may seek divorce but it is not so for the wife. Under special circumstances the wife who seeks separation may have to forgo her claim to the *mehar* amount. Remarriage of widow, widower and divorcee is socially approved. Levirate and sororate may also be practised. A man is, however, not allowed to marry his wife's sister in the lifetime of his wife. A widow can remarry only after observing the *iddat,* a period of seclusion. This also holds true when a woman contemplates a second marriage after divorce. In the event of divorce, the custody of the children goes to the husband. Infants and small children may be allowed to stay with the mother only to be returned to the father when they grow up.

The extended pattern of joint families was mostly prevalent but due to urbanization and industrialization, bringing about socioeconomic changes, it has largely affected the traditional joint family system. As a result nuclear families are emerging to suit the changed socioeconomic milieu. Inheritance and succession is patrilineal. Daughters do have a share in the father's property but more often than not the same is surrendered in favour of the brothers. A widow has a right to maintenance. The interpersonal relations among the members of a household are those of love and respect and are governed according to age, sex and kinship status of the respective member. Women observe purdah in the presence of senior male members of the husband's household and generally maintain distance from the male relatives, whereas relationship existing with femalefolks of a household is free from restraint and inhibition. They share in each others' moments of joy, anxiety and fear.

Women do not enjoy an equal status with men in many respects. They do not have the power of decision-making in economic matters. They do have a share in the ancestral property but this right is hardly ever exercised. The women generally do not work outside the house but of late in the urban areas due to greater educational opportunity, with freedom of movement and contact women have also started moving forward. In the domestic field they exert a considerable say in the household management. They actively participate in the rituals and festivals. The women do not hold any religious office and normally do not go to mosques for offering prayers and discharge their religious duties within the campus of their houses. Their role in the political field is also fairly restricted. The majority of the women do not show any interest in political life.

The life-cycle rituals observed by the Sayyads in accordance with Muslim customs and practices. As soon as the child is born it is considered important that the child be attuned to the divine call. The words of *azan* are, therefore, whispered into both his ears. Post-birth restriction and pollution lasts till the fortieth day. Between this period a purificatory bath is given to the mother and the child at frequent intervals. *Sunnat* is an important event in the life of the child which formally initiates him into the Islamic fold. Another ceremony named *aqiqa* is observed during childhood in which the hair of the child is shaved off. Thereafter, a goat or sheep, customarily two, are sacrificed and the meat is distributed among friends, relatives and among the poor. When the child is old enough to go to school the ceremony of *bismilah* (I begin in the name of the God) is observed. The child is dressed in new clothes and he is made to recite a few lines from the Quran.

Nikah is solemnized in the presence of the *maulvi* and the *gawah*.

The Sayyads bury their dead. The body is first given a bath and is wrapped in white. A special prayer is offered for the departed soul before the body is lowered into the grave. The mourners fill the grave with earth and after offering the prayer for the depated soul return to the house of the bereaved family. On the third day *tija* rite is performed. People again assesmble for the *fatiha*, invoking God's mercy for the dead. Food is cooked and distributed among the poor. This is followed by *daswa* (the tenth day) and *chaliswan* in which relatives and friends are called. Food is cooked and distributed among those who are present. Food is also given to the poor in charity. This practically marks the end of the pollution period. The widow however has to observe *iddat.* During *iddat* she is not expected to go out or mix with outsiders. At the end of this period, sweet rice is prepared and distributed among children, and life returns to normal thereafter.

The Sayyads are in different pursuits like agriculture, business, service and in a wide variety of white-collar professions such as medicine, engineering, law and teaching. Those inhabiting the rural areas practise agriculture. In villages traditional patron-client relationship exists with Nai (Hajjam), Chamar and Bhisti, and certain artisan castes like Lohar, Trikhan and the like. These castes receive a certain share of the produce at each harvest and also on certain important socioreligious occasions. In urban areas this kind of an obligatory system of patron-client linkages does not operate. The traditional pattern of exchange through barter has considerably weakened even in rural situation.

For breach of social conduct the Sayyads refer the matter to their respective council and its decision is taken to be final. In rare cases when consensus is not reached, the matter is referred to law courts and is governed under the Muslim Personal Law. The nature of punishment is mostly in the form of cash. For serious breach of social conduct the offender may be socially boycotted. Minor conflicts are taken care of by the elders of the *biradari* whose efforts are for mutual reconciliation. Gram Panchayats and Mahila Mandals also exist, the latter taking up issues relating to women.

A true Muslim must fulfil four basic obligations towards God and fellow beings. These are offering of Namaz five times a day, keeping fast for the whole month of Ramzan, giving a part of his salary as charity for the poor and making the pilgrimage to Mecca for performing certain rituals at least once in one's lifetime. Besides they celebrate all the Muslim festivals in accordance with Muslim beliefs and practices. They also visit the shrines of famous pirs and saints of which the Dargah of Baba Dadeshah is of special importance.

The continuous interplay of what is preached and practised influences the attitude of one group towards the other. Ideologically, in practice differences do exist on the basis of sects, different religious schools, various occupational groups and between the indigenous converts and the immigrants, each trying to maintain endogamy at its level on the pretext of the nobility of descent. The Sayyads try to contract marriage from amongst their own. For commensal norms, social distance is evident in respect to the Hindus. The latter would not accept any cooked food, *pucca* or *kachcha,* from them unless it is cooked by a member of an upper caste Hindu. Similarly the Sayyads would not accept anything from lower caste Hindus. Among the Muslims there are no restrictions on the exchange of food and water. In the religious sphere there is no discrimination against high or low or rich or poor in mosques and religious congregations.

The Sayyads have responded favourably to development activities in the

State. In the field of education, there has been a significant improvement. With the setting up of Anganvadis, young children receive their first valuable training in schooling. They are also provided with nutritious meals. Such organizations also impart training to mothers in child care. Under the State literacy programme, there is emphasis on adult education so that those desirous of availing themselves of education may do so after returning from work. More schools and colleges have come up and people have enthusiastically reacted to these changes.

Health is another aspect which has received their attention. Health care clinics are provided even in remote areas. Family welfare activities have also been received favourably in the cities and towns. In the sphere of economic development, economic grants in the form of loans and subsidies have been greatly beneficial to the people. There are schemes of providing loans to the maximum of Rs. 25,000 to the unemployed youth. There are vocational guidance centres for training people in the craft of carpentry and blacksmithy and mechanical engineering to equip them to earn their livelihood. All these development programmes, in addition to the existing facilities of transport, communication, electricity and water have significantly improved the quality of life in general.

Vatsala Sarkar

SEOK

The Seok, Sewak or the Sheok is distributed in a vast terrain including Chhota and Bara Bhangal and Palampur and Joginder Nagar tehsils of Kangra and Mandi districts of Himachal Pradesh. Negi (1976) writes about the community that the Kanets or Seoks of Chhota and Bara Bhangal have remained so secluded and insulated by reason of geographical and topographical barriers that they deserve to be a scheduled tribe. He further writes: "The advisory committee (Lokur Committee) and the Joint Selection Committee of Parliament have proposed four new tribes to be added to the Schedule, namely, Beta (Beda), Chahan, Domba (or Gara or Zoba) and Kanet or Seok (of Chhota and Bara Bhangal). All these tribes have to be studied at length to judge the justification for their being Scheduled." Chuhar Ghati forms a part of Chhota Bhangal and the four main subsections, namely, Kotgarh, Dev Garh, Hastpur and Amar Garh. The whole area lacks facilities and to cross over to Bara Bhangal is considered hazardous and difficult even today. Due to lack of outside influence the people have maintained their age-old customs which are little known to the outside world.

They belong to the Kanet group of Rajputs who have been mentioned as Kulind, Kunind, Kulindrin, Kulinda or Kanait in our scriptures and other books. The Kanets have been referred to in *Punjab Castes* (Ibbetson,1916) also. General Cunningham (vide Ibbetson, 1916) divides the Kanet community in three principal clans, namely, Mangal, Chauhan and Rao. According to him the Chauhans are Khasia/ Khasa and Kanet are from different stocks and there are differences in the costumes and local traditions of both the communities. Parmar (1975) in his book mentions the Kanets as the yeomen of the State. On the west they extend as far as Baghal and on the eastern portions of the Kangra Valley, and in the east they occupy the whole of Kullu, Mandi, Suket, the Shimla Hills and Sirmaur. They form more than half of the population of the Shimla Hills and Sirmaur. The Seoks might have had some relations with ancient Shaka tribe but the situation has to be studied in depth as nothing is definitely known in this respect. According to Alaxander Cunningham (vide Ibbetson, 1916), "the Kanets were the descendants of Kunindas or Kulindas, a rich and powerful people who ruled about 1500 B.C. between the Beas and Tons rivers and that they were the original inhabitants of the lower slopes of the Himalayas from the back of the Indus to the Brahmputra." It can thus be said that Kanets have, since proto-historic times, been a powerful ethnic entity in the region and with the passage of time got amalgamated with other communities. The Seoks or Sewaks of Bara Bhangal and Chhota Bhangal have since maintained their old traditions and can thus provide important links to the study of this community. These people address themselves as Seok but the origin of this term is not exactly known. It might have been that the community was subjugated to serve the rulers and thus acquired the nomenclature of very polite and humble people called Sewaks or Seoks or they might have got some connection with Shaka tribe of ancient times. The Gaddis who live in the adjoining area of Dhauladhar and Bharmaur address themselves as 'Miter' (friend) and these people are called Sewaks or Seoks. The culture of both the communities is common in many ways and their costumes are almost identical.

The clans of the community are almost the same as quoted by Ibbetson (1916).

The areas of Bhangal remain under the snow for a long time and thus the outside influence is minimal but the Seoks who reside in parts of Palampur and Joginder Nagar tehsils in lower areas, have intermixed with other inhabitants in such a way that they are not easily identifiable. The dialect of the Seok is the local form of Kangri, Kulvi, or Mandiali, as the case may be. Earlier their script was Tankri but now they use Devanagari as their script. The community is a *savaran* Rajput caste.

The Seok are non-vegetarian but do not eat beef, buffalo meat or pork. Their staple food is wheat, maize, rice,. barley, pulses of *rajmah, urad, chana, roongi, masur* and oil seeds. Roots and tubers are used according to seasons and occasions. Green vegetables and milk are consumed in plenty. Alcoholic drinks are also prepared and taken by male members of the community. Liquor is also available in the local market like other commodities and is sold locally. *Lassi*, squash, curd, apple juice are also used. *Khichri, bare, bhalle, sattoos* of barley and *moon* (locally called *mori*) are prepared after parching wheat and other grains.

The Seoks address themselves as Thakur, Chauhan, Kashyap, Kasib, etc. Surnames are used by the younger generation.

Three types of marriages are common among the Seoks. Arranged marriages are most common, but marriages by symbolic elopement are also prevalent. Exchange marriages and the custom of bride price are also prevalent. *Jhanjrara* also takes place. Second marriages of divorced or widows are permissible. Dowry system is gaining ground. Avoidance relationship and joking relationships are prevalent as in the case of other societies of the area. There is no *purdah* system but avoidance from elders is a must. *Pagband* and *chundaband* systems are in vogue and the property is divided equally among all the male members (sons) at the time of division.

Interfamily relations are quite cordial. Joint family system is prevalent but nuclear families are also coming up. Women command respect in the community. They are given an equal share in the property of their husbands. They contribute to family income and collect fuel, food and water and attend to all the family duties including rearing of children.

Important events for rituals include birth, marriage and death. The birth of a male child is considered auspicious. There is a function after seven or eight days after the birth in which a feast is served to villagers and neighbourers. *Sutak* and *patak* are observed. *Sutak* is the pollution at the time of birth of a son in the family and *patak* is pollution after death in the family. In the *patak* period the family does not use *heeng, haldi*, oil or anything chewable. The mourning period lasts for about six months during which no sacred activity is performed by the family. *Chauka baithana* is an important ritual on the thirteenth day after the birth of a child. Image of *Bitau* (Bhattarila) is made. It is a clay model signifying the blessings of the mother of fortune and death called *Bidhi-mata.*

On this day the child and the mother are brought out for the first time. *Shudhikaran sanskar* is conducted after the thirteenth day after the occurance of death in a family. The dead are cremated. The offering of a cow at the time of death is considered important and it is called *Vitarni dan* (offerings to river). The dead are given a bath and clay is put around the private parts of the female body. The Nath, a person from a particular caste, accepts the offerings at the time of death and helps to conduct the rituals. *Kumkum, teeka* and red costume are offered to the *suhagin* (women having living husbands) at the time of their death. *Phaska* (grains offered in the name of the dead that are on the way while the dead body is being taken to the cremation ground) is offered. The person attending the last rites at the cremation ground are called *kathyahe.* During *panchka* (constellations of five stars) images are made to avoid further deaths in the village or family before cremating the dead. *Bhailkal* plant is taboo and is not kept near the cremation ground. *Ghogar ki dhar* is a mysterious place where the witches and supernatural spirits are supposed to arrange a fight once a year. The winning of witches is considered auspicious for crops and the general prosperity of the people of the area. The fight between witches of the neighbouring areas and other spirits take place in *dagwans amavasya* (black night of Bhadrapada) day. *Ghogar ki dhar* is a hill range near Joginder Nagar.

Land, water and forests are individual properties and also controlled by Government agencies. Grazing of herds is the main profession of the people. The community is receptive to all sorts of development schemes and cooperates in initiating various schemes in the region. They are Hindu by religion and their major fairs and festivals are Lohri, Diwali, Saranahuli,

Manimahesh Jatra, Shivaratri, Baisakhi, Sair and Holi, etc.

Traditional intercommunity linkages are very cordial. *Dharam bhai* system is popular in the region.

B.R. Sharma

SHEIKH

Literally, Sheikh means a chief or a leader and is used in its Arabic form as an honorific title for the head of a tribe, lineage or family. In India and throughout the subcontinent, the term refers to the persons who claim to have descended from the tribe to which Prophet Mohammad belonged and connotes a status group (Ahmad, 1978 : 179) which with the passage of time has acquired a community status.

History testifies that the Arab invasion of India was led by Mohammad Ibn-e-Kasim into Sind in the eighth century, which was only partially successful. On the other hand, by the end of the eighth century, Persia, Central Asia and parts of Afghanistan were all included in the Arab empire. The invaders later married the natives of the various countries in which they had made their homes. When the Turk, Afghan and Mughal invaders poured into India, the descendants of these Arab settlers followed to carry out the same pursuits that had been carried out in Persia and elsewhere. Various district gazetteers show that from the time of Sultan Mohammad to the late Mughal emperors there was a constant influx of individuals and families, some classed as Sayyad, others as Sheikh, but all claiming Arab descent.

The Sheikhs in the country, according to Ahmad (1978), are actually of foreign origin. The total number of persons claiming that they belonged to the Sheikh caste was well over 1,800,000 in 1931 and this represented an increase of over 150 per cent over those who made this claim in 1901. It is on record that no immigrations took place from Arabia during the period 1901-31. This remarkable increase could not have been possible but for the slow and gradual induction of members of other castes into the Sheikh category—the pseudo-Sheikh. This has been well described in the Persian proverb—*peshaiyan qussab budem, badazar gushten shaikh: ghalla chun arzan shawad, imsal sayyed meshawem* meaning, "Last year I was a Julaha; this year I am a Sheikh; next year if prices rise, I shall be a Saiyad" (Ibbeston 1916:222). In other words, there was a tendency for a person to claim a higher lineage than his own. And this was, and is, especially marked amongst converts from Hinduism.

The Sheikhs are widely dispersed throughout the whole subcontinent with somewhat larger concentration on the Indo-Gangetic plains. There has been influx of the Sheikhs in Himachal Pradesh from the Jammu and Kashmir side and one finds a sizeable Sheikh population inhabiting the low hills especially the districts of Chamba, Kangra, Una, Hamirpur, Mandi, Bilaspur, Solan and Sirmaur.

The language/dialect spoken by the Sheikhs among themselves is Urdu and their script Persio-Arabic; but with members of other communities they speak Hindustani and use the Devanagari script. They have also picked up the dialect of the area where they live, and often use it while conversing with the locals.

The younger generation of the community is unidentifiable in the general mass of the population, but the older generation can be spotted through their dress. The typical male dress consists of a *lungi* and an *angerkha* (shirt) or *kurti* with a round white cap on the head, often made of crochet. The younger generation, however, wears westernised shirt and pants.

The community is non-vegetarian, and they take meat of sheep, goat and chicken and fish occasionally. Beef is not available in the State and hence not consumed, but there are no taboos regarding eating it. Those visiting Saharanpur or other adjoining areas, where beef is available, do take it. Restrictions exist on the intake of meat in terms of the mode by which the animal has been killed, i.e., whether by *halal* or by *jhatka*. Muslims in general accept only *halal*.

Their staple food consists of wheat *chapati*, pulses of gram, *urad, moong* and *masur* and seasonal vegetables, which also includes roots and tubers. Mustard and vegetable oil and *ghee* are used as cooking media. Seasonal fruits are also moderately taken. Milk is taken by the adults usually in tea or in its derived forms as curd, *lassi, ghee* and *paneer.* In its original form it is consumed only by the children or invalids. Alcoholic drinks are taboo. Though the older generation abstains from it totally, the younger generation does take it in cities without the knowledge of the family members.

Abstinence from food and water is observed from sunrise to sunset during the period of *roza* and also during the first three days of mourning when in a family food cannot be cooked in the house. Special delicacies like *seviyan* are a must on the festival of Id and preparation of mutton is a must on the Bakrid. Besides, on social and festive occasion delicacies and meat are prepared. Preparation of meat is also taboo during the month of *Ramzan.*

The Sheikhs are divided into a number of subgroups based on descent and source of origin and their members not only identify themselves as members of a separate group, but also try to preserve their separate group identity through a careful use of surnames, who take their names from an eponymous ancestor. These are (a) Abbasi—descendants of Muhammad's paternal uncle, (b) Jafari—cousin of Muhammad Ali's brothers, (c) Alvi—descendants of Ali from the other wife, (d) Hashmi—descendants of the Prophet's great grandfather, (e) Siddiqi named from the first Khalif Abu Baqr-as-Saddiq, (f) Bani Israel—or sons of Israel, (g) Faruqi-from Khalif-Umar nicknamed Faruq, (h) Sulaimani, (i) Usmani-both from the third khalif, (j) Faridi—followers of famous Saint Baba Farid of Pak Pattan, (k) Qidwai—claim descent from Qazi Qidwat, son of the King Rum (Turkey) who came to India via Arabia in the time of Shahad-ud-din Gori, (l) Ansari—name given to the citizens of Medina—after conversion and (m) Qureshi—the Arab 'tribe' to which the Prophet belonged. The largest section among the Sheikhs are Siddiqi and Qureshi (Siddiqui, 1978; Ahmad, 1978).

Each of the subgroups within the Sheikh category are hierarchically arranged on ethnic differentiation, i.e., ranking being based on descent and the degree of distance from the Prophet serves to define the relative standing of subgroups. Highest in the hierarchy are the Qureshi who trace their descent from the tribe of Prophet. Next in order of precedence are the descendants of the three Caliphs followed by the descendants of the close associates or friends of Muhammad, especially those who accompanied him to Medina. Last in the hierarchy are the groups who have supposedly come with the invading Muslim armies. Each of the various sections of the Sheikhs are largely endogamous.

There is ample available evidence which suggests that the Sheikh category always remained somewhat open and fluid. Mobile groups seeking a new status identity frequently used the Sheikh category as a means of raising their status. Consequently, this has led some scholars to make a distinction between the genuine Sheikh and the spurious Sheikh, which is highly ambiguous (Siddiqui, 1978; Ahmad, 1978).

The social hierarchy among the pseudo-Sheikhs (neoconverts) is based on the norm of cleanliness of different occupations which they pursue, and their relative hierarchy differs from area to area.

As mentioned earlier, each of the various sections of the Sheikhs was endogamous, but in recent years they have begun to marry their daughters outside the group within the Sheikh order on the principle of hypergamy. They acquire brides for their sons from one set of families and give their daughters to another set of families. A few of the Sheikhs have also intermarried with the Syyads, Mughals and Pathans. Their religion permits such marriages but these are not in vogue.

Each Sheikh family maintains a *shijra* (genealogy). The social and personal status of the families from which brides' have been acquired and to which girls have been given in marriage are recorded in it. This is used whenever marriages are arranged outside the known kin men, splitting the marriage circle into endogamous and exogamous circles.

The former is restricted to within the kinsmen and the latter to outside the kin-group. The member of the latter marriage circle distinguish themselves on the ground that they have married outside the group and they do not marry with the former. The former consider the latter as having lost the ritual purity by marrying outside. Marriages with cross-cousins and parallel-cousins form the preferential marriages. Marital restrictions exist only to the boy and girl sharing the same mother's breast milk.

The *mehar* forms an indispensable part of the marriage contract. The amount of *mehar* differs from family to family and depend upon the economic status of the boy, but in no case can it be less than Rs. 32.25, i.e., *Sikka riazul wakht*, the amount of which was fixed for Fatima Bibi. This is a deferred payment and has to be paid on the dissolution of marriage. Dowry is also given and usually consists of clothes, jewellery and utensils. The amount of dowry given depends on the economic status of the bride's family.

Talaq or *khula* is permitted among the Sheikhs. It is effected by the utterance of the word *talaq* by the husband or the wife three times in the presence of a witness. From this time the women has to observe a period of *iddat* which is of three months and ten days. Only after the expiry of the term of *iddat* the divorcee women can be remarried. The divorce can be initiated by either of the aggrieved parties on grounds of cruelty, maladjustment and adultery. In the case of a husband divorcing his wife, the *mehar* has to be paid to the wife which acts as a maintenance allowance during the period of *iddat* (Roy, 1979).

The woman can demand back the dowry brought by her in marriage. In the event of the wife divorcing the husband, she forfeits her claim of *mehar*, but has the right to ask for the dowry. The children of estranged parents remain a liability of the father.

Widow remarriage is permitted with the only difference that the widow has to observe a period of *iddat* before remarriage. Junior levirate and sororate or those falling within the proximity of these relationships are preferred.

The residence after marriage is patrilocal. The families are vertically extended and all the members living under the same roof share the hearth. The eldest male member is the head of the family, and his decision on all family issues, which are arrived at after consultations among the members, is final and honoured. He is held in great respect. Age, sex and paternal and filial affection form the basis of mutual love and affection. Purdah is not observed in a strict sense, for its observance depends on one's economic conditions. However, in a majority of the households, avoidance is observed between a wife and her husband's elder male relatives and all such relations in that line, at least in the initial years of marriage. Joking relationship freely exists within cousins, husband's and wife's younger relatives.

"The incidence of close family endogamy and close cousin marriages, especially of the father's brother's daughter type, has usually been assumed to be associated with the desire to maintain property within the family in the face of the Koranic rule of inheritance" (Granquist,1931:78; Zarina Ahmad, 1960:48) which entails upon women a certain portion of share (1/4th) in the parental property which is equally divided among all sisters. More often than not, their respective shares are bequeathed in favour of brothers in order to maintain family harmony and good relations.

On the contrary, many of the Sheikh families follow a customary law, which is similar to those of the Hindus, wherein a daughter has no right of inheritance if there is a son. If a woman is unmarried at the time of father's death, she has the right to receive her share of dowry from the ancestral estate, and if she is a widow, she has the right to maintenance. Even if a divorcee reverts to the father's house, she enjoys maintenance.

Whatever the general law of inheritance may be, it is male equigeniture which is practised. The succession is also always in the male lines.

Women's position under the Islamic law and especially among the Sheikhs is infinitely superior to that of her Hindu sister. She remains under the parental care till she comes of age and during her childhood her father has the right to give her in marriage without her consent. He forfeits this right when she becomes an adult. Then she acquires her own independent right and cannot be married without her consent. She has the right to marry a man whom she likes. It is true that the women are kept in purdah, but history is testimony to the fact that women of Prophet's own family enjoyed considerable freedom ranging from leading troops to holding political discussions. Purdah appears to have come in vogue in about A.D. 744 as a safeguard against the habits of the deprived and tyrannical debauchee, Omayyad Khalif Walid II (Roy, 1979).

Traditionally the women held a subordinate status. In contrast, men were the bread winners. With economic development and change in the attitude and value system of the people, many families have started giving equal education opportunity to girls and, preparing them to be economically independent in case of distress in the family. Eventually this led to their gainful employment in various institutions which was consequent to the urge for better standards of living. They are now working as teachers, doctors, scientists and clerks. The uneducated are well versed in stitching, embroidery and tailoring, and earn money and contribute to the family income. In this arena also, they have now stood by the side of the men sharing an equal status.

The religious status of women is nevertheless low, for a Sheikh woman cannot offer prayers in the mosque, though, she can offer *namaz* at home. They are also not permitted to attend religious congregations. The elderly women do however attend religious discourses, but they must sit in the back rows at a distance from the men. During the month of Ramzan, however, discourses for ladies are held exclusively in the *jenankhana* (lady chamber). Traditionally Muslim women enjoyed political independence. The participation in the political activities of Sheikh women save a few who have started contesting elections is very low. Most Sheikh women are largely restricted to the exercise of their franchise. The Sheikh women are the virtual managers of the house and carry out other household chores.

The birth of a son, as among other patrilineal communities, is greatly rejoiced over. Restsrictions do exist on the enceinte mother. She is not allowed to go alone out of the house at night, or visit a burial ground. She is also not allowed to cut any fruit or vegetable or go out of the house during eclipse. Immediately on the birth of a child, a *maulvi* is called who whispers *azan* in the child's ears and names him, for even a child born dead cannot be buried without being named. A period of pollultion is observed for forty days in which the mother and the child are prevented from coming out of the house. However, she starts working in the house immediately after three days. *Aqiqa* is observed on the sixth day, but at times it is deferred for economic reasons. In the event of the birth of a son, *kurbani* of two goats, and in case of the birth of a daughter of one goat is made. Thereafter, the child's head is shaved off. *Khatna* or *sunnat* is performed for males before the age of six years by a barber-surgeon.

Marriage is performed by *nikah* at the bride's residence. Immediately afterwards, a marriage document *nikahnama* is signed in the presence of witnesses who are usually paternal and maternal uncles and *maulvi*. A copy each of the document is kept with the boy, the bride's parents and the *maulvi*.

The dead of the community are buried in a common burial ground and a tomb is later erected over the grave. The economically well-off make concrete tombs while the poor make a mud tomb, *kachcha mazar*. *Matam* is observed for a period of three days. The death rituals vary from family to family according to the *firqa* to which they belong. The two *firqa*, Deobandi and Barelvi, are very common among the Sheikhs. While a Deobandi will observe only *tija*, a Barelvi will observe *tija, daswan, biswan,* and *kul* on the third, tenth, twentieth and a month after death. Every year on the day of death, the family members go to the *mazar* and offer prayers for the peace of the departed soul.

In the matter of marriage, the customs of the communities from Hindu converts and described as Sheikh, are often a curious mixture of Hindu and Muhammadan customs.

The Sheikh is an agricultural, but also a landless community. A few of them who possess land, form a negligible percentage. They are in varied fields of occupations right from teaching, administration, scientists, clerks to shopkeepers, ironsmiths and craftsman. A few of those who have meagre landholdings, often till the land of the large landholders whether on sharecropping or *batai* or 1/3 *teha* or *theka*. While in the former two, the division of crop is primary, in the last the land is held for farming in consideration of a fixed amount of money. They have total dependence on the market for marketing their produce without middlemen and cash forms the usual medium of exchange. Children below the age of 15, and especially those who are poor, often find jobs as agricultural labour or in road construction for which they are paid in cash.

Each constituent occupational community of the Sheikh category has its own traditional council called as Biradari Panchayat, which assures the pattern of guild-cum-caste council and consists of community elders, who are invited to be on the panel of jury for deciding a particular issue. Such nominations are by the general consensus. The council looks after the maintenance of traditional norms and prevents any infringement of rules. Each family is linked up with a particular *firqa*, and are governed by the rules laid down by the said *firqa*. In case of difference of opinion regarding interpretation of Koranic rules, a letter is sent to the headquarters of the *firqa*, stating the facts of the case, and their opinion is solicited. A few moderate ones invite opinion from two different schools and then arrive at a conclusion. Cases that are put up before the council, usually relate to disrespect for traditional norms, adultery, rape or matters relating to the payment of *mehar* and dowry on divorce. The offenders are punished by cash fines which are utilized for defraying expenses of the (religious institutions) *madarsa*.

Although after Independence statutory Gram Panchayats have come into existence to look after planning and implementation of various welfare schemes, yet their traditional council still continues to hold its way over the community.

A variety of sects have come up, the primary ones being the Sunni and Shia sects, which are further subdivided into Barelvi and Deobandi in the first order and Ashari, Bahra and Ismaili in the second order. Among the Sheikhs, the Sunnis constitute the largest sectarian group. "These sects cut across regional and ethnic division and are strong dividing force in a society in the sense that inter-sect marriages within the same ethnic group, though permissible, are often resisted" (Siddiqui, 1978:253). The sectarian affliation of the groups within the category is largely related to the history of their recruitment to Islam. In Himachal Pradesh the decisive bulk of the Sheikh belonging to the Sunni sect are of Deobandi variety followed by Barelvis. The community believes in the doctrine of five fundamentals, viz., unity of God, the prophethood of Muhammad, *namaz*, fasting in Ramzan and payment of *zakat*.

The recruitment of religious functionaries like *imam* and *maulvi* is made on the basis of the capability of the individual for the job irrespective of the ethnic group he belongs to. The *imam* or *maulvi* is responsible for conducting religious functions, congregations and officiating at life-cycle rituals.

Besides the sects, a number of hereditary mystic orders affiliated to *silsilah* (various orders) also characterize the Sheikh community. This differs from family to family. Some do not consider their attachement to *silsilah* necessary whereas others consider it necessary for salvation. These *silsilah* act as an intermediary between man and God. Individuals and families also have individual affiliation to Pirs who are mystics rather than theologians and are believed to have hereditary powers rather than acquired characteristics. The community performs special rituals either in the form of *urs* or *fateha* at the tomb of the revered Pir to whom they pay their obeisance to.

The sacred shrines of the community are Mecca, Medina and the Dargah of Salim Chisti and Ajmer Sharif. It is the cherished desire of every devout Sheikh to pay a visit to these shrines at least once in his lifetime. The major fairs celebrated by the community are at *urs* which are held in the honour of their Pir all over the State. Prominent among them is the Gugga Pir and the Nau Gaza Pir, who are held in reverence all over the State. The major festival of the community is Id'ul fitr, Id'ul zuha, Barawafat, Shabebarat and Ramzan, which have socioreligious significance and are celebrated with fervour and enthusiasm.

The community has been in the thick of various socioreligious movements which have resulted in the recruitment of new members to their order. The neo-converts from Hinduism though they have changed their faith have only partially changed their social customs.

The women of the community are well versed in the art of thread embroidery, *kashidakari*. Songs are also not community specific, and are sung on festive and social occasions. Devotional songs known as *marsia* are sung on *urs* at the tombs of the Pirs. The women also indulge in dancing on social occasions within the four walls of the house purely for amusement purposes. As the Sheikh is a fluid category and a number of occupational communities are included in it, each occupation group practises its own craft in which it is deft.

Despite the obvious existence of ranked groups, the concept of brotherhood of all Muslims remain an ideal and displays a significant functional value. The community obliterates the notion of high and low, and promotes equality. The symbolic ritual equality of the members of an ethnic group is expressed in such acts as eating and smoking together. Expelled community members lose the right to such equality.

Members of groups within these categories do not eat or drink with the Lalbegi, who passively accept their position and often experience difficulty in getting their dead buried in the common Muslim burial ground. Similar avoidance is also observed in matters of acceptance of food from the begging communities like the Mirasi, Dafali and Faqir. A Sheikh would accept any type of food from certain Hindus, but the latter would not accept food cooked in the house of the Sheikh, though they may accept *pucca* food provided it is cooked separately by a Hindu. No restrictions exist among them in the sharing of wells, facilities of road, school, burial, entry to mosque and Panchayat Ghar with the other Muslim communities. The rigidity in matters of acceptance of food is observed more in villages than in urban centres where such restrictions have dissipated.

Political leadership has emerged at the regional level. The community has been producing businessmen, persons in white-collar profession, teachers, Government officials and the like.

The attitude of the community towards various development programmes has been favourable especially in relation to literacy and education. The Sheikhs are sending their children for formal education, though in a majority of the cases, girls are only able to receive primary or middle school education, after which they drop out for want of higher educational facilities, as girls are not allowed to go unescorted out of the village. No such restrictions exist for boys on going outside the village for education, where they can study till they are able to secure jobs.

The people are not averse to modern medicine, but they also use their traditional homemade remedies. Family planning programmes do not find favour with them, as it is believed that nothing should come in the nature's way. A few of the educated are, however, aware of the benefits of a small family and are practising family planning. Loans to educated employed and the rural poor are also available under the self-employment schemes.

Drinking water is available at most of the places through pipes. At other places water is taken from wells or rivulets. Modern means of communication, i.e., metalled roads, television, radio, cinema and newspapers are available and so are road transport, post and telegraph services. Most of the areas of Sheikh inhabitation are electrified. Wood and kerosene continues to be their main fuel. Some of the Sheikhs who are involved in agriculture use chemical fertilizers in addition to the organic manures and irrigate their fields at places by *kuhl*, whereas at others they depend on rain.

Mid-day meal programmes by the school-going children is availed of. The facilities of Integrated Child Development Scheme in which immunization and nutritional food is provided to the children in 0-5 age group and also to the expectant and nursing mothers.

Rajendra Sarkar

SIKH

The Sikh community's whose religious philosophy is a combination of Islamic and Hindu beliefs. It started as a reform movement, and was founded as a separate entity by Guru Nanak Dev, the first *guru* (preceptor), in the late fifteenth century. The community had a following prodominantly in Punjab. The word 'Sikh' is basically derived from the Sanskrit word *shishya*, meaning disciple. Sikhs are disciples of their ten *gurus*, some of whose writings are compiled in the Granth Sahib, sacred book of the Sikhs. An act of the Indian legislature defines a Sikh as one who "believes in the ten *gurus* and the Granth Sahib". The Sikhs formed a powerful State in the Punjab under Maharaja Ranjit Singh, before the British took over the country. The majority of them belonged to agricultural Indo-Scythian stock and have gradually proliferated economically, socially, and politically through their dexterity and ambition. They are mainly distributed in north western India and in other parts of India mainly after partition. Their ambitious nature and hard work paid them well, and to-day they form a prosperous community. They suffer from no inhibition and are a very closely knit community.

In their present habitat at Paonta Sahib, they had been migrants, though that is now history. The natural environment of the region is valley-type surrounded by hills with the river Yamuna flowing by. The Paonta Sahib township is situated on its right bank. It is characterized by the famous Sikh Gurdwara of Paonta Sahib. The climate of the place is moderate, with hot summers, cold winters and a fairly good monsoon season. At a distance from the main township are fairly dense forests. Rainfall is also on the higher side. In the Sirmaur district the Sikhs number 7,558 as per the 1981 Census. The language the Sikhs speak among themselves is Punjabi, using the Gurmukhi script. Among the modern generation youths, usage of English is on the rise. With outsiders they speak in Hindi and English, using the Devanagari and Roman scripts, respectively. Their community identification markers are the male turban, the flag and their emblem. In addition there is an iron bangle on the right hand for both males and females, long hair for the males, along with a small comb attached to the hair coil at the crown, the *kirpan* and the *kachha*. Ladies perfer wearing the traditional *salwar* and *kameez*. Old men folk prefer the traditional *salwar* and *kurta*, while younger men and recenlty girls as well prefer western dresses.

Though generally vegetarian some of them are occasionally non-vegetarians. No non-vegetarian item is taboo, although, having a Hindu heritage, beef is avoided. Pork products are widely consumed, apart from egg, mutton, poultery birds and fish.

Their staple cereal diet is wheat. Rice is occasionally taken in generally in a fried form. Other cereals taken are *jowar, bajra,* maize and barley. Maize bread is generally taken during the winter months. Their traditional cooking medium is *ghee.* Other cooking media occasionally used are mustard oil, groundnut oil and other vegetable fats and oils, depending on the individual economic capacity. Roots and tubers are also consumed. Though their religion advocates avoidance of alcoholic drinks, many men do take alcoholic drinks which are generally purchased from the local market. The intake of alcohol increases during the winter months. Fruit consumption is moderate and universally popular among them. They consume all kinds of pulses and gram. Food habits have not changed among them, but updated and new menus have been included. Milk consumption and milk products are universally popular. Tea and coffee with heavy dosage of milk in them are also taken.

Because of their Hindu heritage they have socially not been able to do away with caste distinctions and other discriminations. Hence, one finds Scheduled Caste Sikhs among them. Social distinctions and discrimination do not have a religious sanction. The differentiation is at the social and economic level—the latter becoming more pronounced today—and these factors are taken into consideration while negotiating marriages. There has been no change in surnames or titles. The title of 'Singh' for men and 'Kaur' for women are popularly and universally used.

The Sikh community considers itself high because of their military and militant qualities and economic achievements and prosperity. They are aware of the varna order but do not recognize it. Being popularly recognized as a martial race and becuase of their enterprising nature and achievements in all spheres, others rate them high.

Endogamy at the community and clan level is preferred. Cross-cousin marriages can take place though are not prescribed and there is no objection to junior sororate or junior levirate. Adult marriages are performed these days, and may be negotiated or can be by mutual consent, elopement, exchange or courtship. Prejudices are limited in the Sikh society. But marriages are preferred with social equals and, more recently, with economic equals but within the community. Marriage is mainly monogamous. In the village, sometimes, a man may take a second wife if the first is issueless, without divorcing the first wife. There are no specific symbols of marriage, however, the married women may wear a plain gold wedding ring. To a lesser extent a married man may also wear a plain gold ring. Married women usually wear finger rings, ear rings and gold bangles. Widows do not put on lipstick. Dowry in cash and kind is given by many people today, but it is neither universal nor compulsory. Dowry does not have religious sanction nor a social one, but is not refused if given. The bride is given away by the father, and in his absence an uncle or even the mother can play the vital role.

Residence is patrilocal giving way to the neolocal form. Divorce is permissible and is usually with judicial approval. Divorce may be due to adultery, barrenness, impotency, chronic illness, cruelty or insanity. It has social and religious sanction. The aggrieved party is compensated. If the female divorces and has a paramour due to whom she asks for a divorce, the paramour compensates the husband. In any case, either party can divorce. In case of divorce, children are the liability of the father. However, it is mutually decided upon as to who should keep the children and how long and under what circumstances and conditions. Infants and small children are usually given in the custody of the mother until they come of age, provided the mother does not resent being the custodian.

Widow remarriage is permissible and so is widower remarriage. Male divorcee remarriage, female divorcee remarriage, and sororate and levirate in this context are all permissible.

Among the educated and urban Sikh, incidence of divorce shows an increase. Avoidance relationships are getting reduced, though some avoidance relationships are maintained between the daughter-in-law and father-in-law and with husband's elder brother, especially in the rural areas. Joking relationship persists as usual with younger in-laws in either case and between grandparents and grandchildren. Points of conflict and confrontation arise on property matters, check on the freedom of youngsters and challenge to the authority of elders. The Sikh youth of today is independent minded, ambitious and unrestrainable and as such resent any obstacle that may come in their way. Traditional elders like to assert authority, which is resented under present circumstances by the youngsters due to the opening up of avenues of economic independence. Inheritance is through equigeniture legally, but usually landed property and assets are equally divided among the sons and the daughters being adequately compensated on marriage. Unmarried daughters who have not been compensated otherwise, however, assert their right to parental assets. Succession is by the eldest son. There has been a rise in the formation of nuclear families and decline of the extended family system.

Rural women have a role in agricultural operations, except ploughing. Animal husbandry, poultery keeping, collection of fuel, bringing potable water and tending the household are some economic activities performed by them. In this last sphere, urban woman are also quite active. They also have a role in social functions, rituals and political spheres, though not in religious spheres. Nowadays they are playing a limited role in mechanisms of social control also. They have equal and high status, are assertive and also have decision-making powers. In case they are engaged in any economic activity and profitable profession, they contribute to the family income. In any case, they control the family expenditure, taking a keen and active interest in the economic activities of their husbands.

Since Sikhism was meant to be a simple religion, rituals and regulations as such were done away with due to their cumbersomeness. Hence, there are no strict pre-delivery rituals as such, nor any post-delivery ones. Naming ceremony may be observed on the eleventh day but it is optional and is usually held according to convenience. There are no other prescribed childhood ceremonies. However, Sikh boys and girls have to undergo an initiation ceremony of the baptism type as soon as they attain puberty. The initiation ceremony is to make them responsible for the five Ks, upon which the boys take the additional name of Singh and the girls, the additional name of Kaur.

Marriage rituals can be performed at the Gurdwara or at the bride's place to the accompaniment of the *Granth Path* (reading of the Holy scriptures by ecclesiastics) and *kirtan* (choral singing of religious hymns). There are no elaborate rituals. Both sides feast the occasion on respective days. Nupitals are usually held at the groom's residence. Observation of pollution on death is limited. The dead are usually cremated. Prayers for the repose of the soul of the dead are held on any day convenient to the affected parties, and not necessarily on the eleventh or the thirteenth day. This is also held to the accompaniment of the Granth Path, *kirtan* and is followed by a *bhog* ceremony (common simple feast). Rituals are limited and optional and hence without any burden.

The economy of the Sikh in this region revolves mainly around agriculture and business. In agriculture, land and water are the main resources and are controlled by the community as well as individual proprietorship subject to government regulations. They are also a landowning and landholding community with individual proprietorship. A fair number of them also have business establishments of various kinds.

Agriculturists have settled cultivation and practise animal husbandry. Some specialize only in the latter. Others in the urban area have business and some are self-employed. Some are in Government service, others in private ones. Some are skilled labourers. Poultery keeping has also made a dent with quite a few of them having this as a full-time profession. Link with the market is direct. The market is daily and is fully regulated. The form of transaction is cash, and sometimes both cash and credit. Payments are usually made in cash.

The panchayat settles some cases in the village. Election to such bodies is by a voice vote. There is a statutory panchayat after Independence. In the urban areas the role of such panchayats is performed by the Gurdwara Sabha. However, if the decisions are not pleasing to the parties concerned, they are free to go to courts of law. Village panchayats are heterogeneous. Forms of punishment are social boycott and a cash fine. In urban areas it is excommunication by the religious body or a cash fine. Crimes or offences dealt with are adultery, rape, elopement, disputes over land and water and theft.

Sikhism advocates belief in one God who is not represented by idol worship or images. It is also a belief in the preachings and teachings of their ten *gurus* compiled in the Granth Sahib. Deities do not exist among them. They venerate their *gurus* only. Sacred specialists are from the same community and are responsible for worship, religious teaching and life-cycle rituals. Festivals are of religious significance to them and, apart from recitation of the *Granth Sahib* on such occasions and *kirtan* singing, are not much celebrated. The ancestors of the present-day Sikhs were converts to this new religion from Hinduism and some even from Islam. Some of the Sikh are recent converts from Hinduism. The religion being simple, pre-change practices as such do not survive except as per personal choice. The Sikhs observe some of the Hindu festivals of importance by performing some ceremonies, especially the Granth Sahib recitation and *kirtan* singing, in their Gurdwaras. The community was involved in socioreligious movements and that is how they came into being as a separate entity. In course of time and especially after the annexation of the Sikh empire by the British, several movements—religious, social and political—were started among the Sikh themselves. The Nirankari sought to reform certain religious rituals. The Namdhari or Kuka under Ram Singh sought to re-establish the spartan traditions of the early Khalsa and restore Sikh rule. The Singh Sabha movement was basically educational and literacy-oriented.

Embroidery on cloth with silver and gold thread are popular especially with Sikh women. Folksongs are sung by both the sexes and their folkdance, the *bhangra*, is very popular. *Gidda* is also a popular womans' dance.Their folktales consist mainly of deeds of bravery performed by their *gurus*, chieftains and forefathers and lovers. The harmonium is a popular musical instrument with them, used mainly for singing of *kirtan*. Other musical instruments used by them are percussion, wind and string instruments used mainly in connection with devotional songs. The drum is played with the *bhangra* dance. Traditional music is used for devotional songs. Light music and pop music are popular with the younger generation. Western classical and Indian classical music have some listeners.

The Sikhs maintain a very cordial and cooperative inter-community relations. They have no inhibition in accepting and exchanging food and water with other communities on caste or creed lines. And, though they prefer marriages within their community, especially nowadays, they have no objection to intercommunity marriages, especially among urban Sikhs if the Sikh tradition is respected and maintained by the non-Sikh party. They share wells and water sources, as well as cremation ground with other communities. They visit their own as well as the others' religious shrines for specific purposes. The Sikhs commemorate the Hindu festivals by performing ceremonies in Gurdwaras, and they also celebrate their own holy days, such as the birthdays of some of their main *gurus* and observe solemnly the martyrdom day of Guru Teg Bahadur. On such occasions, Granth Path and *kirtan* singing are held in the Gurdwaras and sometimes the Granth Sahib is taken in a procession through the streets. Some of them observe Diwali by lighting lamps on that day, bursting crackers, lighting other fireworks, and exchanging sweets with the Hindus as a sign of fraternity. Baisakhi and Holi are popular festivals. The community has entrepreneurs/businessmen, scholars, members holding white-collar jobs, teachers, administrators, engineers, doctors, political leaders at the village panchayat, regional and state levels and members in the defence services.

Formal education is favoured for both boys and girls and they are given the option to study up to college and post-graduate levels. Boys may drop out to reap the harvest of more renumerative pastures and girls to get married, but seldom does anyone give up studies before passing the high school at least.

Their attitude to indigenous traditional medicare is favourable, especially in the villages, where modern medicare is not widely available, but they have a preference for modern medicare. The attitude towards family planning is favourable, especially in the urban areas where modern methods of family planning are availed of, including sterilization, irrespective of sex preference. In the rural areas they have improvised their own ways and means of sex gratification without enlarging the family, if so desired. Drinking water is available within the locality in urban areas and within easy reach in rural areas. In urban areas, homes have their private taps. In rural areas, dug-wells, hand-pumps or tube or bore-wells serve this purpose. Rural development is voluntary, Their self-employment includes agriculture, poultry, animal husbandry, small-scale industry, confectionary, general merchandise, transport, contractorship and various other industrial enterprises. They listen to radio, watch television and occasionally visit cinema. Electricity is widely used. Fuel resources are fuelwood, sawdust, cowdung cakes and *gobar* gas in rural areas, and kerosene and LPG in urban areas.

T.K. Ghosh

SIKLIGAR

The Sikligar or Saiqalgari is an occupational group of ironsmiths who are engaged in making and repairing agricultural implements and utensils of domestic use. During the times of princely states they used to sharpen swords. The word Sikligar is from the Arabic word *saiqal,* meaning a polisher. They are a semi-nomadic group who live in temporary settlements, and move from place to place in search of work. The Sikligar population in Himachal Pradesh is very sparsely distributed. Their total population according to the 1981 Census is 795 persons. They enjoy the constitutional status of a scheduled caste.

The history relating to their migration and origin is vague. Many of them embraced Sikhism during the reign of Ranjit Singh. They came from across the frontier from the district of Dera Gazi Khan and Dera Ismail Khan at the time of partition and settled in parts of Punjab, Haryana and Uttar Pradesh. In Himachal Pradesh they are mostly found scattered in the foothills in the districts adjoining Punjab and Haryana.

The men wear *tamba* (loin cloth) and *kameez*, whereas the women wear *jampar* (shirt) and *salwar* along with *odhani* to cover their head. Since the Sikligars are both Hindu and Sikh, the Sikhs wear turbans and sport a beard, but the younger generation is not particular about keeping long hair or sporting a beard. During death and mourning the women wear a white *odhani.* A widow, as long she does not remarry, wears a white *odhani* as a sign of widowhood.

They are non-vegetarians who eat pork, meat of rabbit, chicken and mutton. Eating beef is a socioreligious taboo. Their staple diet consists of maize, wheat and pulses of *masur, mah* and *channa*. They consume alcoholic drinks which are procured from the market. The Hindu Sikligars smoke *bidi, hukka* or chew tobacco. Among the non-alcoholic beverages, tea is consumed by the men, women and children. At the time of death, they observe certain restrictions like preparing simple food without using oil and spices. Non-vegetarian food is also not cooked during the period of mourning.

Since the Sikligars are both Hindu and Sikh, differences on account of different religious backgrounds do occur. The two groups used to intermarry, but nowadays some reservations have been observed in this regard. They have a number of exogamous *gots* which denote their descent and regulate matrimonial alliances. Socially they rank among the artisan castes. Their perception of the varna system of hierarchy is extremely vague. Other communities do not have connubial and commensal relations with them.

The Sikligars consider themselves superior to Bagri, Sansi, Dumna, Chamar and Chuhra.

The Sikligars are an endogamous community practising *got*-based exogamy. Marriages are settled through negotiation with the help of a middleman. The boy's side goes to the girl's side to offer the proposal for marriage. The usual age at marriage is 15 to 16 for the girls and 20 to 25 years for the boys. A girl may be slightly older then the boy but now this is not considered proper.

A married woman would be usually dressed in bright clothes with more jewellery than those who are unmarried. The Hindu Sikligars do not demand dowry but gifts are customarily given to the girl by her parents at the time of marriage. A Hindu Sikligar woman puts a vermilion mark and uses bangles and nose-pin as the symbols of marriage.

After marriage, the couple sets up a separate residence. Remarriage and divorce are permissible for both men as well as women. A widow may remarry her deceased husband's brother or anyone outside the family. But in that case she forfeits her claim to her husband's property. The children also remain in the custody of the father. A mother is only allowed to keep infants with her till the time they grow up. A divorce, though rare, is sought on the grounds of adultery, impotency, frigidity, cruelty and chronic mental sickness. If a woman is divorced without any tangible cause, she may appeal to the panchayat for compensation. Similarly, if a woman divorces her husband to marry someone else, the latter may also claim compensation from her father. A second marriage in the lifetime of the first wife, though rare, is sometimes resorted to for getting a heir, but it does not necessitate divorcing the previous wife.

A family normally consists of married couples and their unmarried children. As soon as the son gets married, he moves out into a separate home. It is also true that all such relations live in the same settlement close to each other. The old parents usually live with the youngest child. The interpersonal relations within the family are based on mutual love and cooperation but instances of conflict and quarrel over petty domestic issues also occur. The women observe purdah by partly covering their head in the presence of the father-in-law and other elder relatives of their husband's side. With husband's younger brothers, sisters and between husband's and wife's younger sisters and brothers, the relations are of joking nature. The family gets together at the time of some family occasion, like birth, marriage or death, and on festivals or rituals.

Inheritance and succession of property is in the male line. Daughters do not get any share from the parental property except in the absence of a male issue. Usually there is no immovable property like land or house which can be divided equally among the sons, but those who have landed property try to divide it. Among the Sikh Sikligars, jewellery whatever little of it there is, is given to the youngest male child and the parents normally live with the youngest child. The son who really looks after the parents, gets whatever movable wealth they leave behind.

The status of women, though not at par with the men, is also not very low for they contribute to the family's economy significantly. They make mats of straw for roofing, weave cots and help in the traditional occupation of the Sikligar, namely blacksmithy. The men go to the market to sell their products whereas women take the entire burden of the household chores bringing water and fuel, besides helping in fashioning iron implements. In the domestic sphere, they are the controlling authority and senior women in the household wield considerable influence in making domestic decisions, but economic decisions are left to the men. The women take active part in religious festivals and in performing domestic rituals but cannot be religious functionaries. Women also do not find any place in the local panchayat.

The life-cycle rituals are performed as per the religious beliefs of the community. The Hindu and Sikh Sikligars observe their respective rites at the time of birth, marriage and death. The birth of the son is a happy occasion and is celebrated accordingly. Both Hindus and Sikhs observe purificatory rites by giving bath to the child and the mother. The pollution following birth lasts for 21 days, up to the maximum of 40 days. Thereafter, the mother and the child are free to move out and attend to normal work. Among Hindus, *mundan* is observed for the boy. The Sikh Sikligars observe *pagri* ceremony when the boy attains 10 to 12 years of age. A sweet pudding is made and offered to all the relatives and neighbours. And in the presence of Guru Granth Sahib, a turban is tied to the boy signifying his enterance into the Sikh fold.

The young boys who have undergone the *pagri* ceremony do not adhere strictly to the religious practices calling for every Sikh to keep long hair and a comb, wear loin cloth, carry a *karpan* (dagger) and wear a *kara* (iron bangle). Many of them have got their hair cut, and even those who had long hair did not wear turban. The Sikh Sikligars also observe the christening ceremony, and on this occasion the child is taken to the Gurudwara and the priest suggests a befitting name. Thereafter a *karah prasad* (sweet pudding) is distributed among all the members of their *biradari* and in the neighbourhood.

Hindu and Sikh rites differ in the marriage ceremonies. The Sikh marriages are performed in the Gurudwara amidst the chanting of hymns from the Guru Granth Sahib. The marriage ritual is known as *lame* which consists of circumambulation around the Guru Granth Sahib four times after tying the nuptial knot. Among Hindus, this consists of seven *phera* around the sacred fire while the *pandit* recite the appropriate verses or *mantra* from the Vedic texts.

Both the Hindu and Sikh Sikligars cremate their dead but children below 10 years of age are buried. On the third day, the bones and ashes of the dead are collected from the cremation site and immersed in the river at Kiratpur or in the Ganges at Hardwar. On the thirteenth day, the Hindus feed the *biradari* and this marks the end of the period of death pollution. The Sikhs on the other hand observe *bhog* ceremony in which verses from the Guru Granth Sahib are recited for the peace of the departed soul and thereafter the house is considered pure.

The traditional economy of the Sikligars consists of making and repairing of iron implements for both domestic and agricultural use. Earlier they were deft in sharpening swords and other implements used in warfare, but nowadays they have shifted to making articles of common use like utensils, knives, artisan's tools and agricultural implements. They sell their finished products in the local market on cash payment. Barter or exchange is not prevalent. The men move in the village for selling their goods directly while women prepare mats of straw, weave cots and help their men in economic activities. They however do not go out to sell the products. Besides their traditional occupation, those who have attained some education are going out in search of jobs in Government and semi-Government organizations and are working as contractors, drivers and mechanics.

Child labour is present to some extent because of extreme poverty and deprivation. The children are trained in the ironsmithy by their parents from a young age to enable them to function independently as early as possible. Their economic activity is a joint venture and all the members in the family play their part effectively. It should be mentioned that because of the market being already flooded with the products which are far too superior in shape and finish the Sikligars are facing a very tough competition to survive in the industrial market. This phenomenon, which is a natural outcome of industrialization, is pushing many artisan groups, including the Sikligars into a deep economic crisis forcing them to change their age-old profession and seek alternative means of livelihood.

For effective management of their code of conduct, social norms, moves and ways, they have their own Biradari Panchayat. This body comprises elder male members of their *biradari* who take up the responsibility of decision making. Whenever there is a breach of social norms, for instance, elopement, rape, adultery, theft, quarrel, divorce, etc. the fine may be imposed both in cash or kind. Elopement with a person outside the *biradari* may result in excommunication. Mostly, the cases are settled by their own council.

The Hindu Sikligars worship the gods and goddesses of the larger pantheon but have more faith and reverence for the local deities, and they pay frequent visits to their shrines. They also have a village deity which is worshipped by all the inhabitants of the village irrespective of caste or creed.

Each year a large feast is arranged in honour of the village deity by collecting contributions from each family.

The Sikligars still have faith in evil spirits, magic, charms and amulets. The specialist who can remove the evil effects of the spirits is known as *sayana*. He can be from any community. Any chronic ailment or mishap is attributed to be the handiwork of the evil spirits.

The Sikligars are trained ironsmiths and deft in polishing and grinding of iron objects which may include implements of agriculture and domestic use. Earlier they used to sharpen weapons like swords and daggers for use in the warfare. The women know embroidery. Their folksongs and folktales are not different from those of other communities of the region. The women sing song and dance at the time of birth, marriage and other happy occasions.

The Sikligars largely fall under the artisan group and maintain social ties with Tarkhan, Lohar and Saini, with whom they may exchange *pucca* food. From castes like Brahman, Rajput, Khatri and Mahajan they may accept *kachcha* food, but the latter do not accept anything cooked, *kachcha* or *pucca*, from the Sikligars. The Sikligars, on the other hand, would not dine with the members of the Bagri, Sainsi, Doom, Chamar, Chuhre and Muslim communities.

The traditional *jajmani* systsem is steadily losing ground and the Sikligars no longer work for other communities on *jajmani* basis. They generally accept cash for the service they render or the articles they sell. All the communities commonly share public taps. But wells are separate for certain castes. The entry of the members of the Sikligar community to temples and shrines is open and no differentiation is practised. With wider communication network and frequent contacts with urban population, the distinctions based on caste are becoming less distinct.

The effect of development after Independence has been significant in the field of health and family welfare, communication, electricity and water supply and to some extent in bringing about a level of literacy among the Sikligars. However, they are still lagging far behind in education for their children do not show much interest in education due to the fact that from the very childhood they are trained in their traditional occupation of blacksmithy. The preoccupation of men and women in their work and their habitat and surroundings leave little scope for formal education. Besides, the Sikligars also shift their settlements in search of work which leads to a semi-nomadic existence. Their houses, made of straw and bamboo *palu*, can be easily dismantled and erected.

The Sikligars get freeship in schools and economic aid under various economic programmes launched by the Government. Some of the families of the Sikh Sikligars in Una district have been provided with *pucca* houses as a part of the rehabilitation drive for the homeless. Loans are also made available to them for buying tools and implements, for setting up cottage industries, for shops and for various other purposes. Some of them have also acquired land under the *nautor* scheme. These benefits are enjoyed by a small section of the people because of lack of awareness and understanding.

Vatsala Sarkar

SIPI

The Sipi or Sippi is one of the indigenous commnities of the hills, included in the list of scheduled caste and lives chiefly in Chamba and Lahaul and Spiti districts of Himachal Pradesh. Their total population in the state according to the 1981 Census was 14,294. Rose (1914:247) describes them as a "weaver of the Gaddi tribe, found in Bharmaur wizarat of the Chamba state and virtually the same as Hali. A low hill-caste who are professional sheep rearers. They are now cultivators and also assist Swanglas and Bodhs at marriages and funerals and are given food and clothes on these occasions". The status of the Halis ascribed to them by Rose is disputed by them, but they all belong to the lower order.

The Sipis live at high altitude in hilly terrain, where the climate is extremely cold and winter months are prolonged with heavy snowfall. The rainfall is scanty, the forest dense and humidity low. They live in homogeneous nucleated villages. There is a touch of Sanskrit in their dialect. They speak Gadiali amongst themselves, whereas with others they converse in Pahari /Himachali. Most of them are illiterate and cannot write, but those who have got education write in Devanagari.

The community is non-vegetarian, but eating beef and buffalo meat is taboo. Their staple food is *makki-di-roti* and *ain-da-sag. Rongi* and *masur* are also used along with *roti* and rice. Vegetables and edible roots and tubers are also moderately consumed, which are cooked in mustsard oil. They smoke tabacco and drink homemade alcoholic drink, *lugri,* though occasionally liquor is also purchased from the market. The use of milk is limited to tea. The seasonal variation in food is observed in winter months when the intake of non-vegetarian food increases along with the use of alcoholic liquor. There is also a shift from non-vegetarianism to vegetarianism, because of the high cost of non-vegetarian food, consequently giving rise to increase of consumption of pulses and vegetables.

Information on genetical and population structure is available on the community (See bio-anthropological report).

The community is endogamous and is subdivided into a number of exogamous *gotras,* viz., Bamari, Baumetu, Bhamere, Dilwar, Dubni, Katte, Khaschi, Nagatwar, Pulan and Sachal. At the time of contracting marriages three generations on father's side and one generation on mother's side are avoided. There is no hierarchy among the *gotras*, the differentiation occurs on social or territorial basis. Hypergamy is permitted. The community occupies the lowest place in the local social hierarchy and this fact is admitted by all. They are neither aware of the varna *vayavastha* nor do they place themselves in it.

A few decades back child marriages were practised, but now they have been replaced by adult marriages. Of the various types of acquiring mates, marriage by negotiation, *byah* or *dharam puna,* is the most common of all, the other types being *batta-satta*, by *kamash* (service) or *ghar jawantri* and *jhind-phunk* (elopement). Though monogamy is the general rule, occasionally polygyny is also practised when the first wife is unable to give a family heir. Junior and senior levirate and junior sororate are allowed. The symbol of marriage for women is nose-ring, which however is not strictly adhered to.

Traditionally giving of *reet* or *lag* was prevalent, but now it is being replaced by dowry, which is not demanded, but depends on the economic status of the family, and is usually in kind. *Chhadi* (divorce) is permissible by either of the aggrieved parties with socio-judicial approval on grounds of extra-marital relations, maladjustment and inability to feed the wife. Compensation by way of returning the marriage expenses is born by the erring party. The children however are the liability of the father.

Khewat (divorcee remarriage) and *qudani* (widow remarriage with unmarried brother of the deceased husband) are also permitted. However, if a widow remarries a married brother, it is known as *balu-jharara.* Widower remarriage is also permitted. The residence is patrilocal. The family is of vertically extended type. The interpersonal relationships within the family are that of love, respect and cordiality. The head of the family who is usually the eldest male member of the family commands great respect; and his decision in family matters is final. Avoidance exists between daughter-in-law and all her husband's male senior kinsmen for a few days after marriage, after which it is not feasible, as they work together in the fields. Joking relationship also exists with all younger brothers and sisters of the husband and wife.

Property is inherited according to the *mundaband* law of inheritance, wherein male equigeniture is followed. An illegitimate child, *chakhandu,* also has the right of inheritance like a legitimate child. The eldest male member succeeds his father as the head of the family.

The women have no right of inheritance, but has the right of maintenance. Her status is regarded as low, but she is an indispensable part of their economic life, for she carries out all agricultural operations, in and outside the household. In addition to this, she is also responsible for bringing fodder for the animals, and also stacking it for winter months. She also brings firewood, potable water and also takes part in economic activities by working as an agricultural labourer or as a labourer in road-making or road-cleaning with the Public Works Department, where she is paid in cash. She has a role in social functions and in various rituals. She participates in political activities also. She also manages all household affairs, doing all household chores, but has no decision-making powers or role in the mechanism of social control.

In the sphere of life-cycle rituals, pre-delivery rituals are observed. The enceinte woman worships the goddess Kali for the well-being of the child to be born. Her movements are also restricted: she is not allowed to go outside the house along after dusk or visit a dreadful sight. *Sutak* is observed for 13 days, until which time the woman is not allowed to do any work. *Sugru* ceremony for naming and for the first cereal-feeding is observed six months after the birth of the child.

The marriage is a simple ceremony and is performed at the bride's residence, with the feast being given by her father. Marriage is solemnized by performing circumambulation around the fire seven times, with the bridal knot having been tied to the apparel of both the bride and the groom. The consummation of marriage however takes place at the groom's residence.

The dead are cremated with the last rites being performed by the eldest male member of the house. The mortal remains are disposed off in a river. The house remains polluted for 13 days. Rituals connected with the dead are also observed on each anniversary, *barkhi,* and a special rite is observed on the fourth anniversary, *chaubarkhi*.

The major economic activity of the community is agriculture. The land is individually owned. They also hold land of the others on a share cropping basis. Because of the meagre landholding and poor yields they also supplement their income by agricultural-labour, labour, acting as *chela* and by other unskilled occupations like herding and skinning sheep and goat and acting as drummers. A few of the Sipis even today have continued their traditional occupation of skinning and making a long rope of sheep hair.

The Sipis use middlemen for marketing their agricultural produce, as the marketable surplus is too little. Barter and cash both form the medium of exchange. Children below 15 years are also employed both in organized and unorganized sectors, where they are paid either in cash or in kind.

The social norm is maintained in the community by their traditional council, *bhai-chara* panchayat. The composition of each panchayat is different, and the members are elected by a voice vote. The panchayat dispenses justice in matters relating to family disputes, theft, black magic, adultery, elopement and insult to the panchayat. The guilty is punished by social boycott and cash and kind fine. Though both the Nyay and the Gram Panchayats exist for maintaining law and order and for planning and implementing welfare activities, yet it is the *bhai-chara* panchayat which has a greater hold on the community.

The community professes Hinduism, with a strong emphasis on the Shakti and Shaiva cults. They believe in *autar* and spirits, which are appeased and worshipped for the well-being of the village community in general and the family in particular. Kailung or Kailu Bir is the demon responsible for abortions. The spirit associated with soil—Khetr Pal—is propitiated for a good yield and Banbir for curing illness. Water sources are believed to be the abode of Nag Devta, and are worshipped by all villagers. Their regional deity is Chamunda Devi. Besides, they also have faith in other deities of the Hindu pantheon.

The *chela* is from the community and is a worshipper of Shiva. It is believed that a *chela* during a *khel* (hypnotic trance) gets possessed by the presiding deity, and whatever he utters is believed to be the utterance of the deity. The *chelas* are consulted in distress to ward off misfortune. However at family rituals the *purohit*, who is also a sacred specialist from other communities officiates.

The important fairs of the community are the Sui fair (which is celebrated on the first day of *Baisakhi*), Bharmaur Jatra (celebrated a day after Janamashtami), Manimahesh fair and Minjar fairs (celeberated during the monsoon). The important festivals of the region are Biswa, Baisakhi, Chinnj, Janamashtami, Diwali, Lohri, Shivratri, Holi and Dholru. All these fairs and festivals have socioreligious significance.

The community has been influenced by the Arya Samaj and Nirankari movements. Of the two, the former has been very effective in the uplift of the people.

A traditional graphic art is practised by the *chela*s wherein they make certain line drawings on the ground, when preparing for exorcism. Weaving of *gardu, pattu* and weaving of *dora* is done by every person of the community. Folksongs are sung by the community. Oral traditions do exist. The community plays drums at social and festive occasions whereas some also excel in playing the *shehnai*.

The community accepts water, *kachcha* and *pucca* food from all the *savarna* communities. The latter on the other hand accepts only *pucca* food from a Sipi provided it is cooked by a person of the *savarna* community. From members of the same community and others of the same rank they would accept both *kachcha* and *pucca* food. They would also accept *sidha* from all communities. Traditionally, no *savarna* would accept anything from a Sipi, but this is not so now.

Putative kinship is established with persons of similar ranking and such kins are known as *mitar bhai*. The traditional restrictions like walking on the roads, entering the house, sitting at a distance and bringing their own utensils is not rigidly observed nowadays, due to the loosening of commensal norms and greater awareness. The traditional *jajmani* relationship exists in which they act as *pohal* (shepherd), and sheep and goat shearers for their clients. They also act as drummers for which work they receive payment in kind and cash from their patrons. With their gaining employment in various other occupations, the relationship of landlord-tenant, cultivator-labour and employer-worker has developed. Other than these, *kamin-bartani* (symbiotic) ties also exist between the Sipi and other communities.

The various development programmes of the Government have made a dent in their lives in spite of all the odds. Their attitude towards education is favourable and they have started sending their children to schools. Girls study up to the secondary level, after which they drop out, as higher education facilities are at a distance. Boys, however, receive education up to the college level. The people make use of modern system of medicare in addition to traditional systems of medicine, but their attitude is not favourable to family welfare programmes, as they consider children to be a gift of god.

Drinking water is available from perennial snowfed streams. Many Sipis have secured loans and assistance by way of subsidy for poultry farming, rearing sheep and goat, and other self-employment programmes.

Their villages are poorly connected through roads and public transport. Post offices exist far off. Some have radio and transistors. In villages the accessibility to cinema is through the extension agencies. Electricity is availed of by some. Firewood is used as the usual cooking medium. Some also use kerosene. For irrigation people have to depend on rainwater. Manure is preferred to chemical fertilizers and pesticides due to scarcity of irrigation water.

Mid-day meal programme for school-going children is availed of and so is the immunization scheme and nutritional programmes for infants and expecting and nursing mothers. They also avail themselves of the public distribution system.

Rajendra Sarkar

SOOD

The Sood or Sud is a community of traders and clerks. Similar to the hill Mahajans, the money-lenders and merchants, the Soods also constitute an important cluster of the traditional traders and shopkeepers like the Bania, Khatri and Mahajan. They are considered at par with the Kayastha or Kayath, the traditional Babu/Munshi (clerk). The community's name is derived from the Punjabi word *sood* or *sud* meaning interest acquired on the principal amount by the moneylenders. A popular legend mentioned by Rose (1914) and Ibbetson (1916) speaks about the origin of the community from the word *sood.* According to the legend a person took a debt from a Bania but was unable to return the interest on it. In lieu of interest he offered his daughter to the Bania. Such offering were known as *sood*—those that came by way of interest. 'Karar' is also used as a synonym for Sood which means 'hard people' who would not spare interest. The honourable title used to address them are, however, Lala, Shah and Bahu. Rose (1914) mentioned two broad groups among the Sood in Punjab, namely Uchandia (Sood of the hills) and Newandia (Sood of the plains) almost equivalent to Kihara or Dasa Bania and the Gola/Daghla/Chichar or Gata Bania. In Himahal Pradesh also there are two broad groups known as the Jaswal Sood and the Palmu Sood. Earlier there was social distinction in terms of hypergamons marriages but these are not in vogue at present.

The community perceives its distribution in 10 out of 12 districts. However, the major concentration of the Sood is seen is district Kangra, followed by Hamirpur, Una, Bilaspur, Shimla, Chamba, Mandi, Kullu, Sirmaur and Solan districts. They inhabit different climatic area—warm and temperate to cold and dry, hills and dales with thin forest canopies and medium rainfall. They speak regioal dialects of the Pahari or Himachali, e.g., Kangri, Bilaspuri, etc. and use Devanagri script. The official language for their trade was Urdu in the past or Pahari (Hindi) with Tankri script but now they have switched over to Hindi. The older men used to wear a white *kurta*,a *chooridar pyjama* and a *safa*. Women dress is *kurta* and *salwar* with *dupatta/ chunni*. They used to wear a *chak* on head, *har* or *kantha, bali, tili, pajeb* and *gajra/kara* as ornaments.

The Soods are occasionally non-vegetarian; some affluent members consume meat, fish and eggs along with liquor quite frequently. But there are also vegetarians and also those who do not take alcohol. Staple cereal food is wheat, maize and rice along with different types of pulses like *arhar, urad, moong, kulthi, masur, moth*, grams, beans and green vegetables, roots and tubers. The cooking medium is mustard and groundnut oil or vegetable *ghee*. Common fruits consumed frequently in the seasons are orange, mango, apple, plum, peach guava, banana, melons and walnuts. Their dietary habits are changing from non-vegetarian to vegetarian food due to religous/ sectarian influence of the Arya Samaj and Radhaswami missions. Milk and its products are taken in plenty. Festival foods are *halwa* and *kheer, dahi* and *bhalle, ankli* (of rice flour), *seviyan*, etc. Non-vegetarian items are taboo on birth and death pollution, fasts and religion occasions.

The broad divisions like Palmu Sood and Jaswal Sood are not effective unlike in the past when hypergamy existed between the two. They usually identify *gotra* and sub-*gotra* or *al* or septs. Rose (1914) states that the Soods have 52 *gotras* including Augarh, Baddhu and Baggha. But they are not aware of all such *gotras* and recall some like Wahil, God, Bhagra, Patoee, Kodel, Kalandar, Chimre, Butel, Bante, Chab, Takarpy, Bagle, Mehdudiye, Parkhoee, Maggwaloh and Gupta. The *gotras* are used to regulate exogamous marriage and many also use them as surnames. The community name is also often used as surname by many. In varna order they place themselves in the middle in the Vaishya varna. Sectarian division into Radhaswami, Arya Samaji and Sanatani have not created social differentiation of a hierarchical nature. The social position of the community is below Bania and Mahajan though their affluence sometimes surpasses these communities.

The Soods are endogamous, though there are spordic cases of marriage with the Mahajan, Khatri, Kayath etc. Village exogamy may be maintained in rural settings but not in the urban settings where locality/*mohalla* endogamy may occur but clan/*gotra* exogamy is retained and they avoid marriage upto the second cousin level. Marriage age has gone up to above 20 years for the girls nowadays, though a few decades back pre-puberty marriages occurred. Marriage usually takes place though negotitaion and ocasionally through exchange of sisters called *batta satta* when suitable mates were available in two families. Monogamy is the practice and only in rare cases of childlessness, can a man go for a second wife with the consent of the first wife. Marriage symbols are *sindur*, glass bangles, *bindi* on forehead, ear and nose ornaments. Bride price is not taken and *kanyadan* is performed. Dowry is given in both cash and kind and sometimes also demanded. As per Vedic traditions, they disfavoured divorce and usually society did not allow it except in exceptional situations. But recently it has taken a legal shape and may occur with judicial approval on various grounds. In such cases, the dependent wife may seek compensation and the children also become the father's liability. Widow and divorcee marriage are allowed. Junior sororate may occur with the consent of the girl.

Vertically extended families are fewer at present and have given way to nuclear families. Avoidance relationship of the *bahuti* exists with her *saurah*, *jeth* and *nandoi*. Joking relations are informal as in many Hindu communities of the region. Property is normally inherited by all sons equally, but sometimes the elder brother gets a little more share called *jathunda*. In rural setting women have a role in agriculture, animal husandry, and fetching potable water. They participate in economic activities, business entrepreneurship and seek Government jobs as teachers, clerks, etc., and also work in banks. They participate in political activities and in the mechanism of social control, besides religious, ritual and other social ceremonies. They have an almost equal status and manage family affairs and expenses.

Vedic or other sectarian rituals are observed during the lifecycle. Birth pollution called *sutak* is maintained for 13 days. *Shudhi* is observed by taking *panjap* that includes Ganges water and cow's urine. Naming ceremony may be observed and a Brahman priest is consulted to give a particular name as per the zodiac sign. *Khirpu* cerenony is observed in the sixth month and feast is offered to children. *Mundan/jamalu* ceremony is observed on an odd year and performed by *mama* or *nana/nani* of the boy. The hair is offered to clan or *kuldevi*. *Kaan chhedan* (ear piercing) ceremony is observed for young girls on Gauntri day following Lohri festival and sweets are distributed. The *janeu* ceremony occurs at the time of marriage.

Sagai, thakha and ring-wearning are the betrothal ceremonies. The usual Vedic ritual are performed by a Brahman priest at the bride's place like *ved* and *agni phere* when the bride and groom cricumambulate the sacred fire. The bride's parents perform *kanyadan* and give a feast. *Muklawa* occurs on the following day and marriage is consummated.

The death rituals of the Soods are also similar to that of most of the Hindus. The dead are cremated and their ashes are immersed in the Ganges at Hardwar and *pind dan* is made to a Panda. Death pollution called *patak* is observed for 16 days. An Acharaj officiates to perform ancestral worship and seeks offerings. The family Brahman priest performs *havan* and ancestral worship and seeks offerings. The Arya Samajis usually finish all death rituals with the *uthala* ceremony within a week. Rituals in them are considerably curtailed to save time and money.

The Soods are essentially merchantile but some people possess landholdings for horticultural and agricultural purposes. Some also have tea estates as individual properties. A few have taken up animal husbandry as well. They have assimilated various merchantile occupations ranging from shopkeeping to industries. Many people are in Government as well as in private jobs on various posts.

They have their community council called Sood Sabha that resolves their social disputes and other socio/economic problems. The problems of dowry are usually discussed in the council to discourage the growing trend. The statutory Gram Panchayat or municipal committee looks after the usual area-oriented developmental activities.

As Hindus they follow the Sanatana, Arya Samaj and Radhaswami sects. The Sanatani have faith in pantheon trinity and in other gods and goddesses, and worship them on various festive occasions. They also worship family or clan deities like *jathore* (ancestors) for whom a space is allotted in the courtyard. Brajeshwari or Kangra Mata, Darsh Devi, etc. are also propitiated as Kul (clan) deities, besides Ashapuri, Baba Balak Nath, Chamunda, Garhi Wali Mata, Balakrupta Chintpurni, Jawalamukhi, Guga etc. Lakhdata is propitiated as Jakh which safeguards their milking buffaloes. They celebrate various Hindu festivals, like Lohri, Baisakhi, Holi, Sair, Chiran, Dussehra, Diwali, Shivratri, Nag Panchami, Krishan Janamashtami, Rakhi, etc. Various fairs of deites including the local Bhikh Shah, Lidwar, Dari, Halir and Dussehra fair, etc. are visited. They share Kangri or Pahari folk songs, tales, music and dance.

As a dynamic community, the Soods have favourably responded to the modern developmental programmes. Literacy level is quite high and they provide college/post-graduate education to both boys and girls without any sex discrimination or favouratism. Modern health and medicare facilities are availed of but sometimes, as the need arises, traditional methods are also utilized. Family planning has been accepted. Sterilization is the common way of restricting the family size after two or three children. Their houses are electrified and most of them avail themselves of or possess modern mass media (radio, T.V., V.C.R., newspaper, cinema) facilities. Road network is at their doorsteps. They are employed and self-employed and generally lead a respectable and prosperous life.

A.R. Sankhyan

SUNAR

The Sunar/Sonar/Sanyar or Swarankar, derived from the word *sona* (gold), is a well-known community of traditional goldsmiths (and silversmiths) popular as jewellers in the cities. Soni and Kapila are also synonyms for this community though other synonyms such as Jargar or Zargar are also used elsewhere (Rose, 1919; Ibbetson, 1916). They have two main subgroups, namely the Tank or Tonk and Mair, of which the former are mostly of Khatri origin and the latter of Rajput ancestry (Rose, 1919). In the higher hills of Shimla district they are also called Bharira. They claim Kshatriya origin. The legendary origin of the Mair or Maipotra Sunar is traced to goddess Durga. It is said that a demon created troubles for the Devi, but was killed by a Mair and so the Devi was pleased and blessed him. Some ethnographic accounts are available for the community in old literature.

The community is known at the national level and in the area of study people perceive their distribution at regional and interregional (interstate) levels. They are distributed in most of the districts, e.g., Bilaspur, Kangra, Hamirpur, Una, Mandi, Solan, Shimla and Kullu, but their exact population figure is not recorded. They live in the rural as well as urban setting but a majority live in the urban and suburban areas, inhabiting the hills and dales of varied climates ranging from warm and temperate to cold and dry. The community is identified by its ocupation. These people have come to the State from outside, mainly from Punjab during the past and have been living here for centuries but fail to recall their migration history. Some also came at the time of India's partition as well as later, who may be distinguishd from the original or earlier inhabitants of the area. Most of them have been living there since time immemorial and have assimilated the regional culture. They speak local dialects like Bilaspuri, Kangri, etc. of the Pahari and write in Devanagari script both within and outside the community. Some also speak Punjabi and the older men can read and write in Urdu (Perso-Arabic script).

The men's dress is a shirt and *pyjama* or presently *pants* and on festive/ marriage occasions and they also wear a *safa*. The women wear *kurta* and *salwar* and a *dupatta/chunni/chadru*. In the upper hill areas men wear *loi, achkan* and *suthan* while women put on *chapkan* and *dhathu*. The common ornaments put on by the women are *bali, koka* or *nath*, chain with a locket on the neck, finger and toe-rings and *pajeb*. Some also wear golden bangles.

They share the food habits of the area. The main staple food in the rural areas is maize, wheat and rice. All different types of pulses-*urad, moong, masur, kulthi, moth, arhar*, peas and beans (*raungi* and *rajmah*) and grams are eaten frequently. The cooking medium is mustard or groundnut oil or vegetable *ghee*. Various types of seasonal vegetables, roots and tubers are eaten frequently. Fruit intake is moderate and seasonal fruits are eaten, the more common of which are mango, banana, apple, peach, guava, papaya and orange. In rural area mulberry, *ber* (berries) and figs are also sometimes eaten. Milk and milk products are frequently consumed. Festive preparations are *halwa, kheer, seviyan, babru* or *kachauri, ankli, bhalle* and *khichri*. Spinach or *sag* of mustard leaves with butter and maize *roti* are enjoyed during winter months. Food taboos are observed during certain fasts and *sutak* period. They are generally non-vegetarian in food babits but occasionally consume eggs, fish and meat. But the followers of Radhaswami mission do not consume non-vegetarian food and liquor, and this trend is gradually catching up in the community in the post-Independence period. The men smoke *bidi*, cigarette or loose tobacco in a bronze-made indigenous pipe called *hukka* or *kali*.

Their social stratification is usually into two subgroups—the Tank and the Mair. The former claim a higher place in social hierarchy over the latter but practically this hierarchy has lost its significance and is known to the older persons only. They usually distinguish themselves into *gotras,* like, Saul, Kaplash, Handa, Varma, Mehta, Soni, etc. which serve to regulate marriages and denote ancestry/descent. There is also some sectarian differentiation as some Sunars folllow Radhaswami sect. But generally this has not resulted in matrimonial discrimination in the community.

In the regional social hierarchy, the Sunar rank at par with the Khatri and claim Kshatriya or Vaishya varna status. The clan names are usually used as surnames. Soni is a more common surname.

The institution of the marriage is similar to that of other Hindus. Marriages usually occur in adulthood and through negotiation by the parents. The community is generally endogamous but also marries with Khatris of equivalent economic status. Clan/*gotra* and village exogamy is maintained. Exchange marriage and bride price did not exist in the community and *dharam punne* marriages occur through *kanyadan* and dowry is given in the form of household articles, ornaments, clothes, furniture, and some also give cash. There are also demands for costly items and dowry has become a status symbol. Monogamy is practised but in case of chidlessness, a man can remarry. The bride lives patrilocally. The marriage symbols are *sindur*, glass bangles or golden bangles and nose and ear ornaments of gold.

Widow remarriage or junior levirate is usually not liked socially but a young widow without children may remarry though not a junior levirate. The widower can remarry any girl or a junior sororate. Divorce is also not approved socially and is looked down upon. But it may occur on judicial approval if the couple cannot adjust. In such cases, the man bears the liability to compensate the woman and supports the children. Both the divorcees can remarry. The institution of marriage witnesses a general increase in age at marriage and giving of dowry and some awareness in respect of acceptance of remarriage.

The family pattern is both nuclear and vertically extended. Usually the married sons do not get separated as long as the father is alive or they are broken due to some disputes over common property matters, unequal work load and some favouratism towards certain family members. But normally the elders command respect from the junior members. Avoidance relationships are fading away in the urban families, but in rural area the *lari/bahuti* covers her face from her *saurah, jeth* and *nandoi*. The joking relationship is informal and may be observed as in many Hindu communities of the area between *devar-bhabi, jija-sali, nanand-bhabi* and *jija-sala*. The inheritance of paternal property occurs as per the rule of male equigeniture and the eldest brother succeeds his father. The Sunar families are cohesive and cooperate with each other on festivals and occasions of sorrow. The staus of women remains somewhat lower than that of men. The women usually are not seen in employment and are mainly confined to household chores. But in village they do participate in agricultural and animal husbandry duties and fetch potable water. They take part in social and religious ceremonies, control or regulate family expenditure and also have a say in family decisions. But the mechanism of social control and political spheres are not their concern.

Life-cycle rituals are observed as per the Sanatana Dharma but followers of the Radhaswami mission do not observe elaborate Vedic rituals. Pre-delivery and post-delivery restrictions are imposed on the women. Post-delivery pollution, *sutak* is observed for 13 days and the *gunt/guntrala/punjap* ceremony is observed for purification. Sweets are distributed and women songs are arranged to greet the family on the birth of the son.

In rural areas, sweetened germinated grams are distributed. The young children are given a feast . Name may be given by consulting a Brahman who prepares *janam-patri*. Cereal-taking is not ceremonised. The main childhood ritual is *mundan* ceremony for the boys. The first hair cut is given by the child's *mama* and hair is offered to the clan deity . *Janeu* ceremony is observed at the time of marriage only. Pre-marriage rituals are *sagai, tika* and *thahaka*. When the marriage is fixed the boy and girl are offered some clothes and ceremonial money. Some, mainly those who have come from Punjab in recent years, observe a ring ceremony solemnizing the engagement.

On the day of the marriage the main rituals are *haldi* or *batna, mehndi* and *samuhat*. The marriage rituals called *lagan* and *vedi* are performed at the bride's place when the *pandit* recites Vedic hymns and the bride and groom circumambulate the sacred fire. Finally, the parents of the girl perform *kanyadan*. They give a feast to the *barat*. At the bridegroom's place, the first ritual is *andrera*.

The bride and groom also circumbambulate a *pipal* or pomegranate tree or its branches and the marriage is completed. The groom's parents give *dham* to the gathered relatives and friends. The *muklawa* occurs on the same or the next day when the marriage is consummated. The Radhaswamis do not observe detailed rituals but arrange *satsang* or *kirtan*, and *havan* is performed by the priest. The couple visits the shrine of the Radhaswami Baba at Beas in Punjab to seek blessings.

The dead are cremated and the ashes are immersed in the Ganges at Hardwar or in Beas river by Radhaswamis. Death pollution called *mitak* is observed for 13 days when an Acharaj officiates to perform ancestor worship and seeks alms and offerings. A purificatory *havan* is performed by the family priest and 16 Brahmans are given meals and some offerings. The Radhaswamis perform a *havan* and give meals and clothes of the dead to the poor. They do not observe further death rites but the followers of the Sanatana observe *barkhi* and *chabarkh* death rites and give ceremonial meals to the community and gathered relatives to commemorate the dead. Every year a *shradha* is also observed in *pitr paksha* and a Brahman is given a meal and a piece of meal is offered to the cow and crows.

The community is thriving in its traditional occupation of gold and silversmithy and in towns they run jewellery shops. In the village some possess small landholdings and do agriculture and animal husbandry to supplement their income. Many persons are also employed in Government jobs in different professions — teachers, doctors, engineers and administrators. There is no bonded or child labour, though in the village children assist their parents in their occupation, agriculture and animal husbandry. The links with the market are direct and the market is fully regulated and the dealings are in cash.

Any organized formal community panchayat or council is lacking but the *sayane* resolve their social disputes. In the villages, the Gram Panchayat also helps in solving the socioeconomic or village disputes over land and water. Serious conflicts are taken to the civil court. Swearing in the name of a local deity or *pipal* tree by taking a water pot with *Gangajal* in hand helps to resolve certain disputes due to foul play or theft.

As Hindus they propitiate the gods and goddesses and various family clan, village and local deities. Sauhra Devi or Naina Devi is propitiated as the family or clan deity by some in Bilaspur and Hamirpur districts. Other propitiate Balak Nath, Lakhdata and Nahar Singh as village or local deities. The Radhaswamis do not take much interest in deities but from time to time visit the shrine of their *guru* to seek blessings and arrange *satsang* at different places and listen to the recorded preachings of their *guru*.

Various fairs of the deities are visited and Hindu festivals of socioeconomic and socioreligious importance such as Lohri, Baisakhi, Sair, Chiran,

Rakhri, Guga Navmi, Ram Navmi, Navratre, Dussehra, Shivratri and Diwali are celebrated. On Diwali evening they worship goddess Laxmi as well as their tools and observe fast for one day and do not work on that day. The women observe fast of Karua Chouth and men and women also observe the fast of Satya Narain. The sacred specialists are from Brahman and the exorcists from other communites. They share various regional Pahari and Punjabi folksongs and folktales, music and dance alongwith popular film songs. Jewellery or carvings on gold and silver is both art and craft as also an occupation.

There are persons in business, holding white-collar jobs, in teaching, medical and engineering professions and as administrators. Political leadership has emerged at the regional level.

Modern development programmes have made good impact on the Sunars. The level of formal education has gone up to the post- graduate level and both the sexes seek higher education. The boys may, however, drop out from studies due to traditional self-employment and the girls are usually not supposed to go out for jobs. Modern system of medicare is favourably availed of but indigenous methods are still used to some extent.

Small family size is favoured by them, and modern methods including sterilization are adopted. Their houses are electrified and they enjoy modern mass media (radio and TV) facilities and also visit cinema or video clubs. Transport and postal facilities are available at their doorsteps in the neighbourhood. Potable water is available through taps but in the countryside springs and step-wells are still in use. Only general provisions exist under IRDP and immunization is availed of under ICDS. In the villages firewood and cowdung cakes are used, and in the town coal, kerosene oil, sawdust and LPG are used by them. Rainwater is the only source of irrigation and modern chemical ferilizers asnd organic manure are used. Facilities of public distriution system are availble in the vicinity. They favour savings in banks and post offices.

A.R. Sankhyan

SUNHAK

The Sunhak is a small community of Sunni Muslims belonging exclusively to the Chandel clan of the Rajput. The community name is probably derived from the word 'hawk' and stands for a community of hunters who used to train *jura/vaaz* (hawks) for hunting small game birds like pigeons, partridges and small mammals like wild hare. The Sunhak were traditionally employed by the erstwhile rulers of the princely state of Kahlur (now district Bilaspur) like Raja Kharag Chand (1824-1839) and Bijai Chand (1893-1928) as *shikari* (hunter) of any community but presently the Muslim Chandels have popularly acquired this name. They are also said to be the outcastes from a Hindu Chandel who married a Muslim woman. The community is mainly confined to two villages, namely Chunjhani and Salahon in district Bilaspur and number a few hundred only. A few families also live in areas of Punjab adjoining district Bilaspur.

They speak Bilaspuri dialect of western Pahari and usually write in the Devanagari script, but some persons also know Urdu (Perso-Arabic script) which is also taught in Government schools. The men wear *kurta* and *pyjama* or *pant* and the women wear *kurta* and *salwar* like other people and do not wear *burka*, typical of many Muslims. Like others, they eat maize as a common staple food during most of the winters supplemented by rice and wheat in most of the summer season. Festive foods are *krah/halwa, kheer, babru, seviyan,* and *gosht* (*halal* meat). Some men take liquor purchased from market and smoke tobacco in *hukka* or *kali* or *bidi*/ cigarettes. Milk and milk products and tea are taken frequently.

The Sunhaks are almost known by a single Chandel clan and by the title of Mian as is commonly enjoyed by the higher Rajputs of the area. They however, consider themselves superior in regional social hierarchy to the Muslim Faqir, Teli, Bharyai/Bharai and Mirasi by virtue of their superior Rajput ancestry. They usually do not marry within their clan and village but marry with the Kulal, Bhatti, Lodhi Pathan, Qureshi and Chaudhari clans of Muslims in district Mandi and Una.

Marriage at cross-cousin (MBD x FSD) level is practised. Presently adult marriages occur through negotiation by parents and relatives. Exchange of sisters, *batta-satta,* may also occur but is not a common practice. Monogamy is practised. Bigamy existed sporadically in the older generation. *Tili* or *koka* and *bali* and glass bangles are the marriage symbols. Bride-price does not exist but *mehar* generally of about Rs. 1500 or above or equivalent to the traditional silver Rs. 32.25, is given to the girl on demand. Dowry in the form of utensils, clothes and furniture is also given. The bride lives patrilocally. Divorce is a rare event but may occur as per the socioreligious tradition of Islam on grounds of malajustment. Widow remarriage is also rare and is disliked. Junior levirate does not occur but sororate may occur. Increase in marriage age and amount of *mehar* and dowry are the noticeable changes during post-Independence period in the marriage customs and institution.

The family pattern is traditionally vertically extended joint but presently such families are breaking down. The married sons usually do not separate as long as the father is alive and junior members are obliged to pay respect to the elders though conflict on property matters are not uncommon. But still families are cohesive on festivals, festivities and occasions of sorrow.

The inheritance is practically as per the rule of male equigeniture though unmarried daughters may claim a part of father's property. The eldest son succeeds the father. The *lari* keeps avoidance from *saurah* and *jeth*. Joking relationship, as in Hindus, exists. The women participate in domestic, agricultural and animal husbandry duties, social rituals and ceremonies but lack a role in the mechanism of social control and in Islamic assemblies. They however enjoy freedom on domestic decision-making matters. The women on the whole have a low status.

The Sunhaks observe major life-cycle rituals as per the Islamic tenets. On the birth of male child *azan* is uttered in his ear. Post-natal restrictions on woman are observed and she remains impure for 40 days after which the pollution is over. Some have started celebrating *chhati* of the male child at present and disribute sweets on the day. Christening and cereal-taking are not ceremonised but the Maulvi suggests the name. Circumcision of the male child before eighth year of age is called *sunnat* and is the major ritual performed by a Faqir or Abdal. Presently, a doctor may also perform circumcision. They arrange a big feast on this day.

Karmai is the first ritual when marriage is contracted. Oil and turmeric ceremony (*batna* and *mehndi*) like Hindus are observed on the marriage day. The *niqah* is the major ritual when the *maulvi* takes *kaul-karar* of the boy and girl three times to approve the marriage amidst all relatives and friends. A feast is given by the bride's parents to the groom's party and the latter reciprocate the same at the bridegroom's place. The *muklawa* of the bride occurs on the third day of the marriage.

The death rituals are typical of the Islamic prescriptions. The dead body is thoroughly cleaned before it is buried. The pollution period lasts for 40 days. Ancestor worship is observed on *teyia, sata, dasa, bisa* and *chalia*. On the last day, offerings in terms of clothes and a few utensils are made to a Faqir, and the gathered relatives are served a meal which may be non-vegetarian.

The community at present practises agriculture and rears cattle, sheep and goats. Hunting with the help of the hawks is a practice of the by-gone days.

Until a decade back, they used to keep mules to trade rock salt, slates, *Balh ka gur* (jaggery of Balh) and other goods. Besides agriculture, some are employed in Government-run hydroelectric projects as *beldar*, foremen, electricians, and a few are in military and police as well. Some run petty shops and a few others earn by trading in cattle or sheep and goats. Some have taken up masonry and tailoring as secondary occupations.

The children also assist their parents in agriculture and animal husbandry pursuits in spare time. The links with the market are direct and the market is regular and the dealings are in cash. The community resolves its social and interfamily disputes among themselves through the intervention of the elders. Major social problems are taken up in the Islamic committee constituted by various Muslim communities of the area elected by a voice vote. This committee also apprises the people of the Islamic preachings and rituals. Economic village disputes are taken up to the statutory Gram Panchayat which deals with the welfare and development of the villages.

The Sunhaks have faith in Allah but they also propitiate various village and regional deities like Balak Nath, Guga and Lakhdata, whose shrines are visited yearly during the local and regional fairs. Their sacred specialists (often a *maulvi*) are from the Faqir community, who also acts as a *chela* and cures diseases of supernatural origin. They mainly celebrate Id and Bakrid, and keep *roza*. They also partake in the Hindu festivals like Lohri and Diwali. The community lacks any art, craft and oral traditions of its own. But pahari folktales, folksongs and popular film songs are rejoiced over. Folk songs are sung by the girls and boys seperately on festive occasions and generally by women at marriages. Simple dances are usually performed on marriage or festive occasions by young boys and girls seperately.

The commensal norms of the community exist with Hindus as well. They accept *kachcha* and *pucca* food as well as water from the Brahman, Rajput, Lohar, Khatri and Jat except from the Chamar and Julaha. But the Brahman, Rajput, Khatri, etc. accept *sukka* or *suchi rasoi* from the Sunhaks. Water sources are shared but the Sunhaks would not touch the drinking water pot of the Hindu. Some Hindus may accept *halal* meat from the Sunhaks but the latter do not accept the *jhatka* meat from the Hindus. Putative kinship exists with the Hindus as well.

Their burial ground is separate and located outside the village. Religious shrines of the village and regional deities are common. A Sunhak would not enter into the kitchen of a Hindu. Patron- client relation exists with a *maulvi,* Nai, Chamar and Lohar. The Sunhaks also till land on a contract basis. Cultivator-labour and other symbiotic relationship also exist. Members work as petty shopkeepers or businessmen, Ayurvedic doctor (one), persons in defence services and holding white-collar jobs. Political leadership has evolved at Gram Panchayat level and the Sunhaks now gained considerable influence in the village or local political activities and are also divided on regional/state political lines.

Formal education is generally favoured for boys and partly favourable for girls for social reason. However, only a few boys entered college due to lack of interest and job security and opt for short technical courses. Modern medical treatment is usually taken but indigenous medical and excorcist media are also made use of.

Their attiude towards family planning is becoming favourable and people consider more children as unwanted and a liability though desire for a son still prevails. There is the instance of a person among the Sunhaks having seven daughters but unfortunately his desire of a son is still not fulfilled. Younger people use modern contraceptive methods. Piped water is available these days but its supply is insufficient and irregular and the traditional sources like natural wells or springs and step-wells are still commonly used. General provisions of IRDP (Integratd Rural Development Programme) exist but people are mostly self-employed in agriculture and animal husbandry and some are involved in general merchandise, contractorship, and in other regular employment.

Modern mass media (radio, television) facilities are enjoyed by them and road communication also exists in the village but the post office is a few kilometres away. They burn wood and cowdung cakes as fuel. Some do have bio-gas/*gobar* gas facilities. Rain water is generally the source of irrigation for the crops. They use organic manure and chemical fertilizers regularly. Immunization facilities are availed of. Ration is available through the public distribution system and banking and postal facilities are also availed of for savings.

A.R. Sankhyan

SWANGLA

The Swangla is a scheduled tribe exclusively living in the Pattan valley tract, along the Chandra Bhaga in Lahaul-Spiti district. It is a generic term which includes Brahman and Rajput groups. According to the legend, when Taimur conquered this part of the country, he drove the Buddhists out and occupied the territory, and the people came to be known as Swangla from 'Swanl', the earlier name of the area. N.G.Nag has described them to be mostly immigrnts from Chamba, displaying Mediterranean features. This conjucture can have possible jusification in the light of Chamba being the adjacent district to Lahaul-Spiti. According to yet another theory, these people have originally migrated from Sangla valley in Kinnaur, which was subjected to Tibetan oppression (Negi, 1976)

Presently, the total population of 7162 (according to the 1981 Census figures), resides wholly in this tract of the Lahaul- Spiti. The Swanglas occupy the remote and inaccessible tract along the banks of Chandra Bhaga. Along with the Swangla, the other communities living with them are the Lohar, Sipi and Dagi which are scheduled castes. They live on flat lands or on hill slopes near water channels.

There are two types of languages spoken by the Swanglas. The first is Manchhad or Manchad, which is Tibetan and Hindi mixed, and is spoken by the Brahmans, Rajputs and Swanglas. The other is Chinali which is spoken by the Sipi and the Lohar. Bhoti too is prevalent but is spoken only by the Bodh inhabitants of the valley. Yet another dialect known as Tinan or Tinent is spoken in the Sissu area. It is worth mentioning that the linguistic researches indicate that in earlier times (200 B.C.), the country was inhabited by an aboriginal tribe, in language and perhaps also in stock analogous to the Munda-speaking tribes of Bengal, Bihar and Central India. Hindi is commonly spoken with the people of other communities. The literate use Devanagari and English for written communication.

The Swangla wear the same dress as others do in the valley.

The Swanglas are non-vegetarian, and they take meat of sheep, goat or chicken. The women cook and eat meat. Their staple food consists of wheat, beans, *chapati* and *rongi* and pulses of *masur*. Millet baked bread *chilra* is also commonly taken. A recent trend is their inclination towards eating rice, which is purchased. Salted buttered tea is very popular and is often taken at regular intervals. The intake of non-vegetarian food increases in winters nearly every day. Milk in its actual form is taken by infants only.

The elders take milk in tea and its by-product like curd. Edible roots and tubers which are locally available in the jungles or grown in kitchen garden are also consumed. Fruits are seldom consumed as they are not available. There is a moderate consumption of green vegetables which are grown by almost all the families in their kitchen gardens, besides potato which is widely grown in the area. *Chhang* is consumed almost daily by men. The women also take alcoholic drinks occasionally. This is usually distilled at home but sometimes purchased from the market. The bulk of distillation takes place during marriage and other social ceremonies. The men also smoke *bidi* and hubble-bubble.

Bio-anthropological Report contains biological information on the community.

As mentioned above, Swangla is generic term and is used for Brahman, Rajput and Rana, living in the Pattan valley, the Brahmans are said to have come from Chamba to serve as official and family priests at religious functions in the temples and in the houses of Rana and Thakur. For the reason, the Swangla Brahmans are also called *pandit.* The other communities like Rathi, Hali, Lohar, Sipi and Chanal, though living in the valley, are not yet included in the term Swangla.

The Brahmans occupy the most prestigious postion in the hierarchical order, followed by Rana, and Thakur. The chief function of these groupings is to regulate the marriage alliances, and the basis for differentiation is purely occupational, the Brahman being the priestly class and the Ranas, the Rajputs, ruling class. Besides these groups there are two other groups, the Garu and Mundro which are believed to have come up as a result of Rajput marrying a Bodh and Rajput marrying a girl of socially lower strata.

Endogamy at the class level is prevalent, with everyone marrying within their respective classes. Marriage outside one's own social class is not recognized, and all such persons are ostracized. Hypergamy is not recognized. Children of hypergamous union are known as Mundro, and Garu, those marrying outside the social class lose their original Swangla status. Marriage with father's sister's daughter, mother's sister's daugher and mother's brother's daughter is prohibited. Marriage is also prohibited within three degrees of relationship both on the father's and mother's side. Junior sororate and levirate are also practised in some of the cases.

Earlier the girl was usually older than the boy. The boys were generally married at the age of 15, whereas the girls were between 20-25 years. However, there is now a reverse trend, with the boys getting married at 18 and the girls at 16.

There are various modes of acquiring mates among the Swanglas, out of which marriage by exchange existed in families of poor economic resources. Marriage by elopement, *rusa-te-byah,* exists where the boy and girl fall in love with each other. *Kua-byah* (marriage by capture) is also pracised when the boy develops a liking for a married or unmarried girl, but the husband or parents are unwilling. The boy forcibly picks up the girl with the help of his friends and brings her to his house. *Mazmi byah* (*ad hoc* marriage) is a typical form of marriage, in which if the boy is unable to bear the marriage expenditure, sends his sister to bring the girl, and starts living with her. The actual marriage is solemnized when they boy is able to bear the marriage expenses.

Fraternal polyandry was the usual practice of marriage, with the modification that one wife cannot be shared by more than three brothers. In the event of there being more than three brothers, the fourth and subsequent brothers within the family get another wife for themselves. But recently polyandry is giving way to monogamy among the educated. Polygyny, is not completely absent. A husband, within the lifetime of his wife can marry again, in the event of the barrenness of the first wife. Both junior levirate and sororate are practised.

Chheti was prevalent in the community, wherein a certain amount of money is given to the bride and deposited in her name. But this is now not given and nothing is being demanded or paid.

Among the Swanglas, the rules of residence are usually patrilocal, but recently there is tendency of setting up neo- local residence. In some of the case where there is no male issue in the family, a son-in-law is invited to look after the property.

Tsud-thvagchi (divorce), a distorted form of the Bhoti word *thagchod-pa*, is permitted. It takes place with social approval. The couple holds a thin thread that signifies the breaking of matrimonial bonds. The common grounds for divorce are strained relations, change of religion by either of the spouses and mutual consent. In the event of divorce, due to infidelity of the wife and her subsequent remarriage, the *izzat* money is to be paid back, to her earlier husband by her paramour. The bride-price in the even of divorce is known as *izzat*. Either of the party can seek a divorce. In the event of divorce, the primary responsibility of bringing up the children rests with the father, but in the event of the children being very young, the child may accompany the mother. Remarriage of widow, widower and divorcee are permitted.

As polyandry was the prevalent form of marriage, polyandrous families existed in order to prevent the fragmentation of land. But today, with the youth getting educated, and with diversified field of occupation, nuclear families are becoming more popular.

All the members of the family live together and have certain kinship bonds that keeps them together. Joking relationship exists freely. Avoidance relationship also exists between the daughter-in-law and father-in-law. The daughter-in-law always hides her face whenever she is front of the father-in-law. This is mark of respect for the elders.The children have love and respect for their biological and sociological fathers.

The property is inherited in the male line with all the sons inheriting the faher's property equally. This is known as the law of *pagwand*. In case a person dies issueless, his wife inherits the property for the lifetime. In the event of there being no widow or male issue, the property is inherited by the daughters. If the daughter does not want to come back to her parents, the property passes on the next collaterals. A step-son succeeds his natural father and has no right to succeed his stepfather. A stepfather cannot assign any share of ancestral property except for his self-acquired property to his stepson. The eldest son succeeds his father as head of family, and after the death of the father, he takes all important decisions in the family affairs.

The role of a woman in the Swangla society is very important. She carries out all the economic activities in the agricultural fields. She even ploughs, weeds and harvests the crop. She collects fodder not only for the immediate use of the cattle, but also stacks it for use in winters. Similarly she collects fuel, both for immediate use and also for winters. She also takes part all socioreligious, and social festivals. Though she takes part in political activities, it is limited only to casting of votes. Her role in the family management is also very important, for she is also responsible for the cooking of meals, bringing up the youngsters and carrying on other household chores. She also grows vegetables in the kitchen garden. Though she is all-round incharge of the family, and does all the work, and makes direct contribution to the family income, reserves the right to control family expenditure.

A son is preferred to a daughter especially if it happens to be the birth of the first child. Pre-natal restrictions are observed by the expectant mother. She is not allowed to lift heavy loads, after five months. She is also not allowed to go in the open during solar or lunar eclipse. Post-natal restrictions and observance of pollution is reported for 20 days. Six months after birth, *chhati* is celebrated. This is also known as *annaprashana* ceremony, wherein the child is fed with cereal food for the first time. On completion of one year, the *kratricti* or *kramog* (tonsure) ceremony is observed. This is normally done in the house by either the mother's brother or the mother's father. *Nanched* (puberty rites) are observed for females among the Swanglas. The onset of the menses is the sign of attaining puberty among the Swangla females. She is secluded for five days, and is not allowed to come near the hearth. On the last day the house is cleaned, and the girl given a bath, and then she is allowed to enter the kitchen.

The marriage rituals are performed at the bride's place. In a polyandrous marriage, all brothers dress up in ceremonial attire and proceed in a marriage procession to the bride's house. Except for the elder brother, all other brothers return from mid-way. On the eldest brother's reaching the girl's house he is invited for a feast and a drink. The bride's elder brother applies a mark on the forehead of the bride and the groom. With this the marriage ceremony ends. On return of the bride to the groom's place, she becomes a common wife of all the brothers. The nuptial ceremony is performed in the groom's house.

The dead are cremated, with the death rites being performed by the eldest male member in the house. The unburnt portion of bones and ashes are immersed in the river. The period of pollution is observed for 13 days, when purificatory rites are observed. A widow puts on the deceased husband's clothes for eight days, which are the main days of mourning.

The major economic resources of the community have been and are land and agriculture. The land is jointly held by the family, in order to avoid fragmentation. Even though there is a trend towards monogamy, still land is not getting divided. Presently the Swanglas instead of devoting more land to the production of cereal crops, devotes it to the production of cash crops like potato and hops. But as the produce does not suffice for the year, they have to supplement their income by doing other jobs like working as labourers, or in business (tea shops), small trading and other available jobs.

The cereal crop produce is barely sufficient for self-consumption. The cash crops potato and hops which are widely grown, do find a market outside the valley through local cooperative society on partly deferred payment. They either purchase commodities of their daily use directly from the local shops or for the entire year from *mandi,* through cooperative members on cash payment which they receive from the sale proceeds of cash crops.

Children below the age of 15 years render a helping hand to the family. The boys assist the parents in agricultural operations and in tending the cattle, whereas girls assist in agriculture and household activities. Since the working season in the valley is limited, they have symbiotic relationship with other as far as economic activity is concerned.

For the maintenance of social norms in the community, the Swanglas have a traditional council of their own headed by a *Sehna* (chief) and assisted by four other elected members by a voice vote. The office of the *Sehna* is not hereditary. His nomination depends on his ability to impart justice impartially, and of course, the age and his social position are the other contributory factors in his election to this office. The cases that come up before it usually relate to divorce, petty quarrels and thefts or breach of community rules. The decision given by the *Sehna* in consulation with the members is final and is binding on all. Sometimes fines in cash or kind are levied on the offender, and the money is utilized towards defraying the expenditure on the panchayat. Though after independence, statutory panchayats have come up for the maintenance of law order and for planning welfare activites still people prefer their traditional panchayat in sorting the disputes.

The community professes Hinduism though some of them also have converted to Buddhism. Those professing the Buddhist faith belong to the

Gelugpa sect. Those professing Hinduism propitiate their dead ancestors as their family deities, and their blessings are invoked on all family festivals for the well-being of the members. They have a separate room in their house for the memory of their ancstors, called *man* and make pictures on wall stones of *man* in the memory of their ancestors. They also have a village god who is represented by Nag Deota (serpent deity). They also worship gods and goddess of the wider Hindu pantheon. In the valley there are two temples, one at Triloknath, and the other at Markula at Udaipur, which are worshipped by all the Swanglas. The Brahmans (Swangla) also perform sacredotal services in the temple and family rituals. They also believe in ghosts and evil spirits. To ward them off they go to Sippis who act as exorcists.

The major sacred centre of the Swanglas is Manimahesh in Bharmaur tehsil of the adjoining Chamba district, across the Kugti Pass. The major fair is the Triloknath fair celebrated by them in the month of August-September. According to Buddhist doctrine none can make a sacrifice of animals to please any Buddhist deity. The other festivals are almost the same as are observed in other parts of the country like Holi, Diwali, Janamashtami, Navratri, Shivratri, Ramnavmi and Dussehra which have a socio-religious significance. Those converted to Buddhism observe both Hindu and Buddhist rituals, with the only difference of *lama* officiating in place of the *pandit.*

The community share the regional oral traditions. The women sing folksongs and dance at social or festive occasions.

The different communities of the Swangla valley have traditional intercommunity linkages. The Sipi, Lohar, Dagi and Chanal render their specialized services to their clients and in return they get a fixed quantity of foodgrains at harvest time.

A Swangla Brahman would accept only *pucca* food and water from a Rajput or Rana. The Lohar and Chanal can accept both *kachcha* and *pucca* food from the hands of a Brahman and Rajput. The Brahman and the Rajput would traditionally not eat *kacchcha* or *pucca* food cooked in the house of Garu or Mundro, except the food cooked by a Brahman. The concept of *sidha* food does not exist. While smoking the *hukka*, the Brahman and the Rajput can share the same pipe. But while sharing with a Chanal or Sipi, the nipple is removed. The system of ceremonial kin exists, known as *mitr-bhai.* He is expected to behave in the same manner as a real kin. All the members living in the village have access to common water resources, roads, schools, crematorium, temple, houses and Panchayat Ghar. People now are holding jobs in occupations like business, administration and other white-collar professions.

Among the various develpment plans, they avail themselves facilities of free education, books and stationery, scholarships and uniform. Today there is no family in the valley which does not send its children to school. There is one primary school in the village. The girls drop out after primary education for want of further educational facilities nearby. The boys however go for higher education outside the district. There are dropouts as they have to carry out all the economic activity in the limited working season.

Their attiude towards allopathic medicines and health care is favourable. In the event of illness, ayurvedic medicines are tried after allopathic medicines, the last resort being health centres. The attitude of the younger generation is favourable towards family planning, but the people are hesitant about sterilization, and they resort to other methods of family planning.

Drinking water through natural streams is available. In winters, when the streams are frozen, ice is melted to make water. With the reservation policy of the Government many have got jobs through the reserved quota. A few of them have also been benefited by the Integrated Rural Development Programme scheme and secured loans for animal husbandry and for setting up shops.

The people listen to transistors and watch films shown through extension agencies or in the private video parlours. Roads do not exist in most of the villages. Post office facilities are available at some distance. There is no electricity in the whole of the valley. Firewood and kerosene are the usual fuel sources. Irrigation of the fields and kitchen gardens is by perennial snowfed streams. Generally the people use only organic manure for crops, but for potato they use a hybrid variety of seeds and chemical fertilizers. The mid-day meal scheme for the school-going children is availed of, wherein nutritional food is made available to children in the 0-5 age groups and nursing and expectant mothers under the Integrated Child Development Scheme. The facility for food and ration is available at Government depots, where it is provided at subsidized rates.

Rajendra Sarkar

TELI

The Teli is an occupational group, consisting of both Hindus and Muslims. Muslims Telis are larger in number and were studied at Chamba, where they are listed as the scheduled caste. The combined population of the two groups of the Telis was 3,768 in Himachal Pradesh according to1981 census. The history relating to their origin and migration is not known. nor do the informants remember anything about it. The Telis are scattered practically in all the districts of the State. In the study area, i.e., Chamba distict, they speak Chambiali—a dialect spoken in Chamba district while in other disticts other local dialects are spoken. The script used is Perso-Arabic which is the script of the whole region. Those who are literate can read or write in Hindi (Devanagari). They share regional dress pattern.

The Telis are non-vegetarian. Eating of pork is taboo. Their staple diet consists of *chapati* of maize or wheat, rice, *mah* along with moderate consumption of vegetables, roots and tubers which are usually cooked in mustard oil. Locally grown fruits are also taken seasonally. Taking of alcoholic drinks is widesprad among the men. These drinks are sometimes locally brewed but mostly purchased from the market. Smoking *bidi* and *hukka* is also quite popular among the men. Chewing of *pan* is not so common but tobacco and betelnut are chewed by both men and women alike. Tea is most commonly taken.

They are mostly Sheikh and Pathan. Intermarriage among other groups of Muslims can take place but the Sayyad Muslims would not marry their daugthers with the Telis. The Sayyad can, however, take a daughter from them in marriage. As per the version of the local people, the Telis were originally Hindus but some were later converted to Islam. Some of the practices also speak of their Hindu origin. For instance, unlike Muslims, they refrain from parallel-cousin marriage. Marriage can take place with father's sister's children and mother's brother's children but not with mother's sister's children.

The marriages are settled through negotiation and offer of marriage must necessarily come from the boy's side. Exchange marriage can also take place. When the marriage is settled, the amount of *mehar* to be paid to the wife is also settled. The amount is normally paid to the wife in the event of the dissolution of marriage. This amount can vary from person to person depending upon the social status of the family. Dowry in the form of clothes and jewellery and items of domestic use is also given to the daugher at the time of marriage. Both divorce and remarriage of widow and widower are allowed. As per the Law of Islam, a man can marry four times, provided he has the consent of the first wife. But in practice this is not so and monogamy largely prevails. Divorce can be sought on grounds of adultery, mental sickness, practice of witchcraft and sorcery and cruelty. A widow can marry her husband's younger brother but can also marry outside her husband's family if she so wishes. A man can also take his wife's younger sister after her death. In the event of divorce, the amount of *mehar* is to be paid to the wife and then only the formalities of divorce can be completed. If a widow marries outside the family, she does not get a share in her husband's property, but her offsprings from the first marriage are entitled to a share from their father's property.

Joint families still hold good among the Telis, but nuclear families are also coming up gradually due to rifts arising out of the paucity of space, unequal division of labour in the extended household and also the unequal earnings of the individual members within a household. Purdah is observed by women in the presence of their father-in-law and husband's elder brothers and other male relatives elder to the husband, but with the younger ones and peer group members joking relationship exists. The eldest male member is the head of the household, but the authority and respect the members of the older generation wielded in the past is gradually declining.

Inheritance of property and succession is in the male line. The sons get an equal share in father's property. Nevertheless,a son who looks after the aged parents is likely to receive some extra share. In the absence of a male issue a daughter may inherit the same.

The women do not enjoy the same socioeconomic status as the men. Economically also they are dependent on men. The women take part in agricultural operations but they refrain from working in others' field. They take active part in rituals and festivals. Socially and politically they are not aware of their rights.

The life-cycle rituals are broadly the same as observed by other Muslim communities but the regional influence is profound. After birth a number of ceremonies are held from time to time. As soon as the child is born, a knowledgeable person from among the *biradari* or a *maulvi* is called to whisper the sacred lines from the holy Quran in the child's ears. The child and the mother are given their first purificatory bath on the fifth and subsequently on tenth, twenty-first and fortieth day. Thereafter, she and the child are free from all impurities. The first feeding of cereal food to the child is held at the age of six months and is locally known as *khirpo*. The child is given some rice pudding to gradually initiate him to a cereal diet. The first shaving of the head is known as *jattu* and is normally performed for boys.

Marriage, known as *nikah,* is performed as per Muslim rites. Prior to marriage the most important ceremony is *mehndi* which is performed on both the sides, in which henna is applied to both the bride and the bridegroom by their sisters and sister-in-law. Marriage songs are sung on this occasion and the sister-in-law and sisters are suitably rewarded. The actual marriage ceremony takes place at the bride's rsidence and a *maulvi* presides over it. The *nikahnama* mentioning the amount of *mehar* is read out and the marriage is solemnized.

Death rites are also observed as per Muslim religious practices. They bury their dead. On the seventh day, known as *sata*, clothes and certain personal belongings of the dead are distributed to the poor. The mourning period lasts for 40 days, during which simple food is cooked. When the husband dies, the widow does not go out of the house for three months and 10 days. This is known as *iddat*. After a year, the *maulvi* is called to read the holy text for the peace of the dead.

The Telis are an occupational caste of oil pressers but nowadays, most of them practise agriculture and also cultivate the land of others on sharecrop basis or on payment of wages. Some have also gone out and taken up jobs in order to supplement their earnings. Some, however, still continue their age-old traditional calling and side by side supplement it with other part-time or full-time occupations like service, labour and business.

The Telis earlier had the *jajmani* relationship with other castes, but gradually such relations are being replaced by modern economic relations based on the principle of *quid pro quo*. The traditional *jajmani* system persists with the Nai and the Dhobi. There is a town market for the supply of goods. There are few permanent shops in the village which cater to the daily requirements of the people.

The Telis have their own *biradari* councils which take up the issues of divorce and compensation claims, and also deal with cases of elopement, adultery, rape and petty theft. In case a settlement is not reached, the party can approach the courts of law. Generally efforts are to sort their problems within themselves, but if the matter goes beyond, other alternatives are resorted to. The nature of punishment is usually in the form of a feast given to the *biradari*.

The Telis follow the Muslims religious beliefs and practices and have faith in Pirs and *mazar* and every Pir has his special day in a week. They propitiate them by lighting an earthen lamp, *chirag*. It would be interesing to mention that the Telis, though Musllim by faith, also take part in certain Hindu festivals like the famous Minjar Yatra. Also, the nomenclature used for many of their life-cycle rituals is the same as used by the local Hindu population.

The women do the famous Chamba embroidery the speciality of which lies in the fact that the stitches look just the same on the reverse side also. Besides, they have a rich heritage of music, folk songs and dance which they share regionally.

The traditional obligatory nature of relationships is gradually giving way to modern economic relationships. However on secular occasions both Hindus and Muslims participate together.

The Telis belong to the scheduled caste category and therefore get the facility of loans and subsidy from the State Government. Many of them are benefited by these welfare programmes.

The facilities of electricity, water transport and communication system exists. The people express their satisfaction at the infrastructural changes which have considerably changed the lifestyle. In matters of education, their children get freeships.

Primary health centres exist in most of the villages. But less equipped with medical and paramedical staff and dispensaries. The overall growth and development of Chamba district has not been up to the mark and the requisite avenues in respect of business and trade are lesser. As such people choose to go out in search of jobs and better economic prospects.

Vatsala Sarkar

THATHIAR

The Thathiar or Thathera is an occupational community of traditional vessel makers. Rose (1919) suggested that a Kasera is one who makes the vessels and a Thathera sells them. But the vessel makers in Kangra (study area) are known by the name Thathera and the distinction between a Kasera and Thathera does not exist. They make vessels mainly of brass, bronze and copper but sometimes also of iron.

The term Kasera is probably derived from *kansa* meaning bronze. The Kasera is a homogeneous caste, an offshoot of the higher mercantile caste, separated from the parental group by adopting a special profession (Crooke, 1896). They trace their ancestry from the hundred-armed Arjuna *sahastraarjuna* among the Kshatriyas.

The hill Kaseras, according to Crooke (1896) , are represented by Tamota or Tamta—a Dom caste. But the Thathera in Kangra denied their ancestry from such a caste and they distinguish many Khatri clans and are both Hindu and Sikhs. They, however, are not aware of their legendary origins and have migrated from the adjoining areas of Punjab, Haryana and Jammu.

The population of the Thatheras in Himachal Pradesh is 709 according to 1981 Census of India and the community is classified among the scheduled castes. The community in the study area is mostly Punjabi. They write both in Devanagari and Gurumukhi scripts and speak Hindi and Punjabi. The area is a valley in the Himalayan foothills with a warm and temperate climate in general and medium annual rainfall and low humidity.

They are identified only by their typical occupation and not by dress or ornaments. Men normally wear a *kurta* and a *tamba* and the Sikh Thatheras wear a *pagri*. The women wear *kurta* and *salwar* and a *chunni*.

The Thatheras share the food habits of the area. The major staple food is wheat and maize and supplemented by rice. The various types of pulses—*urad, moong, masur, kulthi*, peas and beans, *rajmah*, and grams are eaten along with different vegetables like cabbage, cauliflower, lady finger, brinjal, gourds, *tori* and *karela*. The cooking medium used is vegetable *ghee* or mustard or groundnut oil. Their festive foods are *kheer* and *halwa, puri,* fried wheat preparation, *kachauri* and *khichri*. Mustard *sag* is eaten with maize *roti*. Milk and milk products—*lassi*, tea, coffee and fruit juices are frequently consumed. They are occasional non-vegetarians in food habit and eat eggs, fish and meat including pork.

Alcohol puchased from the local market is also consumed frequently by men especially on marriage or other festive occasions. Men (Hindus) smoke *bidi*/cigarette and/or loose tobacco in an indigenous *hukka*. Betel chewing habit is individualistic and not a community trait.

They constitute two main religious groups, Hindus and Sikhs, but lack any hierarchical stratification or distinction. The community is divided into different exogamous *got/gotra*, viz. Wadhavan, Mehta, Uppal, Chadda, Anand and Varma. These clans denote ancestry and regulate matrimonial alliances among themselves. Usually clan names are suffixed as surnames. In the varna system they place themselves among the Kshatriyas and this social position is not denied by other communities.

Marriages take place by the rule of community endogamy. Usually the Sikh group marries within itself, but Hindu-Sikh marriages do occur. Clan exogamy is strictly adhered to but they may marry in the same village if suitable mates are available. Marriages occur through negotiation in adulthood. Monogamy is practised. Marriage symbols are *sindur* or *bindi*, bangles and nose and ear pins. The bride's parents observe *kanyadan* and dowry in the form of domestic items, clothes and ornaments is given. The bride lives patrilocally.

Divorce is not approved socially, but on grounds of maladjustments either of the spouses can seek judicial approval. Compensation is paid to the wife and the father bears the liability of the children. Both the divorcees can marry again. But if the woman remarries, she does not get further maintenance expenditure. Widow remarriages are not socially approved, but if a young childless widow wants to remarry, the community does not stop her from doing so. The man can remarry a junior sororate or any other woman. The main changes in the institution of marriage are an increase in age at marriage and giving of more dowry.

The family pattern is mainly nuclear. Married sons, when employed, establish a separate household. Avoidance relationship is maintained with elder persons only. The *nuh* or *bahuti* covers her face slightly from her *saurah* and *jeth*. Joking is allowed between *jija* and *sali*, *devar* and *bhabi*, *jija* and *sala* and *nanad* and *bhabhi*.

Conflicts may arise at times on property matters and on division of labour in the family. The ancestral property is inherited in male lines by all the sons equally. Legally, the daughters also have a right to the father's property but they usually forego the same in favour of their brothers. After the father's death, the eldest son becomes his successor.

The status of women is usually low even though they participate and assist men in their vessel-making work. They do all the domestic jobs, bring potable water, participate in social and religious ceremonies and regulate family expenditure. They however, have little role in decision-making, political sphere and social control mechanism.

The life-cycle rituals are observed as per the Hindu and Sikh tenets in the two sections of the community. Pre-delivery and post-delivery restrictions exist on a woman. Birth pollution called *sutak* lasts for 13 days. The birth of the son is celebrated by distribution of sweets and singing songs by the ladies.

A name may be given by consulting a Brahman priest as per the zodiac sign in the horoscope of the child. Cereal-taking ceremony is often ignored. *Mundan* of the boy (in Hindus) is performed by the *mama* of the child or by a barber and a feast may be given to friends. The wearing of *janeu* occurs only at marriage.

Marriage rituals are observed as per the Sanatana/Arya Samaj prescriptions among the Hindus and by *anand karaj* as per the Guru Granth Sahib among the Sikhs. *Sagai, thahaka* and ring ceremony are pre-marriage rituals for both the Hindus and the Sikhs. *Haldi, mehndi* and oil ceremonies take place on the day of the marriage. The Arya Samajis perform major rituals at a temple but the Sanatanis perform the *vedic* rites (through a Brahman priest), *lagan* and *ved*, at the bride's place when the bride and groom circumambulate the sacred fire.

Finally, *kanyadan* is performed by the bride's parents who also arrange a feast for the groom's party. After the departure of the *barat*, the younger sister/friend of the bride reads out the *sehra* (written or printed matter on a calendar paper) in which a brief and affectionate description of the bride is printed and instructions are given to the bridegroom to take proper care of the bride. The mother-in-law does *arti* of the bride and the door is worshipped by the bride before she enters into bridegroom's house. The groom's parents also arrange a feast. The *gauna* or *muklawa* follows soon after the marriage.

The death rites of the Thathiars are similar to those among the other Hindu and Sikh communities. The dead are cremated and the ashes are immersed in the Ganges at Haridwar or in the Beas in Kangra and *pind dan* is given to a Panda or to a Bharara at Kaleshwar in Kangra. *Uthala* occurs on the fourth day but death pollution called *patak* lasts for 13 days when *kirya* and *rasam pagri* is performed by an Acharaj and ancestor worship is observed. The Acharaj gets *dan* in cash and *dhoti*. The Arya Samajis usually perform a *havan* on the fourth day and meals and clothes are offered to the poor. *Barsi* is also observed and a ceremonial feast is given to relatives and friends in the name of the dead.

The Thathiars are mostly landless and subsist on its traditional occupational of vessel-making. They make different types of brass pots for domestic consumption like *gagar, patila, purat, baltoi,* plates, buckets etc. They usually work on contract basis for an industrialist who supplies the raw material and purchases the articles. Each adult member usually earns about Rs. 1,000 per month through this work. Some persons are also industrial labourers on fixed wages and other are in Government service in different cadres. The market is of daily nature and fully regulated and the dealings are in cash. Child labour also exists in terms of assisting their parents in their occupation.

The *sayane* of the community often solve their community disputes but there is no formal council. Legal course may also be adopted in disputes beyond the control of the elders of the community. The Hindu Thathiars propitiate various family/clan and local deities, like Baba Achlechar, Vishva karma and Kartik Rishi in particular. The Sikh group worships at Gurudwara Kandh Sahib at marriages besides other Sikh Gurus. Kali and Brajweshwari Devi are of special reverence to both Hindus and Sikhs besides other regional deities like Jawalamukhi.

The Thathiars celebrate various Hindu festivals and Sikh Guruparabs. On Diwali night, they observe fast and worship their tools. Naumi fair and Babe Lal fair at Batala (Punjab) are attended with great zeal. They share various regional or Punjabi folk oral traditions—songs and tales—like *Heer Ranja, Sohni-Mahwal* and *Sasi-Punnu. Bhangra* and *gidda* are favourite dances and *dhol* is a common mucial instrument. Metal work is their traditional craft-cum-occupation.

Modern development programmes have made a little impact on the community. Formal education is favoured but not for girls. The boys also do not normally go in for college education. Reasons for this are both economic and social. The children are supposed to take part in the traditional occupation of metal work and girls are considered a social liability and the sooner they are married, the better it is.

They favour both modern as well as indigenous health and medicare methods. In this respect they are guided more by the availability and accessibility of the facilities within their means and not by the choice of a traditional or modern method. Due to economic compulsions they favour family planning measures and modern sterilization methods are adopted. Socially, however, they desire at least one son as a heir and working hand.

Drinking water is available in the locality through pipelines. They enjoy modern mass media (radio and television) facilities and also visit the cinema. Road and railway connections are also available. Postal and telegraphic facilities are within their reach. Their energy sources are firewood, cowdung cakes, coal, sawdust and kerosene oil. Under the ICDS only immunization is used. The people are quite careful about savings and are not dependent on the local moneylenders or shopkeepers.

A.R. Sankhyan

THAVI

The Thavi is a lesser known and smaller community. They are also identified as Thawin, Raj and Mistri at the regional level. The etymology of the community name is derived from the local word *than,* meaning 'place' or 'shelter' as they construct buildings or houses and temples. They are stone workers and masons of the country and known for preparing various household articles of stone (sandstone), namely pestle-mortar, grinding wheel, grinding bolsters, and *chakla-belan* (plate and roller).

The Thavis trace their origin from the Kshatriya Rajputs and locally like to be identified as Rajput rather than as Thavi/Thawin, as the latter name distances them from the Rajput-fold and points to an inferior social position. In the study area in Nalagarh tehsil of Solan district, they recall their migration from the Jammu area. They say that the Hindur Raja brought them here to construct palace and temples. They are also distributed in Solan, Bilaspur, Kangra, Mandi and Kullu districts.

They live in the hilly terrain with warm and temperate or cold climate and low humidity; the hill ranges are covered with bushes and a thin canopy of forest and receive moderate rainfall. They speak regional dialects, like Hinduri (in Nalagarh) a dialect of the western Pahari. They write in Devanagari script both within and outside the community.

They share the food habits of the region. The major staple food is maize in the winters supplemented with rice and wheat in the summer months. The various types of pulses—*urad, moong, kulthi, masur, moth, tur,* peas and bean and grams, are eaten along with seasonal vegetables, roots and tubers. The cooking medium is mustard oil or vegetable or *desi ghee.* They are non-vegetarians but meat, fish and eggs are eaten though less frequently. They consume country liquor, occasionally. Milk and its products find a place in their daily diet. Their fruit intake is occasional and seasonal like mango, apple, peach and guava. Their festive foods are meat, *kheer, halwa, babru, bhalle, seviyan, ankli* and *ankloo*. Non-vegetarian foods are not consumed during death pollution when the family members do not prepare food for themselves, but the married daughters cook meals.

The Thavis have small *gots* or clans which are similar to those of the Rajputs. The clans recorded in the field are Ranaut, Ludu, Kaundal, Tanghwai, Bhatti, Gunsain, Chandel, Chauhan, Patial, Katoch and Bhanot. The clans denote their ancestry or descent and are used for regulating matrimonial alliances. The clan names are also sometimes suffixed as surnames. The position of the Thavis among Rajputs is however, quite low and equivalent to that of the Kanets because they practise junior levirate and *karewa* (widow remarriages).

The marriages occur by the rules of community endogamy, and *got* and village exogamy. Marriages occur through negotiation and exchange of sisters. A few decades back child marriage was a common practice along with bride price. But, presently the girls are married when they are above16 years and the boys after 20. Bride price has also given way to *dharam punya* marriages without bride price, but *daj dan* is given in the form of household articles, clothes and utensils. Monogamy is practised but a second wife may be acquired and allowed socially in case of no issue from the first wife. The marriage symbols strictly observed are *sindur*, glass bangles, *tili/nath*, *koka* and ear-rings.

The couple live patrilocally. The widow or widower may marry a junior levirate or junior sororate. But, man can marry in other families than that of his wife as well. Divorce is socially disliked but it may occur through judicial approval on grounds of maladjustments, cruelty or adultery. Compensation is usually given to the wife but if the wife divorces and marries another man she gets no compensation or has to refund the bride price (in case it was taken). The children are the liability of father in case of a divorce. A few changes have occurred in the institution of marriage, namely an increase in the marriage age, decline of bride price and advent of dowry system and legislation of divorce rules.

The family pattern of the Thavis is both nuclear as well as vertically extended joint type. The sons usually do not get separated as long as the father is alive or all the sons are married. The junior members are obliged to pay respect to the elders by touching their feet. Avoidance relationship is strong. The *lari* or *bahu* covers face in the presence of her *saurah, jeth, nandoi* and elderly men of the village. Joking is permitted between *devar* and *bhabi, jija* and *sali, jija-sala,* and *nanad* and *bhabi.*

Property matters and other social situations in the family like some bitterness in the *sas-bahu* and *nanad-bhabi* relationships may create conflicts in the family. Also, unequal earning or participation in family or household duties by sons leads to the breaking up of the families. Inheritance of paternal property, is however, on male lines and as per the rule of equigeniture and daughters inherit only if they have no brothers. The eldest son becomes the successor of his father.

The status of the Thavi women remains low even though they do all type of domestic, agricultural and animal husbandry duties. They collect fuel and fodder, fetch potable water and participate in various religious and social ceremonies. They however have little say in the mechanism of social control and the political sphere and also do not contribute to the family income, but regulate family expenditure and have some influcence in decision-making in social matters.

The life-cycle rituals of the Thavis are performed by a Brahman priest as per Hindu Santana tenets. Pre-delivery restrictions on the expecting mother are imposed. The first delivery usually occurs at her parental home. The woman is confined to an interior dark room or corner of the house on the lower storey. The *sutak* lasts for 40 days but purification ceremony occurs on thirteenth day by taking bath and cow's urine called *guntral*a. The birth of the first son is celebrated by singing songs and distributing sweetened germinated grams. On christening and cereal-taking ceremonies sweet meals may be offered to young children. *Jatlu* or *mundan* ritual is the major childhood ritual performed by the child's *mama* on any odd year before three years of age. The clan deity is propitiated and the family priest performs *havan* or *puja* and is given some alms. *Janeu* is put on the day of the marriage only. Puberty rites for girls include ear and nose piercing but without any ritual.

The pre-marriage rituals are *karmai* or *sagai*. The *sand* and *samuhat* rituals start one or two days before marriage when the boy/girls confined and are not to cross a stream. Both a Nai and a Brahman *purohit* play an active role in performing their respective duties. The family propitiates its *kuldevta* and worships a *sill* (stone bolster) and *batta* (grinding stone). The oil ceremony is observed during which the mother's parents offer clothes to the bridegroom. The actual marriage rituals are *lagan* and *ved* performed at the bride's place when the bride and groom circumambulate the sacred and take oath for an ideal conjugal living.

The bride's parents perform *sankala*p or *kanyadan* and offer *daj dan* to the daughter. They arrange a feast for the groom's party and relatives and friends. At the bridegroom's place, the major ritual is tree worship of a *pipal* or *khair* (*Acacia catechu*). The marriage ends with music and dance. The bride returns to her parents the same day followed by the bridegroom in the evening. On the next day the groom brings the bride back and the marriage is consummated. The *lari* does not live with her *sas* during the first Bhadon month of her marriage as this month is considered inauspicious.

Their death rituals are also performed as per the Sanatana beliefs. The dead are cremated and the ashes are collected on the third day and immersed in the Ganges at Hardwar or at Patalpuri near Kiratpur in Punjab. The sons shave off their head. The eldest son performs *pind dan*. Ancestor worship is observed and the Acharaj performs *kirya karam* on the thirteenth day. The family priest performs the purification *havan* which marks the end of the *patak*. The annual *barki* and fourth annual *chabarakh* death rites are also observed. The friends and relatives are given a ceremonial meal. Annual *shradh* is also observed every year to commemorate the ancestors and *roti* is given to the cow and crows.

The Thavis mainly subsist on their traditional occupation of masonry and stone work. Their ancestors were good sculptors and prepared statues and constructed temples. But presently the art of sculpture has been lost and they prepare various objects of sandstone for the domestic use of agricultural communities of the rural areas. They also possess small landholdings and practise agriculture and animal husbandry. The landlessness or insufficient land has led to daily-wage casual labour on roads, forest, dams and building construction. Some are also agricultural labourers or till land on sharecrop or contract basis.

Very few Thavis are in Government jobs or in regular employment. Child labour exists. The market is fully regulated and of daily nature and located at an accessible distance. The dealings are usually in cash terms.

Their social norms are maintained by the *sayanas* of the village or community, or by an informal Biradari Panchayat. The social problems related to marriage and divorce are resolved in this panchayat but the village disputes over land and water are taken to the statutory Gram Panchayat. For serious disputes they also go to the civil courts.

The community follows Hinduism and propitiate gods and goddesses of the pantheon. Hidimba Devi is propitiated as a family or clan deity by some. The village and regional deities of special reverence are Guga, Lakhdata, Balak Nath, Nahar Singh, Naina Devi, Jalpa Devi and Sitla Mata. Their shrines are visited on festive occasions and annual fairs. Various fairs of the area like Sair fair, Baisakhi fair, Peer Than fair, Lohri fair, Chhinj fairs, Sitla Mata fair and Guga and Baba Barbhag Singh fairs, are notable.

Various Hindu festivals of socioreligious and socioeconomic importance like Lohri, Baisakhi, Sair, Rakshabandhan, Navratre, Shivratri, Ramnaumi, Dussehra and Diwali, are celebrated. A few Thavis follow Radhaswami and Nirankari sects and pay visit to the shrines of their patron *gurus*. Oral traditions—folksongs and tales—of the region are shared. Rock art and craft has presently dwindled. They do, however, make objects of stones which are basically for domestic use. *Bhajan* and *kirtan* find a greater place in folk traditions and *dhol* is used in music and dance. Dance is popular during marriages.

The inter-community linkages are differently exhibited with the various communities of the village or area. The exchange of *kachcha* and *pucca* food and water occurs traditionally with the certain communities but not with the Chamar, Julaha and Dumna. From these they may accept a *suchchi rasoi* or a *sukka/sidha*. The water resources are similarly shared. The Thavis, however, cannot smoke from the pipe of a Brahman. The cremation grounds are common. Putative kinship-based friendship may occur with other communities. The temples/religious shrines and other public places are common.

Traditional *jajmani* relationships exists with a Lohar, Chamar, Brahman priest and Nai, and sometimes with a Kumhar as well.

Modern development programmes have made little impact on the community. Formal education is not much favoured for girls but the boys study up to secondary school level though higher education cannot be afforded due to economic reasons. The boys usually adopt masonry as their means of livelihood for which they have not to spend anything. In the sphere of health and medicare, both modern as well as indigenous methods are used. Modern system of medicare is, however, regarded quite as being costly.

The attitude towards family planning is favourable but usually they do not go in for it, though some persons have adopted sterilization. At least one son is desired socially even though more daughters are born in the process. Drinking water is available through pipes as well as the traditional sources like springs and step-wells.

Their houses are electrified and modern mass media (radio & T.V.) facilities are availed by some and accessible in the vicnity. Road communication and postal facilities are at a short distance. The energy sources are firewood and cowdung cakes. The source of irrigation is only rainwater. They use organic manure and fertilizers. Immunization is availed of under ICDS. Public distribution system provides ration at subsidized rates. People generally favour savings and are not dependent on moneylenders.

A.R. Sankhyan

THUANA

The Thuana, locally called as Thohnu, are the Kanets belonging to the Ranot or Ranaut and Kaundal *gotra* of the Rajputs. It is the least known community which is only mentioned as a sept of the Kanet Rajput of Hindur by Rose (1919). Hindur is an old name for present Nalagarh (in Solan district). The community is mostly confined to the northwestern border of Nalagarh adjoining district Bilaspur around Swarghat.

The name 'Thuana' is taken from a village known as Thohan or Thuan and its inhabitants are called Thohnu or Thuanu or Thuana. This village however has at present only five households of these Ranaut/Kaundal Kanets. But probably the community has been popularly named after this section of the Kanets. There are other sections too named after the names of the villages. These are Bhalsagu, Kulahu, Jukhar, Jagarwal, Machyane, Kotwal, Dadhwalu and Nandwal. Among these the Bhalsagus are more in number followed by Kulahu and Tohnu (Thuana).

The Thuanas live easily in the hilly terrain difficult of access. The climate is generally warm but cold in winter with moderate annual rainfall and low humidity. The terrain is covered with a thick cover of bushes and thin forest of pines. They perceive their distribution at the local level in areas bordering Bilaspur and Solan district.

The Thuanas speak the local Hinduri dialect of the Pahari and write in Devanagari script like other people of the area. Identification markers in dress/ornaments are lacking. But older men wear a *kurta* and a *pyjama* and a safa. The younger men wear pants and shirts. The women wear a *kurta* and *salwar* with a *dupatta* or *chadru*. The traditional ornaments were a conical silver chak on head, *murki* or *laung, bali, gajra, har* and *pajeb*.

They share the dietary habits of the region. The common staple food for winters is maize supplemented with rice, whereas wheat and barley are consumed frequently during summers. Various types of pulses—*urad, moong, masur, kulthi, moth*, gram, peas and beans are frequently consumed along with local and seasonal vegetables like lady finger, *tori, lauki, kaddu* (all gourds), brinjal, *karela* and roots and tubers and mustard leaves. The cooking medium used is mustard oil or desi or vegetable *ghee*. Milk and its products find place in the daily diet. Fruits like mango, banana, apple, guava, mulberry and figs are consumed seasonally and moderately.

They consume country or local liquor of sugar molasses occasionally. The men smoke tobacco in an indigeneous pipe called *hukka* or *kali* or smoke *bidi* and occasionally cigarettes. Non-vegetarian foods like meat of sheep and goat are consumed occasionally and/or during festivities. Other festive foods are *halwa, kheer, seviyan, babru, bhalle* and *ankli. Heeng* and non-vegetarian foods are not consumed during death pollution in the family.

The Thuanas identify only *biradaris* or lineages which are treated as exogamous sections of the society. There is no hierarchy in these sections which regulate the matrimonial alliances and denote descent. Some have sectarian discrimination by following a Radhaswami sect but this difference does not create social distinction. In the Rajput hierarchy these Kanets are treated at the lowest position by the Mian community. This is so because they practise widow remarriage. The community is endogamous and rarely marries outside. They also follow the rule of village exogamy.

Marriages are negotiated, and at present post-puberty marriages occur. Earlier, child marriage was prevalent along with the custom of bride-price or exchange of sisters. The exchange marriages still occur but bride-price is not taken or socially regarded as a symbol of poverty, and persons taking bride price are not respected in the society. The Thuanas now adhere to the *kanyadan* marriages of girls and also give *dahej*. Earlier, *dahej* was given to the girl in the form of household and agricultural articles and was regarded as *dan*, but at present it has become a status symbol and a social compulsion particularly among the economically well-off.

Monogamy is the practice though a man can marry another woman in case the first wife is sterile or has not given birth to any male child. The symbols of marriage are *sindur* or *bindi*, glass bangles and nose ornament. The *lari* lives patrilocally in her father-in-law's home. On the death of spouse, widow as well as widower remarriages are socially approved. Widow remarriage which is commonly a junior levirate is called *karewa* or *jhanjara* and is solemnized by a simple ritual called *nath-chadar dalna* in which her husband's younger brother offers her a nose ring and a shawl. A small feast is given to the villagers.

With the advent of literacy, junior levirate marriages are usually not accepted by the youngsters, and a widow (with children) may not remarry. Divorce is socially approved on grounds of maladjustments, witchcraft and sorcery. The divorced woman is paid Rs. 1000 and her ornaments are returned by her husband. But in case bride price was taken, and the woman divorces her husband and marries another man, the latter pays compensation called *reet* to the first husband. This custom was common in the past but has almost died out at present.

They live in vertically extended joint families and the families usually do not break up until all the sons get married or till the father is alive. Avoidance relationship of *lari/bahu* exists with her *saurah, jeth, nandoi* and elderly male members of the village. Joking relations exist between *devar* and *bhabi*, *jija* and *sali, jija* and *sala* and *nanad* and *bhabi*.

Conflicts in family may occur on property matters, unequal division of labour and on prejudiced social attitudes of *sas, nanad* and *bhabhi* towards *bahu*. The paternal property is inherited as per the rule of male equigeniture. On the death of the father, the eldest son becomes his successor. Interfamily relationships are based both on occasional confrontation as well as cooperation in socioeconomic and socioreligious pursuits.

The status of the Thuana women is by and large lower than that of men but for practical purposes they are not less than men socially, religiously and economically. They participate in agriculture and animal husbandry work and are more loaded with work than men. They perform all household chores, collect fuel and fodder, fetch potable water and participate in social and religious ceremonies. They however do not seek money-earning jobs and have little say in the matters of social control and political activities and lack decision-making power in vital matters. They, however, regulate family expenditure.

The life-cycle rituals are observed as per the Sanatana prescriptions. The pre- and post-delivery restrictions on mother exist. The *sutak* is observed for 13 days when the women takes bath and purification occurs by taking cow's urine with the water of Ganges. The birth of a son is celebrated by distributing boiled maize and germinated grams coated with sugar. The ladies of the neighbourhood are invited to sing greeting songs. A virgin's feet are washed and she is offered meals.

The *mama* of the boy offers clothes and *kangnu*. Cereal-taking and christening are not ceremonised. But a name may be given to the boy by consulting a Brahman. The *jamalu* of the boy is the main childhood ritual when the hair is cut by the *mama* or by a barber at the clan deity's (Naina Devi) temple. Some arrange a small feast for young children. Some also perform a *tola* in which the child is weighted in cereal grains and iron pieces, to seek protection from the ill-effects of evil spirits and stars. This *dan* is given to a poor man. Thread-wearing ceremony is performed at the time of marriage.

Karmai or *sagai* are the pre-marriage rituals. The marriage rituals are similar to the those of other Hindu communities of the region and are performed by a Brahman as per the Vedic rites. The major rituals occur at the bride's place are called *ved* and *lagan* when the bride and groom circumambulate the holy fire and take oath for an ideal living. The parents of the bride perform *sankalp/kanyadan*. They arrange a feast for the groom's party. At the groom's place both the bride and groom worship and circumambulate a *khair* (*Acacia catechu*) or *pipal* tree and tie a white thread around it. Putative kinship-based friends are also made at this time. The marriage ends with music and dance. The marriage is consummated after the *muklawa* ritual which presently occurs on the following auspicious day of the marriage. Earlier the *muklawa* used to occur after the girl had attained puberty.

The Thuana death rituals are also similar to those in most of Hindu communties of the area. The dead are cremated and the ashes are immersed in the Ganges at Hardwar by the eldest son who performs the *pind dan* and makes offerings to a Panda. Ancestor worship is observed and the pollution period lasts for 13 days. On the tenth day, called *dashang*, the clothes are washed. On the thirteenth day the *kirya* rite is performed by a Charaj/Acharaj who seeks offerings in the name of the dead. The family Brahman priest performs the purification *havan* and also gets his dues in the form of clothes, utensils and cot. Sixteen invitees from among the married daughters and their husbands (*dhyan and jamai*) are offered a steel/aluminium glass, a *parna* (scarf) and a few coins. The exchange of meals becomes open with other people by offering a ceremonial feast called *solia* on the sixteenth day. The annual and fourth annual death rites called *barkhi* and *chabarakh* respectively are also performed and ceremonial feasts are given to commemorate the dead.

Their traditional as well as present occupation is agriculture and animal husbandry. Horticulture has presently become a secondary occuaption for some. A few persons having small landholdings also till the land of big landlords on cash or half share-cropping basis. Some also seek agriculture, road and forest casual labour on daily-wage basis. Some of them are in permanent jobs in the Government as teachers, junior engineers, peons/ chowkidars and in the army. Some run petty shops and tea stalls. Child labour exists in the community and usually the children assist their parents in agricultural and animal husbandry pursuits. The market is located at a short distance and is of daily nature and provides essential commodities of daily consumption. The dealings of the community in the market are mainly on cash terms. Some also sell out cereals to purchase special items.

The community-specific formal panchayat is lacking but the *sayane* of the multi-ethnic village or of the community usually resolve their social disputes as the nature of the disputes remains fairly similar in different communities of the area. Many socioeconomic or village disputes over land and water are resolved by the statutory Gram Panchayat. The earlier tradition of a headman and punishment by excommunication has almost ended though people may stop taking and giving meals from a particular family on certain personal differences.

The Thuanas are all Hindus and propitiate various deities of the local and the wider pantheon. Naina Devi, also a regional deity, is regarded by many as a family or clan deity. Various local deities like Jalpa Devi, Balak Nath, Lakhdata and Nahar Singh are specially propitiated on the arrival of the crop and festivities. Chintpurni and Kali goddesses are also propitiated by many. Some persons follow the Radhaswami sect and visit its main shrine at Beas in Amritsar district (Punjab). These followers do not observe elaborate life cycle rituals of the Sanatana and also do not propitiate different dieties.

The Thuanas celebrate various national and regional festivals of socio-economic (Baisakhi, Sair, Chiran) and socioreligious importance (Lohri, Rakshabandhan, Shivratri, Diwali, Ramnaumi, Navratre). Various fairs held every year in the area or region are visited, namely, Chhinj fairs of Lakhadata, Markand fair, Sair fair, Barader fair, Naina Devi fair and Jawalamukhi fair. But Guga fairs, quite typical of Bilaspur district, are uncommon in the area. They sing pahari folksongs called Himachali *gane* and share regional folktales and lore, music and dance.

Modern inter-community linkages have developed because of the community members, involvement in various professions like teaching, engineering and military services. Political leadership has emerged at the Gram Panchayat level.

Modern development programmes have made an impact on the community. Formal education is favoured for boys but many still do not go for higher education due to economic reasons and lack of proper guidance, interest and job security. For girls, education up to secondary school level only is favoured due to social, economic and geographical reasons (college are far off). The social attitude towards girl is that they do not have to seek jobs and are to be just married off.

In the sphere of health and medicare both modern and indigenous methods are used. Modern health care facilities are not adquately available in the area. They still believe some diseases to be of supernatural origins and magic-cum-medicine men are consulted for treatment. Their attitude towards family planning is becoming favourable and they usually prefer three children that should include at least one son for continuation of the *vansh* (lineage) and seeking salvation. Sterilization has been adopted as a modern method for restricting the family.

Modern mass media (radio and television) facilities are availed of by some. Road communication is at a few kilometres' distance, and so is the postal facility. Their houses are electrified. Drinking water through pipelines is available in the village but due to inadequate supply, traditional sources like springs and *bauri* are also used. The source of irrigation is usually rainwater.

The fuel resources are traditional firewood and cowdung cakes. ICDS programmes provide immunization to children and the Anganwadis are recently opened. Public distribution system for purchase of essential items on subsidized rates is available in the area. The Thuanas generally favour savings and are not dependent much on village moneylenders.

A.R. Sankhyan

TOORI

The Toori/Turi, the players of a musical trumpet *turi* are also known as Dhaki or Bajgi. They are also known as Dayal in the Kiran area of Chaupal tehsil of Shimla district, where their women are famous for the black magic they perform. They mainly occupy the trans-Giri tract of Sirmaur district but are also scattered in the adjoining Shimla district, where they have adopted a new name, Nai. They also stich the clothes of the people inhabiting the area for which they get *khaltha* (foodgrains) at the time of every harvest. When goats are slaughtered in the month of December by their *yajmans* (in public they serve as tailors), one head of a goat per family is collected by them as part of their *khaltha.* The community is a scheduled caste and according to the 1981 census there are 4,556 Tooris. They speak the language of the area they inhabit. Sirmauri is commonly spoken among themselves, whereas, with others, Hindustani is spoken.

The community is non-vegetarian and they take the meat of goat, fish, chicken and pork. Beef, buffalo and meat of sheep and *minda* (ram) is taboo to them. Their staple food consists of wheat *chapati, kodra, cholai, kangni, chinei* (all millets), rice, pulses of beans, *gram, urad, moong* and vegetables which also include roots and tubers. Mustard and wild appricot oil and lard are commonly used as cooking media. Vegetables are moderately used, but fruit consumption is occasional depending on the local availability. Potato and *kachalu* are also commonly eaten. Drinking alcohol is very common in the hills and also among the Turis. Both men and women take alcohol which is mostly home-brewed. At times it is also purchased from the local market. Tea is very common. The adults only take milk in its derived forms. Smoking of tobacco, *bidis* and cigarettes is also fairly common for both the sexes. No restriction exists on the intake of food, but on special occasions i.e., fairs and festivities, liquor is a must with non-vegetarian preparation. *Sidkes* (steam baked bread), *babru, patanda, anklu, chule, tasmai,* etc., are the favourite dishes.

The community is divided into exogamous *gotras* which denote their ancestry. The chief function of these *gotras* is to regulate marriages. The community is considered low in the regional social hierarchy owing to their taking part in mortuary rites, thereby defiling their status. They are ranked lower than Lohar but higher than the Chuhra and Chamar. Nowadays, many have taken up the occupation of the barber and prefer to call themselves Nai, who are in the middle social order. Such Tooris consider themselves higher than the Lohars.

The community is aware of the varna-*vayavastha* and place their position along with the Sudra, though again a section of them prefer Kshatriya status as, according to them, they are Nay-Thakurs. As a step towards the process of Rajputization they have started using 'Singh' as their surname.

The community is endogamous. They however, practise *gotra* exogamy—in which only self-*gotra* is avoided. Hypogamy is practised. Though they cannot take a bride from the higher communities, a Kanet can take a Turi woman as his wife. Ibbetson (1914:474) writing on the Turis confirms that "a Kanet may not cohabit with a Turi woman, but in the lower hills he could be outcasted for so doing. A Rahu or Kuran Kanet might possibly keep a Turi woman without much risk of excommunication". Junior and senior levirate and junior sororate are also a common practice among them. The age for marriage nowadays is 20 years for boys and 14-15 years for girls, but even earlier a girl of seven years could be married off.

The most prevalent form of acquiring mate is by negotiation where the marriages are arranged by the parents. Other forms are marriage by *batta-satta, jhanjrara* and marriage by *har* which was once very widely practised but which is now on the decline. Monogamy is the prevalent form of marriage, but in the event of there being no male issue in the family, a second marriage can also take place with the consent of the first wife. But this is very rare.

Bishthai or *bishti* or *reet* or *dheri* (bride-price) is prevalent and this has to be returned along with compensation in case of divorce. Besides bride price, gifts in kind are also given to the girl as per the economic condition of the family. The rule of residence is patrilocal, but at times, in the event of no male issue in the family, a son-in-law is invited to stay with the girl in her house and to look after the property.

Divorce is permissible on grounds of infidelity or maladjustment. In case of infidelity on the part of the wife, the bride-price has to be returned to the husband by the wife's paramour. In all cases of divorce the consent of the Biradari Panchayat is essential. Children in divorce cases are the liability of the father. Since women are more in demand in the community as well as outside the community, divorce proceedings are normally initiated by them though it can be sought by either of the partners. *Dingta chorna* (breaking of the straw) or *peeth jharna* (sweeping of back with hands) are symbolic terms for breaking matrimonial alliance after which both the partners are free to enter into fresh wedlock. Widow, widower or divorcee remarriage is permissible. No rituals are observed, the boy and the girl start living together as husband and wife after giving a feast to the Biradari Panchayat.

A gradual change in the institution of marriage is visible among Tooris. Certain customs which were in practice like *batta-satta, jhanjrara* and *har* have nowadays been replaced by negotiation. Marriage symbols which earlier were non-existent have found a place in their society.

The family pattern is of the extended type with all the vertically extended relations living under the same roof and sharing the same hearth. Exception to this rule are the families who have resident sons-in-law. Interpersonal relations in the family are very cordial. The eldest male member of the family is the head and he is held in great respect and honoured by all. His decision on all family matters is final. The parents and children have mutual obligation towards each other. While it is obligatory on the part of parents to bring up their children, it is also obligatory for the children to look after their parents in their old age. There is no avoidance, but joking relationships exist with husband's elder and younger brother and with wife's sister. The situation of conflict and confrontation usually relates to property matters.

The property is divided equally among all the sons and the widow after the death of the father. The share of the widow is known as *jiyoga*, and is passed on to the son who serves her well during her lifetime. The widow has only usufructuary rights in the property. The daughter normally does not have any right of inheritance or a share in the ancestral property as long as there is male issue in the family, but in the event of there being no male issue, she can inherit her father's property, but her husband has to come and stay with her. Out of the landed property the eldest son is entitled to one extra field of his choice as *jetha* which is probably reminiscent of the land of primogeniture that might have existed in the area in the remote past.

A change is noticed in the family pattern of the Tooris which is changing from extended to nuclear due to their shifting from their traditional occupation and taking up the occupation of barber in settings outside the villages.

The status of a Toori woman is high insofar as her social and economic status is concerned. She has complete freedom in the selection of spouse and is not tied to a single man in case she does not want to stay with him. The presence of the bride-price further makes her important. This puts their parents in a bargaining position who are in much demand by their own community people as well as by the Kanets. Similarly, women are considered an economic asset as they take part in all agricultural and other economic activities, both in and out of the house. Excepting ploughing, a woman does all other agricultural activity. She also does all household jobs like bringing fuel, fodder, water, cooking and looking after the young ones, and in addition also tends the cattle. Her political and religious status is not equal to that of a man. She takes part in all family rituals and festivals, yet she is not allowed to worship family deities on days of pollution. She has full rights in family mangement. Though she does not have any decision-making powers, invariably she is able to influence the judgement through her husband.

Among the Tooris, the birth of a first child especially if it is a boy, is greatly rejoiced over. She is not allowed to go near water sources or in the forest at night; for it is believed that evil spirits may overpower the lady which will be harmful for the foetus. Post-delivery rituals are observed on the *chhati*—sixth day of the birth, when the child is brought out from confinement and is given a bath. The child is also named on this day by a Brahman priest. *Dasuthan* is observed on the eleventh day, when a havan is performed by the *pandit*, and in this ceremony the relatives of the mother's side have a very important role to play, who are obliged to bring *gur* and *ghee* for the occasion.

As long as "a woman has not given birth to a child, she is considered impure during her menses; but once she is mother her menstruation is disregarded, and she is not kept apart or prevented from doing her ordinary house work" (Crook, 1896: 131)

The marriage ceremony used to be a simple affair. The boy's father paid the bride-price, and took the girl home and the marriage was recognized by feeding the community members. Nowadays, after payment of the bride-price, the groom goes to the girl's house and the wedding is performed by the seven *pheras* round the fire in the presence of a Brahman priest. The first marriage is very elaborate but in subsequent marriage (remarriage) *pheras* are not performed.

"Persons who die of cholera, small pox or snake-bite, are buried because they are supposed to be under the direct influence of the deities who rule these diseases" (Crooke, 1896: 132). Infants are also not cremated. In the event of a pregnant woman dying, her abdomen is cut open and the child is taken out. While the woman is cremated the child is buried. This job of chalking of stomach is done by the husband. Persons who die a natural death are cremated. The peculiar custom of cremation is that instead of wood, *chir* leaves and *makki* roots are used for burning the body. The last rites are performed by the eldest male member of the house, and in case of wife by the husband. The house remains polluted for a period of 13 days, when a *mrityu bhoj* (funeral feast) is given to friends and relatives and the beards of all the consanguineal relations are shaved off.

The traditional occupation of the Turis was blowing of a long trumpet or 'cholera horn' at weddings, but later they also took to playing drums. Their women acted as midwives. Besides, they also blew their *turi*, ahead of the funeral procession and took the funeral shroud and got fees in proportion to the means of the deceased as a payment for their services. For rendering their traditional services they are now paid in kind, mostly in the form of cereal at the harvest times.

The community was traditionally landless, but today, they have been provided with some land by the Government under the *nautor* scheme which is however, insufficient for the family's survival and they have to work as sharecroppers on the land owned by others, sharing the produce in 1:3 or 1:2 proportion, as agreed upon by the owner. In addition the Tooris have taken to service, contractorship, business and tailoring, alongwith the traditional blowing of *turi*. They have total dependence on regular, regulated market, where they directly market their produce and buy things of their need. Children below the age of 15 years render a helping hand in the fields or work as labourers or tend the cattle. The payments to children are usually in cash.

Whenever any dispute comes up regarding breach in traditional norms, the elders of the community gather and solve the dispute. The cases that are heard by the elders are usually of elopement, desertion or payment of bride-price. Fines are usually imposed in cash and are paid by the offenders which are passed on to the sufferer. Now, with the coming up of the statutory panchayats the hold of the elders is giving way. These councils are heterogeneous in composition and have statutory powers.

The Tooris are chiefly Shakti worshippers and the inhabitants of the trans-Giri tract of Sirmaur district have great faith in Shirgul (Shiva) and those in Shimla district worship Mahasu Devta. Each household has a shelf, on which is placed a *trishul* with an iron lamp and an earthenware vessel containing some beads which represent the goddess. These articles are symbolic of Shirgul. Parsuram is considered their *kuldeota*, and his representation is taken to Renuka on the day of Renuka fair, given a bath in the lake and brought back. The whole night people keep awake and sing songs in praise of Lord Parsuram. They also have faith in the village *deota* who is called as Khera and is represented by flat platform in front of a big banyan or *pipal* tree. He is believed to be the well-wisher of the entire village and is situated at the entrance of the village to safeguard the village from any evil spirit entering the village.

Their sacred centres are Renuka, and Pinol (Uttar Pradesh). Traditionally they had no priest, but now they have started employing a Brahman priest at their family rituals. The major fair of the community is Bissu-ka-Mela which is held on the first Baisakh to mark the new year and also to celebrate the harvesting of the crop. The other fair which has got importance is the Haryali-ka-Mela held in the month of August. The important festivals are Navratra, Basant Panchami and Markar Sankranti which they share with the other communities of the region. Budhi Diwali is celebrated 30 days after the Nai Diwali of the Hindus with pornographic overtures and songs in the dark of the night. Similarly, festivals of lights, Holach or Chireoli is celebrated during monsoon in which people dance around a *agnikund* of wooden logs which is lighted by burning deodar wood.

The women are involved in the art of weaving and knitting purely for domestic use. The community shares regional/oral traditions which are carried from one generation to another in the form of folktales and folklore. Folksongs are sung by women at social and festive occasions. The men are skilled musicians, especially in the art of blowing *turi* and beating drum. The men and women also sing songs and dance. *Rasa* dance is a very popular dance among the community members in which both the males and the females dance together holding each others' hands.

The Tooris had traditional linkages with all the communities of the neighbourhood in terms of their specialized services of providing music on social and festive occasions at the houses of their clients and in fairs. Their women provided the services of midwife to the neighbouring communities.

Traditionally, the Brahman and Rajput will not eat *kachcha* or *pucca* with the Dhaki, but can share the same *hukkah.* The Tooris will not accept any type of food cooked in the house of Chamar, Chuhra or Koli unless the food has been cooked separately by a Brahman or Rajput for them.A Toori boy can only marry a Toori girl, but a Toori girl can marry outside the community. Putative kinship exists and people do adopt *dharam bhai* who are expected to perform obligations as are expected of a real one. There are separate water and crematoria sources for separate communities, but the Turis can share them only with the Brahman and Rajput.

Traditional *jajmani* relationship existed earlier and they were paid a fixed amount at harvest times for rendering their traditional services. In modern times, since they have become agriculturists, it has become necessary for them to approach other communities for their traditional services. The Tooris have *jajmani* relationship with Koli, Dom, Chamar, Badi and Lohar who are paid a fixed amount of foodgrain at harvest time. Because of their diversified occupation the Tooris have also developed new relations. In the village, with members of the same community, symbiotic relationship exists which is locally known as *hela bear* or *sata.* One family which has lent a labour to the other for agricultural purposes has the right to receive the return services from such families when the need arises.

The attitude of the community towards various developmental activities implemented by the Government is favourable. Though the older generation is largely illiterate, the younger generation, both boys and girls have started going to school beause of free education, books and scholarship provided to them. The girls usually study up to primary level after which they drop out for want of schools in the village, whereas the boys may study up to the college level. Thereafter they have to find jobs for themselves in order to support their family.

Their attitude towards modern medicare and small family norms is also favourable and people prefer two to three children and use indigenous methods of contraception. There is no special preference for sterilization. Drinking water is provided to the people through channelization of streams in the remote areas and through pipes near urban locales.

Employment opportunities under various schemes are available. They avail themselves of Integrated Rural Development Programme facilities for procuring loans at nominal rates of interest and subsidy for agricultural purposes and setting up small shops or workshops. The people have also received employment in Government offices and factories against reserved quotas.

The villages are well connected by metalled roads. People in general have transistor radios and also see movies and other documentaries shown to them by extension agencies. Post offices exist near the villages. The houses of the Tooris are electrified. Firewood, and occasionally kerosene, constitute their fuel. At times when wood is not available, they burn maize roots for cooking. Mid-day meal programme for school children are availed of. Infants in the 0-5 age group, expectant and nursing mothers avail themselves of nutrition and immunization schemes through the Integrated Child Development Scheme. Public distribution system is availed of.

Rajendra Sarkar

VAISH-AGARWAL

The Agarwal or Agarwala/Agarawal is the principal trading community, belonging to the Vaishya order of the Hindu varna vayavastha, and they are also referred to as Vaishya-Agarwal, Vaish-Agarwal, and Bania. The word *bania* is derived from the Sanskrit term trader 'banik', and as the name implies, they are engaged in commercial activities. The word Agarwal is derived from the Hindi *agr* and *wal* which means descendants of Agar, hence Agarwal. According to yet another theory, the community in its remote past traded in aromatic wood called 'Agar' which was used by the Brahmans for performing various rituals and hence were called as Agarwals or Agrawals. They trace their origin from Maharaja Agar Sain, who according to Bhat Shivkaran was born on the fifth day of black fortnight, Krishna Paksha, on Saturday, in the month Margheesh as evident from the following:

vadi mangsir shani panchami
treta pahle charan
agrwal utpan bhaiye, suni
bhake shivkaran. (Vidyasankar Satyakehi, 1938)

The progenitor of the Agrawals—Agar Sain—ruled over the territory of Agroha in Hissar (Haryana) where the ruins of his "mighty empire" are still being excavated by the Archaeological Surey of India. According to legends they are of Rajput descent. The Agarwala say that their first ancestor was a Kshatriya king who married a Naga or snake princess (Russel and Hiralal (1916:116). Elliot confirming this writes, "Raja Agar Sen, being a king, must have been a Kshatriya', while Crooke (1896) states, "their appearance indicates good race and breeding, and would lend colour to the theory of Rajput origin". "The memory of the Naga princess who was their ancestor is still", Sir H. Risley (1908) states, "held in honour by the Agarwalas, and they say our mother's house is of the race of snake" (Ibbetson, 1916: 243).

Though references to the fact that the ancestors of Agarwals were Kshatriya are available, the process of how they moved down in the social order to the status of a Vaishya cannot be substantiated by any historical account. However, according to the legend prevalent in the community, Raja Agar Sain, their progenitor was a Kshatriya of Suryavanshi clan and was a ruler of the mighty kingdom of Agroha.

As per the customs of those days, the king in order to prove his supermacy over the territory used to perform horse sacrifice. On each of the *yajna* different saints *rishis* officiated and from them 18 *gotras* of the Agarwals sprang. After the completion of each *yajna* a horse was beheaded. Maharaja Agar Sain performed 17 *yajna* successfully, but when the eighteenth was being performed, and the time came for beheading the animal, he developed a soft feeling in his heart, and could not kill the horse. Thus the eighteenth *yajna* could not be completed. That is why the Agarwals do not account for 18 but only 17 $^1/_2$ *gotras*; the last being counted as half. This incident moved Maharaja Agar Sain so much that he stopped waging wars and left ruling the country and took to the graceful profession of trading. From then on he stopped taking non-vegetarian diet and started leading a simple life.

The Aggarwals are widely spread throughout the country and so also in the State of Himachal Pradesh, primarily in the districts of Sirmaur, Solan, Shimla, Kangra, Bilaspur and Chamba. The language and dialect spoken by the community is of the area which they inhabit. As the community is wholly confined to the urban locale, most of them are educated and converse among themselves and with outsiders in Hindi and English whereas their script is Devanagari and English. The community has a saffron-coloured flag of four feet by two and a half feet in dimension, and in the centre there is a picture of Maharaja Agar Sain. All Agarwals come under this banner, and it is seen flying in their regional and all-India meets and as also in the procession which is taken out during the Maharaja Agar Sain Jyanti.

The Agarwals are very strict about food. They abstain from all kinds of non-vegetarian food and alcoholic drinks. They are strictly vegetarian and many of them do not even take onion and garlic. The Jain Agarwals do not smoke or chew toabcco, while the Vish-Agarwal smoke and chew tobacco. Their staple diet consists of wheat *chapati*, pulses of *arhar, moong, mah* or *urad* etc., and rice and vegetables. Fruits, milk and milk products are also moderately consumed. Though drinking of alcohol and taking of meat is prohibited and is not approved by the community, a trend is seen among the youngsters of taking to these in private without the knowledge of the elders.

They are subdivided into Bisa Agarwals (from *bis*=twenty), i.e., 100 per cent pure, and those of impure origin resulting from the inter-marriage of Agarwals with outside communities, are ten (*dasa*) or half pure, five (*panja*) 25 per cent pure and twelve and a half *(dhanja)* per cent pure. According to a legend, the descendants of Maharaja Agar Sain and his wife are known as Bisa Agarwals. According to yet another theory, when Sikander waged a war against Agroha, some of the families of Agarwals who sided with Sikander were ostracized and were thus called Dasa Agarwal. This theory again does not say anything for the Panja and Dhanja sections.

The Agarwals can further be divided according to the (a) Sections, (b) Territory, and (c) Religion (Vidyasankar Satyakehi, 1938). According to territorial divisions, the community is divided into (a) Deshwali or Vaish-Agarwal and (b) Marwari divisions. After the fall of Agroha, many Agarwals left their ancestral home and started settling in other parts of country. A large section of them settled in Marwar, south of Rajasthan, and they started calling themselves as Marwari Agarwal. Due to acculturation, they took up the language and culture of the local people and imbibed their culture thus differentiating themselves from the core group. Similarly, among the Deshwals, there are number of sections based on territory they occupy, e.g., Maharaja from Mahim, Sahlaha from Sahrola (Ludhiana district) Oswal from Osaingiri, etc. Except for territorial differentiation, there is no division whatsoever. They have connubial and commensal norms with each other.

The third division among the Agarwals is according to the region. The followers of Jain religion are known as Maheshwari, and Vaishnava sectarians are called Agarwal Vishnois. The latter two have a lot of similarity and the division is basically according to the faith the family. Hence, broadly, Agarwals have only two sections, i.e., the Hindu or the Sanatani and the Jain. Inspite of the religious differences, there are no connubial or commensal restrictions.

In addition to these subdivision, as already mentioned, they are further subdivided into seventeen and a half *gotras,* named they are further officiated at *yajna*. The list of these *gotras*, as given by Sherring (1872), Risley (1908) and Crooke (1896) is similar with minor differences in nomenclature.

The seventeen and a half *gotras* as given in *Agra Vaish Vanshanukirtanam* are Garg, Goi, Gaavaal, Vaatsil, Kasil, Singhal, Mangal, Bhandal, Tingspal, Acran, Bhairan, Dhingal, Tittal, Mittal, Tayal, Gobhil and Govan. These names with some variations exist even today. Besides these, they are also divided into numerous *al,* which denote different families like Kedia, Kanungo, Kanodia and Goenka. These *al* are named after village Ked; Tulsian, Jaalan, and Bhojan are named after great men like Seth Tulsiram, Seth Jaliram, Seth Bhoraj and so on.

The function of these subdivision is to indicate their ancestral linkages and to regulate marriages. The hierarchy in the names of the *gotras* is associated with the order of *rishi* who officiated at different *yajna*. The hierarchy of *gotras* does not absolve any person of his obligation to help his brethren at the time of need. It is obligatory on the part of the members to help their fellowmen at the time of need by providing one buck and Rs 5 per house. This rendering of help in business is mutual without any consideration of *gotra*.

Endogamy is practised at the community level, while exogamy is in practice at the *gotra* level. Exogamy is also practised in the *gotra* in which the girl has been given. Earlier endogamy was practised at the sectional level i.e., a Bisa always would marry a Bisa, Dasa, a Dasa, and so on, but nowadays a change in the trend is apparent. Laxity is also visible at the religious level where a Sanatani could marry a Jain and vice versa. Junior levirate and sororate are permitted, but earlier junior levirate was prohibited. Second marriage is permissible only in the case of barrenness but in that the case consent of the first wife is essential.

In earlier days, child marriages were performed, with the *gaona* or *muklawa* being deferred till the girl came of age, but the concept of marriage has changed and the boys are now 22 years and girls 18 years old at the time of marriage. The usual form of marriage is by negotiation, which is performed according to the faith one professes. The typical marriage symbols for the ladies is *chutki*, glass bangles and vermilion in the parting of the hair. Dowry in cash and kind is prevalent and depends on factors like the boy's service or occupation which is taken into account along with the boy's family background.

The rule residence after marriage is patrilocal. The girl comes to stay with the parents of her husband. Divorce is permitted by the community on ground of maladjustment, cruelty or demand for more dowry. The divorce proceedings can be initiated by either of the aggrieved parties. The elders of the *sabha* try to resolve the problems amicably, but where things go beyond their control, the concerned parties move the court of law for seeking divorce. Compensation to be given to the aggrieved party is decided by the *sabha*. The children of estranged parents are the liability of either parents, but often the responsiblity is shouldered by the father, excepting in cases where children are infants. Remarriage of divorcee, widow and widower are now practised, but at one time widow remarriage was prohibited and the widows practised *sati* by burning themselves alive on the pyres of their husbands. Such *satis* are held in high esteem. This practice is no longer in vogue.

The families are of the patrilineally extended type, with all the male relatives of the husband's side living under the same roof and sharing the same hearth. Interpersonal relations in the family are those of love and respect, with age and relationship being given due regard. Avoidance is observed with all elder male in-law relatives. The woman covers her face with the part of her sari when she comes in front of the elder male members. As a mark of respect she also keeps her head covered with a sari in front of elder women also.

Joking relationship exists between a woman and her husband's younger relatives and between a husband and his wife's young male and female relatives. The husband and wife do not speak each other's name but refer to each other teknonymically. The eldest male member of the family is the head of the family. He is given due regard and respect. His decision in family matters is final. The decision is arrived at after consultation with all the adult male members, and is invariably honoured. The situation of conflict is very rare, and it is normally related to the checking of freedom of youngsters or on property matters.

The property is divided equally among all the sons. A widow also enjoys a share in the property for her lifetime, after which it passes on to the sons. The daughters do not have any right in the father's property, as it is believed that they take away their respective share in the form of dowry. Though statutory provisions provide for equal share of property by the daughters, usually it is waived in the favour of brothers. In the event of no sons in the family, the property is either passed on to the daughters or adoption of a male child is resorted to. Interfamily linkages are mutually strong and are best seen in social or religious ceremonies when different families get an opportunity to interact with each other.

The status of a woman differs in different spheres of life. Traditionally they lived in seclusion, and were not permitted to take up independent jobs or move out alone. But, with the changing times and spread of education, they have also gained education, and have taken to employment in Government and private departments, teaching, administration and to other white-collar profession. They take active part in the family rituals and no *yajna* is regarded complete without the participation of both the man and woman sitting together tied with a knot. For women exercising of franchise serves as taking part in politics.

The expectant mother is not allowed to go out alone during the night, cross a river or to see a funeral procession, an eclipse, or cut fruit or vegetable during the peiod of eclipse lest the child should be born with a deformity. The house remains polluted for a peiod of 9 days in case of girls and 11 days in case of boys, after which the purificatory bath is given to the parturient mother and from then onwards she can take part in housework, but still she is not allowed to go out of the house with the child for 40 days. This period of pollution is known as *sutak. Chhati* ceremony is observed on the sixth day and the child and mother are given the purificatory bath. New clothes brought from the mother's family are put on by the child and leaf soot is applied to the eyes of the child. The mode of observance of *chhati* differs from family to family, but a purificatory bath on the sixth days is essential in all cases. *Dasuthan*, literally meaning the tenth day ceremony, is seldom performed on the desired day. In case of the birth of a girl, it is performed and observed on the ninth day and in case of boys is postponed to the eleventh day. This ritual is again associated with the purificatory bath and *havan*. On this day the *pandit* suggests some name for the child and the elders of the family also give a nick name to him. This is followed by *bal-utarna* or *mundan* ceremony, in which the child's first hair shave is done at a desired place for the fulfilment of wish. This is done on odd years, but preferably before the age of five. The people from Sirmaur go to Trilokpur or Renuka temples for head shaving which is done by the Nai. A small tuft of hair (*chola*) is left on the occiput. In other areas also, getting the tousure ceremony arranged at some sacred place is a common belief.

The next ritual connected with the wearing of sacred thread, *yajnopavit*, for which there is no rigid time for observance. It is either performed before five years or with marriage rituals before the actual marriage, but sometimes it is not performed at all as the community is not rigid about it. *Kanchhedan* (ear-piercing) and *nakchhedan* (nose-piercing) is performed at the age of five or seven years. *Nakchhedan* concerns only the girls but *kanchhedan* is done for both the sexes. It is performed at home by the mother or by any elderly lady. Small *nanti* (earings) are put on by the men, while the women prefer putting on a nose pin.

The marriage rituals are performed according to the Sanatan Dharma doctrines, which include a series of rituals consisting of betrothal, *tilak, kanyadan* by the father of the bride, putting of vermillion in the parting of hair five times and circumambulating the fire five times.

The Sanatanis cremate their dead. The dead who have grand-children are carried in a wooden box to the cremation ground and a feast is given to the *biradari*, whereas the other are carried on a bier. The *antyesti* (last rites) is performed by the eldest son, and, in his absence, by the youngest son. The mortuary rites are observed on the third day, when unburnt portion of bones are collected and are dispersed in the Ganga at Hardwar. The Acharaj helps in performing the offering of *pind-dan*. On the tenth day *dasai* is observed, when the male agnates take a bath and get their hair shaved off. The Acharaj again officiates, and makes an offering of boiled rice and pulses, *khichri* and *kheer* in the name of the deceased. *Kriya* ceremony is performed on the eleventh day when the Acharaj is given almost all the belongings of the deceased.

The *pagri* ceremony is performed on the thirteenth day but it deferred in case of old persons to the seventeenth day. On this day the Brahman in equal numbers matching the days on which it is observed are served with meals. The mother's brother brings a *pagri* and ties it on the head of the eldest male member of the family or gives Rs. 5 for the *pagri* and Rs. 21 in cash. This ceremonial tying of *pagri* signifies succession and transfer of authority. This marks the end of the period of *patak*. Every month on the date according to Hindu calendar, *tithi*, a Brahman is fed for a year, till the time when anniversary *barsi* is performed and the entire *biradari* is feasted. A similar ritual of feast is also repeated on the *chaubarsi*.

The major economic activity of the community continues to be business. Presently, a trend is visible for change of occupation, as a result of which many men and women have taken to white-collar profession, and are working as engineers, scientists, Government officials, administrators and teachers. This has primarily been due to no aptitude for business, insufficient funds for business and also for reasons of family businesses not being able to meet the growings demands of the family.

The Vaish Aggarwals are totally dependent on the market, with cash and barter system forming the medium of exchange. For the maintenance of community rules, they have two levels of judicature; first, at the regional level, known as Agarwal Sabha, and second, at the national level, known as Akhil Bhartiya Vaishya Maha Sabha. The newly formed councils are now being named as Vaishya Sabhas, which have a wider connotation and include all the sections of the Agrawal community . In Himachal Pradesh, the Agarwal or the Vaishya Sabhas exist at Nahan, Solan, Shimla, Kangra, Bilaspur and Chamba, and the Akhil Bhartiya Vaish Maha Sabha at Delhi. The composition and the function of the Sabhas and the Maha Sabha are identical. They consist of an elected body of functionaries like the secretary, vice-president, treasure and executive members. These also control social evils like dowry. Whenever a case is not decided by the regional council or its decision not upheld by the members, it is referred to the national council.

Traditionally, severe punishment like excommunication, was awarded to the guilty according to the nature of the guilt which resulted in the upcoming of the sections like Dasa, Panja and Dhanja according to the degree of degradation. But today the situation has considerably changed and people are shunning the age-old sectional diversity and feelings of separation. The reformist attitude within the Agarwal communities has resulted in intermarriage with the other sections, resulting in their assimilation into the wider whole—the community. Offenders of the norms are now required to pay cash fines which is utilized for the welfare of the community.

Despite the statutory panchayats, the traditional community councils hold sway and exercise no less than statutory powers in the field of social control.

They are largely Hindu, professing Vaishnavism and a section of the Agarwals also profess Jainism of which the majority are of the Digambar sect. The Sanatan Dharami Agarwals have a *kuldevi* or *ist-devi,* who differs from family to family, and similarly every family is associated with a *sati,* who are worshipped for the well-being of the community. They have faith in and reverence for the gods of the wider Hindu pantheon. The Vaishnavas are worshippers of Vishnu in form of Ram and Sita, and worship Shiva in the phallic form. The Arya Samajis believe in the *nirankar* form of god. Their community deity is Lakshmi. They also venerate ancestors at the usual *shradhs.* The sacred centres of the community are Hardwar and Gaya, where they go to perform the last rites, and for immersion of the mortal remains. Brahman commonly referred to as *purohit* officiates at the festivals, family rituals and rituals connected with the life-cycle.

The major festival of the community is Maharaja Agra Sain Jayanti, which is held on the first day of Navratra in the month of Asuj, in honour of the founder of Agarwal dynasty. A chariot *rath yatra* procession is carried out in the streets, singing hymns in his praise, in which the entire Vaishya *biradari* takes part. They also worship snakes at Nag Panchami, making offering of milk to the snake god. Among trees they venerate the *pipal, kadam* and *babul.*

The Jain Agarwals celebrate Mahavir Jayanti. Another festivals, held in honour of the Agarwal *sati* is observed on the *amavasya* (Diwali day) when *puris* and other delicacies are offered to the young girls in the name of the *sati*. Besides, they also celebrate other regional fairs and festivals. The women in certain areas used to make pictures of a Nag in the courtyards. Music and dance are used only for recreational purposes and are confined to women within the four walls of the houses and are displayed on festive or social ceremonies. The community has folktales of *sati* are especially the *satis* who are held in high esteem. The community continues its traditional social and occupational linkages with others.

In terms of commensal norms they accept cooked food, both *kachcha* and *pucca* only from certain Brahmans but not from Acharaj and Bujhru. They also accept water and sweet meals from the Rajputs. Exchange of hubble-bubble is governed by the rules in force for water and sweet meals. The rigidity of commensal norms is nowadays restricted only to the elderly population, whereas those of modern generation do not observe them so rigidly. *Jajmani* system exists with occupational communities like the Chuhra, Dhobi and Nai, who were given food and clothes besides being paid in cash at social and festive occasion in lieu of the services rendered by them. This system is now dying out.

As the Vaish Agarwals are wholly urban, there are more avenues for education and consequently one finds a higher percentage of literacy among them, with both the boys and girls receiving academic, professional and technical education. The availability of modern medical facilities and family welfare schemes have resulted in the betterment of the families and adoption of small family norm through modern family planning devices.They have procured loans through banks and other agencies under provisions of loan for unemployed educated youths for setting up shops, coattage or small-scale industries.

Rajendra Sarkar

Appendix A

(Communities studied later)

BEDA (HINDU)

The Beda is an entertainer who performs one of the most spectacular ceremonies of the Himalyan region, i.e., the rope sliding ceremony or Bhunda. The Bhunda or *Bihunda* is called Bedarat, Barta, Badwar or Barat in Tehri and Garhwal but in Himachal Pradesh, the ceremony is known as Bhunda. The Badhi, a separate commuity in Himachal Pradesh is sometimes identified with the Bedas in Uttar Pradesh but they are not identical with the Bedas. There is only one family of this community in Nirmand village in Outer Seraj of Kullu district and two families in Rohru tehsil of Shimla district. The Bedas are also called 'Jyali' or 'Jyayi'. The ceremony of Bhunda or Bedarat is observed in Garhwal district and the Satluj valley on both sides of the border between Central and Western Pahari speaking areas.

Bhunda is the term related to and derived from 'Bihunda' or 'Bihund' in the remote past. During the epic age Bihund was an Asura, killed by the Devas. The festival is held at Nithar, Dalash, Dansa, Nandla, Nirath, Datanagar and some other places situated in the slopes of river Satluj and in erstwhile Bushehr state.

On finding, through the oracle of the concerned village, that the appropriate time for arranging Bhunda ceremony has approached and that various troubles in the habitat are cropping up due to the wrath of the village god and other celestial beings which can be appeased by way of arranging the ceremony, the villagers start making arrangements and send an invitation to the Beda for preparing a rope for the purpose. In most of the villages where rope-sliding ceremonies are arranged, Lord Parshuram is said to have stayed during the course of his meditation. In Nirmand village, the ceremony is believed to have been arranged by the sage himself for the first time. Lord Parshuram made 1600 Brahmans settled there who accompanied him in Kanchanpuri (now Kao village in Mandi), Mayapuri (Mumail village in Mandi), Duttanagar in Shimla district and Nirmand in Outer Seraj of Kullu district. In the present times, the ceremony is arranged in about 10 villages in Shimla and Outer Seraj areas but in the past, the number of the places was much higher. The prominent places among them include Nirmand, Kharahan, Sholi, Spail, Bachhunch, Pujarli, Naina, Chuhar valley, Kulgaon, Ralsa, Dansa, etc., etc.

Among all fairs and festivals, the Bhunda festival deserves a special mention as this is the festival of exclusive importance to the Bedas. Being a sacrificial type of the ceremony now in most of the villages in upper Shimla district, Bhunda is the name given to a festival in which the goats and rams are offered to appease the village gods even without having the rope sliding activities attached to it. Such types of Bhunda festival, are a regular feature of the villages in the region. Earlier the ropesliding ceremony might have been associated with such functions but now this system has emerged only as a social gathering in a particular village. The real and great Bhunda festival in its original form is arranged after a long interval and a Beda-the ropeslider— is invited to perform at this function.

In outer Seraj valley of Kullu district the village Nirmand is famous for Ambika Devi temple. There is a legend that Lord Parhuram meditated at the place. The Parshuram temple and his cave in which he meditated are at Nirmand. Now the cave forms a part of the Parshuram temple. He is the presiding deity of Bhunda festival as it is believed that it was during his life time that the festival was started. In ancient times various types of yajnas were performed. These included Narmedh or Purushmedh, Gaumedh and Ashvamedh. Bhunda, though called a Narmedh yajna by some, is in fact a ceremony associated with the winning of Sura and Asura (Devasur) battle by the allies of Lord Indra. The rope prepared for use by the ropeslider Beda is alled 'Barat', 'Barto' or 'Balohar'. These terms indicate 'Vritra'- the Asura of Vedic period who was killed by Lord Indra. Earlier, Bhunda was held after every twelve years' interval but now it is arranged only after a directive is received through the oracle of the village god. The festival is associated mostly with the worship of Lord Parshuram but in the villages of Sholi and Kharahan and some others, the village gods arrange it at their own level inviting the Kalash of the village gods of the villages where Bhunda is arranged. It is of some interest to note that even 'Ravin Pothi', a sacred manuscript ever since undeciphered and uninterpreted, is worshipped during this featival. The manuscript is preserved by the Brahamans of Ravin village near Sarahan in Shimla district. It is written in Sharda script. During the festival, a clay image of 'Hirbani' (Hidimba) goddess is made and worshipped. This is associated with Kali worship.

The ceremony in its original form consisted of stretching a long rope of *moonj* (a wild grass) from the top of the hill or precipice and letting a man of the Beda community seated on a saddle to slide down the rope in a sitting posture. Keeping in view the risk involved in the feat, a goat is substituted for a man at Nirmand but in some other villages, the rope is tied to two poles placed in such a way that there is no risk of life during the course of rope - sliding by the Beda.

Moonj grass is cut by the villagers on an auspicious time about three months before the fair. The Beda himself prepares the rope performing constant obulations while working at it. It is usually 100 to 200 feet in length or even more, and when ready, is placed in a room where none is allowed to approach without the permission of the Beda.

The rope is considered very sacred and a symbol of the spirit of a serpent god. Like a snake it has a hood and a tail. A piece of red cloth tied to the tail and the hood is made thicker as compared to the tail. No one should approach it in an unclean position wearing shoes or cross it, lest it should get defiled. One defiling it is fined a goat, which is sacrificed and in that case the rope is required to be remade. On the day of the fair it is taken to a nearby pond or *baoli* (water source) bathed and taken to the upper pole by the people of a particular community, on their shoulders. On reaching the cliff it is fastened to the upper pole and its other end lowered down to be tied to the lower pole. The Beda is taken to the *havan kund* and made to sit before the image of Hirbani. Later he is escorted to the place of sacrifice, the upper pole located at the cliff. Panchratna (five precious things) is put in his mouth to indicate that in case of any eventuality, he should be ready to face death. He is then clothed in *pagri* (turban) and white *chola* with a funeral music played in the background.

The relatives of the Beda stay around the lower pole, a place to which he comes sliding down. He sits on a sort of a wood saddle called *ghori* secured to the rope and is supported by another rope tied to his waist with which he is held back on the slope rope. Sand bags are also tied to his legs to balance hm. At the signal by the *gur* (oracle), the cord holding and balancing him is cut and he slides down with a fast speed to reach the lower post.

The Beda, on reaching the lower pole is taken off and the rejoicing people take him on their shoulders and dance with him. He is placed in *dhure* (leading place) in the dancing party as if elevated to the status of a higher community. He is offered gifts and money and at this time he blesses people by distributing and offering some straws of *moonj* grass to each one of them as his gesture of goodwill to them. He visits the villages of the nearby area and collects offering and gifts from the people for a pretty long time. In earlier days, the Beda after the feat, was allowed so much of liberty that any ornament or costly garment touched by him would have to be offered to him as a token of gift by the concerned persons as otherwise it was considered a sign of bad luck for the possessor.

The Beda is a non-agriculturist community and has a very meagre source of income excepting taking part in such rituals where they get handsome amount and earn the right of approaching people of the neighbouring villages after the ceremony to reward them of their horrific deed of sliding down the rope. Some scholars including Waddell L. Austine, Charles Bell and James G. Fraser have found out that this type of rope sliding ceremony was held annually in the premises of the Potala at Lhasa also. According to a manuscript available in Mumail village in Mandi district, the Beda community is said to be the illegitimate progeny of saint Bhrigu and Mamlesha, a Kinnari and the sects of saints suggested Bhunda eremony to be arranged to get rid of the male members of the community, who were feared to die at the time of rope-sliding during the ritual. Both these versions don't find the support of popular beliefs, as according to tradition, the Beda is not allowed to die while sliding the rope and if at all, this happened, the village god is cursed for it by the villagers.

The community does not have special costumes but at the time of the ceremony the performer is given white shirt and *pajama* and a white robe to be used. After the ceremony, the Beda is adorned with silken gown and his wife and family members also get colourful garments.

The Bedas are non-vegetarian. They take the meat of goat, ram and sheep and take fish. Beef and buffalo meat are prohibited but the Beda community of Kinnaur, Lahul and Spiti had less aversion to these things in the past according to the reports. Beef and buffalo meat are taboo among the Bedas of the tribal areas and Bedas of rope sliding community these days. Their staple food is barley, rice and maize with cereals, all kinds of pulses and oil seeds. Vegetables and fruits available in the region are also consumed by them. They like parched barley and wheat which is called *mory*. *Sattu* prepared out of barley flour is also consumed. Milk and other local drinks are also popular. They like *siddu* in Shimla.

There is no major social divisions in the community. They have cordial kinship relations. Their hierarchical order is akin to other communities of the area in which they live.

The Beda marriage in Shimla and Outer Seraj is called *gader*. In this type of the marriage, the bride goes to house of the bridegroom in a marriage party and all the rituals relating to the ceremony are performed in his house. The bride stays in her in-laws' house for some days. The word *gader* appears to be a corruption of the ancient system of marriage known as *gandharva vivah* or 'love marriage' with a difference. Love marriage in these areas is called *praino (pranay)*. *Vyah* and *har* are other forms of marriage. Divorce is also permissible among the Bedas.

The Bedas prefer to stay in a joint family. They have happy inter-personal relationship among the members of the family. The property is divided equally among the sons but now even the daughters have share in the ancestral property. The women collect fuel and fodder and perform religious, social and ritualistic activities but are not interested in political activities.

Shivratri is the most important festival of the Bedas. Lord Shiva and his consort Parvati are worshipped on this occasion. Sacrifice of a number of goats is an integral part of the ceremony. Lohri, Diwali, Boorhi Diwali, Sair, Holi, Phag etc. are other important festivals of the Bedas.

The family is considered polluted for 11 days after the birth of a child. The blessings of the village god are sought at an appropriate time when the mother and child are in a position to be taken to him.

The Bedas are not a land owning community. They mainly serve as orchardists and farmers at the time of need. Ritual performance of rope sliding is their main occupation. The Bedas are artisans in preparing good quality ropes of *moonj* (a type of grass). Some of them prepare local handicrfts also. Gohria was a famous rope slider in the community. He performed Bhunda six times at various places.

There is no Biradari panchayat of the Bedas. They form a part of the village panchayat. The communtiy is Hindu by religious faith. In Lahul and Spiti their counterparts are known Bedas but they don't perform rope sliding feats. They are Buddhist by faith. The Hindu Bedas go to the village god temples of Lord Parshuram, goddess Ambika, Hatkoti and Durga and to Tirthas such as Haridwar, Jagannathpuri and other places.

The community has inter-community linkages with other people. The *savarna* accept only uncooked food from them but scheduled caste people consider them equal in status. This tradition of separation is now fading away and the sense of equality among the people of various communities is visible. There is no *jajmani* system among the Bedas but according to their population, they have divided areas for performances among themselves. This division too is not very rigid one.

They have a positive attitude towards development schemes of the government.

B.R. Sharma

GARA

The Gara, also known as Domba or Zoba live in Lahul and Spiti district of Himachal Pradesh. They form a single community of the blacksmiths in the area which is addressed by different names in various valleys of the district. In Khoksar valley the blacksmiths are called Gara. Negi (1976: 111) has given the following account of the communtiy of the Dombas:

> "This community is called Domba, Lohar, Zo and Gara. The people of the Pattan Valley and the Dombas themselves call them Lohar whereas the people of Lower Chandra Valley and the lower Bhaga Valley call them Gara. In Spiti Valley they are called Zo. Their professional work is blacksmithy but in Gahar and Chandra Valley they work as communtiy musicians also. Their language in Lahaul is vey akin to the language of the Chahans, but in Spiti they speak Bhoti. Two or three families of Dombas will be found in every village of the district. Their chief profession being blacksmithy, they make and repair all the agricultural implements of the villagers from whom they get a fixed quantity of grain at each harvest. Some of the Dombas are professional gold smiths and silver smiths.
>
> They marry and dine within the community. The other communites, such as Swanglas and Bodhs, treat them as low as Chahans. The Dombas, have however, interrelations with them because Chahans consider them lower than themselves. In the Spiti sub-division Domba (Zo) have interdining relations with Bodhs or Bhots but no inter-marital relations.
>
> Their rituals and ceremonies are performed by the Chahan in the Lahul sub-division, but in Spiti sub-division by the lamas. Dombas have small land holdings"

Some scholars are of the opinion that Lohars come from Kullu and other adjoining areas. Tobdan (1984:20) says:

> "This is evident from their language also as they speak a speech which belongs to Aryan Sanskritic family. But there is also equally strong evidence which connects them with the Bhotia race. The Lohars of Gumrang belong to the *rus* of Merupa and that of Khangsar and Tino to *Yeshe-ras-pa*. There are many Bhotia families who also belong to the same *rus*. This relation is not only asserted by the Lohars but is also respected by the Bhotia families of the same *rus*. It must be borne in mind that the relationship of *rus* is the most sacred relationship between the two families in Lahul. No new family can enter this relationship unless it is one of the branches of the same *rus*. On the other hand, the *rus* becomes

extinct and all the familes belonging to that particular *rus* become without *rus* at the moment the sacred relationship is broken, that is if marriage relationship is estiblished between two families of the same *rus*. Therefore, it is difficult at the present state of knowledge to which particular race they should be related. Their physical features, however, tend.to place them nearer to the Bhotias".

The opinion expressed by Negi (1976: 60-61) amply clarifies the position of Domba or Lohars and we can easily infer that they belong to two separate stocks. The Lohars of Spiti and parts of Lahul have got so much intermixed with the original inhabitants that they speak fluent Bhoti also, and possibly some blacksmiths have come from Tibetan areas to settle down in Spiti.

In the District Gazetteer of Lahul and Spiti (1975) the following account on Lohar is available.

" Lohars are called Gara in the local language of Keylong and Khoksar villages, Domba in Bhaga and Chandra valleys and Lohar only in Pattan valley. They have land which was originally given to them by the village people in consideration of their customary service as blacksmiths. This allotment of land was called *grazhing*. They are given food for smiths' work and grains at harvest according to the size of the holding of their employer. There is a legend, which has been written down in Bunan dialect by the Morovians, that Garas were imported from Kulu with corn-seed. The Garas are the local jewellers and musicians as well as blacksmiths.

Caste toboos have loosened greatly. Swanglas who despised Bodhs as *Bhot-zat* no longer do so. They now do not mind eating, drinking and smoking with Bodhs and accept Bodh girls in marriage. Similarly, Shipis regarded themselves as superior to Lohars and did not in the past eat with them or give their daughters in marriage. Now these distinctions have disappeared and Shipis eat and drink with Lohars and also give their daughters in marriage to them. There is a legend that Swangla and Shipis belong to the same caste. According to this legend when two Swangla brothers started for Lahul from Chamba their rations gave out on the way and some one offered them beef. The elder brother did not accept it, but the younger brother took it. On reaching Lahul the elder brother called him Chandal and refused to eat with him. The legend does not appear to be true since the mother tongues of both the castes differ materially. Had they been brothers they would have spoken the same language. Shipis and Lohars who are Harijans are not treated as untouchable by Bodhs and Swanglas."

The population of the community is not much but it is scattered throughout the length and breadth of the district. The areas, in which the community is located are land-locked and surrounded by high mountain ranges clad with snow throughout the year. They speak Bhoti and Indo-Aryan languages but their mother tongue in Lahul is mainly distinct Indo-Aryan. There are no indentification marks with typical forms of dress.

The Garas are non-vegetarian and use of alcohol is in plenty. Locally prepared wine and other forms available from the market are used. The staple food of the community includes rice, maize, wheat, barley and other local products including a variety of pulses.

Social divisons within the society do not exist. According to the local customs, the Lohars in Spiti believe in primogeniture and the eldest son is entitled to the property, but in Lahul the ancestral property is divided in equal parts among all the sons. The community is an integrated one.

The institution of marriage is like that in other communities of the region especially like Chahan or Shipis. Marriages generally take place in the childhood but now there is a change in the age and girls of about 15 to 18 years and boys of 18-21 years of age get married. The community is of Sudra varna and they accept it as such. Bride price is prevalent. The family system is polyandrous and dowry in cash and kind in prevalent. *Sindur* and ornaments are the symbols of marriage for the women. Rules of residence after marriage are partilocal. Remarriage is allowed for divorced husband and wife. Divorce is simple and is as in other communities of the area.

Joint family system is prevalent. Interpersonal relations, rules of inheritance and succession are similar to those of other communities. Inter-family linkages are strong and help is extended at the time of necessity.

The women have a respectful place in the family and contribute to major decisons in the family. They have an equal right with their husbands in the family property. The women collect fuel and fodder and participate in rituals and social activities, but they are least interested in political activites. They contribute to family income indirectly.

Life-cycle rituals are observed. Birth of a son is considered a matter of joy for the family. Name-giving ceremony is not solemnised. Childhood and adolescence ceremonies are not arranged but tonsures are done at the age of one year. Consummation of marriage is arranged in house of the bridegroom but no ceremony is organised. The dead are cremated. The local Lamas are consulted in Spiti before the disposal of the dead.

The community in not a holder of landed property and water resources are common. There are no forests in Spiti but in Lahul the forests exist near the villages and people make use of this government property, and in some cases private forests also exist. The occupation of the community is rearing of sheep and goat, blacksmithy and agriculture. The wages are paid in cash and kind. Child labour is also prevalent. The life of the people is very hard and they have to toil much. With the advent of roads and other facilities, the change in economic activities is visible. There are no bonded labourers but labour in the village can be arranged on a contract basis.

Traditional (Jati) panchayats exist. These are establised on mutual understanding and respect. Statutory Gram panchayats also function.

The community professes Hindu faith but some families are believers of Buddhism also and they have faith in monasteries and local deities. Their major fairs and festivals include Phaguli, Losar (New Year function), Halda, etc.

The community is of artistic nature. The blacksmiths prepare various types of tools and ornamanets. Their art is typical and useful. The women also engage themselves in preparing woollen socks and blankets, etc. Folksongs, dances, and folk tales exist, but these are common with other communities of the region.

Inter-community and inter-ethnic linkages exist. *Yajmani* system is also prevalent. Inter-community marital exchange is not common. Putative kinship based relations are found with other communities. Landlord-tenant relationship also exists. Employer-worker relationship is also a part of the community.

The attitude of the Garas towards development schemes is positive and helpful. The community is very useful for the area and serves a bridge between various communities of the region.

B.R. Sharma

KANGHERA

The Kanghera is a little known community in Kangra district. It derives its name from *kan* (ear) as its members were the traditional ear repairers/ surgeons. It carries the synonyms of Kangyarhia and Kangehra also. There are only three families which have been reported respectively from Kangra, Dharamshala and Mandi towns of the State. The ancestors of the community worked as plastic surgeons in the past and were experts in replanting the nose, ear and other limbs on the bodies of the mutilated/maimed culprits according to customary and Muslim systems of punishment. In the remote past they are said to have migrated from Hastinapur, the capital of the Pandavas, to Kangra. They belong to a separate *savarna* community whose clan is 'Shukla' and consider themselves, in social hierarchy, equal to Bhatnagar and Kayastha with whom they also have matrimonial alliances in Pathankot. The total approximate population of the community is less than one hundred.

The three families which have been identified at Kangra, Dharamshala and Mandi are nature lovers. They have no landed property these days but own only residential accommodation. However, it is learnt that a Katoch ruler of Kangra issued them a *patta* for getting revenue from Jamanabad area near the Kangra town. It was a vast piece of landed property which was grabbed by the cultivators gradually. The 'Hukamnama' showing the offer of the landed property and entitlement receipt of the revenue of Jamanabad area is still with the family.

It has been mentioned in (Kangra Gazetteer 1924-25: 33-44) that during AD 1905 a severe earthquake rocked Kangra which destroyed the whole of the old Kangra Bazar with a death toll of 12,669 persons out of a total of 18,313. The Mohalla of Kangehra was also destroyed in which fifteen persons of this community were killed. Since then only three families are reportedly surviving in the region. The community name may also be associated with Kangra as the ancient name of Kangra is also believed to be 'Kangarh' or 'Kankat'. It is said that the ear of demon 'Jalandhar' fell here and later a big fort was built with the name of 'Kangarh'. The historians have referred to this fort with the name of 'Kangra fort'. The nomenclature of the valley and the place was later changed to 'Nagarkot'. We find the references of 'Nagarkot' even in Rig Veda. It is presumed that the fort belonged to the king 'Shambar' who fought against the Aryan ruler 'Divodasa' in the first epic war known as 'Shambar Divodasa Yuddh'. Shambar's father was 'Kulitar' and some scholars infer that the place might have been inhabited by Kolarian people during those days. The inhabitants at that time were known as 'Dasyus' who were ruled by their mighty king 'Shambar', the master of 99 forts situated in the Himalayan ranges.

The Kangehras speak Kangri or Pahari dialect and know Hindi and English also. Their script is Devanagari. The Kangra area had a number of Muslim families who practised the law of their religion which allowed punishment of mutilation of hands, ear and nose for various offences. The last operation of replanting the ear on a patient who came from Lahore for the purpose was conducted by Late Shri Dina Nath, the father of the informant, during the year AD 1932 at Kangra. The members of the community wear usual type of dress, i.e. *kameez, salwar* and *dupatta* by the women and cap, shirt and pants or *pajama* by the men . Traditionally a turban was worn but now a cap is worn on various occasions by the men. Ornaments like nose rings, ear rings, bangles, etc. made of gold or silver are worn by the women like those of other communities.

The people of the community are non-vegetarian but their staple diet is rice, wheat, maize and various pulses like *urad* . They eat various green vegetables like cabbage, *sag,* carrot, tomato, etc. The women generally don't like non-vegetarian food. The meat of goat is preferred, besides chicken. Locally available fruits are consumed.

The men have a taste for alcoholic drinks. It is said that their ancestors used to prepare drinks with certain Ayurvedic herbs which were also provided to the patients before being operated upon. Presently on various occasions they purchase the beverages from the local market. They usually take milk and other non- alcoholic drinks. Special foods prepared on various occasions like other people are *ankloo* on Diwali *seviyan* on Sair, and on 'Lohri' they eat *khichri.*

The Kanghera practise *dharm* or *pun* marriage in adulthood through negotiation. Betrothal ceremony is arranged with pomp and show and the bridegroom accompanies the marriage party in a palanquin or car as the case may be. Married women use the symbol of *sindur* on their hair parting. The eldest son, according to the customary law of inheritance has the first option to a particular portion of the property. In case of inheritance by sons by more than one wife, the *chundavand* rule is followed. It means that first the property is divided among mothers and then to the respective sons. In some cases the mothers and their sons get equal share according to total heads which is called *pagvand,* literally the division according to turbans. Dowry is not demanded, but is voluntarily given, mostly in kind. The residence is patrilocal, but if the space in the parental accommodation is not enough, the new couple, with the consent of the parents or elders can establish a separate household. No case of divorce is recorded. Remarriage of widower is permissible but that of a widow is not permitted but presently the attitude towards remarriage of widows is changing.

Joint family system is retained and the interpersonal relations among the members are cordial, respectful and full of love. The sister-in-law can share jokes with the younger brother of her husband but respects the elder brother and doesn't like to talk in a light mood with him. Inter-family linkages are also cordial ones.

Womenfolk attend to the household chores and their right of inheritance is in accordance with the rules of other communites for the purpose. Residing in towns, they don't have to worry about the collection of fuel and fodder. They take part only in social, ritualistic and religious activities and don't feel interested in political activities. The educated women serve in the offices and thus add to the family income.

Birth, marriage and death are the main *sanskara* among the Kangehras. The family in which child is born remains polluted for about 10 days or till the day of the *punjap* or *guntrala* performed by the *pandit*. A feast is arranged on this occasion and the child is also named on the very day. The marriage ceremony is a function, not only of the concerned family, but of the whole village or mohalla. In order to help the family, the neighbourers and relatives come to do various jobs relating to the arrangement of marriage. The marriage ceremony of a girl is of special significance in the mohalla and each one of the family invite the girl to dine with the members before the marriage and at the time of the ceremony gifts are given to the bridegroom and the bride. The *vivah muhurat* (the auspicious day for marriage) is fixed by the pandits of both the sides. On *samuhat* day, the family priest of the bridegroom family goes to the bride's family with ornaments, clothing, dried fruit, *mehndi* and *batna*, etc. The ancestors are worshipped before *shanti havan*. On *parsahi* day the bridegroom is shaved and made to bathe and is dressed up in new clothes and wears *sehra* of golden lace. *Sreshtachar milni, sirgundi* of the bride are other important ceremonies before the departure of the *barat*.

The family remains polluted for about 13 days after the death of a member in it. On 9th day, the clothes are washed and on 11th day, *kirya* ritual, in which an Acharaj performs special *pooja*, is organised. After 40 days, in some cases, a *yajna* in the name of the deceased in organised. The dead body is cremated and the remains are immersed in Ganges at Hardwar.

The young boys and girls are averse to dowry system and want to minimise the expenditure on marriage. The joint family system is getting deteriorated and intercaste marriages are increasing. The community is economically sound and all the families have their own houses in towns. The traditional occupation of the community has been medical treatment and surgery. They were experts in Unani and Ayurvedic systems of medicine and handicrafts were also their source of income. The aforesaid Late Shri Dina Nath was a skilled and known bamboo craftsman as well. The Late Pratap

Singh Kairon, former Chief Minister of Punjab honoured him for making a model of a Japanese ship. The Kangheras also prepare *jhankis* for processions on various religious occasions like Dussehra, Janamashtami and Durga Pooja etc. The Kangheras were known for plastic surgery and only the boys of the family were allowed to enter the operation theatre at the time of operation. This was done keeping in view the secrecy and sanctity of the profession. The surgeons of the community conducted worship of the goddess of Kangra, Brajeshwari Devi before conducting operations. It is said that 'Ashwasthama' the Mahabharata war hero who was deprived of 'Mani' (lighting pearl) on his head by Lord Krishna, approached one of the Kanghera to cure his wound. The physician told him that they could cure any thing excepting the wound caused by Lord Krishna due to extraction of 'Mani' from Ashwasthama's body. On hearing this the spirit of Ashwasthama disappeared immediately. Dina Nath planted a new nose on the face of one Shri Raina Jatly of Rawalpindi and his uncle Sunder Lal was also a plastic surgeon.

A reference about the practice of plastic surgery in Kangra district is available in the *Kangra District Gazetteer 1924-25* p. 62:

> "Frequent mention is made in the Muhammadan histories of the cutting out of tongues at the Devi temple in Bhawan a practice that was common in former times and happens occasionally even now. The act was done by the worshipper and the cut tongue was believed to be restored in an hour or two or in a few days. (For references see *Ma'asir-ul-Umara,* Vol. II, p. 186; *Hadiqat- ul-Alglin*; Archaeological Survey of India Reports, Vol. V, p. 168-9; and *Vigne travels* Vol. I, p. 140-1).
>
> Akbar was told that Kangra was famous for four things:
>
> 1. The manufacture of new noses. 2. The treatment of eye diseases. 3. Basmati rice, 4. The strong fort.
>
> The operation on nose for which Kangra was long famous, is said to have been introduced by a surgeon of Akbar. A criminal who had his nose cut off as a punishment by order of the emperor, appeared soon afterwards with a new nose. On being asked by Akbar how it was restored, he said that a surgeon of his own had done the operation. The surgeon was rewarded by receiving a Jagir in Kangra, with a little deed, but the grant is said to have been resumed a long time ago, under the Sikh rule. The operation continued to be practised till long after the beginning of British rule in the Punjab."

It becomes thus clear that the surgeon who conducted operation on the nose of the culprit belonged to Kangehra community and hailed from Kangra. There is a common saying in Kangra -

Suhnana bhai suhnana, bhate kane khana, nak paya badhana, kangre jayee lagana."

'Suhnan' is a particular type of local tree found in the Shivalik ranges. People of Kangra and other regions prepare sauce of its flowers which is used without putting salt in it as its flowers contain enough salt. The raw fruits of the tree are used for making pickles. The trunk of the tree produces a special type of gum which when chewed, joins the upper and lower teeth to the extent that it is difficult to separate them with ease. A free rendering of the saying quoted above is that 'Suhnan' should be taken with rice and if nose got cut off, it can be replanted at Kangra. It appears that the surgeons of Kangehra community might have been using 'Suhnan' in one form or the other for the purpose of surgery.

There are no caste council of the community and in case of any feud statutory Panchayats and Municipal Committees or legal courts are approached. All the families of Kangheras live under the jurisdictions of Municipal Committees of their respective towns.

The Kangheras are great worshippers of the goddess Brajeshwari Devi besides other Hindu gods. They believe in the mystic powers of the goddesses and Lord Shiva. They do not have any ritual specialist of their own but the local Brahman *pandits* perform their rituals and social ceremonies.

The Kangehras celebrate Navratri Pooja when the goddess is worshipped and fasts observed. Lohri, Diwali, Vishwakarma Pooja, Krisna Janamastmi, Shivratiri and Sair are their religious and social festivals. On Dusseshra, they take part in *jhankis* and attend all functions arranged in the Devi temple and other sacred places.

The ancestors of the community were good bamboo craftsmen but the present generation is not interested in it. Carving, engraving, medicine making and doing research in various traditional systems of medicine remained their interest. The unique art of plastic surgery was practised by them, with the advent of modern system of medicine and advancement of science, it is no longer a paying profession, and as such, the present generation does not learn it. There is a painting available with one of the families in which an ancestor of the family was shown at work preparing some medicine. They also have a manuscript available containing diagnoses and formulae for various ailments. The Kangehras share the music and dance of the area.

They have traditional inter-community linkages with other communities of the region without marital exchanges. They have pulative kinship-based relations with the people of other communities and believe in making ritual-based friendship relations. These is no *Jajmani* relationship among them. Some of their members take part in political activities also.

The Kangheras are engaged in business entrepreneurship and government employment. There is an optician, a pharmacist and even a Municiapal Commissioner in the community.

The community is actively interested in the various development programmes initiated by the Government. Almost all the members of the community are educated and respond to health and medical care. Family welfare programmes have been patronised by them. It is interesting to note that some of them have retained their traditional medical profession.

B.R. Sharma

KEER

The Keer, a small community whose members are engaged in agricultural pursuits, and doing various odd jobs is distributed in Kummi and Dadaur villages of Mandi district. They are Hindus and recall their links with the Rajputs but have marital relations with their own community in Punjab. They worked as agricultural labourers with village landlords prior to Independence and had no right on landed property but with the post-Independence land reforms they were declared owners of land which was under their possession. They are not skilled craftsmen but most of them are engaged in illicit distilation of wine outside their hamlets and earn their livelihood by setting up the breweries secretly.

Some of them associate themselves with the Nungars of Punjab. Though, presently they are not engaged in salt business, earlier extracted it from the salt mines near Mandi, yet their linkages with the Nungars of Punjab hint that their ancestors might have got something to do with salt extraction in erstwhile Punjab province. About the Nungar community Ibbetson (1916: 317) writes:

> "Nungar or as it is often called Nunia or Lunia or Nunari, is derived from *nun* or salt and denotes an occupation rather than a true caste. This is true also of the Shoragar or saltpetre-maker, who is sometimes called Rehgar from *reh* or saline efflorescence. But the two terms are commonly applied to the same class of men, who indeed, now that the making of salt is prohibited in most parts of the Punjab, manufacture either saltpetre from the debris of old village sites, or crude soda (*sajji*) from the *barilla* plant which is found in the arid grazing grounds of the Western Plains. Many of them have settled down to agricultural pursuits, and this is especially true in the Multan and Derajat divisons. They also appear to carry goods from place on donkeys, which would seem to indicate a very low social status, though these men are said to consider themselves superior to the Nungars who still work at their hereditary calling, and to refuse to intermarry with them. They are generally Hindus in the east and Musalmans in the west of the Province."

The Keers of Himachal Pradesh don't associate themselves with activities related to salt making and don't keep donkeys as the Nungars of other areas mentioned. About their relationship with the Nungar of Punjab, they don't know much about it, but some did have marital relations with the Nungar of Ropar and other districts in Punjab. They claim that their ancestors fled from Rajasthan after the defeat of Maharana Pratap and settled in the area adjoining Delhi and at various places in Haryana. In some of the areas in Punjab and Haryana they are known as 'Shishodiya' Rajput. Later they were called 'Sambhar' Rajput as some of their community men were engaged in saltmaking, but those who took up ironsmithy were called as 'Bagriya'. During the sixteenth century, Raja Madansen of Suket, captured some parts of Mandi state and got hold of the salt mines at Drang and Gumma. He established his capital at Lohara in Mandi and it was perhaps at that time that the Keers were invited to take up the job of saltmaking in the state. At that time, the *begaar* system was prevalent in the state.

They trace their origin from their ancestral links with Prithvi Raj Chauhan of Kannauj. According to the history of Punjab Hill states, the Keers invaded Bharmour area of Chamba district during the 8th-10th century. They invaded Chamba area during the regime of Laxmi Verman who was killed in the encounter. Later his son Mushak Verman who is said to have been guarded by rats at the time of birth, fought against the Keers and defeated them. Mushak Verman was brought out by the ruler of Suket state and was allowed an estate at 'Pangna' in that state. It is presumed that the Keers might have ruled Chamba state for sometimes. There is no proof to establish the links of the Keers of Mandi district with the people of the same tribe of the remote past. Some say that the Keers who invaded Chamba belonged to Mongoloid stock whereas some others are of the opinion that they were the natives of some parts of Punjab. It is also worthwhile to mention that the Keers are associated with 'Kirgram' (the present Baijnath). Maha-pandit Rahul Sankrityayan calls them 'Kirata' of our scriptures. Some scholars are of the opinion that the Keers inhabited the north-western part of Kashmir and originally belonged to Yarkand or Tibet. They have been mentioned as inhabitants of Kashmir in *Raj-Tarangni* and *Brahat-Samhita*.

The Keers are mainly found in Mummi and Dadaur villages of Balh valley of Mandi district but are also found in the Syohali and Bheora villages of the valley. According to the historical records they migrated from Punjab and some of their clansmen are found in Ghanauli, Kiratpur and Kurali villages of Ropar district. They are found in other parts of Punjab and Haryana.

The habitat of the community is generally located in open spaces. They are nature lovers and like to have an open courtyard and a spacious compound around the house. They prefer hill tops for community dwelling. The climate of the areas is temperate and moderate. There is some influence of Punjabi and Rajasthani in their tones, but they write in Devanagari. Shirt, *pajama* and cap are the common dress items for men of the community. Some of them use turban also. Jacket, coat, and *lungi* are also used. The women wear *salwar, sari* and *chunni* similar to other communities of the area. The Keers are not considered to be outcastes, so their women could use gold ornaments in the past also.

They are non-vegetarian but don't take beef or buffalo meat as well as pork. Their staple food is cereals, pulses and oilseeds. Roots of some wild edible plants like *tarari* and *drehgal* are also used at times but barks are not used. They eat local vegetables like *gobhi, kaddu, karela, ghiya* etc. and local fruits including banana, citrus and other available fruits are also used. *Patroru* prepared out of leaves of *arabi* are also relished.

The home-made wine is a common drink and it is extracted almost by the whole community. They use it freely and also sell to customers from sorrounding areas. Special dishes and *pakwans* are prepared on special occasions. On Lohri festival, *khichri* of rice and moong pulse is taken with *lassi*, curd and *ghee;* on Diwali, *ankali* and *ankloo* are prepared. *Ankloo* and other preparations of rice are not made during rainy season as it is considered taboo to prepare baked *pakwans* of rice at a time when the rice crop is in the fields. On Phag (Holi), bread fried in ghee is liked. The people take food of better quality with the change in status and sources of income.

The community claims to have Chauhan, Sisodia and some other Rajput clans. There is no social differentiation but the economic position of a particular family is an important consideration for settling marital alliances. Some educated persons use their clan names as surnames. The other communities of the adjoining villages place the Keer in the lower social order. But the community considers itself in the Kshatriya varna.

During the past child marriages were a common practice but this custom has faded away with the passage of time. Marriages are now settled through negotiations by the parents from both the sides. The marriage day is decided by the priests and the bridegroom goes to the house of the bride in a marriage party. Red coloured clothes are considered auspicious and the married women use *bindi* on their foreheads along with ornaments as symbols of the married women. The instances of divorce are very uncommon and in case of remarriage, the husband receives compensation from the second husband. Bride price in some cases is accepted and dowry system is not very conspicuous. The community follows the joint family system and the young couple has to share the limited accomodation in the same house. Changes in joint family system are visible and in some cases the newly wedded sons want separate family houses. These are cases when the boy and girl don't like their marriages to be settled by their parents alone.

Joint family system is a common rule of the community. The youngsters respect the elders and obey them. Avoidance relationship exists with grand-parent-in-laws and elder brothers of the husband. Elderly people of the village are respected. Joking relationship exists between *devar-bhabhi* and *jija-sali*. In some cases conflict and confrontation is noticed between daughter-in- law and mother-in-law. All the sons get equal share in the family property but the eldest brother is the custodian of property of the family after the death of the father and mother. Inter-family linkages are given due weightage and girls are given a share in the property according to the law of the land.

The women attend to household jobs and command respect in the family. They collect fuel and fodder and attend to the social and religious activities but don't take part in political activities which are the monopoly of menfolk. Since the women are mostly uneducated, they don't contribute much to the family income by way of service but assist family members in preparing wine and attending to other household jobs. They take part in social ceremonies and rituals.

Life-cycle rituals observed by the community have three main *sanskaras*, i.e., birth ceremony including purification ceremony after seven or eight days, *namkaran* (name giving ceremony), *mundan,* marriage and death ceremonies. The family remains polluted for 11 days after the death, and after 16 days a *sanskar* called *solha* is arranged. The remains of the dead are immersed in the Ganges. Consummation of marriage is not considered to be a special ceremony in the community. No change is noticed in the practices but people are trying to simplify the marriage ceremony.

Land and preparation and marketing of wine are the main sources of income. Some members of the community work as labourers and some of them earn their livelihood by way of collecting fuel wood and selling it to the town people nearby. They have now individual proprietorship, landed property and are now a land-owning community though a few are landless or don't have enough landed property. The community is dependent on the market to some extent as they sell illicit wine and get things of every day use by doing so. Child labour is prevalent in the community. Payment of wages is made in cash and kind according to the situation.

There are *jati* Panchayats and Sabhas in the community. Such councils are based on understanding and mutual respect and formed by the elderly persons for solving social disputes. Statutory gram panchayats are playing vital roles in settling the cases these days which also punish the guilty.

The community professes Hinduism and worships the gods of the Hindu pantheon. They have faith in life after death and reincarnation. They go to Hindu *tirthas* and visit temples. Rewalsar is their nearest sacred place. They go to Hardwar and other places sacred to the Hindus. The sacred specialists from other communities perform their ritualistic ceremonies. Shivratri at Mandi is their biggest fair and festival. They also celebrate Baisakhi, Sair, Diwali, Dussehra and Lohri festivals. The folksongs and folktales of the area are shared by them. The members of the community are interested in music and dance but the community doesn't have specific music and dance patterns.

Traditional marital linkages exist within people of the community or with the Nungars living in Punjab, Haryana and other parts of the country. But some exceptions have been noticed in the system that the young boys are trying to have marital relations with girls of other communities. People of other communities accept *kachcha* food from them and exchange water. Putative relations are established with other communities. Facilities of roads, schools, crematorium, entry to temples, panchayat *ghar*, etc. are jointly shared with other communities. There is patron-client relationship with the barbers, priests, ironsmiths, etc. The people of this community are interested in political parties. Since the electorate of the commuity remains almost united so the candidates try to appease them.

The community is interested in literacy and educational programmes. They attend to health and medical care programmes. They respond to family planning programmes. They avail themselves of drinking water facilities and employment programmes such as IRDP and employment guarantee schemes. They are self-employed. They avail themselves of electricity, irrigation facilities and use chemical fertilizers. Public distribution system is also availed of. They respond to banking facilities, saving and investment system and nutrition programmes.

There have been no men of letters or of any other distinction in the community. The Keers are thus a community struggling for existence and adaptation to the changing situations in the area. Being a small community, they sometimes feel isolated and seek the help of their kith and kin outside Himachal Pradesh but they form an important part of the inhanbitants of the area.

B.R. Sharma

MAHANT

The Mahant are known by this name but some people address them as Pandit also. The term 'Mahant' carries the meaning of 'one who holds a temple or is an ascetic who has renounced the world' but according to the present study, the Mahant community in Kullu, is neither the sole proprietor of any temple or ashram nor has it the practice of renouncing the world and reside in temples or other established social or spiritual centers.

The Mahant community lives in various parts of Himachal Pradesh. The community is of two types: the Mahant who manage various temples and maths established by sages, and those who had renounced the world and devoted their lives to spiritual and social services who are mainly ascetics and the successors of the head saints of the ashrams concerned. But the Mahant community, which belongs to the normal social order of the inhabitants in Kullu region is the successor of temple priests who came to that area with the principal deity Raghunath Ji from Ayodhya. They are still the managers of various activities relating to god Raghunath Ji, the presiding deity of the ruling family of erstwhile Kullu state and principal deity of the famous Kullu Dussehra festival held during October every year. They are family holders and have got landed property also.

There is a legend that some three hundred years back a ruler of Kullu suffered from leprosy and could not be cured even after consulting the best healers in the region. At last he was advised by sage, named Krishan Dass Payehari who stayed at Naggar, the then capital of Kullu state, that he should install an image of Raghunath Ji after managing to get in from a temple at Ayodhya. The ruler managed to have an image of Raghu Nath Ji as desired by the saint and established it in Raghunath Temple at Kullu. Raghunath ji is Lord Rama and his consort Sita is also adorned in another image accompanying the image of the presiding deity. Various local gods in their wooden palanquins are brought to Dhalpur Maidan in Kullu to pay their homage to the presiding deity during the days of Dussehra festival.

The Mahant community is not restricted only to Kullu town but it is distributed in some other villages of the state also. The Mahants who act as managers or head-saints of various temples or ashrams which are established on the Jagir offered to saints by the rulers or Jagirdars of previous times are not many in the state. Some Mahants however manage the goddess and god temples in Kangra, Bilaspur, Una and Hamirpur areas but they are not the sole proprietors of the shrines and their role is almost similar to the family holding. Their number is very limited.

In Daroh village (Kangra) there are two families of this community. They have landed property and are holding the status of household families with married people in the household. People address them as Gosain or Baba and they bury their dead. They are the *pujari* of the local Shiva temple and are entitled to the income of the temple. They are endogamous and have their marital relationship with Mahants or Gosains settled at Chowari in Chamba, Sunder Nagar in Mandi and some other places in Kangra. They have their relationship with the Gosain settled at Bara in Hamirpur district. The Gosains have started writing their surname as 'Goswami'. People address them as Mahant also. They bury their dead in 'Samadhi' posture i.e. in Padmasan and recite some *mantra* before the ceremony. It is believed that some of their ancestors had renounced the world but their progeny started leading a settled life and acquired landed property also. Perhaps they are called 'Mahant' as they manage the affairs of the local temple which is a gifted property. They also consider themselves Brahman

The Mahants of Kullu believe that their ancestors came from Ayodhya and other parts of the country in the service of Lord Raghunath ji and later some of them attended the other local village gods who with the installation of the Lord as the presiding deity of the State were attending his Darbar as subordinate deities.

The community is found in villages of Kullu, Sultanpur, Dobhi, Naggar, etc. Though it is not a farming community, it has got some landed property and own permanent settlements in all the villages where it is found. No census figures relating to total population of the Mahants are available. These people speak the Kullui dialect and can converse in Hindi and Urdu also. The educated ones have knowledge of English also. They use Devanagari script for all their written communications with their kin and others.

They wear Kullui dress as is worn by people of other communities in the area. The area is hilly and woollen clothes such as shawls, coats, woollen long coats, trousers, sweaters, pullovers and leather coats, etc. are used during winters. Colourful Kullu shawls and designed woollen garments decorated with border laces and linings are the special favourites of the people of the area as also of the Mahant women and menfolk.

The community is vegetarian but some of them consume eggs. They take staple food consisting of maize, wheat, rice, cereals, pulses and oil seeds etc. Roots of some wild plants like *taradi* (a type of tuber) are also taken. They are fond of green vegetables grown by them. These include cabbage, potatoes, *saag*, lady finger, *arabi,* etc. Fruits like banana, apple, chestnut, ground nut, Japani fruit, almond, and a number of other local fruits are consumed. Local drinks are also used by some of them. Milk is popular in the community. Alcoholic drinks are rarely consumed.

There are no major social divisions in the community. They place themselves among the Brahmans but the higher clan Brahmans don't accept them for matrimonial alliances as their economic status, according to them, lags behind their own. The Mahants however consider themselves superior to others and form an endogamous community.

The marriage set-up of the community is not separate in any way. The marriage settlements are generally through negotiations initiated by the parents. The parents of girls through some medium or mediator express their desire for matrimonial settlements with the parents of the suitable boy. The marriage age is generally 20 years for a boy and 18 years for girl. Exchange marriages are not common and divorce is also very rare. Bride price is not paid but a tolerable dowry, according to the economic conditions of the family, is permitted but not demanded. In case of *haari* or marriage after leaving the first husband, the second husband has to make good the loss of money suffered by the first husband as negotiated by local or Biradari Panchayat as the case may be. Post-divorce maintenance system is not prevalent as the divorce takes place only in case of second marriage by a woman and in that case the new husband pays some compensation to the first or former husband. In that case, the children by the first husband are either taken by him or the wife takes her children with the consent of her new husband to his house. In some cases on seeing the plight of the mother, her parents also take the responsibility of bringing up the children. But a change is being noticed in the marriage system and it is becoming simpler and without the involvement of the parents of both the sides. However, their consent is not totally done away with. The friends of the boy and girl are now playing greater role in the settlement of marriages.

The Mahants have a joint family system. They have cordial and affectionate relationships within the family. Their interpersonal relations are based on respect and regards to the elders, avoidance among women especially those who have entered the family after having been married to its fold, mutual understanding among the members and sharing of joys and sorrows among all. Inheritance is according to the rules of equal shares to all the brothers and sisters but the married sisters don't want to share the property in the family of their parents and offer their shares to brothers. The eldest son is the head of the family after the death of the parents. Women also have to head and direct the family in the absence of aged and experienced men if necessary.

The Mahant women enjoy a respectable place in the family with the status of dominance and they mix with others freely and without hesitation but are loyal to their life partners. They are not much inhibited but are god-fearing, affectionate, good devotees to the local gods, expert in handling household affairs and are gay and cheerful in nature. They help the family in agriculture, horticulture and preservation of culture. By working in the fields and apple orchards, they relieve the economic tension in the family. They knit, spin and even weave their woollen garments. They are hospitable and social in nature and take good care of their children and are not touchy about the menfolk of the household who are stuck up outside in connection with their jobs and other errands.

The Mahants observe life-cycle rituals as are observed by people of other communities residing in the area. Pollution after birth is observed for seven or nine days as per the instructions of the oracle of the local deity or the priest and generally 13 days are considered polluted after the death in the family. During this period and up to 40 days in case of birth in the family, the local deity is not lifted or touched. During their menstruation period the women avoid going to the temples and do not touch the palanquin of the village god. They observe fast on various auspicious occasions. Name giving ceremony is performed without pomp and show. According to the local traditions, however, the tonsure ceremony is performed at some temple and the father of the child has to perform some joking feats such as shooting an arrow towards a fixed target on a long pole fixed in the temple premises especially belonging to Jamloo god. But this practice is not found in all the villages. So the name giving and tonsure ceremonies are performed on a smaller scale as compared to birth, marriage and death ceremonies. Marriage is a occasion of joy so the Mahants arrange special feasts to their near and dear ones.

The members of the community are the managers of shrines but they are considered inferior to Pujari Malis (oracles) and work like other *kardar* of village temples. Their duties are restricted to arranging various rituals and working according to the wishes of the oracle or Pujari. They know about the ritual aspect of the ceremonies and help in arranging the ceremonies in traditional ways.

During Dussehra festival, when the presiding deity Raghunath ji is brought out to Dhalpur Maidan in a wooden palanquin and worshipped in a traditional way in the shrine, the Mahant had to play a prominent role in performing the ceremony. Some years back a Mahant youth was expected to rub *sindoor,* oil and different colours to his body so that he could act as Hanuman and symbol of an evil spirit together. He used to smear *sindoor* in such a way that his appearance would not be recognised by even his known people for some time. After doing so used to sit on one side of the multitude or at a secluded place visible conspicuously to the gathering and behave like Hanuman. At the time of the chariot of Lord Raghunath being dragged to the center of Dhalpur Maidan, he sometimes gets up and rubs his body with whosoever comes his way. To make the ceremony more jovial, he would rush towards the men and women and they, in fright would avoid him as otherwise he would spoil their clothes while rubbing his body with them. It was believed that it would be better to avoid the rubbing but if it was unavoidable in any case, it was a common belief that those who are caught in the hobnob would be blessed with a son during the period of one year starting from Dussehra. It was a good source of recreation for the people attending the festival. Now this practice has been abandoned as the Mahant youth are not ready to take part in the performance. From this it appears that the community was not taken seriously by the controllers of various rituals of the shrines and were allotted jobs at their wishes.

The Mahants have their community panchayat and take decisions regarding any dispute whatsoever in their panchayat. The Jati Panchayat settles disputes relating to divisions in the family, marriage disputes and any other break disgrace to the community or family by having done injuries to the prestige or tradition of the people.

The Mahants consider themselves special devotees and attendants of Lord Raghunath, so they make it a point to be present on all ceremonies relating to the deity. They have their assigned jobs to perform at the time of various rituals. In order to make their both ends meet, they practise astrology, palmistry, have expertise in herbal medicines and performing worship with *mantras* and guide people in socioreligious activities. They are associated with all the fairs and festivals related to Lord Raghunath.

The Mahants are respected and invited by the people of other castes as they act as priests also. They are however, not oracles of any of the deities in the valley.

Now with the spread of education, the youth of the community is changing its attitude towards the traditional approach of the community towards their performance, and their knowledge in the fields where their older generation remained involved is limited. As such the community is feared to lose its original identity in future and their *yajman* (clients) would be less interested in their involvement in various household rituals. There has been no hero or a big saint or priest in the community to perform remarkable historical or religious event.

They have good relationships with the members of other communities, and a positive approach towards development programmes. They take part in all the programmes initiated by the government.

The community, with the passage of time, is becoming more and more keen about the education of their children and some of the members have entered in government or private jobs.

B.R. Sharma

MAWI

The Mawi or Mawis is an ancient community which is almost extinct but some of its families are located in outer Seraj and the hilly areas of Kullu district. The ancestors of the community were owners of the forts which they constructed on high mountain tops. The people of this community were against the local rulers who are known as 'Thakurs' or 'Rao' or 'Rahu' and wanted to oust them with the help of the local population and through Greek warfare strategy known as 'Dheeng' during 6th to 10th century AD.

According to this technique, the upper portion of the trunk of a tree was made full of cavities where big stones were inserted. These stones or boulders were used with a bang to kill the enemies. One such fort still exists near Sarpara village in 15/20 (*pandra beesh*) area of Shimla district. There is a legend in the area that the Mawis wore a Greek dress and did not allow any one to come near the fort. A Mawi family still resides in the above mentioned area but it has no typical system of living and does not know much about the Dheeng— the system of warfare. It was reported by the President of the Gram Panchayat that some years back there was a circular from the Deputy Commissioner, Shimla to all the panchayats of the area to find out some man who knew the techinque of 'Dheeng' but after a thorough probe none could be found, and the system remains a legendary one.

The Mawis are a revolutionary people who did not get reconciled to their contemporary rulers. The families of the community have intermingled and amalgamated with the local people so much so that no difference in customs, rituals and other aspects of life is ascertainable now. It is, however, said by the people of the area, where the forts in a dilapidated condition are located that when they visit the sites of the forts, bugs who are otherwise in a dying condition come out and start sucking the blood of the visitors. After sometime these tiny insects grow fat and start running on the walls of the forts. This is a strange phenomena that on hill tops where snowfall is very heavy, these creatures remained alive since time immemorial and wait for the visit of human beings.

The Mawis are now known as Rajput and in the Rajput community fold but people of the area keep them in high esteem because they were from the warrior class. The other community in the area which tried to capture power in parts of the hilly region, is 'Rao' or 'Rahu'. This community is from the Kanet stock and had enemity with the Khasas of ancient days. Raos are found in plenty in remote areas and in village Diyar in Kullu. They did not like to dine with the Khasas, who are their neighbourers in that very village. The Rao or Rahu do not have a separate social identity these days and it has become a clan or subgroup of some of the Rajputs in the area.

B.R. Sharma

NAGVANSHI

The Nagvanshi use Nag as their surname and Khadpa as a synonym in district Kangra. In their language Khadpa means one who strikes back in anger or is revengeful. However, Khadpa, Pundrik and Goslu are also regarded as subgroups by some. As far as the history of their origin is concerned the informants could only mention that there is reference to Nags and their kingdom in Mahabharata. W.E. Crooke's (1896: 39) writes:

> "Nagvanshi are a sept of Rajputs in Gorakhpur, of whom Dr. Buchanan writes 'there are in this district a good many Nagbansis, some of whom call themselves merely by that name, while others call themselves Vayasas, a name which in the account of Shahabad has been written as Vais. The Vayasas or Vais, however, universally admit that they are Nagbansis, and that they assumed the name of Vayasas from Vayaswara, a town between Lucknow and the Ganges, where they were long settled, and from whence they came to this district, some generations ago, in consequence of a famine. Some of these, with whom I conversed agreed with the account which I received at Shahabad, and looked upon themselves as descended of the great dragon (*nag*)'".

Informants from Himachal Pradesh report that the Nagvanshis migrated from Bengal during first Muslim invasion of Bengal. They also mention that there are Nag in Jammu and Kashmir, Bengal, Assam and South India. One informant from Shimla is of the opinion that they are called Nag as they are *nag pujak* or worshippers of *nag* (serpent). They mention that there was one Nag king, Bhagsu Nag, in the district of Kangra who was very famous, and till date he is worshipped. There is a temple of Bhagsu Nag in the district of Kangra near Dharamshala. They live in undulated terrain. They speak Pahari and Kangri at home and Hindi outside. They also use English with outsiders. They use Devanagari and Roman scripts. They do not have any identification mark.

The Nag eat both vegetarian and non-vegetarian food items. Those who are non-vegetarian consume meat, fish, egg, chicken and pork. But they do not consume beef and buffalo flesh. Rice, wheat and maize are their staple cereals. They consume all sorts of pulses. They use mustard oil as a cooking medium. They consume patato, ginger, onion, garlic, etc. All sorts of locally available seasonal vegetables and seasonal fruits are consumed. They consume milk, curd, *lassi* and tea. They do not take alcoholic drinks.

Two groups of the Nagvanshis are noted: Brahman Nag and Thakar Nag. The Thakars claim to be Rajput. The Brahman Nags are divided into *gotras* like Kashyap, Bharadwaj, Sukalyan. The Nag Brahmans belonging to Sukalyan *gotra* consider themselves lower in socioreligious status in comparison to the Brahman Nag belonging to Kashyap and Bharadwaj *gotra*. The basis of differentiation among the Thakar Nags and the Brahman Nags is Hindu varna system. They are also occupationally different. The Brahman Nag do not practise agriculture personally but the Thakar Nag do involve themselves in agriculture. Though the former do not cultivate their holdings by their own hands, they do supervise agricultural operations in their land. The social divisions of Nag control marital and commensal relations. The Thakar Nag marry among other Rajputs and abide by the rule of *gotra* exogamy. The Brahman Nag consider themselves superior to the Thakar, Bania and others. The Thakar Nags claim equal status with other septs of the same community.

The Nag are exogamous at *gotra* and lineage levels. They practise adult marriages. A Nag boy generally gets married between the age of 22 and 28 years and a Nag girl between the age of 18 and 22 years. Marriage by negotiation is the most preferred and prevalent mode of acquiring mates. But sometimes marriage by exchange is also practised. Monogamous form of marriage is the most prevalent form. Married women use *sindur*, nose stud and *chak* on the forehead as symbols of marriage. Bride price is absent in the community. But the girls' parents give marriage gifts to their daughters in kind. After marriage, the newly married couple live either with the boy's parents or they set up their new home near to the place where the husband works. Divorce is not socially permitted but one can seek divorce through legal procedures. Remarriage of both widow and widower is generally permitted among the Nag excepting the Brahman where it is not a common practice.

Both nuclear and extended families exist among the Nag. Interpersonal relation is of love, respect, avoidance and joking exist. The wife respects the husband and she avoids him in presence of elder relatives. Brothers develop relationship of conflict on sharing of paternal property. Grandparents and grandchildren have joking relationship. Paternal property is equally shared by the brothers. Sisters do not get a share of paternal property. Succession follows male primogeniture. Interfamily relations are cordial and every family takes part in socioreligious occasions of neighbouring families.

Nag women are also employed as teachers, doctors and do all household chores. They also look after cattle, and collect fuel and fodder.

The Brahmans among the Nag observe 11 day birth pollution called *sutak*. On the eleventh day of birth the priest prepares *tipra* (horoscope) of the child and finds out the auspicious letter to name the child depending on the time of birth. On that day *kuldevta* (Nag) is worshipped and pollution gets over. A feast is arranged by the father of the child on the occasion. *Mundan* ceremony is performed either on first, third or fifth year. *Janeu* ceremony is performed on the thirteenth or fifteenth year of age. No adolescence ceremony is observed for girls. The Thakar Nags observe 21 days' birth pollution. On the twenty-first day of birth, a *purohit* comes and invokes *kuldevta* by performing *havan.* An auspicious letter is found out from the alphabet by the *purohit* to name the child depending on the time of birth of the child. A feast is given by the father of the child on this day and birth pollution ends. *Annaprashan* ceremony is performed between the age of six months and one year. *Mundan* is performed either in the first or third year.

Marriage is called *bivah* by the Nag. On completion of marriage negotiation, the family priest is called in to find out the auspicious date and time for both *sagan* (betrothal) and *bivah.* A day before marriage a paste of turmeric powder and musturd oil is applied on both the bride and the groom called *batna.* The bridegroom boards a *palki* to reach the bride's place. On arrival, the groom's party, *baratis,* made to sit in some other house or a specially raised *pandal* for the purpose. A Brahman *purohit* presides over the ceremonial part of marriage. *Havan* is performed and both the bride and the groom circumambulate the sacred fire. They take the vow of remaining lifelong partners. A feast is given to the *barat*, relatives and friends by the bride's father. On the next day of marriage the newly married couple and *barat* return to groom's village. A feast is given by groom's father to his relatives, friends and neighbours.

The Nag cremate the dead. Death pollution is observed for 10 to 12 days. In case of 10 day pollution the sons shave off their heads and *shradha* and *pind dan* is performed on the eleventh day. *Mundan,* the shaving off of head as a symbol of mourning is done on the day of the death in the family after the cremation of the dead. Similarly, in case of 12 day death pollution, *mundan* is done on the twelfth day and *shradh* and *pind dan* are performed on the thirteenth day of death and a Brahman *bhojan* is performed. Yearly death ritual is performed for three years. On the fourth year the final death ritual is performed and a feast is given to the villagers. After fourth year, two death rituals are performed annually, one on the day of death and the other during *shradh paksha.*

Land is the major economic source for the Nag. The Nag Brahman however, do not till their land but either engage tillers from castes practising agriculture or they engage crop sharers to cultivate their plot of agricultural land. There are both landowning and landless families among the Nag. The teaching of astrology and advisory work was their traditional occupation. They are dependent on the local trade market.

No traditional caste council or modern regional association of the Nags exists. The is statutory village panchayat looks after various developmental and welfare works of the village. The Nag follow Hinduism and are Shaivites and Shaktas. Nag Devta is worshipped by them as *kuldevta* in general. They also worship Jawalaji, Balak Nath, Chintpurni, Brajeshwari, etc., as regional deities. Besides, they worship deities of the wider Hindu pantheon. Sacred specialists perform birth, marriage and death rites. Some women do cloth embroidery. Folksongs are sung during birth and marriage. They use percussion and windblown musical instruments.

The Nag have traditional *jajmani* with various service groups like Nai, Kumhar, Lohar, Barhai, Chamar, etc. They serve various castes as priest, astrologer, etc. The Nag Brahmans accept food and water from other Brahman, Rajput, Bania, etc. but not from Chamar and Dholi, etc. They accept *sidha* from Thakar Nag and Kumhar. The Thakar Nags accept food and water from Brahman, other Rajputs, Bania and Kumhar but also not from Chamar, Dholi, etc. Inter-caste marriage has not been reported among the Nags. Putative kinship relations like *kangan bhai* and *kangan bhan* are reported. They share water sources with other castes of the area.

They have modern linkages with other castes of the area as Government servants, teachers, doctors, etc. They take part in local political activities. As landowners they have relations with other castes of the area as employers. Among the Thakar Nag those who are landless agriculturists or daily labourers have relations with other castes of the locality as employees.

They are eager to get their children educated. Health and medical facilities are available to them. Family welfare programme has been accepted by the Nags. They get drinking water either from hand-pump or from piped source. Some of them are self-employed as lawyers, shop owners, agriculturists, etc. They listen to radio and watch television. Electricity is available to them. They use firewood, kerosene and LPG as fuel. Irrigation facility is available to them. They use chemical fertilizers and insecticides. Foodgrains at fair price is available to them through the public distribution system. They have a positive attitude towards savings.

Mukul Hazra

NATH

The Nath is distributed in various parts of Himachal Pradesh. It is divided into two sub-sects. One sect is of hermits who have renounced the world and live like saints practising meditation and useful mystic practice including traditional method of treatment, relieving people of magic effects, spirits, evil effects of ghosts and other mental and physical ailments. They practise palmistry, astrology and spiritual pursuits. The other sect of the community consists of household people who have landed property in various villages of Kangra, Mandi, Kullu and some other districts.

Those who are non-householders are not so many in number as the Dashnami Akharas and the other shrines which they are associated with are not very many. Their biggest concentration is at Jawalamukhi where they are managing the 'Gorakh Dibi' (the boiling water potlike formation associated with Guru Gorakh Nath). At Bharmaur in Chamba the legend of the visit of nine Naths and eighty-four Siddhs during the ancient times, is recorded in the history of erstwhile Chamba state and there are various fables relating to miracles and unusual feats performed by the Naths or Kanphatta Yogis. Nawala festival, a ceremony arranged to worship Lord Shiva and Mani Mahesh Jatra (the festivals of Mani Mahesh) as well as some other fairs and festivals arranged in Chamba region even upto the present time are associated with the Nath cult. Some *mantras* (chants) to cure a snake-bite and warding off poisonous effects of various types on the body, are still prevalent in various parts of the State in the name of Nath Yogis, especially Guru Gorakh Nath. The Naths are revered as great mendicants and realized saints. It is said that Charpat Nath, one of the nine Nath Yogis belonged to Bharmaur village of Chamba district. He was the Guru of Sahil Verman, the founder ruler of Chamba state. His temple is situated in the town of Chamba and his disciple Champa, who is worshipped as goddess and whose temple is situated near Chamba Chaugan, is considered the spirit behind the establishment of the capital of the state at Chamba. Numerous disciples of nine Nath Yogis running various Dasnami Akharas in the region establish their strong faith in the cult and the *Chhari* (mace) for Mani Mahesh Jatra, a sacred lake located at an elevation of about 14000 feet above the mean sea level, is taken in a procession in the name of Yogi Charpat Nath from Chamba to Mani Mahesh every year.

The Nath community, residing in Kullu has taken to agriculture as other activities such as singing legends and songs of Bhartrihari, helping in the performance of traditional festivals like Shant and Bhunda (ropesliding ceremony), etc. In Kullu district the people of this community reside in the villages of Parshi, Khokhan, Ganakhal, Dhunju, Bhaikhali, Kharahal, Jhaul, Dobhi, Jawani, Pari and some other villages. They prepare rosaries of flower and flower cases and present and sell them to those in need. They also beg alms by reciting 'Alakh Niranjan', a slogan popular with the Nath Yogis. They perform the last rites of the people of other castes also.

During the month of Magh (January-February) the male members of this community putting long sticks of wood to their heads and covering it with a piece of red cloth, while playing with a bell and a musical instrument, known as *kansi* go from village to village singing a song called 'Bahatwara'. They say the word 'Bahatwara' at the end of every line of the song. This term is not clear to others and is taken as an opening rhythm only to add a mysterious cover to the presentation. They present the song in a duet form. A portion of the song is as under:

Kungu dori Bahatwara.

First person: *Hua biana Bahatwara.*

Second voice: *Kungu dori Bahatwara.*

Ghar Ghar dori Bhatwara.

'*Bahatwara*' is a character in some other presentations. He performs the role of 'Sravana' in the folk theatre of Ramayana presented by the artists of the community.

The community has not received the attention it deserved. The members of the community are artists by nature and use ancient and traditional musical instruments; *kinnari veena* (Kindari) and *singi* (horn) are the rare and mystic instruments used by Nath and Siddha Yogis to produce enchanting tunes. These instruments are only used by Nath artists while presenting ballads and ritualistic songs. The community is located in mountainous regions in the state and it is believed that they are the followers of Nath Yogis who settled in these areas and were forced by the circumstances to serve the inhabitants of other communities continuing the tradition of their mentor Sadhus. They use their musical instrument and ballads while earning their livelihood. They speak local dialects and the script used by them is Devanagari.

The Naths are usually vegetarian but keeping in view the local climate some of them are non-vegetarian also. They don't consume buffalo or cow meat. Pork is also not consumed by the community. The staple food of the Naths is cereals, pulses and oilseeds. They take local products such as maize, rice, wheat, barley and pulses of different types. Roots of some edible plants are also consumed but this is just an occasional and casual type of arrangement. Fruits are consumed in plenty.

The Naths generally don't consume liquor but this is not taboo. Milk and other non-alcholohic drinks are used. Those who are interested in taking drinks, like homemade as well as *desi* and English brands of wine.

Change in food habits is being noticed as with the improvement in transportation and communication system things are becoming more and more accessible to common people of even remote villages.

There are no social divisions among the Naths. All the Naths settled in various villages are endogamous. The community is considered outcaste by others but falls between upper and lower castes and communities. During various festivals, they are given alms. They consider themselves to be in line with some great Yogis like Guru Gorkh Nath and don't easily want to part with the knowledge and mystic powers they might have got from their ancestors. During the rope sliding ceremony (Bhunda) a Nath was made to occupy the throne of Lord Parshuram, kept in Parshu Ram temple at Nirmand in Kullu district for some time. He was worshipped and his body painted in different colours. He was then made to lead a procession through the streets of the village followed by *mashal* (wooden torches) and basket full of grains and other eatables during the year 1981 when Bhunda ceremony was held thereafter a span of nineteen years. The Nath left the village at the sunset with the objects offered to him and didn't come back to stay during the night as it was believed by the villages that by allowing him to stay in the village again would mean that the evil spirits, who might have come to see the fair of Bhunda after hearing the tunes played on musical instrument, would come back with him again not to leave the village. The Nath, this way, represented the deity and was sent out of the village during the odd hours to drive away the spirits haunting the village during the festival period. People in some village feel that the Naths are capable of driving away the spirits and help people fighting evil spirits who inflict illness on them, with their magical powers.

The Naths, as already said, marry within their community. The age of marriage for the boys is about twenty years and for girls about eighteen years. The marriage is performed in a simple way without any demand of dowry. This is done through negotiations by parents of the boy and the girl. Exchange marriages though not very common are also not an exception. *Sindur* is applied on the forehead of the bride at the time of marriage by the bridegroom. The bride stays in the house of her in-laws after the marriage. Divorce is uncommon but both the spouses are at liberty to break the marriage after completing some formalities and decide to remarry.

The Naths prefer joint family system but deviation from this is also not an exception. All sons get an equal share in the property. The eldest son is the head of family after the death of his parents. Inter-personal relationship is quite cordial. Respect and affection as well as fear of elders and avoidance from in-laws and elder brother of the husband are common practices. Change in the family system is noticeable and the small family concept in gaining ground. Women have a place of respect in the family. According to the latest arrangements, they enjoy the right to the property of the parents but they prefer to leave it at their own will to their brothers. The women are a great help to the men in smooth running of the household affairs. They attend to the household chores and take keen interest in bringing up children and making arrangements of their proper education.

The life-cycle rituals are observed like other communities of respective areas. The idea of pollution after the birth of a child is kept in view for 5,7 or 9 days according to the instructions of the priest or village god. After death in a family, it is considered polluted for 13 days but complete sanctification is reached after 40 days. *Yajnopavit* is worn by the community and tonsure is done by the brother of the mother or some other person who becomes god-maternal uncle after this ceremony.

The dead body is cremated but those families in which some body has taken *sanyas* during his lifetime or those who are the Nath Yogis, are buried. The graves of those who are buried are also worshipped with incense from time to time.

Economic activities of the Naths are dependent on education, business, but earlier on *yajmani* (patron-client) and traditional system of healing, astrology, magic, driving away the spirits, playing musical instruments, singing ballads and wishing happy new year and performing rituals in the villages. Their traditional knowledge is now limited only to the older generation, who believed in ghosts, evil spirits and folkloristic trends. The community is mainly landless but some of them have small landed property. They serve as manual and skilled labourers. The following account is available about the community in Ibbetson (1916:236):

> "The Naths of the higher hills, where the worship of Siva is prevalent, correspond very closely with the Jogis of the plains, though they make little pretence to an ascetic character and live chiefly by growing vegetables; but they also perform certain semi-sacredotal function, taking the place of the Acharj of the plains in the funeral ceremonies of the Kanets, and receiving like him the clothes of the deceased. They also consecrate new houses, and purify them when they have been defiled. They now form a true caste and are not recruited from without. One or more in almost every Nath household has his ears pierced in honour of Siva, and is called a Kanphatta Nath. They occupy much the same social position as the Jogi-Rawal of the plains. They are understood to have returned themselves as Jogis."

Jogis are also found in Hamirpur, Kangra, Una and some other parts of the State. Under the head Jogi Ibbetson (1916:235) included two very distinct classes of persons:

> "First are the Jogis proper, a regular religious order of Hindus, which includes both the Augar Jogis and the Kanphatta Jogi ascetics, who are followers of Gorakh Nath and priests and worshipers of Siva. These men are fully as respectable as the Bairagis, Gosains, and other religious orders".

He further writes about the Jogis at page 228 as follows:

> "The Jogi will presently be discussed under the head of Minor Professional Castes. It will there be explained that the word originally means nothing more than one who has by the practice of mental abstraction acquired the power of clairvoyance and similar faculties. But besides the low-class Jogi Rawal there described there are two sets of exceedingly respectable Jogi Faqirs, the Kanppatta who pierce their ears and the Augar who do not. The former are priests of Siva and are generally to be found in Shivalas. The latter too are Saiva but are more secular. The Kanppatta is also called Darshana.... The Jogis bury their dead in a sitting posture."

It is clear from the above description that the Nath, Jogi and Rawal have been clubbed together. But, it is not clear whether when Rawals after whose name the town of Rawalpindi was ascribed, migrated to Himachal Pradesh, but the two remaining communities, the Jogi and Nath are found at various places. A separate study of the Bairagi community has since been conducted. The Jogis who run the family and household affairs are permanently settled in various parts of the State now, and associate themselves with Brahman community like Bairagi but the Naths are considered to be of the lower strata of society. Though, ascetic the Naths are respected as mendicants and considered capable of driving away the ill effects of spirits and magic, etc., but the permanent settlers among them are not considered of that status. The assessment made about them in the paragraph referred to above appears to be correct. There is however, some commonness between the two communities, viz, they are a departure from their ascetic ancestors, so until an indepth study is made in the subject they may be placed together.

The Gosain community has also the same type of set-up, i.e., a part of the community belongs to the ascetics and the other one to the permanent settlers. About them Ibbetson (1916:227) says as follows:

> "The Gosain is a Saiva order corresponding in many ways with the Bairagis among Vaishnavas. Like them the Gosains are often collected in monasteries, while many of them officiate as priests in the temple of Siva. They are also like the Bairagis, one of the most respectable of the Hindu orders. They are very commonly but not all necessarily celibate."

The Naths have their traditional Biradari Panchayats and are receptive to the programmes initiated by the government. They are good artists and honest and upright people. They are storehouses of myths and legends and present various ballads including Ramayana, Mahabharata, Bhartrihari, Gopichand, Shravan, etc. on scheduled times, in their *yajmani* village. During winter they present these ballads and epics during the night singing and performing.

B. R. Sharma

A BIO-ANTHROPOLOGICAL REPORT

Bio-anthropological variation in humankind is the result of four evolutionary agents, mutation, selection, hybridization and genetic drift. Himachal Pradesh provides ample scope for the action of all these forces in view of enormous diversity of all types, geographical, climatic, ecological, social and cultural. Prolonged seclusion of many communities in Himachal Pradesh in remote areas practising endogamy resulted in enhanced frequencies of certain biological traits and elimination of others through selection and genetic drift. However, relaxation of community endogamy under various constraints both in geographical seclusion or in the mainstream urbanized centres, provides opportunity for different traits or genes to contribute to the gene pool of a community resulting thereby in a wide range of variations. History of migration and socio-political events acted as catalysts to change the original biological composition of ancient communities in Himachal Pradesh. The introduction of the Indo-Aryan ethnic element from Indo-Gangetic plains, right from proto-historical to recent times into the ancient Caucasoid populations (like the Khasa) and the ancient Australoid or proto-Australoid ones (like Koli, Dom, etc), has brought about considerable bio-anthropological diversity in Himachal Pradesh, especially in the lower and middle eco-cultural regions. In addition, the Tibeto-Burman Mongoloid people, who entered into H.P. during recent historical times, also brought about changes in the biological make up of the Himachalis, especially in the upper eco-cultural region. The interplay of all these natural, social and historical phenomena/events can be glimpsed in bio-anthropological traits of the people of Himachal Pradesh, briefly presented below.

Bio-anthropological information is provided here on various traits under the following five major categories: (I) somatometric, (II) dermatoglyphic (III) certain genetic, (IV) serological, and (V) biochemical characters. The compiled data tables from different sources are given in Singh *et. al.* (1994). In view of limited sample size and/or technical reasons a few studies are ignored here.

I. SOMATOMETRIC VARIABLES

Common characters like stature, head types, nose and facial forms are considered for understanding somatometric variability .

1. Stature: Only 10.4 % people are *tall* on an average (i.e. above 170 cms), and the Muslim Gujjars (174.2 cm) are among them. The *above medium tall* (167.0-169.9 cms) are also fewer (12.2 %). The *medium tall* (164.0-166.9 cms) are relatively more frequent (16.5 %), namely, the Tibetan (Dharamshala), Rajput (Barot and Chamba) and Kanet (Kalpa- Kinnaur and Pattan valley). The common stature (27.4 %) category is of the *below medium tall* (160.0-163.9 cms) people, like Rajput (Mandi and Manali), Gaddi (Dharamshala), Kanet (Lahaul, Parvati Valley and Malana), the Kinnaura, various social groups of the Gorkha, and the Manchati (Chamba). More commonly (31.7%) however, the Himachalis are of *short* average stature (150.0-159.9 cms), but very few (1.8 %) are of *very short stature* (below 150 cms).

The average stature for all Himachalis, however, is 162.2 cms (in the *below medium tall* category), and points to a mixed character with preponderance of Indo-Aryan and ancient Caucasoid ethnic element.

2. Head Type: The maximum head breadth and length index called Cephalic Index (CI) speaks of four head types. Above half (53.5 %) people with CI 71.0-75.9 are long and narrow-headed (*dolicocephalic*) - an Indo-Aryan/Caucasoid ethnic trait noticed among the Rajput, Gaddi, Kanet (Kullu, Malana, Parvati & Pattan valleys) and Manchati (Chamba). However, the Kinnaura are exceptionally very long and narrow-headed (*hyper dolicocephalic*) with low Cephalic Index (65.5)—also a Caucasoid character. Nearly 1/4th (25.76 %) Himachalis have medium head type (*mesocephalic*) with higher Cephalic Index (76.0-80.9) as reported for the Rajput sections of the Gorkha (CI 77.1-78.8) though Brahman and Newar Gorkha (Dhauladhar-Chamba area) are relatively long-narrow headed (CI 75.1-75.6). Other *mesocephals* are the Kanet of Kalpa (CI 76.5) and Lahaul (CI 77.5), and the Tibetan of Dharamshala (CI 78.4-79.0). The short and broad head type (*brachycephalic*) typical of the Eastern/North Eastern Mongoloids (CI above 81) is just 3.5 % in Himachal Pradesh.

The over-all average Cephalic Index of 74.2 for Himachalis speaks for the preponderance of the Indo-Aryan/Caucasoid ethnicity.

3. Nose Type: Almost half (48.1%) of the people have narrow (*leptorrhine*) nose, with 55.0-69.0 Nasal Index (NI). Nearly the same (48.4%) have medium (*mesorrhine*) nose type (NI 70.0-84.9). But people of very narrow (*hyper leptorrhine*) nose (NI below 54.9) are rare (2.1%), and that of the broad (*chamaerrhine*) nose (NI above 85) are rarer still (1.3%). The Manchati (NI 63.8), Gaddi (NI 65.0), and the Kanet at large (NI 63.6-65.6) (except those of Kullu, who are *mesorrhine* with NI 74.1) are *leptorrhine* type. The Gorkha are *mesorrhine* (NI 69.3-76.4), whereas the Tibetan are *lepto-mesorrhine* (NI 68.3-70.9).

Leptorrhiny is an Indo-Aryan/Caucasoid trait, but *chamaerrhiny* occurs in certain Austro-Asiatic Mongoloids and Australoids, and also among Dravidian Caucasoids, while *mesorrhiny* is quite prevalent in India. The average Nasal Index for Himachalis (68.95) falls at the threshold of *leptorrhiny* and *mesorrhiny*, suggesting unique/mixed character.

4. Facial Type: About 1/3rd Himachalis (33.1%) have a broad (*euryprosopic*) face with Total Facial Index (TFI) ranging between 79.0-83.9. Almost the same (32.4%) have a medium (*mesoprosopic*) face (TFI 84.0-87.9). The narrow-faced (*leptoprosopic*) people (TFI 88.0-92.9) are 22.8%, and a half (11.8%) of the same have a very broad (*hyper-euryprosopic*) face (TFI below 78.9). The very narrow-faced (*hyper-leptoprosopic*) category (TFI above 93.3) is altogether lacking in Himachal Pradesh.

The narrow face is observed in the Gaddi (TFI 89.4), Manchati (TFI 90.4), and the Kanet of Kullu (TFI 88.0-90.0) and Kinnaur (TFI 88.0). The broad face characterises the Tibetan (TFI 85.9- 86.4) and the Gorkha at large (TFI 84.6-87.3) as well as the Malaneese (TFI 82.6). But while the Rajput of Manali have both broad and narrow face (TFI 83.7-90.1), the Gorkha-Newar of Dhauladhar-Chamba region have a narrow face (TFI 88.5).

Narrow and narrow-medium faces are generally Indo-Aryan/Caucasoid traits while broad to very broad faces occur among the Mongoloid people. However, the average Total Facial Index for Himachalis (85.1) suggests a preponderance of medium face, i.e., a considerable admixture.

II. DERMATOGLYPHIC CHARACTERS

The distal phalanges of human fingers have dermal ridges whose total count as well as the patterns (loop, whorl and arch) they form show variation in different communities.

1. Finger Patterns: Himachalis have general preponderance of loops (54.0%) over whorls (43.1%), the arches (3.0%) being low. The higher incidence of loops (50-60%) is reported for many communities, namely, the Brahman, Rajput, Gaddi (both Brahman and Rajput), Chowdhary (Ghirath), Kanet, Arya (Hali), Gorkha and Nepali. The Chamar and the Pangwal, however nearly have equal averages of loops (48.4%) and whorls (44.2%). The Lahaulis show a reverse trend, i.e., the whorls (53%) being higher than the loops (44.2%).

This discriminates the Indo-Aryan/Caucasoid and the Tibeto-Burman Mongoloid populations in Himachal Pradesh as is also seen in other parts of India. It is further reflected in the average percentage frequency of these patterns for the Indo-Aryan (loops 52.7%, whorls 43.0%) and for the Tibeto-

Burman (loops 44.0%, whorls 53.3%) tribes.

Arches more than 5% are reported for the Brahman (Shimla), Khatri, Gaddi Brahman & Rajput and Muslim Gujjar (all Chamba), the Kanet (Shimla) and the Nepali (Dharamshala).

2. Pattern Intensity Index (PII): This tells about the proportions of the whorls and loops. It ranges between 13 and 15 in Himachal with an average of 13.9. Most of the Indo-Aryans in Himachal Pradesh have lower mean value than the Lahaula, Pangwala, Rajput (Manali) and the Gaddi (Dharamshala) where this index is above 14.4. It appears that the Indo-Aryans in this area are under the Mongoloid influence.

3. Total Ridge Count (TRC): This is known for a few communities. The Gaddi Rajput have lower (below 121) ridge count, the Brahman showing an intermediate value (126-136), whereas the Muslim Gujjar show the highest (above 140) ridge count.

III. CERTAIN GENETIC TRAITS

In this category three genes are considered, namely, colour blindness, taster and secretor genes.

1. Colour Blindness: Some persons are genetically unable to distinguish green or red colours. The gene for this colour vision anomaly is located on one X (sex) chromosome, therefore expressed in males (XY), who have single X-chromosome, but the females (XX) with two X-chromosomes carry the gene. The frequency of this gene ranges from 0 to 6.5% with an average value of 3.68%. The Pangwal, Sipi, Gaddi (Kangra), Brahman (Kullu & Shimla), Rajput/Kanet (Kinnaura), Koli and Bodh, all show less than 2% incidence. The Brahman and Rajput reported from different areas, however, fall on the average, but high (or above 5%) frequency is reported for the Brahman and Rajput of Bilaspur, and for Gaddi of Chamba.

In India, the Muslims and Tibeto-Burman speaking Mongoloids are reported with higher colour blindness. But, in Himachal Pradesh this trend is not yet confirmed or refuted due to paucity of data.

2. Taster gene of Phenyl Thio-Carbamide (PTC): The tasting and non-tasting of this compound is controlled by a pair of alleles, *T* (taster) and *t* (non-taster) alleles. In India the taster-gene (T) is generally above 60% among Tibeto-Burman Mongoloids, and below 50% in the Indo-Aryan and Dravidian people.

But in Himachal Pradesh the T-gene is higher both in the Mongoloids as well as the Indo-Aryans in the Mongoloid belt.

3. *ABH* Secretor Gene (Se): This gene is tested through saliva and splits people into secretors (Se) and non-secretors (se) to a varying extent, usually secretors being higher than the non-secretors. High percentage frequency of Se gene is reported in the Tibetan (66.4) and the Bodh (63.9) followed by the Kanet or Kinnaura (59.5-59.9). Then come the Rajput of Bilaspur (58.6), Mandi (58.2) and Barot (55.6), followed by Brahman at Bilaspur (53.3) and Shimla (52.4). Variable and lower incidence is recorded in certain pockets of Rajput in Kullu, Shimla and Rampur (42-49) as well as of the Gaddi Rajput (40- 47). The Muslim Gujjar (42.6) and Gaddi Brahman (40.0) present low secretor gene.

In general, high mean secretor gene (63.9) is recorded for the Tibeto-Burman Mongoloids than for the Indo-Aryan family. The latter exhibits three grades of low incidence of Se gene, lowest being in the scheduled castes (37.9), followed by the scheduled tribes in the middle (44.1), and the others (55.1) in the moderately high category.

IV. SEROLOGICAL CHARACTERS

The commonly used serological parameters for population studies are of ABO, Rh, MN, MNSs, Kidd, P and Duffy systems.

1. *ABO* Blood Groups: There are three main genes A (A_1+A_2), *B* and *O*, which are also designated as p (p_1+p_2), q and r respectively. Evolutionary forces resulted in different frequencies. Relative *A* and *B* gene frequencies made striking differences in the North-West Indian people who show a general preponderance of *B* over *A*, among the Mongoloids and the *vice versa* among the Indo-Aryans. A_1 gene is also generally high among the Indo-Aryans of the Himalayan belt, where A_2 is specifically low among the Tibeto-Burman Mongoloids. *O*-gene usually prevails among the Austro-Asiatic tribes in India.

Lower *A* (17.3-22.9) and moderate to high *B* (23.1-32.2) with fairly stable *O* (49.55) genes are reported for the Brahman (Kangra, Bilaspur, Chamba and Rampur Bushahr). However, Brahman of Kullu, Shimla and some in Rampur Bushahr have moderate to high *A* gene frequency (21-30) where *B*-gene also increases further (24-36) but *O* falls down below 50 per cent. The Brahmans of Lahaul & Spiti have strikingly higher *O* gene (above 60) at the cost of lower *A* (below 20) as well as *B* (18). A similar pattern is noticed in the Tibetan of Lahaul & Spiti as well as Dharamshala, viz., *A* 14-16, *B* 18-21, *O* 64-67.

However, the Swangla, Bodh and the Lahaula, in general, follow a consistent pattern of high average *B*-gene (30), but both *A* (about 22-25) and *O* (42-49) in moderate intensity.

The Gaddis (both Brahman and Rajput) show a general trend of moderate to high *A* (24-29), and *B* (26-30) and moderate *O* (44-48). But the Gujjar Muslims (Chamba) are noted for very low *A* (13), whereas *B* (28) and *O* (59) are moderately high.

There is a considerable variation in the Rajputs. At Bilaspur they present a consistent pattern of moderately high *A* (25-26) as well as *B* (27-29) genes, *O* being moderately low (46-48). But in the Kangra - Palampur-Dharamshala terrain *A* (18-23) lowers down and *B* (27-34) increases; similar situation in the Rajputs prevails at Rampur and Shimla, i.e., low *A* (11-22) and higher *B* (24-32), but slight more fall in *A* and rise in *O* (54).

A gene rises further (than what it is in Bilaspur Rajputs) in the Rajputs of Kullu (28-30), Manali and Lahaul & Spiti (31-32) while *B* (25-28) retains moderate character. Certain pockets of Rajputs in Kullu show very high *A* (34-36), which rises to exceptionally high degree at Barot (41) where both *B* (20) and *O* (39) drop sharply—a typical Caucasoid feature.

The Kanets have two pockets of *A* gene: A moderate to moderately high (24-32) at Shimla, Manali and Kinnaur except Puh where *A* gene shows sharp decline (11-18). *B* gene generally remains low in Kanet of Manali and Kinnaur (14-21) except a moderate rise at Kalpa (27), Nachar (29) and Shimla (27-29), but a steep rise at Puh (36-37) is at the cost of low *A* suggesting Mongoloid admixture. The Kolis at Puh also show low *A* (10) but also low *B* (22) at the cost of very high O (69). Low *A* (12- 15) and high *O* (59-62) but moderate to high *B* (21-35) are reported for the Koli in Kinnaur in general, though at Nachar and Kullu a general moderacy is recorded *A* (20-24), *B* (21-35), *O* (44-58) in *A* and *O* but rising tendency in *B*. A_2 gene also occurs in high frequency in the Kanet (4.1-5.5) as well as Koli (5.1) at Nachar. But higher A_2 gene is noticed in the Barot Rajputs (9.3) and Gaddi Brahmans of Kangra (6.9).

The Chamars at Kangra present slight increase in *A*(24) overtaking *B* (22) and slight increase in *O* (54). *B* (47) and *O* (32) gene relationships are reversed in the Harijans of Rampur Bushahr with moderacy in *A* (21) indicating Mongoloid influence. The Aryas retain moderate *A* (23), moderately higher *B* (29) and moderately low *O* (47).

The Chamba Mahajans show a Tibetan-like pattern of low *A* (14), moderate *B* (23) and high *O* (63), whereas the Chowdhary (Ghirath) of Kangra present a moderate picture of *A* (24-25), *B* (27-28) and *O* (47-49).

Different levels of convergence and divergence among communities are revealed from the *ABO* blood group gene frequencies.

2. *MN* Blood Group System: Generally M-gene remains higher (above 50 per cent) in North Indians with a southward decline, and N-gene remains lower (below 50 per cent) with a southward increase. In Himachal Pradesh highest M-gene is recorded in Barot Rajput (92.2), followed by the Lahaula (84.5), Rajput of Bilaspur (82.2), Brahman of Shimla (76.1) and the Bodh (70.6) with the higher frequencies.The moderate M-gene frequency is reported in the Chowdhary (60.0) and Brahman of Kangra (59.0) and low reports are for the Chamar (53.6) and the Koli (54.5).

3. *MNSs* Blood Groups: These genes occur in four combinations (haplotypes), viz., MS, Ms, NS and Ns.

MS Haptotype: The observed range is 20-28 per cent. Communities with high frequencies are the Swangla (28.1), Pangwal (27.2) and Bodh (26.7). Moderate occurrences are in Gaddi Rajput (24.0-26.0), Koli (24.3), Brahman (23.6) and Rajput (22.9) of Kullu, and the Kanet/Kinnaura (22.8). Low is reported for the Gaddi Brahman (20.6-21.3). In general Mongoloids present higher, and the Indo-Aryan/Caucasoids moderate to low in Himachal Pradesh.

Ms Haplotype: The observed range is 30.4-40.1, the highest being in the Brahman (40.1) and Rajput (38.1) of Kullu, the Swangla (38.8) and the Bodh (37.9), and the lowest in the Gaddi Rajput of Chamba (30.4), Gaddi Brahman of Kangra (32.4) and in the Koli of Kullu (32.9). Moderate value is reported for the Kanet/Kinnaura (35.4), Pangwal (35.5), Gaddi Brahman of Chamba (35.1) as well as the Gaddi Rajput of Kangra (33.7-36.2).

NS Haplotype: The observed range is 5.3 to 18.4 the lowest for the Swangla and the highest for Gaddi Brahman of Chamba recorded so far. Low-moderate incidence is seen in Gaddi Rajput (8.9-11.4), Kullu Brahman (11.3) and the Bodh (12.1), while higher-moderate is in the Gaddi Brahman of Kangra (13.3), Kullu Rajput (13.2) and Koli (13.8), and the Pangwal (14.2).

Ns Haplotype: Observed range is 23.1-35.0 shown by Pangwal and the Kanet, respectively. The Bodh (23.3), Rajput (25.7) and Brahman (25.0) of Kullu and the Chamba Gaddi Brahman (25.2) also show low values. Moderate incidence is reported for Gaddi Rajput of Kangra (29.1-30.8), Swangla (28.1) and the Koli (29.0), whereas Gaddi Rajput (34.6) of Chamba as well as Gaddi Brahman (33.7) of Kangra have higher frequency.

4. Rh Blood Group System: Eight genetic haplotypes have been identified in this system with five antisera (-D,-C, -c, -E and -e), namely, R_z (CDE), R_1 (CDe), R_y (CdE), R' (CDe), R_2 (cDE), R_o (cDe), R" (cdE) and r (cde). More important haplotypes with higher frequencies in India are R_1 (43.4-86.8 per cent) and r (0-34.7 per cent).

R_1 Haplotype: Its observed range is 45.5-77.9. High incidence is shown by the Chowdhary (77.9), Chamar, (71.2), Gaddi Brahman of Kangra and Chamba (64.8-68.4) and Gaddi Rajput of Kangra (66.4). Moderate incidence is recorded for many communities, viz., the Swangla (61.0-63.6), Pangwal (62.4), Bodh (61.4-63.7), Kullu Rajput (62.9) and Koli (61.4), Kangra Brahman (62.9), Chamba Gaddi Rajput (57.8-63.6), and the Sipi (59.0). Low incidence is noticed in the Kinnaura (47.6-52.6) or Kanet at Puh (44.5), Kalpa (46.8-53.5), Nachar (48.5) and Sangla (55.1). The Rajput of Rampur (53.3) also have low R_1 gene.

r Haplotype: The observed range is 0.3-29.2, the lowest in the Puh Kanet and the highest in the Koli. The others in the low category are the Chowdhary (11.0) and the Chamar (11.1); in the high category come Chamba Gaddi—both Brahman (22.0-27.6) and Rajput (24.9-26.8), Kangra Brahman (23.4) and the Kinnaur Koli (29.2). Other than that of Puh, the Kanet (17.7-22.7) along with the Bodh (15.8-18.2), Swangla (17.7-22.7), Pangwal (18.7), Kullu Brahman (17.5) and Rajput (18.5), Rampur Rajput (20.1) and the Kullu Koli (20.7), all show moderate r-gene frequency.

Other Rh Haplotypes: Ry is rarest and lowest and reported for Rampur Rajput (0.47 per cent) only. R" is also rare and of low incidence reported in the Chowdhary (2.78), Rajput (1.86), Koli (1.20-1.80), Kanet (1.80) and Chamar (0.02). Rz is relatively common than Ry and R", with an observed range of 0.51-5.50. High frequency of Rz is reported for the Kanet (5.50) and Rajput (4.65) of Kalpa, whereas Bodh (0.51-0.81), the Rajput of Kullu (0.58) and Rampur (1.79), the Sipi (1.40) and the Swangla (1.87) show low incidence.

R' haplotype ranges from 0.01 to 6.50. Like Rz, it is also high in the Kanet (4.60-6.50) and Rajput (4.01) of Kalpa and in the Chamar of Kangra (6.16). Other communities like Koli (2.30-2.90), Sipi (2.30) and Kangra Brahman (1.88) have relatively moderate value, but it becomes rarer in the Rajput of Chamba and Kangra (0.50-1.10) and Muslim Gujjar (0.88).

5. *Kidd* Blood Group: Two genes (Jk^a and Jk^{b+jk}) are known in this system. The JK^a gene occurs more frequently (52.0-81.7 per cent), lowest being in Kullu Brahman and highest in Kangra Gaddi Brahman. The Kanet of Puh (71.3) and the Lahauli Rajput (72.3) also have higher Jk^a gene frequency with slight decrease in Chamba Gaddi Brahman (65.0) and Kangra Gaddi Rajput (68.5), followed by moderate incidence among the Bodh (60.0), Pangwal (59.2), Gaddi Rajput of Chamba (58.3), the Kanet of Kalpa (58.0) and Koli of Kinnaur (57.8). Low incidence is encountered in Kullu Brahman (51.0), Kanet of Nachar (52.0) and moderately low at Sangla (55.7) and in the Swangla (55.3).

6. *P* Blood Group (P^1 gene) : This is studied only in a few communities. The Kanet (14.20-26.10) and the Koli (22.1-29.6), both show low incidence in Himachal Pradesh in comparison to other Indians.

7. *Duffy* Blood Group (Fy^a & Fy^b genes) : The observed range for six communities is 40.8-86.7. The Koli (40.8), Brahman (43.8), Rajput (44.0), Swangla (42.7) as well as Bodh (48.3), all of Lahaul & Spiti have low Fy^a gene frequency. But in Kinnaur the Koli (79.3-81.2) as well as the Kanet (70.5-86.7) show high to the highest incidence.

V. BIO-CHEMICAL CHARACTERS

(A) Protein Polymorphisms

1. Haptoglobins: Two genes Hp^1 and Hp^2 are studied for six communities. Hp^1 gene presents a range of 12.3-33.1. The lower incidence is in Puh Kanet (12.3) and Kinnaur (14.7) and Lahaul & Spiti Koli (14.4). Moderate incidence is shown by Bodh (17.4) and Rajput (18.7) of Lahaul & Spiti, Muslim Gujjar of Chamba (18.9), Swangla (20.0), Kullu Brahman (21.9), while in other Kanets of Kinnaur (20.7-24.3) Hp^1 gene rises further, but only Gaddis show the high (33.1) incidence.

2. Transferrins : Three genes of this system, viz. Tf^C, Tf^B and Tf^D show ethnic variation, but only Tf^C is most frequent (usually 98-100 per cent) while the other two are rare (0-2 per cent). Tf^D is reportedly lacking in Himachal Pradesh where Tf^B is present in low frequency and that too present in the Kanets (0.70-1.80). The other studied communities, namely, Brahman (Kullu and Lahaul & Spiti), Rajput (Kullu), Koli (Lahaul and Kinnaur), Bodh and Swangla (Lahaul & Spiti), the Gaddi (Kangra-Bharmaur) and Pangwal, all have 100 per cent Tf^C gene.

3. Group-Specific Component (GC System): GC^1 and GC^2 genes are more common. GC^1 ranges from 70.0 to 86.3 per cent whereas the rest is GC^2 gene. Higher GC^1 gene is recorded in the Gaddi Brahman of Chamba

(85.3) and Bharmaur (84.6-85.9), followed by Kanet of Sangla (81.6), the Koli of Kinnaur (80.8-80.9), and Gaddi Rajput of Bharmaur (79.1) and Palampur (78.5). The Pangwal (75.4) show moderate, and other communities like the Rajput of Chamba (71.6-72.4), Gaddi Rajput of Kangra-Chamba region (about 70), and the Kanets of Puh, Kalpa and Nachar (71.0-71.6) show a lower incidence.

(B) Enzyme Polymorphisms

1. Phosphoglucomutase (PGM): PGM^1-gene shows a range of 58.5-81.2, lowest shown by the Chamar and the highest by the Koli (80.8-81.2). Next high incidence is seen among Gaddi Rajput in general (78.80). Moderate frequency is common (67.5-73.7) in Brahman/Gaddi Brahman, Khatri, Mahajan, Chowdhary and Pangwal. The Kanets usually retain low to moderate (60-73) gene frequency.

2. Adenylate Kinase (AK): The observed range for AK^1 gene is 80.3-100. The Koli show lower values (80.3-87.3), whereas most of the communities of Indo-Aryan ethnicity, namely Brahman, Gaddi, Khatri, Mahajan, Chowdhary, plus the Chamar, and scheduled castes of Bharmaur, all show moderate (88-93) values. The Pangwal (95.2), Bodh (94.7), Kanet (95.8-96.4) of Kinnaur in general present high value. The Puh Kanet (99.3) and Swangla (100) show the highest. As such AK^1 gene is higher among Mongoloids or under their influence.

3. Red Cell Acid Phosphatase (RCAP): P^a and P^b genes of this system are higher in frequency, $P^b > P^a$. P^a gene has a range of 6.8 to 36.1. The Pangwal exhibit exceptionally low (6.8) frequency, while general low (18.2-21.2) occurs in the Kanet, and in the Koli (23-27.8) as well. The Gaddi Rajput show variably low to moderately high (21.5-29.3) in Kangra-Chamba area, but a higher frequency of P^a gene is noticed especially in the Khatri of Chamba (36.1), Rajput of Kangra (34.2), scheduled castes of Bharmaur (32.7) and the Brahman (30.3) and Rajput (29.2) of Chamba.

4. Esterase-D (ESD): ESD^1 is more frequent than ESD^2 gene. The observed range of ESD^2 is from 12.4 to 33.6. Lower incidence is noticed in Bharmaur Gaddi Rajput (12.4) and Gaddi Brahman (17.9), the Pangwal (12.8), Gaddi Rajput of Kangra-Palampur (20.7-21.5) area, Rajput (20.1) and Khatri (20.9) of Chamba. Moderate frequency (22-26) is observed for Chamba Brahman (22.9) and Mahajan (23.8), Rajput (23.2), Gaddi Brahman (25.6) and Gaddi Rajput (24.3) and the Kanet in general (22.2-25.4). High frequency is encountered in the Koli (27.6-33.6) and the Gaddi Rajput of Chuwari-Chamba (32.5).

A general biological blending of the various ethnic elements is strikingly exhibited by the Himachalis, though there is also seen a tendency to maintain ethnic distinctions in certain pockets.

A.R.Sankhyan

GLOSSARY

aapi: mid wife (Kinnaura)
achkan: a long coat
adha-batai: half share-cropping
agàng: cremation, fire
agni-phere: circumambulation of fire at the time of marriage or a ritual
along: gold ear-ring
als: family names
alta: red paint
amchi: indigenous medicine-man
amrit-chakhna : ritual taking of sweets after being offered to the diety/holy saints
anand karaj: a term for marriage performed as per Sikh rituals
anderera: entering into the house of in-laws after marriage by the bride
anderli jat: upper caste/inner caste
androd: bride observing purdah-system on reaching the house of in-laws
androl: confinement in purdah/ to remain in veil
anjuman: traditional council of the Muslims
ankli: rice flour chapati
anklu: rice flour cakes
annaprasana: first cereal feeding
aqiqa: ritual connected with the sixth day after birth/tonsure (Muslim)
arak: local whiskey
armi: middleman; traditional council of Bodh
ashwamedh yajna: A Vedic politico-ritual tradition of sending a horse to different kingdoms, which, if returned unapposed signifies subjugation of those kingdoms, consequently bestowing the title of a Chakravarty Raja (sovereign emperor) upon the sender king. Mistakenly taken as 'horse sacrifice'.
asthi/astu parwah: immersion of ashes
asudh/ashudh: polluted
athwasa: 8th month ceremony in pregnancy
autar: issueless man/woman
awaranda: swaying a coin over the head of the bride and groom.
azan: calling of Lord's name (Muslim)
babru: fried sweet cakes of wheat flour

badhaee: greetings
badi kathi: death anniversary
bagma: normal type of marriage (Bodh)
bahar ke: outer caste/lower caste
bahu jharara: Junior levirate
bahu/bahuti: son's wife
bainth/painth: row/line (for taking food)
baithak: sitting room
baithana: Junior levirate/widow remarriage
bajantri: musical band party
balda : tonsure ceremony (Bodh)
bali: ear-ring
balmi/bami: a serpent's hole
bama : priest (Bodh)
bar/birlap: death ballads
bara ghar: big house
barat-ka-khana: marriage party feast
barghes: sticks
barhi: twelfth day purificatory rites after death
bariana/breena/brina: bride price
barikcha: annual death purificatory rites
barkhi/barsi/barkhadi: ritual connected with first annual death anniversary
barni : betrothal
barni: bride price
bartan: social exchange
baswai: putative kinship
batlami: symbiotic/mutual exchange
batna: applying turmeric paste on the bride and groom
batoi: share cropping
batta-satta: a term for marriage by exchange of sisters
baturu/bhaturu: baked cakes of wheat flour
baur/bohar/baud: upper storey of the house
bauri/bauli/bavli/bowli: step well
be-dawa: approved written divorce
bedi/vedi: platform for ritual performance
begar: forced labour
beri: wild goose berry
bhabi/bhab/bharjai: elder brother's wife
Bhadon: a month according to Hindu calender which corresponds to August-September
bhadran/chhilbhadran: shaving off the head - a death ritual
bhaikhal: a wild herbal and magical plant
bhandari: treasurer
bhat khulai: ritual feeding of boiled rice items to the groom and party

bhalle: fried cakes of pulses
bhoara: a system of mutual obligation among the relatives (Kinnaura)
bhojpatra: birch
bhunda: rope sliding ceremony of the Bedas
bhoot./bhut: male evil spirit/ghost
bichhia: toe-ring
bidai: ritual departure of the bride
bicholia: middle man/negotiator
bidi/biri: indigenous cigarette of leaf
binana: patron-client/landlord-tenant relationship
bindi: mark put on forehead by women
bingri: naming ceremony of the Bodhs
biradari panchayat: community council
bisthai/bishti: bride-price (Toori)
burka/burqa: veil worn by Muslim women
bulak: studded nose ring
byah/bivah/biah/vivah: a term for marriage among Hindus
cha-zhang: land in the ownership of the monasteries
chabarkh: fourth death anniversary
chadar: a sheet of cloth
chadar dalna: Junior levirate/widow remarriage
chak: conical scalp ornament; potter's wheel
chakhandu: a child born to a widow without getting remarried/a bastard child
chaku: iron knife
chamukurti: jacket of the Kinnaura
chana: gram
chank: decoration of floor on festive occasions
chapati/roti: unleavened bread
char-bhai: traditional council of the Kinnaura (literally four brothers)
chara: fodder
charbi: lard
charkha: spinning wheel
chauk bithana: 13th day birth purificatory ritual
chauth: fourth day ceremony after marriage
chawa: fourth day mortuary rite among the Bodhs
che-che: divorce
chechlam/chaliha: fortieth day mortuary rites among Muslims
chela: exorcist medium
chera: gown
chewar: a term for tonsure among the Gorkha
chhad-chhada: divorce
chhadi : term for divorce among the Sipis
chhah : *lassi* or butter milk/whey
chhaj: winnowing fan
chhalian/challi: maize

chhang: local alcoholic drink/millet beer
chhati: sixth day purificatory rites after birth
chhauli: shawl
chheti: a term for bride price among the Swanglas
chhota ghar: small house
chhuba: coat
chhut-chhurawa: divorce (Gorkha)
chhut/chhoot/chhutta-chhutti: divorce
chila: period of pollution
chilra: millet baked bread
chhinj: wrestling
chir: a variety of plums; pine tree
chizik: fourth day death ritual (Khampa)
chola: a gown of the Gaddis
choli: blouse
cholu: an overcoat
chomo: nun
choora: a big size wrist ring of silver
chorde: divorce
chorten/chosten: a structure to ward off the evil eyes/evil spirits
choti: cue
chowdhary: head of the community council
chua: long gown
chulah: hearth
chulli: apricot
chundaband: customary law of inheritance or division of property
churel: female evil spirit/witch
churi/choori/bang: bangles
churu : a cross between a yak and a cow
dab-dab: a term for marriage by elopement (Kinnaura)
dag/daag: lighting the funeral pyre; dead cattle
dagle: figs
dahi: curd
daj/daz/daj-dan/dahej/dan-dahej: dowry or gift to the bride
dal: pulses
damchaltshis: love marriage (Kinnaura)
darati: sickle
dargah: mausoleum, tomb of the saints
darwaza-ka-char/dwar char : receiving of marriage procession at the doorstep
dashmi: tenth day mortuary rite
dasthon/dasuthan: birth purificatory bath after 10 days
daswa/daswan/daspindi/dasa: tenth day mortuary rite
dawat-e-walima: marriage feast given by the groom's side (Muslims)
deori pujan : door worship
desil: a sweet preparation of rice and curd (Khampa)

devar: husband's younger brother
dhaja: an exorcist's ritual/ a folk theatre (Chamar/Nichar)
dham: marriage feast
dhamam uthana: a ritual marking the end of birth pollution (Punjabis)
dharam bahin: ceremonial sister/putative kinship
dharam bhai: ceremonial brother /putative kinship
dheri: a term for bride price among the Tooris
dhom: sari
dhori: money given to the bride's parents for defraying marriage expenses (Kinnaura)
dhruwali: a rice liquor (Nar)
dhuwaju: marrying second time
dhyan/dhian: married daughter of the lineage
dingi: a term for small stick among the Kinnaura
diyodari : marriage by exchange of sisters (Pangwal Rajput)
dohru: woollen sari (Kinnaura)
dolangchim: money offered at mother-in-law's feet by the bride-groom (Kinnaura)
doli: ritual departure of marriage procession of the bride
dori: pig-tail/thread tied around the waist
dud lugru: cereal feeding of the child
damchaltshis: a term for love marriage among the Kinnaura
durries: carpets
duzik: seventh day mortuary rite (Khampa)
fateha/fatiha: prayer for the dead (Muslims)
firqa: sect/school of thought (Muslims)
fung-pao: a term for gifts in the Chinese
gachhang:: waist band
gadda-gadolu: share of the service renderer in the crop in patron-client relationship
gadpo: headman of the community council among the Bodhs
gagakache: a ritual ceremony among the Bodhs in which a compensation is demanded by the bride's friends from the groom
gaini: learned man or the chief Lama of Yellow sect (Bodh)
gajra: wrist ring
galicha: carpet
gaon: village
gaon deota: village deity (male)
gaon devi: village deity (female)
gaona/gouna: ritual departure of the bride to the groom's house/ consummation of marriage
gardu: woollen rugs
gawah: witness
ghanti: a local liquor
ghar-jamai/ghar javantri: resident son-in-law

ghaar: share-cropping
gharat: water-mill
gharki-panchayat: community council
gharmoj/ghadoj/gharoj/gharonj : widow re-marriage
ghee: clarified butter
ghori: a term for combination of villages over which a deity rules
ghund/ghood.ghunghat: covering the face in avoidance
ghural: hill goat
gidda: a type of women's dance
god bharai: a pregnancy ritual blessing the woman
gompa/goupa: monastery
got khana: thirteenth day death rite (Gorkhas)
gotra/got: lineage/social division
gova/goba: a chief of the Khampa community council
grokch/grokcha: a medium between a deity and a man, oracle (Kinnaura)
gulgula: a fried sweet preparation of jaggery and wheat flour
gunt/guntrala/guntsala: post-delivery purificatory ritual of taking cow's urine
gur/goor: a custodian of the deity/exorcist medium
gyut: members descended from a common ancestor/clan
haar: remarriage by elopement with a paramour
haari: compensation for divorce
hakuks: privileges/rights
hal: plough
hala: a term for land tenure system
halda: a term for tonsure among the Bodhs
haldi charahna: application of turmeric on bride and groom at marriage
hallad: a bastard child
halmandi: an office-bearer of the traditional council (Kinnauras)
hanging: shirt
haq mehar/mehar: dower (Muslims)
harsho: a flag to ward off evil eyes
hatya: woman of the lineage who committed suicide
hibba: legal will
hom: sacrificial offering to fire
hookah: hubble-bubble, smoking device
hukka pani band: excommunication/abandoning social exchange
icchhadhari: capable of changing forms
iddat: period of avoidance and abstinence on divorce or death of the husband (Muslims)
izzat: compensation in the form of bride-price
jagrata: to keep awake at night singing Devi songs/a religious musical night
jajmani: patron-client relationship

jal-pravah: immersion in water
jamai: son-in-law
janeu: sacred thread investiture ceremony
jarrah: barber-surgeon (Muslims)
jathere: ancestors/ancestral mound
jathong: eldest brother or customary right of the eldest brother (Kinnaura)
jathunda: rules of inheritence by which the eldest brother gets a little more share
jatolna: tonsure
Ja-tsari-kha-dal-va : a term for divorce (Khampa)
jattu/jatlu/jaulu: tonsure
jau: barley
jaul: bridal knot
jayasthang: village council (Malaneese)
jeptan: shawl worn by women around their shoulders (Bodh)
jestha: juryman
jha-cho-che: a term for divorce (Khampa)
jhanjrara/jhanjra: Junior levirate/widow-remarriage
jhatka: slaughtering with one stroke
jhind phuk/brar phuk: elopement and marriage by circumambulation of burning bushes
jiyoga: widow's share (Toori)
jiyuk: parents' share given to the eldest son for paying off their debts
jokheya: term for ceremonial friendship between a man and woman (Kinnaura)
jokheya un: garland of fruits for establishing ceremonial friendship between a man and a woman
kabar kuninde: grave diggers
kachcha/cuchcha khana: boiled food
kachha: underwear
kahika: a Narmedh ceremony and a function of the Nars
kale-urad: black gram/pulses
kameej: shirt
kanchhong: youngest brother (Kinnaura)
kangha: comb
kanisthong: rules of inheritance for the younger brother
kanji: *a* pre-delivery ritual
kankani: village gate
kanya: young girl before puberty
kanyadan: marriage ritual giving away of the daughter in charity
kara: wrist ring
karbala: burial ground for tazia (Muslims)
karewa: widow remarriage
karmai.: betrothal

karodi/kharodi: middleman or negotiator
karu-kranori: a term for tonsure
karuwa chauth: a festival of women among Hindus
kashidakari: embroidery
kathi: death ceremony
kathyache: person attending cremation rites (Seok)
kaya: body
keera: long overcoat
kesh: hair
khachchar: mule
khadu: ram
khaka: a Chinese dialect
khallar: wallet
khamba zumche: a term for junior levirate among the Bodhs
khandan: lineage/a social division among the Kinnauras
khang-chen: big house
khang-chen-pa : occupants of the big house (Bodh)
kharpan: Wazir of the Bodh king
khatal je: a term for divorce (Khampa)
khatna: circumcision
kheje: a term for divorce (Khampa)
khel: status group (Kinnaura); hypnotic trance during an exorcist's performance
khewat: marriage of the divorcee (Sipi)
khindum: a term for love marriage (Bodh)
khing-chung: small house (Bodh)
khing-chung-pa: residents of *khing-chung*
khirpu: first cereal feeding ceremony of the child
khir/kheer: rice porridge/sweet preparation of rice and milk
khotansa: white flag (Bodh)
khuchis/khukichimo: marriage by elopement (Kinnaura)
khukhri: dagger
khumb: wild mushroom
khunt: a term for combination of *ghori* (deity's village area)
kinshu: household deity
kirpan/karpan: dagger
kirri/kilta basket
koka: nose-pin
kokheya: ceremonial brotherhood (Kinnaura)
konech: a term for ceremonial friendship between two women (Kinnaura)
konech-un: garland of fruits for establishing ceremonial friendship between two women
kramog/kra-tricti : a term for tonsure among the Swanglas
kua-byah: a term for marriage by capture
kuhl: water channel

kunn: Chamar/Nichar's place of work/worship
kuram: daughter-in-law's and son-in-law's father
kuri/kudi: term for girl in Punjabi
kursim: a term for exorcism (Bodh)
labrang/Lagang: monastery
laddar: persons accompanying bride
lagaan: revenue
lagan: marriage ritual during circumambulation of the fire
lajoru: companion of the bridegroom
lama: Buddhist monk
langar: common eating
lara: bridegroom
lari: bride
lassi: diluted stirred curd or butter-milk - a drink
lefo: a term for marriage by exchange
lepha: a term for village guard (Bodh)
lhu: a malevolent spirit among the Bodhs
logar: annual death anniversary (Khampa)
lulan: a term for inheritance
madarsa: religious institution/school (Muslims)
mah: urd or black grams (pulses)
mahel: bracelet
maida: fine wheat flour without bran
makpa/magpa: resident son-in-law (Bodh)
mamla: bride-price
mamla -de-dena: return of bride price
manch deothiya: gods once in human form
mandap: platform for marriage rituals
mane: a tomb
mang bharna: putting vermilion in the hair parting of the bride
mangni: engagement/betrothal
masand: priest from one's own community
masankhri/shamshanghat: cremation ground
mashak: a skin bag
matam: mourning
matar: peas
math: rituals connected with sacrificial offerings; religious shrine
matra: bride-price
matri-havan: a type of worship
maynali: engagement ceremony
mazar: tomb
mazmi-byah: ad hoc marriage among the Swanglas
mehar: dower (Muslims)
mehndi: henna
migeur chhang: betrothal ceremony
mitr-bhai: ceremonial kin brother

mokomo-kheyasimig : a system of mutual obligation among the neighbours (Kinnaura)
momo: boiled meat stuffed in dough; festive food (Khampa)
mool nakshatra: a kind of inauspicious star in Hindu astrology
moong: green pulses
moonga: ruby
moulvi/maulvi: Musilm priest
muh dishta/muh ghudan: a marriage ritual when bride and bridegroom see each other's face
mukhiya: a village chief
muklawa: departure of the bride for the groom's house
mundan: tonsure
murki: coiled nose ring
musalmani: circumcision (Muslims)
naing: a term for umbilical cord
nak-ki-tilli: nose pin among the Kinnauras
nakh: a variety of pears
nalki: nipple
nalmandi: the Koli member of council of the Kinnauras
namaz: prayer (Muslims)
nanad: husband's sister
nanched : a term for puberty rites (Swangla)
nankiye: relatives from mother's side
nanti: small earring
narmedh/narkhand/nar-bhedi yagya: liiterally human sacrifice/ritual offering of a person to the deity
nasrawan: foodgrains offered to the priest
nath-chadar dalna: a term for simple marriage of a widow
nautor: a scheme initiated by the government for distribution of land to the landless
newang: seventh day birth rite (Kinnaura)
nihali: Lohar's working place
nikah: a term for marriage (Muslims)
nikahnama: marriage agreement (Muslims)
nishan: emblem, sign
nuh: daughter-in-law
nyay: justice
nyog: a woman engaging a person for childbearing when her husband is incapable of the same
obal: garland
obra : inner room of the house
oom-ya-che: Chinese New Year festival
orhni/odhni: female headgear
pagga: cue
pagri ki rasam: ritual of succession/a death rite
pagwand : customary law of inheritance (male equigeniture)

pahu: tenant/cultivator
pai-pujji: worship of feet
pakki-roti: fried food
pam-phera: first return of the bride to her parents' house after marriage
pan: betel leaves
panch: members of the judicial council
panchami: fifth day of the lunar-month fortnight
panchap/panjap: birth purificatory rite by taking cow's urine and holy water
panchayat: council
panchayat-ghar: council house
panchmasa: fifth month
pandit: priest
pangmo thauka: irrigation
pangrokhna: midwife (Kinnaura)
panigrahan: a marriage ritual of giving the bride's hand to the groom
parojan: initiation
parsahi: wearing of the ornaments with crown by the bridegroom
patak: death pollution
patroru: steamed preparation of arbi (*Colocasia*) leaves
patta: a unit of measure (Bodh)
pattu: woollen blanket
phaktun: marriage by negotiation (Khampa)
phaska: grains offered to the dead
phangma: a term for bride among the Bodhs
phera/phere/lawan: circumambulation
phironi: first return of the bride/consummation of marriage (Pangwals)
pind dan: death offerings to a Panda
pingree: name giving ceremony (Bodh)
pir/peer: holy persons/saints
pitar/pitr/pitra: ancestors
pith-chuk : marriage by capture (Pangwals)
pitra-paksha: fortnight devoted to ancestor worship
pitri puja: ancestor worship
polali: toe ring
pooja: sacredotal performance
poolas: strand shoes
pote: bead necklace (Gorkha)
prasad: giving of sweets after offering them to the deity
praurh roti: big loaf of unleavened bread.
pret: spirit of the dead
pugree/pagri: turban
punthi: sacred text

puranda: colourful threaded hair locket of the women/pig tail/hair ribbon
purdah: avoidance, veil
purohit: traditional ritual officiant-in-charge of the Hindus
putande: dosa-like wheat flour preparation
qudani: junior levirate (Sipi)
rabara/rabaru: marriage negotiator/middleman
ral chang/raldak: tonsure ceremony (Khampa)
randi-byah: a term for widow-remarriage
ranjhunana: greeting songs sung at the birth of a son
rasham pagri: succession of the son - a death ritual
reet/rit: bride-price or amount paid by the new husband to the old husband
reje: marriage by negotiation (Bodh)
retti: a tern for bride price among the Pangwals
rinkchje: ceremonial sisterhood (Kinnaura)
rinpochie: chief lama
rishi: saint
rongi: red beans
roza: days of abstinence (Muslim)
rumal: an embroidered cloth/handkerchief
rusa-te-byah: a term for marriage by elopement
sag/saag: spinach of mustard or other leaves
sand/saand: a marriage ritual in which stars and clan deity are worshipped
sabha: association
safa : turban
sagai: betrothal
sala : wife's brother
sali : wife's sister
salwar : female trousers
sami momo: wife's younger sister (Bodh)
samuhat : purificatory ritual at marriage
sang: 3rd day birth purificatory ritual of the Kinnauras
santhong: temple premises (Kinnaura)
sarguddi: widow remarriage
sarpanch: chief of judicial panchayat
sarson: mustard
sartora: son of a keep/concubine
sas : mother-in-law
satmasa: seventh month
sattu: a preparation of parched barley flour
saurah : father-in-law
savarna: inner/clean or upper caste
sayana: elderly person of the village/headman or representative in community panchayat

seedha/sidha: raw cereals /uncooked grains
sehna: chief of the community council
sehnai/shehnai: clarionet
sehra: a ceremonial headgear of the bride groom/wedding crown
sekhor/skhor/skor: birth pollution
seppy: patron-client relationship (Saini)
sewai/sevian/seviyan: vermicellis
shaman: exorcist or oracle
shavan: amulets to ward off evil eyes (Bodh)
she: share-cropping
shik-vade: tonsure ceremony (Pangwals)
shingtickashimig: a term for divorce (Kinnaura)
shingmo: a term for land tenure system
shipchu sherku: fortyninth day mortuary rite (Khampa)
shrad/sarad/shradha: annual death rite; ancestor worship during Pitr Paksha
shuddi/suddi: purificatory rite
shuzan chungi: traditional council of the Khampa
siapa: expression of mourning
siddu: baked balls of wheat flour
sikka-riazul wakht: silver rupee coin
sindur: vermilion
siring kingar: cap
soaim: alms
sog: death ceremony
solia: sixteenth day death rite
sota: bride-price
suchchi rasoi: clean food prepared by a *savarna* caste
sugru: naming and cereal feeding ceremony
sui-binana: a system of patron-client relationship in which clothes are given for stitching
sukdan : woollen bed sheet (Khampa)
sukhna: a wish kept in the name of a deity
suktu: woollen body shawl (Khampa)
sunnat : circumcision (Muslim)
sup: winnowing fan of bamboo
sutak/sootak: post-delivery pollution
suthan: trousers
talaq: divorce
tamol: presentations to the bridegroom
tanamana: exorcism (Bodh)
tanglang: local manure
tazia: ratha or chariot (Muslim)
tel-talwai: oil ceremony at marriage
terahi/terhyi/terhaee: 13th day death rite
teu: maintenance for the widow (Bodh)

thag-chocha: a term for divorce (Kinnaura)
thahaka: betrothal
than/thaan: place of the deity
thatha: a ceremony to ward off evil spirits
theka: contract
thepang: cap of the Kinnaura
thippu/thipu: a female scarf/headgear
thodkar: white turban (Khampa)
thugpa/thukpa: thick stem of roasted barley flour (Khampa)
thwachi: a term for divorce
tika: head ornament
til: seasum
tilak: tattoo mark on forehead
timde-luh: question-answer songs
tithi: the day according to Hindu calender
tockche: hand hoe
tokniya: an office bearer of the traditional council of the Kinnaura
tong: bushel
tonglong: wish of a dying man (Kinnaura)
toriya: a variety of oil seeds like mustard seeds
tsud-thvagchi : a term for divorce among the Swanglas
turan: seventh day head shaving ceremony after tonsure leaving a cue on the occiput
tuzi: 39th day mortuary rites (Bodh)
upnayan: thread wearing
urad/urd: black grams (pulses)
uthala: ritual marking end of death pollution
vaitarni dan: offerings to river - a death ritual
vyavastha: order
yagopavit: sacred thread investiture ceremony
yajmani/jajmani: patron-client relationship
yajna: offerings to the fire
yanva: marriage songs (Bodh)
yatra/jatra: religious procession
ying-yung: smaller house
yogni/jogni: fairies
yogshie: share
yu-la: village deity of the Bodh
zakat: giving a part of one's income in charity to the poor
zanekang/zanchang: marriage by arrangement/settlement among the Kinnauras
Zo : a Bodh blacksmith
zumba : a cross between a yak and a cow

SELECT BIBLIOGRAPHY

Agarwal, B.C. (ed.). *Tribe, Caste and Peasantry*. Lucknow: Ethnographic and Folk Culture Society, 1974.

Ahmad, Imtiaz (ed.). *Caste and Social Stratification among Muslims of India*. Delhi: Manohar Publications, 1978.

Ahmad, Zarina. *Muslim Caste in Uttar Pradesh*. M.A dissertation (Unpublished). London: University of London, 1960.

Anonymous. *Encyclopaedia Britannica*. Chicago: Encyclopaedia Britannica Inc, 1969.

Anonymous. *Himachal Ke Lok Jeewan Aur Paramparanyen* (Hindi). Shimla: Himachal Kala, Sanskriti aur Bhasha Akademi, 1988.

Bahadur, K.P. *Castes, Tribes and Culture of India*. New Delhi: Ess Ess Publications, 1978, Vol. VI.

Bailey, T.G. 'Dialects of Kulu', in *Studies in North Himalayan Dialects*. Calcutta: Baptist Mission Press, 1905, pp. 35-65.

Baines, J.A. *General Report (Census of India, 1891*). London: Eyre and Spattiswoode.

Bajpai, S.C. *Kinnaur in the Himalayas*. New Delhi: Concept Publishing Company, 1987.

Bhattacharya, J.N. *Hindu Castes and Sects*. Calcutta: Editions India, 1968.

Bingley, A.H. *History, Caste and Culture of Jats and Gujjars*. Calcutta: Superintendent Government Printing, 1904; reprint 1978, New Delhi: Ess Ess Publications.

Blunt, E.A.H. *The Caste System of Northern India*. London: Oxford University Press, 1931; reprint Delhi: S. Chand and Co., 1969.

Campbell, George. 'Ethnology of India', in *A Glossary of Tribes and Castes of Punjab and North West Frontier Province*. Comp. H. A. Rose, Lahore: Government Printing Press, 1919, Vol II.

Chitrav, Siddeshwara Shastri. *Bharatvarshiya Prachin Charitrakosh*. Pune: Bhartiya Charitrakosh Mandal, 1964.

Chopra, S.R.K. and L.S. Siddhu. 'Distribution of ABO Blood Group in Lahaulis', *The Eastern Anthropologist*. 1970, Vol. 23, No. 1.

Chowdhury, A.K. Bio-Anthropological Study of the Lahaulis (Unpublished report. Calcutta: Anthropological Survey of India) *n.d.*

Crooke, W. *The Tribes and Castes of the North-Western Province and Oudh*, Calcutta: Superintendent of Government Printing, 1896, (4 Vols); reprint, Delhi: Cosmo Publications, 1974 & 1975.

Diack, A.H. 'The Kulu dialect of Hindi', in *Census of India* (1891), ed. E.D.

Maclagan. Calcutta: Superintendent of Government Printing, 1896, Vol I, Part I.

Fanshawe, H.C. 'Kulu Language Spoken at Malana', in *Punjab Notes and Queries*, ed. R.C. Temple. Allahabad.: Pioneer Press, 1881, Vol.I., No. 4-6.

Farewell, Byron. *The Gurkhas*. London: Penguin Books Ltd., 1984.

Francke, A.H. *A History of Western Tibet: One of the Unknown Empires*. London: S.W. Patridge & Co., 1907.

Gill, M.S. *Himalayan Wonderland: Travels in Lahul-Spiti*. Delhi: Vikas Publishing House Pvt. Ltd., 1972.

Gispert Sauch, G.S.J. 'Christianity', in *Religions of India*, ed. Karan Singh. Delhi: Clarion Books, 1983.

Granquist, H. *Marriage Condition in a Palestinian Village*. Helsinki Societas Scnebtuaryn Fenrica, commentationes Humanurum Litterarum III. B., 1931.

Grierson, G.A. (ed). 'Tibeto Burman Family', in *Linguistic Survey of India*. Calcutta: Superitendent of Government Printing, Vol. III. Part I, 1909.

Grierson, G.A. *Linguistic Survey of India*. Calcutta: Superintendent of Government Printing, 1976, Vol IX, Pt IV.

Haimendorf, C. von Furer (ed.). *Caste and Kinship in Nepal, India and Ceylon*. New York: Asia Publishing House, 1966.

Harcourt, A.F.P. *The Himalayan District of Kooloo, Lahaul and Spiti*, London: W.H. Allen, 1871; reprint, Delhi : Vivek Publishing House, 1972.

Hutchison, J. and J.P.H. Vogel. *History of Punjab Hill States*. Lahore: Superintendent of Government Printing, 1933, (reprinted 1982), Shimla: Department of Language and Culture, Himachal Pradesh.

Ibbetson, D. *Punjab Castes*. Punjab: Government Press, 1916, reprint 1974, Delhi B.R.Publishing Corpn.

Ibbetson, D.C.J. 'Outlines of Punjab Ethnography' ,in *Census of the Punjab* 1881. Calcutta: Superintendent of Government Printing, 1883.

Jasta, Hari Ram; *Himachal Ki Lok Sanskriti* (Hindi). Delhi : Sanmarg Prakashan, 1986.

Kaushal, R.K. *Himachal Pradesh : Socio-economic, Geographical & Historical Survey*. New Delhi : Reliance Publishing House, 1988.

Khosla, G.D. 'Republic within Republics', in *Of Mountains & Men*. New Delhi: Allied Publishers Pvt. Ltd., 1980.

Mamgain, M.D. *Himachal Pradesh District Gazetteers. Bilaspur*. State District Gazetteers, Shimla: Himachal Pradesh, 1975.

Mamgain, M.D. *Himachal Pradesh District Gazetteers, Lahaul & Spiti*. Chandigarh: Greater Punjab Press, 1975.

Mathur, K.S.and B.C. Agarwal (eds). *Tribe, Caste and Peasantry*. Lucknow : Ethnography & Folk Culture Society, 1974.

Mc Lagan, E.D. (ed.). 'The Punjab and its feudatories', in *Census of India* 1891. Calcutta: Superintendent of Government Printing, 1892, Vol. 19 Part I.

Mian Amar Singh. *Report Kanuni Bandobast, Riasat Kahlur (Bilaspur), Zila Shimla* (in Urdu). Lahore: Munshi Gulab Singh & Sons, 1907.

Mushir-ul-Haq. 'Islam', in *Religions of India*. ed. Karan Singh, Delhi: Clarion Books, 1983.

Negi, T.S. *Himachal Pradesh District Gazetteer, Chamba*. Batala: Standard Printing Press, 1963.

Negi, T.S. *Himachal Pradesh, District Gazetteers - Sirmur*. Aligarh: Oriental Printing Press, 1969.

Negi, T.S. *Scheduled Tribes of Himachal Pradesh - A Profile*. Meerut: Raj Printers, 1976.

Newell, W.H. *Report on Scheduled Castes and Scheduled Tribes, Bharmaur Tehsil of Chamba District, Himachal Pradesh*. Delhi: Manager of Publications, 1967, Vol. XX, Pt. V-B.

Northey, W. Brook and C.J. Morris. *The Gurkhas: Their Manners, Customs and Country*. London: John Lane, 1928; reprint 1974, Delhi: Cosmo Publications.

Parmar, Y.S. *Polyandry in the Himalayas*. Delhi: Vikas Publishing House Pvt. Ltd., 1975.

Prince Peter, H.R.H. *A Study of Polyandry*. Netherlands: Mouton and Company, 1964.

Raghviah, V. *Nomads*. Secunderabad: Adim Jati Sewak Sangh, 1968.

Raha, M.K. 'The Khandan System of the Kinnaura of the Western Himalayas', In *The Himalayan Heritage*, ed. M.K. Raha. Delhi: Gyan Publishing House, 1987.

Raha, M.K. and S.N. Mahato. *The Kinnaurese of Himalayas*. Calcutta: Anthropological Survey of India, 1985.

Rahul, Ram. *The Himalayan Borderland*. Delhi: Vikas Publishing House Pvt. Ltd., 1970.

Risley, H.H.. *The People of India*. Calcutta: Thacker, Spink, 1908.

Rose, H.A. (Comp.). *A Glossary of the Castes and Tribes of Punjab and North-West Frontier Province*. Lahore: Government Press, 1914, Vol. III.

Rose, H.A. (Comp.). *A Glossary of the Castes and Tribes of Punjab and North-West Frontier Province*. Lahore: Government Press, 1919, Vol. II.

Rosser, C. 'An Aspect of political organisation of Malana', in *Tribe, Caste and Peasantry*. eds. K.S.Mathur and B.C. Aggarwal. Lucknow: Ethnographic and Folk Culture Society, 1974, pp. 199-210.

Roy, Shibani. *Status of Muslim Women in North India*. Delhi: B.R. Publishing Corporation, 1979.

Saraswati, B.N. *Brahmanic Ritual Traditions in the Crucible of Time*. Simla:

Indian Institute of Advance Studies, 1977.

Sashi, S.S. *Himachal : Nature's Peaceful Paradise.* Delhi: Indian School Supply Depot, 1971.

Sashi, S.S. *The Gaddi Tribe of H.P.: A Sociological Study.* New Delhi : Sterling Publishers Pvt. Ltd., 1977.

Shah, V.P. 'Jainism,' in *Religions of India.* ed. Karan Singh, Delhi: Clarion Books, 1983.

Sharma, Banshi Ram. *Kinnar Lok Sahitya* (Hindi). Lehri Sarail (Bilaspur): Lalit Prakashan, 1976.

Sharma, Banshi Ram. *Himalaya Ki Pauranic Jan Jatiyan* (in Hindi). Delhi : Arya Prakashan, 1985.

Sharma, Banshi Ram, *Himachal Lok Sanskriti Ke Srot* (in Hindi). Delhi : Arya Prakashan, 1986

Sharma, D.D. *Lahul Samaj aur Sanskriti.* Manuscript, n.d.

Sharma, P.C. 'Group Differentiation in Isolation: A Comparative Morphometric study of Malaneese in relation to some neighbouring populations of Himachal Pradesh, Ph.D. Thesis, (Unpublished) Chandigarh: Punjab University, 1985.

Sharma, P.C. 'A Demogenetic Profile of Malaneese : An isolated community in Malana glen. District Kulu,' H.P., M.Phil (Anthropology) Thesis (unpublished), Chandigarh: Punjab University, 1977.

Sharma, P.C. and V. Bhalla. 'Malaneese of Malana Glen: Analysis of Morphometric data and ethnic relationship with some neighbouring populations of Himachal Pradesh'. India, *Anthropologischer Anzerger,* Germany, Jg. 45(4), 1987, pp. 337-350.

Sharma, Raj Bahadur. *Christian Missions in North India* 1813-1913. Delhi : Mittal Publications, 1988.

Sharma, Vidyasagar. *Himachal Pradesh Ki Anusuchit Jatiyan* (in Hindi). Salogra: Himgiri Prakashan, (n.d.).

Sher, S.S. *The Sansis of Punjab.* Delhi: Munshilal Manoharlal, 1965.

Sherring, M.A. *Hindu Tribes and Castes.* Calcutta: Thacker Spink, 1879; reprint, Delhi: Cosmo Publications, 1974, Vol III.

Siddiqui, M.K.A. 'Caste among the Muslims of Calcutta', in *Caste and Social Stratification among Muslims in India,* ed. Imtiaz Ahmad. Delhi: Manohar Publications, 1978.

Singh, A. *Census of India 1971, H.P. Series-7, Social and Cultural Tables.* Simla: Directorate of Census Operation, 1971, Part II-C(2).

Singh, A. 'Pojana—A village survey, Himachal Pradesh', in *Census of India 1961.* Simla: Directorate of Census Operations, 1964, Vol. XX, Pt. VI, No. 17.

Singh, Kavi Ganesh. *Shastri Vansh Vinod* (in Hindi). Varanasi: Bharat Jeewan Mudranalay, 1892.

Singh, K.S., V. Bhalla and V. Kaul. *The Biological Variation in Indian Populations, People of India, National Series*. Anthropological Survey of India, Delhi: Oxford University Press, 1994, Vol X.

Singh, Mian G. *Himachal Pradesh—History, Culture and Economy*. Simla: Minerva Book House, 1988.

Singh R.C. Pal. 'A village Survey-Kupha, Parmas, Thamoh and Nalet, Pangi sub-Tehsil, Chamba district, H.P.', in *Census of India,* 1961. Simla: Government of India Press, 1964, vol. XX, Part VI No 7.

Sinha, S.B. 'Twelve Sons of Lord Chitragupta' in *Souvenir of 61st,* All India Kayastha Conference. Calcutta, (n.d.).

Swinson, Arthur. *North-West Frontier*. Delhi: U B S Publishers, 1967.

Thornton, D.M. *Parsi, Jains and Sikhs-Some Minor Religious Sects in India.* Delhi: Mittal Publications, 1987.

Tobdan. *History and Religions of Lahul: From the Earliest to circa A.D. 1950*. New Delhi: Books Today, 1984.

Tribe, W.H. 'The Kunawari Languages' in *Punjab Notes and Queries,* ed. R.C. Temple. London: Trubner and Company,1884, Vol I, No. 9-11, pp. 104, 114, 127.

Vidyasankar, Satyakehi. *Agarwal Jati ka Prachin Itihas* (Hindi). Bombay: Akhil Bhartiya Marwari Jati Kosh, 1938.

Young, G. M.. 'Malana and the Akbar-Jamlu legend', *Journal of Punjab Historical Society*. Vol. 4, 1916, pp. 98-111.

MAP 1: LOCATION OF COMMUNITIES/LOCALE OF STUDIES

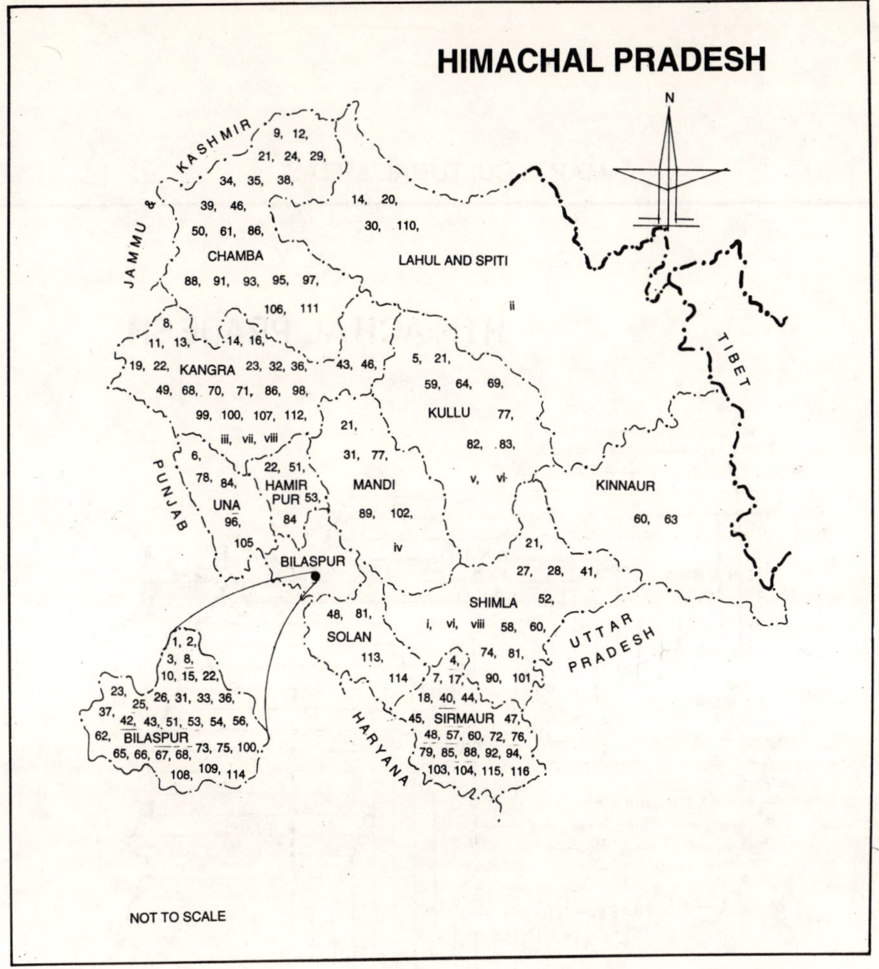

1. Abdal
2. Acharaj
3. Ard Popo
4. Atishbaz
5. Badhai
6. Bairagi
7. Bangali
8. Banjara
9. Bansi
10. Bard
11. Battarha
12. Batwal
13. Bazigar
14. Beda (Bodh)
15. Bharai
16. Bharare
17. Bhat
18. Bhisti
19. Bhojki
20. Bodh
21. Brahman
22. Bujru
23. Chamar
24. Chanal
25. Chandel Rajput
26. Chhimba/Dhobi
27. Chinese
28. Christian
29. Chuhra/Balmiki
30. Dagi
31. Dagoli
32. Darain
33. Daule
34. Dhogri
35. Dosali
36. Dumna/Bhanjra
37. Faqir
38. Gaddi Brahman
39. Gaddi Rajput
40. Gaderiya
41. Gaur Brahman
42. Ghai
43. Ghirath
44. Gorkha
45. Gosain
46. Gujarati Brahman
47. Gujjar (Hindu)
48. Gujjar (Muslim)
49. Hadi
50. Hali
51. Hesi
52. Jain
53. Jat
54. Jheewar
55. Jogi
56. Julaha
57. Kanghigir
58. Kayastha
59. Khampa
60. Khasa
61. Khatik
62. Khatri
63. Kinnaura
64. Koli
65. Kumhar
66. Labana
67. Lohar
68. Mahajan
69. Malaneese
70. Masku
71. Megh
72. Mehra
73. Mirasi
74. Nagalu
75. Nai
76. Nalband
77. Nar
78. Nichar
79. Noongar
80. Od
81. Pajiara
82. Pangwal Brahman
83. Pangwal Rajput
84. Pathan
85. Penja
86. Pharera
87. Punjabi
88. Punjabi Refugee
89. Raeen
90. Rajput
91. Rana
92. Rangar
93. Rathi
94. Rawat
95. Rihara
96. Saini
97. Sanhai
98. Sansi
99. Sansoi
100. Sarehde
101. Sayyad
102. Seok
103. Sheikh
104. Sikh
105. Sikligar
106. Sipi
107. Sood
108. Sunar
109. Sunhak
110. Swangla
111. Teli
112. Thathiar
113. Thavi
114. Thuana
115. Toori
116. Vaish-Agarwal

i. Beda (Hindu)
ii. Gara
iii. Kanghera
iv. Keer
v. Mahant
vi. Mawi
vii. Nagvanshi
viii. Nath

MAP 2: CULTURAL AREAS

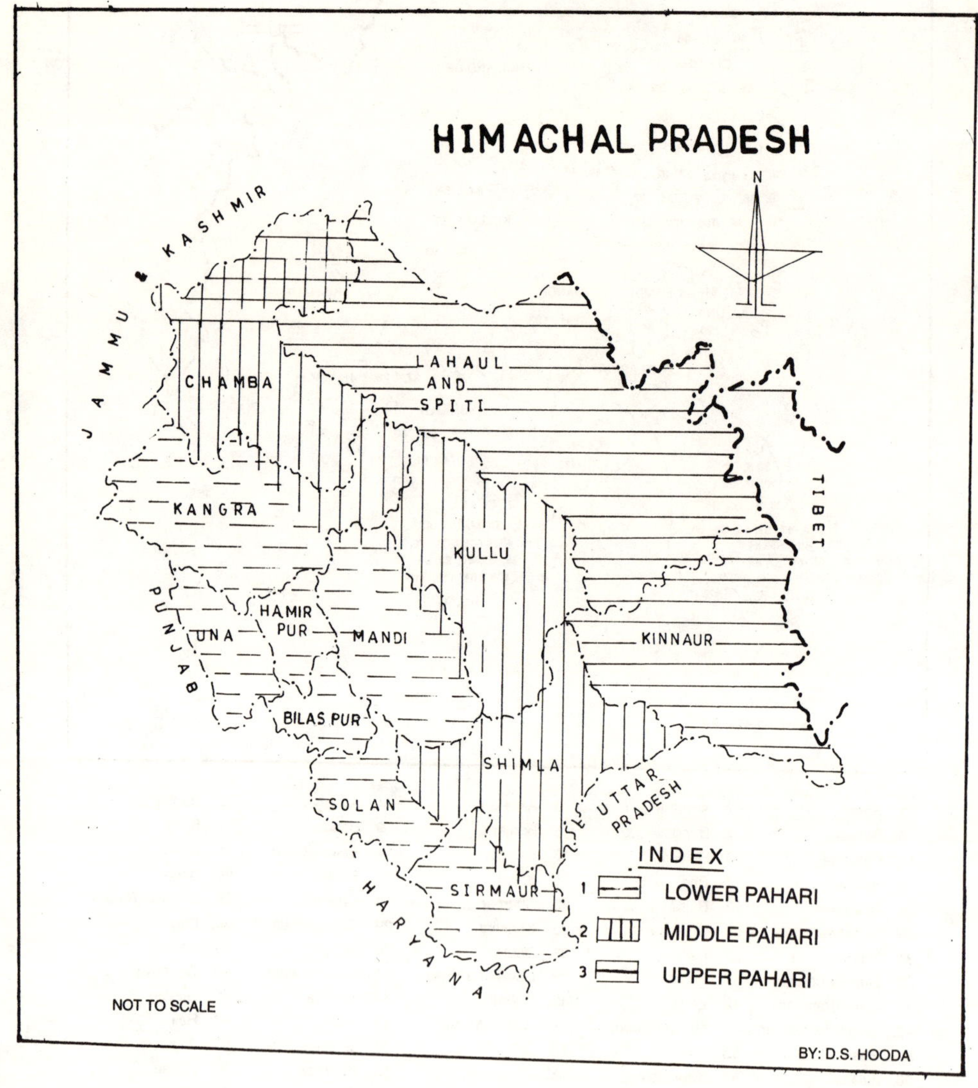

INDEX